Nick Engler's
Woodworking Wisdom

Nick Engler

SPECIAL EDITION FOR THE

HANDYMAN
CLUB OF AMERICA

The author and editors who compiled this book have tried to make all of the contents as accurate and as correct as possible. Plans, illustrations, photographs, and text have all been carefully checked and cross-checked. However, due to the variability of local conditions, construction materials, personal skill, and so on, neither the author nor Reader's Digest assumes any responsibility for any injuries suffered or for damages or other losses incurred that result from the material presented herein. All instructions and plans should be carefully studied and clearly understood before beginning construction.

Printed in the United States of America

Library of Congress Cataloging in Publication Data

Engler, Nick.
    [Woodworking wisdom]
    Nick Engler's woodworking wisdom/Nick Engler.
    p.   cm.
    Originally published: Emmaus, Pa.: Rodale Press, 1997.
    Includes bibliographical references (p.).
    ISBN 0-7621-0178-4
    1. Cabinetwork. 2. Furniture making. I.Title. II. Title:
Woodworking wisdom.
TT197.E56 1999
684'.08—dc21   99-39197

We're always happy to hear from you. For questions or comments concerning the editorial content of this book, please write to:
    Reader's Digest
    General Books Editors
    Reader's Digest Road
    Pleasantville, NY 10570

Credits and Thanks

America's Best Tool Company, Inc.
West Milton, Ohio

Jon Arno
Berkley, Michigan

Richard Belcher
Dayton, Ohio

Richard & Susan Burman
Eaton, Ohio

CMT Tools
Oldsmar, Florida

Colonial Hardwoods
Springfield, Virginia

Della International Machinery Corp.
Pittsburgh, Pennsylvania

Franklin International
Columbus, Ohio

Garrett Wade
New York, New York

Georgia-Pacific Corporation
Atlanta, Georgia

Good Wood Alliance
Burlington, Vermont

Manny's Woodworker Place
Lexington, Kentucky

Frank Miller Lumber Company
Union City, Indiana

Miller Logging and Lumber Sales
West Manchester, Ohio

Nemeth Engineering
Crestwood, Kentucky

North American Plywood Corporation
Jersey City, New Jersey

The Olson Saw Company
Bethel, Connecticut

Paxton Beautiful Woods
Cincinnati, Ohio

Scott Phillips
Piqua, Ohio

Pierson-Hollowell Company
Lawrenceburg, Indiana

Don Reuter
Columbus, Ohio

Robertson's Cabinets
West Milton, Ohio

Israel Sack, Inc.
New York, New York

Shopsmith, Inc.
Dayton, Ohio

U.S. Forest Products Laboratory
Madison, Wisconsin

George VanderVoort
Reading, Pennsylvania

Wertz Hardware
West Milton, Ohio

Woodcraft
Parkersburg, West Virginia

Woodwerks
Columbus, Ohio

Woodworker's Supply of New Mexico
Albuquerque, New Mexico

The Workshops of David T Smith
Morrow, Ohio

Dr. & Mrs. Evan Young
Greenville, Ohio

Your Floor Store
West Milton, Ohio

Contents

PART ONE: WOODWORKING DESIGN AND CONSTRUCTION

iii

PART TWO: WOODWORKING TOOLS

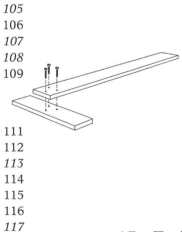

PART THREE: WOODWORKING TECHNIQUES

GENERAL METHODS

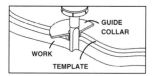

PART FOUR: WOOD AND WOODWORKING MATERIALS

APPENDIX: WOODWORKING SOURCES

At last, Dennis,
An Answer to Your Question

Several years ago, an accomplished woodworker, Dennis Rollins, wrote to me asking, "How do I become a master craftsman?" I sweated over his letter more than any I have received before or since. It's a perplexing question, and an important one. Although *Handyman Club of America* members may not all share Dennis's ambition to be a master, we certainly hope to produce masterful results. But how do you ferret out the necessary experience and wisdom from the overabundance of woodworking information that surrounds us? And how do you know that you've gotten correct and complete information?

To answer Dennis, I studied European guilds that set standards of craftsmanship and still confer the title "master craftsman." (Here in America, it's an honorific bestowed by publishers to help sell books.) A master must understand four areas of woodworking lore – *wood and woodworking materials, design and construction, tools, and techniques.* Each subject is necessary to the others. A craftsman who knows tools and techniques but doesn't grasp the subtle properties of wood and how they affect an assembly cannot consistently do good work.

I searched for a reference to help Dennis with his quest, but no one book would serve. There are several excellent texts on general woodworking that provide an overview of this essential knowledge. But none take you to the next level, showing you how to progress beyond the basics and gain the know-how to do truly masterful work.

Well, if you can't find it, make it. So I began to collect information for the book that Dennis needed. This *Handyman Club of America Special Edition* is the result – an answer to his question and many others that I've received. It's not a "complete" book of woodworking; there's no such thing. Woodworking is too vast a subject to squeeze between just two covers!

This is, however, a *comprehensive* book, covering every facet of the craft. Dozens of professional craftsmen and experienced amateurs have told me what they felt was necessary information, and from this I collected what most agree is the *core* woodworking knowledge necessary for good work. If you are new to the craft, this book will give you the firm jumping-off point you need for a good start. If you are a veteran craftsman, it will provide crucial information to round out your woodworking education. Either way, it will answer your most pressing questions.

But that's just for starters. As I was writing this book, I imagined it as a signpost in the middle of a vast country: "This way to an in-depth understanding of lathe turning; that way to some excellent plans for Shaker furniture." Although we all need general woodworking knowledge, every craftsman has unique ambitions and needs *specific* information. So I've included important woodworking *resources* – books, videos, organizations, institutions, schools, museums, and publications – showing you how to explore the parts of the craft that you wish to master.

I was flattered that Dennis asked me how to become a master craftsman. I've never claimed to be one, although enough booksellers have claimed it for me. I am, however, a master of research and of what journalists call "boiling it down." This is the distilled wisdom of hundreds of true masters whom I have read or talked to, and the sources from which they gained their wisdom.

A parting thought for Dennis and *Handyman Club of America* members who have the same dream: No, reading this book won't make you a master craftsman. But this is where you begin.

With all good wishes,

Nick

This **Appalachian Dulcimer**, built by craftsman/author Nick Engler, was displayed at the Kennedy Center for the Performing Arts during America's Bicentennial (1976). In addition to making traditional American musical instruments, Nick holds several patents on woodworking tools. He has taught wood technology and craftsmanship at the University of Cincinnati and was a contributing editor to **American Woodworker** magazine. This is his 48th book on woodworking.

PART ONE

WOODWORKING DESIGN AND CONSTRUCTION

The Nature of Wood

Three unique properties affect everything you build from wood – its grain direction, movement across the grain, and strength along the grain.

The virtues of wood as a building material are legendary. It's attractive, abundant, and easy to work. Pound for pound, it's stronger than steel. If properly cared for, it will last indefinitely. And you can use it to make almost anything, from a tiny box to a huge building.

It's also a complex (and often perplexing) material. Unlike metals and plastics, whose properties are fairly consistent throughout, wood is wholly inconsistent. It's stronger along the grain than across it. It expands and contracts more in one direction than another. Its color, weight, and grain pattern vary not only from species to species but from board to board.

To work with wood – and have it work for you – first learn its complex nature. In particular, you must understand three unique **properties**[1] that affect everything you build. These are grain, movement, and strength.

WOOD GRAIN

Wood grows in concentric layers around the trunk, limbs, roots, and other woody parts of the tree. You can see these layers when you slice through a trunk.

The **Postmodern Cabinet** remains the pinnacle of the woodworking craft. Its ingenious design, developed over centuries, shows off the beauty of the wood grain, takes advantage of its strength, and allows for its movement.

SPECS: 69″ high, 36″ wide, 23″ deep

MATERIALS: Walnut and walnut veneer

CRAFTSMAN: Randall Patterson
Stanley, NC

Photo by Rick Echelmeyer

HOW WOOD GROWS

At the very center is the *pith.* In some trees, this is much softer and possibly a different color than the surrounding *heartwood.* Heartwood is made up of dead cells that no longer serve any purpose except to support the tree. Next is the *sapwood,* which carries water, minerals, and plant sugars between the roots and the leaves. This is often lighter in color than the heartwood. Outside the sapwood, close to the surface, is the *cambium,* a thin layer of living cells. These cells manufacture the wood as they grow. The cambium is covered by a protective layer of *bark.* The cambium grows rapidly at the beginning of each growing season, creating light-colored *springwood.* As the climate warms, it slows down and produces darker *summerwood.* This later growth is somewhat denser and harder than the early springwood. As the weather turns cold, the cambium becomes dormant until the next spring. This cycle produces distinctive *growth rings.*

MORE *INFO*

Although woodworkers usually prefer heartwood for its richer color, this is not always the case. When working with light-colored woods such as maple, many folks fancy sapwood for its consistent creamy white hues.

GRAIN STRUCTURE

As the cambium grows, it generates two types of wood cells. Most of these are long, narrow *longitudinal cells* that align themselves with the axis of the trunk, limb, or root. These are what give the wood its grain. The cambium also produces a smaller number of *ray cells* that line up in *rays* extending out from the pith, perpendicular to the axis.

As the wood grows outward, the living protoplasm inside the cells dies and deteriorates, leaving behind just the cell walls. These walls are composed mostly of *cellulose fibers,* which give the wood its strength.

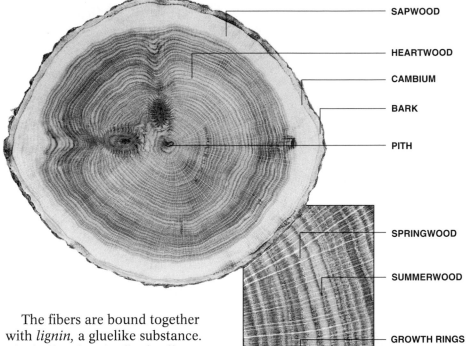

SAPWOOD
HEARTWOOD
CAMBIUM
BARK
PITH

SPRINGWOOD
SUMMERWOOD
GROWTH RINGS

Wood grows in concentric layers, or **growth rings.**

The fibers are bound together with *lignin,* a gluelike substance. The hollow longitudinal cells become part of the sapwood, conducting the sap up and down the tree. The hollow rays store plant sugars.

After several seasons, the older sapwood turns to heartwood. The sap dries up, and mineral compounds called *extractives* form on the cell walls. These chemicals turn the wood darker, giving it the characteristic color of its **species**[2]. They also affect its strength, stability, and hardness.

TYPES OF GRAIN

Because of the manner in which wood grows, every board has a definite *grain direction,* parallel to the length of the longitudinal cells. The grain appears differently depending on how the board is sawed.

■ When you cut a board across the grain (perpendicular to the grain direction and the growth rings), you reveal *end grain.*

■ Cut wood parallel to the grain direction and tangent to the growth rings, and you'll see *flat grain* (also called tangential or plain grain).

■ Cut it parallel to the grain direction but through the radius of the growth rings to see *quarter grain* (also referred to as radial grain).

■ Both flat grain and quarter grain are sometimes called *long grain.*

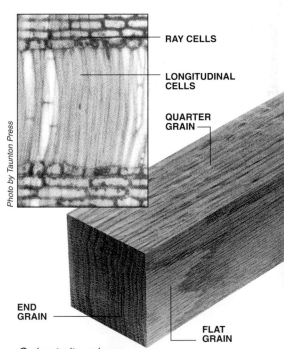

Photo by Taunton Press

RAY CELLS
LONGITUDINAL CELLS
QUARTER GRAIN
END GRAIN
FLAT GRAIN

Owing to its unique structure, wood grain appears differently depending on how the board is cut.

SEE *ALSO:*

[1]Mechanical Properties   347
[1]Physical Properties   352
[2]Chemical Attributes   346

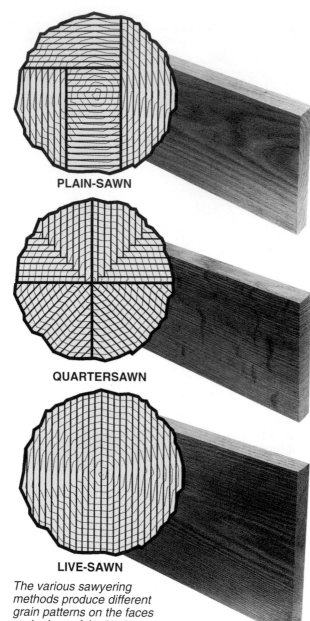

PLAIN-SAWN

QUARTERSAWN

LIVE-SAWN

The various sawyering
methods produce different
grain patterns on the faces
and edges of the lumber.

WOOD GRAIN IN LUMBER

Sawyers[1] use several methods to cut up a tree, each of which reveals different grain patterns.

■ The most common method is *plain sawing* because it produces the highest quantity of usable lumber. The sawyer begins by sawing several boards from one side of the log, turns it 90 degrees and saws several more, and continues in this manner "sawing around" the log. Plain-sawn boards show flat grain on their faces and quarter grain on the edges.

■ The sawyer might also *quarter saw* a log. First, he saws the log in quarters, then slices each quarter into boards, either by cutting boards from the two flat sides alternately or by *gang-sawing* the quarter (making parallel cuts). Quartersawn boards show mostly quarter grain on their faces and flat grain on the edges.

■ On special request, a sawyer will *live saw* a log for a woodworker, gang-sawing the entire log. (This is sometimes called *sawing through and through.*) Live sawing produces much wider boards than other methods, and these boards show mostly *mixed grain* — flat grain near the center of the face and quarter grain near the edges.

PRO*TIP*

If you have a log live-sawn, ask the sawyer to number the boards as he cuts them. When you dry them, stack the boards in the same order in which they were cut. This makes it easier to match boards for grain and color when the wood is ready to work.

TEXTURE AND PATTERN

The size, type, and arrangement of the wood cells differ with the species, and this also affects the appearance of the grain. The *texture* of the wood is determined by the relative size of the longitudinal cells. Wood species with large cells are said to have a coarse texture, while those with smaller cells have a fine texture.

Hardwoods[2] have *vessel elements,* a special type of longitudinal cell much larger in diameter than the surrounding cells. When these vessels are sliced open, they leave tiny hollows in the wood called *pores.* These pores give the hardwoods a distinct look from **softwoods**[2], which have none. Some hardwoods have a larger concentration of pores in the springwood — these are known as *ring-porous* woods. Hardwoods in which the pores are distributed evenly throughout the springwood and summerwood are *ring-diffuse.* The arrangement of pores has an enormous effect on the grain. Ring-porous hardwoods have a pronounced or *strong* grain pattern, while the grain pattern of ring-diffuse stock is much less distinct.

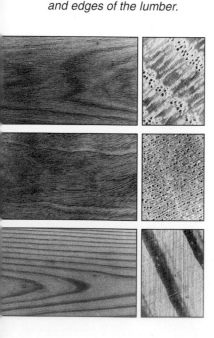

The pores in **ring-porous** hardwoods such as red oak create a strong grain pattern.

The pores in **ring-diffuse** hardwoods like mahogany are more evenly distributed and the grain pattern is less distinct.

Softwoods such as yellow pine have no pores. The grain pattern is due to the color difference between the springwood and the summerwood.

FIGURED WOOD

Wood grain isn't always straight and even. The longitudinal and ray cells sometimes grow in unusual patterns, many of which are strikingly beautiful. These are known as *figured grain*.

A few wood species, such as white oak, have especially prominent rays. When quartersawn, these produce **silver grain.**

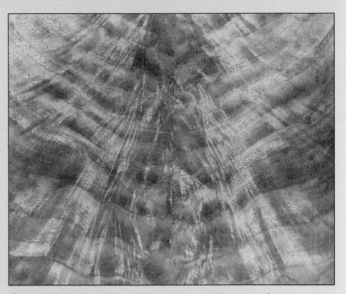

Crotch figure, *such as this walnut crotch, is cut from the part of a tree where the trunk divides into smaller limbs and branches.*

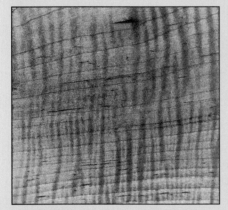

Curly grain *occurs when the longitudinal cells grow in waves. This occurs in many species but is especially striking in maple.*

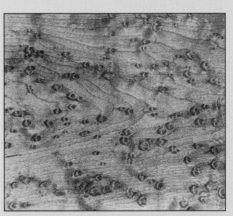

Bird's eyes *like those in this maple are caused by small dimples in the layers of cells. These are thought to be caused by a fungus that affects the growth of the longitudinal cells.*

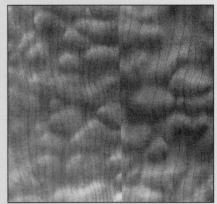

Larger dimples result in **quilted figure,** *like the quilting in this soft maple. This, too, is the result of a fungus.*

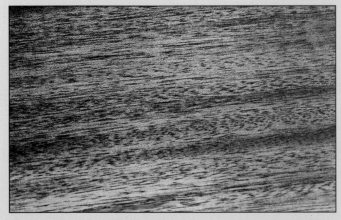

The longitudinal cells of certain species, such as mahogany, sometimes spiral around the trunk, reversing direction every few growth rings. This creates **ribbon figure.**

Sometimes a tree produces a large growth on the side of the trunk or a branch. The cells seem to swirl around each other inside these growths. When sliced, these produce a **burl figure** *such as this elm burl.*

WOOD MOVEMENT

Wood moves. Because of its unique structure, it's constantly expanding and contracting. And you must cope with this movement in every project you build.

MOISTURE CONTENT AND MOVEMENT

Wood moves as its *moisture content* changes. In a tree that's just been felled, the wood is "green" – sap fills the cell cavities. This *free water* (as the sap is sometimes called) accounts for 72 percent of the total moisture content, although this percentage may vary from species to species. The remaining 28 percent saturates the wood fibers in the cell walls. This *bound water* in the fibers causes them to swell, just as a sponge swells when you wet it.

As wood dries, the free water evaporates first, then the bound water. The wood is dimensionally stable (it doesn't shrink or swell noticeably) as it loses free water, but once it begins to lose bound water, it contracts.

Wood dries to an average moisture content of between 4 and 11 percent, depending on the area of the country, but *it never really comes to rest!* The amount of bound water in the wood continually changes with the amount of moisture in the surrounding atmosphere.

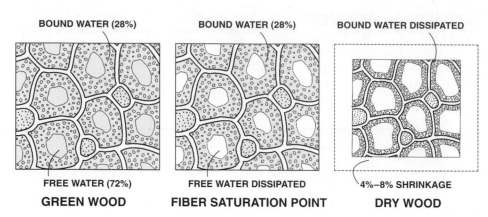

BOUND WATER (28%)   BOUND WATER (28%)   BOUND WATER DISSIPATED

FREE WATER (72%)   FREE WATER DISSIPATED   4%–8% SHRINKAGE

GREEN WOOD   **FIBER SATURATION POINT**   **DRY WOOD**

*In green wood, **free water** fills the cell cavities and **bound water** saturates the fibers in the cell walls. As it dries, the free water evaporates first, then the bound water. The wood doesn't move until it begins to lose bound water.*

On the average, wood gains or loses about 1 percent moisture content for every 5 percent change in the *relative humidity.*

The wood fibers swell as they absorb moisture and shrink as they release it, causing the wood to expand and contract. In the Northern Hemisphere, relative humidity increases in the summer and decreases in the winter. And due to the effects of heating and air conditioning, the relative humidity is generally different indoors than out. Additionally, the relative humidity may vary from one building to another if the indoor temperatures differ. Consequently, wood tends to move with the seasons or whenever you change its location.

MORE *INFO*

When wood is at 28 percent moisture content, it's said to be at its *fiber saturation point,* where the wood fibers have absorbed as much water as they possibly can. This is also the point at which the wood fibers are swollen as big as they're going to get.

MYTH *CONCEPTIONS*

HUMIDITY Wood doesn't always move with changes in humidity, just the *relative humidity.* The relative humidity is the ratio of the actual moisture in the air *(absolute humidity)* to the maximum amount of moisture the air will hold at its present temperature. The warmer the air, the more moisture it will hold. Because of this, it's possible for the absolute humidity to change while the relative humidity remains the same. If both the absolute humidity and the air temperature rise at the same time, the relative humidity will remain constant — and the wood won't move.

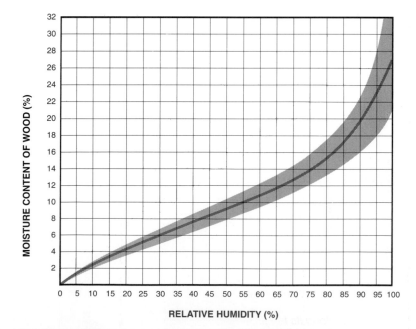

*The **moisture content** of the wood varies with the relative humidity of the surrounding air, as this chart shows. Once the wood has been dried, the moisture content never again rises above 28 percent (its **fiber saturation point**) from the effects of humidity alone. For this to happen, the wood must be immersed in water.*

DIRECTION OF MOVEMENT

Although it's constantly expanding and contracting, wood does not move equally in all directions. The grain structure causes it to move differently in three different directions.

■ Wood is fairly stable along its *longitudinal direction,* parallel to the grain. Green lumber shrinks only 0.01 percent of its length as it dries. An 8-foot-long board will move only ³/₃₂ inch.

■ Wood moves much more *across* the grain, tangent to the growth rings. Green lumber shrinks as much as 8 percent in this direction.

■ But it shrinks only half as much (4 percent) in the *radial* direction, extending out from the pith along the radius of the growth rings.

For this reason, **quartersawn lumber¹** is more stable than **plain-sawn lumber¹**. Quartersawn lumber is cut radially and moves only half as much across its width as plain-sawn lumber, which is cut tangentially.

CHANGING SHAPE

The difference in tangential and radial movement has other important consequences. Depending on how it's cut from the tree, a board may change shape as it dries:

■ If the annual rings run side to

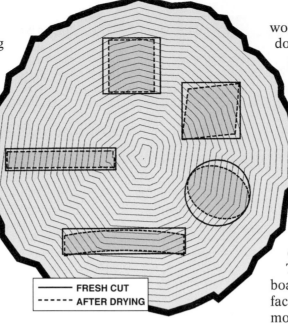

FRESH CUT
------ AFTER DRYING

Because of the difference in tangential and radial movement, boards change shape as they expand and contract. The way in which they change depends on how they are cut from the tree.

side in square stock, the stock will shrink to a rectangle.

■ If the rings run diagonally from corner to corner, the stock will become diamond-shaped.

■ Round stock becomes oval as the tangential diameter shrinks more than the radial diameter.

■ Plain-sawn lumber tends to cup in the opposite direction of the growth rings because the outside face (the face farthest from the pith) shrinks a little faster than the inside face.

■ In quartersawn lumber, both faces shrink equally and the board remains flat.

And there are other forces that may cause a board to move or change shape. Stress sometimes develops in the tree as it grows or in the lumber when it's **improperly dried²**. Internally stressed wood (called *reaction wood*) moves when you cut it. Cutting relieves some of the stress, and the wood reacts by changing shape. This is quite different from normal wood movement, however. Once the stress dissipates, it no longer affects the

wood. But there's nothing you can do to stop radial and tangential movement. As long as there's weather, the boards will continue to shrink and swell.

ESTIMATING WOOD MOVEMENT

It's also useful to know *how much* a board is likely to move. You must anticipate the movement when fitting drawers and doors, inserting panels in frames, and dozens of other operations.

The rule of thumb is that if the board shows mostly flat grain on its face, allow for ¼ inch *total* wood movement for every 12 inches across the grain. If it shows mostly quarter grain, allow for ⅛ inch movement. This will accommodate an annual change of 8 percent moisture content – much more than is common in most areas.

Also consider the time of year. Wood shrinks to its smallest dimension in the winter and swells to its maximum in the summer. The wood in winter projects will expand; the wood in summer projects will contract. In the spring and fall, remember that the wood will expand half your total movement allowance and contract the other half.

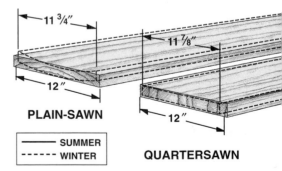

PLAIN-SAWN

SUMMER
------ WINTER

QUARTERSAWN

Quartersawn lumber is more stable than plain-sawn, expanding only half as much across its width. Additionally, quartersawn boards remain relatively flat, while plain-sawn boards tend to cup when they move.

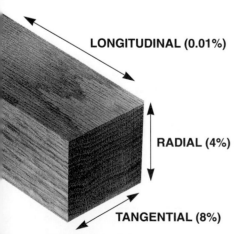

LONGITUDINAL (0.01%)

RADIAL (4%)

TANGENTIAL (8%)

Wood is fairly stable along its length, moving only 0.01 percent as it loses its bound water. However, (on the average) it moves 8 percent tangentially and 4 percent radially.

RELATIVE WOOD STRENGTHS

Wood has several kinds of strength. For a rough, general estimate of strength, refer to the *specific gravity* or density of the wood. When you need more detailed information, there are several additional choices.

Engineers measure the *com-pressive strength* by loading a block of wood parallel to the grain until it breaks, and the *bending strength* by loading a block perpendicular to the grain. Both are measured in pounds per square inch (psi). *Stiffness* is determined by applying a load to a beam until it deflects a certain amount, and it's measured in millions of pounds per square inch (Mpsi). To find *hardness,* engineers drive a metal ball halfway into the wood's surface. The force used is recorded in pounds (lb). In each case, the higher the number, the stronger the wood.

Wood Species	Specific Gravity*	Compressive Strength (psi)	Bending Strength (psi)	Stiffness (Mpsi)	Hardness (lb)
DOMESTIC HARDWOODS					
Alder, Red	0.41	5,820	9,800	1.38	590
Ash	0.60	7,410	15,000	1.74	1,320
Aspen	0.38	4,250	8,400	1.18	350
Basswood	0.37	4,730	8,700	1.46	410
Beech	0.64	7,300	14,900	1.72	1,300
Birch, Yellow	0.62	8,170	16,600	2.01	1,260
Butternut	0.38	5,110	8,100	1.18	490
Cherry	0.50	7,110	12,300	1.49	950
Chestnut	0.43	5,320	8,600	1.23	540
Elm	0.50	5,520	11,800	1.34	830
Hickory	0.72	9,210	20,200	2.16	†
Maple Hard	0.63	7,830	15,800	1.83	1,450
Maple, Soft	0.54	6,540	13,400	1.64	950
Oak, Red	0.63	6,760	14,300	1.82	1,290
Oak, White	0.68	7,440	15,200	1.78	1,360
Poplar	0.42	5,540	10,100	1.58	540
Sassafras	0.46	4,760	9,000	1.12	†
Sweetgum	0.52	6,320	12,500	1.64	850
Sycamore	0.49	5,380	10,000	1.42	770
Walnut	0.55	7,580	14,600	1.68	1,010
DOMESTIC SOFTWOODS					
Cedar, Aromatic Red	0.47	6,020	8,800	0.88	900
Cedar, Western Red	0.32	4,560	7,500	1.11	350
Cedar, White	0.32	3,960	6,500	0.80	320
Cypress	0.46	6,360	10,600	1.44	510
Fir, Douglas	0.49	7,230	12,400	1.95	710
Hemlock	0.45	7,200	11,300	1.63	540
Pine, Ponderosa	0.40	5,320	9,400	1.29	460
Pine, Sugar	0.36	4,460	8,200	1.19	380
Pine, White	0.35	4,800	8,600	1.24	380
Pine, Yellow	0.59	8,470	14,500	1.98	870
Redwood	0.35	5,220	7,900	1.10	420
Spruce, Sitka	0.40	5,610	10,200	1.57	510
IMPORTED WOODS					
Bubinga	0.71	10,500	22,600	2.48	2,690
Jelutong	0.36	3,920	7,300	1.18	390
Lauan	0.40	7,360	12,700	1.77	780
Mahogany, African	0.42	6,460	10,700	1.40	830
Mahogany, Genuine	0.45	6,780	11,500	1.50	800
Purpleheart	0.67	10,320	19,200	2.27	1,860
Rosewood, Brazilian	0.80	9,600	19,000	1.88	2,720
Rosewood, Indian	0.75	9,220	16,900	1.78	3,170
Teak	0.55	8,410	14,600	1.55	1,000

*After kiln-drying. Specific gravity may be slightly higher in green wood.

†Rating not available — species has not been tested.

WOOD STRENGTH

When building with wood, consider how each part will bear the load that will be placed upon it.

GRAIN DIRECTION AND STRENGTH

To take full advantage of a wood's strength, pay attention to the grain direction. Wood is a natural polymer – parallel strands of cellulose fibers held together by a lignin binder. These long chains of fibers make the wood exceptionally strong – they resist stress and spread the load over the length of the board. Furthermore, cellulose is tougher than lignin. It's easier to split a board with the grain (separating the lignin) than it is to break it across the grain (separating the cellulose fibers).

Remember this when you lay out the parts of a project. Always orient the grain so the fibers support the load. Whenever possible, cut the parts so the grain is continuous, running the length of the board.

PRO TIP

Straight-grained boards are stronger than those with uneven grain, knots, and other defects. Parts such as shelves will support a heavier load if the weight rests on straight grain.

SPECIFIC GRAVITY

When strength is paramount, grain direction may not be your only consideration. Some species of wood are naturally stronger than others. **Chairmakers**[1], for example, typically use maple, birch, and hickory for legs, rungs, and spindles. These parts are fairly slender, and weaker woods won't hold up.

A good indicator of a wood's strength is its *density* – the weight for a given volume. This is measured by its **specific gravity**[2] – the weight of a volume of wood divided by the weight of the same volume of water. Generally, the higher the ratio, the denser and stronger the wood. This is not always the case, but specific gravity is a useful reference nonetheless.

ADDITIONAL MEASUREMENTS OF STRENGTH

In some woodworking situations, "strength" is an ambiguous term. To say oak is strong doesn't tell you whether an oak shelf will sag when loaded with heavy objects, or whether its surface is hard enough to resist scratches and dents. You may need better information. Engineers have devised ways to measure specific types of strength.

■ *Compressive strength* tells you how much of a load a wood species can withstand parallel to the grain. How much weight will the legs of a table support before they buckle?

■ Bending strength (also known as the *modulus of rupture*) shows the load the wood can withstand perpendicular to the grain. How much weight can you hang on a peg?

■ The *stiffness* or *modulus of elasticity* indicates how much the wood will deflect when a load is applied perpendicular to the grain. How far will those shelves sag?

■ The *hardness* reveals how resistant the surface of the wood is to scratches, dents, and other abuse. How long will that kitchen counter stay looking new and unmarred?

To compare the strengths and specific gravities of common domestic and imported woods, refer to the chart "Relative Wood Strengths" on page 8.

MORE *SOURCES*

Understanding Wood, by R. Bruce Hoadley, Taunton Press, 1980

Wood Handbook: Wood As an Engineering Material, by the U.S. Forest Products Laboratory, U.S. Government Printing Office, 1987

SEE *ALSO:*

[1] Chairs   21
[2] Mechanical Properties   347

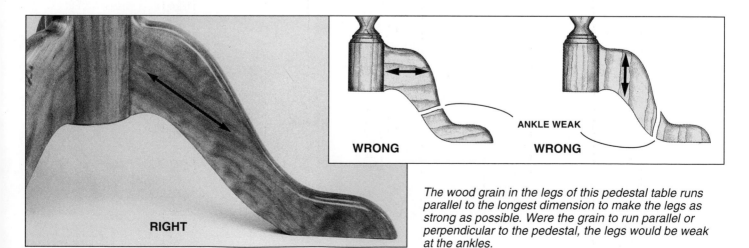

RIGHT   **WRONG**   **ANKLE WEAK**   **WRONG**

The wood grain in the legs of this pedestal table runs parallel to the longest dimension to make the legs as strong as possible. Were the grain to run parallel or perpendicular to the pedestal, the legs would be weak at the ankles.

2

Joining Wood

There are three simple rules for choosing the right joinery: Support the load, let the wood move, and provide a good gluing surface.

Joinery is the very heart of woodworking. As woodworkers, we spend a great deal of our time joining one board to another in the hopes of making something useful. To a great extent, the soundness and the integrity of our joints determine the value, utility, and durability of our craftsmanship. This, perhaps, is why early woodworkers referred to themselves as "joiners."

CHOOSING THE RIGHT JOINT

The first step in **making a sound joint**[1] is choosing the right one. This can be a daunting task; for every wooden assembly, there are dozens of possible ways to fit the members to one another. To sort through the possibilities, you must apply what you know about the **special nature**[2] of your building material – the wood grain, how it moves across the grain, and its strength along the grain.

To help you do this, there are three simple rules of thumb for selecting joinery. Every wood joint must:

■ Support the load
■ Let the wood move
■ Provide a good gluing surface or a suitable anchor for a fastener

*Although the primary purpose of joinery is to hold the wooden assembly together, many craftsmen also use it as a design element. The exposed mortise-and-tenon joints on this **Art Deco Bed** testify to the skill of the craftsman who made them, transforming an otherwise plain piece into an elegant work.*

Photo by Lee Fatherree

SPECS: 87½" long, 67½" wide, 43" high at the headboard, and 37" high at the footboard

MATERIALS: Nara and gaboon ebony

CRAFTSMAN: David Fay, San Francisco, CA

SUPPORT THE LOAD

Every woodworking joint is under some *stress*. This stress is a force that pushes or pulls on the wooden members, trying to tear them apart. For example, the weight of an object resting on a table stresses the table's joinery. When you lift up on the table or scoot it across the floor, you stress the joinery. Even the weight of the tabletop and other wooden parts, no matter how small, creates stress.

TYPES OF STRESS

There are four types of stress that can affect a wood joint. They differ by the direction from which the forces push or pull the wooden members.

■ *Tension* pulls the joined boards apart. If you were to draw arrows to indicate the directions in which the forces were pulling, they would be parallel and pointing away from one another.

■ *Compression* squeezes the boards together. The forces are parallel, pointing toward one another.

■ *Shear* pushes the boards past one another in opposite directions. The forces are parallel, but not aligned as they are with tension and compression.

■ *Racking* rotates or bends the boards around one another.

> **MORE** *INFO*
>
> Of the four types of stress, racking is the most destructive. It bends one wooden member like a lever, magnifying the force and popping the joint.

STRESS SYSTEMS

Additionally, the joints in a woodworking project work together in what engineers call a *stress system*. Each joint helps to distribute the load to other parts of the assembly. In that way, several members can support a load that would be too large for any one of them individually. The compression generated by a heavy object on a table is transfered through the joinery to all four legs, so each leg supports just a

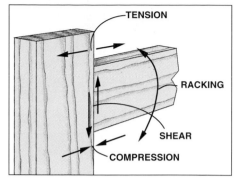

*Four types of stress will tear a wood joint apart — **tension, compression, shear**, and **racking.***

quarter of the weight. When you push against the edge of a table, the racking force is transferred to the adjoining aprons, and from them to all four legs – all the parts share the load. Consequently, the joinery makes the assembled table much stronger than the individual parts by themselves.

SEE *ALSO:*
[1] Making Wood Joints   230
[2] The Nature of Wood   2

*The joinery in a woodworking system comprises a **stress system**. The joints transfer the load from one part to another, redistributing it so no one part is stressed to the breaking point.*

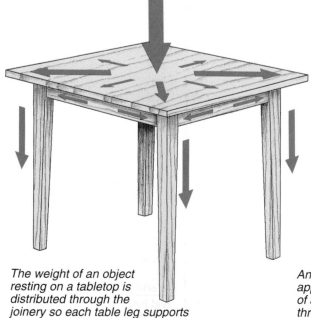

The weight of an object resting on a tabletop is distributed through the joinery so each table leg supports just a quarter of the burden.

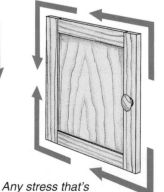

The action of opening and closing a drawer generates stress at the drawer front. The corner joints distribute this load to the other parts of the assembly.

Any stress that's applied to one member of a paneled door is transferred through the corner joints and shared by the other members.

The weight of the books on the shelves of a bookcase are transferred to the supports through the joinery.

DESIGNING FOR STRENGTH

When selecting the joints for an assembly, consider the entire system. Don't just imagine the stress that will be placed on a single joint; consider how that stress will be distributed to the surrounding members.

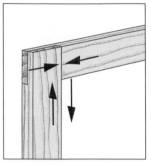

*Even before it's glued or fastened, a **butt joint** will withstand compression.*

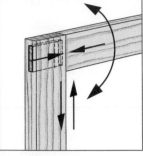

*A **lap joint** will withstand compression and shear in one direction.*

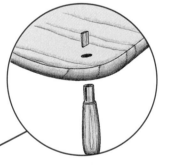

*A **mortise-and-tenon joint** will withstand compression, shear, and racking.*

■ As much as possible, pick joints that will withstand the anticipated stress even before they're glued or fastened. Don't depend on the glue or the hardware alone to hold the joint together.

■ Orient the wood grain properly to withstand and transfer the stress. Remember, wood is *strongest along the grain*. In a **mortise-and-tenon joint**[1], for example, the tenon is much stronger when the wood grain runs through its length. When the grain is perpendicular to the length, the tenon can be easily broken.

■ Use a suitable material. If a joint must stand up to heavy use, the parts must be made from a hard, durable wood. The legs and rungs of **turned chairs**[2], for example, are traditionally made from hard maple, birch, or hickory so the joints will withstand the weight of a person.

■ Size the parts in the assembly properly. A thick shelf is less likely to sag than a thin one; a fat tenon will take more abuse than a slender one.

■ When a large part would look clunky or out of **proportion**[3], use several smaller ones. Turned chairs often use several thin spindles (and multiple mortises and tenons) in place of a solid back attached by a single joint.

■ Add bracework, particularly if the joint will be subjected to large racking forces. The rungs and stretchers on a turned chair brace the legs and keep them from splaying.

The back is composed of many slender spindles. Although no one spindle is strong enough to keep from breaking when you lean back, together they can withstand the load.

The thick seat may be made from pine or poplar, but the slender legs, rungs, and spindles are turned from hard maple, birch, or hickory. The racking forces would compress softer woods, loosening the joints.

The legs are braced by rungs and stretchers to help control racking.

Most of the parts are joined by round mortises and tenons to resist the racking forces that are generated when you sit in the chair.

The wood grain for the turned parts is as straight as possible for maximum strength.

*The traditional **Windsor chair,** a centuries-old design, is a classic example of a woodworking assembly that's engineered for strength. Although many of the parts appear delicate, the assembly is remarkably strong.*

Crafted by George Ainley, Perkinsville, VT; photo by Rich Frutchey

LET THE WOOD MOVE

Wood moves with changes in **relative humidity**[4], expanding and shrinking with the seasons. This motion will stress a wood joint like any other force. Consequently, you must plan the joinery to accommodate or control it. If you don't, the joints will eventually fail. In fact, more joints fail from the stress generated by wood movement than from any other cause.

When considering its motion, remember that wood moves in three directions. You can disregard the longitudinal movement (parallel to the wood grain) because it's so small, but you must accommodate the tangential movement (across **flat grain**[5]) and the radial movement (across **quarter grain**[5]). Additionally, it's important to remember that the radial movement is generally half of the tangential movement.

COPING WITH WOOD MOVEMENT

There are several important joinery techniques that either allow the wood to move or limit its movement without unduly stressing the assembly.

■ Orient the wood grain so the parts move in unison – align the wood grain *and* the annual rings.

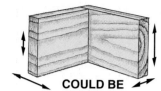

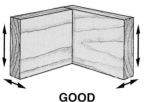

POOR
The wood grain is mis-aligned, so the two boards move in different directions, stressing the joint.

COULD BE BETTER
The wood grain is aligned, but the annual rings are not. The boards expand in the same direction but not at the same rate.

GOOD
Both the wood grain and the annual rings are properly aligned.

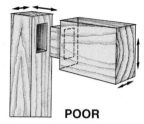

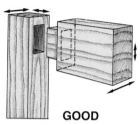

POOR
The wood grain is aligned as well as possible, but the annual rings are not. Tangential movement in the tenon is opposed to longitudinal movement in the sides of the mortise, the broadest surface in the joint.

COULD BE BETTER
The arrangement of the annual rings is slightly better — radial movement in the tenon is opposed to longitudinal movement in the mortise.

GOOD
This is the best possible arrangement with the least amount of stress — radial movement in the tenon is opposed to radial movement in the mortise.

The members of a wooden joint should expand and contract in the same direction. Additionally, the tangential and radial planes should be arranged so they don't fight each other.

MYTH CONCEPTIONS

GLUE STEPS Joinery that has been planed and sanded flush sometimes develops *glue steps* — tiny changes in the surface levels from one board to another. These are especially noticeable in tabletops where two or more boards are joined edge to edge. The common misconception is that these steps are caused by improper gluing technique, but they are actually the result of uneven wood movement. Sometimes a craftsman fails to **shop-dry**[6] the lumber. The individual boards have different moisture contents when they are joined, and the moister boards move more than the drier ones. Or the craftsman glues flat grain to quarter grain, opposing tangential movement to radial movement. The flat-grain edge moves at a different rate than the quarter-grain edge. In both cases, a step results.

12% MOISTURE CONTENT **10% MOISTURE CONTENT**
When two boards of different moisture contents are joined edge to edge...

8% MOISTURE CONTENT **8% MOISTURE CONTENT**
...the board with higher moisture shrinks more, and a glue step develops.

QUARTERSAWN FLAT-SAWN
Something similar happens when you join boards with different grain orientation.

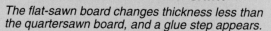

QUARTERSAWN FLAT-SAWN
The flat-sawn board changes thickness less than the quartersawn board, and a glue step appears.

■ Orient the grain so the parts move as little as possible. When stability is critical, use quartersawn stock since wood moves less across quarter grain than across flat grain. Or, rip flat-grain lumber into narrow strips, rotate the strips 90 degrees, and glue them back together with the quarter grain showing.

■ When you must fasten two boards together with opposing grain directions, make sure the boards are as narrow as possible. As a rule of thumb, most craftsmen put a *3-inch* limit on the width of lap joints, mortise-and-tenon joints, and other joints in which the grain directions of the members cannot be parallel.

■ Use floating joints to let the wood move. When you must join a wide board to another with the grain directions opposed, do *not* glue the boards to each other. Instead, let one board float in the assembly, free to expand and contract. There are several ways to do this. For example, cut a groove or a slot in one board and rest the other board in the recess – this is the principle behind **frame-and-panel construction**[1]

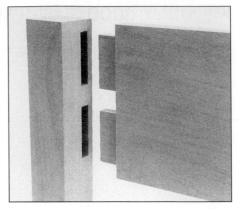

"Butcher-block" countertops and table tops are glued up from strips of wood for maximum stability. Each strip is turned so the quarter grain shows on the face of the assembly. Since wood expands and contracts across quarter grain only half as much as it does across flat grain, this reduces the total movement.

When you must glue two boards together with the grain directions opposed, limit the width of the adjoining surfaces to 3 inches to keep the stress at a minimum. I prefer to split wide tenons into two or more smaller ones. This reduces the stress in the joint without significantly reducing the strength of the tenon or the area of the gluing surface.

PRO*TIP*

Use small nails to apply moldings when the grain direction of the molding is opposed to the board to which it's applied. The nails bend slightly as the wood moves, letting the parts float.

Also remember that wood often changes shape as it moves. Although you cannot prevent the wood from moving, you can often keep it from deforming. For example, when you're making a table, a well-placed brace or fastener will prevent the table top from cupping.

*In a frame-and-panel door, the panel "floats" in the frame. It rests in grooves in the inside edges of the frame members, but **it's not glued in place**. It's free to expand and contract, and it's cut slightly smaller than the available space so it has room to move.*

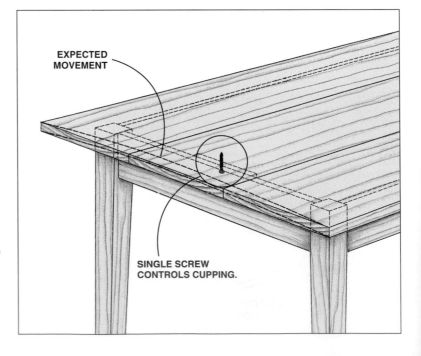

EXPECTED MOVEMENT

SINGLE SCREW CONTROLS CUPPING.

When gluing up a wide table top from plain-sawn boards, turn the boards so the annual rings cup up. Because wood tends to cup in the opposite direction of its rings, the table top will want to rise in the middle. Prevent this by fastening the top to the aprons near the middle of the assembly.

PROVIDE A GOOD GLUING SURFACE OR ANCHOR

Most wooden assemblies are either glued together or fastened with hardware. In a **glue joint**[2], the mating parts provide surfaces for the glue to grip. In a fastened joint, they provide anchors for the fasteners.

MATING SURFACES OF GLUE JOINTS

The strength of a glue joint is proportional to the *amount* of gluing surface. The larger the surface area, the stronger the joint. A finger joint is stronger than a butt joint because the fingers provide more gluing surface.

This isn't the whole story, however. There are several ways to glue one board to another, and some produce a stronger joint than others, depending on the orientation of the wood grain. You can glue wood:

■ **Long grain**[3] to long grain, with the grain parallel. This is the strongest arrangement.

■ Long grain to long grain, with the grain perpendicular. This is strong, but the parts move in opposite directions, stressing the joint.

■ Long grain to **end grain**[3]. This is fairly weak because the end grain on one surface absorbs much of the glue, "starving" the joint.

■ End grain to end grain. This is the weakest arrangement because both surfaces absorb the glue.

When choosing joinery, consider both the amount of gluing surface and the type of grain. Look for joints with a high proportion of long-grain-to-long-grain surfaces. If the mating long-grain surfaces are perpendicular, don't make them too broad. (Remember, 3 inches is about the limit.) Also consider using dowels, splines, or biscuits to increase the long-grain gluing surfaces.

> ### PRO*TIP*
>
> To increase the strength of an end-grain glue joint, seal the ends. Paint them with a thin coat of glue; wait 30 minutes; apply more glue and clamp the parts together. The first coat of glue prevents the second from being absorbed.

MATING SURFACES OF FASTENED JOINTS

When designing a fastened joint, the grain is important for a different reason. **Nails**[4] and **screws**[5] hold better when driven into face grain (perpendicular to the grain direc-

Much of the reason that a finger joint is stronger and more durable than a butt joint is that it offers a great deal more gluing surface.

tion) than when driven into end grain (parallel to the grain direction). If you must drive them into end grain, use longer fasteners than you would otherwise. The extra length helps hold them tight.

Also make sure there is enough material in the joint to anchor the fasteners properly. If the wood is too narrow or thin, it will split easily.

*The **strength of a glue joint** depends on both the amount of gluing surface and the orientation of the wood grain.*

*The **strongest** glue bond occurs between long-grain surfaces with the grain parallel.*

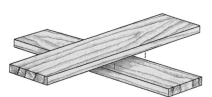

*The **second-strongest** glue bond occurs between long-grain surfaces with the grain perpendicular.*

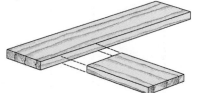

*The **second-weakest** glue bond occurs between long-grain and end-grain surfaces.*

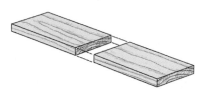

*The **weakest** glue bond occurs between two end-grain surfaces.*

*When **fastening a joint with nails**, drive the nails at different angles to lock the parts together.*

*In this butt joint, the nails are driven at **alternating angles,** up and down.*

*In this miter joint, the nails are driven at **right angles** to one another.*

TYPES OF WOODWORKING JOINTS

Once you understand the principles of wood joinery, it's much easier to sort through the choices. There are hundreds of ways to fit one board to another, and some of the most common woodworking joints are shown here. These are organized into four broad categories.

SIMPLE JOINTS

Most **simple joints**[1] are made by making a single cut in each of the adjoining parts. There are three types – *primary, housed,* and *halved.*

REINFORCED JOINTS

A **reinforced joint**[2] joins two boards with a third part such as a dowel or spline.

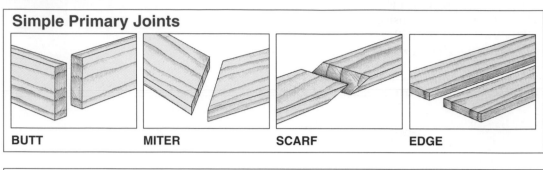

Simple Primary Joints

BUTT   MITER   SCARF   EDGE

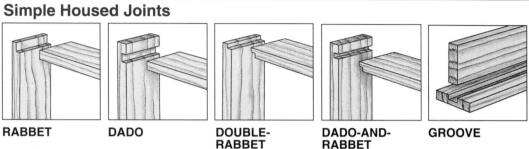

Simple Housed Joints

RABBET   DADO   DOUBLE-RABBET   DADO-AND-RABBET   GROOVE

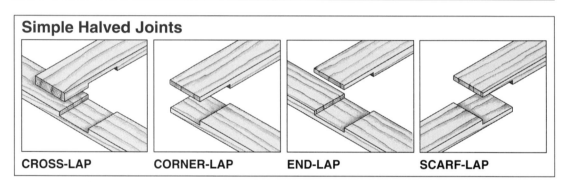

Simple Halved Joints

CROSS-LAP   CORNER-LAP   END-LAP   SCARF-LAP

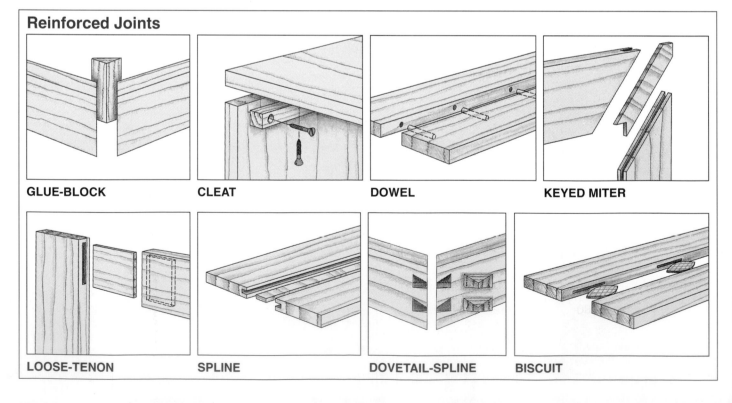

Reinforced Joints

GLUE-BLOCK   CLEAT   DOWEL   KEYED MITER

LOOSE-TENON   SPLINE   DOVETAIL-SPLINE   BISCUIT

MORTISE-AND-TENON JOINTS

In a **mortise-and-tenon joint**[3], one part is cut with an extension (a *tenon*) and the other with a recess to fit that extension (a *mortise*).

INTERLOCKING JOINTS

The adjoining parts in an **interlocking joint**[4] have multiple tenons that form interlocking extensions and recesses.

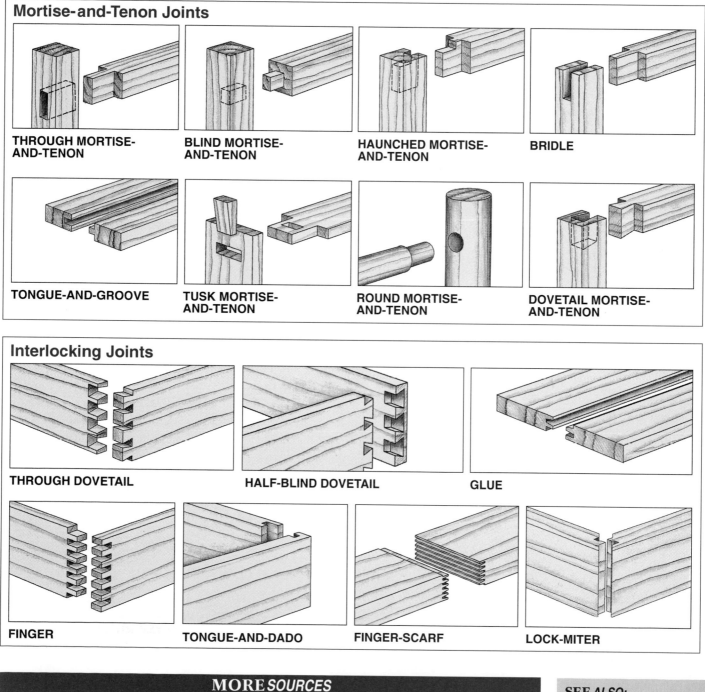

Mortise-and-Tenon Joints

THROUGH MORTISE-AND-TENON

BLIND MORTISE-AND-TENON

HAUNCHED MORTISE-AND-TENON

BRIDLE

TONGUE-AND-GROOVE

TUSK MORTISE-AND-TENON

ROUND MORTISE-AND-TENON

DOVETAIL MORTISE-AND-TENON

Interlocking Joints

THROUGH DOVETAIL

HALF-BLIND DOVETAIL

GLUE

FINGER

TONGUE-AND-DADO

FINGER-SCARF

LOCK-MITER

MORE SOURCES

Understanding Wood,
  by R. Bruce Hoadley,
Taunton Press, 1980

Wood Joiner's Handbook,
  by Sam Allen,
Sterling Press, 1990

Joining Wood,
  by Nick Engler,
Rodale Press, 1992

SEE ALSO:

[1] Making Simple Joints 232
[2] Making Reinforced
   Joints 234
[3] Making Mortise-and-Tenon
   Joints 238
[4] Making Interlocking
   Joints 244

Furniture Construction

The craft of furnituremaking incorporates every major woodworking material and method.

For almost five thousand years, woodworking and furniture have developed hand in hand. Furnituremaking incorporates every major woodworking material and assembly method. Consequently, a working knowledge of furniture construction is invaluable no matter what kind of woodworking you do.

METHODS OF CONSTRUCTION

Although there are hundreds of furniture forms, they all use similar assemblies, based on just four methods of construction:

■ *Box construction* joins the boards that make up a box, chest, or drawer. The four sides are attached at the corners, while the bottom and top are captured in a **floating joint**[1]

■ *Frame-and-panel construction* lets wide panels move without stressing an assembly. The panels float in grooves in the rails and stiles.

■ *Case construction* joins the sides, back, top, shelves, and frame members of cupboards and cabinets.

■ *Leg-and-rail construction* connects the legs of a table or chair to stretchers, aprons, and seats, typically using **mortises and tenons**[2]

Often, a piece of furniture combines several methods of construction. In **chests of drawers**[3], for example, the drawers are box constructions and the enclosure is a case construction.

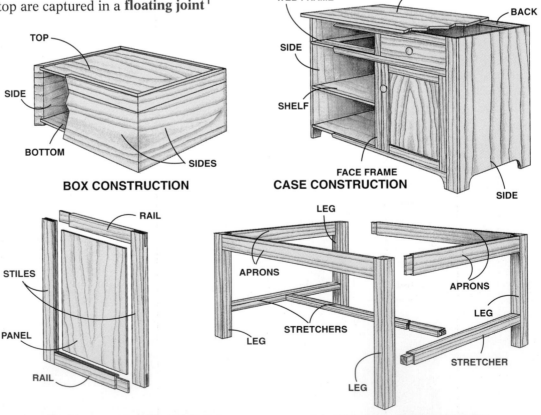

BOX CONSTRUCTION

CASE CONSTRUCTION

FRAME-AND-PANEL CONSTRUCTION

LEG-AND-RAIL CONSTRUCTION

TABLES

Although there are tables for every conceivable purpose, when you boil a table design down to its essence, it's just a flat surface (a table top) supported at a comfortable height and angle for whatever activity you have in mind – eating, writing, working, and so on.

TABLE TOPS

There are three common types of table tops.

■ A *slab top* is fashioned from a single wide board, several boards glued edge to edge, or a sheet of material such as plywood.

■ A *folding top* consists of one or more "leaves" hinged to a slab. With the leaves folded, the table occupies less space than a same-size slab top.

■ An *extension top* has detached or sliding leaves. Often, the top is split into two halves that pull apart so you can insert the leaves between them.

TABLE SUPPORTS

Additionally, there are three ways to support a top.

■ In a leg-and-apron table, several legs are joined by aprons. The top rests on this assembly.

■ In a pedestal table, the feet are joined to a central post and the top rests on the post.

■ In a trestle table, the top rests across trestles, like a plank laid across sawhorses. Often, the trestles are joined by rails.

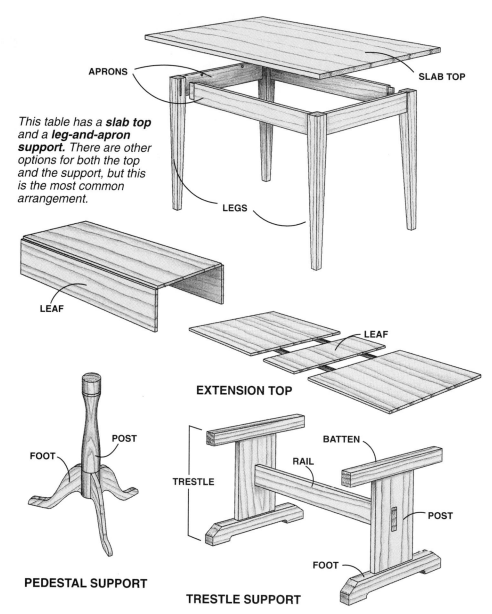

APRONS

SLAB TOP

LEGS

This table has a slab top and a leg-and-apron support. There are other options for both the top and the support, but this is the most common arrangement.

LEAF

LEAF

EXTENSION TOP

POST

FOOT

PEDESTAL SUPPORT

BATTEN

RAIL

TRESTLE

POST

FOOT

TRESTLE SUPPORT

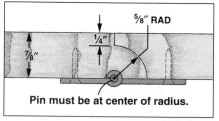

⅝″ RAD

¼″

⅞″

Pin must be at center of radius.

Drop-leaf hinges *join the leaves to the fixed portion of a folding top. They are commonly used with a rule joint, as shown.*

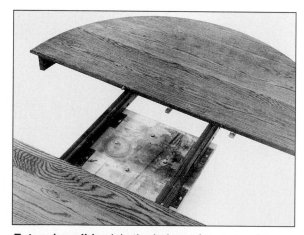

Extension slides *join the halves of an extension top, allowing you to pull them apart to insert leaves. When the top is supported by a pedestal, use* ***equalizer slides*** *— as you pull on one half of the table top, the other moves the same distance in the opposite direction.*

Table clips *fasten a table top to a supporting assembly yet still allow it to expand and contract. Cut a groove in the inside face of the aprons or battens, and fasten the clips to the underside of the top so they hook into grooves.*

SIZING A TABLE

Suitable dimensions for a table depend on its function. Size the piece to make it useful for its intended purpose.

■ *Dining tables* should be 27 to 30 inches high. Allow 23 to 26 inches of elbow room and 12 to 15 inches of space in front of each person. Also provide 18 to 24 inches of toe room under the table, and place the table legs and other supports where people won't bump into them. The bottom edges of the aprons should be no lower than 24 inches above the floor to provide adequate knee clearance.

■ *Worktables*, such as **workbenches**[1], may be anywhere from 30 to 40 inches high depending on the type of work, although most are between 34 and 36 inches. The tops can be any size, but most are 15 to 30 inches wide and 30 to 72 inches long – large enough to hold the work but small enough that you can reach everything on the surface easily. Since you normally stand at a worktable, knee clearance is not a consideration. Toe space is minimal – allow the top to overhang the aprons 2 to 4 inches.

■ The dimensions of *occasional tables* and *specialty tables* depend on their use. Remember, if you must sit at these tables, they should offer adequate toe space and knee clearance.

STANDARD TABLE DIMENSIONS

The following dimensions are averages, intended as guidelines only. Use them as a jumping-off point for designing your own tables.

	Seats	Height	Width/Dia.	Length
DINING TABLES				
Square	2	27"–30"	24"–26"	24"–26"
	4	27"–30"	30"–32"	30"–32"
	8	27"–30"	48"–50"	48"–50"
Rectangular	2	27"–30"	24"–26"	30"–32"
	6	27"–30"	30"–36"	66"–72"
	8	27"–30"	36"–42"	86"–96"
Oval	4	27"–30"	28"–32"	42"–48"
	6	27"–30"	32"–36"	60"–66"
	8	27"–30"	48"–52"	72"–78"
Round	2	27"–30"	24"–26" dia.	
	4	27"–30"	30"–32" dia.	
	6	27"–30"	42"–45" dia.	
	8	27"–30"	62"–66" dia.	
WORKTABLES				
Food preparation		34"–36"	23"–24"	30"–72"
Serving		36"–42"	15"–18"	42"–60"
Workbench		30"–40"	24"–30"	30"–72"
OCCASIONAL TABLES				
Coffee table		15"–18"	22"–30"	30"–60"
End table		18"–24"	18"–24"	18"–24"
Hall table		34"–36"	16"–20"	36"–72"
Nightstand		24"–30"	18"–20"	18"–20"
Side table		18"–24"	18"–20"	24"–28"
Candlestand		24"–32"	15"–24"	15"–24"
SPECIALTY TABLES				
Child's table		20"–22"	18"–22"	26"–30"
Computer table		25"–28"	22"–30"	36"–60"
Drafting table		32"–44"	23"–44"	31"–72"
Dressing table		29"–30"	18"–22"	40"–48"
Game table		28"–30"	30"–32"	30"–32"
Writing table		28"–30"	20"–24"	36"–42"

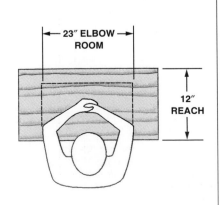

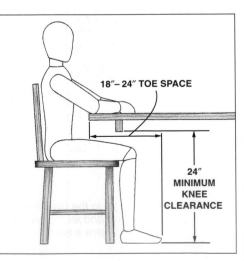

*When you design a dining table, you must provide adequate **reach, elbow room, toe space,** and **knee clearance** for each person you want to seat. Additionally, the table top should be a comfortable **height** above the floor. This height depends on both the height of the chair seats and the feeling you want to create. The higher the table and the chairs, the more formal they feel.*

23" ELBOW ROOM

12" REACH

18"–24" TOE SPACE

24" MINIMUM KNEE CLEARANCE

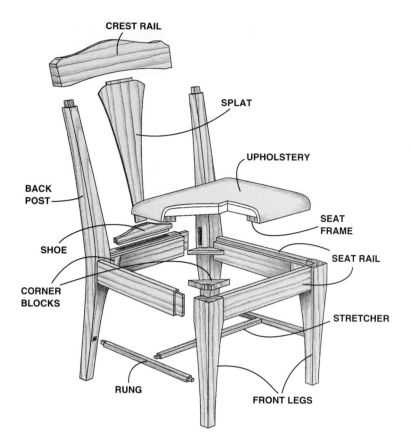

CREST RAIL

SPLAT

UPHOLSTERY

BACK
POST

SEAT
FRAME

SHOE

SEAT RAIL

CORNER
BLOCKS

STRETCHER

RUNG

FRONT LEGS

*This dining chair is made in the **joiner's tradition.** The members of the supporting frame are mostly rectangular and joined with square mortises and tenons. It has a **frame seat** — an upholstered frame supported by four rails.*

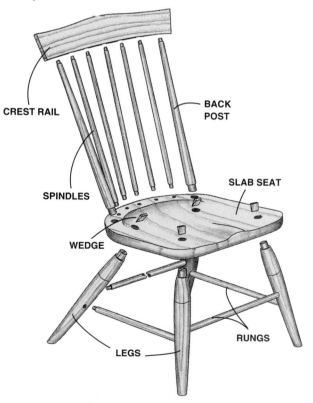

CREST RAIL

BACK
POST

SPINDLES

SLAB SEAT

WEDGE

LEGS

RUNGS

*A Windsor chair is made in the **turner's tradition.** The frame members are mostly turned round and joined with round mortises and tenons. Traditionally, Windsors have a **slab seat** scooped from a solid block of wood.*

CHAIRS

Like tables, chairs have two major component assemblies – the *seat* and the supporting *frame,* including the legs, rungs, stretchers, and back.

CHAIR SEATS

There are two common methods to fashion a chair seat.

■ Cut the seat from a solid slab of wood. Windsor chair *slab seats* are traditionally sculpted or scooped to fit your backsides. Scooped seats are known as saddles.

■ Attach the seat to the chair frame. *Frame seats* incorporate four rails, joined at the ends. The seat is often a pliable material, such as cloth or leather, stretched over the frame. Or, it may be an upholstered board that rests on the frame members.

CHAIR FRAMES

There are also two ways to make a chair frame.

■ Cut the legs, rails, and other parts (roughly) rectangular, and join them with **square mortises and tenons**[2]. This is the *joiner's tradition* of chairmaking.

■ Turn the legs, rails, and other parts round, and join them with **round mortises and tenons**[2] This is the *turner's tradition* of chairmaking.

CHAIR MATERIALS

The wood species used to build a chair is crucial, more so than in any other woodworking project. The joinery is subjected to the worst kinds of stress; many surfaces suffer continual abrasion. The wood must be able to stand up to the punishment, or the chair won't last.

Always use a hard wood (a species with a fairly high **specific gravity**[3]) for legs, posts, rails, and other frame members. Ash, beech, birch, cherry, hickory, maple, oak, and walnut are all good picks. Use lighter, softer woods such as pine, poplar, and mahogany for the seat and other thick parts. If your design includes bent parts, select **woods that bend**[4] easily – ash, birch, hickory, maple, and oak are traditional choices.

SIZING A CHAIR

More than any other project, a chair must fit a person *comfortably*. To design a comfortable chair:

■ Make the seat slightly wider at the front than at the back.

■ Adjust the seat height to allow the occupant's feet to rest flat on the floor.

■ Slant the chair back *slightly* (5 to 15 degrees for most chairs) to prevent it from pressing against the shoulder blades.

■ Don't make the seat so low or tilt the back so far that the occupant has trouble getting into and out of the chair. Make the seat level or sloped slightly backwards so the occupant doesn't slide forward. As the slant of the back increases, it becomes more important to give the seat some slope.

■ If the occupant must sit for long periods of time, cushion the seat. A frame seat is more comfortable than a slab seat; an upholstered seat is more comfortable than a frame seat.

■ Create an opening in the chair back where it meets the seat to make room for the buttocks.

■ If the chair has arms, position them so they support the occupant's arms without making it necessary to raise his or her shoulders.

It's impossible to design a single chair that will fit everyone for every occasion. The optimum size for a chair depends on both the size of the occupant and what the person's doing while seated. For this reason, there are subtle but important differences in the sizes and configurations of side chairs, arm chairs, easy chairs, and rockers. Refer to the chart of "Standard Chair Dimensions" below for guidelines.

MORE *INFO*

A child's chair is built to the same proportions as an adult's, but about two-thirds the size. On the average, the seat is 13 inches high, 14 inches wide, and 13 inches deep. The back is 24 inches high.

STANDARD CHAIR DIMENSIONS

The following dimensions are averages, intended as guidelines only. Use them as a jumping-off point for designing your own chairs.

SIDE CHAIR

Seat height	14"–19" (16"–17" average)
Seat width (front)	17"–18"
Seat width (back)	15"–15½"
Seat depth	16"–17"
Back slant	5°–15° off vertical 90°–105° from seat (95° average)
Overall height	28"–35" (32" average)

ARM CHAIR

Seat height	14"–19" (16"–17" average)
Seat width (front)	19"–20"
Seat width (back)	16½"–18½"
Seat depth	16"–17"
Arm height	8" above seat
Arm length	14"–15"
Back slant	5°–15° off vertical 90°–105° from seat (95° average)
Overall height	28"–35" (32" average)

EASY CHAIR

Seat height	13"–18" (15½" average)
Seat width (front)	19"–20"
Seat width (back)	16½"–18½"
Seat depth	18"–20"
Arm height	8" above seat
Arm length	16"–18"
Back slant	5°–30° off vertical 95°–115° from seat (105° average)
Overall height	25"–39" (30" average)

ROCKER

Seat height (front)*	15½"–16"
Seat height (back)*	12"–12½"
Seat width (front)	19"–22"
Seat width (back)	16½"–19½"
Seat depth	16"–18"
Arm height	8" above seat
Arm length	14"–16"
Back slant	25° off vertical (at rest) 95°–115° from seat (105° average)
Seat slant	10°–15° (at rest)
Rocker length	30"–35"
Rocker radius	40"–50"
Overall height	40" average

Above the floor with the rocker at rest.

ADJUSTING FOR HEIGHT

The most comfortable seat height changes with the height of the occupant. If you are designing a chair for a specific person, adjust the seat height accordingly.

OCCUPANT'S HEIGHT	SEAT HEIGHT
60"	14"
63"	15"
66"	16"
69"	17"
72"	18"

BEDS

A bed is a large wooden frame that supports bedding, such as a mattress and box springs or a futon. The frame rests on four legs or *bed posts*. Typically, there is a large *headboard* at the head of the frame and a smaller *footboard* at the foot.

BED JOINERY AND HARDWARE

Because a bed is so large, it's made to be knocked down. Otherwise, it would be extremely difficult to get it through a bedroom door. Typically, the frame comes apart into four components – two *bedsteads* (the headboard and footboard) and two *bed rails*. Traditionally, bed rails were attached to the bedsteads with **mortise-and-tenon joints**[1] and held in place with *bed bolts*. The bolts were driven through the posts and into nuts embedded in the rails. As the bolts were tightened, they drew tenons on the ends of the rails into mortises in the posts.

Today, craftsmen commonly use interlocking *bed rail fasteners*. Each fastener consists of a *bracket* and a *standard*. The bracket is mounted on the end of a rail and hooks into the standard, which is **mortised**[2] into a post.

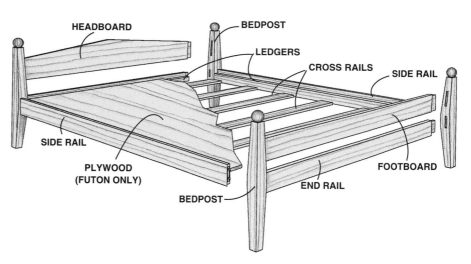

A bed is a large knockdown frame that holds a mattress or a futon.

SIZING A BED

Bed frames are usually designed to hold standard-size mattresses, box springs, and futons. The *interior* dimensions of the frame should be 1 inch wider and 2 inches longer than the bedding to make room for the bedclothes. When the bed is assembled, the top of the mattress should be about 24 inches above the floor. Futons are typically held lower, 12 to 15 inches above floor level. Refer to the chart of "Standard Bed Dimensions" below for guidelines.

*Old-time beds were assembled with **bed bolts**. The heads of these bolts were sometimes hidden by a decorative cover.*

*Contemporary bed frames are held together with interlocking **bed rail fasteners**.*

STANDARD BED DIMENSIONS

Bed frames are designed to support mattresses, box springs, and futons with ample room for bedclothes. Although these dimensions are based on standard bedding sizes, the actual measurements may vary slightly with the manufacturer.

WIDTH AND LENGTH

Bedding Style	Interior Frame Width (Bedding Width)	Interior Frame Length (Bedding Length)
Crib	28″ (27″)	55″ (54″)
Single	37″ (36″)	77″ (75″)
Twin	40″ (39″)	77″ or 82″ (75″ or 80″)
Double	55″ (54″)	77″ or 82″ (75″ or 80″)
Queen	61″ (60″)	82″ or 86″ (80″ or 84″)
King	77″ (76″)	82″ or 86″ (80″ or 84″)

HEIGHT

Bedding Type	Height above Floor	Thickness of Bedding
Mattress	24″–27″	7″ each for mattress and box springs (14″ total)
Futon	12″–15″	3″–6″
Crib Mattress	31″–39″ *	

Cribs should be designed so the height of the mattress is adjustable.

BOXES AND CHESTS

In their simplest form, boxes and chests are made from just six boards – four *sides*, a *bottom*, and a *lid*, all assembled with common **box construction**[1] methods. The sides are rigidly joined at the corners, while the bottom rests either in grooves or on a ledge so it can move independently of the other parts. The lid is either fitted or hinged to the assembly so it opens easily. Large chests often rest on a *frame base* or *bracket feet*.

WOOD GRAIN IN BOXES

There are many joints you can use to join the corners of a box or chest, from simple miters to intricate dovetails. However, the actual joinery isn't as critical as the orientation of the wood grain and annual rings. The sides must move in unison so there is no stress in the corner joints. Additionally, the annual rings should cup toward the outside of the assembly. Remember, **plain-sawn stock**[2] has a tendency to cup in the opposite direction of its rings. If the rings cup in, gaps may develop at the corners.

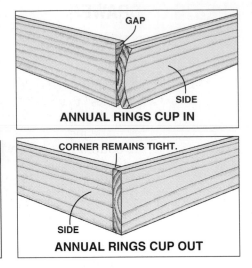

ANNUAL RINGS CUP IN

GAP
SIDE

ANNUAL RINGS CUP OUT

CORNER REMAINS TIGHT.
SIDE

> **PRO*TIP***
>
> When making a decorative box, cut the sides from the same board. Join them so the wood grain appears continuous, as if you had bent the board around the corners.

SIZING BOXES AND CHESTS

A box or chest can be built to any size. For some common pieces of box-constructed furniture, the range of possible dimensions is very broad, as the chart of "Standard Box and Chest Dimensions" below shows. Practically, a chest should be big enough to hold the items you want to store with enough room left over to get your hands around or under those items. However, it shouldn't be so deep that you can't easily reach the items in the *till* (as the inside of a chest is called). Nor should it be so large that it's difficult to move.

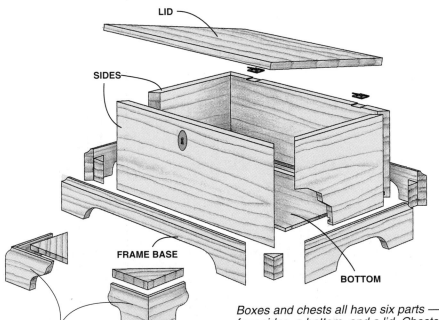

LID
SIDES
FRAME BASE
BRACKET FEET
BOTTOM

Boxes and chests all have six parts — four sides, a bottom, and a lid. Chests sometimes rest on a base or feet.

*Lids are commonly attached to their boxes with **hinges.** The hinges on this stationery box are mortised into the lid and side so only their knuckles show when the box is closed.*

*Lids don't have to be attached with hardware; some are simply **fitted** to their boxes. The fitted lid on this knife box slides in and out of grooves in the sides.*

STANDARD BOX AND CHEST DIMENSIONS

The measurements given are intended as guidelines only — boxes and chests can be built to any practical size.

	HEIGHT	LENGTH	WIDTH
Blanket Chest	15"–24"	30"–60"	12"–24"
Jewelry Box	6"–12"	12"–24"	8"–16"
Lap Desk	3"–8"	16"–24"	12"–16"

CHESTS OF DRAWERS

Chests of drawers evolved from chests. Folks found it difficult to retrieve items that were buried at the bottom of the till, so they began to install "drawing boxes" that could be pulled out horizontally from the chest. At first, they made just one drawing box at the bottom of a chest. Then they added another and another until the chest was nothing but an enclosure for drawing boxes or *drawers*.

DRAWER CASES

As the chest filled with drawers, it became a **case**[1]. A drawer case is a rectangular assembly with openings at the front. Typically, it consists of two *sides*, a *top*, a *back*, a *face frame*, and several horizontal members such as *web frames*, *shelves*, or *rails*. Commonly, these horizontal parts rest in **dadoes**[3] in the sides. The back fits in **rabbets**[3] along the back edges of the sides.

DRAWER JOINERY

Drawers are simple boxes, open at the top. The drawer *fronts* join the *sides* with lock joints, dovetails, or other sturdy joinery that will withstand the stress of being pushed and pulled. There isn't as much stress at the back of the drawer, so the joints between the *backs* and the sides are usually simpler, often just dadoes. The drawer *bottoms* float in grooves. In some designs, drawers have separate *faces* attached to the fronts.

Drawer construction also depends on how the drawer fits the case. A drawer may be *inset* so the front surface is flush with the front of the case. The front can also *overlay* the case, partially covering the case parts. Or, the drawer may be *lipped* – that is, the front is rabbeted all around the perimeter so only the shoulders of the rabbet fit inside the drawer opening. The lips created by the rabbet overlay the case.

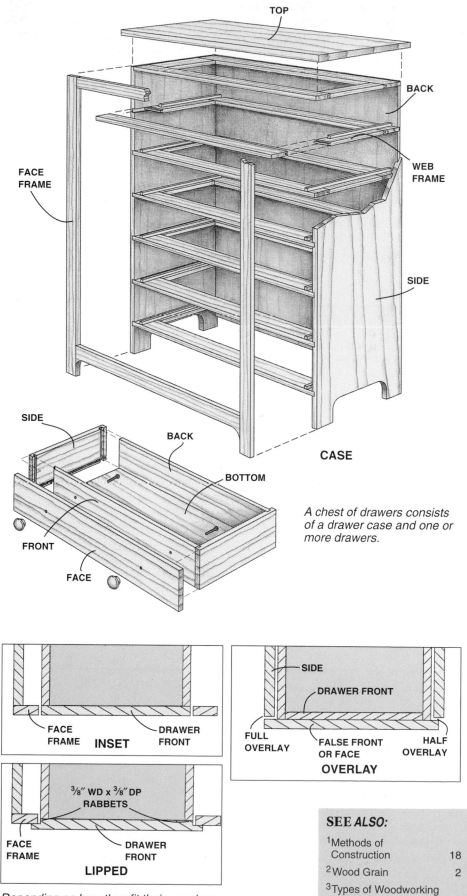

A chest of drawers consists of a drawer case and one or more drawers.

INSET

LIPPED

³⁄₈″ WD x ³⁄₈″ DP RABBETS

OVERLAY

FULL OVERLAY   FALSE FRONT OR FACE   HALF OVERLAY

*Depending on how they fit their openings, drawers may be **inset, overlay,** or **lipped.***

HANGING DRAWERS

Drawers are *hung* in a case, either supported from the bottom or suspended by their sides. To support a drawer from the bottom, let it rest on L-shaped *support brackets* attached to the case sides. Or, use *web frames* dadoed into the case sides or *bottom-mounted slides* that span the distance between the front and back of the case. To suspend a drawer from its sides, attach *drawer guides* to the case sides and cut grooves in the drawer sides to fit the guides. Or, use *side-mounted slides*.

Metal slides[1] consist of a channel and a roller that rides inside it – the channel mounts to the case and the roller to the drawer. When using this hardware, you must build the drawers slightly smaller than their openings to allow room for it.

PRO*TIP*

When designing a project in which the drawers stack vertically, place the deepest drawers on the bottom and the shallowest on top. Otherwise, the piece will be top-heavy and may tip over.

SIZING A CHEST OF DRAWERS

Although chests of drawers may be any size, there are some practical considerations that govern their measurements. The drawers mustn't be too large – when loaded, they become too heavy to open and close easily. Nor should they be too deep – stuff gets lost near the bottom. The case shouldn't be too big to move easily, although you can build a large piece such as a highboy in two sections. Check the chart of "Standard Chest of Drawers Dimensions" below for guidelines.

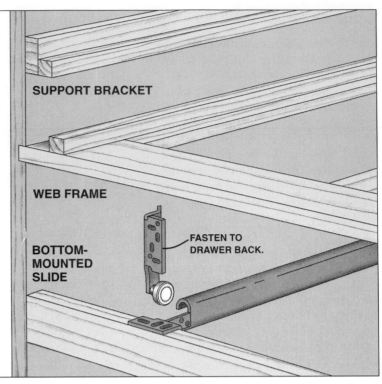

You can hang a drawer by supporting it from the bottom with a **support bracket, web frame,** or **bottom-mounted slide.**

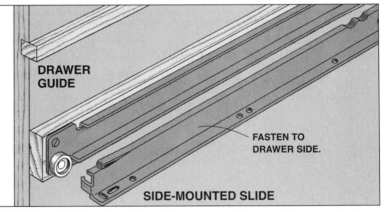

Or, suspend it from the sides with **drawer guides** or **side-mounted slides.**

STANDARD CHEST OF DRAWERS DIMENSIONS

These measurements are intended as guidelines only — chests of drawers can be built to any practical size.

	HEIGHT	WIDTH	DEPTH
Chest of Drawers	42"–56"	34"–40"	18"–21"
Bureau/Dresser	29"–34"	36"–48"	18"–24"
Double Dresser	29"–34"	60"–72"	18"–24"
Lingerie Chest	48"–54"	22"–24"	16"–18"
Highboy	80"–96"	36"–48"	21"–24"
Chest-on-Chest	72"–84"	36"–48"	18"–24"
Filing Cabinet			
Letter, 2 drawers	28"	15"	22"–28"
Legal, 2 drawers	28"	18"	22"–28"
Letter, 4 drawers	52"	15"	22"–28"
Legal, 4 drawers	52"	18"	22"–28"

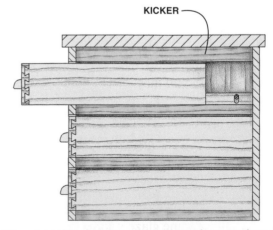

When hanging drawers, you must make sure they don't tip forward as you pull them from the case. When necessary, install kickers above the drawers to prevent tipping.

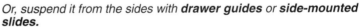

SHELVING

Every shelving unit has two things in common – horizontal *shelves* held by vertical *supports*.

TYPES OF SHELVING

Beyond that, however, there is much variety.

■ The simplest type of shelving is a *rack*. Racks have shelves, supports, perhaps a few horizontal *braces* to provide stability, and little else. The structure is open front and back.

■ Open *shelves* also have a *back* and a *face frame* to add stability. With the shelves and the supports, these parts form a simple **case**[2]

■ A *cupboard* adds solid *doors* to the case, enclosing the shelves. Dry sinks and linen presses are typical cupboards.

■ A *display case* is built in the same manner as a cupboard, but it has *glazed* (glass) doors. A bookcase is a good example.

Additionally, there are two types of shelves you can install in a shelving unit. *Fixed* shelves are joined to their supports permanently – typically, the supports are **dadoed**[3] to hold the ends of the shelves. *Adjustable* shelves rest on movable pins or brackets. You can add, remove, or change the height of adjustable shelves as needed. A shelving unit always has at least two fixed shelves – top and bottom – for stability. Tall units often have an additional fixed shelf near the middle of the assembly.

DOOR JOINERY

The doors on cupboards may be made from solid wood or sheets of plywood. More often, they are simple **frame-and-panel**[2] assemblies. The frame members are joined with **mortises and tenons**[3], and wooden panels float in the frames – you cannot see into the case. In a display case, panes of glass replace wooden panels. These panes rest in **rabbets**[3] in the inside edges of the frame members. Some glazed doors have several glass panes separated by *muntins*.

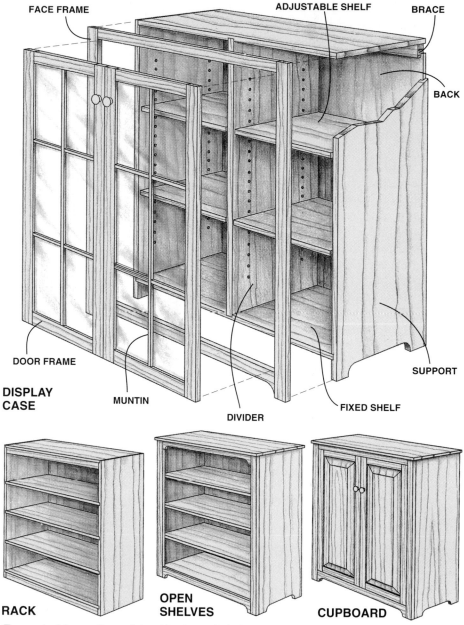

Every shelving unit consists of horizontal shelves held by vertical supports. The other parts in a bookcase add stability, versatility, protection, and decoration.

*The two most common ways to support adjustable shelves are with **shelving support pins** (left) and with **standards and brackets** (right). The standards are often inset in grooves in the shelving supports.*

Door construction also depends on how the door fits the case. Like the **drawers**[1] in a chest, a door may be *inset* so the front surface is flush with the front of the case. The front of the door can also *overlay* the case, partially covering the case parts. Or, the door may be *lipped* – rabbeted all around the perimeter so only the shoulders of the **rabbet**[2] fit inside the door opening. The lips created by the rabbet overlay the case.

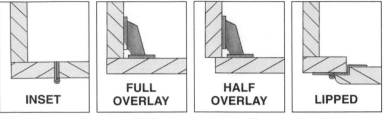

| INSET | FULL OVERLAY | HALF OVERLAY | LIPPED |

*Like drawers, doors may be **inset**, **overlay**, or **lipped**, depending on how they fit their openings.*

SIZING SHELVES

You can make a shelving unit to any size, depending on what you want to store in it. Practically, however, there are some limits. You should not make the shelves so deep or so tall that it becomes difficult to reach the objects stored on them. For these reasons, shelving is rarely over 24 inches deep or 84 inches tall.

One of the most important dimensions is the *span* of the shelves – the distance between the supports. If the span is too long, the shelves will sag. The proper span depends on the load the shelves are expected to support and the material they're made from. The stiffer the wood (the higher its **modulus of elasticity**[3]), the longer you can make the shelf span.

PRO*TIP*

When the span of the shelves is too long, break it up with *dividers* — intermediate supports between the two outside supports — to prevent sagging.

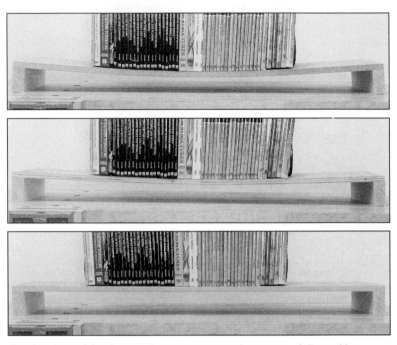

Particleboard (top) sags the most over a given span, followed by plywood (middle). Solid wood (bottom) sags the least.

STANDARD SHELVING DIMENSIONS

The size of a shelving unit depends on many factors — what you want to store on the shelves, the shelving material, and whether the unit stands on the floor or hangs on a wall. The measurements given are intended as guidelines only.

OVERALL HEIGHT

Standing unit	30"–84"
Hanging unit	30"–42"

LEVEL OF SHELVES

Highest shelf	72"–78" above floor*
Lowest shelf (standing unit)	3"–4" above floor
Lowest shelf (hanging unit)	36"–54" above floor

DEPTH OF SHELVES

Small or narrow objects	6"–8"
Books[†] or large objects	10"–12"[†]
Dishes (above counter)	12"–13"
Linens, clothes	15"–18"
Audio components	18"–20"
Video components	18"–24"
Cooking utensils (below counter)	24"–25"

SPACE BETWEEN SHELVES

Small objects/paperback books	7"–8"
Medium objects/hardcover books	10"–12"
Large objects/tall books	13"–15"

MAXIMUM SHELVING SPAN[‡]

¾"-thick particleboard	24"
¾"-thick plywood	30"
¾"-thick softwood	36"
1"-thick softwood	48"
1½"-thick softwood	66"
¾"-thick hardwood	48"
1"-thick hardwood	54"
1½"-thick hardwood	78"

To reach the shelves from a seated position, the highest shelf should be no more than 58" to 60" above the floor.
[†] *The standard depth for bookshelves is 11½".*
[‡] *Assuming the shelves must support no more than 25 pounds per running foot.*

CABINETS

Cabinets are complex case pieces that combine elements of simpler furniture, particularly **chests of drawers**[1] and **shelving**[4] units such as cupboards. In fact, cabinet construction methods borrow so much from cupboards that the terms are sometimes used interchangeably. There are subtle differences between them, however. A cabinet usually includes cupboard space (shelves enclosed by solid doors), but it also offers drawer space. Also, some shelves may be enclosed by **glazed doors**[4]. Finally, cabinets are typically formal pieces of furniture, while cupboards tend to be more utilitarian.

CABINET FORMS

Cabinets take several different forms.

■ A *low cabinet* (such as a sideboard) is less than 40 inches tall. The top is often used as a serving table.

■ A *tall cabinet* stands more than 72 inches tall. Wardrobes, armoires, corner cabinets, and most entertainment centers are all examples of tall cabinets.

■ A *step-back cabinet* is a tall piece that's divided horizontally into two sections. The top section is not as deep as the bottom, forming a step between the two. Hutches and china cabinets are step-back cabinets.

■ A *breakfront* is divided vertically into three sections. The middle section is deeper (and often taller) than the two flanking sections.

■ A *hanging cabinet* is a small cabinet that hangs on a wall. It usually has several small drawers, as well as shelves enclosed by glazed doors.

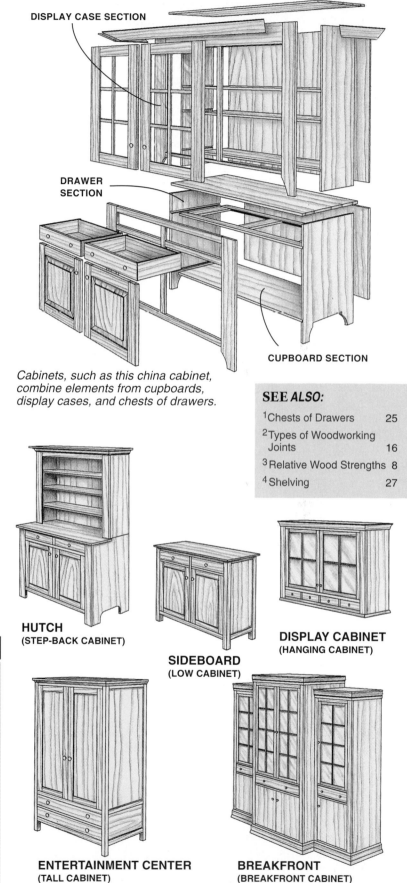

DISPLAY CASE SECTION

DRAWER SECTION

CUPBOARD SECTION

Cabinets, such as this china cabinet, combine elements from cupboards, display cases, and chests of drawers.

HUTCH
(STEP-BACK CABINET)

SIDEBOARD
(LOW CABINET)

DISPLAY CABINET
(HANGING CABINET)

ENTERTAINMENT CENTER
(TALL CABINET)

BREAKFRONT
(BREAKFRONT CABINET)

Although there are many types and sizes of cabinets, their construction is similar. They all have enclosed shelving space and drawers.

STANDARD CABINET DIMENSIONS

The measurements given are intended as guidelines only — cabinets can be built to any practical size. When sizing the shelves in cabinets, also refer to the chart of "Standard Shelving Dimensions" on page 28.

	HEIGHT	WIDTH	DEPTH
Sideboard	30"–36"	40"–72"	15"–21"
Wardrobe	72"–80"	36"–48"	18"–24"
Hutch	70"–84"	48"–60"	18"–24"*
China Cabinet	70"–84"	48"–66"	19"–24"*
Breakfront	78"–84"	48"–84"	18"–20"†
Hanging Cabinet	30"–42"	24"–36"	6"–13"

*The top sections are shallower: 10"–15" deep.
†The flanking sections are shallower: 12"–16" deep.

DESKS

Desks, as we know them, are a relatively recent invention. For hundreds of years, simple desk **boxes**[1] (such as lap desks) stored paper, ink, and other writing materials. But as literacy – and paperwork – increased, so did desks.

DESK FORMS

Today, there are many types of desks. Like cabinets, these are hybrids of several furniture forms – **shelving**[2] pieces, **chests of drawers**[3], and **tables**[4].

■ A *writing desk* is a leg-and-apron table with several drawers beneath and open shelves or a cupboard on top.

■ A *pedestal desk* is made like a trestle table. However, instead of trestles, the desk top is laid across two chests of drawers (the "pedestals"). Often, the sides and backs of the pedestals are made using **frame-and-panel construction**[5].

■ A *secretary* is a cupboard or a cabinet with a built-in writing surface. In some designs, the upper doors drop down to make the desk top. In others, they open up and the desk top folds or slides out.

■ A *computer workstation* combines a table and shelving to hold the components of a personal computer – central processing unit, keyboard, mouse, monitor, and printer – in a convenient configuration. The working surface is usually several inches lower than other desks to provide a comfortable height for using the keyboard and mouse.

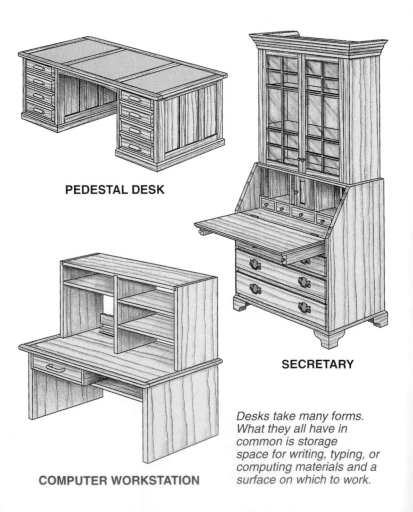

*A typical desk, such as this **writing desk,** combines elements of a table, cupboard, and chest of drawers.*

PEDESTAL DESK

COMPUTER WORKSTATION

SECRETARY

Desks take many forms. What they all have in common is storage space for writing, typing, or computing materials and a surface on which to work.

STANDARD DESK DIMENSIONS

Desk dimensions are governed by many of the same rules that apply to tables — you must provide adequate reach, elbow room, toe space, and knee clearance. (See "Sizing a Table" on page 20.) In addition, different desk forms commonly fall within standard size ranges.

	HEIGHT	WIDTH	DEPTH
Writing Desk			
Work surface	28″–30″	30″–48″	20″–30″
Shelving section	10″–36″*	30″–48″	10″–15″
Pedestal Desk			
Work surface	28″–30″	48″–72″	24″–30″
Each pedestal	28″–30″	15″–24″	24″–30″
Secretary			
Work surface	28″–30″	36″–42″	18″–24″
Shelving section	48″–54″*	36″–42″	12″–15″
Computer Workstation			
Work surface	24″–28″	24″–60″	20″–30″
Shelving section	24″–30″*	24″–60″	12″–18″

*Above work surface.

MORE *SOURCES*

Cabinetmaking and Millwork,
   by John Feirer, Bennett, 1982
*Designing Furniture from Concept
   to Shop Drawing,* by Seth Stem,
   Taunton Press, 1989
The Encyclopedia of Furniture Making,
   by Ernest Joyce, Sterling Publishing,
   1987
Furniture and Cabinet Construction,
   by William P. Spence and L. Duane
   Griffiths, Prentice Hall, 1989

Making Boxes and Chests, by
   Nick Engler, Rodale Press, 1994
Making Desks and Bookcases,
   by Nick Engler, Rodale Press, 1993
Making Spectacular Furniture for Kids,
   by Peter Sylvester, Sterling Publishing,
   1987
Making Tables and Chairs, by
   Nick Engler, Rodale Press, 1995
Working in Wood, by Ernest Scott,
   Putnam Pub. Group, 1980

DESIGNING A COMPUTER WORKSTATION

The personal computer has introduced a whole new wrinkle in desk design — the *workstation.* The purpose of a workstation is to hold the computer components in the proper relationship to each other and to the computer operator.

CPU. The placement of the central processing unit, or CPU — the heart of the computer — is, surprisingly, the least of your concerns. You must be able to reach the switches and drives, but you can put the CPU anywhere within an arm's length.

Many operators place the CPU on the desk top, but this takes up valuable work space. It's often better to place it under the desk top or on the floor beside the workstation.

KEYBOARD. The closer you put the keyboard to your lap, the more comfortable you will be. If it's too high and you must hold your arms up when you type, you'll tire quickly. Mount the keyboard 24 to 28 inches above the floor, the same height as a typing table. If you spend long stretches at the computer, invest in a *keyboard shelf* that can be adjusted up and down. By adjusting the keyboard level from time to time, you forestall fatigue.

MONITOR. There are two schools of thought on where to put the monitor. At eye level, the strain on your neck is at a minimum, but the monitor and the keyboard are separated by as much as 60 degrees. It gets tiring as you glance back and forth between

your hands and the screen. If you place the monitor as close to the keyboard as possible, there's more neck strain but less eye strain. Some workstations incorporate a monitor shelf that drops *below* the keyboard and tilts the monitor upward so you see it just over the keyboard's edge.

Wherever you place the monitor, the screen should be at least 28 inches from your eyes to eliminate possible unhealthful effects of electromagnetic radiation generated by the monitor.

PRINTER. The printer is best placed below the work surface, 18 to 24 inches above the floor. This lets you reach the printer controls easily and read the copy as it comes out of the machine.

Many workstations provide a separate stand for the printer. If you have limited office space, you can also store it in a slide-out shelf beneath the desktop.

MOUSE. Include a flat area next to your keyboard for the mouse. It should be about 10 inches square to give you adequate maneuvering room. If both right- and left-handed people will use the workstation, provide space on *both* sides of the keyboard.

FLEXIBILITY. The most important feature you should include in a workstation is *flexibility.* Make it easy to rearrange the position of computer components by making the workstation modular or making the shelves adjustable. This helps you keep up with rapidly changing computer technology.

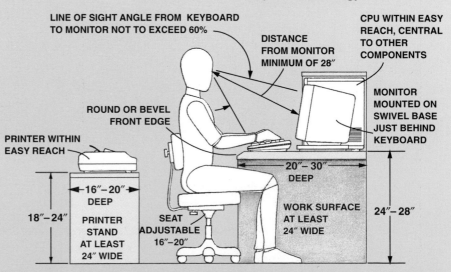

LINE OF SIGHT ANGLE FROM KEYBOARD TO MONITOR NOT TO EXCEED 60%

DISTANCE FROM MONITOR MINIMUM OF 28″

CPU WITHIN EASY REACH, CENTRAL TO OTHER COMPONENTS

ROUND OR BEVEL FRONT EDGE

MONITOR MOUNTED ON SWIVEL BASE JUST BEHIND KEYBOARD

PRINTER WITHIN EASY REACH

16″–20″ DEEP

18″–24″

PRINTER STAND AT LEAST 24″ WIDE

SEAT ADJUSTABLE 16″–20″

20″–30″ DEEP

WORK SURFACE AT LEAST 24″ WIDE

24″–28″

The purpose of a workstation is to hold all the computer components in an efficient and comfortable arrangement. If poorly arranged, even the best of systems will be tedious and tiring to use.

4

Built-In Construction

Large built-ins are made up of small modules, each designed to be simple to build and easy to install.

There was once a time when most home furnishings were built-in. A typical medieval house might have had a few crude tables; but shelving, cupboards, even beds were constructed as part of the walls. Only royalty or the very rich had any furniture to boast of. It wasn't until the Renaissance that common folks began to furnish their homes with stand-alone pieces.

Then, early in the twentieth century, the popularity of built-ins rebounded. Today's homes are often furnished with permanent work surfaces and storage units. Unlike the old medieval cupboards, however, these built-in counters and cabinets are not an integral part of the architecture. They are made separately, then fastened to the structure of the building.

BUILT-IN BUILDING BLOCKS

The assembly methods for modern built-ins borrow a great deal from **furniture construction**[1]. A built-in kitchen cabinet, for example, is similar in construction to a traditional stand-alone cabinet.

There are important differences, however. The most striking is that built-ins, unlike stand-alone furniture, are often made up of smaller *modules* to simplify construction and installation.

*The American Arts and Crafts Movement, which lasted from the 1890s to the 1920s, did much to popularize built-ins. Modular, permanently attached cabinets were a common feature in "Craftsman" homes from the period. These **Craftsman Bookcases** and **Entertainment Center** were built to restore an 1895 dwelling.*

SPECS:	60" high, 36" wide, 14" deep (bookcase module)
	18" high, 36" wide, 14" deep (window seat module)
	60" high, 36" wide, 28" deep (entertainment center)
MATERIALS:	Oak and oak-veneer plywood
CRAFTSMAN: Chris Walendzak Centerville, OH	**DESIGNER:** Mary Jane Favorite West Milton, OH

STANDARD BUILT-IN UNITS

Built-in modules are building blocks or *units* arranged to fit the available space. You can use as many or as few of these units as you wish when designing a cabinet system. You can also make them any size you want, but you'll find that for most built-in projects, you need only three basic types.

■ A *counter unit* rests on the floor. The top is waist-high to provide a table or a work surface, and the space below it contains drawers and shelves. The shelves are usually enclosed by doors.

■ A *wall unit* hangs on the wall at eye level and may extend up to the ceiling. It contains only shelves since it would be difficult to see the contents of drawers that hang at eye level or above.

■ A *tall unit* rests on the floor and extends above eye level, often to the ceiling. It's filled with drawers and enclosed shelves.

There are two common configurations for each unit. One lies flat against a wall and has a *rectangular* footprint. The other turns an inside corner and has either an *L-shaped* or a *pentagonal* footprint.

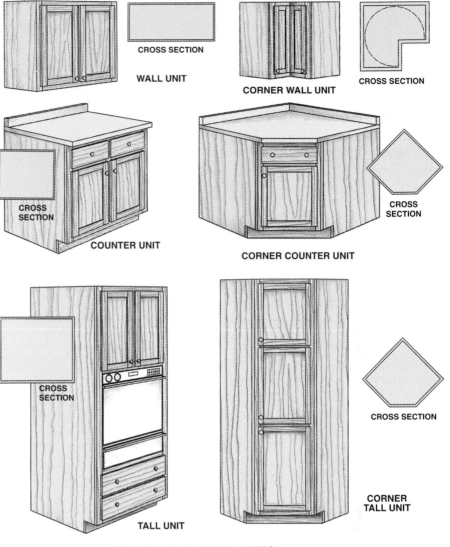

CROSS SECTION

WALL UNIT

CORNER WALL UNIT

CROSS SECTION

CROSS SECTION

CROSS SECTION

COUNTER UNIT

CORNER COUNTER UNIT

CROSS SECTION

CROSS SECTION

TALL UNIT

CORNER TALL UNIT

STANDARD BUILT-IN UNITS

SEE *ALSO*:

[1]Furniture Construction   18

These built-in kitchen cabinets consist of 12 modules — 5 counter units, 6 wall units, and 1 tall unit. Two of the counter units are configured to turn a corner.

UNIT CONSTRUCTION

Making a built-in unit is similar to making stand-alone **case**[1] furniture – most units have two sides, a top, a back, a face frame, and horizontal members such as shelves or web frames. The differences are in materials and design.

■ To a large extent, built-ins are made from sheet materials such as **plywood and particleboard**[2] to simplify construction and make them more stable. Stability is important – once the units are installed, they mustn't shrink or swell too much.

■ Built-ins rely on the building to which they're attached for much of their structural strength. Complex joinery and bracework are often unnecessary. This, too, simplifies construction.

■ Built-in units usually have *nailing strips* or *hanging strips* to fasten them to the wall.

PRO *TIP*

To compensate for the irregularities in walls and floors, build your cabinets with a **fitting allowance** at the back and sides. When you install the cabinets, trim this extra stock to fit the adjoining surfaces.

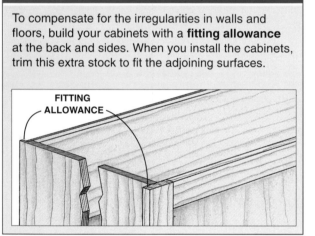

FITTING ALLOWANCE

Your choice of a drawer suspension system also affects construction. For example, if you support drawers on web frames, your cabinets will require more complex framework than if you suspend the drawers from bottom-mounted slides.

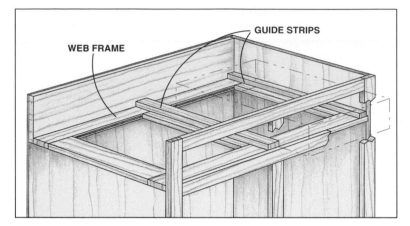

WEB FRAME
GUIDE STRIPS

The drawers in this built-in case are supported on a **web frame.**

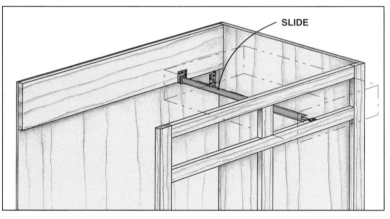

SLIDE

The drawers in this built-in case are supported by **bottom-mounted slides.**

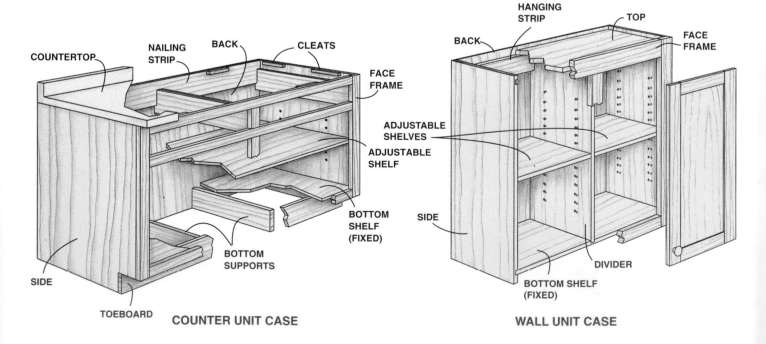

COUNTERTOP
NAILING STRIP
BACK
CLEATS
FACE FRAME
ADJUSTABLE SHELF
BOTTOM SHELF (FIXED)
BOTTOM SUPPORTS
SIDE
TOEBOARD

COUNTER UNIT CASE

HANGING STRIP
BACK
TOP
FACE FRAME
ADJUSTABLE SHELVES
SIDE
DIVIDER
BOTTOM SHELF (FIXED)

WALL UNIT CASE

COUNTERTOPS AND TOE SPACE

Counter units also have some unique features. Countertops in wet areas such as kitchens and bathrooms are commonly covered with a waterproof material such as **plastic laminate**[3]. The laminate is very thin and must be installed over a sub-strate of plywood or particleboard. This substrate is known as the *underlayment.* The front edge of the underlayment is often faced with a wooden *banding,* while the back is built up to make a *splashguard.* Both the banding and the splashguard are covered with laminate.

When the counter is designed to be used while standing, the unit usually includes a *toe space* just below the bottom shelf. This lets you stand close to the work surface without stubbing your toes on the case. The toe space is faced with a *toeboard.*

SEE *ALSO:*

[1] Methods of Construction 18

[2] Plywood and Particleboard   362

[3] Veneers and Laminates   368

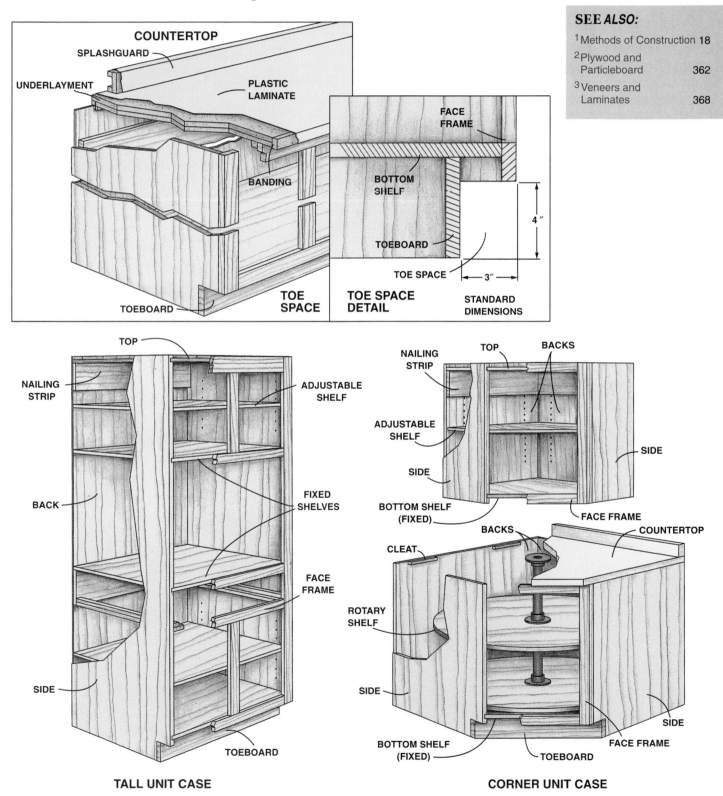

TALL UNIT CASE

CORNER UNIT CASE

CONSTRUCTION METHODS

Up until the 1950s, most built-ins were made with traditional case-construction methods. Then designers introduced a simpler way with fewer parts.

TRADITIONAL AND CONTEMPORARY CONSTRUCTION

There are two common ways to design and build the standard built-in units.

■ *Traditional* built-in cases have face frames. The doors that enclose the cupboard spaces are hinged to these frames.

■ *Contemporary* built-in cases have no face frames. The doors are hinged directly to the sides. Often the parts are assembled with special hardware rather than glued joints.

The **doors**[1] and **drawers**[2] in traditionally constructed built-ins are usually inset or lipped. Occasionally they overlay the face frame, but this is rare. However, doors and drawers in contemporary-constructed built-ins overlay their cases more often than not.

You may wonder whether traditional built-ins, because of their face frames, are stronger than contemporary assemblies. They are, but only to a small degree. Remember that a built-in derives much of its strength from the structure to which it's attached. Once installed, a contemporary built-in is sufficiently sturdy.

MORE *INFO*

When the term *contemporary* describes construction, it means something altogether different than when describing style. Contemporary-style furniture and built-ins are highly functional with no unnecessary parts or ornament, as described in "Styles of Craftsmanship" on page 52. Contemporary-constructed pieces have no face frames. Contemporary construction is used to make contemporary-style pieces, but it can also be used for other styles.

SEE *ALSO:*

[1]Shelving	27
[2]Chests of Drawers	25

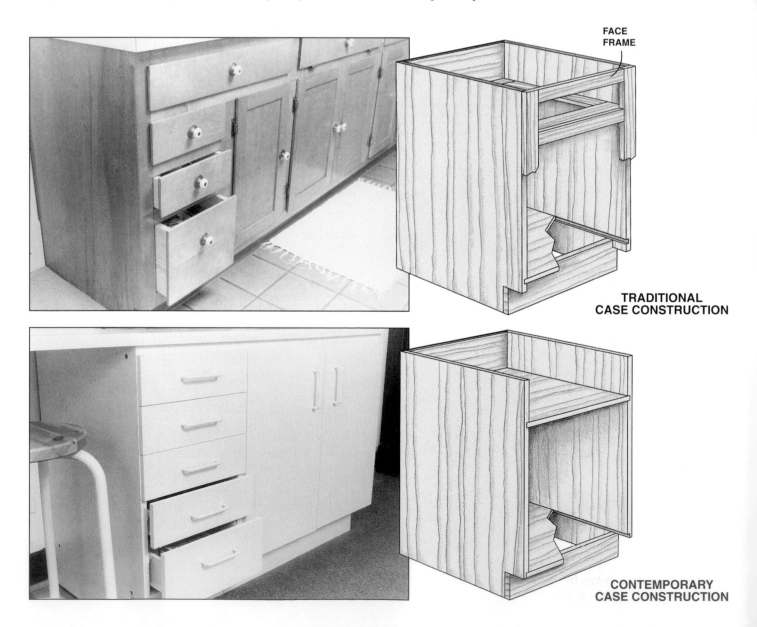

FACE FRAME

TRADITIONAL CASE CONSTRUCTION

CONTEMPORARY CASE CONSTRUCTION

STANDARD BUILT-IN DIMENSIONS

These dimensions are intended as guidelines only. Design the complete built-in assembly to fit the available space, and size the individual units to be easy to handle and install.

COUNTER UNIT

Depth	24"–25"
(Commercial countertops are made to fit units 24", 30", and 36" deep.)	
Height	36"
Width	12"–96"
Countertop thickness	
Kitchens/bathrooms	1"–2"
Elsewhere	1"
Countertop overhang	1"–2"
Backsplash height	4"–12"
Toe space depth	3"
Toe space height	4"

WALL UNIT

Depth	
Kitchens	12"–13"
Elsewhere	8"–15"
Height	30"–42"
Width	12"–96"
Height above countertops	16"–18"

TALL UNIT

Depth	12"–25"
Height	60"–84"
Width	12"–96"

CORNER COUNTER UNIT

Diagonal depth	43"–45"
Width	26"–38"

CORNER WALL UNIT

Diagonal depth	25"
Width	23"–24"

DOORS

Height	
Counter units	26"
Elsewhere	Varies
Width	12"–18"

DRAWERS

Height	
Top drawer	5"–6"
Middle/bottom drawers	6"–10"
Width	12"–18"
(Often matches door above or below.)	

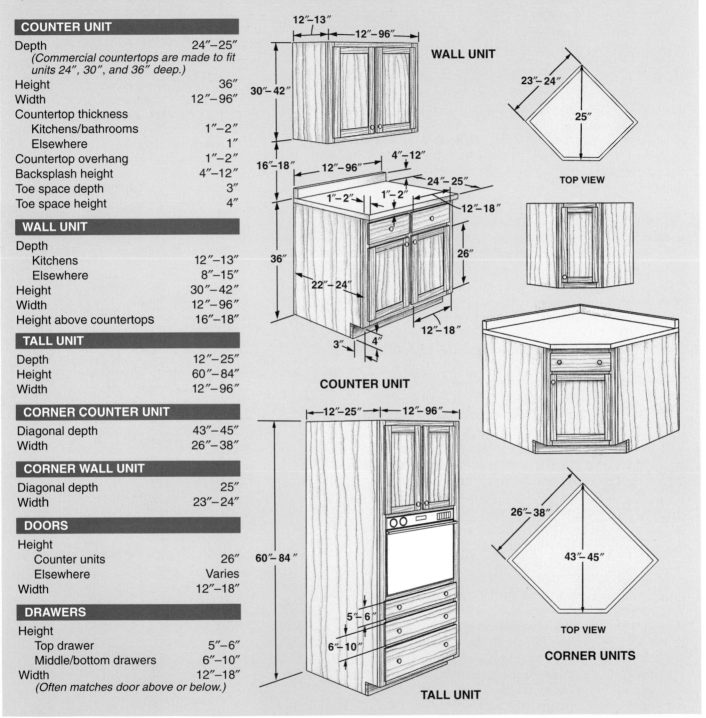

WALL UNIT

COUNTER UNIT

TALL UNIT

TOP VIEW

CORNER UNITS

MORE SOURCES

Building Traditional Kitchen Cabinets, by Jim Tolpin, Taunton Press, 1994

Cabinets and Built-Ins, by Paul Levine, Rodale Press, 1994

Cabinetmaking and Millwork, by John L. Feirer, Bennett Publishing, 1989

Furniture and Cabinet Construction, by William P. Spence

and L. Duane Griffiths, Prentice Hall, 1989

Making Built-In Cabinets, by Nick Engler, Rodale Press, 1992

5

Architectural Trim and Finish Work

*In finish carpentry, there is less emphasis on **building** a piece and more on **installing** it.*

Medieval woodworkers, called *joyners,* adapted carpentry techniques to build furniture. Mortises and tenons, frames and panels, shaping and molding were all used to construct buildings before they were employed in smaller projects. Antique collectors sometimes point out that Gothic chests and cupboards from this era resemble small mansions.

Contemporary furniture is less likely to look like a building, but architecture and woodworking have remained intimately connected. Finish carpenters and cabinetmakers still share many of the same methods of construction. Building a door is not so very different from other frame-and-panel constructions.

On the other hand, there are some important differences. Finish carpenters work with a great variety of manufactured products — very few finish carpentry projects start with raw lumber. These products require installation rather than assembly. With the machining and initial assembly done for you, the skill that you must bring to the job is in attaching the products to the structure.

MATERIALS: Quartersawn oak

CRAFTSMAN: Lloyd Bowser
Brookville, OH

*The trim that graces this **"Coffered" Ceiling** was made using the same techniques that any cabinetmaker might use to make moldings for a piece of furniture. Installation, however, requires a working knowledge of carpentry and building construction.*

DOORS AND WINDOWS

Doors and windows are a case in point. Although carpenters once built these architectural elements on site, this is no longer common practice. Most contemporary windows and doors are manufactured as units and prehung in a *case*. All you do is install the case in an opening.

DOOR CONSTRUCTION

Doors are classified by their materials and construction. *Solid-core* doors, for example, are made from strips of solid wood. *Hollow-core* doors are thin sheets of plywood glued to a frame. *Paneled* doors are made from wood using traditional frame-and-panel construction, while clad doors are created by covering rigid foam insulation with thin sheets of metal or fiberglass.

A door case is a simple **box**[1] – *side jambs* on the left and right, a *head jamb* above, and a *threshold* below. On most prehung interior doors, there is no threshold, just a temporary cleat nailed to the side jambs to keep them properly spaced.

WINDOW CONSTRUCTION

The glass in each window is held by a *sash*, a **frame**[1] made of stiles and rails. Some windows are divided into smaller panes by horizontal and vertical *muntins* within the sash. The sash are hung in a case consisting of two *side jambs*, a *head jamb,* and a *sill*.

Windows are classified by how the sash is hung in the case. *Sliding* windows slide horizontally; *double-hung* windows have two sash, both of which slide vertically. *Casement* windows are hinged like doors to swing out. *Awning* windows have a large sash that pivots horizontally; *jalousie* windows have many small pivoting panes. *Fixed* windows don't open at all.

Windows and doors come as preassembled units, prehung in a case and ready to be installed in an opening.

SEE ALSO:

[1]Methods of Construction 18

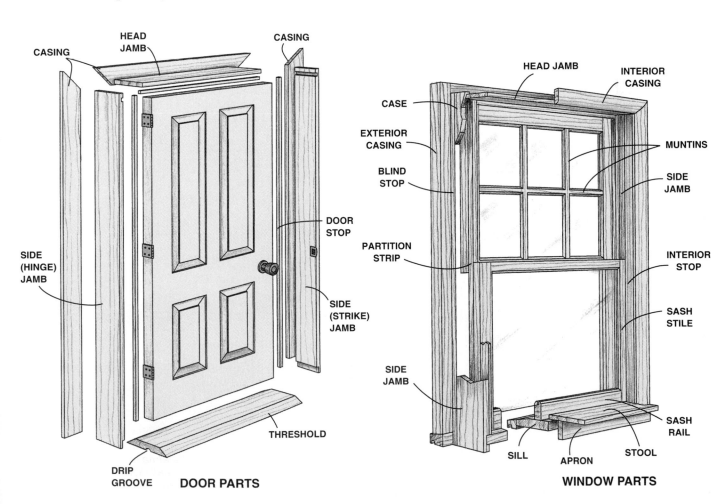

DOOR PARTS

CASING · HEAD JAMB · CASING · SIDE (HINGE) JAMB · DOOR STOP · SIDE (STRIKE) JAMB · THRESHOLD · DRIP GROOVE

WINDOW PARTS

HEAD JAMB · INTERIOR CASING · CASE · EXTERIOR CASING · BLIND STOP · MUNTINS · SIDE JAMB · PARTITION STRIP · INTERIOR STOP · SASH STILE · SIDE JAMB · SASH RAIL · SILL · APRON · STOOL

DOOR AND WINDOW CASINGS

The **trim or molding**[1] that surrounds a door or window is called a *casing*. The casing frames the opening and covers the joints between the wall covering and the jambs.

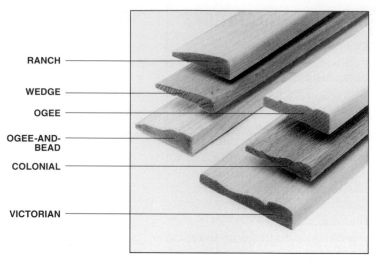

Casing trim is available in dozens of different profiles; shown are a few of the most common. Most casings have a slight recess in the back surface so the board will lie flat even if it cups slightly.

REVEAL

The casing is attached directly to the jambs with **finishing nails**[1]. Typically, the casing is positioned so a portion of the jamb edge shows. This is called the *reveal*. The *reveal opening* – the door or window opening plus the revealed portion of the jambs – is what you must frame with the casing.

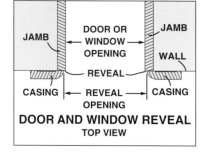

DOOR CASINGS

The trim used to make casings is available in dozens of different **profiles**[2], from simple rectangles to intricately molded shapes. Additionally, casings can be installed in many different configurations around an opening. When installing a door casing, you can butt the trim strips together, miter them, or join them with rectangular pieces called *plinths* and *corner blocks*. You can use a single molded profile or combine profiles to create more intricate shapes.

WINDOW CASINGS

Window casings are similar to door casings – they can be butted, mitered, or joined with blocks. Most are installed with a shelf or stool attached to the interior portion of the sill and an *apron* under the stool. In some newer homes, window casings have no sills or aprons; they are installed like a picture frame.

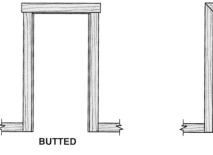
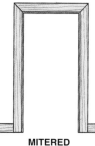
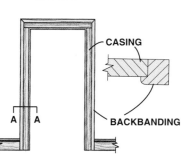

COMMON DOOR CASING DESIGNS

| PICTURE FRAME | STOOL-AND-APRON WITH BUTTED TOP | STOOL-AND-APRON WITH MITERED TOP | STOOL-AND-APRON WITH CORNER BLOCKS | STOOL-AND-APRON WITH CABINET HEAD |

COMMON WINDOW CASING DESIGNS

MOLDINGS AND TRIM

In addition to trimming the doors and windows in your home, it's also customary to trim floors, walls, and ceilings to tie the architectural elements together. This trim is customarily attached to the house framing with finish nails. Occasionally, it's necessary to attach *grounding* to the framework, then attach the trim to the grounding.

BASEBOARDS

Baseboards disguise the joints between the floor and the walls. Contemporary baseboards are made from a single piece of trim, but traditional baseboards were made from two or three – a *base*, a *shoe*, and a *cap*.

MORE *INFO*

While the base is typically attached to the framing in the wall, the shoe is nailed to the floor. This disguises any gaps that might open up as the house ages and the floor settles.

CHAIR AND PICTURE RAILS

Chair rails (once called *dado rails*) prevent the backs of chairs from rubbing against walls; *picture rails* provide a ledge from which to hang framed pictures. They are no longer as common as they once were, but some craftsmen install them when restoring older homes or to create visual interest in newer ones.

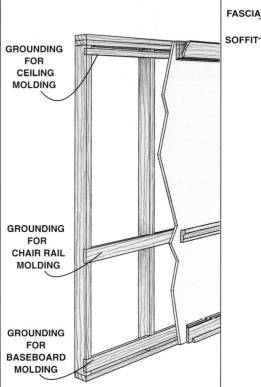

When installing complex trim, it helps to add **grounding** to the framework. This wood strip provides additional support and nailing anchors.

CEILING MOLDINGS

Ceiling moldings not only add visual interest, they can make a ceiling look higher or lower. Although they can be as simple as a single piece of trim, they are often built up from several profiles – vertical *fascia* and *flat moldings*, horizontal *soffits*, and diagonal *sprung moldings*.

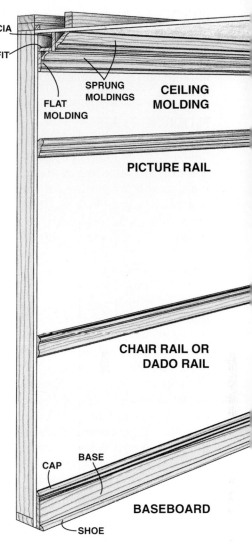

SEE *ALSO:*

[1] Nails   372
[2] Shaping and Molding   288

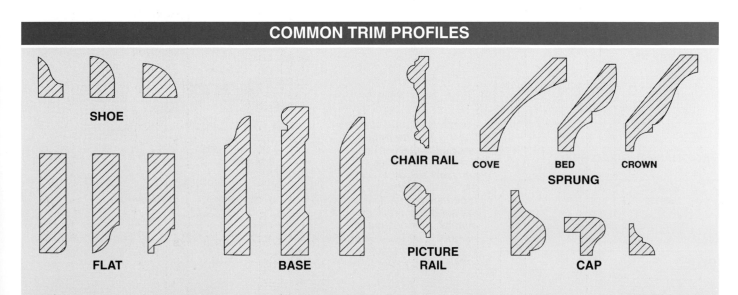

COMMON TRIM PROFILES

SHOE

FLAT

BASE

CHAIR RAIL

PICTURE RAIL

COVE

BED

CROWN

SPRUNG

CAP

WOODEN FLOORS

The floors of older homes and many newer ones are covered with durable hardwood or softwood *flooring.*

FLOORING TYPES

There are three types of wooden flooring: *strip, laminated,* and *parquet.* Strip flooring comes in long, narrow strips of solid wood less than an inch thick. Laminated flooring is made by gluing thin layers of hardwood to plywood strips. Parquet flooring comes in preassembled squares or *tiles,* 9 to 12 inches square.

UNDERLAYMENT

You must install all three types over a *subfloor.* Some also require *underlayment* – wooden boards or plywood decking that creates a smooth surface. There are special types made to be applied directly to a concrete slab, which serves as the subfloor and underlayment. Although the flooring is durable and attractive, it provides little structural strength. The subfloor and underlayment support the load.

FLOORING JOINERY

A typical piece of flooring has a tongue cut in one edge and one end, and a matching groove cut in the

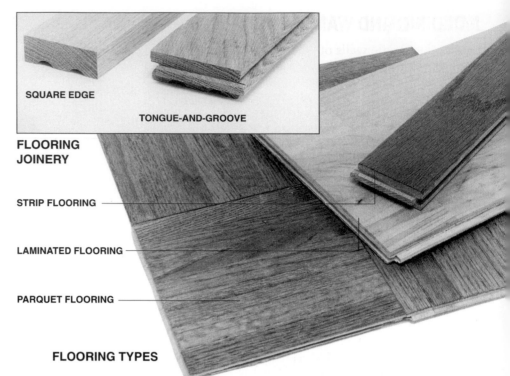

FLOORING JOINERY

SQUARE EDGE

TONGUE-AND-GROOVE

STRIP FLOORING

LAMINATED FLOORING

PARQUET FLOORING

FLOORING TYPES

other edge and end. These **tongues and grooves**[1] interlock, helping to keep the surfaces of the pieces aligned. Some flooring is made with "square edges"; the pieces are simply butted against each other. Square-edge flooring doesn't stay as well aligned as tongue-and-groove, but it's simpler to install.

Ordinarily, you **blind-nail**[2] and **face-nail**[2] strip flooring to its base. Laminated and parquet flooring are glued in place with mastic adhesives.

MORE *INFO*

Some laminated flooring products are designed to *float* above the base. The tongues and grooves are glued together, but the strips simply rest on the underlayment; they aren't attached. Typically, these products are backed with a thin layer of foam.

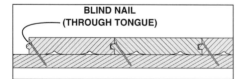

BLIND NAIL
(THROUGH TONGUE)

BLIND-NAILED

FACE NAIL

FACE-NAILED (HEAD SET)

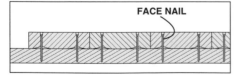

GLUE OR MASTIC

GLUED

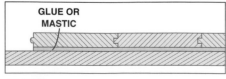

*For the most part, strip flooring is **blind-nailed** in place. The nails are driven through the tongues so you can't see them. When this isn't practical, it's **face-nailed** and the heads are set below the flooring surface. Laminated and parquet flooring are **glued** in place with mastic adhesives.*

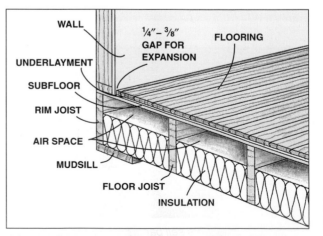

WALL

UNDERLAYMENT

SUBFLOOR

RIM JOIST

AIR SPACE

MUDSILL

¼" – ⅜"
GAP FOR
EXPANSION

FLOORING

FLOOR JOIST

INSULATION

*Wooden flooring is installed over a **subfloor.** If the floor is relatively thin, it also requires a smooth **underlayment** of boards or plywood.*

PANELING AND WAINSCOTING

You can cover the walls of your home with plywood or hardboard *sheet paneling* or solid wood *wainscoting*.

SHEET PANELING

Paneling is commonly available in 4 × 8-foot sheets covered with wood veneer or another decorative surface. If the sheets are thick enough, you can **face-nail**[2] them directly to the house framing; thinner sheets must be nailed and glued over walls that are already covered with drywall or sheathing.

Most sheet paneling is cut with square edges as if the sheets were meant to butt against one another. In practice, however, you must leave a small gap in the seam between each sheet to allow for **expansion and contraction**[3]. It's also a good idea to paint or stain the material under the seams a dark color so the seams won't show when the panels contract.

When the panels meet at corners, the sheets are typically lapped and the rough seams are covered by trim. Cover inside corners with *cove* or *quarter-round* moldings, and outside corners with *corner guards*.

PLANK WAINSCOTING

Solid wood "plank" **wainscoting**[4] consists of strips of wood similar to strip flooring. These can be nailed directly to the framing or glued over another wall covering. Nailing often requires horizontal *grounding* to provide a suitable anchor.

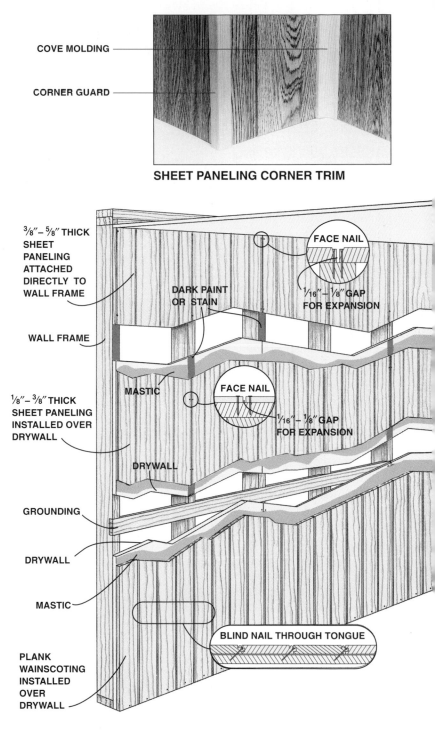

SHEET PANELING CORNER TRIM

- COVE MOLDING
- CORNER GUARD

- ⅜″–⅝″ THICK SHEET PANELING ATTACHED DIRECTLY TO WALL FRAME
- WALL FRAME
- ⅛″–⅜″ THICK SHEET PANELING INSTALLED OVER DRYWALL
- MASTIC
- DRYWALL
- GROUNDING
- DRYWALL
- MASTIC
- PLANK WAINSCOTING INSTALLED OVER DRYWALL
- FACE NAIL
- DARK PAINT OR STAIN
- ¹⁄₁₆″–⅛″ GAP FOR EXPANSION
- FACE NAIL
- ¹⁄₁₆″–⅛″ GAP FOR EXPANSION
- BLIND NAIL THROUGH TONGUE

Sheet paneling ⅜ inch thick or thicker may be nailed directly to the naked studs in a wall frame. Thinner sheets, however, must be applied to a covered wall. Face-nail the thin sheets to the frame and adhere them to the wall covering with mastic.

Because **wainscoting** comes in narrow strips, you must first install horizontal grounding before you can nail it to a wall frame. Or, you can glue it to a wall covering with mastic.

Several manufacturers sell paneling and wainscoting "systems" — sheets or planks plus matching trim — that you can tailor to your needs. The wainscoting in this room was assembled from a packaged system.

SEE *ALSO:*

[1]Types of Woodworking Joints	16
[2]Nails	372
[3]Wood Movement	6

The edges are joined with either tongues and grooves or overlapping rabbets. Where the planks meet at an inside corner, butt the edge of one plank against the face of another. At outside corners, either butt the planks or miter them.

PANELED WAINSCOTING

Paneled wainscoting is a **frame-and-panel**[1] wall covering. The panels are usually small sheets of veneered plywood or hardboard held in place by wooden rails and stiles. The horizontal rails are nailed to wall studs, the vertical stiles are joined to rails, and the panels float between these frame members.

There are several different **joinery systems**[2] you can use to assemble the parts of paneled wainscoting. Traditionally, rails and stiles are joined by mortises and tenons, but contemporary installations are more likely to use loose tenons or biscuits. The panels may rest in grooves in the frame members, or they may rest in rabbets and be held in place by moldings.

The corners are treated like plank wainscoting. At inside corners, the frame members are butted edge to face. At outside corners, they are either butted or mitered.

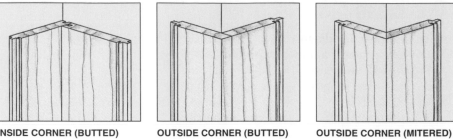

INSIDE CORNER (BUTTED)   OUTSIDE CORNER (BUTTED)   OUTSIDE CORNER (MITERED)

PLANK WAINSCOTING CORNERS

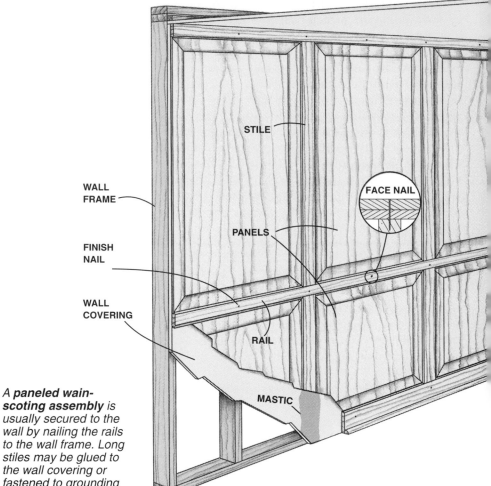

WALL FRAME

FINISH NAIL

WALL COVERING

STILE

FACE NAIL

PANELS

RAIL

MASTIC

*A **paneled wain-scoting assembly** is usually secured to the wall by nailing the rails to the wall frame. Long stiles may be glued to the wall covering or fastened to grounding for additional stability.*

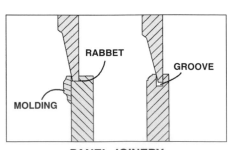

RABBET

GROOVE

MOLDING

PANEL JOINERY

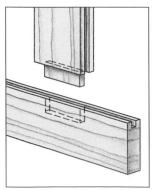

MORTISE-AND-TENON JOINT

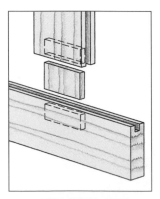

LOOSE-TENON JOINT

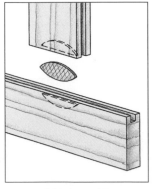

BISCUIT JOINT

RAIL-AND-STILE JOINERY

STAIRCASES

A staircase stretches diagonally between the floors of a home. The total height of a staircase is its *rise,* and its horizontal length is its *run.*

TREADS AND RISERS

The staircase itself is made up of horizontal *treads* and vertical *risers,* held by diagonal sawtooth *carriages* or stringers. The sides are trimmed by sawtooth *skirts,* which overlap the drywall or plaster. The treads overlap the skirts, protruding an inch or two beyond. The risers are cut even with the skirts, butting against them or joining them with miters.

The vertical distance from the top surface of one tread to the top surface of the next is called the *unit rise.* The horizontal distance from the front surface of one riser to the front surface of the next is the *unit run.* When you add up these units, they equal the total rise and run.

PRO TIP

Housing codes normally dictate that the unit rise of a staircase be no more than 8 inches and the unit run no less than 9 inches.

BALUSTRADE

To be safe, each staircase requires a *handrail.* This is often supported at the top and bottom of the staircase by a *newel post.* The handrail may be mortised into the post or attached to it with wood screws. *Balusters* fill in the space between the handrail and the treads. The top ends of the balusters rest in a groove in the underside of the handrails, spaced apart by filler blocks. The bottoms join the treads with mortises and tenons. Together, the handrails, newel posts, and balusters make up the balustrade.

SEE ALSO:

[1]Methods of Construction   18

[2]Types of Woodworking Joints   16

MORE SOURCES

Basic Stairbuilding, by Scott Schuttner, Taunton Press, 1990

Carpentry and Building Construction, by John L. Feirer, and Gilbert R. Hutchings, Bennett Publishing, 1981

Hardwood Floors, by Don Bollinger, Taunton Press, 1990

Trim Carpentry Techniques, by Craig Savage, Taunton Press, 1989

HANDRAIL
GROOVE
NEWEL POST
FILLER BLOCKS
WOOD SCREW
BALUSTER

BALUSTRADE DETAIL

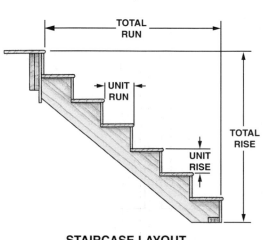

GOOSENECK
HANDRAIL
BALUSTER
NEWEL POST
HANGERBOARD
SKIRT
RISER
TREAD
CARRIAGE
KICKBOARD
SKIRT

STAIRCASE CONSTRUCTION

TOTAL RUN
UNIT RUN
TOTAL RISE
UNIT RISE

STAIRCASE LAYOUT

6

Special Constructions

No matter what you build from wood or how it's constructed, you must consider wood's unique properties.

Although furnituremaking, cabinet-making, and finish carpentry are the core of woodworking, they don't comprise all of the craft – or even the bulk of it. There are many other branches, each with its own special designs, techniques, and construction methods. Wooden toys, for example, are constructed as simply as possible, with no sharp edges that might endanger a child. Marquetry designs include hundreds of tiny pieces fitted together like a puzzle. Outdoor furniture is built to withstand the weather, musical instruments to produce pleasing sounds, and clocks to keep time. Each type of project is substantially different in construction and purpose.

However, they are all made from wood, and the same characteristics that govern your work when making a chair or cabinet also affect you when making a clock or a violin. The following pages give an overview of several special constructions to show how **grain, movement, and strength**[1] affect a structure, no matter what you build. The list of books and videos on page 51 will help you obtain in-depth information on most woodworking branches.

*A **Noah's Ark** is a traditional "Sunday toy" — a plaything that parents once gave their children to discourage boisterous play on the Sabbath. This particular ark combines three woodworking specialties: toy making, box making, and carving. The ark is constructed like a box, while the toy animals are carved.*

SPECS: 14¼" high, 8" wide, 18" deep (ark)

MATERIALS: Poplar (ark) and jelutong (animals)

CRAFTSMAN: Mary Jane Favorite
West Milton, OH

TOY MAKING

Toy construction is usually simple and straightforward – there's rarely a need for complex joinery or intricate design. However, you must put some careful thought into the project to make it safe and durable.

■ *Grain* – The appearance of the wood is rarely important; figured grain and exotic grain are wasted on a child's toy. It's more important that the grain be straight and clear for strength and stability.

Also choose a closed-grain species without visible pores. Children's toys are handled continually; open grain collects dirt and grime. Closed-grain woods such as maple are easier to keep clean. They are also less likely to throw splinters.

■ *Movement* – Typically, the smaller the toy, the smaller your concern about wood movement. In toy designs where the parts are linked by pivots or other moving joints, wood movement is of no concern – the linked parts are free to move independently.

■ *Strength* – Because toys are subject to heavy use (and occasional abuse), wood strength is critical. Not only must the wood withstand unusually heavy stress, the surface must resist wear and abrasion.

This is especially important in toys with moving parts. These parts rub against each other continually. A dense wood such as maple or beech holds up much better than lighter species.

■ *Toxicity* – The extractives in some woods are **potentially toxic**[2] to humans. These species must be avoided for toys or other projects that someone might put in their mouth or rub against their skin. This same concern applies to other materials such as glue and **finishes**[3] These, too, should be nontoxic.

MAKING BOXES

Standard box construction consists of four sides joined at the corners, with a floating top and bottom. This, however, is just one way to make a box. In its simplest form, a box is an enclosure. There are no limits to the number of parts in an enclosure. It may have any number of sides, and the interior can be subdivided into compartments. You can even make a one-piece box, turning, routing, or sawing the enclosure from a single block by hollowing the interior.

■ *Grain* – Part of the appeal of a small box is its beauty, so the appearance of the grain is extremely important. Figured grain and exotic woods are frequently used. Craftsmen often mix grain types and wood species for effect.

■ *Movement* – Although the parts are small, movement is an important concern. Small boxes often have close-fitting lids and drawers. If the movement isn't carefully controlled, the box may distort, ruining the fit of the parts. To avoid this problem, you must diligently align the grain where you can and use **floating joinery**[4] where you can't.

■ *Strength* – The smaller the box, the less important wood strength becomes. Only when a part is subject to unusual stress (such as a wooden hinge) does strength become an issue in box making.

*The moving parts on this **Toy Tyrannosaurus** are made of cherry and are joined with hard maple pegs. Both hardwoods are reasonably strong and resistant to wear and tear. This helps make the toy as durable as possible.*

SPECS: 10½″ high, 4¼″ wide, 10½″ long

MATERIALS: Cherry and hard maple

CRAFTSMAN: David Wakefield
Millfield, OH

CLOCKMAKING

A clock case is either a **box construction or case construction**[1] designed to hold mechanical clockworks. When building a case for a clock, you must completely enclose the works to protect them from dust. And you must be able to reach the works easily for cleaning and maintenance. Beyond that, the construction concerns are the same as for fine furniture.

■ *Grain* – Pick straight, clear grain for parts that must remain straight and true, such as door stiles and rails. If the clock design includes any carved finials or moldings, use straight grain for these parts, too – they will be easier to carve. Reserve figured wood for large, flat panels.

■ *Movement* – Traditional box and case construction allows for wood movement, but you need to take special care when making an ornate clock case. Classic clock designs typically include many moldings, and these are often applied perpendicular to the grain direction of the wood that supports them. You must devise **floating joints**[2] for these parts.

■ *Strength* – Many clock movements are quite heavy. The case must provide adequate support for these. Beyond that, the structure only needs to support itself.

MUSICAL INSTRUMENTS

A musical instrument is a sound chamber – a box or tube designed to amplify the vibrations of a string or your own breath. The design may seem complex, but the construction techniques are usually very simple.

■ *Grain* – Sound travels faster and with less distortion in a dense, consistent material. Also, thin stock will not dampen vibrations as much as thick stock. So sound chambers are best made from dense woods with even grain, planed as thin as possible. Species such as maple and sycamore, with closely spaced growth rings and little difference in density between springwood and summerwood, also produce better sounds.

■ *Movement* – This can be a tricky problem in musical instruments. The parts of a sound chamber should be solidly joined to transmit vibration; you cannot use **floating joints**[2] to compensate for wood movement. To keep movement to a minimum, luthiers (stringed-instrument makers) use quartersawn stock for wide parts. They have also developed designs such as an hourglass-shaped guitar soundbox that allow some expansion and contraction.

■ *Strength* – There is considerable stress in a stringed musical instrument when the strings are drawn taut. The wide, thin parts on a soundbox are often braced to withstand enormous loads. Long, narrow parts such as the neck of a guitar may be reinforced with a metal rod. Fingerboards and other parts that must stand up to continual handling are made from extremely hard, dense woods.

*The metal strings on this **Hammer Dulcimer** create enormous stresses on the thin sounding board when they are drawn taut. To withstand the load, the board is crisscrossed with bracework on the inside of the instrument.*

SPECS:	6″ high, 19″ wide, 43″ long
MATERIALS:	Maple, teak, purpleheart, walnut, bocote, rosewood, and vermillion
CRAFTSMAN:	Harlan Olson Bozeman, MT

MARQUETRY AND PARQUETRY

In marquetry, you inlay tiny bits of **wood veneer**[3] to form ornamental pictures. In parquetry, you make geometric patterns.

■ *Grain* – Because both are decorative techniques, the appearance of the wood is paramount. Exotic species are often preferred to ordinary species; figured grain, to plain grain. The color of a veneer and how it contrasts with neighboring pieces are also important.

■ *Movement* – Surprisingly, the movement of the wood veneers is of little concern. The pieces are sliced so thin that they expand and contract with whatever material they are bonded to. Consequently, you must choose this material (called the *core*) to be as stable as possible. If it moves too much, gaps will open up in the veneer assembly.

■ *Strength* – Because the veneers are so thin, a marquetry or parquetry piece derives all its strength from the core material. The core must be sufficiently strong and its grain oriented properly to withstand the stresses that will be put upon it.

WOOD CARVING

Unlike most wood crafts, carving is a *reductive* process. Instead of assembling parts, a carver cuts wood away to create something useful or decorative. There are many types of carving, such as figure carving, wildlife carving, relief carving, and chip carving. They all have similar requirements.

■ *Grain* – The choice of wood is extremely important. While all woods can be carved, very few offer the grain structure needed to produce fine results.

The carver's main concern is not necessarily the ease with which the wood can be cut, but *control*. In many species, the **summerwood**[4] is a good deal denser than the **spring-wood**[4]. When carving these materials, you must apply considerably

*To carve the intricate details in this **Decorative Plate**, a carver needs a clear wood with a consistent density. This gives the carver much more control than a species in which the summerwood is denser than the springwood.*

SPECS:	12″ in diameter
MATERIALS:	Basswood
CRAFTSMAN:	Wayne Barton Park Ridge, IL

more pressure to cut through the dense parts. When the knife suddenly exits the summerwood, there will be too much pressure behind the blade and the knife will plow ahead into the springwood. This makes it difficult to control the cuts. Consequently, a carver looks for woods such as basswood, butternut, and mahogany that have an even grain and consistent density.

It's also important to choose straight grain. When carving, you must cut with the grain for best results. If you cut against it, the blade will dig in and may chip or tear the wood. When carving irregular grain, it's difficult to tell when you are cutting with the grain direction. Straight grain is easier to "read."

■ *Movement* – Carved figures and patterns expand and contract like any other wooden object. Consequently, a carver gives considerable thought to movement. When gluing up stock for large carvings, you must align the wood grain so the pieces all move in the same direction. You must also align tangential and radial grain directions to prevent the com-

pleted carving from developing unsightly glue steps.

■ *Strength* – When laying out a carving, the same considerations apply as when laying out a table leg or a chair rung – the grain must run through the long dimension of the wood for maximum strength. However, carvings often have protruding parts that cannot be aligned with the grain. When this is the case, carvers sometimes inlay metal reinforcing rods in the block as they glue it up. Or they leave a "bridge" to reinforce the protrusion while they work, then remove it as they near completion.

Wood strength is also the reason behind the carver's maxim, "Carve the details last." Protruding parts, crisp edges, and other details may be broken or rounded over if handled too much.

OUTDOOR FURNITURE

Outdoor furniture is built with the same concern for comfort and utility as **indoor furniture**[1]. However, it must also withstand continual exposure to rain and sun and large fluctuations in relative humidity. Consequently, outdoor furniture construction is very different.

■ *Grain* – Straight, clear stock is less likely to distort or split as it adapts to changes in the weather. Closed-grain hardwoods (which have microscopic pores) and softwoods (which have no pores at all) shed the water better than open-grain species with large, deep pores.

■ *Movement* – This is your number one concern when building outdoor furniture. Rain soaks the construction, causing the wood to expand much more than it would indoors. Furthermore, standard joinery often captures the rainwater. A mortise-and-tenon joint, for example, holds water and lets it soak into the wood. The tenon swells up inside the mortise, crushing the wood fibers. When the tenon dries and shrinks, it's loose. To prevent these problems, you must design the structure so that it sheds water. Space the boards so the wood can dry quickly, and use joinery that is unaffected by wood movement. A simple butt joint, reinforced by a rust-resistant fastener, captures little water and holds tight as the wood moves.

■ *Strength* – Overall, the construction of a piece of outdoor furniture must be stronger than its indoor counterpart. Not only must it stand up to the ravages of bad weather; it's also likely to suffer hard use during good weather.

■ *Durability* – Left outdoors, wood is likely to decay and rot. However, some wood species, such as cedar, teak, and mahogany, have antibiotic extractives that limit the growth of bacteria and make them more **resistant to decay**[2]. Avoid "pressure-treated" softwoods that have been soaked with toxic preservatives such as chromated copper arsenate. Your skin comes in intimate contact with these woods, especially when you're wearing shorts, short-sleeve shirts, and other summer attire.

To help this **Adirondack Chair** better weather the elements, it's constructed entirely with butt joints so there are fewer cracks and crevices to trap rainwater. It's also made from cedar, a decay-resistant wood.

SPECS: 38" high, 33¾" wide, 37¼" deep

MATERIALS: White cedar

CRAFTSMAN: Jim McCann
Brookville, OH

DESIGNER: Mary Jane Favorite
West Milton, OH

ANALYZING CONSTRUCTION

You don't need vast experience to do well in a woodworking specialty that's new to you. To develop a workable design – or better understand someone else's design – ask yourself some pertinent questions.

■ What type of wood grain would be most suitable for the structure? Does it require the strength and workability that you get from straight grain? The stability of quarter grain? The homogenous appearance of an even grain? Or the striking beauty of a strong grain or figured grain?

■ How will the movement of the wood affect the structure? Can you compensate for the movement by using stable materials, properly orienting the wood grain, or carefully choosing the joinery? Will your joinery choices adversely affect the appearance or utility of the project?

■ Does the project have unusual strength requirements? If so, would it be best to beef up the construction with stronger materials? Thicker, heavier parts? More parts? Bracework? Can you use a different design that better absorbs the stress?

■ Finally, are there any special requirements? Where will the structure be used? And for what purpose? Does the environment, purpose, or another special circumstance affect construction?

Many books are available on the specialities I've mentioned, and on others like green woodworking, boatbuilding, and whirligigs. I've included a listing of my favorite books on these subjects on the next page to help narrow your search for detailed information on these special constructions.

MORE *SOURCES*

Birdhouses and Feeders
Beastly Abodes Book and Kit, by Bobbe Needham, Sterling/Lark, 1995
The Bird Feeder Book, by Thom Boswell, Sterling/Lark, 1995

Boatbuilding
Canoecraft, by Ted Moores and Marilyn Mohr, Camden House, 1993
How to Build a Wooden Boat, by David C. McIntosh, WoodenBoat Publications, 1988

Bow Making
Bowyer's Bible, Lyons and Burford, 1994

Box Making
BOOKS
The Art of Making Elegant Wood Boxes, by Tony Lydgate, Sterling/Chapelle Publishing, 1993
The Book of Boxes, by Andrew Crawford, Running Press, 1993
Making Wood Boxes with a Band Saw, by Tom Crabb, Sterling Publishing, 1985
VIDEOS
Small Shop Projects: Boxes, with Jim Cummins, Fine Woodworking Videos

Carving
BOOKS
Carving Carousel Animals, by H. Leroy Marlow, Sterling Publishing, 1989
Classic Designs for Wood Carving, by Richard Adam Dabrowski, Sterling Publishing, 1987
Great Carving Projects, National Carvers Museum, 1985
How to Carve Wood, by Richard Butz, Taunton Press, 1984
Realistic Decoys, by Keith Bridenhagen and Patrick Spielman, Sterling Publishing, 1985
Wood: Carving Techniques and Projects You Can Make, Meredith Books, 1993
VIDEOS
Carving Techniques and Projects, with Sam Bush and Mack Headley, Jr., Fine Woodworking Videos
Woodcarving, with Tom Wolfe (series), Mountain Meadows Enterprises

Chip Carving
BOOKS
Basic Chip Carving, with Pam Gresham, Schiffer Publishing, 1993
Begin with Moor, by Dennis and Todd Moor, Dennis and Todd Moor, 1995
Chip Carving: Techniques and Patterns, by Wayne Barton, Taunton Press, *n.d.*
VIDEOS
Chip Carving, with Wayne Barton, Fine Woodworking Videos

Clockmaking
Clockmaking, by John A. Nelson, T A B Books, 1989
Making and Repairing Wooden Clock Cases, by V. J. Taylor and H. A. Babb, Sterling/David and Charles Publishing, 1994
Wooden Clock Cases, by David Bryant, Stackpole Books, 1995

Doll Houses
Making Period Doll House Furniture, by Derek and Shela Rowbottom, Guild of Master Craftsmen Publishing, 1993
The New Doll House Do-It-Yourself Book, by Venus and Martin Dodge, David and Charles Publishing, 1993
The Secret of Doll House Making, by Jean Nisbet, Guild of Master Craftsmen Publishing, 1994

Green Woodworking
Green Woodworking, by Drew Langsner, Rodale Press, 1987
Make a Chair from a Tree: An Introduction to Working Green Wood, by John D. Alexander, Jr., Astragal Press, 1994

Marquetry and Parquetry
Marquetry, by Pierre Ramond, Taunton Press, 1989
Marquetry and Veneer, Taunton Press, 1987
The Marquetry Manual, by William A. Lincoln, Linden Publishing, 1990

Miniatures and Models
Historic Ship Models, by Wolfram zu Monfeld, Sterling Publishing, 1977
Making Miniatures, by Venus A. and Martin Dodge, David and Charles Publishing, 1993
Mott Miniature Furniture Workshop Manual, by Barbara and Elizabeth Mott, Fox Chapel Publishing, 1995

Musical Instruments
The Amateur Wind Instrument Maker, by Trevor Robson, University of Massachusetts Press, 1980
Constructing a Five-String Banjo, by Roger H. Siminoff, Hal Leonard Corporation, 1985
Guitarmaking: Tradition and Technology, by William R. Cumpiano and Jonathan D. Natelson, Chronicle Books, 1994
Make Your Own Electric Guitar, by Melvyn Hiscock, Sterling Publishing, 1986
Making Stringed Instruments, by George Buchanan, Sterling Publishing, 1990
Making Wood Folk Instruments, by Dennis Waring, Sterling Publishing, 1990
Violin Making As It Was and Is, by Ed. Heron-Allen, Sterling Publishing, 1991

Outdoor Furniture
Garden Furniture, by George Buchanan, Sterling/Cassell, 1993
Outdoor Furniture, by Nick Engler, Rodale Press, 1988
Outdoor Furniture, by Bill Hylton with Fred Matlack and Phil Gehret, Rodale Press, 1992

Toy Making
Animated Toys, by David Wakefield, Popular Science Books, 1986
Making Old-Time Folk Toys, by Sharon Pierce, Sterling Publishing, 1986
Puzzle Craft, by Stewart T. Coffin, Stewart T. Coffin, 1985
Toymaking Basics, by David Wakefield, Sterling Publishing, 1993

Whirligigs
Whirligigs and Weathervanes, by David Schoonmaker and Bruce Woods, Sterling/Lark, 1991
The Wonderful World of Whirligigs and Wind Machines, by Alan and Gill Bridgewater, T A B Books, 1990

Styles of Craftsmanship

The artistic traditions of four continents came together in America to form a rich tapestry of woodworking styles.

While construction is an important concern in any woodworking project, it's not your only concern. You must also consider the *style* of a project. If you make a table, how will it look? Contemporary or traditional? Country or classic? Will the top be square or round? Will the legs be tapered or turned? Each of these choices determines the table's style.

And you have plenty of choices. America has a unique history of woodworking design. The artistic traditions of four continents came together in this country, as well as the design philosophies of several unique cultural and religious groups. These diverse designs evolved and intermixed over four centuries, producing a rich tapestry of woodworking styles.

AMERICAN DESIGN TRADITIONS

There are four major woodworking traditions in America – design philosophies that have developed and blossomed since Colonial times. Each has produced one or more distinct styles of furniture and architecture:

- Southwest Tradition
- Eastern Tradition
- Southern Tradition
- Folk Tradition

*While most furniture styles conceal the joinery, Mission furniture flaunts it. On this **Mission Bookcase,** the visible ends of the pegs and tenons become decorative elements.*

SPECS: 59" high, 45" wide, 12" deep	
MATERIALS: Quartersawn oak	
CRAFTSMAN: Jim McCann Brookville, OH	DESIGNER: Mary Jane Favorite West Milton, OH

SOUTHWEST TRADITION 1521 TO PRESENT

The first American furniture was made long before the Europeans colonized America. Aztec and Pueblo craftsmen made *petlatls* (benches for sitting and sleeping), *tollicpalis* (chairs), and several types of low tables.

In 1521, when the Spanish conquered New Spain – the area we know as Mexico, California, Arizona, and New Mexico – they found highly skilled woodworkers among the natives. As part of their missionary efforts, Spanish *ensembladores* (cabinetmakers) taught native craftsmen to build European furniture. The Spanish designs were a unique blend of European and African art forms. When the African Moors ruled Spain during medieval times, the Spanish had adopted their design tradition, the *mujedar*. Native American woodworkers found these geometric designs remarkably similar to their own. These two decorative styles, Islamic and Indian, combined to create the unique *Southwest* style.

In the nineteenth century, settlers from the East brought their own woodworking designs and slowly the old Southwest style began to fade. But as America approached her bicentennial, interest in history and tradition grew stronger. Southwest cabinetmakers resurrected the old designs, using them as an inspiration for the *Southwest Revival* style.

EASTERN TRADITION 1607 TO PRESENT

A century after the Spanish landed in the New World, the English colonized the eastern seaboard and began the Eastern furniture tradition. Because the population and the number of skilled craftsmen grew more rapidly in the East than elsewhere, this tradition is by far the most influential and prolific furniture aesthetic in America, often engulfing other traditions.

SEVENTEENTH-CENTURY STYLES

When the first settlers arrived in Virginia and Massachusetts, they were far more concerned with survival than furniture. They made only the most essential, rudimentary pieces, which we remember as *Primitive* furniture. The primitive style lasted for almost 250 years, marching westward with the frontier.

By 1640, there were a small number of furniture shops in the towns and villages that were springing up along the Atlantic coast. Craftsmen made massive, blocky pieces after English Renaissance designs – "court cupboards," paneled chests, and turned chairs. This was *American Jacobean* furniture, named for King James I and II of England. It's sometimes referred to as the *Pilgrim* style.

SOUTHWEST FURNITURE
1521–1850

SOUTHWEST REVIVAL FURNITURE
1970–PRESENT

PRIMITIVE FURNITURE
1607–1850

AMERICAN JACOBEAN FURNITURE
1640–1690

AMERICAN FURNITURE STYLES: SIXTEENTH AND SEVENTEENTH CENTURIES					
	1500	1550	1600	1650	
Southwest Tradition		SOUTHWEST			
Eastern Tradition				PRIMITIVE	
					AMERICAN JACOBEAN
					WILLIAM AND MARY
Southern Tradition					
Folk Tradition					

**WILLIAM AND MARY
FURNITURE
1690–1725**

**QUEEN ANNE
FURNITURE
1725–1760**

**CHIPPENDALE
FURNITURE
1760–1780**

**FEDERAL FURNITURE
1780–1820**

EIGHTEENTH-CENTURY STYLES

As the eighteenth century dawned, eastern craftsmen continued to copy English styles. From Jacobean they graduated to *William and Mary* pieces and introduced several new forms – the highboy, lowboy, and easy chair. This soon gave way to *Queen Anne* style. Enamored of Chinese furniture, European and American woodworkers incorporated Oriental design elements such as the cabriole leg in their own pieces. The graceful cyma curve or *ogee* was used extensively in Queen Anne.

In 1754, Thomas Chippendale published *The Gentleman and Cabinet-Maker's Director,* a pattern book based on Queen Anne forms but heavier and more ornate. He also resurrected the straight line as a design element, often using straight, untapered legs.

Meanwhile, American chairmakers invented the *rocking chair.* Originally intended to provide old folks with simple exercise, the "rocker" became immensely popular with people of all ages.

After the American Revolution, there was a backlash against all things English, and we looked to our ally, France, for inspiration. Here, designers had revived the principles of classical Greek and Roman architecture. The *Federal* style sprang from these "neoclassical" aesthetics. These were light, graceful pieces, often sporting tapered legs and exotic veneers.

NINETEENTH-CENTURY STYLES

As Napoleon established his empire in France, neoclassical design became heavier, more severe, and geometric. *American Empire* furniture followed these trends. But Americans eventually mended fences with England and took a renewed interest in English styles. The Victorian era brought the *Gothic, Rococo,* and *Renaissance Revival* styles, each more ornamental than the last.

At the same time, we became fascinated with the gadgetry of the Industrial Revolution, including *Patent* furniture – mechanical pieces that folded, swiveled, or converted from one form to another. As more and more furniture was produced in factories, styles developed that lent themselves to

**AMERICAN EMPIRE
FURNITURE
1815–1840**

**VICTORIAN REVIVAL
FURNITURE
1840–1880**

**PATENT
FURNITURE
1860–1910**

AMERICAN FURNITURE STYLES: EIGHTEENTH CENTURY

	1700	1725	1750	1775
Southwest Tradition	SOUTHWEST			
Eastern Tradition	PRIMITIVE			
	WILLIAM AND MARY			
				FEDERAL
		QUEEN ANNE		
			CHIPPENDALE	
Southern Tradition	SOUTHERN			
Folk Tradition		WINDSOR		
		PENNSYLVANIA GERMAN		
				SHAKER

OAK FURNITURE
1870–1925

INTERNATIONAL
FURNITURE
1920–1960

machine production. One of the most popular was *Oak* furniture, so-called because it was made mostly from oak and oak plywood. Oak pieces typically had straight or lightly curved legs, band-sawed pediments, applied carvings, and ornate hardware.

Toward the end of the century, there was a reaction against excessive ornament and mass production. Charles Eastlake and his followers created *Art* furniture as a tasteful alternative to the ornate Victorian Revival styles. The *Eastlake* style, as it's remembered, used simple geometric surface decorations and moldings. The woodworkers who built *Arts and Crafts* (or *Mission*) furniture revived old medieval forms and advocated a return to individual craftsmanship.

EASTLAKE FURNITURE
1870–1890

MYTH *CONCEPTIONS*

MISSION FURNITURE Despite its name, the Mission style didn't originate in Spanish missions. This misunderstanding apparently began when Joseph McHugh, a small-time manufacturer of Arts and Crafts furniture, advertised a new line "designed along the lines of old mission chairs." Actually, the chair that inspired McHugh was only a few years old, built for the Swedenborgian church in San Francisco in 1894. Although McHugh's line had little success, the name "Mission" stuck. No one since has been able to set the story straight.

ART DECO FURNITURE
1925–1940

TWENTIETH-CENTURY STYLES

After the turn of the century, the reaction against factory-made furniture subsided, but the swing away from ornament continued. It culminated in the aesthetic of functionalism – "form follows function" – and the ultra-functional *International* style. However, not all designs were completely devoid of decoration. *Art Deco* furniture used exotic veneers and materials for embellishment.

After World War II, the International style spawned lighter, more versatile, and more economical furniture forms that have come to be called the *Contemporary* style. More recently, since the 1970s some designers have rebelled against the lack of

MISSION FURNITURE
1895–1925

CONTEMPORARY
FURNITURE
1950–PRESENT

AMERICAN FURNITURE STYLES: NINETEENTH CENTURY				
	1800	**1825**	**1850**	**1875**
Southwest Tradition	SOUTHWEST			
Eastern Tradition	PRIMITIVE			
	FEDERAL			PATENT
		AMERICAN EMPIRE		EASTLAKE
			VICTORIAN REVIVAL	MISSION
				OAK
Southern Tradition	SOUTHERN			
Folk Tradition	WINDSOR			
	PENNSYLVANIA GERMAN			
	SHAKER			

POSTMODERN FURNITURE 1975–PRESENT

SOUTHERN FURNITURE 1718–1803

WINDSOR CHAIRS 1725–1830

PENNSYLVANIA GERMAN FURNITURE 1730–1840

ornament. They have combined older Baroque and neoclassical elements with newer forms to create an innovative *Postmodern* style. Additionally, many individual craftsmen are exploring new designs, techniques, and materials in a riot of personal creativity, collectively called the *Studio* style because many of its adherents work in small one-man shops or studios. It's also referred to as the *Handicraft Revival* style.

SOUTHERN TRADITION, 1718 TO 1803

When the French established New Orleans in 1718, it quickly became a booming trade center, complete with its own furniture industry. The French-inspired *Southern* style was copied throughout much of the South during the eighteenth century, then blended into the Eastern tradition when France sold Louisiana to the United States.

FOLK TRADITION, 1725 TO 1935

There are several American furniture styles that did not follow prevailing trends. For religious, cultural, or personal reasons, the craftsmen who made these styles developed their own aesthetics and stuck to them.

Windsor chairs, for example, are based on English folk traditions, but American craftsmen made the style their own and introduced many new forms. American Windsors are distinguished by a thick seat, steeply sloped legs, and spindle backs.

German and Swiss immigrants banded together in tight enclaves outside of Philadelphia, where they preserved their own traditions. Among these were painted *Pennsylvania German* furniture, decorated with colorful folk designs.

The United Society of Believers in Christ's Second Appearing (the Shakers) founded their religion on the principles of celibacy, equality, communal living, and asceticism. Believing that "beauty rests in utility," they made *Shaker* furniture – carefully crafted, functional pieces devoid of almost all ornament.

STUDIO FURNITURE 1970–PRESENT

SHAKER FURNITURE 1790–1935

AMERICAN FURNITURE STYLES: TWENTIETH CENTURY

	1900	1925	1950	1975
Southwest Tradition				SOUTHWEST REVIVAL
Eastern Tradition	PATENT	ART DECO		
	MISSION		CONTEMPORARY	
	OAK			STUDIO
		INTERNATIONAL		POSTMODERN
Southern Tradition				
Folk Tradition	SHAKER			

A PHOTOGRAPHIC HISTORY OF AMERICAN FURNITURE STYLES

Courtesy Christopher Ferguson, Santa Fe, NM

SOUTHWEST STYLE, 1521–1850

As part of the Spanish missionary efforts in New Spain, immigrant ensembladores (cabinetmakers) trained native craftsmen to make furniture in the conquistadors' style. The Spanish designs were a unique blend of European and African art forms, remarkably similar to the Indians' own. These two decorative traditions combined in the distinctive Southwest style, exemplified by this antique table and chairs.

Courtesy Israel Sack, Inc., New York, NY

Courtesy Virginia Museum of Fine Arts, Richmond, VA

PRIMITIVE, 1607–1850

The pioneers who settled America were more concerned with survival than furniture. They made only the most essential, rudimentary pieces. This primitive style spread westward across the continent with the frontier, fading away when an area acquired enough people to support a woodworking trade. Folks sometimes held onto a primitive piece, even when they could afford better, decorating or updating it to suit their tastes. This chest of drawers, for example, may have been painted much later than it was made.

AMERICAN JACOBEAN, 1640–1690

By 1640, there were a small number of furniture shops in the newly established towns and villages along the Atlantic coast where cabinetmakers made oak and pine "Pilgrim" furniture after English Jacobean designs. As this "court cupboard" shows, these were often massive pieces, decorated with incised carvings, applied bosses, and spindles. Turned parts, such as chair rungs and table legs, were intricate and exaggerated.

A PHOTOGRAPHIC HISTORY OF AMERICAN FURNITURE STYLES

Courtesy Israel Sack, Inc., New York, NY

WILLIAM AND MARY, 1690–1725

William and Mary was lighter than preceding styles, often sporting scrolled skirts and intricately turned legs. "Trumpet" shapes and "turnip" feet, as shown on this lowboy, were common.

Courtesy Israel Sack, Inc., New York, NY

Courtesy Israel Sack, Inc., New York, NY

QUEEN ANNE, 1725–1760

Early in the eighteenth century, cabinet-makers became enamored of imported Chinese furniture. They began to use Oriental design elements such as cabriole legs, ball-and-claw feet, and shell carvings, as shown on this highboy.

CHIPPENDALE, 1760–1780

In 1754, Thomas Chippendale's English furniture designs were highly ornate, but the American interpretation was much more restrained. This blockfront desk, attributed to Edmund Townsend of Newport, Rhode Island, is an example of some of the very best American Chippendale furniture.

A PHOTOGRAPHIC HISTORY OF AMERICAN FURNITURE STYLES

Crafted by Lance Patterson, Boston, MA

FEDERAL, 1780–1820

After the American Revolution, American craftsmen looked to France for inspiration and found them experimenting with ancient Greek and Roman forms. The American interpretation of these "neoclassical" forms gave rise to Federal furniture. As this sideboard shows, Federal pieces were light and graceful, often veneered with exotic woods.

Crafted by George Ainley, Perkinsville, VT; photo by Rich Frutchey

Courtesy Louisiana State Museum, New Orleans, LA

WINDSOR, 1725–1830

American turners adapted this English folk form and invented several new twists, including the rocking chair. As this continuous-arm chair shows, the American Windsor style is distinguished by thick seats, steeply sloped legs, and spindle backs.

SOUTHERN, 1718–1803

After the French founded New Orleans, craftsmen throughout the South copied French colonial pieces such as this armoire. But after Louisiana was sold to the United States, these designs were absorbed by the Eastern tradition.

A PHOTOGRAPHIC HISTORY OF AMERICAN FURNITURE STYLES

Courtesy Israel Sack, Inc., New York, NY

PENNSYLVANIA GERMAN, 1730–1840

Immigrant German and Swiss craftsmen banded together in conservative communities outside Philadelphia to preserve their Old World traditions. Among these was a style of painted furniture adorned by brightly colored folk designs. This six-board chest shows tulips, a favorite motif.

Courtesy Hancock Shaker Village, Pittsfield, MA

SHAKER, 1790–1935

The Shaker faith was founded on celibacy, equality, communal living, and asceticism. Reflecting their beliefs, Shaker craftsmen created a purely functional style. These Shaker rockers use a minimum amount of materials and are almost devoid of ornament, yet they are surprisingly comfortable and durable.

A PHOTOGRAPHIC HISTORY OF AMERICAN FURNITURE STYLES

Courtesy The Hermitage: Home of President Andrew Jackson, Nashville, TN

Photo by Brad Simmons Photography

AMERICAN EMPIRE, 1815–1840

As Napoleon established his empire in France, neoclassical design became more severe and geometric. American furniture from this period, such as this canopy bed, was more massive and ornate.

VICTORIAN REVIVAL STYLES, 1840–1880

With the emergence of the British empire, Victorian craftsmen revived three older design philosophies from Britain's past. The Gothic revival resurrected medieval forms; the Rococo revival, Baroque; and the Renaissance revival, Renaissance. Pieces such as this Gothic Revival table were copied for fashionable upper-class Americans.

Courtesy Richard and Eileen Dubrow Antiques, Inc., Bayside, NY

PATENT, 1860–1910

America found the gadgetry of the Industrial Revolution fascinating, including "patent" furniture — ingenious pieces such as this "Wooton" desk that offered substantial improvements on old forms. This furniture was not so much designed as it was invented.

A PHOTOGRAPHIC HISTORY OF AMERICAN FURNITURE STYLES

Courtesy The Chicago Historical Society, Chicago, IL

EASTLAKE, 1870–1890

Toward the end of the nineteenth century, there was a reaction against excessive ornament and mass production. Charles Eastlake and his followers created Art furniture, a simpler alternative to the revival styles, characterized by simple geometric shapes and moldings, as shown on this rolltop desk.

Courtesy Linda Watts

OAK, 1870–1925

As more and more furniture was produced in factories, styles developed that lent themselves to machine production. These became known as Oak furniture, so-called because oak was the preferred material for production. These pieces often had contoured pediments and applied carvings. Many popular designs, such as this dresser, were asymmetrical.

Courtesy Don Treadway Gallery, Inc., Cincinnati, OH

MISSION, 1895–1920

Mission or Arts and Crafts furniture also grew out of a reaction against industrialization. Its proponents emphasized simplicity, utility, and "honest craftsmanship." They resurrected many old medieval forms and invented some new ones, such as this "Morris" chair and "flower" table.

A PHOTOGRAPHIC HISTORY OF AMERICAN FURNITURE STYLES

Courtesy Herman Miller, Inc., Zeeland, MI

INTERNATIONAL, 1920–1960

The first "modern" style grew out of the aesthetic of functionalism, which stressed the utility of form and materials. International furniture was characterized by simple structure and minimal decoration. The forms — such as the pleasing curves of these chair seats and backs — were considered adequate adornment.

Courtesy The Chicago Historical Society, Chicago, IL; photo by Abramson-Culbert Studio

ART DECO, 1925–1945

Craftsmen who worked in the Art Deco style also used simple shapes and structures. But their designs were not as austere. They often employed restrained stylized ornament and exotic materials, such as the imported veneers that were used in this sideboard.

Crafted by Jesse Woodworks, Salem OR; photo by Steve Viale

CONTEMPORARY, 1950–PRESENT

The Contemporary style was the direct descendant of International design. The furniture grew lighter, more elegant, and even more functional, as this chest of drawers shows.

A PHOTOGRAPHIC HISTORY OF AMERICAN FURNITURE STYLES

Crafted by Larry Templeton, Dallas, TX; photo by Cutter-Smith Photographic

Crafted by Lynette Breton, Brunswick, ME; photo by John Tanabe

SOUTHWEST REVIVAL, 1970–PRESENT

As the American Bicentennial renewed interest in our history, Southwestern craftsmen revived the old Southwest style. Today, these designs are often blended with modern forms to produce highly stylized pieces such as this arm chair, with both contemporary and Southwest characteristics.

STUDIO, 1970–PRESENT

This term encompasses the multitude of highly individual designs that are built by craftsmen today. If there is any central theme at all, it's technique. Studio craftsmen have invented many new woodworking techniques and have pushed traditional methods to new frontiers. For example, the book-matched veneered panels and the leaded glass that echoes them on this bookcase are a powerful display of craftsmanship.

POSTMODERN, 1975–PRESENT

Rebelling against the dearth of ornament in Contemporary designs, some craftsmen have begun to mix modern forms with classical design elements from older styles. This has produced a contemporary style with a traditional touch. This writing table, for instance, echoes the Queen Anne form, but there are many modern touches such as the carved drawer pull.

Crafted by W. Richard Goehring, Gambier, OH

MORE SOURCES

BOOKS

Overviews and Mixed Styles

American Antiques from the Israel Sack Collection, Volumes 1 through 7, Highland House Publishing, 1981

American Furniture, by John S. Bowman, Crown Publishing Group, 1995

American Furniture in the Metropolitan Museum of Art, Volumes 1 through 3, by Morrison H. Heckscher, The Metropolitan Museum of Art, 1985

The Best of Fine Woodworking: Traditional Furniture Projects, Taunton Press, 1991

Dictionary of Furniture, by Charles Boyce, Henry Holt & Co., 1988

Fine Woodworking Design Books (One through Six), Taunton Press, 1977–1992

Four Centuries of American Furniture, by Oscar P. Fitzgerald, Gramercy Publishing Company, 1996

Furniture Treasury, by Wallace Nutting, MacMillan Publishing Co., 1928

The Knopf Collectors' Guides to American Antiques: Furniture, Volumes 1 and 2, Alfred A. Knopf Inc.,1982

The New Fine Points of Furniture: Early American..., by Albert Sack, Crown Publishing Group, 1993

Chippendale

Chippendale, by Nathaniel Harris, Chartwell Books, 1989

Thomas Elfe: Cabinetmaker, by Samuel A. Humphrey, Wyrick & Co., 1995

Country Furniture

American Country, by Mary Ellisor Emmerling, Clarkson N. Potter Inc., 1980

American Country Furniture: Projects from the Workshops of David T. Smith, by Nick Engler and Mary Jane Favorite, Rodale Press, 1990

American Painted Furniture 1660–1880, by Dean A. Fales, Random House Value Publishing, 1991

Country Pine, by Bill Hylton, Rodale Press, 1995

The Heritage of Upper Canadian Furniture, by Howard Pain, Key Porter Books, 1984

Pine Furniture of Early New England, by Russell Hawes Kettell, Dover Publications, 1956

Empire Furniture

Duncan Phyfe and the English Regency, by Nancy McCloud, Dover Publications, 1980

Federal Furniture

Federal Furniture, by Michael Dunbar, Taunton Press, 1986

Mission Furniture

Making Authentic Craftsman Furniture, Collected from The Craftsman magazine 1901 to 1916, Dover Publications, 1986

Mission Furniture: How to Make It, by Popular Mechanics Company Staff, Dover Publications, 1980

Oak Furniture

Furniture Made in America: 1875-1905, by Richard and Eileen Dubrow, Schiffer Publishing, 1982

Golden Oak Furniture, by Velma Susanne Warren, Schiffer Publishing, 1992

Pennsylvania German Furniture

Decorated Furniture of Mahantongo Valley, by Henry M. Reed, Bucknell University Press, 1987

The Pennsylvania German Collection, by Beatrice B. Garvan, Philadelphia Museum of Art, 1982

Postmodern Furniture

Measured Shop Drawings for American Furniture, by Thomas Moser, Sterling Publishing, 1988

Queen Anne Furniture

Master Craftsmen of Newport, The Townsends and Goddards, by Michael Moses, MMI Americana Press, 1981

Queen Anne Furniture, by Norman Vandal, Taunton Press, 1990

Shaker Furniture

The Book of Shaker Furniture, by John Kassay, University of Massachusetts Press, 1980

Making Authentic Shaker Furniture: With Measured Drawings of Museum Classics, by John G. Shea, Dover Publications, 1992 (originally published as *The American Shakers and Their Furniture,* by John G. Shea, Van Nostrand Reinhold Co., 1971)

Religion in Wood, A Book of Shaker Furniture, by Edward and Faith Andrews, Indiana University Press, 1971

The Shaker Chair, by Charles Muller and Timothy Rieman, University of Massachusetts Press, 1992

Shaker Design, by June Sprigg, Whitney Museum of American Art, 1980

Shop Drawings of Shaker Furniture and Woodenware, Volumes 1 through 3, by Ejner Handberg, Berkshire House Publishers, 1991

Southern Furniture

Neat Pieces, the Plain-Style Furniture of 19th Century Georgia, Atlanta Historical Society, 1983

Southwest Furniture

The Encyclopedia of Spanish Period Furniture Designs, by Jose Claret Rubira, Sterling Publishing, 1984

Hispanic Furniture, by Sali Katz, Architectural Book Publishing Co., 1986

New Mexican Furniture, 1600-1940, by Lonn Taylor and Dessa Bokides, Museum of New Mexico Press, 1987

Studio Furniture

The Best of Fine Woodworking: Modern Furniture Projects, Taunton Press, 1991

Contemporary American Woodworkers, by Michael A. Stone, Peregrine Smith Books, 1986

Furniture Projects, by Rod Wales, GMC Publishing, 1991

Victorian Furniture

The Victorian Cabinet-Maker's Assistant, Dover Publications, 1970

Windsor Chairs

Make a Windsor Chair with Michael Dunbar, by Michael Dunbar, Taunton Press, 1984

Windsor Style in America, by Charles Santore, Running Press, 1992

MUSEUMS

Art Institute of Chicago, Chicago, IL

Baltimore Museum of Art, Baltimore, MD

Colonial Williamsburg, Williamsburg, VA

Henry Ford Museum and Greenfield Village, Dearborn, MI

High Museum of Art, Atlanta, GA

The Metropolitan Museum of Art, New York, NY

Museum of Early Southern Decorative Arts, Winston-Salem, NC

Museum of Fine Arts, Houston, TX

Museum of International Folk Art, Museum of New Mexico, Santa Fe, NM

National Museum of American History, Smithsonian Institution, Washington, DC

Old Salem, Winston-Salem, NC

Old Sturbridge Village, Sturbridge, MA

Philadelphia Museum of Art, Philadelphia, PA

Shaker Museum, Old Chatham, NY

Shakertown, Pleasant Hill, KY

Wadsworth Atheneum, Hartford, CT

William Penn Memorial Museum, Harrisburg, PA

Winterthur Museum, Winterthur, DE

Planning a Project

Plan your work; work your plan.

No matter what types or styles of woodworking projects you like to build, the first step is always to get or make a *plan* – a road map that helps you decide what materials to buy, how to cut them, and how to fit them together.

It's impossible to overemphasize the importance of a plan. Few craftsmen can visualize all the design and construction details of a project unless it's fairly simple. Drawing or studying a plan helps you work out whatever problems you might encounter without wasting precious wood or shop time. In effect, a plan lets you build the project on paper and see what it will look like before you make your first cut. For this critical step, craftsmen have developed a simple "language of lines." You may know this language as engineering drawing, architectural drawing, or simply *drafting*.

READING A PROJECT PLAN

Every time you open a woodworking magazine or book with project plans, you are reading this language. It's an intuitive, "user-friendly" method of communication, straightforward and easy to follow, even for a novice.

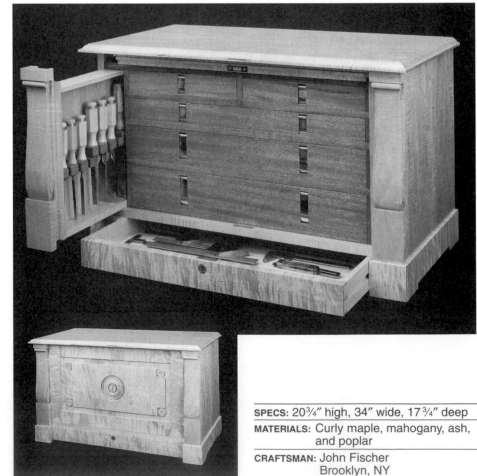

Photos by Lance Patterson

*Every **Tool Chest** is an exercise in precision planning, practicality, and proportion. In designing this bench top chest for hand tools, the craftsman started with a "golden rectangle" (a rectangular shape with especially pleasing proportions) and filled it in with drawers that grow progressively deeper from top to bottom. Then he hid three additional drawers in the chest — two in the sides and one in the bottom — without disturbing the simple proportions in his design.*

SPECS: 20¾" high, 34" wide, 17¾" deep

MATERIALS: Curly maple, mahogany, ash, and poplar

CRAFTSMAN: John Fischer
Brooklyn, NY

ORTHOGRAPHIC PROJECTIONS

Woodworking projects such as this country-style "Porringer Table" are commonly presented in an *orthographic projection,* showing face-on views from the front, side, and top. This is commonly called a *three-view.* A simpler project may require only two views; more complex pieces may need four or more. Important details, such as the mortises and tenons that join the legs and aprons, may be shown in sections, in cutaways, or by themselves. Each view and detail is drawn to *scale* so you see the true proportions of the parts. A good projection

will tell you everything you need to know to build the project – the size and shape of the individual parts, how they fit together, even the fasteners used to assemble them.

A LANGUAGE OF LINES

The lines and symbols in the plans all have precise meanings. Thick, solid lines, for example, are *object lines* – they outline a solid object. Thin lines terminating in arrows indicate dimensions; dotted lines show hidden parts. Important details are described in call-outs; common words and phrases are often abbreviated. *FHWS,* for

example, denotes a "flathead wood screw," while *RAD* is the radius of a curved shape. *TYP* stands for "typical," and indicates similar features in the drawing are the same size.

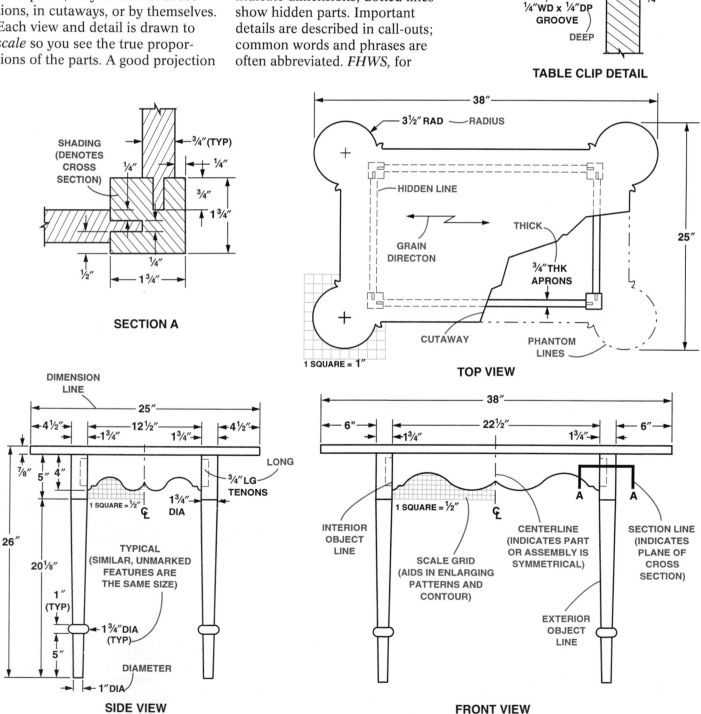

LISTS

Project drawings are usually accompanied by one or more lists – lists of wooden parts, hardware, and raw materials.

BILL OF MATERIALS

The most important of these is the *bill of materials,* or materials list. This is actually two lists – a *cutting list* to indicate the final size of each wooden part, and a *hardware list* that describes the non-wood materials. Often, the bill of materials is keyed to a three-dimensional *exploded view* of the project.

A bill of materials is essential because it allows you to *check the plan for errors.* Much of the information in the drawings is repeated in the bill of materials, but in list form.

SHOPPING LIST

A *shopping list* tells you the amounts of materials needed to build a project. You can figure this from a bill of materials.

To calculate the amount of solid stock, look down the cutting list and decide the **rough thickness of stock**[1] needed to make each part. (For example, you'll need 4/4 [four-quarter] stock to make ³/4-inch-thick parts.) Multiply the length and width of each part (in inches) to get the *surface area* (SA) in square inches. Total the surface area of those parts that are the same thickness, and convert the total to square feet by dividing by 144. Then multiply by the thickness of the rough-cut lumber in quarter inches (X/4). This will give you the number of **board feet**[2] (BF) required. Here's the equation:

$$(SA \div 144) \times X/4 = BF$$

To figure the amount of sheet materials, calculate the surface area (SA) in square inches for each thickness required. Divide these totals by 4608, the surface area of a standard 48-inch by 96-inch sheet. This will tell you the number of sheets needed. The equation is:

$$SA \div 4608 = \text{\# of sheets}$$

PRO *TIP*

After figuring the board feet of solid stock or the amount of sheet materials required, add an extra 20% for wastage and round up to the next highest whole number. If you're working with **common grades**[3] of stock, add 30% or more.

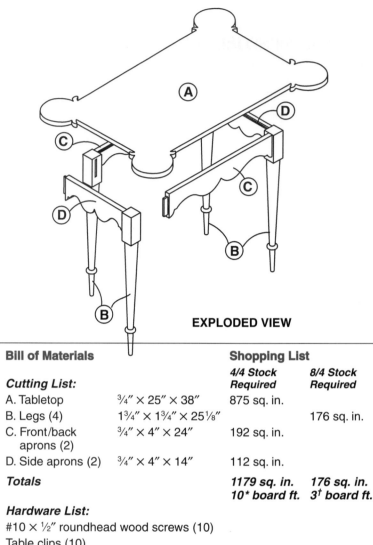

EXPLODED VIEW

Bill of Materials		Shopping List	
Cutting List:		**4/4 Stock Required**	**8/4 Stock Required**
A. Tabletop	³/4″ × 25″ × 38″	875 sq. in.	
B. Legs (4)	1³/4″ × 1³/4″ × 25¹/8″		176 sq. in.
C. Front/back aprons (2)	³/4″ × 4″ × 24″	192 sq. in.	
D. Side aprons (2)	³/4″ × 4″ × 14″	112 sq. in.	
Totals		**1179 sq. in.** **10* board ft.**	**176 sq. in.** **3† board ft.**

Hardware List:
#10 × ¹/2″ roundhead wood screws (10)
Table clips (10)

*(1179 ÷ 144 × 4/4) + 20% = 9.8, or 10 when rounded up
†(176 ÷ 144 × 8/4) + 20% = 2.9, or 3 when rounded up

CUTTING DIAGRAMS

When figuring shopping lists, it often helps to make *cutting diagrams,* sketching out how you would cut up the stock to make the parts. This is especially helpful when making projects from plywood. The cutting diagram below shows how to make a "Parsons" coffee table from a half-sheet of plywood. Remember to allow for the width of the saw kerf (usually ¹/8 inch) between the parts.

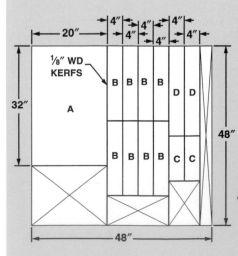

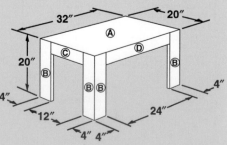

DRAWING A PROJECT PLAN

When building an original project or adapting a design, you must make your own scale drawings. This requires very little artistic talent; just patience and a few simple drafting tools.

SCALE

You'll find that quarter scale (¼ inch = 1 inch) works well for most woodworking projects. Extremely large projects may require a slightly smaller scale; smaller projects may need a larger one. You can count off the fractions on an ordinary ruler, but this gets old. An *architect's rule* (available at office supply stores) provides a selection of easy-to-use scales.

Many craftsmen prefer to draw *full-size* plans. These have several advantages. You can better evaluate a design when you see it life-size. You can also make direct measurements on a full-size drawing and use it to trace templates and patterns.

DETAIL

The amount of detail you put in your drawings depends on the design and your experience. If your project is assembled with mortises and tenons that you've made many times before, there's probably no need to detail this joinery. But if the project includes unfamiliar parts, drawing them gets you acquainted with their construction. At the very least, your plan should include enough detail to enable you to evaluate the design and — presuming you find it to your liking — put together a bill of materials.

SEE *ALSO*:

[1]Sawyering	336
[2]Purchasing Lumber	342
[3]Softwood Lumber Grades	340
[3]Hardwood Lumber Grades	341

TRADITIONAL DRAFTING TOOLS

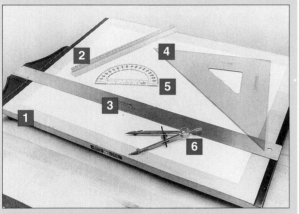

Basic Equipment You can produce sophisticated plans with simple drawing tools. At a minimum, you need:

1 A **drawing board**   4 A **right triangle**
2 A **rule**   5 A **protractor**
3 A **T-square**   6 A **compass**

Scales An **architect's rule** makes it simple to draw to scale. This rule may be flat or triangular and is marked with several useful scales as well as full-size measurements.

Templates To save time, use templates to create simple shapes. **French curves,** for example, help draw fair curves and contours. A **circle template** will make small circles.

BASIC DRAFTING KNOW-HOW

Tape the paper down securely to the drawing board so it can't shift as you work.

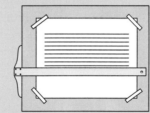

Horizontal Lines Use a T-square to draw horizontal lines.

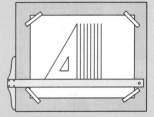

Vertical Lines Use a T-square and triangle to draw vertical lines or lines at common angles.

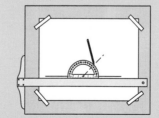

Angles Use a protractor to draw lines at odd angles.

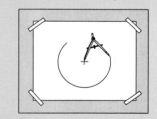

Circles Use a compass to create circles and curves.

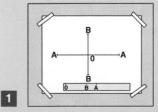

1

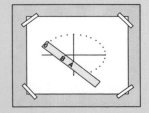

2

Ellipses Draw the major (long) and minor (short) axes. On a straightedge, mark point "0" and lengths A and B. Then place the straightedge so the A-mark falls on the minor axis and B on the major axis. Make a dot at "0." Change the straightedge angle, realign the marks with the axes, and make another dot. Repeat until the dots form an ellipse.

SHOP MATH

To plan a project, you must know a little math. You must be able to read a ruler and a protractor and understand how to add and subtract fractions and degrees. Beyond that, there are several useful formulas – mathematical shortcuts – that help you make precise plans.

PLANE GEOMETRY

Most woodworking problems can be solved with *plane geometry,* the branch of mathematics that describes two-dimensional shapes. These calculations are often so straightforward, you may not realize you're doing geometry.

When you're planning a picture frame, for example, and you want to know how much molding to make, you figure the perimeter of the rectangular frame – 2 times the width plus 2 times the length. When making a shopping list, you figure the area of the rectangular boards by multiplying width times length.

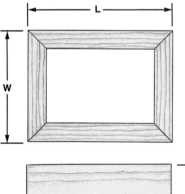

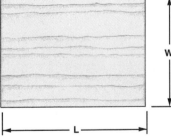

Plane geometry divides a circle into 360 degrees. This system of *angular* measure is as indispensable as *linear* measure (inches and feet). To figure the angle between the sides in an octagonal box, divide 360 by the number of sides: 360 ÷ 8 = 45 degrees. To find the

miter angle that you must cut to join the sides, divide the angle between the sides by 2 and subtract from 90: 90 - (45 ÷ 2) = 67½ degrees.

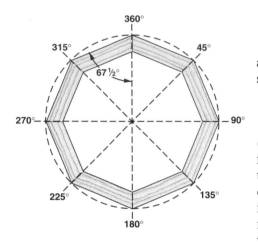

Plane geometry also provides a method for figuring the circumference and area of circles and arcs. Should you need to know how much banding to buy to cover the edge of a round table top 48 inches across, multiply the diameter by the value of *pi,* 3.1416: 48 × 3.1416 = 150.8 inches, approximately.

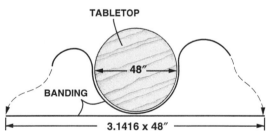

TABLETOP

48"

BANDING

3.1416 x 48"

TRIGONOMETRY

Not all woodworking problems are quite so simple, however. Occasionally you need to resort to a mathematical system with a little more firepower.

Trigonometry is a special type of geometry that describes *right triangles.* A right triangle has three parts – a *side* (a), a *base* (b), and a *hypotenuse* (c). The angle (C) between the side and the base is always 90 degrees, while the other two angles (A and B) always total 90 degrees. Also, in a right triangle the square of the hypotenuse c is

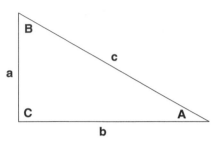

always equal to the sum of the squares of side a and base b:

$$c^2 = a^2 + b^2$$

This is the Pythagorean Theorem (after the Greek philosopher who formulated it), and it's what gives trigonometry its teeth. Often, you can divide the design of a project into right triangles to calculate missing dimensions. Any rectangular wooden piece, the mitered end of a board, even complex shapes such as tapered legs and dovetails, can be divided into triangles. Applying the theorem, you can calculate the dimension of any part of a right triangle, provided you know the length of the other two.

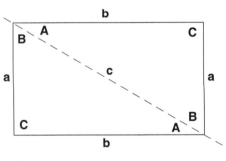

There is also a proportional relationship between the parts of a right triangle and the *angles* at the corners. Mathematicians call these relationships the *sine, cosine,* and *tangent* (usually abbreviated *sin, cos,* and *tan*). It's not important to understand how these values are figured. Just know that you can use them to find any dimension or any angle in a right triangle, provided you know either the length of two parts or the length of one part and the angle of one corner other than the right (90-degree) corner. The formulas for figuring dimensions and angles are listed in "Indispensable Shop Formulas" on the opposite page.

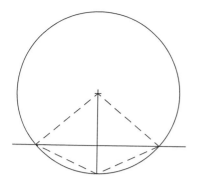

You can also use trigonometry to decribe circles and arcs. This makes it possible to figure the dimensions or the radius of curved parts, such as a rocker on a rocking chair. These formulas are also listed at right under **Circles and Arcs.**

MAKING CALCULATIONS

To use many of these formulas, you must be able to figure square roots or look up the sines, cosines, and tangents of angles. You'll find tables of these values, as well as instructions for calculating square roots, in most trigonometry and algebra books, but a *scientific* calculator will do the job more easily and will cost less.

To find a sine, cosine, or tangent with a scientific calculator, enter the degrees on the numerical keypad, then push the appropriate SIN, COS, or TAN key. To find the degree that corresponds to a sine, cosine, or tangent, punch the value on the numerical keypad, press the INV or SHIFT key, then the appropriate SIN, COS, or TAN key.

INDISPENSABLE SHOP FORMULAS

Plane Geometry

Triangles

Perimeter = a + b + c
Area = a × b ÷ 2

Circles

Circumference = 3.1416 × d
Area = 3.1416 × r^2

Rectangles

Perimeter = 2a + 2b
Area = a × b

Ellipses

Perimeter =
3.1416 (1.5 [a + b] - $\sqrt{ab}$)
Area = 3.1416 × a × b

Regular Polygons *(all sides equal)*
N = Number of sides

Perimeter = N × a
Area = (N × a × r) ÷ 2

Corner Angles
N = Number of sides

Angle between sides = 360 ÷ N
Miter angle = 90 - (360 ÷ 2N)

Trigonometry

Right Triangles

Parts and Angles Known	Formulas for Parts and Angles to Be Found		
Side a, base b	c = $\sqrt{a^2 + b^2}$	tanA = a ÷ b	B = 90° - A
Side a, hyp. c	b = $\sqrt{c^2 - a^2}$	sinA = a ÷ c	B = 90° - A
Base b, hyp. c	a = $\sqrt{c^2 - b^2}$	sinB = b ÷ c	A = 90° - B
Side a, angle A	c = a ÷ sinA	b = a ÷ tanA	B = 90° - A
Side a, angle B	c = a ÷ cosB	b = a × tanB	A = 90° - B
Base b, angle A	c = b ÷ cosA	a = b × tanA	B = 90° - A
Base b, angle B	c = b ÷ sinB	a = b ÷ tanB	A = 90° - B
Hyp. c, angle A	b = c × cosA	a = c × sinA	B = 90° - A
Hyp. c, angle B	b = c × sinB	a = c × cosB	A = 90° - B

Circles and Arcs

r = (l^2 + $4h^2$) ÷ 8h
h = r - ($\sqrt{4r^2 - l^2}$ ÷ 2)
l = 2 $\sqrt{h(2r - h)}$

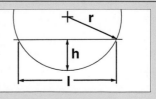

PROPORTION

Although precision is important, it's not enough. A good woodworking design must also have *pleasing proportions.*

GOLDEN SECTION

What constitutes pleasing proportions is not just a matter of taste. There are concrete guidelines, and one of the most widely used is the *golden section.* Ancient Greek architects found they could better satisfy the public sense of proportion by dividing lines and shapes into sections so the smaller part (a) was to the larger part (b) as the larger part was to the whole (a + b):

$$a \div b = b \div (a + b)$$

The only ratio that satisfies this condition is 1 to 1.618. To figure the larger length, multiply the smaller by 1.618. To find the smaller, divide the larger by 1.618. You can also use this ratio to construct a *golden rectangle* in which the long sides are 1.618 times the length of the short ones.

This sketch of a dry sink shows how to apply the golden section.

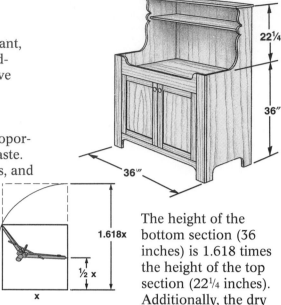

The height of the bottom section (36 inches) is 1.618 times the height of the top section (22¼ inches). Additionally, the dry sink's outline, as seen from the front, is a golden rectangle (36 inches by 58¼ inches).

SYMMETRY AND ASYMMETRY

Most woodworking designs are symmetrical. If you divide them in half vertically, the right half is a mirror image of the left half. There's a good reason for this – it makes them easier to build. However, a little asymmetry is good for the soul. It helps balance shapes and creates visual interest.

Consider the following two cabinet designs. In one, both the cab-inet and its doors are symmetrical. Where the doors swing together, the two interior stiles appear as a wide, disproportionate strip. A designer might say the doors are "overbalanced." In the other, the cabinet remains symmetrical, but the doors are not. The width of the adjoining stiles has been reduced to balance the doors.

CABINET AND DOORS SYMMETRICAL   **CABINET SYMMETRICAL, DOORS ASYMMETRICAL**

PROGRESSION

Repetitive elements in a design, like drawers in a chest or shelves in a case, often look better if they are sized or positioned according to a mathematical progression.

Consider a chest of drawers in which all the drawers are the same size. It looks top-heavy. In a well-proportioned chest, the drawers might follow a simple *arithmetic progression.* Each drawer is a constant amount deeper than the one above it. This makes the piece look more stable.

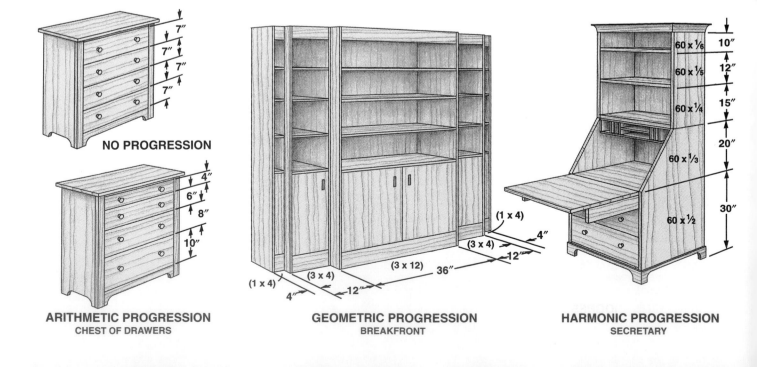

NO PROGRESSION

ARITHMETIC PROGRESSION
CHEST OF DRAWERS

GEOMETRIC PROGRESSION
BREAKFRONT

HARMONIC PROGRESSION
SECRETARY

Arithmetic progression is one of several possible systems. You might also use:

■ *Geometric progression,* which builds on a constant ratio. The series 4, 12, 36, builds on a ratio of 3 – each number is three times the preceding number.

■ *Harmonic progression,* in which the ratios are reciprocals of a sequence. You obtain a reciprocal by dividing a number into 1. The sequence $\frac{1}{2}$, $\frac{1}{3}$, $\frac{1}{4}$, $\frac{1}{5}$ is the harmonic of 2, 3, 4, 5.

■ *Hambridge progression,* in which the ratios are successive square roots – 1, 1.41, 1.73, 2 are the square roots of 1, 2, 3, 4. Multiply the roots by the width of the piece as shown in the drawing below.

MORE *SOURCES*

Designing Furniture, by Seth Stem, Taunton Press, 1989

Machinery's Handbook, by Eric Oberg, Industrial Press, 1996

Measure Twice, Cut Once, by Jim Tolpin, Betterway Books, 1993

Technical Drawing, by George Stegman and Jerry Jenkins, Macmillan Publishing, 1986

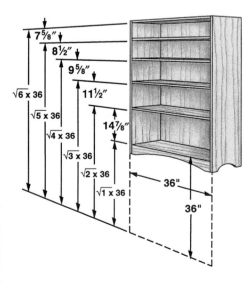

HAMBRIDGE PROGRESSION
BOOKCASE

FROM PHOTOGRAPH TO PROJECT PLAN

How many times have you seen a photo of a striking piece of furniture and wished you had a project plan? It's not difficult to draw plans from a photo — just apply a few tricks and some intelligent guesswork. Suppose you'd like plans for a Mission bookcase you saw in a book. Make several photocopies of the picture to draw on.

REFERENCE DIMENSION

1 *To start, you need a reference dimension — the height, width, or depth of the bookcase. If there's no clue in the caption or story, search the photo. In this case, there are books on the shelves. The average height of a book is about 10 inches. Measure the height of one of the books in the picture — it's about $\frac{3}{4}$ inch tall. Divide this into 10 and you get a ratio of 13.3. Measure the height of the bookcase **at the same position as the book** — 4$\frac{1}{2}$ inches. Multiply this by the ratio and you find that the bookcase is 60 inches tall.*

ROUGHING OUT A FRONT VIEW

2 *Draw a long vertical line on a piece of paper. Place the photo several inches to one side of the line, arrange it so the side of the bookcase and the line are parallel, and tape the photo to the paper. Use a straightedge to extend the horizontal lines in the front of the bookcase (top, rails, and shelves) to the vertical line. Where the extended lines meet the vertical line, draw parallel lines out from those points, perpendicular to the vertical line and away from the photo.*

(continued)

FROM PHOTOGRAPH TO PROJECT PLAN — CONTINUED

VERTICAL MEASUREMENTS

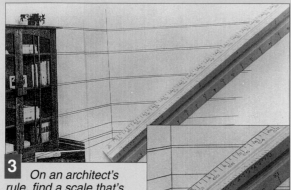

3 *On an architect's rule, find a scale that's close to, but just a little larger than, the photo. Place the rule diagonally across the parallel lines and position it so "0" is on the bottom line and 60 (on the scale) aligns with the top line. Draw a diagonal line across the parallel lines. Using the same scale, measure the distance between parallel lines along the diagonal. This will tell you the vertical measurements of the bookcase — distance between shelves, width of the rails, length of the legs, and so on.*

HORIZONTAL MEASUREMENTS

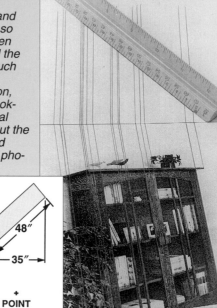

4 *Draw a horizontal line and tape the photo to the paper so the top is parallel with it. Then repeat Steps 2 and 3 to find the horizontal measurements such as the widths of the doors.*

For a reference dimension, estimate the width of the bookcase. If you apply the original ratio, you'll get 35 inches. But the width appears foreshortened because the bookcase was photographed at an angle. A better guess would be 48 inches.

Remember this when you make the measurements. The near door will appear wider than the far one, even though the two are the same width. Use your common sense to adjust the results.

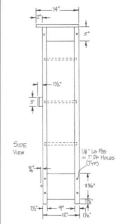

48"

35"

+ POINT OF VIEW

REFINING THE FRONT VIEW

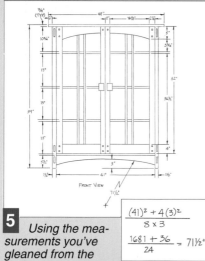

Front View

5 *Using the measurements you've gleaned from the photo, draw a rough front view to scale and study the results. Check it against the architectural and engineering data at your disposal. Are 48-inch shelves too long? Will they sag? No; according to the chart of "Standard Shelving Dimensions" on page 28, the maximum shelving span for ¾-inch-thick hardwood is 48 inches.*

$$\frac{(41)^2 + 4(3)^2}{8 \times 3}$$

$$\frac{1681 + 36}{24} = 71\frac{1}{2}''$$

*Fill in any missing measurements. What are the radii of the arcs on the door frames and the apron? Using a formula under **Circles and Arcs** in "Indispensable Shop Formulas" on page 71, you'll find they are 71½ inches.*

SIDE AND TOP VIEWS

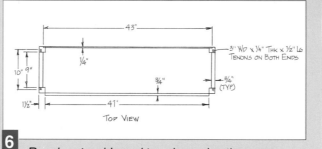

Top View

6 *Rough out a side and top view using the same process. Or, take a shortcut. "Standard Shelving Dimensions" on page 28 tells you the accepted depth for bookshelves is 11½ inches. It's a fair bet that this bookcase is about that deep on the inside. With this dimension and the information already accumulated, it's a simple matter to draft the missing views.*

Side View

ASSEMBLY DETAILS

7 *Finally, decide on how you will assemble the bookcase. You don't have to know how this one is assembled as long as your reproduction looks like the original. Consult the section on "Shelving" on page 27 for some simple constructions. Study plans of other shelving to evaluate alternatives. When you've designed a good joinery system, add the assembly details to your drawings.*

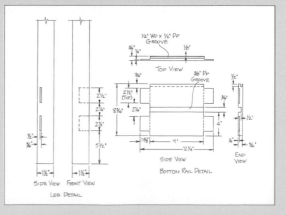

Side View   Front View
LEG DETAIL

Side View   End View
BOTTOM RAIL DETAIL

WOODWORKING TOOLS

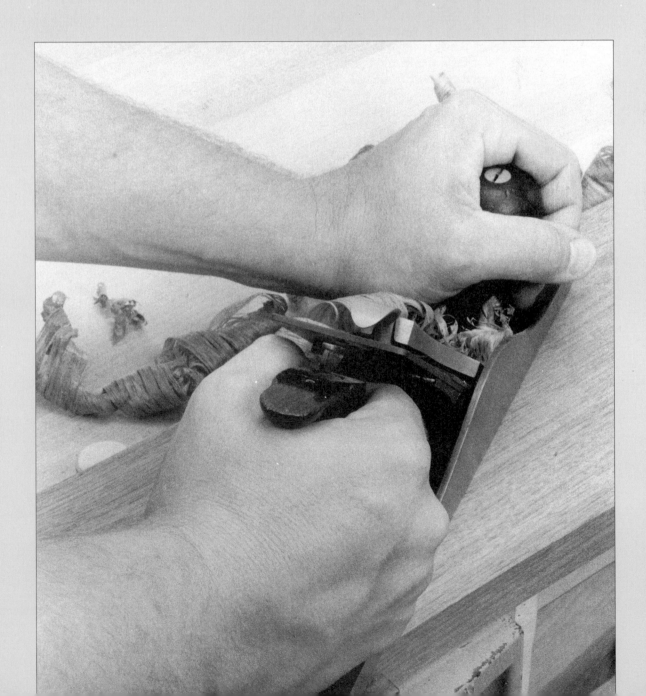

The Workshop Environment

A workshop is a unique environment – careful layout and planning make it comfortable and safe.

The most precious commodity in your workshop is the space in which you work. If that space is comfortable and efficient, you'll want to spend more time in the shop and enjoy it more. Consequently, you'll get more done and do better work.

So how do you put together a comfortable shop? There is no single answer. Many different configurations will work, although some will work better than others. Furthermore, a design that works well for one woodworker may not work at all for another. A good design depends on

- How you like to work
- What you like to build
- The available space

SHOP ORGANIZATION

All the major fixtures in your shop – workbenches, tool cabinets, and stationary tools – require two kinds of space. They occupy *physical space,* which is determined by the actual dimensions of the item. And they also require *working space,* the room needed to work at a bench, open a cabinet, or use a tool.

For example, to rip 8-foot-long boards on your table saw, there must be 8 feet of unobstructed space in front *and* in back of the saw – this is the working space that surrounds it. Not only do you need the physical space in your shop for a table saw, but you must also have adequate working space *around* the tool to use it.

*Part of the attraction of woodworking is the mystique of the workshop environment. Few craftsmen understand this better than **Scott Phillips,** the host of television's **American Workshop,** who consciously designed his workshop to be comfortable and conducive to woodworking. "I want my viewers to feel at home," says Scott. "A workshop should be a place you want to visit again and again."*

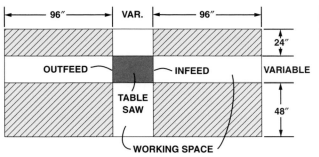

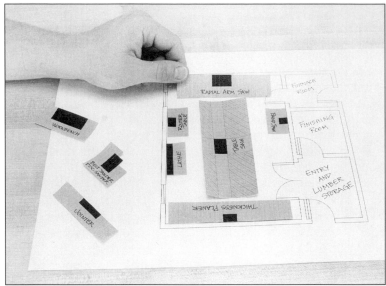

*Draw a scaled **floor plan** to properly arrange your shop and ensure enough working space. On a separate piece of paper, sketch the top views of your tools and fixtures, as well as the working space that surrounds them. Arrange the paper outlines on the floor plan. Remember, the working spaces can overlap each other, but you must not obstruct the working space of one tool by placing it too close to another.*

ARRANGING SHOP FIXTURES

Whenever you add a major new fixture to your shop, consider *both* types of space. Can you make the new tool fit *and* leave enough space around it to maneuver materials safely and easily? You can overlap working spaces, but you should not place one tool inside another's working space.

If you can't find an arrangement that provides adequate space, try arranging several fixtures in a *cluster*, making one working space serve for all. To do this, you must modify **stands and supports**[1] so all the work surfaces in the cluster are the same height. Or, consider making your tools **mobile**[2], and use a central area in your shop as a common working space. When you need a machine, move it into the working space and store the others out of the way.

WORKSTATIONS

Also consider *work flow* when arranging tools. You can work more efficiently if you keep related tools and accessories together in a *work-station*. For example, you might place a router table on a stand that stores router bits and other accessories. Whenever you need to rout, all your routing tools will be close at hand and easy to find.

However, it's not always a good idea to keep *all* related tools together, particularly if you must stuff your workstations to the gills to do so. You can free up working space and eliminate clutter by keeping only *frequently* used tools in a workstation. Store occasionally used items in out-of-the-way locations.

SEE *ALSO:*

[1]Tool Stands   96

[2]Making Shop Furniture
Mobile   97

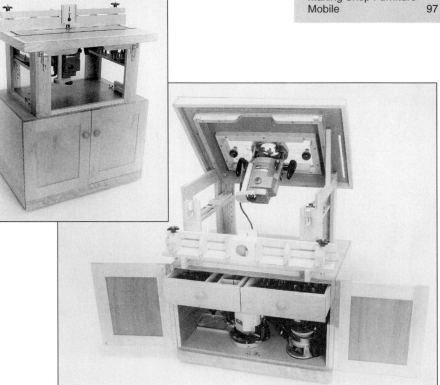

*This router table and cabinet form a routing **workstation**. All the frequently used routing tools — hand-held router, table-mounted router, router bits, router accessories — are stored and used at the same location.*

SHOP STORAGE

In addition to the physical and working space, every workshop needs an adequate amount of *storage space*. In addition to the tools themselves, you must store

- Lumber and sheet materials
- Hardware and fasteners
- Expendable supplies such as glues, abrasives, and finishes
- Unfinished projects

STORAGE SPACE

Space for these items needn't eat into your working area. In fact, most shops have an abundance of unused space that can be used for storage. The walls, for example, offer a vast storage area for small and medium-size items. Corners often make good places for **tool cabinets**[1] and wood racks. And there's often plenty of room **under a tool**[2] or around it that doesn't include the working space.

VISIBILITY AND ACCESS

The keys to good storage are *visibility* and *access*. You must be able to see what's in storage and retrieve it easily. This is why walls make such good storage spaces – a hanging item is visible and (provided there's a clear path to the wall) accessible.

Give this careful thought when designing storage systems. There is nothing that eats up good shop time quicker than having to search for a tool, then having to move dozens of items to reach it.

*These **storage cabinets** show how you can make use of the area under and around a tool without sacrificing working space. The counter units rest under the working space for the radial arm saw. In fact, the countertops provide additional support for the work. The wall units hang above the work.*

The shelves in this tool cabinet are angled, making it easier to see and reach the hand planes stored on them. Shelves are great storage devices, but small items often hide behind larger ones. To prevent this, either angle the shelves or make narrow ones.

Not even the best storage system can keep everything in plain sight. When things are hidden, it helps to label items. In this wood storage rack, the wood species and figure are carefully marked on the board ends to save digging through the stack. To help identify the fasteners stored in these bins, samples have been attached to the front surfaces.

JIGS & FIXTURES

LUMBER RACKS AND BINS

Next to your stationary tools, materials take up the most room in your shop. Long boards, sheet materials such as plywood, and *shorts* — cut-off boards and small pieces of plywood that are too large to throw away — all require different storage fixtures.

Long boards are best stored in a *rack,* either horizontal or vertical. It's okay to store boards vertically for short periods of time, but they begin to bow after a few weeks. Storing them horizontally helps keep your stock flat.

If possible, make an *open rack* rather than a *closed rack.* Open

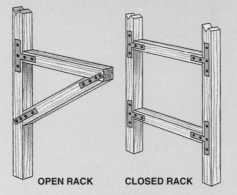

OPEN RACK   CLOSED RACK

racks allow easier access — you can remove the boards sideways. With a closed rack, you must pull the boards out end first. This can be time-consuming, particularly when

you need to retrieve a board from the middle of a stack.

Sheet materials are usually stored vertically, on edge, in a rack that holds them upright like files in a folder. This makes it easy to retrieve a single sheet from the middle of a stack. Some materials, particularly thin stock, must be stored horizontally to keep them from bowing.

Shorts should be stacked vertically in a bin. Place the shorter stock in front and the taller in back so you can see what you have. This arrangement also allows you to flip through the boards and retrieve them easily.

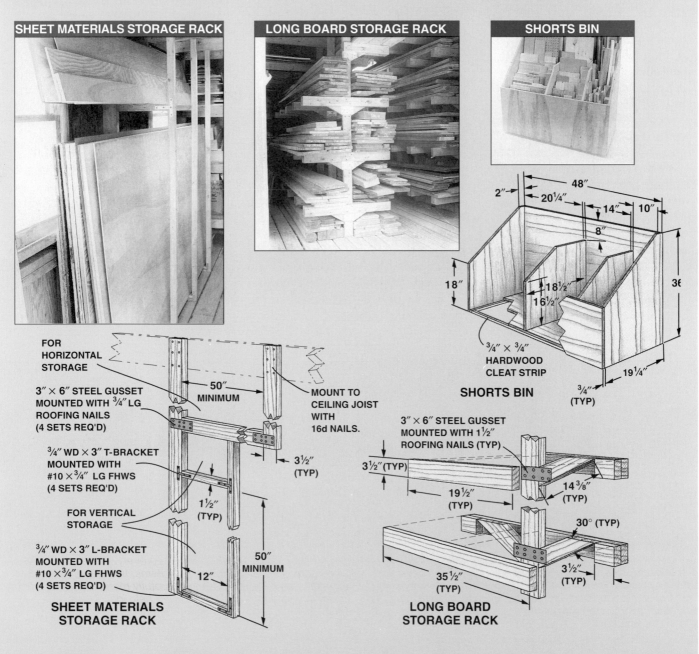

SHEET MATERIALS STORAGE RACK

LONG BOARD STORAGE RACK

SHORTS BIN

SHORTS BIN

FOR HORIZONTAL STORAGE

3″ × 6″ STEEL GUSSET MOUNTED WITH ¾″ LG ROOFING NAILS (4 SETS REQ'D)

¾″ WD × 3″ T-BRACKET MOUNTED WITH #10 × ¾″ LG FHWS (4 SETS REQ'D)

FOR VERTICAL STORAGE

¾″ WD × 3″ L-BRACKET MOUNTED WITH #10 × ¾″ LG FHWS (4 SETS REQ'D)

50″ MINIMUM

MOUNT TO CEILING JOIST WITH 16d NAILS.

3½″ (TYP)

1½″ (TYP)

50″ MINIMUM

12″

SHEET MATERIALS STORAGE RACK

¾″ × ¾″ HARDWOOD CLEAT STRIP

3″ × 6″ STEEL GUSSET MOUNTED WITH 1½″ ROOFING NAILS (TYP)

3½″ (TYP)

19½″ (TYP)

14⅜″ (TYP)

30° (TYP)

35½″ (TYP)

3½″ (TYP)

LONG BOARD STORAGE RACK

SHOP SYSTEMS

There's more to a shop than work space. It requires several essential *systems* – electrical wiring, heating and cooling, lighting, and ventilation.

SHOP WIRING

The wiring in your shop must be adequate to run stationary power tools. The amount of current depends on your machines, but generally the 120-volt circuits should handle 20 amps. The 240-volt circuits should deliver at least 30 amps to run motors up to 3 horsepower. All circuits should be grounded, of course.

How much total current do you need? A 50-amp service is the minimum for a small, one-person shop. If the shop has a separate heating and cooling system, you need at least 100 amps. Additionally:

■ Locate outlets conveniently near workbenches and power tools. To run power tools in the middle of your shop, install floor outlets or ceiling drops.

Use armored electrical cable (BX) if there is any risk of accidental damage to the wire. For long runs, use rigid conduit or electrical metallic tubing (EMT).

■ Install "slow-blow" fuses or delayed circuit breakers to prevent unnecessary power interruptions. Electric motors often draw large amounts of current when starting,

*To keep from running power cords across the floor of your shop, install a **retractable electrical ceiling drop** over workbenches and stationary power tools. They are expensive, but the safety and convenience make them well worth the money.*

but this quickly tapers off as they come up to speed.

■ Make sure the tools and the lights are on *separate* circuits. You don't want to be left in the dark if one of your tools overloads a circuit in the middle of a critical cut.

HEATING AND COOLING

It's important to heat and cool a shop not just for comfort but because woodworking operations such as gluing and finishing are sensitive to temperature. Any reliable heating and cooling device will work, provided you keep it dust-free. Clean radiators, baseboards, and filters regularly. Sawdust destroys the efficiency of heat exchangers and ruins blower motors.

PRO*TIP*

If your shop is heated or cooled with forced air, install an air return with a two-stage filter to clean the air before it gets back to the furnace or air conditioner.

Avoid open-coil electric heaters, kerosene heaters, and open-flame heaters of any sort. These may set fire to sawdust, wood shavings, and flammable finishes in a shop.

In humid locations, dehumidify your shop to **stabilize the wood**[1] and to prevent tools from **rusting**[2]. In dry environments, humidify the air to keep the wood from **overdrying**[3] and developing checks or splits.

SHOP LIGHTING

The work areas in your shop should be as well lit as a surgical theater. You perform many potentially dangerous tasks in a workshop, and you must be able to see what you're doing. Storage areas need good lighting, too, so you don't have to search for supplies in the shadows. Besides, a comfortable light level improves your mental outlook.

Don't depend on natural lighting alone. Sunshine is unreliable in most locations. Even if you live in a sunny area, direct sunlight and the harsh shadows it casts are hard on the eyes.

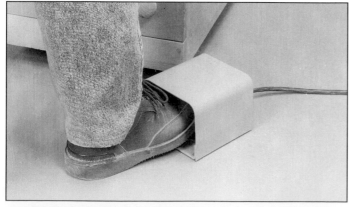

*A **shielded foot switch** makes some woodworking operations safer by allowing you to keep both hands on your work as you turn a power tool on and off. If anything goes wrong during the operation, simply step away from the machine to shut it down.*

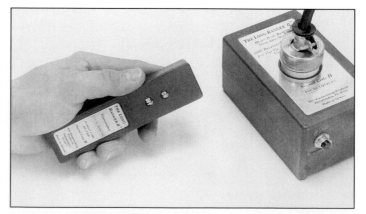

*A **remote control electrical switch** lets you turn on a dust collector, an air compressor, or other electrical devices from any point in your shop.*

Artificial lighting is more reliable and you can put it where you need it. Fluorescents are the most efficient source, but common "warm white" and "cool white" bulbs make colors look washed out. To see true colors, purchase bulbs with a color rating index (CRI) of 80 or more from a lighting store. (Ordinary fluorescents are between 50 and 70 CRI.)

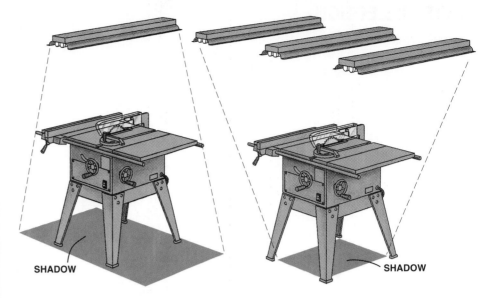

SAFE *GUARDS*

Fluorescent lights flicker faster than the eye can see, and this flicker may synchronize with a moving blade or cutter, making it look like it's standing still. An incandescent or tungsten-halogen light eliminates this dangerous optical illusion.

Position lighting directly over the work area to keep shadows to a minimum. If possible, light work areas from all directions to eliminate shadows.

Incandescent and tungsten-halogen bulbs are best used where you need extra light on an operation, especially for supplemental lighting on power tools.

VENTILATION

Most one-man shops are relatively small. The air quickly fills with fine sawdust particles or **finishing fumes**[4], making the environment unhealthy and unsafe.

This problem is easily remedied with ventilation. And because the shop is small, you don't need an expensive system. You can quickly exchange the bad air in the shop for good with a window fan or attic fan.

If the shop air is heated or cooled, constantly exchanging indoor air for outside air will run up the utilities. When this is the case, *filter* the air by using a fan to pull the air through a fine filter and return it to the shop.

Unfortunately, filtering does little to remove the noxious fumes from the air. And it may not be able to keep up with especially dirty operations like sanding. For this reason, you need *both* an air exchange system and an air filtration system. Use the filter as much as you can, but when the air quality deteriorates, turn on the ventilation system before the air becomes unhealthy.

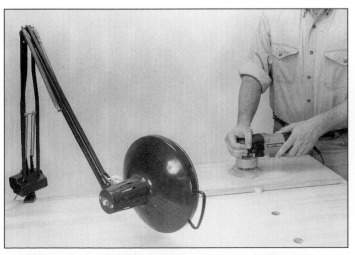

A bright, oblique light aids sanding, scraping, and finishing operations. Shine a light across the work at a steep angle to reveal imperfections in the surface.

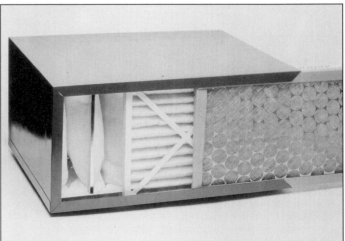

Commercial air filters are available to clear the dust from shop air. A powerful fan inside this metal box pulls the air through a three-stage filter.

Courtesy CMT Tools

DUST COLLECTION

Sawdust is an unpleasant and potentially dangerous part of the shop environment. Not only is it a nuisance, it can be a **health hazard**[1]. Dust in the air irritates your skin, nose, and throat and aggravates respiratory ailments. The minerals or *extractives* in the wood are **fine abrasives**[2] that can ruin bearings and electrical switches.

Ventilation and filtration are only partial solutions. To keep the sawdust under control, you must collect the dust at its source.

DUST COLLECTORS

Power tools produce a high *volume* of sawdust. To keep this dust from piling up, you need a machine that can evacuate the waste as fast as the tool can make it. A *dust collector* moves a constant volume of air, measured in cubic feet per minute, or CFM. To keep up with the wood shavings generated by most home workshop tools, you need a collector that moves at least 350 CFM. Especially "dirty" tools, like the planer and band saw, require 400 CFM or more.

*Although they both suck air, a **shop vacuum** (left) and a **dust collector** (right) are two different machines. Shop vacs draw a low volume of air with an extremely high force to quickly clean up small messes. Dust collectors generate less force but move a much larger volume of air so they can evacuate sawdust as fast as you can make it.*

> ### MORE *INFO*
>
> The force with which a dust collector moves the air is called static pressure, and it's measured by the number of inches the machine can pull a column of water up a tube of a given diameter.

DUST PICKUPS

In addition to a high-volume dust collector, you also need a *dust pickup,* a collection point on the power tool where you can attach a collector hose. Many tools come with built-in pickups; others require that you build your own.

To build a pickup, first decide where you should attach the collector. The best collection point is usually as close to the cutter as possible. Watch the cutting action of the tool and note where the cutter flings the sawdust. A band saw, for example, directs it down, under the table. Consequently, the best collection point is under the table, near the blade.

What if the tool flings sawdust over a wide area? Build a chute or a funnel to collect the wood chips, positioning it so they settle in the narrow end. Connect your dust collector at the narrowest point.

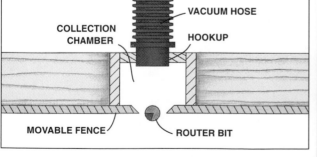

VACUUM HOSE

COLLECTION CHAMBER

HOOKUP

MOVABLE FENCE

ROUTER BIT

The box-shaped chamber on the back of this router table fence catches wood chips and funnels them toward the vacuum hose hookup. Note that the opening at the front of the fence is adjustable, allowing you to close it down around the bit. This improves the efficiency of the dust pickup — as the opening gets smaller, the air velocity increases.

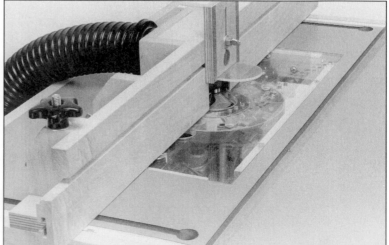

AIR VELOCITY

The size of the opening through which the dust is collected is extremely important. If the opening is too large, the dust collector won't be able to move the air fast enough to carry away the sawdust. But if it's too small, the collector won't be able to draw in enough air.

The smaller the opening, the higher the air *velocity* required to keep up with the rated volume of the dust collector. And high velocity is just what you need — the air must flow at least 3,500 feet per minute (FPM) to move the sawdust with it. Use this equation to calculate the largest useful opening for your collector:

$$(CFM \div 3,500 \text{ FPM}) \times 144 = \text{Area (in square inches)}$$

For example, if your collector is rated at 400 CFM, then the largest opening you should use for a dust pickup is about $16\frac{1}{2}$ square inches: $(400 \div 3,500) \times 144 = 16.46$. This is roughly equal to the area of a hole 5 inches in diameter. If the opening is any larger than that, the air velocity won't be high enough to pull sawdust into the opening.

DUST RUNS

This consideration also applies to the enclosed path (called a *run*) through which the sawdust travels. The cross section of the run at any point must be no greater than the largest useful opening. If the air is drawn through a wide chamber (such as a box), the velocity will drop inside the chamber and the dust will settle out, possibly clogging the pickup. To create a narrow run through a wide chamber, install airtight baffles that enclose the path inside the larger space.

COLLECTION EFFICIENCY

By the same token, you shouldn't make the opening too small or the velocity too high. Your collector has limits — it can move only so much air with so much force. As the size of the pickup opening decreases or the run narrows, the collector reaches a point where it just can't pull the air fast enough to keep up with the necessary volume, and its efficiency declines. A good rule of thumb is to size dust pickups and runs to pull air between 4,000 and 8,000 FPM.

The length of the run also affects the efficiency of the collector. The static pressure drops over distance, and the force with which the collector pulls the air dwindles. If the run is too long, you won't have the volume or the velocity needed at the pickup.

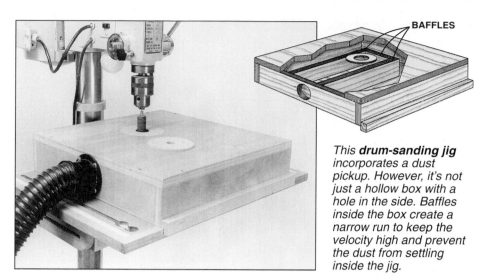

*This **drum-sanding jig** incorporates a dust pickup. However, it's not just a hollow box with a hole in the side. Baffles inside the box create a narrow run to keep the velocity high and prevent the dust from settling inside the jig.*

MORE *SOURCES*

Woodshop Dust Control, by Sandor Nagyszalanczy, Taunton Press, 1996

Workbenches and Shop Furniture, by Nick Engler, Rodale Press, 1993

The Workshop Book, by Scott Landis, Taunton Press, 1991

SEE *ALSO:*

[1] Health Hazards from Woods — 361

[2] Cleaning Power Tools — 163

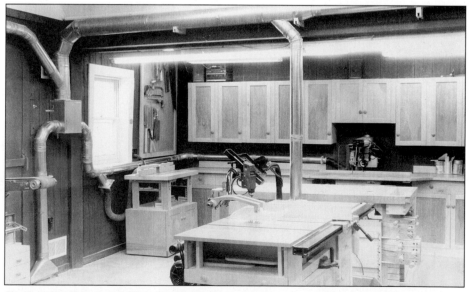

***Dust collection systems** incorporate long runs that channel the sawdust to a central collector. When installing these systems, you must (1) size the ducts to keep the air velocity above 3,500 FPM and (2) make the runs as short as possible to keep the static pressure up. Long runs typically start out at the largest efficient diameter at the collector, then taper down as you near the pickup. This prevents the velocity and the pressure from dropping too much.*

DUST COLLECTION PICKUPS

Make the hookups in these fixtures by cutting 2¼-inch-diameter holes with a hole saw. Standard (2½-inch-diameter) dust collection hoses have tapered ends that friction-fit holes of this size.

TABLE SAW PICKUP

This collector depends on gravity as much as air movement to work. The wood dust slides down the sloping bottom of the chute and is funneled to the vacuum hookup in the back.

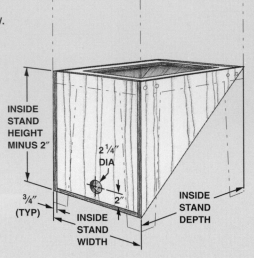

INSIDE STAND HEIGHT MINUS 2″

2¼″ DIA

2″

¾″ (TYP)

INSIDE STAND WIDTH

INSIDE STAND DEPTH

JOINTER PICKUP

The jointer pickup works much the same way as the table saw pickup (above), but the chute is built into the stand. The whirling knives fling the chips down the chute to the vacuum hookup. This hookup is cut in a door that covers the lower end of the chute. The door is necessary because the jointer sometimes produces large shavings that can clog the pickup. When this happens, open the door and clean out the chute.

#8 × 1½″ LG RHWS (2 REQ'D)

½″ × ½″ × 3″ LG SWIVEL CATCH ON ½″ × ½″ × ½″ SPACER BLOCK (2 SETS REQ'D)

½″ WD PIANO HINGE

1″ TALLER THAN OPENING

2¼″ DIA

1″ WIDER THAN OPENING

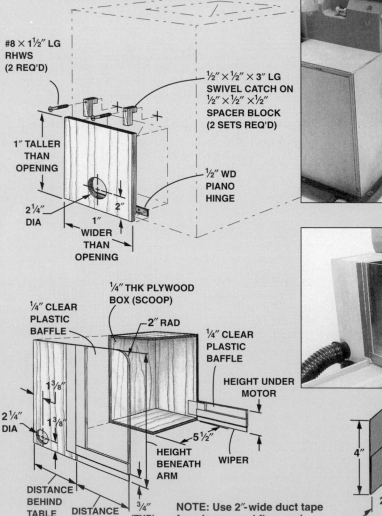

RADIAL ARM SAW PICKUP

As the saw cuts, it flings most of the sawdust back into this scoop. The clear plastic baffles can be adjusted to direct the sawdust no matter what the angle of the arm. When the dust hits the back of the scoop, it settles to the bottom and a vacuum hookup whisks it away. A 2-inch-long "mud flap" (made from duct tape) on the back of the saw guard keeps the sawdust from being thrown up and over the collector.

¼″ CLEAR PLASTIC BAFFLE

¼″ THK PLYWOOD BOX (SCOOP)

2″ RAD

¼″ CLEAR PLASTIC BAFFLE

HEIGHT UNDER MOTOR

1³⁄₈″

1³⁄₈″

2¼″ DIA

5½″

HEIGHT BENEATH ARM

WIPER

DISTANCE BEHIND TABLE

DISTANCE BEHIND FENCE

¾″ (TYP)

NOTE: Use 2″-wide duct tape for wipers, mud flap, and baffle hinges.

4″

2″

2″

MUD FLAP DETAIL

JIGS&FIXTURES

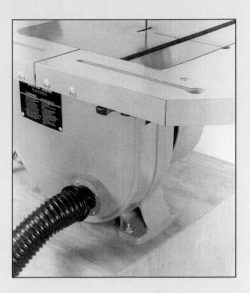

BAND SAW PICKUP

As the band saw cuts, the blade throws sawdust toward the bottom of the frame. A vacuum hookup in the lower housing, next to the blade, picks up most of this dust before it has a chance to settle.

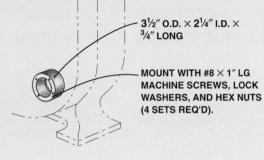

$3\frac{1}{2}$" O.D. × $2\frac{1}{4}$" I.D. × $\frac{3}{4}$" LONG

MOUNT WITH #8 × 1" LG MACHINE SCREWS, LOCK WASHERS, AND HEX NUTS (4 SETS REQ'D).

DISC SANDER PICKUP

This simple box encases the lower half of the sanding disc — the portion below the work surface. Since you sand on the side of the disc that rotates down, the abrasive flings the dust into the pickup. The angled side on the pickup allows the worktable to tilt.

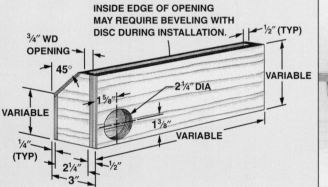

INSIDE EDGE OF OPENING MAY REQUIRE BEVELING WITH DISC DURING INSTALLATION.

$\frac{3}{4}$" WD OPENING

45°

$\frac{1}{2}$" (TYP)

VARIABLE

VARIABLE

$1\frac{5}{8}$"

$2\frac{1}{4}$" DIA

$1\frac{3}{8}$"

VARIABLE

$\frac{1}{4}$" (TYP)

$2\frac{1}{4}$"

$\frac{1}{2}$"

3"

DRILL PRESS PICKUP

This pickup is a nozzle that you can place in different positions on the drill press worktable, depending on the drilling operation. Clamp the nozzle to the table or weigh it down so the opening partially surrounds the bit.

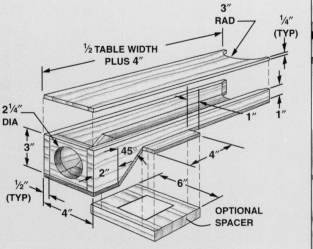

3" RAD

$\frac{1}{4}$" (TYP)

$\frac{1}{2}$ TABLE WIDTH PLUS 4"

$2\frac{1}{4}$" DIA

1"

1"

3"

45°

2"

4"

$\frac{1}{2}$" (TYP)

6"

4"

OPTIONAL SPACER

NOTE: To raise pickup above stock, attach spacer with carpet tape.

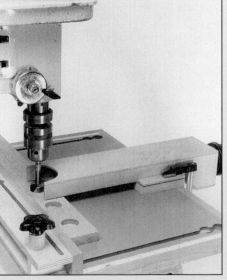

10

Workbenches and Shop Furniture

The heart of every workshop is its workbench. This is where all your woodworking ambitions are realized.

The furniture in your shop defines its purpose. Just as a bedroom needs a bed for sleeping, so a workshop requires a workbench and tool storage for working with wood. Furthermore, the quality of your shop furniture influences the quality of your work. You sleep better on a comfortable bed; you work better at a capable bench.

Photos by John Hamel

*Professional craftsmen often invest as much time and creativity in making a **Tool Cabinet** as they would a fine piece of furniture. Besides its usefulness, a finely made tool cabinet is a showpiece that a woodworker can use to impress prospective clients. And beyond these practical concerns, it's inspiring to work amidst some of your best craftsmanship.*

SPECS: 84″ high, 36″ wide, 18″ deep

MATERIALS: Honduran mahogany, tiger maple, and birch plywood

CRAFTSMAN: Andy Rae, Associate Editor *American Woodworker*

WORKBENCHES

Ask a roomful of woodworkers what's the best design for a workbench, and no two will give you the same answer. The fact is, there is no single answer. Many different designs will work, although a design that works well for one craftsman may not work for another. A workbench is a highly personal piece of furniture, and a good design depends on how you like to work.

TYPES OF WORKBENCHES

Some benches are no more than a table. Others are complex work centers, built to a specific size and a comfortable height with different **vises**[1], special fixtures, and customized storage spaces. Between these two extremes, there are five broad categories of workbenches.

■ A *worktable* is a sturdy table on which to work. You can clamp work to the surface, but there are no built-in vises. Despite this deficiency, worktables are handy for layout, assembly, and finishing.

■ A *utility workbench* has a single vise mounted on the front or an end. It's a modest design, but very capable. And for many craftsmen, there's nothing to be gained by building anything more grandiose. After all, how many vises can you use at one time?

■ A *cabinetmaker's workbench* is based on a classic design that first appeared in the eighteenth century. It has two vises, a *face vise* mounted on the front edge and a *tail vise* on an end. There is a single row of holes for **bench dogs**[2] along the front edge, which are used in conjunction with the tail vise.

■ A *carver's workbench* is similar to a cabinetmaker's bench but has a second row of dog holes along the back edge to increase holding capacity. Instead of a tail vise, there is a wide face vise or two separate vises mounted on one end.

■ A *workstand* has a small work surface, making it easier to reach the work from all sides. It sometimes sports a specialized vise.

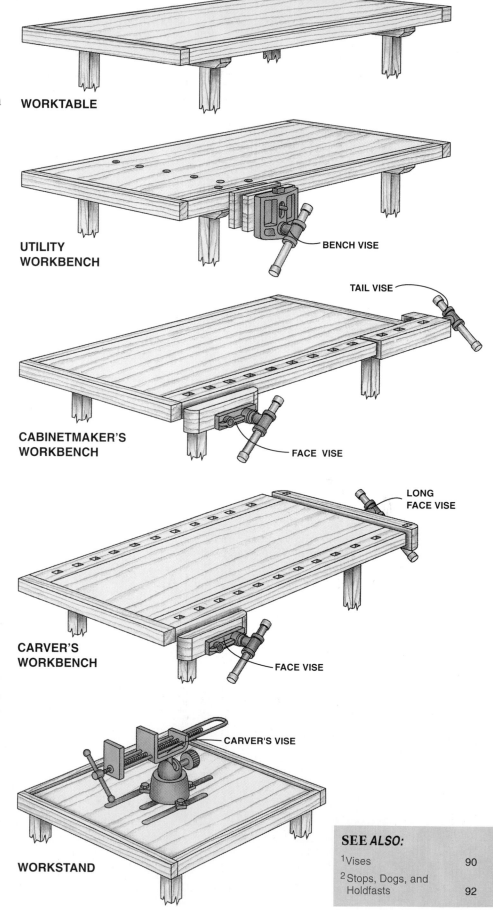

WORKTABLE

UTILITY WORKBENCH — **BENCH VISE**

CABINETMAKER'S WORKBENCH — **TAIL VISE** / **FACE VISE**

CARVER'S WORKBENCH — **LONG FACE VISE** / **FACE VISE**

WORKSTAND — **CARVER'S VISE**

SEE ALSO:

[1] Vises   90

[2] Stops, Dogs, and Holdfasts   92

WORKBENCH CONSTRUCTION

The configuration of the bench top, vises, and dog holes are just a few of the options you have when designing a workbench. You can also choose the surface on which you work, how that surface is supported, and how to store tools in the bench.

WORK SURFACES

Traditionally, the tops of workbenches are made from strips of maple, beech, or oak glued edge to edge to form a "butcherblock" slab. Each strip is straight-grained and turned so the **quarter grain**[1] shows on top. The straight grain makes the top as strong as possible, while the grain orientation makes it more stable, since the wood **expands radially**[2]

You can also make a bench top from clear dimensional lumber. Joint 2 × 4s to remove the rounded edges and laminate them face to face. This isn't as durable as a hardwood top, but it's less expensive and easier to resurface.

Hardwood-core plywood[3] is very stable and reasonably durable. So is **particleboard**[4], especially when covered with **tempered hardboard**[4]. The particleboard provides mass and strength; the hardboard makes a smooth surface. When making a gluing or a finishing bench, you may wish to cover plywood or particleboard with **plastic laminate**[5] for easy cleanup.

> **PRO TIP**
>
> Keep bench tops waxed. This will prevent glue from sticking and chemicals from staining.

SUPPORTING FRAME

There are three common methods for supporting a bench top, all of which are borrowed from standard **furniture construction**[6]

■ *Leg-and-apron* – The top is supported by four legs. The legs are joined and braced by aprons and stretchers.

■ *Trestle* – The top lies across two simple frames or trestles. These are joined and braced by stretchers.

■ *Cabinet* – The top rests on a sturdy case that can also be used for tool storage.

LEG-AND-APRON SUPPORT

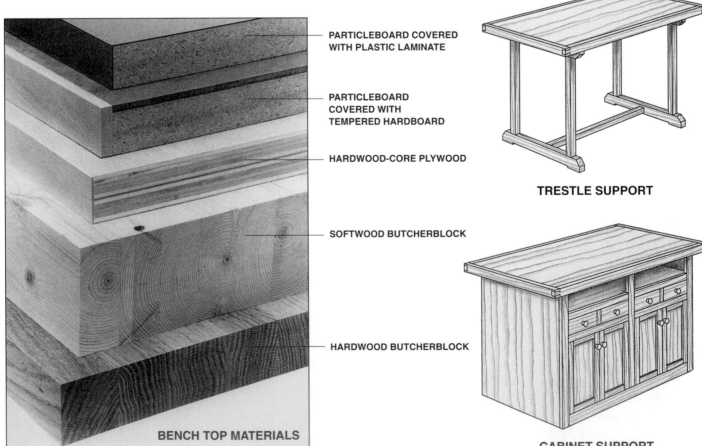

PARTICLEBOARD COVERED WITH PLASTIC LAMINATE

PARTICLEBOARD COVERED WITH TEMPERED HARDBOARD

HARDWOOD-CORE PLYWOOD

SOFTWOOD BUTCHERBLOCK

HARDWOOD BUTCHERBLOCK

BENCH TOP MATERIALS

TRESTLE SUPPORT

CABINET SUPPORT

BENCH STORAGE

Because you do so much work at a bench, it's a logical place to store the hand and portable power tools that you use often. There are several common storage devices.

■ *Open shelves* are the simplest type of workbench storage – just lay a few boards between the legs and stretchers. Tools stored on the shelves are easy to find and reach, although they collect dust.

■ *Cupboards* are enclosed shelves. They require more time and materials to make, but they protect the tools from dust.

■ *Drawers* also protect tools. They are the most difficult kind of storage to build, but they also provide the easiest access and the best means of organizing tools.

■ *Bins* are often built into bench tops to keep small tools handy but *just below the surface,* where they won't interfere

with the work. You can also make portable bins that rest in drawers or on shelves. These let you carry the tools in the bins wherever you need them.

■ *Pegboard* and the wide variety of metal pegs, hooks, and racks that fit it comprise one of the most versatile workshop storage devices. Mount pegboard on the wall behind your workbench or to the inside surfaces of cupboard doors.

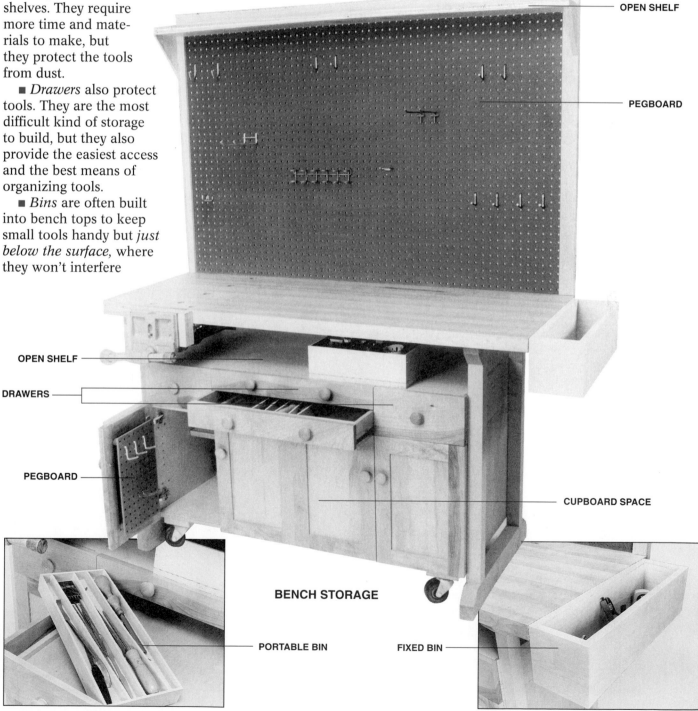

OPEN SHELF

PEGBOARD

OPEN SHELF

DRAWERS

PEGBOARD

CUPBOARD SPACE

BENCH STORAGE

PORTABLE BIN

FIXED BIN

VISES

An old woodworker's pun goes, "You can't have too many vices." That may be true in a large shop, but most small shops can get away with just one or two. The trick is to choose a vise that will handle the types of woodworking you enjoy.

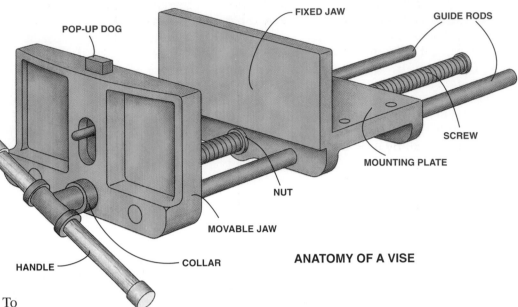

ANATOMY OF A VISE

Labels: POP-UP DOG, FIXED JAW, GUIDE RODS, SCREW, MOUNTING PLATE, NUT, MOVABLE JAW, COLLAR, HANDLE

HOW A VISE WORKS

A typical woodworking vise has a movable jaw that clamps the work against either the edge of the bench top or a *fixed jaw*. To open and close the jaws, turn a *handle* (also called a *tommy bar*) to spin a large *screw*. This screw passes through a *collar* (which is fastened to the movable jaw) and a *nut* (which is fastened to the fixed jaw or the bench top). As the screw turns in the nut, the collar drives the movable jaw in or out. *Guide rods* keep the movable jaw aligned with the fixed jaw as the vise opens and closes. A *mounting plate* secures the vise to the workbench.

GENERAL-PURPOSE VISES

There are five common types of woodworking vises:

■ A *bench vise* is the most popular. Both the screw and the jaws are made of metal, although craftsmen line the jaws with wood to prevent them from damaging the work. Most bench vises have a *pop-up dog* in the movable face. When used with **bench dogs**[1], the holding capacity of the vise can be as long or as wide as the workbench itself.

■ A *face vise* has just one movable wooden jaw or "face" that clamps the work directly to the edge or end of a bench top. Usually, it has just one screw, although long face vises may have two.

MORE *INFO*

The jaws of most vises are angled slightly to meet at the top first. Because there is always some slop in the screw mechanism, the movable jaw will tilt slightly as you tighten it. The pressure spreads evenly across the angled jaws, and the entire holding surface contacts the work. If the jaws were parallel to begin with, they would apply more pressure at the bottom than at the top.

BENCH VISE

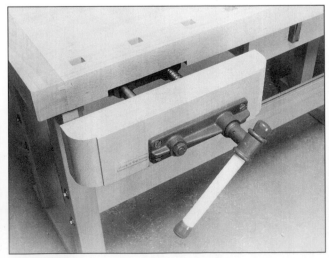

FACE VISE

■ A *shoulder vise* is designed to clamp the face of a board against the bench top so you can work its edge. However, it holds stock end up and face up as well.

■ A *tail vise* holds a board so you can work its face. There are dog holes in the movable wooden jaw and along the edge of the bench top where it's mounted. By inserting a dog in the jaw and another in the bench, you can secure a workpiece almost as long as the bench itself. *Interesting note:* A tail vise appears to be made from solid wood, but it's hollow. The screw and nut mechanism is inside.

■ A *leg vise* has a long, vertical movable jaw that pivots at the bottom. The pivot is attached to a horizontal bar that slides in and out of the vertical fixed jaw. (Sometimes the workbench leg becomes the fixed jaw.) This arrangement provides an adjustable, large-capacity vise.

SPECIALTY VISES

Besides these general-purpose vises, several specialty vises are useful to woodworkers.

■ A *mechanic's vise* is handy when you need to do a little metalworking. It's made completely of metal, mounts on top of the workbench, and holds the work well above the surface of the bench. On some models the base swivels, allowing you to approach the work from any side.

■ A *carver's vise* tilts and rotates to hold the work at almost any angle. These are usually designed to hold small and medium-sized work only.

■ A *patternmaker's vise* is the most versatile of all. It has a large capacity, pop-up dogs, and jaws that tilt and swivel to hold a variety of shapes, and the entire device rotates to hold work at almost any angle.

SEE *ALSO:*

[1]Stops, Dogs, and Holdfasts   92

SHOULDER VISE

TAIL VISE

LEG VISE

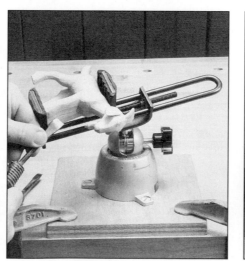

MECHANIC'S VISE

CARVER'S VISE

PATTERNMAKER'S VISE

STOPS, DOGS, AND HOLDFASTS

Several other workbench accessories are designed to hold the work to the bench.

STOPS

A stop is a strip of wood or metal that fastens to the workbench to keep a board from sliding across the surface as you work. To use it, place the board on the bench top and against the stop. Plan your work so the action of the tool forces the board against the stop.

BENCH DOGS

Bench dogs are small, movable jaw faces used in conjunction with vises. They mount in holes in the bench top to extend the capacity of a vise. They may be round or square, wood or metal. Square dogs are more stable, but round ones can be turned to accommodate odd shapes. Metal dogs are more durable, but wooden ones are less likely to mar the work.

Most **bench vises**[1] have pop-up dogs designed to be used with bench dogs. When using **a face or a tail vise**[1], however, you must mount bench dogs in the bench top and the movable vise jaw.

HOLDFASTS

A *holdfast* presses down on a board, clamping it to the bench surface. A traditional holdfast is a thick iron shaft with a long, protruding arm. Mount the shaft in a hole in a bench top and whack it with a mallet to set the holdfast and press the arm against the board. On a *screw hold-fast*, the arm pivots at the end of the shaft. Turn a screw to apply pressure.

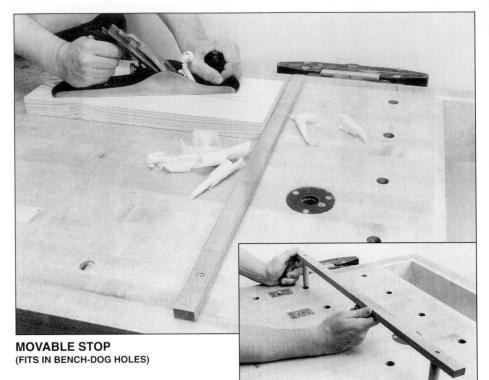

MOVABLE STOP
(FITS IN BENCH-DOG HOLES)

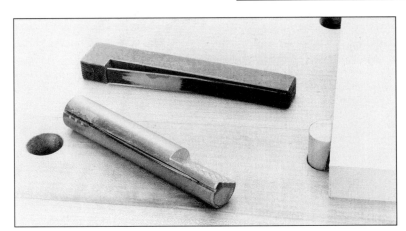

BENCH DOGS

SCREW HOLDFAST

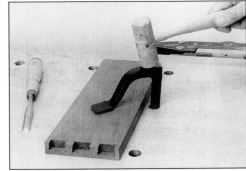

TRADITIONAL HOLDFAST

SEE *ALSO:*

[1]Vises   90

JIGS & FIXTURES

SHOP-MADE WORKBENCH ACCESSORIES Sometimes you need extra hands when you're working in your shop. Here are several accessories that you can make to help hold workpieces on your workbench.

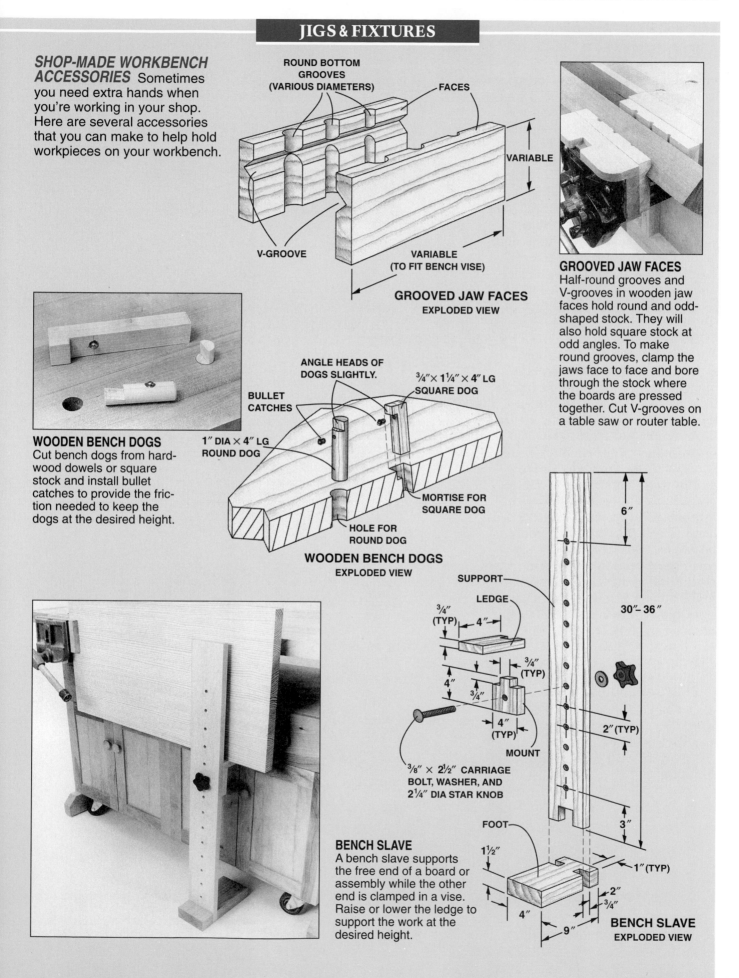

ROUND BOTTOM GROOVES (VARIOUS DIAMETERS)

FACES

VARIABLE

V-GROOVE

VARIABLE (TO FIT BENCH VISE)

GROOVED JAW FACES
EXPLODED VIEW

GROOVED JAW FACES

Half-round grooves and V-grooves in wooden jaw faces hold round and odd-shaped stock. They will also hold square stock at odd angles. To make round grooves, clamp the jaws face to face and bore through the stock where the boards are pressed together. Cut V-grooves on a table saw or router table.

WOODEN BENCH DOGS

Cut bench dogs from hardwood dowels or square stock and install bullet catches to provide the friction needed to keep the dogs at the desired height.

ANGLE HEADS OF DOGS SLIGHTLY.

BULLET CATCHES

$\frac{3}{4}'' \times 1\frac{1}{4}'' \times 4''$ LG SQUARE DOG

$1''$ DIA $\times 4''$ LG ROUND DOG

MORTISE FOR SQUARE DOG

HOLE FOR ROUND DOG

WOODEN BENCH DOGS
EXPLODED VIEW

SUPPORT

LEDGE

$\frac{3}{4}''$ (TYP) $4''$

$\frac{3}{4}''$ (TYP)

$4''$

$\frac{3}{4}''$

$4''$ (TYP)

MOUNT

$\frac{3}{8}'' \times 2\frac{1}{2}''$ CARRIAGE BOLT, WASHER, AND $2\frac{1}{4}''$ DIA STAR KNOB

$6''$

$30''-36''$

$2''$ (TYP)

$3''$

$1''$ (TYP)

FOOT

BENCH SLAVE

A bench slave supports the free end of a board or assembly while the other end is clamped in a vise. Raise or lower the ledge to support the work at the desired height.

$1\frac{1}{2}''$

$4''$

$9''$

$2''$

$\frac{3}{4}''$

BENCH SLAVE
EXPLODED VIEW

TOOL CHESTS, CABINETS, AND CARRYALLS

In addition to a bench on which to work, you need a place to keep your tools. A clever chest or cabinet not only stores small tools, accessories, and materials, it also helps keep track of them.

A workshop can be a crazy place when you have a project in high gear – small items grow legs and wander away. From time to time, you have to round up your tools and take inventory. If you have a tool storage unit with a designated place for everything, it's easy to tell when something strays.

TOOL CHESTS

The classic storage unit for tools is the tool chest. Old-time woodworkers packed up their implements in a large **six-board chest**[1] with a deep *till*. This till was fitted with dozens of lift-out trays and bins to organize the many hand tools on which craftsmen once depended.

This chest has evolved over the years, becoming smaller and more accessible. Today, the standard tool chest is what was once commonly known as a *machinist's chest* – a small **chest of drawers**[2] with a shallow till at the top. The drawers in the bottom section are various sizes and depths, and the till often has a lift-out tray.

*Old-time woodworkers often kept their tools in large six-board chests. This is a reproduction of an early-nineteenth-century **tool chest** that once belonged to Duncan Phyfe, a New York cabinetmaker who acquired an international reputation.*

*H. Gerstner & Sons, of Dayton, Ohio, is the only tool chest manufacturer still producing wooden chests. This small **machinist's chest** is one of several models available.*

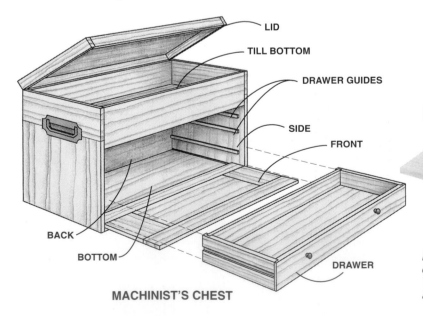

LID
TILL BOTTOM
DRAWER GUIDES
SIDE
FRONT
BACK
BOTTOM
DRAWER

MACHINIST'S CHEST

STANDING CABINETS

Craftsmen with larger storage requirements typically prefer a standing **cabinet**[3] to a large chest. A cabinet displays tools at eye level, making them easy to find and reach. And though a cabinet occupies about the same footprint in your shop as a large chest, it offers more storage space.

You can put an enormous amount of effort into building a cabinet – and many craftsmen do – but these don't have to be complex pieces of furniture to be useful and attractive. Many are just large **boxes**[4] fitted with shelves, drawers, and doors.

CARRYALLS AND TOTES

Many craftsmen prefer to keep at least some of their tools in portable storage. Small bins that fit inside a drawer or a cupboard can be carried from place to place in your workshop. A simple carryall or carpenter's tote lets you carry often-used tools from location to location for jobs outside the shop.

SEE *ALSO:*

[1] Boxes and Chests   24
[2] Chests of Drawers   25
[3] Cabinets   29
[4] Methods of Construction   18

Although elegant in appearance, this **tool cabinet** is simple to construct. The case is made up of three boxes — one large box fitted with shelves and drawers, and two smaller boxes which serve as doors.

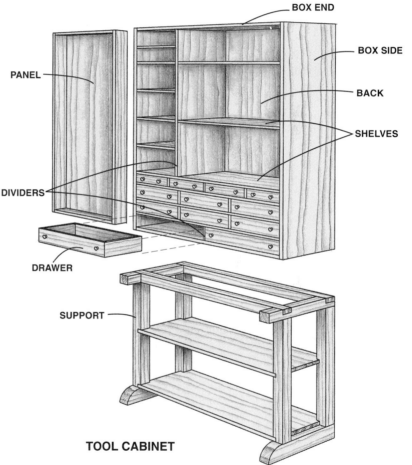

TOOL CABINET

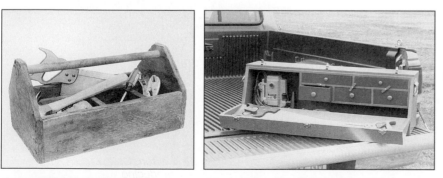

A **carryall** (left) holds tools in an open bin, while a **carpenter's tote** (right) encloses them in a box. Typically, there are drawers inside the box.

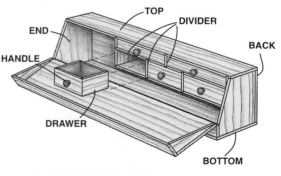

CARPENTER'S TOTE

TOOL STANDS

You can create an enormous amount of storage in your shop by using the space under your stationary power tools. *Storage stands* not only store small items, they also improve work flow and efficiency by keeping cutters and accessories close by the tools where they're used.

STAND CONSTRUCTION

A storage stand must properly support the power tool as well as provide storage space. This, in fact, is your most important consideration – it should be at least as sturdy as the commercial stand it replaces.

One of the strongest and most versatile structures you can make is a **box**[1]. A simple plywood box, properly joined and braced, will support all but the heaviest power tools. Besides being simple to build, boxes are easy to outfit with shelves, doors, and drawers.

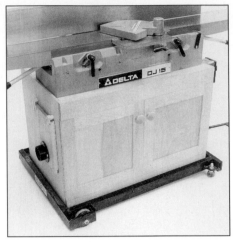

This custom **jointer stand** offers cupboard storage only.

A box-constructed storage stand looks like a cabinet, but it's much stronger and easier to build. This **band saw stand** has been divided into both cupboard and drawer storage space.

The top portion of this **scroll saw stand** is fitted with drawers, while the bottom section is filled with sand. The sand adds mass and helps dampen the vibration of the saw.

⅜″ WD × ⅜″ DP
GROOVE

⅜″ WD × ⅜″ DP
RABBET AND TONGUE

SIDE

BACK

BOTTOM

¾″ WD ×
⅜″ DP DADO

(ALL STOCK ¾″ THICK)

JOINERY DETAIL

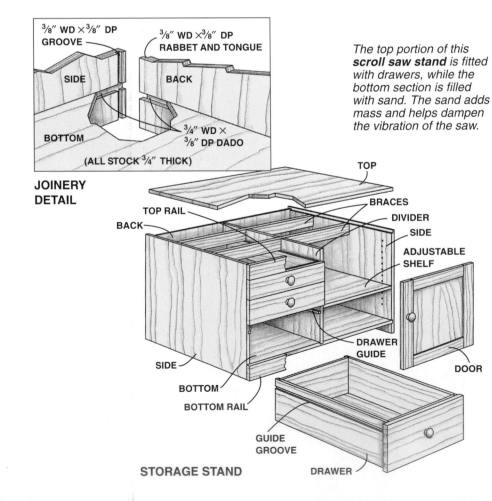

TOP

TOP RAIL

BRACES

DIVIDER

BACK

SIDE

ADJUSTABLE SHELF

SIDE

DRAWER GUIDE

BOTTOM

DOOR

BOTTOM RAIL

GUIDE GROOVE

DRAWER

STORAGE STAND

MORE SOURCES

The Next Step, by John McPherson, T-Line Design, 1992

The Toolbox Book, by Jim Tolpin, Taunton Press, 1995

The Workbench Book, by Scott Landis, Taunton Press, 1987

Workbenches and Shop Furniture, by Nick Engler, Rodale Press, 1993

SEE ALSO:

[1]Methods of Construction 18

[2]Shop Organization 76

MAKING SHOP FURNITURE MOBILE

You can make workbenches, tool cabinets, and stationary power tools mobile simply by mounting heavy-duty casters on the bottoms of the supports or stands. This lets you move fixtures in and out of storage easily or **rearrange your shop** [2] whenever the need arises.

However, casters create problems. The points at which they contact the floor are somewhat smaller than the footprint of the stand itself. If the distance between the casters is too small, the tool will be top heavy. To prevent this, make the stand a little larger than you would otherwise.

Tools mounted on casters also tend to "walk" as you use them. This can be annoying and dangerous. To prevent walking, make either retractable casters that swing up and let the stand rest on the floor, or retractable feet that swing down and lift the casters.

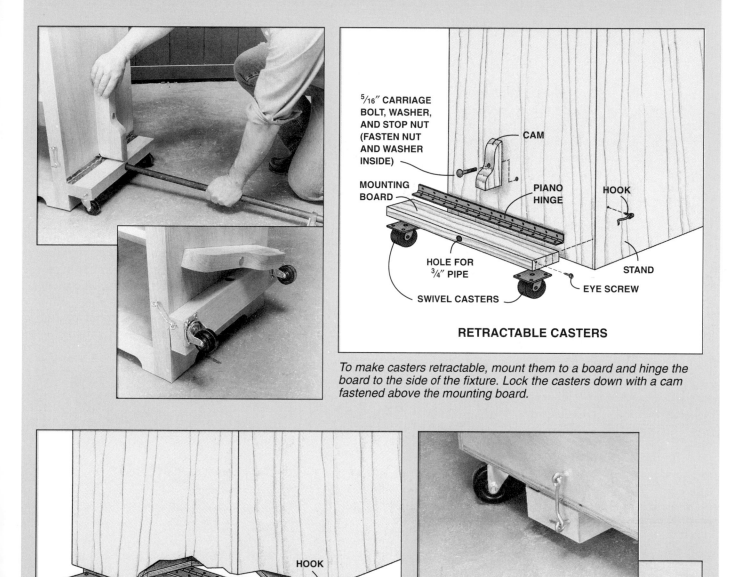

⁵⁄₁₆″ CARRIAGE BOLT, WASHER, AND STOP NUT (FASTEN NUT AND WASHER INSIDE)

CAM

MOUNTING BOARD

PIANO HINGE

HOOK

HOLE FOR ³⁄₄″ PIPE

STAND

EYE SCREW

SWIVEL CASTERS

RETRACTABLE CASTERS

To make casters retractable, mount them to a board and hinge the board to the side of the fixture. Lock the casters down with a cam fastened above the mounting board.

HOOK

SWIVEL CASTERS

PIANO HINGE

EYE SCREW

FOOT BOARD

RETRACTABLE FEET

To make a retractable foot, hinge a board to the bottom of the fixture. The board must be slightly wider than the casters are tall to hold the casters off the ground.

11

Stationary Power Tools

To use a power tool to your best advantage, learn how it works, what dangers it poses, and how to fine-tune it for precise results.

Most contemporary craftsmen rely on electric power tools for jobs that would otherwise be tedious and labor-intensive. These tools are normally lumped into two large categories – *stationary power tools* that rest on the floor, a stand, or a bench, and *portable power tools* that can be carried to the work. Although both are important, stationary tools are best suited for precision work. Their mass and stability help produce more accurate cuts.

There are diverse machines for sawing, planing, sanding, drilling, and shaping. You don't need all of these tools, of course, just a few carefully chosen machines. To select the tools that are right for you and to get the most out of them, learn what they do, how they work, how they are aligned and adjusted, and what blades, bits, and cutters are available for them.

TABLE SAWS

More often than not, the pivotal power tool in a woodworking shop is a table saw, and for good reason. There is no faster, more accurate tool for cutting large boards into little pieces. In addition to **crosscutting**[1], **ripping**[1], and other straight cuts, table saws are also used for **dadoing**[2] and molding.

*Although most modern power tools are driven by electric motors, electricity was not the first power source. Water-powered saws first appeared in the 1300s, and steam-powered tools were invented in the late 1700s. Gasoline power developed about 100 years later, followed quickly by electric power. As late as the 1930s, tool manufacturers made stationary power tools that could be run by several different power sources for craftsmen who lived in areas where electricity was scarce. This **1932 Delta "Workshop Unit,"** for example, can be driven by either an electric or a gasoline motor.*

BASIC OPERATION

The most distinguishing feature on a table saw, of course, is its *table*. This is often enlarged by *table extensions*. A *circular saw blade* protrudes through a removable table *insert* set flush with the table surface. Removing the insert lets you reach the *arbor* on which the blade is mounted. The arbor, in turn, is mounted in a *blade carriage* that changes the blade height and angle.

To raise or lower the blade, turn the *elevation crank*. To change the blade angle, turn the *tilt crank*. The blade and arbor are powered by an electric *motor*.

When crosscutting, a *miter gauge* guides the wood. The gauge travels in *miter gauge slots* in the table, one on either side of the blade. When ripping, a *rip fence* guides the wood. The fence is mounted on *fence rails*. During both operations, a *saw guard* protects you from injury. This guard is often mounted on a *splitter* which keeps the wood from pinching the blade after it's cut.

SAFE *GUARDS*

When using a table saw, never stand in line with the blade. Position yourself to one side in case the wood kicks back.

NECESSARY IMPROVEMENTS

The Achilles' heel of every table saw is its miter gauge. It's too small to crosscut long boards accurately. A **sliding table**[3] or a *cut-off box* cures this deficiency. A *precision fence* system is also a good investment.

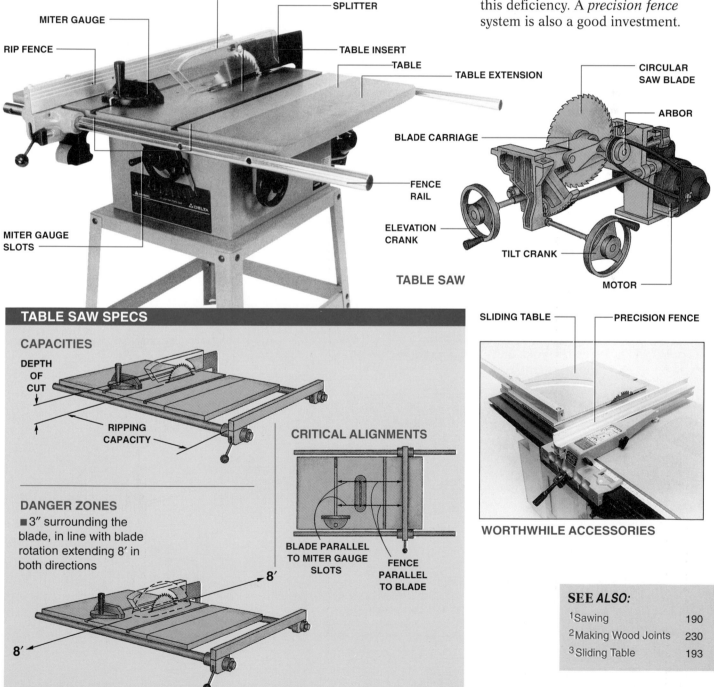

SAW GUARD
MITER GAUGE
RIP FENCE
SPLITTER
TABLE INSERT
TABLE
TABLE EXTENSION
CIRCULAR SAW BLADE
ARBOR
BLADE CARRIAGE
FENCE RAIL
ELEVATION CRANK
TILT CRANK
MOTOR
MITER GAUGE SLOTS

TABLE SAW

SLIDING TABLE — PRECISION FENCE

WORTHWHILE ACCESSORIES

TABLE SAW SPECS

CAPACITIES

DEPTH OF CUT

RIPPING CAPACITY

DANGER ZONES

■ 3" surrounding the blade, in line with blade rotation extending 8' in both directions

8'

8'

CRITICAL ALIGNMENTS

BLADE PARALLEL TO MITER GAUGE SLOTS

FENCE PARALLEL TO BLADE

RADIAL ARM SAWS

Like a table saw, a radial arm saw reduces large boards to little ones. Some craftsmen prefer this tool because it makes it easier to **crosscut**[1] long stock. However, the **ripping**[1] capacity is limited and you must keep a constant watch on the alignment.

SEE *ALSO*:
[1]Sawing   190

PRO *TIP*

If you just want a saw to make cutoffs, a **power miter saw** will save you money and space.

BASIC OPERATION

On a radial arm saw, the *circular saw blade* is mounted directly to the shaft of a *motor* and covered by a *blade guard.* The motor is held in a *yoke.* These four parts make up the *cuttinghead.* This assembly travels along a *track arm,* which is suspended above the *table* by a telescoping *column.* A *fence* in the table backs up the work for crosscutting and guides it when ripping.

Tilt the blade by loosening the *bevel lock* and swiveling the motor in the yoke. Or adjust the miter angle by loosening the *miter lock* and swinging the track arm left or right. You can also adjust the depth of cut by turning the *height adjustment* to raise or lower the column. A *yoke lock* between the yoke and the arm lets you rotate the motor so the blade is parallel to the fence for ripping, and a *cuttinghead lock* clamps the cuttinghead in one position on the track arm.

SAFE *GUARDS*

When ripping, tilt the blade guard back until it almost touches the work.

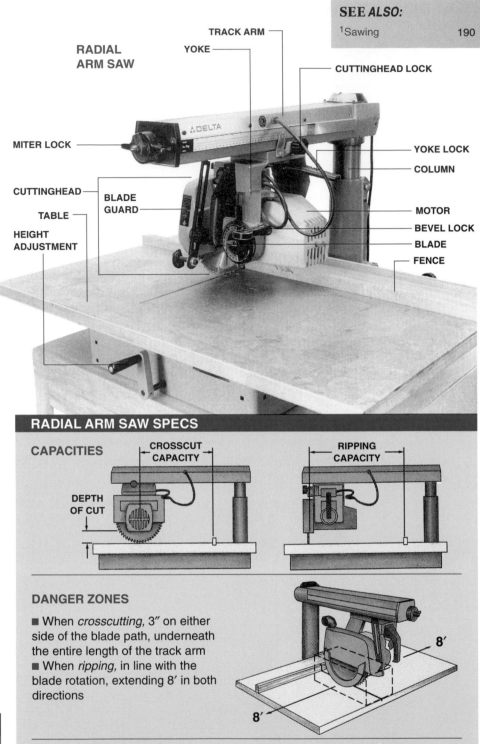

RADIAL ARM SAW — TRACK ARM — YOKE — CUTTINGHEAD LOCK — MITER LOCK — YOKE LOCK — COLUMN — CUTTINGHEAD — BLADE GUARD — TABLE — HEIGHT ADJUSTMENT — MOTOR — BEVEL LOCK — BLADE — FENCE

RADIAL ARM SAW SPECS

CAPACITIES

CROSSCUT CAPACITY — DEPTH OF CUT — RIPPING CAPACITY

DANGER ZONES

■ When *crosscutting,* 3″ on either side of the blade path, underneath the entire length of the track arm

■ When *ripping,* in line with the blade rotation, extending 8′ in both directions

8′ · 8′

CRITICAL ALIGNMENTS

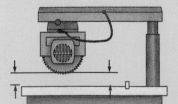

■ Blade travels parallel to table

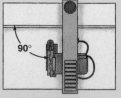

CROSSCUTTING

■ Blade travels perpendicular to fence

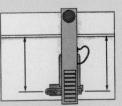

RIPPING

■ Blade is parallel to fence

CIRCULAR SAW BLADES

The *sawteeth* may be cut into the steel *plate,* or they may be bits of carbide attached to it. The teeth are ground to attack the wood at a specific *hook angle* — larger angles take bigger bites and feed more aggressively. *Gullets* between the teeth clear saw-dust from the cut, while *expansion slots* keep the blade from distorting as it heats.

Each tooth is arranged so the *kerf* that the blade cuts is wider than the plate. (This prevents the plate from rubbing in the cut.) On all-steel blades, the teeth are either *set* (bent) left and right, or the plate is *hollow-ground* to be thinner than the teeth. Carbide teeth are made wider than the plate.

The cutting edge of each tooth is ground to a specific *profile* that controls how it cuts. *Flat* teeth shave the wood fibers like a plane, *beveled* teeth cut them in two like a knife. *Triple-chip* teeth are mixed with flat teeth to cut tough materials in small bites. The mix of teeth on a blade is known as the *grind.*

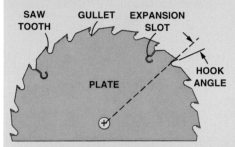

PARTS OF A BLADE

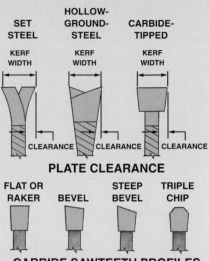

PLATE CLEARANCE

CARBIDE SAWTEETH PROFILES

BLADE TYPE AND USES	CONFIGURATION	GRIND
RIP Cutting parallel to wood grain, ripping to width	Because it's easier to cut with the grain, rip blades have a *large hook angle* (20 to 25 degrees). This cuts aggressively and removes large chips, so there are *fewer teeth* and *wide gullets* to clear the waste. STEEL CARBIDE	*Flat-Top Grind* (FTG). The tooth profiles are all flat. STEEL CARBIDE
CROSSCUT Cutting across wood grain, cutting to length	It's harder to cut across the grain, so crosscut blades have a *small hook angle* (5 to 10 degrees) to take smaller bites. Because the chips are smaller, these blades can have *more teeth* and *narrow gullets.* STEEL CARBIDE	*Alternate Top Bevel* (ATB). The teeth alternate right bevel and left bevel. *Steep Alternate Top Bevel* (SATB). Reduces chipping and tear-out. STEEL CARBIDE
COMBINATION Ripping and crosscutting woods and wood materials	The teeth are arranged in sets of five — first a *ripping tooth* preceded by a *wide gullet,* then four *crosscut teeth* with *narrow gullets.* The hook angle varies between 5 and 25 degrees depending on the tooth. STEEL CARBIDE	*Alternate Top Bevel and Flat* (ATBF). The crosscut teeth alternate right and left, the rip tooth is flat. STEEL CARBIDE
PLYWOOD Cutting plywood; carbide-tipped blades will also cut composites	To make a smooth cut, plywood blades usually have 80 or more *small teeth* with *narrow gullets.* Each tooth has a small hook angle (5 to 10 degrees) to take small bites. STEEL CARBIDE	*Steep Alternate Top Bevel* (SATB). Typically steel blades. *Triple-Chip Grind* (TCG). Carbide-tipped blades only. STEEL CARBIDE
HOLLOW GROUND PLANER Joinery, moldings, and sawing operations requiring a smooth cut	Hollow-ground planer blades have the *same hook angle and tooth arrangement as combination blades.* However, the teeth have no set. These blades are available in steel only. STEEL	*Steep Alternate Top Bevel* (SATB). Leaves a very smooth surface, reduces chipping and tear-out. STEEL
THIN KERF Ripping or crosscutting hardwood	Available in rip, crosscut, and combination configurations, carbide-tipped only. The plate and the teeth are approximately *two-thirds the width of ordinary blades.* Because the blade removes less stock, the saw makes a quicker cut. RIP CROSSCUT COMBINATION	*Flat-Top Grind* (FTG). Thin-kerf rip blades. *Alternate Top Bevel* (ATB). Thin-kerf crosscut blades. *Alternate Top Bevel and Flat* (ATBF).Thin-kerf combination blades. RIP CROSSCUT COMBINATION

JOINTERS

A jointer cuts a wood surface **straight and flat**[1], at a precise angle to an adjoining surface.

BASIC OPERATION

The jointer has two long, narrow tables – an *infeed* table and an *outfeed* table. Between them is a *cutterhead* that holds several *knives*. These are covered by a *cutterhead guard*. A *fence* guides work over the jointer.

This assembly is mounted on a *base*. The base rests on a *stand*, which holds the *motor*. The stand may also incorporate a *chip chute* to carry the waste away from the jointer as you work.

Adjust the depth of cut with the *infeed table adjustment* to raise or lower the infeed table. Release the *fence locks* to tilt the fence and

change the angle at which the work passes over the knives. Better jointers also have an *outfeed table adjustment* to align the outfeed table with the knives.

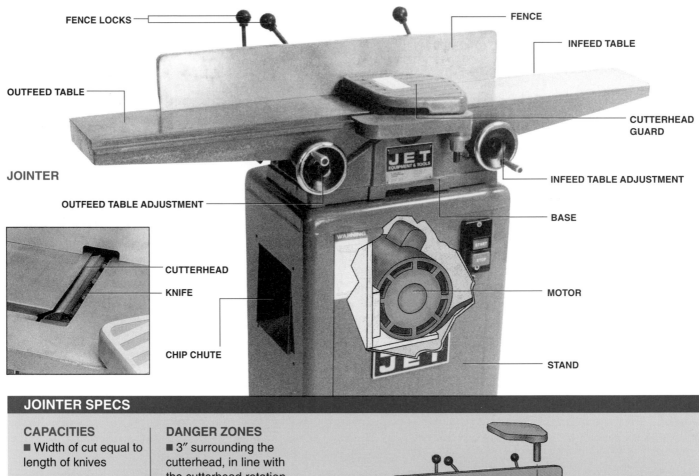

FENCE LOCKS

FENCE

INFEED TABLE

OUTFEED TABLE

CUTTERHEAD GUARD

JOINTER

INFEED TABLE ADJUSTMENT

OUTFEED TABLE ADJUSTMENT

BASE

MOTOR

STAND

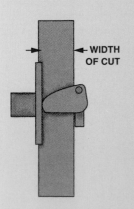

CUTTERHEAD

KNIFE

CHIP CHUTE

JOINTER SPECS

CAPACITIES
■ Width of cut equal to length of knives

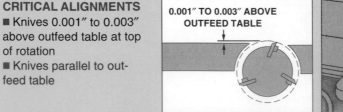

DANGER ZONES
■ 3″ surrounding the cutterhead, in line with the cutterhead rotation extending 8′ toward the infeed direction

8′

WIDTH OF CUT

CRITICAL ALIGNMENTS
■ Knives 0.001″ to 0.003″ above outfeed table at top of rotation
■ Knives parallel to outfeed table

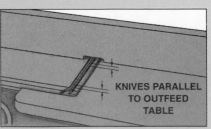

0.001″ TO 0.003″ ABOVE OUTFEED TABLE

KNIVES PARALLEL TO OUTFEED TABLE

THICKNESS PLANERS

A thickness planer cuts one surface of a board parallel to another surface, **reducing the thickness**[1] or the width (depending on how you feed the board through the machine).

BASIC OPERATION

The sturdy planer *bed* supports and guides the wood under a *cutterhead.* Like a jointer, this cutterhead holds several long *knives.* An *infeed roller* and an *outfeed roller* feed the stock and keep it flat against the bed. Better planers also have a *pressure bar* to help hold the wood on the bed.

Turn the *thickness adjustment* to change the distance between the cutterhead and the bed. This, in turn, changes the thickness of the planed stock. As the knives shave the wood, a *chip breaker* breaks up the shavings and directs them away from the stock. *Anti-kickback pawls* prevent the work from kicking back. Better planers also have *bed rollers* to reduce friction and keep the stock gliding smoothly over the bed.

A single *motor* typically turns both the cutterhead and the feed rollers, although some planers use separate motors.

SAFE *GUARDS*

Never put your hands inside the planer housing when the machine is running.

SEE *ALSO:*

[1]Jointing and Planing   182

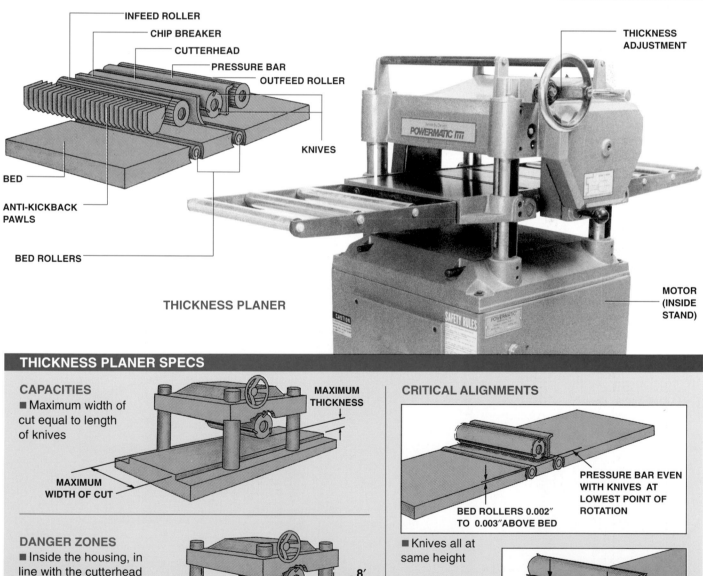

INFEED ROLLER
CHIP BREAKER
CUTTERHEAD
PRESSURE BAR
OUTFEED ROLLER
THICKNESS ADJUSTMENT
KNIVES
BED
ANTI-KICKBACK PAWLS
BED ROLLERS
POWERMATIC

THICKNESS PLANER

MOTOR (INSIDE STAND)

THICKNESS PLANER SPECS

CAPACITIES
■ Maximum width of cut equal to length of knives

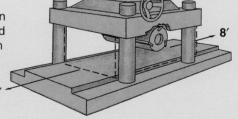

MAXIMUM THICKNESS

MAXIMUM WIDTH OF CUT

DANGER ZONES
■ Inside the housing, in line with the cutterhead rotation extending 8′ in both directions

8′

8′

CRITICAL ALIGNMENTS

PRESSURE BAR EVEN WITH KNIVES AT LOWEST POINT OF ROTATION

BED ROLLERS 0.002″ TO 0.003″ABOVE BED

■ Knives all at same height

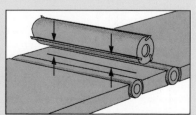

■ Knives parallel to bed

BAND SAWS

Of all the saws available, the band saw is the most versatile. Most craftsmen use it for **cutting curves and contours**[1], but it can also be used for **resawing**[2] and **creating three-dimensional shapes**[3] like cabriole legs.

BASIC OPERATION

The *band saw blade* is a continuous band of flexible steel. This blade revolves on a *drive wheel* and one or more *idler wheels.* A *motor* turns the drive wheel and the blade. A *tension adjustment* keeps the blade taut, and a *tracking adjustment* positions the running blade on the wheels.

The blade travels down through a *table.* An *upper blade guide* above the table and a *lower blade guide* below it keep the blade running straight and true. Each guide consists of *guide blocks* to keep the blade from twisting and *thrust bearings* to back up the blade. By loosening the *guide lock,* you can raise or lower the upper blade guide to accommodate the work. A *blade guard* on the upper blade *guide post* covers the unused portion of the blade above the work.

The wheels, guides, and table are mounted on a *frame.* A removable *cover* gives you access to the wheels and blade.

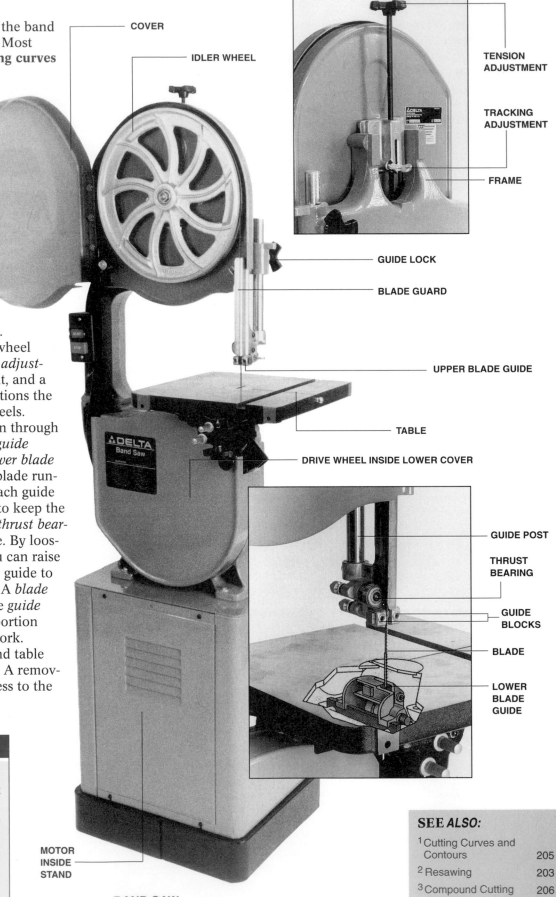

COVER

IDLER WHEEL

TENSION ADJUSTMENT

TRACKING ADJUSTMENT

FRAME

GUIDE LOCK

BLADE GUARD

UPPER BLADE GUIDE

TABLE

DRIVE WHEEL INSIDE LOWER COVER

GUIDE POST

THRUST BEARING

GUIDE BLOCKS

BLADE

LOWER BLADE GUIDE

MOTOR INSIDE STAND

BAND SAW

SAFE *GUARDS*

Keep the upper blade guide as close to the work as possible. It's not safe to leave more than ¼ inch of the blade exposed. Besides, the closer the guide to the work, the better the blade will be supported in the cut.

BAND SAW SPECS

CAPACITIES

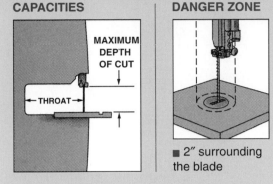

DANGER ZONE

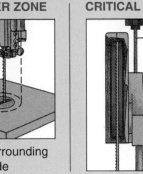

■ 2″ surrounding the blade

CRITICAL ALIGNMENTS *(These must be performed in the order shown.)*

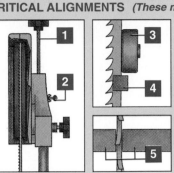

1. Blade tensioned properly.
2. Blade tracking properly.
3. Position thrust bearing 0.005″ from back of blade.
4. Position front edge of guide blocks even with bottom of gullets in blade.
5. Position the guide blocks 0.002″ to 0.003″ (a paper's thickness) away from blade.

BAND SAW BLADES

Every band saw blade is made from a flexible metal band called the *body*. The *gauge* is the body thickness — the thinner the body, the more flexible it is. The body is joined in a continuous loop by a *weld*. The *teeth* and *gullets* are ground in the front edge of the body, while the *back* remains flat. Each tooth is designed to attack the wood at a specific *rake angle*. The spacing between the teeth is called the *pitch* and is measured in teeth-per-inch (tpi).

When selecting a band saw blade for a specific operation, consider the blade *width, grind,* and *set.*

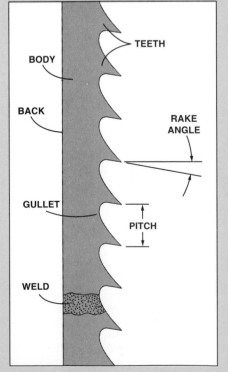

WIDTH The distance between the tips of the teeth and the back is the *width* of the blade. The blade turns slightly in the kerf, allowing you to cut curves, but it stops turning when the back rubs against the sides of the kerf. For this reason, the narrower the blade, the smaller the radius you can cut with it.

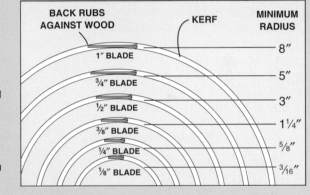

	MINIMUM RADIUS
1″ BLADE	8″
¾″ BLADE	5″
½″ BLADE	3″
⅜″ BLADE	1¼″
¼″ BLADE	⅝″
⅛″ BLADE	³⁄₁₆″

GRIND There are three different tooth profiles or *grinds.* A *standard-tooth* grind has more teeth per inch. This arrangement cuts slower and smoother than other grinds. In a *skip-tooth* grind, the teeth have roughly the same profile but are spaced much farther apart. This cuts faster but coarser. In a *hook-tooth* grind, the pitch is the same as skip teeth, but the rake angle is about 10 degrees to cut more aggressively.

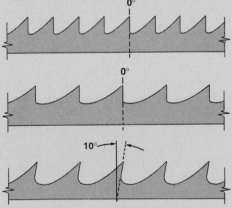

STANDARD TOOTH Best used for crosscutting, joinery cuts, smooth surfaces

SKIP TOOTH Best used for cutting curves and contours, thick stock, fast cuts

HOOK TOOTH Best used for ripping, resawing, cutting green or resinous wood, thick stock, fast cuts

SET The teeth are *set* left and right so the kerf left by the blade will be wider than the gauge. An *alternate set* produces the smoothest cut because more teeth contact the sides of the kerf. A *raker set* produces a rougher surface, but it clears sawdust more effectively, making it better for cutting thick stock.

ALTERNATE SET Best used for joinery cuts, smooth surfaces, thin stock

RAKER SET Best used for resawing, thick stock, fast cuts

DRILL PRESSES

A drill press **bores precise holes**[1] in wood. It will drill completely through the wood or stop at a preset depth. It can also drill at various angles or create **round mortises**[2]

BASIC OPERATION

A drill press has four major assemblies – the *head*, which holds, turns, and feeds the *drill bit*, the *table*, which supports the work, and the *column*, which supports both the head and the table. The column is held upright by a *base*.

The head holds the *motor*, which turns a *spindle* in a movable *quill*. The bits are mounted in a *chuck* on the bottom end of the spindle. Adjust the *speed changer* to increase or reduce the rate at which the bit turns. Move the quill up and down with the *quill feed;* limit its travel with the *depth stop,* or secure it in one position with the *quill lock.*

Use the *table tilt adjustment* to tilt the table to the desired angle. Raise or lower the table on the column with the *table height adjuster,* and secure it at the desired height with the *table lock.*

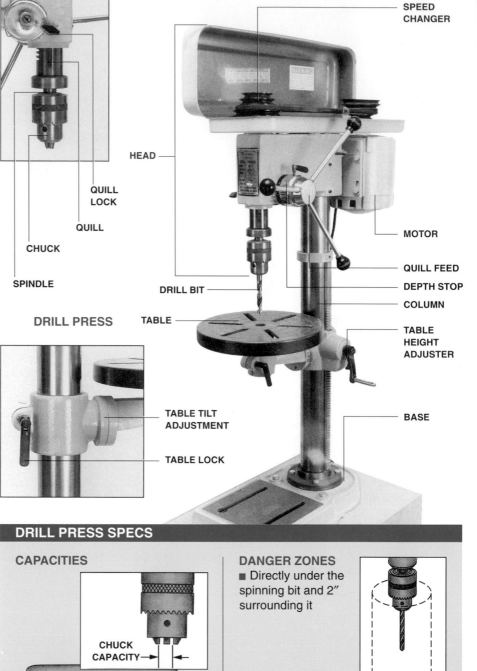

QUILL
LOCK

QUILL

CHUCK

SPINDLE

DRILL PRESS

SPEED
CHANGER

HEAD

MOTOR

QUILL FEED

DEPTH STOP

COLUMN

TABLE
HEIGHT
ADJUSTER

DRILL BIT

TABLE

BASE

TABLE TILT
ADJUSTMENT

TABLE LOCK

SAFE*GUARDS*

Always secure the work on the table before you drill. Back it up with a fence or hold it down with clamps. Otherwise, the drill bit may catch on the work and spin it around.

NECESSARY IMPROVEMENTS

A typical drill press table is too small to support large boards. And, if it tilts at all, it tilts from side to side, limiting the size of the work when drilling at an angle. (The column gets in the way.) An auxiliary table remedies these problems.

DRILL PRESS SPECS

CAPACITIES

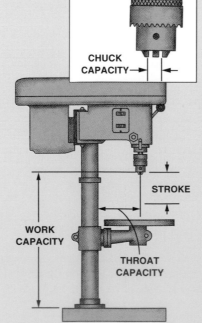

CHUCK
CAPACITY

WORK
CAPACITY

STROKE

THROAT
CAPACITY

DANGER ZONES
■ Directly under the spinning bit and 2″ surrounding it

CRITICAL ALIGNMENTS

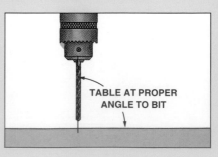

TABLE AT PROPER
ANGLE TO BIT

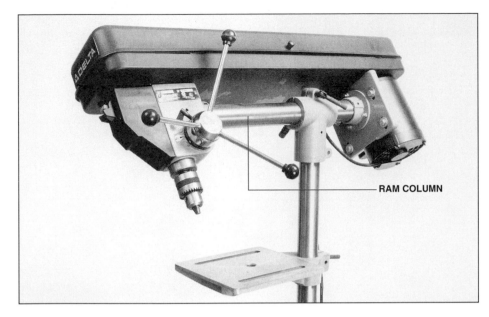

RAM COLUMN

A **radial drill press** has a much larger throat capacity (up to 17 inches) than a standard drill press. The head travels forward and backward on a **ram column,** making the throat adjustable. The head and the ram column also rotate, letting you change the angle at which you feed the bit. Although this design is much more versatile, it's less accurate. The flex in the ram column makes it difficult to drill a hole to a precise depth.

SEE *ALSO:*

[1] Drilling and Boring   208

[2] Making Round
    Mortises and Tenons   242

DRILL BITS

Each bit has a *shank* that mounts in the chuck, while the body extends out from it. At the *tip,* the *lips* cut the wood, creating a hole. Most bits also have a *lead point* at the tip to keep the bit running true. Some have *spurs* to score the circumference of the hole ahead of the tip. Some also have *flutes* to lift the wood chips out of the hole.

DRILL BIT

SHANK
BODY
TIP
FLUTE

SPUR
LEAD POINT
LIP

DRILL BIT TYPES	COMMON USES	DIAMETERS
TWIST BIT	Best all-around multipurpose bit. Designed to drill metal, but also works well in wood or plastic.	Fractional and decimal sizes from 0.014″ dia. to ½″ dia. Metric sizes also available.
BRAD-POINT BIT	Best for general drilling tasks in wood. Lead point and spurs help cut clean, accurate holes. Will also drill plastic, but not metal.	Fractional sizes from 1/16″ to 1¼″. Metric sizes also available.
SPADE BIT	Quick, rough holes; also good for boring end grain. You can regrind profiles to make holes of odd sizes and profiles.	Fractional sizes from ¼″ to 1½″.
BORING BIT	Quick, smooth holes. More expensive than spade bits and not as readily available.	Metric sizes from 15 to 40mm. A few fractional sizes also available.
FORSTNER BIT	Flat-bottom holes with smooth sides. Best used for small holes (1½″ diameter or less).	Fractional sizes from ¼″ to 3″. A few metric sizes also available.
MULTI-SPUR BIT	Flat-bottom holes with smooth sides. Best used for large holes (1½″ diameter or more).	Fractional sizes from 3/8″ to 4″.

JIGS & FIXTURES

TILTING DRILL PRESS TABLE

Although a drill press is essential for precision woodworking, most presses are designed for metal-working and have some serious shortcomings in a wood shop. The most glaring problem is the table — it's too small, has no fence, and tilts in the wrong plane (side to side).

You can mend this by building an auxiliary table that mounts to the existing one. The table shown offers a generous work surface that tilts up to 55 degrees front to back. It also has a movable fence that can be mounted face up (when you need a short fence) or edge up (when you need a tall fence).

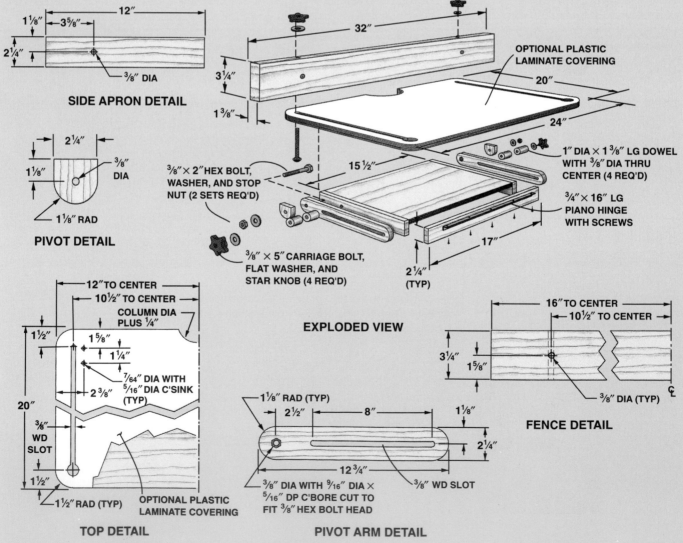

SIDE APRON DETAIL
- 12"
- 1⅛"
- 3⅝"
- 2¼"
- ⅜" DIA

PIVOT DETAIL
- 2¼"
- 1⅛"
- ⅜" DIA
- 1⅛" RAD

TOP DETAIL
- 12" TO CENTER
- 10½" TO CENTER
- COLUMN DIA PLUS ¼"
- 1½"
- 1⅝"
- 1¼"
- 2⅜"
- ⁷⁄₆₄" DIA WITH ⁵⁄₁₆" DIA C'SINK (TYP)
- 20"
- ⅜" WD SLOT
- 1½"
- 1½" RAD (TYP)
- OPTIONAL PLASTIC LAMINATE COVERING

EXPLODED VIEW
- 32"
- 3¼"
- 1⅜"
- OPTIONAL PLASTIC LAMINATE COVERING
- 20"
- 24"
- ⅜" × 2" HEX BOLT, WASHER, AND STOP NUT (2 SETS REQ'D)
- 15½"
- 1" DIA × 1⅜" LG DOWEL WITH ⅜" DIA THRU CENTER (4 REQ'D)
- ¾" × 16" LG PIANO HINGE WITH SCREWS
- ⅜" × 5" CARRIAGE BOLT, FLAT WASHER, AND STAR KNOB (4 REQ'D)
- 2¼" (TYP)
- 17"

PIVOT ARM DETAIL
- 1⅛" RAD (TYP)
- 2½"
- 8"
- 1⅛"
- 2¼"
- 12¾"
- ⅜" DIA WITH ⁹⁄₁₆" DIA × ⁵⁄₁₆" DP C'BORE CUT TO FIT ⅜" HEX BOLT HEAD
- ⅜" WD SLOT

FENCE DETAIL
- 16" TO CENTER
- 10½" TO CENTER
- 3¼"
- 1⅝"
- ⅜" DIA (TYP)

SANDING MACHINES

There is an amazing variety of sanding machines available, each designed to remove stock and **smooth wood surfaces**[1] For the most part, these are categorized by the shape of the abrasive.

DISC SANDER

On stationary disc sanders, the abrasive is mounted to a spinning *disc* 6 to 24 inches in diameter. A small *worktable* in the front of the disc supports the work. You can also align the work to the disc with a *miter gauge*. Use the *tilt adjustment* to change the angle of the table to the disc.

Disc sanders are useful for quickly removing stock from flat and convex surfaces, sanding up to a mark or line, fitting joints, and sanding wooden joints flush after they've been assembled.

BELT SANDER

A stationary belt sander runs an *abrasive belt* in a continuous loop over two *drums*. Track the belt on the drums with a *tracking adjustment*. A *platen* backs up the belt where you press the work against it, and a *backstop* supports the work. Change the angle of the backstop to the belt with the *tilt adjustment*.

Because the abrasive surface travels in a straight line, you can sand with the grain. This makes belt sanders useful not only for removing stock, but also for surfacing and smoothing wood. These tools come in many sizes, from small bench-top units to huge stroke sanders with a sanding surface as large as a door.

SEE *ALSO*:

[1]Sanding, Scraping, and Filing   260

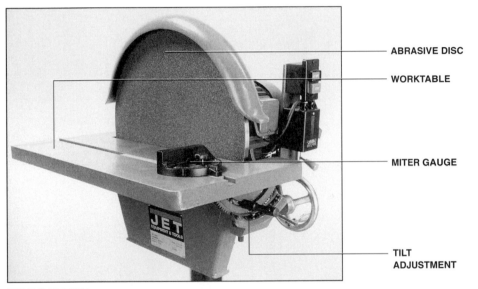

ABRASIVE DISC

WORKTABLE

MITER GAUGE

TILT ADJUSTMENT

DISC SANDER

TILT ADJUSTMENT

BACKSTOP

ABRASIVE BELT

PLATEN

DRUM

TRACKING ADJUSTMENT

BELT SANDER

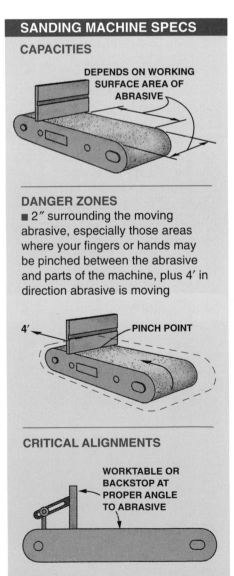

SANDING MACHINE SPECS

CAPACITIES

DEPENDS ON WORKING SURFACE AREA OF ABRASIVE

DANGER ZONES

■ 2″ surrounding the moving abrasive, especially those areas where your fingers or hands may be pinched between the abrasive and parts of the machine, plus 4′ in direction abrasive is moving

4′   PINCH POINT

CRITICAL ALIGNMENTS

WORKTABLE OR BACKSTOP AT PROPER ANGLE TO ABRASIVE

STRIP SANDER

Strip sanders drive narrow *abrasive belts* (between ½ inch and 2 inches wide) over several *wheels*, similar to a band saw. A *platen* backs up the abrasive, and a *worktable* supports the work. Track the belt on the wheels with the *tracking adjustment,* and change the angle of the table with the *tilt adjustment.*

Strip sanders are commonly used for sanding and shaping small parts. Some can be set up to sand the edges of interior cuts.

SPINDLE SANDER

Spindle sanders turn *abrasive drums* of various diameters on a *spindle,* while a *table* supports the work. On better machines, the spindle oscillates up and down as it spins. This motion helps clear sawdust. The abrasive cuts faster and leaves a smoother surface.

Spindle sanders are typically used to shape or smooth edges.

THICKNESS SANDER

A thickness sander uses a long, horizontal *abrasive drum* to smooth broad surfaces. It works like a thickness planer. Raise or lower the drum with the *height adjustment* to change the thickness of the sanded stock. Pass the stock underneath the drum on the *feed belt.*

Use this machine not only to smooth surfaces, but also to reduce the thickness of stock.

SAFE *GUARDS*

When using sanding machines, be especially wary of **pinch points** — places where your fingers or hands may be pinched between the moving abrasive and the edge of a table or backstop.

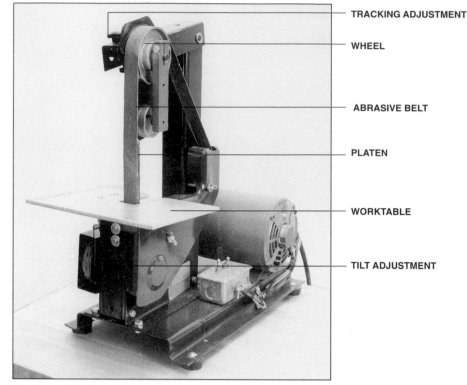

TRACKING ADJUSTMENT

WHEEL

ABRASIVE BELT

PLATEN

WORKTABLE

TILT ADJUSTMENT

STRIP SANDER

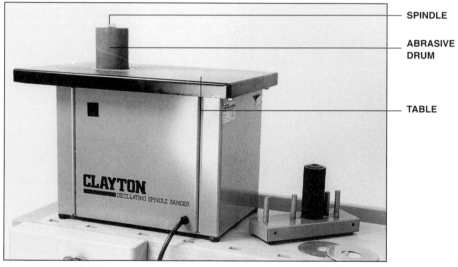

SPINDLE

ABRASIVE DRUM

TABLE

SPINDLE SANDER

HEIGHT ADJUSTMENT

ABRASIVE DRUM INSIDE COVER

FEED BELT

THICKNESS SANDER

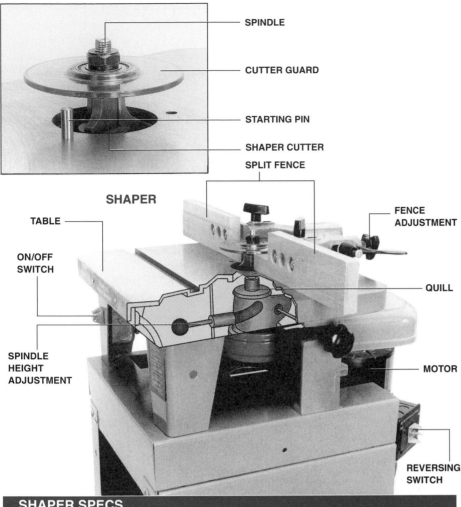

SPINDLE

CUTTER GUARD

STARTING PIN

SHAPER CUTTER

SPLIT FENCE

SHAPER

FENCE
ADJUSTMENT

TABLE

ON/OFF
SWITCH

QUILL

SPINDLE
HEIGHT
ADJUSTMENT

MOTOR

REVERSING
SWITCH

SHAPERS

The shaper cuts **molded shapes**[1] in the edges of boards. These shapes may be decorative beads, ogees, and other ornamental shapes, or functional joints such as tongues and grooves.

BASIC OPERATION

The shaper *motor* turns a vertical *spindle* which protrudes above a *table*. The spindle is surrounded by a *split fence* and protected by a *cutter guard*.

Mount the *shaper cutters* on the spindle and adjust their vertical position with the *spindle height adjustment*. This moves the *quill*, which houses the spindle, up and down. The spindle can be set to rotate either clockwise or counterclockwise with the *reversing switch*. Use the *fence adjustment* to position the infeed and outfeed fence halves. (Normally the fence halves are either even with one another, or the outfeed half is slightly in front of the infeed half.) When shaping curved edges, remove the fence and use a *starting pin* to help start the cut and guide the work.

SHAPER SPECS

CAPACITIES
(with spindle at highest position)

WORKING
CAPACITY

DANGER ZONES

■ 3″ surrounding the cutter, above it and on all sides

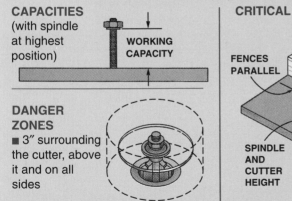

CRITICAL ALIGNMENTS

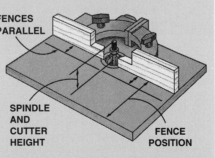

FENCES
PARALLEL

SPINDLE
AND
CUTTER
HEIGHT

FENCE
POSITION

SEE *ALSO:*

[1]Shaping and Molding   288

SHAPER CUTTERS

Shaper cutters commonly have three cutting **flutes** attached to a central **hub**. They are usually mounted on the spindle with **rub collars** to limit the depth of cut. The flutes can be cut to almost any shape.

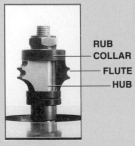

RUB
COLLAR

FLUTE

HUB

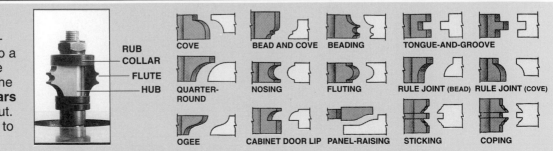

COVE

BEAD AND COVE

BEADING

TONGUE-AND-GROOVE

QUARTER-ROUND

NOSING

FLUTING

RULE JOINT (BEAD)

RULE JOINT (COVE)

OGEE

CABINET DOOR LIP

PANEL-RAISING

STICKING

COPING

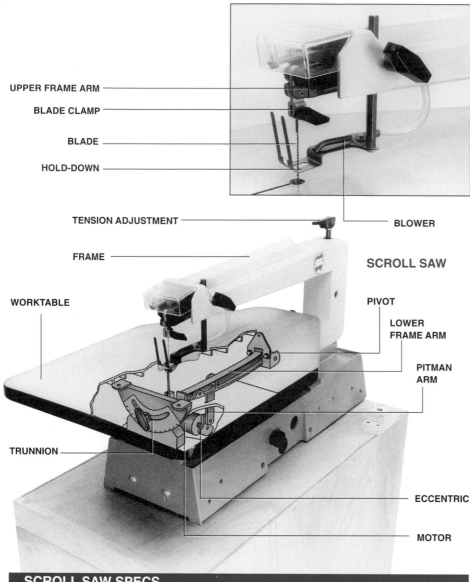

UPPER FRAME ARM

BLADE CLAMP

BLADE

HOLD-DOWN

TENSION ADJUSTMENT

BLOWER

FRAME

SCROLL SAW

WORKTABLE

PIVOT

LOWER FRAME ARM

PITMAN ARM

TRUNNION

ECCENTRIC

MOTOR

SCROLL SAWS

A scroll saw cuts fine, **intricate profiles and patterns**[1] such as fretwork, marquetry, and inlay. It will also cut interior shapes without having to cut through the stock from an outside edge.

BASIC OPERATION

A scroll saw holds a narrow *blade* vertically in a *frame*. The frame and the blade reciprocate – move up and down as the saw cuts. The blade extends through a *worktable* and is attached to the front ends of the *upper frame arm* and the *lower frame arm* by *blade clamps*. When you tighten the *tension adjustment*, the blade draws taut. The frame rocks up and down on one or more *pivots*. The lower arm is connected to the *motor* by a *pitman arm* and an *eccentric*. As the motor turns, the eccentric drives the pitman arm up and down. This, in turn, drives the lower arm and all the linked parts, including the blade.

The worktable is mounted on *trunnions* so it can be tilted. A *hold-down* keeps the work firmly against the table as you cut. Some scroll saws have a *blower* that directs a stream of air to clear the sawdust away from the pattern lines as you work.

NECESSARY IMPROVEMENTS

Because the moving parts reciprocate, scroll saws vibrate more than other tools. This interferes with the machine's accuracy and exhausts the craftsman working with it. To reduce vibration, mount your scroll saw to a **heavy stand**[2]

SCROLL SAW SPECS

CAPACITIES

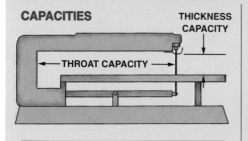

THICKNESS CAPACITY

THROAT CAPACITY

DANGER ZONES

■ 1″ surrounding the blade on all sides

NOTE: The scroll saw is one of the safest woodworking tools because it cuts so slowly. However, there are dangerous pinch points on some saws — places where your fingers could be pinched between the moving frame and other parts of the machine.

CRITICAL ALIGNMENTS

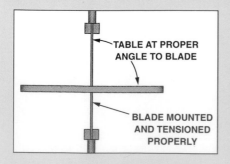

TABLE AT PROPER ANGLE TO BLADE

BLADE MOUNTED AND TENSIONED PROPERLY

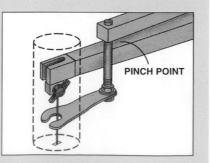

PINCH POINT

SCROLL SAW BLADES

TYPES OF BLADES. There are five types of blades for scroll saws:

■ *Scroll blades* for heavy-duty work in wood and soft metals.

■ *Fret blades* for fine work in wood and soft metals.

■ *Precision-ground blades* for cleaner cuts and better control.

■ *Metal-cutting blades* for work in metals.

■ *Spiral blades* for omnidirectional cuts in wood and soft metals.

Each type is available in different sizes, tooth styles, and tooth spacings.

BLADE SIZE. The size of a blade refers to its width and thickness. Most blades are classified in a numbering system that runs from 8/0 (0.012 inch wide and 0.006 inch thick) to 12 (0.062 inch wide and 0.024 inch thick). Larger blades are available up to 0.250 inch wide and 0.028 inch thick, but these are not numbered.

TOOTH STYLE. There are three different tooth styles.

■ *Standard teeth* are spaced close together and are used mostly for scroll and metal-cutting blades.

■ *Skip teeth* are used for fret blades to help clear the sawdust.

■ *Double-skip teeth* are also used for fret blades. They cut slower and smoother than skip teeth.

Additionally, skip-tooth fret blades are available with several *reverse teeth* near the bottom of the blade. This reduces *feathering,* tiny splinters that occur on the bottom of a workpiece.

TOOTH SPACING. The number of *teeth per inch* (tpi) on a blade depends on its size and tooth style. The greater the tpi, the slower and smoother the blade cuts.

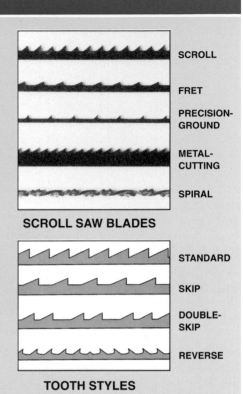

SCROLL SAW BLADES

SCROLL
FRET
PRECISION-GROUND
METAL-CUTTING
SPIRAL

TOOTH STYLES

STANDARD
SKIP
DOUBLE-SKIP
REVERSE

BLADE TYPE AND STYLE	SIZE	SPACING	USES
SKIP-TOOTH FRET BLADES	From: 0.022″ wd, 0.010″ thk To: 0.048″ wd, 0.018″ thk	From: 28 tpi To: 8 tpi	General cutting of wood, wood products and plastics between ¹⁄₁₆″ and 2″ thick. Use smaller blades for thin stock.
SKIP-TOOTH PRECISION-GROUND BLADES	From: 0.040″ wd, 0.018″ thk To: 0.048″ wd, 0.018″ thk	From: 12 tpi To: 8 tpi	Smooth cuts and precise control in wood and other soft materials from ⅛″ to 2″ thick.
DOUBLE-SKIP TOOTH FRET BLADES	From: 0.026″ wd, 0.013″ thk To: 0.061″ wd, 0.022″ thk	From: 30 tpi To: 10 tpi	Smooth cuts in wood and other soft materials between ¹⁄₁₆″ and 2″ thick. Use smaller blades for thin stock.
REVERSE SKIP-TOOTH FRET BLADES	From: 0.038″ wd, 0.016″ thk To: 0.100″ wd, 0.022″ thk	From: 13 tpi To: 9 tpi	Reduces splintering and feathered edges when cutting wood and plywood.
STANDARD-TOOTH METAL-CUTTING BLADES	From: 0.024″ wd, 0.012″ thk To: 0.070″ wd, 0.023″ thk	From: 48 tpi To: 20 tpi	Cutting soft metals between 0.020″ and 0.060″ thick and other hard materials between ¹⁄₆₄″ and ¼″ thick.
STANDARD-TOOTH SCROLL BLADES	From: 0.110″ wd, 0.022″ thk To: 0.250″ wd, 0.028″ thk	From: 20 tpi To: 7 tpi	Heavy-duty cutting in wood, wood products, plastics, and soft metals.
STANDARD-TOOTH SPIRAL BLADES	From: 0.030″ dia To: 0.051″ dia	From: 51 tpi To: 30 tpi	Omnidirectional cuts in wood, wood products, and plastic from ¹⁄₁₆″ to 1″ thick, and soft metals up to 0.060″ thick.

LATHES

A lathe **turns a piece of wood**[1] allowing you to shave it with special chisels. These chisels cut the wood into a cylinder, then shape it with decorative beads, coves, flats, and tapers. You can also hollow out the wood, making wooden bowls and containers.

BASIC OPERATION

When turning a long workpiece, support the work between the *headstock* and *tailstock.* Mount a *spur center* to the *drive spindle* in the headstock. Slide the tailstock into position and secure it with the *tailstock lock.* Adjust the *tailstock feed,* advancing the *cup center* on the tailstock toward the spur center, clamping the wood between centers.

Slide the *tool rest carriage* along the *bed,* placing it beneath the section of the work you wish to turn. Position the *tool rest* a short distance from the work, then secure the rest and the carriage with the *tool rest lock* and *carriage lock.* Set the *speed changer* to run the drive spindle at the proper speed for the turning task. The *motor* drives the spindle and the spur center, spinning the work. Rest a chisel on the tool rest and slowly advance the cutting edge until it shaves the work.

When turning the face of a workpiece or hollowing it, don't support the work between centers. Instead, mount it to a *faceplate,* then secure the faceplate to the drive spindle.

LATHE

LATHE SPECS

CAPACITIES
■ Swing (maximum turning diameter)
■ Distance between centers (maximum work length)

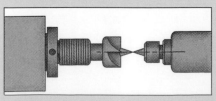

DANGER ZONES
■ 2″ surrounding the spinning work on all sides. There is also a dangerous pinch point between the work and the tool rest.

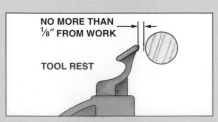

CRITICAL ALIGNMENTS

■ Spur center and cup center aligned

■ Tool rest as close as possible to work

SHARPENING MACHINES

Several power grinders are designed specifically to **sharpen wood-working tools**[2]. These machines turn abrasive stones, which hone the cutting edges of chisels and planes. There are two general types.

HOLLOW GRINDER

A hollow grinder turns an abrasive *grinding wheel* in a vertical plane. A *water reservoir* bathes the stone as it spins, floating away the swarf (metal filings) and keeping the metal tool from overheating. To sharpen a tool, adjust the *tool rest* to hold it at the proper angle to the wheel. Place the tool on the rest and slowly feed it into the edge of the wheel. Because you're working on the circumference of the wheel, the face of the tool will be concave or **hollow ground**[3].

FLAT GRINDER

A flat grinder turns a circular *whetstone* in a horizontal plane. A *water reservoir* drips water onto the stone as it spins to wash away the swarf and keep the metal cool. To sharpen a tool, adjust the *tool rest* to hold the tool at the proper angle to the stone. Place the tool on the rest and slowly feed it into the stone. Because you're grinding the tool on the stone's face, the tool will be **flat ground**[3]

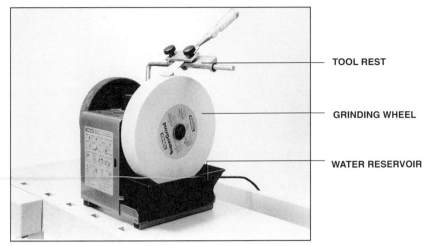

TOOL REST

GRINDING WHEEL

WATER RESERVOIR

HOLLOW GRINDER

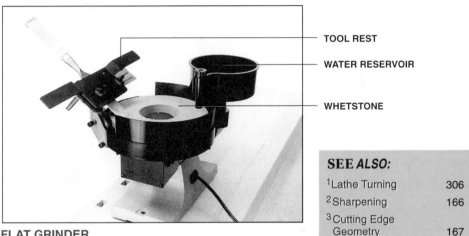

TOOL REST

WATER RESERVOIR

WHETSTONE

FLAT GRINDER

SEE *ALSO:*

MYTH *CONCEPTIONS*

Despite advertising to the contrary, **bench grinders** are not especially useful sharpeners for woodworking tools. They spin very fast and grind dry, so the tool can easily overheat. A wet grinder with a large wheel is a better investment.

SHARPENING MACHINE SPECS

CAPACITIES
■ Dependent on tool rest. Standard rest limits the size of the cutting edge to that of the abrasive surface. Rest with a **sliding carriage** (shown) lets you sharpen a long cutting edge on a small abrasive.

DANGER ZONES
■ Slow-turning, wet abrasives are relatively safe. However, there are dangerous pinch points between the moving abrasive and the stationary parts of the machine.

PINCH POINT

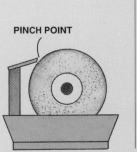

CRITICAL ALIGNMENTS

TOOL REST AT PROPER ANGLE TO ABRASIVE

MULTIPURPOSE TOOLS

In addition to single stationary power tools, there are *multipurpose* designs that combine two or more tools on the same stand. If you have a **small shop**[1], they pack a lot of woodworking capability into a tiny area. And even if you have a large shop, they are a space-efficient way to add tools that are used only occasionally. For example, you might set up a multipurpose tool as a sanding station (which you use often), then convert it to a lathe or a scroll saw on those rare occasions when you need them.

There are two general types of multipurpose tools.

CONVERTIBLE DESIGN

Convertible multipurpose tools, such as the *Shopsmith* and *Total Shop,* are based on a design by inventor Dr. Hans Goldschmidt. They convert to make a table saw, disc sander, lathe, drill press, and horizontal boring machine. Manufacturers have also developed add-on tools such as a jointer, band saw, belt sander, scroll saw, and thickness planer. The machine must be reconfigured before you can use each tool. This takes time, but it's extremely versatile.

COMBINATION DESIGN

Combination multipurpose tools, such as the *Robland,* were first manufactured for the millwork industry. Manufacturers combined a table saw, jointer, planer, mortiser, and shaper to create a workstation for craftsmen making custom windows and doors. This saved steps and speeded up production. There's no change-over time needed to use a tool, but the available tools are limited.

SEE *ALSO*:

[1]Shop Organization	76
[2]Alignment and Adjustment	158
[3]Tool Steel and Carbide	140

MORE *SOURCES*

BOOKS

Cabinetmaking and Millwork, by John L. Feirer, Bennett, 1981

The Complete Book of Stationary Power Tool Techniques, by R. J. DeCristoforo, Sterling Publishing, 1988

The Complete Manual of Woodworking, by Albert Jackson, David Day, and Simon Jennings, Alfred A. Knopf, 1989

Mastering Woodworking Machines, by Mark Duginske, Taunton Press, 1992

VIDEOS

Mastering Woodworking Machines, with Mark Duginske, Taunton Books and Video

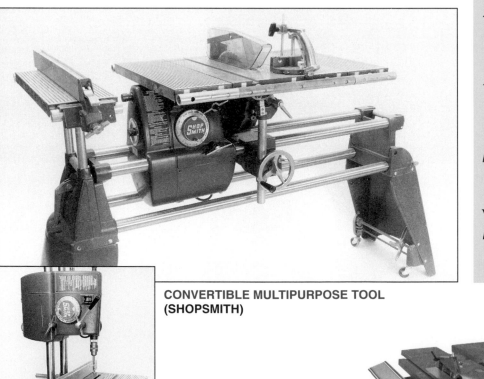

CONVERTIBLE MULTIPURPOSE TOOL (SHOPSMITH)

COMBINATION MULTIPURPOSE TOOL (ROBLAND)

Courtesy Laguna Tools, Laguna Beach, CA

TOOL BUYMANSHIP

Tools are an *investment* — a well-made tool holds its value much better than any other manufactured item you can buy. To make a good investment, you must look beyond capacity and capability and carefully consider the details.

Imports or the real McCoy?

■ Inexpensive imported tools are not necessarily inferior to expensive domestic brands, but there is *less quality control.* Consequently, the quality varies. Buy two identical tools and you may find that one runs perfectly, while the other has serious problems. To avoid disappointment, don't buy these tools sight unseen. Visit a show or a dealer and carefully test the tool. If it passes inspection, *buy the tool you've tested.*

What's it made from?

■ Some craftsmen assume that a quality tool should be made from *heavy materials.* The rationale for this is that mass absorbs vibration and the tool runs smoother. While this is true, improvements in drive train components — motors, belts, and bearings — have reduced the amount of vibration there is to absorb. Newer tools may not weigh as much as older ones, but the better ones run smoother.

■ Moving parts, especially those that affect the accuracy of your work such as trunnions and saw carriages, should be *machined from metal.* Manufacturers often cut corners by making these parts from stamped steel or plastic. This saves money because it requires no machining. But the movements aren't as precise or durable as they might be.

■ Although craftsmen complain about the use of *plastic* in tools, it has its place. Plastics make durable lightweight covers, see-through guards, and comfortable molded handles. However, you should avoid tools that use plastic for structural parts that must support a load (such as work tables) or withstand stress (such as a band saw frame). Plastic *creeps* under a constant load — that is, it deforms permanently. A plastic work table or saw frame may warp, affecting the tool's accuracy.

How is it made?

■ To gauge how much care went into the manufacture of a tool, *inspect the castings.* If someone took the time to knock off the sharp edges and flashings with a file, chances are they paid attention to other, more important details.

■ Carefully test the surfaces that need to be *straight and flat* — work tables, fences, slots, and extensions. Use a *precision straightedge* for this task; an ordinary straightedge won't do. Generally, you shouldn't be able to scoot a crisp dollar bill beneath a 2-foot-long straightedge when it's held against the surface.

■ Test arbors and spindles for *runout.* Use a **dial indicator**[2] to measure how far out-of-true these parts run. In general, the runout should be less than 0.002 inch. If the arbor mounts a large blade (over 10 inches in diameter), the runout should be less than 0.001 inch.

■ Test for *slop and deflection.* Does a miter gauge move from side to side in its slot? If you wrap a single thickness of paper around the bar, it should be too tight to fit the slot. Does a fence or an arm move when you put pressure on it? There should be no discernible movement under *ordinary stresses.*

How does it run?

■ Choose *induction motors* over *universal motors* in stationary power tools. Universal motors run fast and produce lots of power, but they wear out more quickly than induction motors. And because of their high speed and design, they produce a great deal more noise. Universal motors are better suited for intermittent tasks in which they run for brief periods of time, as they do in portable power tools.

■ Check that the machine *runs smoothly.* Place a glass of water, full to the brim, on the table with the motor running. If the water slops out or the glass walks across the table, there's too much vibration.

Is it safe and comfortable to use?

■ Pay attention to *knobs and controls.* Are they easy to reach and comfortable to turn? Are they large enough to get a good grip on them? Do you scrape your knuckles on other parts when you turn them? Can you turn the machine off quickly and easily in an emergency?

■ Can you *align and adjust* the machine easily? Did the manufacturer ignore or eliminate critical alignments? (This happens more often than you'd think, especially on inexpensive tools.)

■ Beware of *work tables with ribs* or ridges on the top surface. Wood catches on the ribs as you feed it across the table. It's also easy to pinch your fingers between the work and the sharp corners of the ribs.

■ Look for a *dust collection hook-up* to make a machine cleaner to use. Check that the hook-up is a standard diameter — $1\frac{1}{4}$ or $2\frac{1}{4}$ inches. Manufacturers sometimes put odd openings on hook-ups, making them frustrating to use.

What about blades and bits?

■ Don't be impressed with advertising claims of *high-speed steel or chromium steel.* These materials offer manufacturing advantages — high speed steel is easier to machine and chromium steel doesn't rust in storage or shipment. But neither have the fine grain necessary for a super-sharp edge that characterizes plain old high-carbon **tool steel**[3]. (That's why they call it tool steel, after all.)

■ Avoid *Teflon-coated blades and bits* — Teflon is a tip-off that the blade or bit bodies are made from cheap steel. To compensate, the thickness is increased. But this reduces clearance in the cut and the body rubs against the wood and burns it. Teflon is a quick fix — it reduces the friction that causes the burning.

■ Even if you must compromise on the quality of a power tool, always purchase *top-notch blades and bits.* A mediocre saw with a great blade cuts infinitely better than a great saw with a mediocre blade.

12

Portable Power Tools

Over the last century, these tools have grown lighter, more capable, more diverse – and more indispensable to the way modern craftsmen work wood.

While stationary power tools offer precision, portable power tools offer *convenience.* You can bring these tools right to your work. Portable tools are also much simpler to set up and use than stationary tools. There are fewer critical alignments, and the operation is more straightforward. Capacity is less important – you can use these tools for large workpieces as well as smaller ones. And because you must hold these tools, often for long periods of time, comfort and balance are paramount.

There is a wide variety of portable machines for all manner of woodworking tasks, and new ones are being introduced all the time.

HAND DRILLS AND DRIVERS

Hand drills are the most popular – and most versatile – portable power tools. They are commonly used to **bore holes**[1] and **drive fasteners**[2]; but with the proper accessories, they can also sand, grind, rasp, and remove rust and paint.

Although there are many types of hand drills, craftsmen generally divide them into two categories:

■ *Cordless drills* are powered by rechargeable batteries.

■ *Power drills* have no on-board power and must be plugged into an electrical outlet.

*As portable power tools have become more versatile, woodworkers have come to depend on them more. Many of the woodworking tasks that once were performed only on stationary machines can now be done with portable power tools as well. The parts of this **Turkey Whirligig** were cut, drilled, shaped, assembled, and sanded entirely with portable power tools.*

SPECS: 16½″ tall, 11″ wide, 17″ long	
MATERIALS: Poplar and European birch plywood	
CRAFTSMAN: Chris Walendzak Centerville, OH	DESIGNER: Mary Jane Favorite West Milton, OH

BASIC OPERATION

Both types of drills operate in the same manner. Mount a driver or drill bit in the *chuck* and pull the *trigger switch* to start the *motor*. In some drills, the motor and chuck are linked by a *gear train* that reduces the motor speed and increases torque (turning power). In others, speed and torque are controlled electronically. A *reversing switch* controls the direction of rotation.

PRO *TIP*

Advertisers have so confused the term *horsepower* that it is almost useless. To better compare power in power tools, refer to the rated *voltage* of cordless tools and the *amps* in corded tools.

FEATURES AND OPTIONS

Beyond these basics, there are many optional features. Some are specific to cordless drills or power drills. Others are shared.

CORDLESS DRILLS ONLY

■ *Battery voltage* is important – 7 to 10 volts will deliver enough power for most woodworking tasks, but you need 12 volts or more for heavy work.

■ An *adjustable clutch* lets you select the proper torque for driving screws so you don't strip them out in softwood or twist off the heads in hardwood.

POWER DRILLS ONLY

■ The motor should draw sufficient *amperage* to provide adequate power – 3 to 4 amps for medium-duty, 4 or more for heavy work.

■ A *trigger lock* holds the trigger down so the tool runs continuously.

■ *Hammer action* delivers several hundred blows per minute to the drill bit, making it possible to drill stone and masonry. To operate a power chisel, adjust the tool for hammer only (so the chisel does not turn).

SHARED FEATURES

■ *Variable speed* allows you to adjust the speed for the task. Drill speeds vary from 0 to 2,000 rpm. The more powerful the drill, the lower the top speed.

■ There are two types of chucks. A *keyless chuck* lets you mount accessories by hand, but you can secure them tighter with a standard *keyed chuck*.

■ *Chuck capacity* is the maximum size shank a chuck can hold.

Common capacities are $\frac{1}{4}$-, $\frac{3}{8}$-, and $\frac{1}{2}$-inch. Most craftsmen consider a $\frac{3}{8}$-inch chuck minimum for general woodworking.

SEE *ALSO:*

[1]Drilling and Boring   208
[2]Screws   373

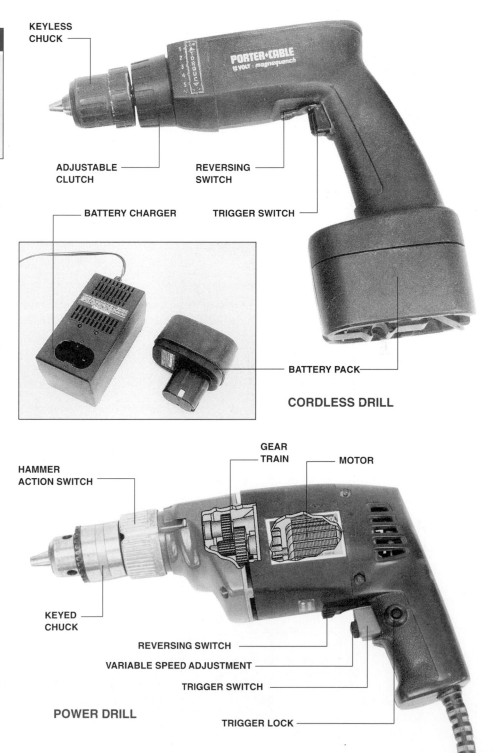

KEYLESS CHUCK

ADJUSTABLE CLUTCH

REVERSING SWITCH

BATTERY CHARGER

TRIGGER SWITCH

BATTERY PACK

CORDLESS DRILL

HAMMER ACTION SWITCH

GEAR TRAIN

MOTOR

KEYED CHUCK

REVERSING SWITCH

VARIABLE SPEED ADJUSTMENT

TRIGGER SWITCH

TRIGGER LOCK

POWER DRILL

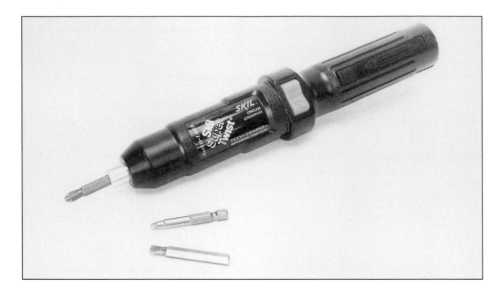

*In addition to drills and drivers with pistol grips, there are also **straight-body power screwdrivers** and wrenches. These have no chuck; instead, they're fitted with quick-change collets that mount drivers with square or hexagonal shafts.*

CORDLESS POWER TOOLS

While cordless drills are the most common type of battery-powered tool, there are many more — circular saws, saber saws, sanders, and grinders, just to name a few of special interest to woodworkers. For the most part, these are used like their corded counterparts. Because of the batteries, however, there are special considerations.

RECHARGEABLE BATTERIES. Most cordless power tools use rechargeable nickel-oxyhydroxide-and-cadmium (ni-cad) batteries, although manufacturers are experimenting with other materials. The battery chemistry is sealed in a steel case or *cell*. A typical ni-cad *battery pack* uses several cells connected in series (negative electrode to positive electrode). The number of cells determines the pack's voltage.

As these cells discharge, the materials inside change chemically. The nickel oxyhydroxide is reduced to nickel hydroxide and the cadmium oxidizes to cadmium hydroxide. Recharging reverses this reaction and restores power. The time to recharge varies with the charger. Most require an hour or so, but there are "fast chargers" available that take 10 to 15 minutes.

BATTERY LIFE. The time between charges depends on the number of cells in the battery pack (how much power it can store) and how you use the tool. The pack can be recharged anywhere from 650 to 3,000 times, depending on how it's used and how it's recharged.

The battery pack begins to die when one or more of the cells develops a short between the nickel and cadmium plates. You can tell a pack is on its last legs when the tool seems to have little energy and the time between charges grows shorter and shorter.

You can extend a battery pack's useful life by keeping it fully charged. Charged cells resist shorts better than discharged cells. Contrary to what many craftsmen believe, ni-cad batteries don't "remember" a low charge if not completely drained before recharging. Manufacturers eliminated this memory effect long ago, although the myth still persists. In fact, draining a battery may

shorten its life. You can charge a battery anytime, but avoid overcharging — this, too, can reduce the life span.

BATTERY SAFETY AND MAINTENANCE. To get the most life from your cordless tools:

■ Keep bits and cutters sharp so the tool does less work.

■ Don't expose the tool to extremely cold or hot environments (below 20 or above 110°F). Ni-cad batteries work best between 50 and 80°F.

■ Don't force the tool — this may cause the battery to overheat.

■ Avoid exposure to moisture and recharge the batteries in a dry location.

■ Be careful how you dispose of dead batteries. Ni-cads may explode in water or fire.

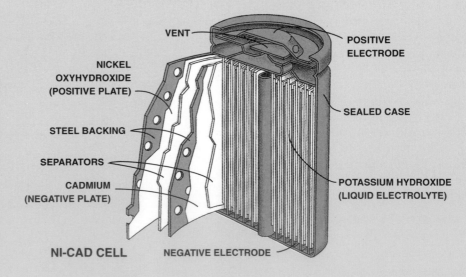

NI-CAD CELL

CIRCULAR SAWS

A circular saw **crosscuts**[1] long boards and **rips**[2] sheet materials. Although it's typically used for carpentry, woodworkers often keep one to reduce sheets of plywood and particleboard to manageable sizes. With the proper **blade**[3] and a long, straight saw guide, you can also make precise finish **cuts in sheet goods**[4].

BASIC OPERATION

The *motor* drives an *arbor,* on which the *blade* is mounted. A *fixed guard* covers the top half of the blade, while the bottom half is shielded by a *retractable guard.* To use the saw, adjust the *blade depth* and *tilt* the blade to the proper angle. Rest the *shoe* on the work and align the *line-of-cut indicator* with the line you want to cut on the work. Pull the *trigger switch* and push the saw forward. The lower guard will automatically retract as the cut progresses.

FEATURES AND OPTIONS

Also consider:

■ The standard *blade diameter* for circular saws is 7¼ inches, but some saws mount blades over 10 inches. Cordless circular saws use blades between 4 and 6 inches.

■ The blade diameter is directly proportional to the *depth of cut* – the larger the blade, the deeper the cut. Average depth of cut for a 7¼-inch blade is 2½ inches.

■ To provide adequate *power,* a corded circular saw should draw at least 10 amps. On cordless saws the battery should provide at least 12 volts.

■ A *blade brake* stops the saw blade a few seconds after you release the switch. This is a worthwhile safety device.

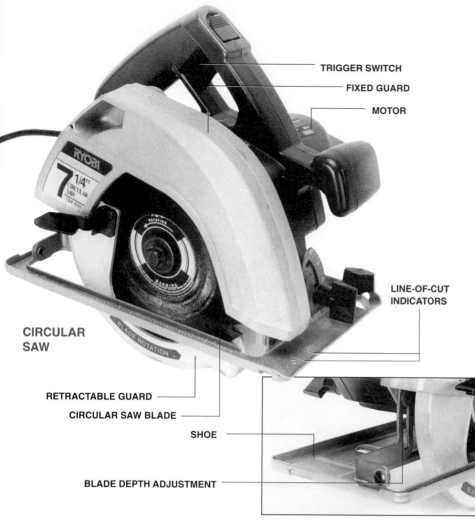

CIRCULAR SAW

TRIGGER SWITCH
FIXED GUARD
MOTOR
LINE-OF-CUT INDICATORS
RETRACTABLE GUARD
CIRCULAR SAW BLADE
SHOE
BLADE DEPTH ADJUSTMENT

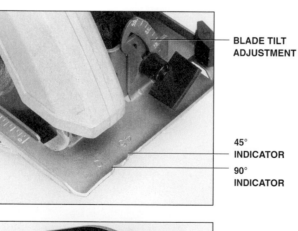

BLADE TILT ADJUSTMENT
45° INDICATOR
90° INDICATOR

Some circular saws have two line-of-cut indicators stamped into the shoe. One notch serves as an indicator for 90-degree cuts, while the other is an indicator for 45-degree cuts.

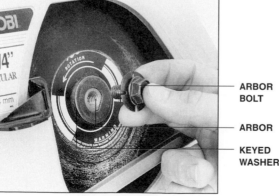

ARBOR BOLT
ARBOR
KEYED WASHER

When mounting a blade, don't overtighten the arbor bolt. When the bolt is snug, the large keyed washer under it acts as a "slip clutch." If you hit a knot or a nail that stops the blade, the arbor will continue to turn. This protects the motor from damage.

SABER SAWS

A saber saw (sometimes called a jigsaw) **cuts curves and contours**[1] It will also **make interior cuts**[2] cut an inside shape without cutting through the work from an outside edge.

BASIC OPERATION

The saw mounts a short, straight *saber saw blade* vertically. The *motor* runs a *drive gear*, which is connected to the *blade holder* by a *drive sleeve*. This arrangement drives the blade up and down in a reciprocating motion. A *counterweight* moves in the opposite direction of the blade holder to reduce the vibration caused by this motion. To use the saw, tilt the *shoe* to the desired angle. Place the shoe on the work, squeeze the *trigger switch*, and push forward.

FEATURES AND OPTIONS

Also consider:

■ Better saber saws let you switch between *straight-line action*, which moves the blade straight up and down, and *orbital action*, which moves the blade in an ellipse. Straight-line cuts produce smoother surfaces with less tear-out; orbital cuts clear the dust more efficiently and reduce friction so the blade cuts quickly.

■ *Variable speed* lets you adjust the cutting speed from 0 to 3,000 strokes per minute to suit the material and the operation.

■ *Blade guides* support the blade during a cut and keep it running true. Most saber saws have a roller to back up the blade, but some also have side guides to keep the blade from twisting. These tools often have a fixed (non-tilting) shoe.

■ A *scrolling control* at the top of the tool lets you turn the blade independently of the saw. This can be useful when cutting patterns.

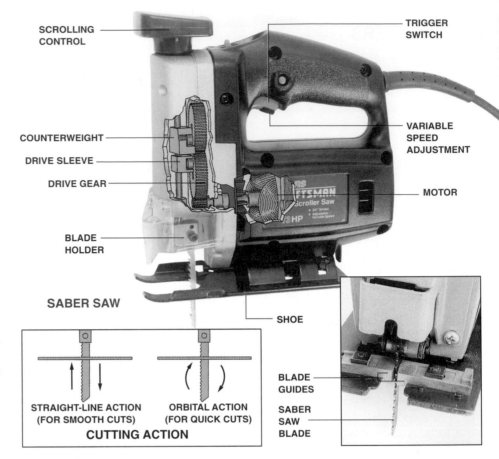

SABER SAW

STRAIGHT-LINE ACTION (FOR SMOOTH CUTS)   ORBITAL ACTION (FOR QUICK CUTS)
CUTTING ACTION

SABER SAW BLADES

Blades vary in their effective cutting length, the number of teeth per inch (tpi), and the manner in which the teeth are set. General-purpose blades are *side set* (alternating left and right). Those designed for cutting hard or abrasive material are *wavy set* so each tooth takes a tiny bite. Fine cutting blades have no set. Instead, the blade body is ground thinner than the teeth.

	CUTTING LENGTH	TPI	SET	USES
General-Purpose	3″	6–8	Side	Rough cuts in wood up to 2½″ thick
Smooth-Cut	3″	6–8	Ground	Clean cuts in wood up up to 2 ½″ thick
Plywood	2″	12–14	Wavy	Cutting sheet materials up to 1¼″ thick
Detail	2″	12–14	Wavy	Cutting intricate patterns in wood and sheet materials up to ¾″ thick
Laminate	3″	10–14	Ground	Reversed teeth to cut laminate-covered materials on downstroke
Offset	3″	6–8	Side	Offset blade for cutting up to a corner

HAND SANDERS

There are many types of portable power sanders, each designed for a different **sanding**[3] task. Shown are the four most common.

PORTABLE BELT SANDERS

Hand-held belt sanders are small versions of stationary belt sanders. Two *drums* run *abrasive belts* 3 to 4 inches wide over a *platen*. The platen backs up the belt and allows you to sand a flat surface. They are best used for quick stock removal and smoothing large surfaces.

RANDOM-ORBIT SANDERS

Random-orbit sanders spin an *abrasive disc.* However, the disc doesn't travel in a perfect circle. A free-spinning *counterweight* just above the disc pulls it this way and that way in a random pattern. Consequently, although it removes stock quickly, it leaves an extremely smooth surface with no circular "swirl" marks.

This makes the tool a versatile general-purpose sander. You can use it for quick stock removal. With a coarse abrasive, it will even grind wood to shape. With fine abrasives, it can be used for finish sanding.

PALM SANDERS

Palm sanders (also called pad sanders and sheet sanders) mount a portion of a standard sheet of sandpaper. (Most hold a quarter sheet.) The cheaper machines vibrate; the better ones oscillate or orbit between 10,000 and 20,000 times a minute. This action removes stock slowly but creates a smooth surface. This, combined with light weight, makes them excellent finish sanders.

DETAIL SANDERS

Detail sanders mount a triangular abrasive pad that will reach into corners and crevices. Like a palm sander, these tools either vibrate or oscillate to produce a smooth surface. They are designed exclusively for finish sanding.

ABRASIVE BELT

PLATEN

DRUM

PORTABLE BELT SANDER

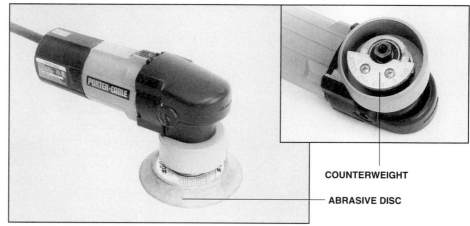

COUNTERWEIGHT

ABRASIVE DISC

RANDOM-ORBIT SANDER

ABRASIVE SHEET

PALM SANDER

TRIANGULAR ABRASIVE PAD

DETAIL SANDER

ROUTERS

The **router**[1] was originally designed as a "hand shaper" for cutting moldings and profiles. But it can do much more. With a modest selection of cutters, you can use it not only for **shaping**[2], but also for **making joints**[3], duplicating, and trimming.

BASIC OPERATION

The router is a simple power tool, nothing more than a *motor* held vertically in a *base*. To use this tool, mount a cutter or *bit* in the *collet* at the lower end of the motor *arbor*. Raise or lower the motor with the *depth-of-cut adjustment* so the bit is at the desired height. Holding the router by its *handles,* place the *sole* on the work and trip the *switch.* (Some routers have trigger switches; others have simple on/off switches.) Guide the router across the work.

FEATURES AND OPTIONS

Also consider:

■ To provide adequate *power,* a light-duty router should draw between 6 and 8 amps; a heavy-duty router, 12 to 15 amps, especially if used for table routing.

■ The *collet capacity* of a light-duty router is usually just ¼ inch; a heavy-duty tool will hold bits with ½-inch-diameter shanks. Better routers have interchangeable collets for both bit sizes.

■ A single-speed router spins between 22,000 and 27,000 rpm, an adequate speed for small bits and most materials. A *variable speed control* lets you reduce this to as low as 8,000 rpm for larger cutters and for materials that are prone to burning.

The soles of most routers are round, but some plunge routers and laminate-trimming routers have a flattened side. This makes a straighter, more accurate cut when guiding the router along a straightedge.

A **collet** is a split or segmented collar that clamps the shank of the bit. Collets with just a few segments make contact at just a few points. Collets with multiple segments are more flexible and make contact all around the shank. This helps keep the bit from slipping.

MOTOR (INSIDE)

DEPTH-OF-CUT ADJUSTMENT

SWITCH

BASE

HANDLE

COLLET

HANDLE

SOLE

BIT

ROUTER

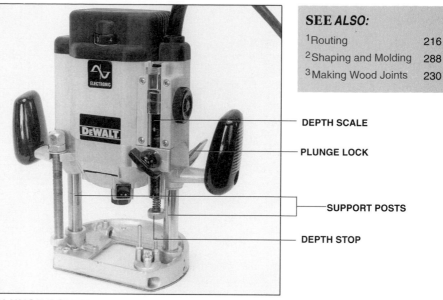

DEPTH SCALE

PLUNGE LOCK

SUPPORT POSTS

DEPTH STOP

*On a standard router, you must adjust the depth of cut before turning on the tool. But a **plunge router** lets you plunge the bit into the work and retract it with the motor running. The motor moves vertically on posts and can be locked or stopped at any height. This is an extremely useful feature, especially when cutting joinery or pattern routing.*

PLUNGE ROUTER

ROUTER BITS

A router bit consists of a cylindrical *shank* and one or more *flutes* that cut the work. On light-duty bits, the flutes are cut from high-speed steel. On bits intended for heavier work, they're tipped with carbide.

TYPES OF FLUTES. Most bits have *straight flutes,* designed for cutting both hardwood and softwood. Bits with *shear flutes* leave a smoother cut and have an easier time plowing through dense woods. *Spiral flutes* help clear the chips from plunge cuts. *Stagger-tooth* and *chip-breaker flutes* are made to cut plywood and particleboard.

PILOTED AND UNPILOTED BITS. Some router bits have *pilot bearings* on the business end to guide the bit along the edge of the work. Unpiloted bits may have *top-cut flutes* or *point-cut flutes* that allow you to plunge the bit into the wood.

TYPES OF BITS. Although there are hundreds of router bits, they can all be organized into just two categories. *Groove-forming bits* cut grooves, dadoes, mortises, and recesses in the work. *Edge-forming bits* cut rabbets and other shapes around the perimeter of the work.

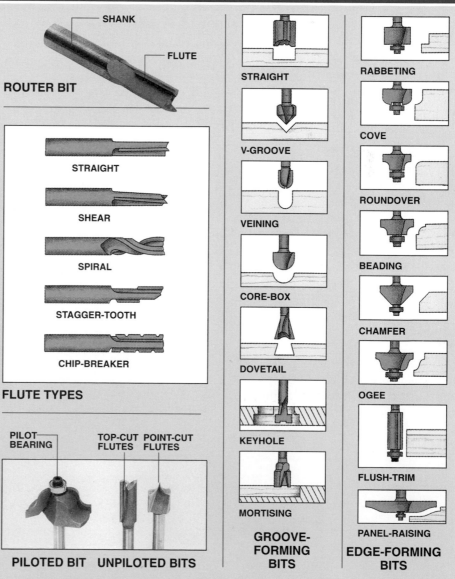

SHANK

FLUTE

ROUTER BIT

STRAIGHT

SHEAR

SPIRAL

STAGGER-TOOTH

CHIP-BREAKER

FLUTE TYPES

PILOT BEARING · TOP-CUT FLUTES · POINT-CUT FLUTES

PILOTED BIT   UNPILOTED BITS

STRAIGHT

V-GROOVE

VEINING

CORE-BOX

DOVETAIL

KEYHOLE

MORTISING

GROOVE-FORMING BITS

RABBETING

COVE

ROUNDOVER

BEADING

CHAMFER

OGEE

FLUSH-TRIM

PANEL-RAISING

EDGE-FORMING BITS

POWER PLANES

A **power plane**[1] shaves the wood surface, removing a thin layer of wood.

BASIC OPERATION

Although it's called a plane, it works more like a hand-held jointer. The *motor* turns a *cutterhead* with two or more *knives*. (In some models, the cutterhead is a solid piece with spiral flutes.) The bottom is split like the tables on a jointer. The *front shoe* adjusts to change the depth of cut, while the *back shoe* stays even with the cutting arc. To use the tool, squeeze the *trigger switch*, place the front shoe on the work, and push forward.

BISCUIT JOINERS

A **biscuit joiner**[2] (also called a plate joiner) cuts matching semicircular slots in the surfaces of adjoining boards. Insert oval-shaped wooden plates or *biscuits* in these slots to reinforce the glue joint between the boards.

BASIC OPERATION

The *motor* in a biscuit joiner turns a small *saw blade* 4 to 4¼ inches in diameter. The blade is enclosed in a retractable *blade guard*. To use the joiner, set the *depth stop* to control how deep the saw cuts. (Most joiners have three stop positions corresponding to three common sizes of biscuits.) Mark the work where you want to cut a slot. Place the *guide fence* against the work and align the *cutting indicator* with the mark. Throw the *switch* and push the machine forward. The guard will retract until it hits the stop. As it does so, the blade will cut a slot to a precise depth.

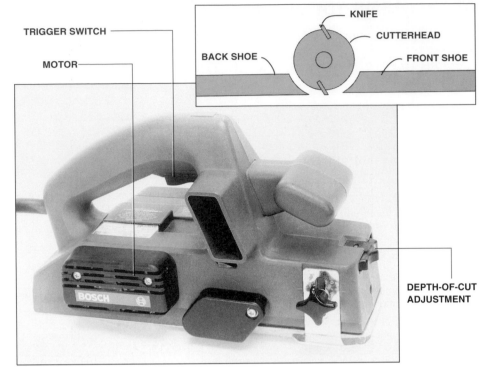

POWER PLANE

BISCUIT JOINER

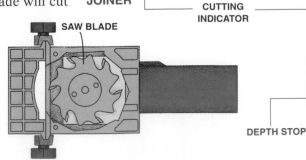

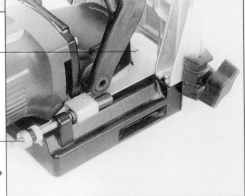

OTHER USEFUL TOOLS

Depending on the type of woodworking you do, there are several additional portable power tools that may be of use to you.

POLISHER/GRINDERS

A polisher/grinder turns a disc at 1,700 to 2,400 rpm. This makes it a useful **finishing tool**[3]. Fitted with a coarse abrasive, it can be used to grind away old paint and finishes. With a polishing bonnet on the disc, you can rub out new finishes.

HAND GRINDERS

A hand grinder is a small motor – small enough to hold and use in one hand – that turns a collet between 20,000 and 30,000 rpm. You can mount various tools in the collet for grinding, routing, cutting, carving, and polishing.

FLEXIBLE-SHAFT TOOLS

On a flexible-shaft tool, a motor turns a long, flexible shaft. Attached to the other end of this shaft are a handle and a collet. The tool mounts the same accessories as a hand grinder and is used for the same purpose. However, the motor is typically larger and more powerful.

GLUE GUNS

A glue gun is a hand-held heater that melts plastic glue sticks. Pulling a trigger squeezes the liquid glue out of the gun's nozzle. Once the glue leaves the gun, it solidifies in moments. There are many types of **hot-melt glue**[4] for various applications. Glue guns aren't typically employed for final assembly, but they are useful for quick repairs and throw-away jigs.

SEE ALSO:

[1] Jointing and Planing   182
[2] Making Biscuit Joints   237
[3] Rubbing Out a Finish   286
[4] Gluing and Clamping   248

MORE *SOURCES*

The Complete Book of Portable Power Tool Techniques, by R. J. DeCristoforo, Sterling Publishing, 1987

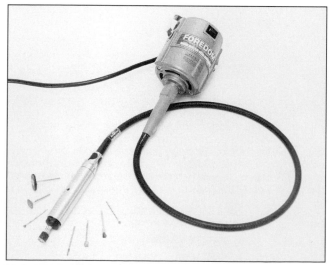

POLISHER/GRINDER

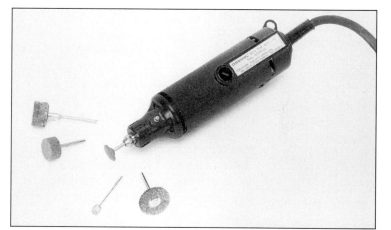

HAND GRINDER

FLEXIBLE-SHAFT TOOL

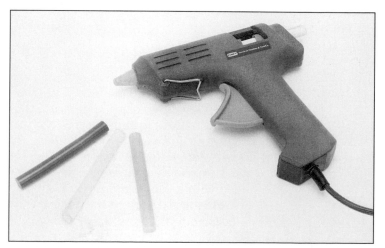

GLUE GUN

13

Hand Tools

Oftentimes they're easier, faster, and more accurate than power tools.

You can't do everything with power tools. Many woodworking tasks, such as measuring, fitting, assembling, and finishing, require some handwork. Sawing small parts or drilling tiny holes by hand is often more convenient than setting up a power tool. Many **scraping and smoothing**[1] tasks are better done by hand. Still others, such as **hand planing**[2], give the wood surface a different look and feel. Hand tools round out your woodworking capabilities, increase your options, and let you tackle a broader range of projects.

There is a common misconception that working with hand tools is doing things the "old way." In fact, most hand tools are products of modern engineering. Old-time craftsmen didn't work with tape measures and dead-blow mallets. Even ancient implements such as chisels have been refined by technology. Knowing how to work with both power and hand tools lets you choose the *best* way to do things.

MEASURING AND LAYOUT TOOLS

While many other shop tasks have been automated to some degree, measuring and marking is still done by eye. And for good reason – the eye is extremely accurate when aided with a good instrument. It's not difficult to measure fractions of degrees or thousandths of inches. The trick is knowing which tools to use.

You can create any wooden shape, no matter how complex, using hand tools alone, as this masterful **carving** of Canadian geese in flight illustrates. Although the birds appear to be carved from solid blocks of wood, they are actually assembled from over 4,000 parts! Each feather was carved separately and attached to the body framework to make the sculpture light and strong.

SPECS:	18″ wingspan
MATERIALS:	Basswood
CRAFTSMAN:	Robert K. Searles Union Center, WI

MEASURING DISTANCES

To measure lengths and widths, craftsmen use *tape measures* and *rulers.* Tape measures gauge long distances – just unroll as much tape as you need. Rulers measure shorter spans, typically under 12 inches. The better ones are very thin or have a beveled edge to bring the scale close to the wood. When you sight a ruler from an angle, your eye projects a line on the scale to a position on the wood's surface slightly beyond it. The closer the scale to the wood, the smaller this *parallax error.*

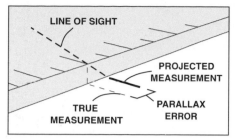

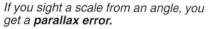

*If you sight a scale from an angle, you get a **parallax error.***

PRO *TIP*

Calibrate your tape measure to your ruler. Measure a short distance with the ruler, then remeasure with the tape. If the measurements differ, bend the hook of the tape measure slightly until they're exactly the same.

MEASURING ANGLES

A square is a fixed gauge that measures 90-degree angles only. There are several types:

■ A *try square* has a thin blade and a thicker base. This provides a shoulder to butt against a surface, automatically squaring the blade to the edge.

■ An *engineer's square* is a small try square, especially useful for layout work and setups.

■ A *carpenter's square* is larger than a try square and can be useful for checking assemblies. It has no base, just a short blade and a long one.

To measure 45- and 135-degree angles, use a *miter square.* Or, use a *combination square,* a tool that measures 45-, 90-, and 135-degree angles. It can also be used as a ruler, level, depth gauge, and marking tool.

TROUBLE *SHOOTING*

IS YOUR SQUARE SQUARE?

To check a square, use it to mark a line perpendicular to the edge of a board. Flip the square so the base or head points in the opposite direction and scribe a second line. The two lines must be parallel. If they aren't, the square isn't square.

1 Draw line.

2 Flop square.

3 Draw second line.

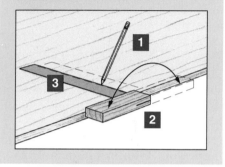

For odd angles, replace the sliding *combination head* on your combination square with a *protractor head.* Or, use a steel *protractor.* A sliding T-bevel lets you copy or transfer an angle.

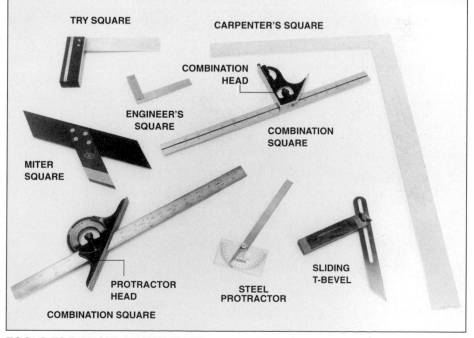

TOOLS FOR ANGULAR MEASURE

TOOLS FOR LINEAR MEASURE

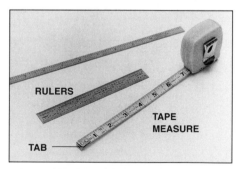

MEASURING THICKNESS AND DIAMETER

Although you can measure thickness and diameter with a ruler, *calipers* are more accurate.

■ A *steel caliper* has two metal jaws that copy or transfer inside and outside measurements.

■ A *sliding caliper* measures inside and outside dimensions up to 6 inches between a sliding jaw and a fixed jaw. Most have a probe to measure depth as well. Depending on its design, you read the measurement on either a scale or a dial.

MARKING THE WOOD

The most common marking device is a *pencil*. Unfortunately, as the pencil point dulls, its line becomes broader and less precise. For this reason, many craftsmen prefer to mark wood with metal tools. The point of an *awl* is designed to scribe a line parallel to the wood grain. A *marking knife* cuts a line across it. A *striking knife* offers both a point and a blade.

PRO *TIP*

If you use a pencil to mark wood, choose one with hard lead, #3 or harder. Roll the pencil between your fingers as you draw each line to help keep the point sharp.

ROLL PENCIL AS YOU DRAW LINE.

To mark a line parallel to an edge or end, use a *marking gauge* or *cutting gauge*. A marking gauge has a point or *spur* (to mark with the grain), while a cutting gauge has a small blade (to mark across it). A *mortising gauge* has two spurs — one fixed, one movable — to mark two parallel lines.

When you need to mark arcs and curves, a *compass* or *circle template* will make a small circle, while *trammel points* will draw larger ones. Use a set of *French curves* to help draw curves and contours. Or, bend a *flexible curve* to the shape you need.

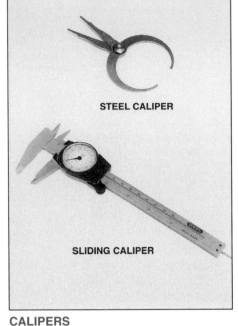

STEEL CALIPER

SLIDING CALIPER

CALIPERS

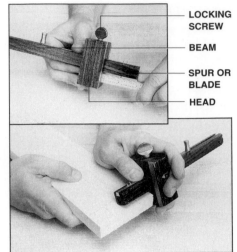

LOCKING SCREW

BEAM

SPUR OR BLADE

HEAD

To use a marking gauge, cutting gauge, or mortising gauge, first adjust the distance between the head and the spur or blade. Hold the head against the work and draw the gauge along it. Press down lightly to scribe a line.

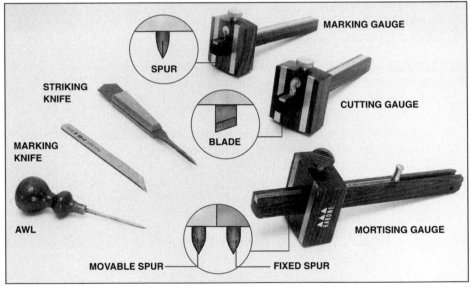

MARKING GAUGE

SPUR

STRIKING KNIFE

BLADE

CUTTING GAUGE

MARKING KNIFE

AWL

MOVABLE SPUR

FIXED SPUR

MORTISING GAUGE

MARKING TOOLS

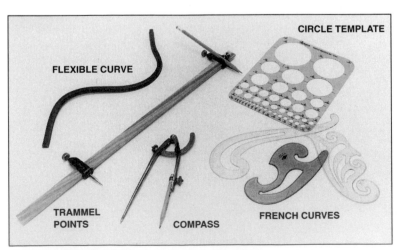

FLEXIBLE CURVE

CIRCLE TEMPLATE

TRAMMEL POINTS

COMPASS

FRENCH CURVES

TOOLS FOR DRAWING ARCS AND CURVES

HANDSAWS

Although most sawing is done with power tools, many woodworking projects involve some sawing tasks that can be accomplished more easily and safely with a handsaw.

CROSSCUTTING AND RIPPING

While all hand-powered saws are *handsaws,* the term usually refers to general-purpose saws 20 to 30 inches long. There are three types:

■ A *crosscut saw* cuts across the wood grain. It has 8 to 12 teeth per inch, sharpened along the edges.

■ A *rip saw* cuts with the grain. It has 3 to 7 teeth per inch, sharpened at the points.

■ A *panel saw* has 7 to 12 teeth per inch, sharpened like those of a crosscut saw. The teeth are hardened to saw plywood and other sheet materials.

> ### PRO *TIP*
>
> Generally, a new handsaw will cut better if you sharpen it. Few manufacturers sharpen their saws; the teeth are just stamped and set.

CUTTING JOINERY

Joinery saws are designed to make short shallow cuts and leave a smooth, flat surface.

■ A *tenon saw* (or *backsaw*) with 12 to 20 crosscut teeth per inch is the basic cutting tool for joinery. Its thin blade is stiffened with a metal spine.

■ A *dovetail saw* is a smaller version of the tenon saw with a thinner blade and up to 26 teeth per inch. It's designed for delicate, **exacting cutting tasks**[1]

■ The teeth of a *flush-cutting saw* are set to one side only. This lets you rest the blade flat on a surface to trim protruding parts.

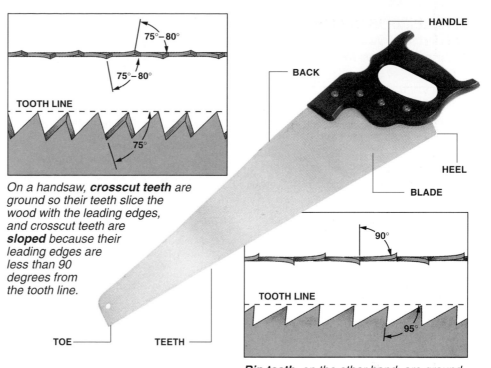

On a handsaw, **crosscut teeth** are ground so their teeth slice the wood with the leading edges, and crosscut teeth are **sloped** because their leading edges are less than 90 degrees from the tooth line.

HANDSAW

Rip teeth, on the other hand, are ground so the points of the teeth are like small chisels, and rip teeth are **hooked** because their edges are more than 90 degrees.

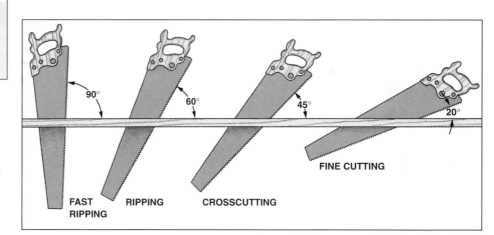

To cut quickly and get the best possible results, hold the handsaw blade at the optimum angle for the sawing operation.

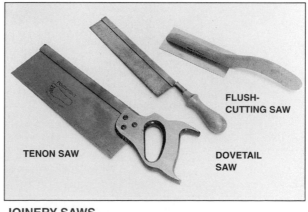

JOINERY SAWS

SEE *ALSO:*

[1] Making Dovetail Joints by Hand   246

CUTTING CURVES AND CONTOURS

In addition to straight cuts, there are also handsaws for **curves and contours**[1]

■ A *frame saw* holds a thin blade in a wooden frame to cut gentle curves.

■ *Coping saws* and *fret saws* hold narrow blades in metal frames for cutting intricate curves. Coping saws have a shallow frame, designed to make coped joints in moldings, whereas fret saws have deeper frames and are used for fretwork, marquetry, and inlay.

■ A *keyhole* (or *compass*) *saw* has a stiff, slender blade mounted in a handle and can be used in places where it would be awkward or impossible to use frame-mounted saws.

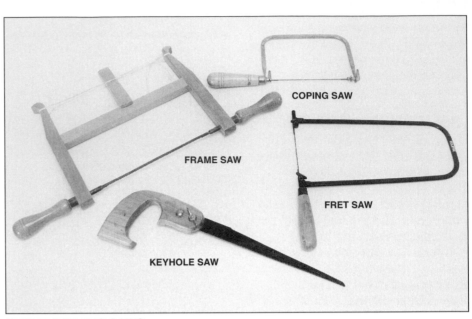

COPING SAW

FRAME SAW

FRET SAW

KEYHOLE SAW

CURVE-CUTTING SAWS

JAPANESE SAWS

The familiar handsaws for general cutting, joinery, and curves originated in Europe and America. Japanese craftsmen, isolated from Western woodworking traditions, have developed vastly different saws for most of the same tasks. These offer significant advantages in some applications.

The blade in a Japanese saw is typically shorter than its European/American counterpart. Many are wider at the toe than at the heel. The handle is a wooden stick wrapped with reed to provide a better grip. The gullets between the teeth are much deeper and sharpened at steeper angles.

The most significant difference, however, is the way in which these saws are used. Japanese saws cut on the *pull* stroke. (European/American saws cut as you *push*.) This puts the saw under tension as it cuts so the blade can be much thinner. This, in turn, produces a finer cut and a narrower kerf.

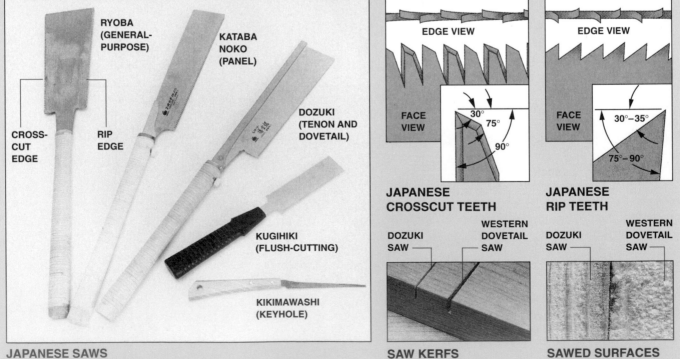

RYOBA (GENERAL-PURPOSE)

KATABA NOKO (PANEL)

DOZUKI (TENON AND DOVETAIL)

CROSS-CUT EDGE

RIP EDGE

KUGIHIKI (FLUSH-CUTTING)

KIKIMAWASHI (KEYHOLE)

JAPANESE SAWS

EDGE VIEW

FACE VIEW

30°
75°
90°

JAPANESE CROSSCUT TEETH

EDGE VIEW

FACE VIEW

30°–35°
75°–90°

JAPANESE RIP TEETH

DOZUKI SAW

WESTERN DOVETAIL SAW

DOZUKI SAW

WESTERN DOVETAIL SAW

SAW KERFS

SAWED SURFACES

CHISELS AND GOUGES

There is no simpler hand tool than a chisel or a gouge; yet with a small selection of these tools, you can create almost any shape.

CHISELS

A chisel blade has a *bevel* and a straight *cutting edge* ground in one face only. The opposite face or *back* is flat.

■ A *paring chisel* has a long, thin blade with beveled edges to reach into tight corners. It's designed to be pushed with your hands rather than struck with a **mallet²**, and it's best used for trimming and fitting.

■ A *firmer chisel* has a thicker, shorter blade, sturdy enough to withstand mallet blows. It may or may not have beveled edges, and it works well for many applications.

■ A *mortise chisel* has a stout blade, sometimes thicker than it is wide. It will withstand hard blows and is used for chopping mortises and other heavy work.

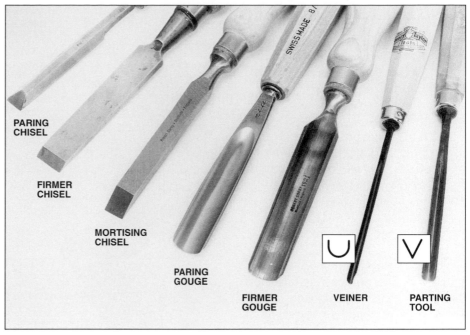

CHISELS AND GOUGES

> **PRO** *TIP*
>
> When driving a chisel without a mallet, use the weight of your body, not your muscles. Lean into the chise and push with your chest, hip, or chin Not only is this technique less tiring, it gives you more control, letting you use your muscles to steer or brake the tool.

GOUGES

Gouges are "hollow" chisels, with blades that curve from edge to edge. Thin-bladed *paring gouges* are designed for light work, while thicker *firmer gouges* can be driven with a mallet.

Gouges come in different widths and radii. The blade radius is the *sweep,* while the curved portion of the blade is the *pod.* Sweeps are numbered from #1 to #12. The higher the number, the smaller the radius and the deeper the pod.

Additionally, there are different shapes available. A *veiner,* for example, has a U-shaped edge for cutting round-bottom grooves. A *parting tool* has a V-shaped edge for making V-grooves.

> **SEE** *ALSO:*
>
> ¹Cutting Curves and
> Contours 205
> ²Hammers and Mallets 138

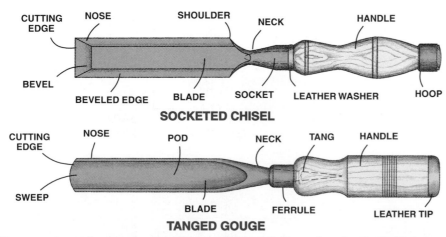

SOCKETED CHISEL

TANGED GOUGE

There are two ways to mount a chisel or a gouge blade to a handle. Some blades are forged with tapered tangs that are forced into the handles; others have sockets that fit the handles. Ferrules, hoops, leather tips, and washers all help the wooden handles weather repeated mallet blows.

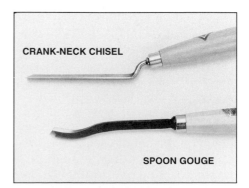

*Some chisels and gouges have bent blades. A **crank-neck chisel,** for example, is bent to keep the handle above the surface. A **spoon gouge** is bent to help reach into recesses.*

HAND DRILLS AND BRACES

Although a portable electric drill performs most **hand-drilling operations**[1], several hand-powered drills are still useful.

BRACE AND BIT

For drilling large holes, a brace and a sharp bit will match the speed of power tools. A brace is a rectangular *frame* with a *shell chuck* on one end. This holds an *auger bit* with a standard-size tapered *tang*. The brace turns the bit as you swing the *grip*.

Auger bits are made with several types of bodies and cutting edges or "noses." A *double-twist* body is best for light work, while a *solid-center* body will stand up to heavy use. A *Scotch nose* will bore rough holes in hard woods, while a *Jennings nose* is preferred for fine woodworking.

MORE *INFO*

Auger bits come in $\frac{1}{16}$-inch increments and are labeled according to their diameter in sixteenths. A $\frac{1}{2}$-inch-diameter bit, for example, is a #8. An $\frac{11}{16}$-inch-diameter bit is a #11.

HAND DRILLS

A hand drill bores small holes using ordinary twist bits and other bits with round shafts. A crank turns a large gear, which rotates a standard three-jawed chuck. Typically, one turn of the crank rotates the chuck ten times, allowing you to spin a bit much faster than you can with a brace.

PUSH DRILLS

A push drill lets you make small holes with one hand. A "spiral ratchet" drives the bit. As you push down on the handle, it slides down a spiral shaft, causing the shaft to rotate. A spring returns the handle for the next push. A push drill typically mounts *drill points* (small bits with straight flutes) in a *collet*.

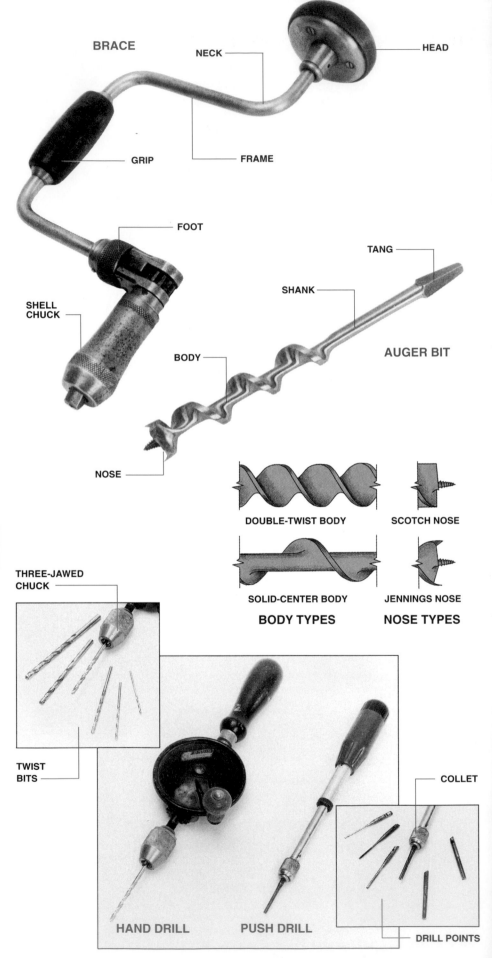

BRACE
NECK
HEAD
GRIP
FRAME
FOOT
TANG
SHANK
SHELL CHUCK
BODY
AUGER BIT
NOSE

DOUBLE-TWIST BODY
SCOTCH NOSE
SOLID-CENTER BODY
JENNINGS NOSE
BODY TYPES
NOSE TYPES

THREE-JAWED CHUCK
TWIST BITS

COLLET
HAND DRILL
PUSH DRILL
DRILL POINTS

SURFACING AND TRIMMING PLANES

A **hand plane**[2] holds a *plane iron* in a metal or wooden body. On many planes, the iron is mounted on a *frog* that lets you adjust the position of the cutting edge in the *mouth* of the plane. The iron is covered with a *chip breaker* to fracture the wood fibers as they're cut and prevent the wood from splitting or tearing.

SURFACING PLANES

There are two common types of surfacing planes. A *bench plane* mounts a plane iron with the bevel side down and is pushed with both hands. A *block plane* holds an iron bevel side up and can be used with one hand.

■ A short bench plane, less than 11 inches long, is a *smooth plane* and is used for smoothing a surface.

■ A *jack plane,* between 14 and 15 inches long, is an all-purpose bench plane.

■ A *jointer* or *try plane* is over 18 inches long. This bench plane is used for truing surfaces of boards.

■ A *standard block plane* is an all-purpose plane that can be used in tight spots.

■ A *low-angle block plane* has a cutting angle 8 degrees lower than other planes to shave hard stock with less effort.

TRIMMING PLANES

Trimming planes are designed to trim the adjoining surfaces of wooden parts to help fit the joints.

■ A *rabbet plane* has an iron as wide as the plane body to trim inside corners. There are several types, the most common being the *shoulder plane.*

■ A *side-rabbet plane* will trim the sides of a dado or groove.

■ A *router plane* trims the bottom of a dado, groove, or mortise.

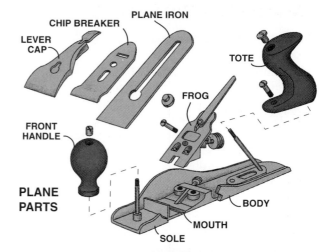

PLANE PARTS — PLANE IRON, CHIP BREAKER, LEVER CAP, TOTE, FROG, FRONT HANDLE, BODY, MOUTH, SOLE

PRO*TIP*

If you're shopping for a plane, the best values are the older Stanleys and Baileys that you find at flea markets and junk stores.

SEE *ALSO:*

[1]Drilling and Boring   208
[2]Using a Hand Plane   188

MYTH *CONCEPTIONS*

SHAVING END GRAIN Block planes are not necessarily better for shaving end grain. The cutting angles of a *standard* block plane and a bench plane are the same; both are designed for general planing. Only a *low-angle* block plane has a slight advantage when cutting end grain because its cutting angle is lower.

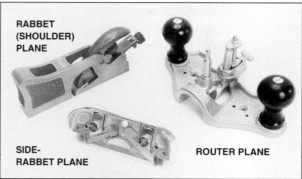

RABBET (SHOULDER) PLANE

SIDE-RABBET PLANE

ROUTER PLANE

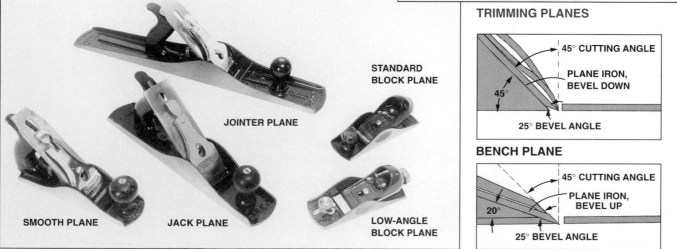

SURFACING PLANES — JOINTER PLANE, STANDARD BLOCK PLANE, SMOOTH PLANE, JACK PLANE, LOW-ANGLE BLOCK PLANE

TRIMMING PLANES

45° CUTTING ANGLE
PLANE IRON, BEVEL DOWN
45°
25° BEVEL ANGLE
BENCH PLANE

45° CUTTING ANGLE
PLANE IRON, BEVEL UP
20°
25° BEVEL ANGLE
BLOCK PLANE

SCRAPERS

Although hand planes leave a smooth surface, the best tools for **smoothing wood**[1] are *scrapers*. These tools have a thin steel blade that scrapes the wood.

■ *Hand scrapers* are blades of various sizes and shapes, designed to be held directly in your hands. They have no handles.

■ A *cabinet scraper* mounts a rectangular scraper blade in a holder with handles on the sides.

■ *Shavehooks* have a handle protruding from the middle of the blade to pull it along. They come in various shapes.

FILES AND RASPS

Files[2] cut the wood with row after row of wide teeth, smoothing a surface. Rasps have hundreds of narrow teeth to remove stock quickly, shaping the wood. Both tools are classified by how fine they cut, their tooth pattern, and shape.

CUT

The way in which a file or rasp cuts is determined by the spacing of the teeth. The more teeth per inch, the finer the cut.

TOOTH PATTERN

The teeth on a file may be *single-cut* (with parallel cutting edges) or *double-cut* (with crossed cutting edges. The double-cut pattern usually works better in wood. Rasp teeth can be *machine stitched* (in an even, geometric pattern) or *hand stitched* (random). Hand-stitched rasps don't chatter as they cut, and they leave a smoother surface.

SHAPE

Files and rasps are available in many shapes – flat, round, half-round, square, and triangular. Sometimes the bodies are bent to fit curved surfaces or reach into tight spaces.

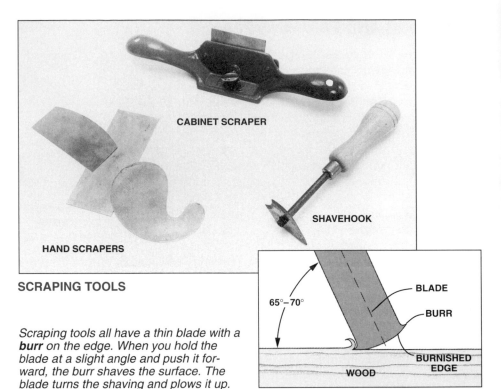

SCRAPING TOOLS

CABINET SCRAPER

SHAVEHOOK

HAND SCRAPERS

65°–70°

BLADE

BURR

BURNISHED EDGE

WOOD

*Scraping tools all have a thin blade with a **burr** on the edge. When you hold the blade at a slight angle and push it forward, the burr shaves the surface. The blade turns the shaving and plows it up.*

MILL FILE (FLAT)

HALF-ROUND FILE

THREE-SQUARE FILE (TRIANGULAR)

SQUARE FILE

RATTAIL FILE (ROUND)

CABINET RASP (HALF-ROUND)

RIFFLER (BENT)

FILES AND RASPS

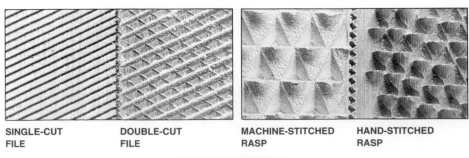

SINGLE-CUT FILE

DOUBLE-CUT FILE

MACHINE-STITCHED RASP

HAND-STITCHED RASP

TOOTH PATTERNS

SHAPING PLANES AND SCRAPERS

Although most planes and scrapers are designed for smoothing, a few are made to create **contoured or molded shapes**[3]

■ A *hollow plane* has a plane iron that curves from side to side, allowing you to plow a wide, round-bottom recess. Some also have a radius front to back, which makes them handy for scooping chair seats and bowls.

■ A *compass plane* cuts a concave or convex surface. You control the radius by adjusting the curvature of the flexible metal sole.

■ A *combination plane* (or *multi-plane*) has adjustable fences, depth stops, and several sizes and shapes of interchangeable cutters. With these, you can plane simple molded shapes – steps, beads, coves, V-grooves, and round-bottom grooves. Or you can use the cutters in combination to create more complex shapes.

■ A *beading tool* scrapes delicate profiles in a board, using small, interchangeable scraper blades of different sizes and shapes. It has two handles to draw the tool along the work and an adjustable fence to guide it.

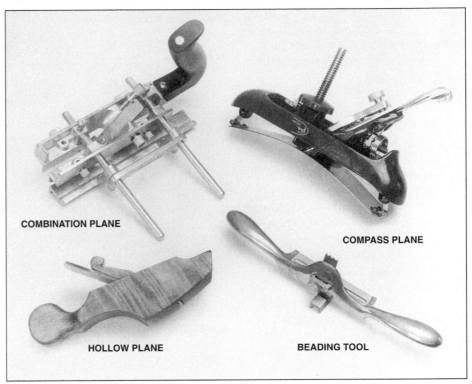

COMBINATION PLANE

COMPASS PLANE

HOLLOW PLANE

BEADING TOOL

SHAPING TOOLS

SEE ALSO:

[1]Scraping   263

[2]Filing   263

[3]Shaping and Molding   288

JIGS & FIXTURES

SCRATCH STOCK A *scratch stock* does the same job as a beading tool, but it's designed to be held in one hand. Cut a blade from an old scraper or find a used hacksaw blade, and grind it to a negative of the shape you want to cut.

Clamp the blade in the slotted handle and set it to cut as deep as necessary. Draw the tool along the work, guiding it against an edge. Make shallow cuts by using light pressure. Don't press too hard; the wood grain will tear. With each pass, the blade will scrape away a little stock, cutting the shape a little deeper.

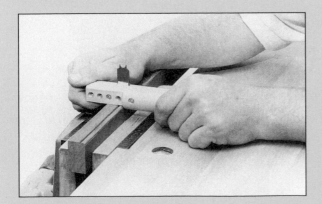

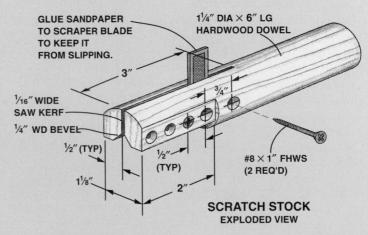

GLUE SANDPAPER TO SCRAPER BLADE TO KEEP IT FROM SLIPPING.

1¼" DIA × 6" LG HARDWOOD DOWEL

3"

¾"

1/16" WIDE SAW KERF

¼" WD BEVEL

½" (TYP)

½" (TYP)

1⅛"

2"

#8 × 1" FHWS (2 REQ'D)

SCRATCH STOCK
EXPLODED VIEW

HAMMERS AND MALLETS

Hammers have metal heads to **drive fasteners**[1], while mallets are made from softer materials and are used to drive **chisels**[2] or to help assemble joints.

■ A *joiner's hammer* has a cylindrical *bell* on one side of the head and a narrow *pane* on the other. Originally, this was a metalworking design that craftsmen found useful for woodworking tasks.

■ The familiar *claw hammer* has a "bifurcated" (split) pane designed to grasp nails and remove them.

■ A *tack hammer* has two faces: a small, magnetized face for holding and starting tacks, and a larger one for driving them.

■ A *carver's mallet* has a round wooden head for driving chisels and gouges. There's no need to orient the mallet before using it; the entire head serves as a striking surface.

■ Use a *dead-blow mallet* for assembly and disassembly. Its heavy head is made of a soft material. This distributes the force of each blow across the surface so it doesn't mar the wood.

■ A *carpenter's mallet* is a general-purpose striking tool. Depending on the size and weight of the square wooden head, you can use it for a variety of tasks.

SCREWDRIVERS

Screwdrivers are classified according to the shape of the tip and the type of **screw**[3] they're intended to drive.

■ A *blade screwdriver* drives slotted screws with a single groove in the head. The tips come in eight widths, from $3/32$ to $1/2$ inch, for different screw sizes.

■ A *Phillips screwdriver* has a pointed, cross-shaped tip to drive Phillips screws. The tips come in five sizes, from #0 to #4.

■ A *square-drive* (or *Robertson's*) *screwdriver* has a square tip to drive screws with square recesses. The tips come in four sizes, from #0 to #3.

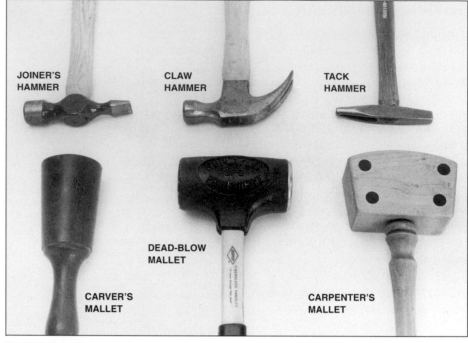

JOINER'S HAMMER

CLAW HAMMER

TACK HAMMER

DEAD-BLOW MALLET

CARVER'S MALLET

CARPENTER'S MALLET

HAMMERS AND MALLETS

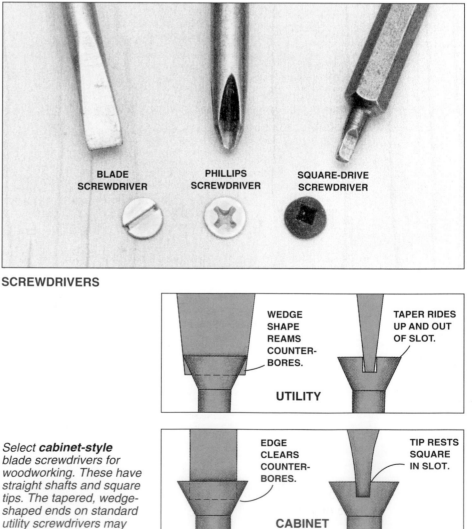

BLADE SCREWDRIVER

PHILLIPS SCREWDRIVER

SQUARE-DRIVE SCREWDRIVER

SCREWDRIVERS

WEDGE SHAPE REAMS COUNTER-BORES.

TAPER RIDES UP AND OUT OF SLOT.

UTILITY

EDGE CLEARS COUNTER-BORES.

TIP RESTS SQUARE IN SLOT.

CABINET

Select **cabinet-style** blade screwdrivers for woodworking. These have straight shafts and square tips. The tapered, wedge-shaped ends on standard utility screwdrivers may not work as well.

CLAMPS

Clamps hold wooden parts together when you're fitting joints or **gluing them together**[4]. There are several types, each with unique advantages.

■ *Hand screws* have a deep reach or *throat*. Their wooden jaws will not mar the work. By turning the screws in opposite directions, you can angle the jaws up to 30 degrees from one another.

> **PRO***TIP*
>
> Wax and buff the wooden surfaces of hand screws to prevent glue from sticking. However, be careful not to get wax on the screws; it will cause them to slip.

■ *Bar clamps* have a wide jaw opening or capacity. This capacity is determined by the length of the bar. The most common are *pipe clamps* – cast-iron fittings mounted on ordinary plumbing pipe. Other choices include *flat bar clamps* and *quick-action clamps*.

■ *C-clamps* have a metal frame with a small throat and capacity. *Deep-throat C-clamps* have a slightly deeper frame. Both are useful for small assemblies.

■ *Spring clamps* work like large clothespins. They also have a small throat and capacity, but they are quick to apply.

■ *Band* (or *web*) *clamps* wrap around assemblies of all sizes and shapes. The nylon strap is drawn taught by a ratchet.

> **PRO***TIP*
>
> Make elastic band clamps from lengths of surgical tubing.

■ *Miter clamps* hold corner joints together. Most are made to hold the wooden parts square to one another, but some allow you to adjust the angle.

■ *Edge clamps* hold bandings and moldings to the edge of a board.

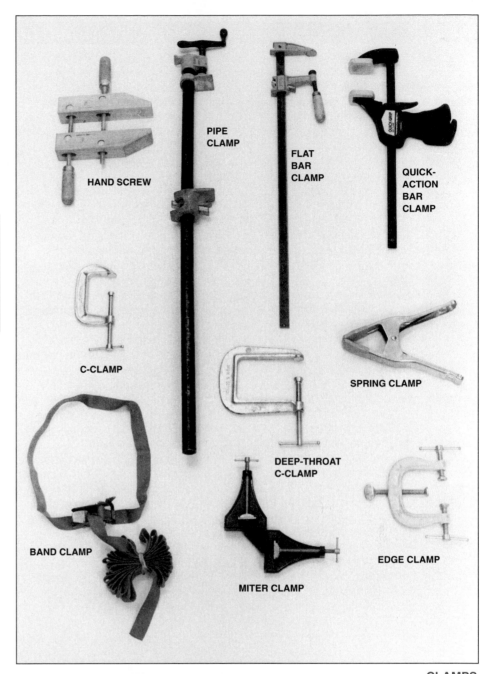

HAND SCREW

PIPE CLAMP

FLAT BAR CLAMP

QUICK-ACTION BAR CLAMP

C-CLAMP

BAND CLAMP

DEEP-THROAT C-CLAMP

SPRING CLAMP

MITER CLAMP

EDGE CLAMP

CLAMPS

MORE *SOURCES*

Dictionary of Woodworking Tools, by R. A. Salaman, Taunton Press, 1990

Japanese Woodworking Tools: Their Tradition, Spirit, and Use, by Toshio Odate, Taunton Press, 1984

Making and Modifying Woodworking Tools, by Jim Kingschott, Guild of Master Craftsmen Publications, 1993

Restoring, Tuning, and Using Classic Woodworking Tools, by Michael Dunbar, Sterling Publishing, 1989

Using Hand Tools, by Nick Engler, Rodale Press, 1995

TOOL STEEL AND CARBIDE

To better understand how to choose and use tools, it helps to know something about the materials from which they are made. The cutting edges of hand tools — the blade of a chisel or the iron of a plane — are made from *tool steel,* a ferrous (iron-derived) metal that will take a sharp edge and retain it. Those of power tools — router bits and saw blades — are often tipped with *carbide,* a substance that holds its cutting edge better than steel.

About Steel
At the molecular level, steel is a *crystal.* The crystals form *grains,* each 0.02 to 0.0001 inch in size. The smaller the grains, the sharper you can grind a cutting edge. The shape and composition of the crystals determine how hard and tough the steel is.

How Tool Steel Is Made
Steel undergoes several fiery reincarnations, and each one adds to its character. It begins as iron ore, which is refined to pig iron in a blast furnace. Then the pig iron is melted a second time in an atmosphere of pure oxygen to reduce *residual elements* (contaminants) and to control the amount of carbon the metal contains. This is *tonnage steel* or *mild steel,* the

stuff that car bodies and bridges are made from. Some steel is made with a high carbon content (0.9 to 1.7 percent). The carbon allows the steel to be hardened, an important characteristic for cutting tools. While it's molten, this high-carbon steel may be mixed with other elements — chromium, vanadium, tungsten, and molybdenum — in varying proportions to make *alloy steels,* each with different working properties.

The high-carbon steel and alloy steel is allowed to cool slowly. It's rolled out as it cools, which helps align the crystals and makes the steel tough, but it remains soft enough to be cut to size and forged (hammered) into rough shape.

After forging, the steel is heated again, not hot enough to melt, but hot enough to transform the crystals into a harder, denser form. The steel is *quenched* (cooled quickly) to preserve this new structure. If it were allowed to cool slowly, it would revert to the softer form of mild steel.

The quenched steel is extremely hard —so hard that it's brittle enough to shatter. So the steel is heated a final time to *temper* the metal and relieve some of its hardness. Cutting tools are normally tempered to between 58 and 61 on the Rockwell C-Scale of Hardness (abbreviated Rc). This makes them hard enough to retain a fine cutting edge but tough

enough to be used. (To give you an idea of the hardness range, mild steel is usually about Rc 20. Tool steel can be as hard as Rc 70 immediately after quenching.)

Types of Tool Steel
There are many types of tool steel, each with different characteristics, depending on the proportion of carbon and alloy elements in the metal. The American Iron and Steel Institute (AISI) labels these compositions for various applications.

■ Ordinary *high-carbon steel* (AISI 1055 to 1095), with no alloys, is used for general toolmaking.

■ *W-type steels* (formulated to be quenched in water) retain a cutting edge better than other types and are often used for chisels and plane irons.

■ *O-type steels* (formulated to be quenched in oil) will not retain an edge as long as W-types, but they are easier to forge. These are used to make cutting tools that require lots of shaping, such as gouges.

■ *D-type steels* (with high amounts of chromium) are best used for knives and tools with thin blades. They are not especially well suited for woodworking tools.

■ *S-type steels* (with high amounts of silicon and manganese) are shock-resistant. These make good cold chisels and tools that must be struck repeatedly.

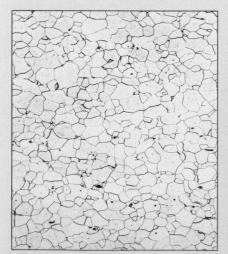

MILD STEEL

HIGH-CARBON STEEL

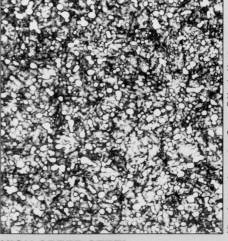

HIGH-SPEED STEEL

Microphotographs courtesy George F. Vander Voort, Carpenter Technology, Reading, PA

Steel has a granular structure, as these microphotographs plainly show. Ordinary **mild steel** *has very large grains, while tool steels such as AISI W1* **high-carbon steel** *and AISI M3T2* **high-speed steel** *have a much finer grain structure.*

■ *M-type steels* (with high amounts of molybdenum) are sometimes referred to as *high-speed steels* (HSS). Although they won't take as keen an edge as most tool steels, they stand up better to heat. They retain their temper even in the high temperatures generated by the friction of high-speed operations. They are commonly used to make cutters for power tools, such as drill bits and jointer knives.

■ *AISI 440C* is a type of stainless (corrosion-resistant) steel that holds an edge almost as well as W-type steels and can be used for cutting tools that will be exposed to water and damp environments.

Choosing Steel

The differences between steels are most apparent when the cutting edges are used continuously or run at high speeds. In hand tools, which are used intermittently at low speeds, these distinctions become very subtle — too subtle, in fact, for most woodworkers to detect. As long as the cutting edge is made from a good-quality steel, the tool should perform well.

On the other hand, how the steel is tempered and the thickness of the cutter can make a noticeable difference. The harder the steel, the better it will hold a cutting edge. But hard steel becomes brittle, and the cutting edge becomes fragile — prone to chipping and breaking.

When selecting tools that are used to pry as well as cut (such as chisels), it's best to stay away from extremely hard steels (above Rc 61). In other tools, like hand planes, you can get away with a hard, brittle steel by increasing the thickness of the cutter. This reinforces the edge.

Don't be swayed by claims that a cutter is made from "high-carbon steel," "Sheffield steel," or the like. These are advertising gimmicks; they don't tell you anything about the quality of the material.

About Carbide

Like steel, carbide has a granular structure. And although it's more durable than steel, the manufacturing process and the resulting character of the material are less complex.

How Carbide Is Made

The individual carbide grains are made by fusing iron, carbon, and an alloy metal (usually tungsten) in a furnace. Then these grains are fused together with a binding metal such as cobalt or nickel. The result is an extremely hard, wear-resistant material that holds a sharp edge when cutting a wide variety of materials, including wood, plywood, and particleboard.

The grains, however, aren't as fine as those in a good tool steel. Consequently, a carbide cutting edge cannot be sharpened to the same degree. It's also fairly brittle. Most carbides are too brittle to be used for the plates or bodies of cutting tools, so just the edges are tipped with carbide.

Types of Carbide

The different types of carbides are designated C1 through C8, and each has different working properties. As the number grade increases, the toughness of the carbide decreases and its hardness increases.

Grades C1 through C4 are straight tungsten carbides with good wear-resistance. These are the materials that are used in most woodworking tools.

Grades C5 through C8 mix tantalum carbides and titanium carbides with the tungsten. This makes the material shock-resistant, but it doesn't wear as well as lower grades.

Choosing Carbide

Look for fine-grain carbides — these will take a sharper edge. Don't be distracted by claims about the hardness of the material. Even the softest carbides (C1 and C2) are plenty hard enough to cut any wood or wood product.

There are two caveats, however. If you do a lot of work with plastic laminates, consider laminate cutters made with C3 and C4. Plastic laminate is a harder substance than wood, and the harder cutting edge holds up better.

If you use carbide-tipped tools to cut wet or green wood, be aware that the phenolic acid in cedar and other softwoods eats at the cobalt binder that holds the carbide grains together. This, in turn, dulls the cutting edges. To prevent this, invest in carbide tools made with a nickel binder. Nickel is unaffected by phenolic acid. (These may be labeled as "corrosion-resistant" or "acid-resistant" carbides.)

Don't worry about acids otherwise. Dried woods and hardwoods contain only small amounts of phenolic acid — too small to harm the carbide.

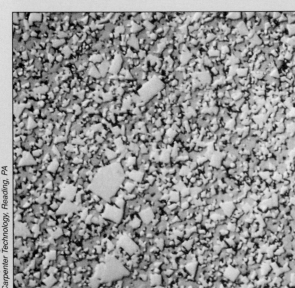

Microphotograph courtesy George F. Vander Voort, Carpenter Technology, Reading, PA

TUNGSTEN CARBIDE

Carbide also has a granular structure, although not as fine as tool steel. The white patches in this microphotograph are grains of tungsten carbide.

14

Jigs and Fixtures

You don't have to be a trained engineer to build effective jigs and fixtures; you just have to think like one.

It's difficult to work wood without making an occasional jig or fixture. By themselves, your hand tools and power tools may not be as accurate or as versatile as you'd like. Even with the best tools available, you will occasionally run across a woodworking task that needs a jig. Well-designed jigs and fixtures increase the accuracy and capability of your tools and make them easier and safer to use.

MORE *INFO*

Although the terms *jigs* and *fixtures* are used interchangeably, there is a difference. Technically, a jig guides a cutting tool, while a fixture holds and guides a workpiece.

DESIGNING JIGS AND FIXTURES

Whenever you build a fixture, begin with a clear idea of what you want it to do. Don't be too ambitious; a good jig extends the capabilities of a tool, but it must not *overextend* it — or you. As you design the fixture:

- Make it *simple to build.*
- Make it *as accurate as possible.*
- Make it *safe to use.*

Photo by Rob Vanmarter

*Occasionally, you need a jig or a fixture even to perform a simple task. For example, it ought to be an easy chore to cut the tapered legs on this **Postmodern Sideboard** — and it is, as long as you have a tapering jig to hold the leg stock as you cut it.*

SPECS: 60" long, 20" deep, 36" high

MATERIALS: Claro walnut, black walnut, Maccassar ebony, mahogany, maple, clear pine, and birch plywood

CRAFTSMAN: Alan McMaster
Dexter, MI

MAKE IT SIMPLE

Experienced craftsmen know that simple jigs work best; complex fixtures are often disappointing. The more complex the jig, the more that can go wrong.

■ Don't design a jig to perform multiple operations unless it will do them simply. Concentrate on making it do one thing well.

■ Use as few parts as possible. Every board and piece of hardware should have a good reason for being there.

■ Build jigs with flat surfaces and square corners. Woodworking machines are best at planing flat surfaces, jointing square edges, and cutting straight lines. Since you'll be building the jig with these machines, take advantage of their strong suits.

■ Use **simple joints**[1] to join the parts.

MAKE IT ACCURATE

Simple jigs are more precise. In mechanical engineering, there is a phenomenon known as *tolerance stack-up*. A good woodworker can cut a part to within $1/64$ inch of a

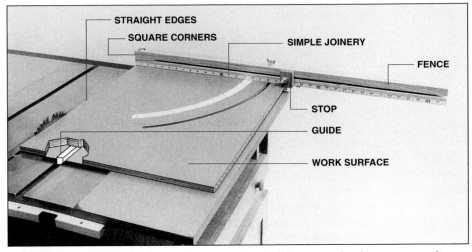

This **sliding table fixture** (sometimes called a **sled**) has one simple purpose — it makes accurate crosscuts on a table saw. The construction is simple, too. There are just four major components — work surface, fence, stop, and a guide to ride in the miter gauge slot. All parts are ordinary rectangles joined with basic joints.

desired dimension. But if there are 64 parts in the assembly, then the last one may be as much as an inch off the mark when they're all assembled.

There are other ways to make your jigs accurate:

■ Make the key parts *adjustable*. If it's important that a fence be fixed at a certain angle, mount it in such a way that you can fine-tune the angle.

■ Make sure your tools are properly **aligned and adjusted**[2] before machining the parts of the jig. You can't make an accurate jig with an inaccurate tool.

SEE ALSO:

[1]Types of Woodworking Joints	16
[2]Alignment and Adjustment	158

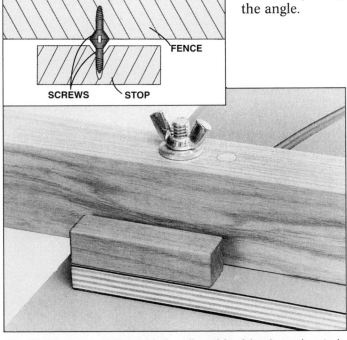

The fence on the sliding table is adjustable. A backstop located behind the fence automatically positions it square to the blade. Where the fence and the backstop come together, two flathead screws meet. Turning one screw or the other lets you fine-tune the position of the fence.

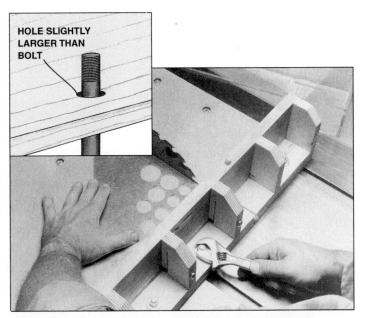

This cutoff box also has an adjustable fence. The mounting holes in the fence base are slightly larger than the bolts that hold it in place. This allows you to adjust the fence just a few degrees right or left to make it perfectly square to the blade.

◼ Give the sawdust someplace to go. Sawdust accumulates on the working surfaces of a jig. This keeps the work from contacting these surfaces and makes the jig hold the work in the wrong position. Provide dust channels, open spaces, or **dust collection**[1] to prevent the sawdust from interfering with the work.

◼ Make critical parts from stable materials. Wood movement will affect the accuracy of the jig.

◼ Acclimate the materials to your shop before cutting them. Let wood, plywood, and particleboard **shop-dry**[2] for a week or two.

◼ Lay out your cuts with a head-band magnifier, loupe, or magnifying lamp. You'd be surprised how much this improves the accuracy of your layouts, even if you have good eyesight.

MAKE IT SAFE TO USE

To design a safe jig, think through the operation you want to perform.

◼ Will the cutter and the workpiece be secure throughout the entire procedure? Do you need to build a carriage for the workpiece or clamp it to the jig?

◼ Will the blade or cutter be exposed during the operation? Can you cover it with a guard or arrange the jig components to cover it?

◼ Will your fingers pass close to the danger zone as you work? Can you add knobs or hand-holds to prevent this?

◼ Could the work kick back? Will a clamp or a backstop prevent this? If there is a kickback, will your body be out of the line of fire?

◼ Will a guard on the power tool catch on the jig? Should nuts and bolts be recessed to prevent this?

*Making a tapering cut can be a risky operation, but this **tapering jig** has features that make it relatively safe. The jig serves as a carriage to hold the wood at an angle to the blade. A clamp secures the work in the carriage, and two handles let you guide the jig while keeping your hands well clear of the blade.*

The edge on the stop attached to this drill press fence has a double-mitered edge to create a point. Instead of piling up against a flat surface and preventing the work from butting against the stop, the dust accumulates behind the point. The work contacts the stop, and the sawdust doesn't interfere with the accuracy of the setup.

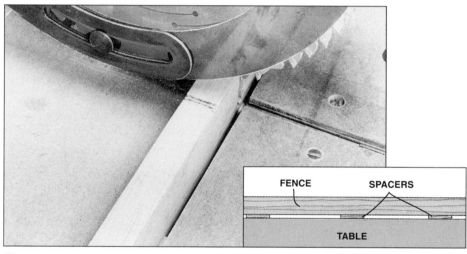

This radial arm saw fence has narrow spacers that hold it ⅛ inch away from the table. Instead of piling up against the fence, where it can ruin the accuracy of a cut, the sawdust drops down through the open spaces.

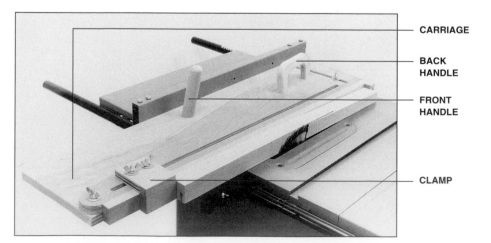

JIG-MAKING MATERIALS

When making a jig or fixture, you must choose your materials for strength, durability, and stability. Don't think you must make every part from the same material. Each part has different requirements; consequently successful jigs are often a blend of wood, plywood, fiberboard, and plastic.

WOOD AND WOOD PRODUCTS

Wood is the strongest material commonly used in jig making. Hard maple and beech are traditional favorites because they wear so well. No matter what the species, however, wood is not particularly stable. You must carefully align the grain so the **expansion and contraction**[3] do not affect the jig.

Plywood is not as strong, but it's just as durable and more stable. Two **types**[4] are suitable for jig making – *hardwood plywood* and *European birch plywood* (sometimes referred to as *Baltic Birch* or *multi-ply*).

Fiberboard[5] is weaker and less durable than plywood, but it's extremely stable and easy to machine. *Tempered hardboard* makes excellent templates and patterns. *Medium-density fiberboard* (called *MDF*) is often used for work surfaces because it's dead flat and remains that way if properly braced and treated.

PLASTICS

There are five types of plastics commonly used in jig making.

■ *Acrylics*, such as Plexiglas, are strong and rigid but somewhat brittle. They are useful for templates and guards. In thicknesses of $3/8$ inch or more, they make good router mounting plates.

■ *Polycarbonates*, such as Lexan, have properties similar to acrylics, but they are less brittle and not as rigid. They flex too much to be used as mounting plates, but they are fine for guards and templates.

■ *Ultrahigh–molecular weight plastics (UHMW)* are flexible, slippery, and very durable. They are a good choice for moving parts, runners, slides, and templates as long as their flexibility doesn't affect the operation of the jig.

■ If you need more rigidity, use *phenolics*. Although not as slippery as UHMW, they are just as long-wearing. Additionally, they are strong, heat-resistant, and chemical-resistant.

■ *Plastic laminates*, such as Formica, cover work surfaces and fences to reduce friction and make them more durable.

PRO *TIP*

To keep laminate-covered wood products perfectly flat, apply laminate to *both* faces. If you leave one face uncovered, it will absorb moisture at a different rate than the covered face, and the stock will cup.

HARD MAPLE

BEECH

HARDWOOD PLYWOOD

EUROPEAN BIRCH PLYWOOD

TEMPERED HARDBOARD

MEDIUM-DENSITY FIBERBOARD (MDF)

ULTRAHIGH–MOLECULAR WEIGHT (UHMW) PLASTIC

PLASTIC LAMINATE

PHENOLIC PLASTIC

POLY-CARBONATE PLASTIC

ACRYLIC PLASTIC

JIG-MAKING MATERIALS

HARDWARE

Because jigs and fixtures are tools, often with moving parts, they use a great variety of hardware.

■ *Threaded fasteners* – Most structural parts are permanently assembled with glue, **screws**[1], and **nails**[2]. Some parts, however, are attached temporarily so they can be adjusted or knocked down. Typically, craftsmen use threaded fasteners such as *carriage bolts*, *hex bolts*, and *machine screws*. Often, these are threaded into *T-nuts* or *threaded inserts* embedded in the wood.

■ *Wing nuts and knobs* – To lock a part down and release it, use *wing nuts* and *thumbscrews*. For a better grip, consider *star knobs*, *T-knobs*, and *ratchet handles*.

■ *Clamps* – To hold a workpiece to a jig, **make a clamp**[3] from a bolt, or purchase ready-made *toggle clamps*.

■ *Pivots* – If you need a part to tilt and swing, make a pivot from a bolt. Secure the pivot bolt with a *stop nut* (also called a *lock nut*) or *jamb nuts* to keep it from working loose.

■ *Slides and tracks* – If a part must slide back and forth, fasten it to a *runner* and let it follow a groove. Or, use a *flange bolt* in a T-slot. If the jig will see a lot of use, consider using a metal *miter gauge track* or *T-track* instead of a wooden groove or slot.

PRO *TIP*

Assemble plywood parts with **sheet metal screws** rather than wood screws. Because sheet metal screws have threads the entire length of the shaft, they are less likely to split the plies.

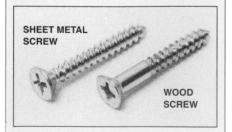

SHEET METAL SCREW

WOOD SCREW

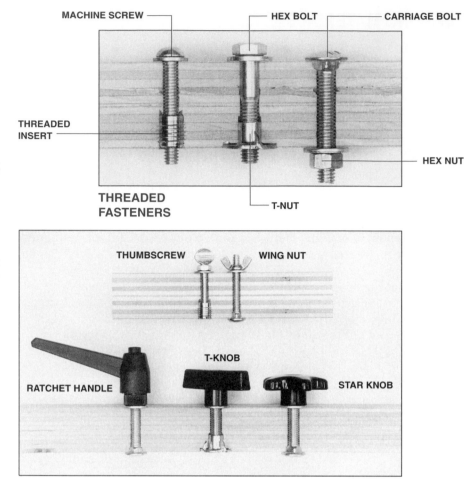

MACHINE SCREW — HEX BOLT — CARRIAGE BOLT

THREADED INSERT

THREADED FASTENERS

HEX NUT

T-NUT

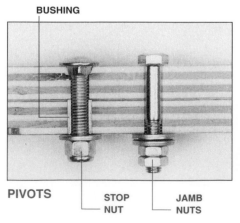

THUMBSCREW   WING NUT

RATCHET HANDLE   T-KNOB   STAR KNOB

WING NUTS AND KNOBS

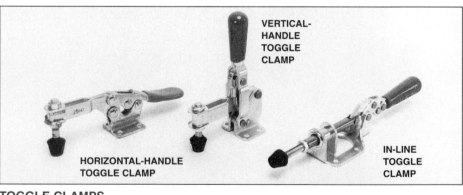

VERTICAL-HANDLE TOGGLE CLAMP

HORIZONTAL-HANDLE TOGGLE CLAMP

IN-LINE TOGGLE CLAMP

TOGGLE CLAMPS

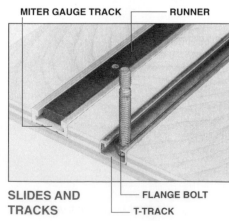

BUSHING

MITER GAUGE TRACK — RUNNER

PIVOTS   STOP NUT   JAMB NUTS

SLIDES AND TRACKS   FLANGE BOLT   T-TRACK

Guard A piece of transparent acrylic plastic guards the bit on this router table. The plastic keeps your fingers away from the spinning bit yet lets you see the cut as it progresses. Make it from a bright orange or red transparent plastic to visually mark the danger zone.

A typical jig or fixture is made up of several *components*. A sliding table, for example, is composed of a work surface to support the work, a fence to hold it at the correct angle to the blade, and a stop to gauge its length. The next few pages show common jig components that you might incorporate into your designs.

SAFETY COMPONENTS

Whenever part of a blade or cutter is exposed, it should be covered with a guard, provided the guard does not interfere with the operation. You must also cover "pinch points" — places where your fingers might be caught between moving parts.

Cover These plywood boxes cover the pulleys and belts that drive a band saw. Belts and pulleys are dangerous **pinch points.** Your hand, if it were to catch on a moving belt, would be quickly drawn between the belt and the pulley, amputating a finger or breaking a wrist.

Hand-holds and knobs, properly placed, give you better control over the work and keep fingers out of danger. Pushers and featherboards hold and guide the work close to the blade.

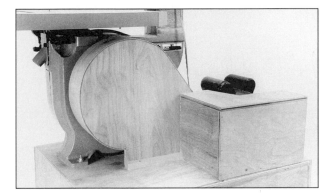

Featherboard The featherboard attached to this jointer holds the wood flat against the fence. This lets you keep your hands on the top edge of the board and away from the cutter as you feed the work.

SEE *ALSO:*	
[1]Screws	373
[2]Nails	372
[3]Clamps and Hold-Downs	152

JIGS & FIXTURES

PUSHERS You cannot work wood safely without *pushers* — simple jigs to help manipulate and feed the wood close to the blades and cutters, keeping your fingers out of danger. Here are two unique designs, each more capable than ordinary push sticks and blocks.

The **reversible push stick** has two notches on the end to help feed the wood. The shaft and head are thin enough to reach into tight spots. Flip the handle right or left so your hand is as far away from the blade as possible.

The **pusher/hold-down** lets you feed the work with the notch at the tip (like a push stick) or hold it down and push it with the dowel at the back (like a push block). The dowel adjusts up and down for different thicknesses of stock.

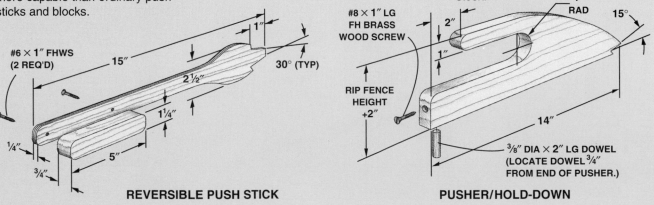

REVERSIBLE PUSH STICK

PUSHER/HOLD-DOWN

TABLES AND WORK SURFACES

When machining a workpiece, you must support it — hold it steady against the action of the power tool on a table or a work surface. When building the work surface, consider the load it will withstand. It must be strong enough to support the work and remain flat.

For some woodworking operations, you must tilt the work surface to adjust the angle of the work. To make a surface tilt, attach it to a fixed base with a hinge or a pivot so it moves through a range of angles. Secure the surface at the desired angle with a slide or trunnion.

Unsupported Work Surface The work surface on this **bar clamp holder** requires no bracework or additional support. The holder rests directly on the workbench.

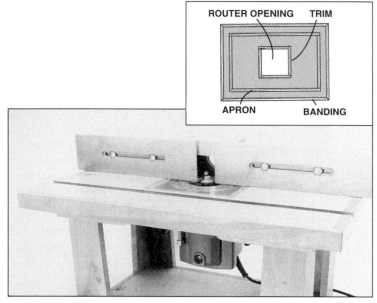

Braced Work Surface The work surface on this **router table** is braced to support heavy loads and remain flat. Three hardwood frames — the **banding** on the edge, the **aprons**, and the hardwood **trim** around the router opening — all strengthen the MDF top.

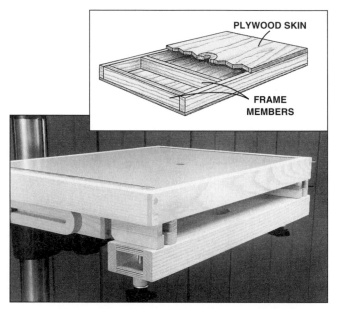

Torsion Box Work Surface A **torsion box** supports an enormous load without massive bracework, making a very rigid work surface. This **drill press table** is a torsion box — a light frame sandwiched between two thin pieces of plywood. One advantage of this design is that you can use the hollow box as a dust collector: The members of the frame become baffles.

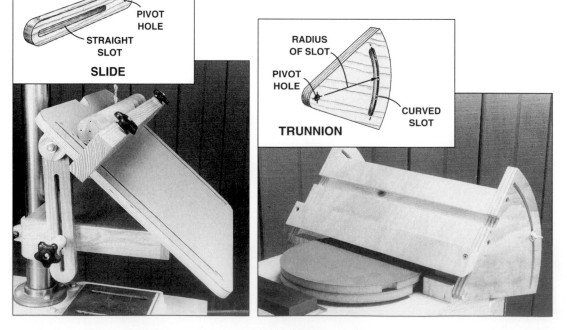

Tilting Work Surface The **drill press table** (left) is hinged to a base so that it tilts. It's secured by pivoting slides with straight slots. The pivoting tool rest on the **shop-made sharpener** (right) is attached to **trunnions,** which hold it at a range of angles. The slot in each trunnion is curved, and the center of the curve is the pivot hole.

FENCES AND GUIDES

In addition to providing support, you must also guide the wood (or the tool) as you work. In most operations, you must guide the wood or the tool in a straight line. This requires a fence or a straightedge.

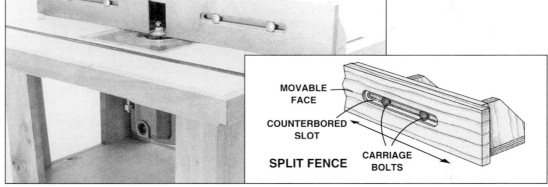

BRACKET FENCE
EXPLODED VIEW

BRACES
FACE
BASE

Bracket Fence A typical fence is a wide, flat, straight surface with bracework to help keep it flat and straight. On this simple bracket fence, the base keeps the face straight, while the braces keep it flat.

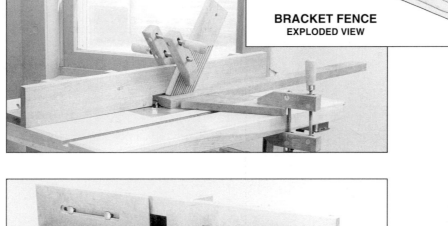

Split Fence Oftentimes, the face of a fence is split to fit around a bit or cutter. On this router table, the fence halves are movable. They slide left and right independently to adjust to the diameter of the cutter. On some split fences, the faces slide forward and back.

MOVABLE FACE
COUNTERBORED SLOT
CARRIAGE BOLTS

SPLIT FENCE

Straightedge At its simplest, a straightedge is just a long, straight piece of wood or metal that guides a tool or a workpiece. This T-square guide adds a crossbar to help square the straightedge to the edge of the work.

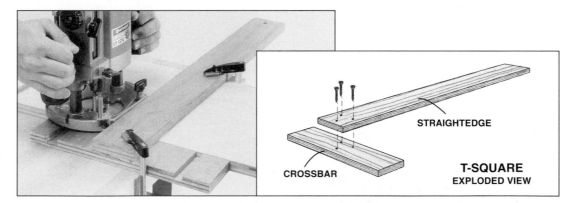

STRAIGHTEDGE
CROSSBAR

T-SQUARE
EXPLODED VIEW

Truing a Fence To make a fence straight, flat, and square to the work surface, joint the face after assembling the parts. If the fence is assembled with screws or bolts, make sure you countersink the hardware deep enough that the knives won't nick them. Hold the base of the fence against the jointer fence as you work.

Some operations require that you move the work or the tool in a precise curve or a pattern. To cut or sand an arc, swing the work or the tool around a pivot. To make a pattern, guide the work or the tool with a template.

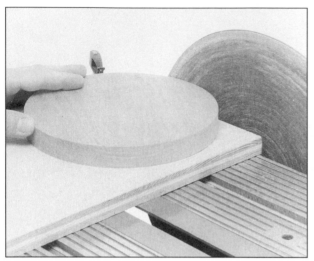

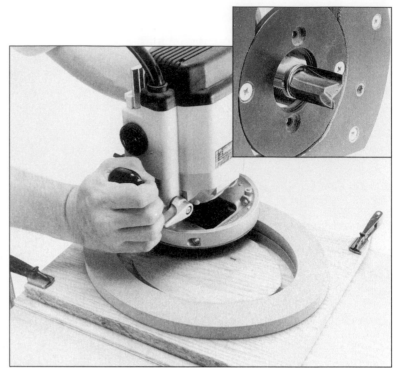

Pivot Jig *A pivot jig lets you cut or sand a perfect circle. Clamp the jig to a band saw, scroll saw, or disc sander so the distance from the pivot to the blade or the abrasive is equal to the radius you wish to cut. Drill a small hole in the center of the work, fit it over the pivot, and rotate the workpiece on the pivot as you cut or sand.*

Pattern-Cutting Bit *To rout a precise shape, cut a template and attach it to the workpiece with double-faced carpet tape. Follow the template with a pattern-cutting bit. This bit has a guide bearing the same diameter as the cutter. As the bearing traces the outline of the template, the bit cuts the shape in the workpiece.*

Guide Collar *You can also follow a routing template with a guide collar. The collar is a hollow metal cylinder attached to the base of the router. The router bit protrudes through the cylinder. Because the collar and the bit are slightly different diameters, you must make the template slightly larger or smaller than the shape you want to cut.*

Drill Guides *To drill holes in a precise pattern, make a drilling template and line the holes with drill guides. These are steel bushings that automatically center the bit and guide it at the proper angle.*

CARRIAGES

Not all workpieces can be supported by a table or guided along a fence. Depending on the shape of the workpiece or the nature of the work you want to perform, you may need to mount the stock in a carriage to support and guide it.

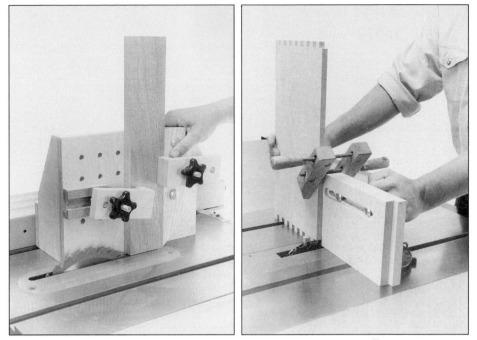

Holding Stock Vertically A **tenoning jig** (left) is a carriage that holds boards vertically to machine the ends. A **finger jig** (right) attached to a miter gauge is another type of vertical carriage.

Holding Odd-Shaped Parts A **notch jig** is cut to a specific shape to hold and position a unique part.

Holding Stock Horizontally A sliding table, such as this **miter jig,** is a carriage that holds boards horizontally. Tapering jigs and cutoff boxes are also horizontal carriages. The jig shown is guided by runners that slide in miter gauge slots. However, carriages can also be guided along a fence or a straightedge.

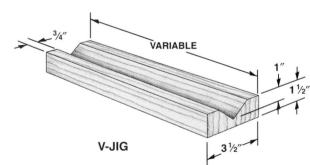

Holding Round Stock A **V-jig** cradles a cylindrical workpiece, such as a lathe turning or a dowel. To cut, drill, or sand the round stock, place it in the jig, then guide the jig across the tool as you would a rectangular board.

CLAMPS AND HOLD-DOWNS

Jigs and fixtures often require clamps or hold-downs to secure the work during a woodworking operation. Clamps and hold-downs hold boards with *pressure*. There are several ways to generate this pressure. The most common are wedges, screws, and cams.

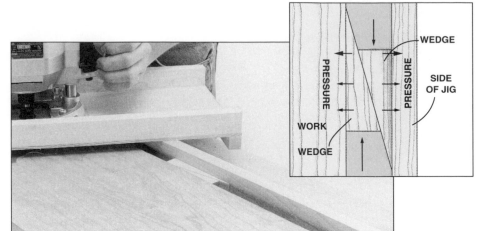

Wedges *The simplest clamping device is a wedge. When you drive a wedge between two objects, it presses against both of them. This* **router planing jig** *uses this pressure to secure the work in the frame. Note that the wedges are used in* **pairs.** *This way, the wedges lie flat, they are less likely to slip, and the pressure is more evenly distributed.*

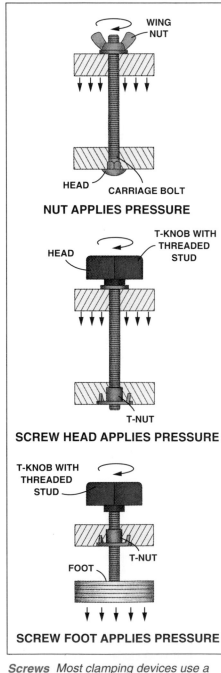

NUT APPLIES PRESSURE

WING NUT

HEAD — CARRIAGE BOLT

T-KNOB WITH THREADED STUD

HEAD

T-NUT

SCREW HEAD APPLIES PRESSURE

T-KNOB WITH THREADED STUD

T-NUT

FOOT

SCREW FOOT APPLIES PRESSURE

Screws *Most clamping devices use a threaded screw and a nut to generate pressure. Above are three basic configurations for a* **screw clamp.**

Compression *In most cases, the pressure generated by a screw clamp* **compresses** *objects, holding them together. For example, as you tighten the wing nuts on the top of the* **clamp bar,** *it compresses the work beneath the bar and holds it to the base.*

NOTE: The springs in the clamping mechanism automatically raise the bar when you loosen the nuts.

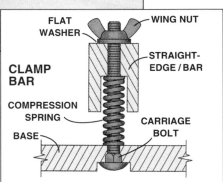

FLAT WASHER

WING NUT

CLAMP BAR

STRAIGHT-EDGE / BAR

COMPRESSION SPRING

BASE

CARRIAGE BOLT

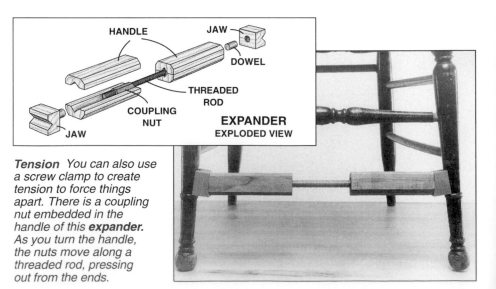

HANDLE

JAW

DOWEL

THREADED ROD

COUPLING NUT

JAW

EXPANDER EXPLODED VIEW

Tension *You can also use a screw clamp to create tension to force things apart. There is a coupling nut embedded in the handle of this* **expander.** *As you turn the handle, the nuts move along a threaded rod, pressing out from the ends.*

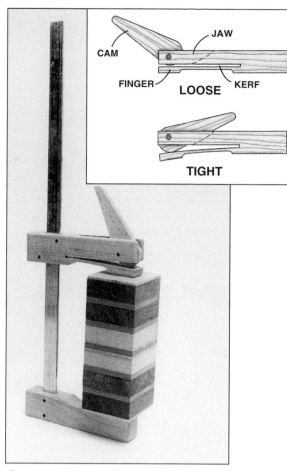

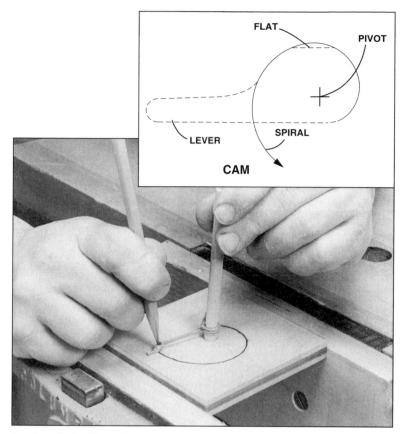

Cams *A cam is a pivoting wedge. As you rotate the cam, the surface bears against neighboring objects with increasing pressure. In this* **cam clamp,** *the cam flexes the jaw to hold the work.*

Laying Out a Cam *To design a cam, you must draw a* **spiral,** *a curve whose radius increases steadily around a central point. Wind string around a dowel and tie the free end to a pencil. Center the dowel on the pivot mark and swing the pencil around it, unwinding the string. The larger the diameter of the dowel, the faster the radius of the spiral increases. Once you've drawn the spiral, add a* **lever** *so you can easily rotate the cam. If you want the cam to turn to the same position every time you use it, add a small* **flat** *at that point in the curve.*

JIGS & FIXTURES

HOLD-DOWNS When you must hold a workpiece in a jig, the common solution is to use a commercial toggle clamp. The trouble is, these clamps are expensive and they don't generate much pressure. For less money, you can build a more powerful hold-down

around a carriage bolt. The shop-made hold-down shown does the same job as a toggle clamp but generates more pressure and spreads it over a wider area.

The hex bolt at the back of the hold-down prevents the jaw from tipping as you apply pressure. Adjust the hex bolt up or down according to the thickness of the work. The spring beneath the hold-down raises the jaw when you release the pressure.

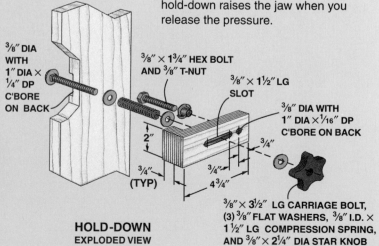

HOLD-DOWN
EXPLODED VIEW

MEASURING AND POSITIONING DEVICES

To do precision woodworking with a shop-made jig, you must measure the work and position it accurately for each operation. Simple scales and stops provide reliable linear measure, angular measure, and positioning.

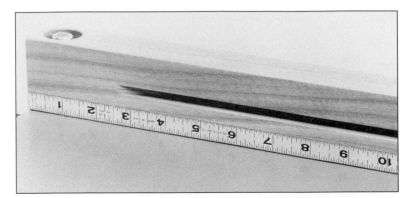

Linear Measure The fence on this sliding table has a tape rule that lets you measure the boards as you cut them to length. The rule is applied in a shallow rabbet slightly below the surface of the fence. (This prevents the rule from wearing.) Also note that the rule is upside down. When you lean over the fence to read it, the numbers appear right side up.

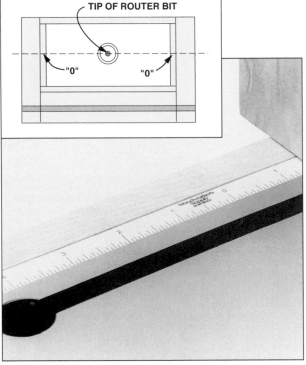

Centering If you need to center something on a fixture, a centering scale reads both left and right from "0." There are two centering scales on this router table. The "0" mark on each is aligned with the center of the router bit — this helps position the fence on the table.

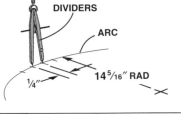

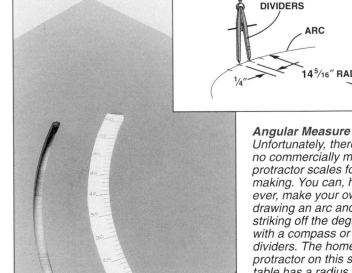

Angular Measure Unfortunately, there are no commercially made protractor scales for jig making. You can, how-ever, make your own by drawing an arc and striking off the degrees with a compass or dividers. The homemade protractor on this sliding table has a radius of 14⁵⁄₁₆ inches. At this dimension, the degrees are exactly ¼ inch apart along the cir-cumference. At a radius of 7⁵⁄₃₂ inches, the degrees are ⅛ inch apart.

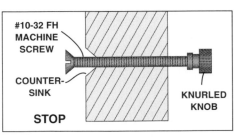

Positioning The all-purpose positioning device is a *stop* — a block of wood that arrests the travel of a work-piece as you slide it along a fence or guide. The stop shown is adjustable. It has a #10-32 flathead machine screw running through it, with 32 threads per inch. One full turn moves the head of the screw exactly ¹⁄₃₂ inch. A knurled knob, epoxied to the end of the screw, lets you turn it easily.

JIG-MAKING TECHNIQUES

Most of the methods required to build jigs and fixtures are the same as those used to build any woodworking project. However, there are several handy techniques that are unique to jig making. Most are concerned with fitting or installing hardware.

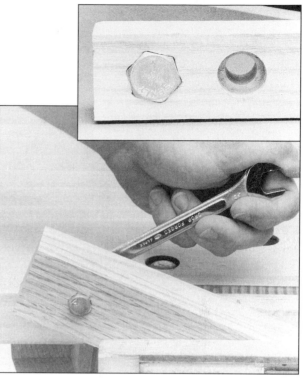

Counterbored Holes Many jig assemblies require that you bury the heads of fasteners or the nuts that secure them beneath the surface. To do this, you must make a **counterbored hole** for each fastener — the head or the nut will rest in the counterbore. Clamp the work to the drill press table, and drill a stopped hole slightly larger and deeper than the head or nut. Then change bits and drill the hole for the fastener shaft **without** changing the position of the wood.

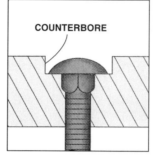

COUNTERBORE

Fitted Counterbores Now and again, you must fit a hex nut or the head of a hex bolt in a counterbore so it won't turn. To do this, make the counterbore the same diameter as the distance from flat to flat on the hex shape. Draw the nut into the counterbore with a bolt. Install a bolt head in the same manner, using a nut to draw it into the counterbore.

Pivot Bolts When selecting bolts to make pivots, make sure that the portion of the bolt inside the pivot hole is **unthreaded**. Otherwise, the threads will eat away at the wood every time the part moves, enlarging the hole. In many cases, you have to purchase much longer bolts than needed and cut away some of the threaded portion.

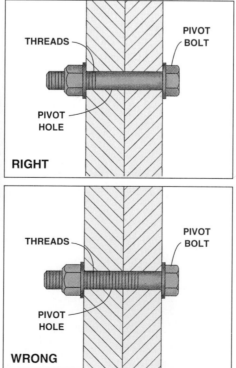

THREADS — PIVOT BOLT

PIVOT HOLE

RIGHT

THREADS — PIVOT BOLT

PIVOT HOLE

WRONG

Bushed Pivot Holes When a pivot will see a lot of use, install a metal bushing in the pivot hole. Drill the hole to the outside diameter of the bushing and press the bushing in place. If it seems loose in its hole, secure it with a cyanoacrylate glue, such as Super Glue. (Bushings are available in limited sizes at most hardware stores. You can find a better selection at businesses that repair electrical motors.)

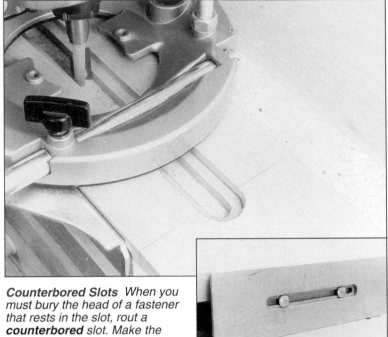

Keyhole Slots

Removable, adjustable parts such as fences and guards are often secured to a fixture with fasteners in **slots.** You can make the part easier to attach by boring an **access hole** somewhere along the slot. This turns an ordinary slot into a **keyhole slot** and lets you insert the hardware in it without having to disassemble the nuts and washers from the bolts. Drill the access hole **before** you rout the slot.

Counterbored Slots

When you must bury the head of a fastener that rests in the slot, rout a **counterbored** slot. Make the counterbore first — select a bit a little larger than the head of the fastener. Position the fence on your router table to guide the work, and rout a groove slightly deeper than the head is tall. Without changing the position of the fence, change to a smaller bit about the same diameter as the fastener shaft. Rout a slot through the stock, down the center of the counterbore groove.

T-Slots

Another technique for burying the heads of fasteners is to cut T-slots for them. The standard method for cutting T-slots is to use a router and a T-slot cutter, as shown at right. However, these cutters are available in limited sizes that will accommodate only flange bolts and small hardware.

To make a T-slot to fit a large carriage bolt or hex bolt, cut grooves in the edges of two separate boards (see below), then cut one side of each groove short. Glue the two boards edge to edge to form the T-slot.

1 Cut grooves.

2 Cut sides short.

3 Glue together.

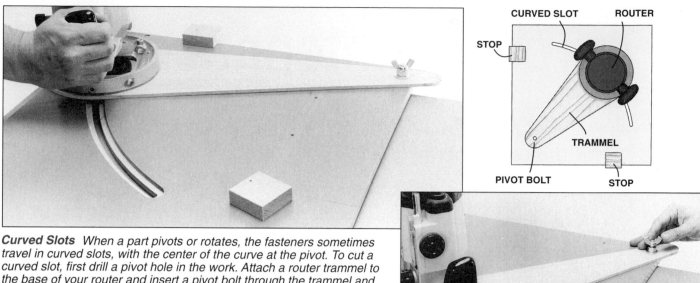

CURVED SLOT   ROUTER
STOP
TRAMMEL
PIVOT BOLT   STOP

Curved Slots *When a part pivots or rotates, the fasteners sometimes travel in curved slots, with the center of the curve at the pivot. To cut a curved slot, first drill a pivot hole in the work. Attach a router trammel to the base of your router and insert a pivot bolt through the trammel and the pivot hole. The distance from the bolt to the center of the router bit must be equal to the radius of the curved slot. Using double-faced carpet tape, attach stops to the work to limit the travel of the router — this will keep you from making the slot too long. Swing the router and trammel back and forth in an arc, cutting the slot a little deeper with each pass.*

Applying a Finish to Jigs *If you want the jig to last, finish it with a penetrating oil such as tung oil. A penetrating finish hardens the surface of wood and wood products, making them more durable. It also slows the absorption and release of moisture, making the materials more stable. Apply at least two coats, then rub out the finish with an abrasive pad (such as Scotch-Brite) and paste wax. The abrasive will create a smooth surface, and the wax will lubricate and protect it.*

TIP: Mix 2 tablespoons of spar varnish and 1 cup of tung oil to make an extremely durable wipe-on finish for jigs.

MORE *SOURCES*

The Woodworker's Guide to Making and Using Jigs, Fixtures, and Setups, by David Schiff and Kenneth S. Burton, Jr., Rodale Press, 1992

Making Jigs and Fixtures, by Nick Engler, Rodale Press, 1995

Woodshop Jigs and Fixtures, by Sandor Nagyszalanczy, Taunton Press, 1994

Woodworking Wisdom, by Rosario Capotosto, Popular Science Books, 1983

JIGS & FIXTURES

ROUTER TRAMMEL To cut circles and arcs with a router, make an elongated sole or *router trammel.* The length of the trammel is variable: It should be at least as long as the largest radius you need to cut. Drill pivot holes along the trammel where you need them. Also drill mounting holes to attach the trammel to the base of the router.

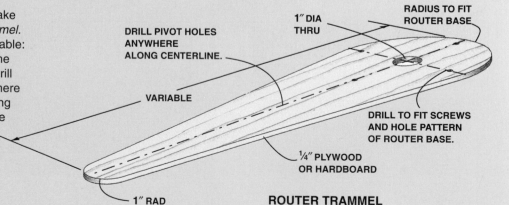

DRILL PIVOT HOLES ANYWHERE ALONG CENTERLINE.

1" DIA THRU

RADIUS TO FIT ROUTER BASE

VARIABLE

DRILL TO FIT SCREWS AND HOLE PATTERN OF ROUTER BASE.

¼" PLYWOOD OR HARDBOARD

1" RAD

ROUTER TRAMMEL

15

Tool Maintenance

Good tools are designed to be easily maintained – with a little care, they will last a lifetime.

Although good tools are remarkably durable, even the best ones require conscientious maintenance. Critical alignments and adjustments drift, lubrication dries up, surfaces collect stains and rust, moving parts become worn. And while each tool has unique maintenance requirements, many share common needs.

This is especially true of power tools. Most of them have a similar power train – an electric motor that drives a shaft or an arbor, either directly through a gear train or using a system of belts and pulleys. **Stationary power tools**[1] also have similar components for guidance and support – worktables, fences, and miter gauges. These are all subject to common problems.

ALIGNMENT AND ADJUSTMENT

The most common maintenance required is realignment – the parts of a tool must be aligned precisely to work correctly. A typical power tool often requires half a dozen separate adjustments.

■ Some parts must be aligned *parallel* to one another.

■ Others must be *perpendicular,* or at some specific angle.

■ Moving parts must have adequate *clearance* between them.

■ Thin blades, drive belts, and abrasive belts must be properly *tensioned*.

■ Bands and belts must *track* correctly.

*Good tools will last a professional lifetime. After more than a half-century of woodworking, this **Delta Table Saw** is still hard at work. George Reid, a master craftsman and furniture historian whose work is displayed in museums throughout the United States, still uses it to repair and reproduce classic furniture. With the exception of an updated fence, all the parts are original. It has never required extensive repairs, just ordinary maintenance.*

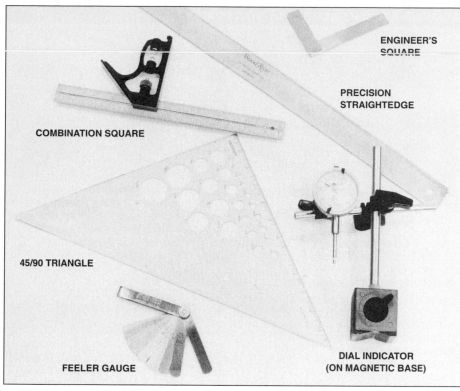

ALIGNMENT TOOLS

ALIGNMENT AND ADJUSTMENT TOOLS

To adjust a power tool, you need measuring tools to gauge the alignment of machine parts.

■ A *precision straightedge* is machined perfectly straight to help gauge when parts are straight, flat, and true. Generally, they are 18 to 24 inches long.

■ An *engineer's square* tells you when parts are perpendicular.

■ A *combination square* gauges 135- and 90-degree angles.

■ A *45/90 metal triangle* gauges 45- and 90-degree angles.

■ A *feeler gauge* measures clearances or gaps between parts.

■ A *dial indicator* measures very small differences in linear dimensions and distances. Often, these come with a magnetic base to mount them to tool surfaces.

CHECKING THE MACHINE

When you align a tool for the first time, or if you have persistent alignment problems, you should check that the critical parts of the machine are *straight* and *flat*. You cannot align a fence parallel to a blade if the fence is bent or bowed. And you cannot set a blade square to a table if the table is not flat. Use a precision straightedge to test that a surface is straight or flat.

By the same token, you may not be able to align a tool if the arbor or shaft that mounts the cutter isn't *running true*. If the arbor isn't perfectly straight, it will wobble as it spins. The magnitude of this wobble is known as the *runout*, and it can be measured with a dial indicator.

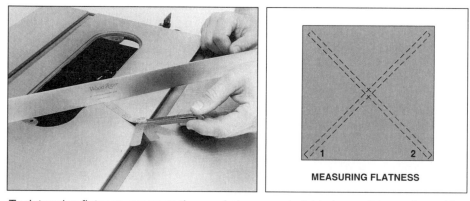

MEASURING FLATNESS

To determine flatness, measure the gap between a straightedge and the surface with a feeler gauge. Measure twice diagonally across the surface so the diagonals cross. For a surface to be considered flat, the gap should be less than 0.003 inch at any point under a 24-inch-long straightedge, or 0.002 inch under an 18-inch-long straightedge.

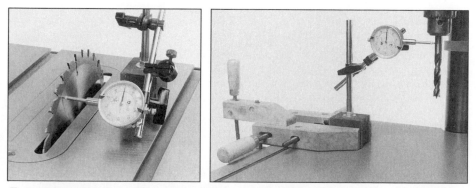

To measure runout, position a dial indicator so the probe rests against the part and rotate it by hand. Watch the indicator as you do so. The amount that the needle swings back and forth is the runout. To be considered true, arbors and shafts should show very little runout — less than 0.001 inch. Bits and blades will show more, especially if you measure the bit at the tip, or the blade near the teeth.

SEE ALSO:

[1]Stationary Power Tools 98

In addition to inspecting the parts, also read the owner's manual for a list of adjustments and how to make them. How you make the same alignment differs from tool to tool, depending on its engineering. It's also important to perform some adjustments in a certain order. For example, blades on **band saws**[1] and abrasive belts on **sanders**[2] must be tensioned before they can be tracked.

PARALLEL ALIGNMENTS

Parallel alignments are common on cutting tools such as saws and jointers. To check that two parts are parallel, measure the distance between them at two locations – the two measurements should be the same.

A **table saw**[3] fence, for example, must be parallel to the blade's plane of rotation. The miter gauge should slide parallel to this plane. If not, the blade will burn the wood as it cuts. Measure the distance from the blade to the fence or the blade to the miter gauge slot. It should be the same at the front of the blade as it is at the back.

On a **jointer**[4], the knives must be parallel to each other *and* the surface of the outfeed table, or the cut won't be smooth and flat. Measure each knife at two locations (near the right and left ends). All measurements should be the same.

ALIGNING A MITER GAUGE SLOT TO A BLADE

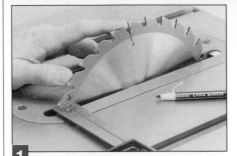

1 To check that a miter gauge slot is parallel to a blade, raise the blade as high as possible and mark a tooth. Rotate the blade until that tooth is near the front of the table. Use a combination square to measure the distance from the tooth to the slot, then lock the straightedge in the square's head.

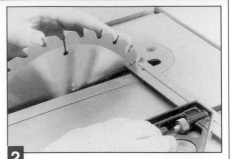

2 Rotate the blade until the tooth is at the back and slide the square adjacent to it. The straightedge should still touch the tooth. By using the same tooth, you eliminate the effects of blade runout on this alignment.

THE WHY OF IT: Why is it important that the miter gauge slot be parallel to the blade? The saw blade cuts a kerf slightly wider than the blade itself. The blade body won't contact the wood as long as the gauge guides the wood parallel to the blade. If it guides it at an angle, the wood will rub on the blade body and burn. Additionally, the teeth at the outfeed side of the cut could catch the wood and throw it back at you.

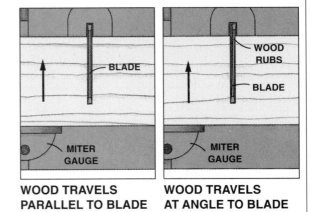

WOOD TRAVELS PARALLEL TO BLADE   **WOOD TRAVELS AT ANGLE TO BLADE**

ALIGNING JOINTER KNIVES

1 To set jointer knives parallel and all at the same height, rest a block of wood on the outfeed table close to a side.

2 Rotate the cutterhead so the knives catch the wood and drag it a small distance (usually 1/8"). Repeat at the other side. Each knife should drag the block the same distance no matter where the block is positioned on the table.

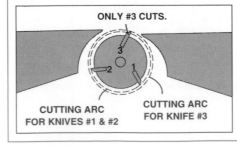

ONLY #3 CUTS.

CUTTING ARC FOR KNIVES #1 & #2   CUTTING ARC FOR KNIFE #3

THE WHY OF IT: Why is it important that jointer knives be parallel and even? If one knife is higher than the others, only that knife will cut and the surface will seem rough. If one knife is set at an angle, the cut won't be square to the fence.

SETTING A 90-DEGREE ANGLE

Use a square or the "right" corner on a triangle to check that two parts are perpendicular to one another. When setting a blade square to a table or a miter gauge, rest the edge of the square or the triangle against the body of the blade. Don't let it contact the teeth.

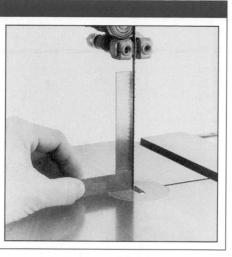

SETTING 45- AND 135-DEGREE ANGLES

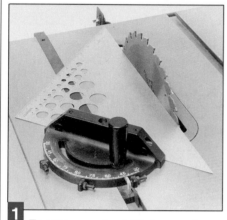

1 *To set two parts at 45 degrees to one another, use the 45-degree corner of a 45/90 triangle.*

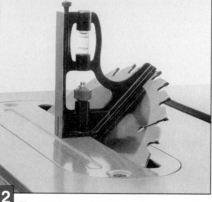

2 *To set them at 135 degrees, use the head of a combination square.*

MEASURING CLEARANCES

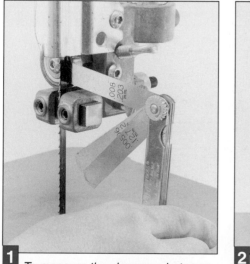

1 *To measure the clearance between two parts, such as the clearance between the blade and thrust bearing on a band saw, probe the gap between the two parts with a feeler gauge.*

2 *When measuring small gaps, it's often handier to use a strip of paper or a dollar bill. Ordinary typing paper is about 0.002 inch thick; a dollar bill is 0.004 to 0.005 inch.*

PERPENDICULAR AND ANGULAR ALIGNMENTS

Many power tools are designed to cut, drill, or sand at an angle, the most common being 90 degrees. In a normal setup, a table saw blade cuts square to the face of the miter gauge. However, the face rotates, allowing you to cut diagonally. On most gauges, there are adjustable stops at the most commonly used angles — 90 degrees, 45 degrees left, and 45 degrees right.

Use a square or the 90-degree corner on a triangle to align cutters perpendicular to worktables or miter gauge faces. To set 45-degree angles, use the 45-degree corner on a triangle or the head of a combination square.

CLEARANCE

For two adjoining parts to move smoothly, there must be some small space or *clearance* between them. For example, the miter gauge bar can't be the same size as the slot it rides in. It must be slightly smaller. The blade guides on either side of a band saw blade can't touch it; there must be a little space between them.

But this clearance mustn't be too large. If it were, the miter bar would move from side to side in the slot and the band saw blade would twist between the guides.

To gauge a clearance, use a feeler gauge. The size of the thickest possible feeler you can insert between the parts (without forcing it) is the distance between them.

TENSIONING

Band saw[1] blades, **scroll saw**[2] blades, abrasive belts, and drive belts must be properly tensioned. On some tools, there is a gauge to measure the tension or the tensioning is done automatically. On others, you must estimate the tension either by pressing against the taut part or plucking it.

There is quite a bit of latitude in tensioning, much more than any other adjustment. Blades and belts will run safely and effectively inside a wide range. And it's easy to tell when a part is improperly tensioned. Loose blades are noisy and produce rough cuts; loose belts slip. Tight blades snap sooner than expected; tight belts bog down the motor.

MORE *INFO*

If a motor bogs down, check the power connections before loosening the drive belt — what appears to be a tensioning problem might be an electrical problem instead. An extension cord that's too long or rated for a lower amperage than the motor will starve the motor for power.

TRACKING

Band saw blades and abrasive belts run over wheels and drums. In most cases, these are *crowned* – their circumference is slightly greater in the middle than at the sides. Additionally, they can be tilted slightly, moving the crowns from side to side. Bands and belts center themselves over a crown as they run. By tilting the wheels and drums, you can track bands and belts on the tool.

Drive belts that run over pulleys must also be tracked. The pulleys must all spin in the same plane. If they don't, the belt will be pulled sideways as it runs. This, in turn, will cause it to wear prematurely and lose its tension. It also requires more power to run.

TENSIONING A V-BELT

When tensioning a V-belt, the rule of thumb is the belt is tight enough when you can't depress it more than ¼ inch with moderate finger pressure. In reality, however, you have more latitude than this.

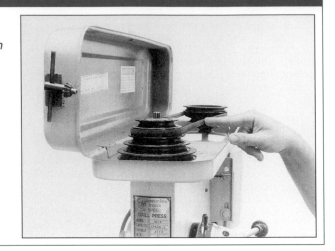

PRO*TIP*

If the power tool vibrates excessively, try replacing stamped pulleys with precision-machined pulleys and V-belts with link belts. Inexpensive belts and pulleys are a major source of vibration.

TRACKING BLADES AND BELTS

A running belt seeks the highest point or **crown** on a wheel. Track the belt by tilting the wheel and moving the crown. **The belt must be running to do this!**

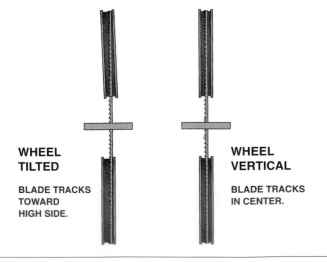

WHEEL TILTED

BLADE TRACKS TOWARD HIGH SIDE.

WHEEL VERTICAL

BLADE TRACKS IN CENTER.

ALIGNING PULLEYS AND BELTS

Pulleys and V-belts must all rotate in the same plane. To a pulleys, loosen the set screws in the hubs and slide them along the shaft or arbor.

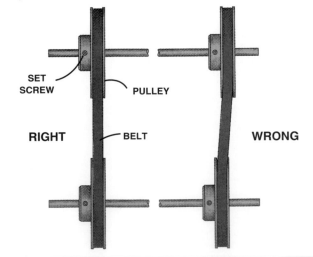

SET SCREW

PULLEY

RIGHT

BELT

WRONG

CLEANING POWER TOOLS

A power tool will run better and longer if kept clean. Sawdust is a **mild abrasive**[3] that wears away electrical switches, saw arbors, and other moving parts. Even sealed bearings are susceptible. Microscopic wood fibers can work their way around the seals.

Sawdust also causes misalignment and runout. If a wood chip becomes lodged in a critical part, it may hold a fence at a slight angle or cause a blade to wobble.

To keep power tools clean:

■ Collect the dust as you work. If the manufacturer provided a **dust collector**[4], use it. If not, make one.

■ Keep a bench brush handy to brush off the dust that settles on the tools.

■ Periodically, remove the fine dust that collects inside your tools.

Unplug the tool, remove the covers, and vacuum as much dust as you can reach. Use a stiff brush to clean racks, gears, and mechanisms where the dust is impacted. Use compressed air to blow dust out of tiny crevices and areas you can't reach with other tools.

LUBRICATION

Parts of your power tools need periodic lubrication to reduce friction and help them wear longer. There are several types of lubricants you can use, depending on the part.

OIL

The most versatile lubricant is a light (10W) machine oil. This is commonly used to lubricate pivots, bushings, and other mechanisms where two metal parts rub against one another. *It must be applied sparingly,* especially in dusty environments. Oil works best as a lubricant when it's only a few molecules thick on the surface of the metal. For this reason, one or two drops go a long way. If you apply too much, the excess oil mixes with dust to form a gummy substance that increases friction and accelerates wear and tear — exactly the opposite effect that you were hoping for.

SILICONE AND GRAPHITE

The parts of some tools are constantly exposed to fine sawdust. The revolving drums of a belt sander or the lower blade guides on a band saw are almost bathed in it. For these mechanisms, any amount of oil, no matter how small, may be too much. Instead, use silicone or graphite — lubricants that don't attract dust. However, the rule of thumb for applying them is the same as machine oil. They work best when used sparingly.

REMOVING IMPACTED SAWDUST

Sawdust packs in racks, pinions, and gears, making them difficult to operate. This is especially common in table saw carriages, the mechanisms that raise and lower planer beds, and quill feeds in drill presses. Remove the dust with a stiff brush such as a toothbrush.

LUBRICATING HARD-TO-REACH PARTS

The long tube on this oil applicator allows you to apply a small amount of oil (less than a drop, if necessary) right where you need it.

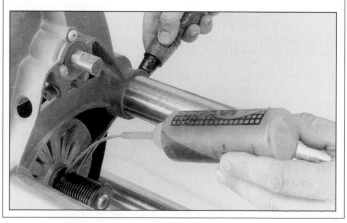

WAX

The work surfaces of tables, fences, and guides – any surface that you pass wood across – also need lubrication. This reduces the effort required to feed the wood and gives you more control over the work. In some cases, it reduces the work that the tool has to do. If you lubricate a planer bed, for example, the feed motor doesn't have to work as hard.

The traditional lubricant for work surfaces is furniture paste wax. (Automotive paste wax does not lubricate.) Properly applied, wax wears a long time and won't rub off on the wood surfaces.

APPLYING PASTE WAX

*Lubricate work surfaces with furniture paste wax. Remember to buff out the excess — **this is extremely important!** If you don't buff, the thick wax will rub off on the wood and interfere with the finish. Or, it will mix with sawdust to form a gummy substance that hinders the operation of the tool.*

CARING FOR ALUMINUM SURFACES

When exposed to air, aluminum oxidizes much like iron or steel. The oxidized aluminum rubs off on the wood, leaving black marks. To prevent this, wax and buff aluminum work surfaces.

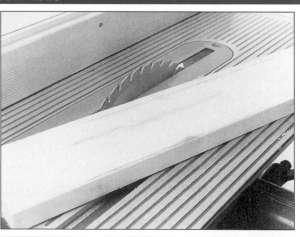

PREVENTING RUST

*Craftsmen traditionally use **camphor** (available at most drugstores) to protect hand tools from rust. A single tablet, placed in a tool cabinet or drawer, slowly evaporates and condenses on metal surfaces. This forms a thin film of camphor oil that insulates tools from moisture.*

RUST PREVENTION

Tools made of iron and steel are susceptible to rust. Contact with water causes the metal surface to oxidize. The oxidized molecules break free from the tight **crystalline structure**[1] of the metal and small pits form in the surface. As the surface continues to rust, these pits grow.

Rust is a problem for all woodworkers, but it especially plagues those that work in humid environments and unheated shops. Moisture in the atmosphere condenses on cool metal surfaces, coating them with water. To prevent this water from rusting your tools:

■ Heat or dehumidify your shop. A heat source keeps the moisture from condensing on the tools; a dehumidifier removes the moisture before it becomes a nuisance.

■ Keep your tools clean and free of dust. Sawdust attracts moisture and holds it in contact with the metal surfaces.

■ Coat metal surfaces with a water-repellent chemical. *Wax*, for example, not only lubricates, it also repels water. So does *camphor*.

■ When storing a tool for an extended period, spray it with a *penetrating oil*. These chemicals include a small amount of paraffin. As the oils evaporate, the paraffin is left behind in a thin film that coats the metal.

SEE ALSO:

[1]Tool Steel and Carbide   140

MORE SOURCES

Mastering Woodworking Machines, by Mark Duginske, Taunton Press, 1992

Restoring, Tuning, and Using Classic Woodworking Tools, by Michael Dunbar, Sterling Publishing, 1989

Fine Woodworking on Woodworking Machines, Taunton Press, 1985

TROUBLE *SHOOTING*

COMMON MAINTENANCE PROBLEMS

Problem	Possible Causes	Solutions
Wood burns as you cut it. Adjusting cutter speed and feed rate do not seem to help.	Blade is not properly aligned with fence or guide.	Align guide parallel to blade's plane of rotation.
	Cutter is dull or loaded with pitch.	Sharpen or clean the cutter.
Cut surface is rough, even when cutting with the grain. Adjusting cutter speed, feed rate, and depth of cut do not seem to help.	Blade is not properly aligned with fence or guide.	Align guide parallel to blade's plane of rotation.
	Cutters are not parallel to one another or at the same height.	Align cutters parallel to one another and set them at the same height.
	Blade is not properly mounted or tensioned.	Mount blade correctly. If necessary, increase blade tension.
	Runout is excessive, due to part not running true, improperly mounted cutter, or wood chip in mount.	Determine cause of runout. Replace parts, mount cutter correctly, or clean tool, as necessary.
Can't make an accurate cut. Blade wants to wander off layout mark or line.	Blade is not properly aligned with fence or guide.	Align guide parallel to blade's plane of rotation.
	Blade is not properly mounted or tensioned.	Mount blade correctly. If necessary, increase blade tension.
	Runout is excessive, due to part not running true, improperly mounted cutter, or wood chip in mount.	Determine cause of runout. Replace parts, mount cutter correctly, or clean tool, as necessary.
Wood pulls to one side as it's fed past blade.	Blade is not properly aligned with fence or guide.	Align guide parallel to blade's plane of rotation.
Wood is difficult to feed past blade or cutter; wood seems to stick.	Blade is not properly aligned with fence or guide.	Align guide parallel to blade's plane of rotation.
	Work surfaces not lubricated.	Clean, wax, and buff work surfaces.
Work surfaces leave dark marks on wood.	Aluminum work surfaces oxidize; oxide rubs off on wood.	Clean, wax, and buff work surfaces.
Machine vibrates excessively.	Pulleys in drive train out of round.	Replace pulleys.
	V-belt in drive train worn.	Replace V-belt.
	Pulleys improperly aligned.	Align pulleys to rotate in same plane.
	Bearing or other moving parts worn.	Replace worn parts.
Machine generates excessive noise.	Moving parts not lubricated.	Apply lubrication sparingly.
	Bearing or other moving parts worn.	Replace worn parts.
Motor slow to start or bogs down easily.	V-belt in drive train improperly tensioned.	Reduce tension of V-belt.
	Pulleys improperly aligned.	Align pulleys to rotate in same plane.
	Extension cord too long or wire gauge too small.	Use shorter cord or one with larger wire gauge.
Blade or cutter seems to slip.	V-belt in drive train improperly tensioned.	Increase tension of V-belt.
	Blade improperly mounted.	Mount blade correctly.
Table, blades, or other moving parts difficult to tilt or adjust.	Moving parts not lubricated.	Apply lubrication sparingly.
	Moving parts clogged with sawdust.	Clean tool, remove all sawdust.
Tool throws wood chips.	Dust channels clogged with sawdust.	Clean tool, remove all sawdust.
Iron and steel surfaces rust.	Environment is wet or humid.	Dehumidify shop and/or coat metal surfaces with wax, camphor, or oil.
	Shop not heated; moisture condenses on cool metal surfaces.	Heat shop or coat metal surfaces with wax, camphor, or oil.
	Tools dusty; sawdust attracts moisture.	Keep tools clean.

16

Sharpening

Sharpening is a simple matter of geometry: Hone a keen edge to the proper angle and shape.

There is no better woodworking experience than working with a truly sharp tool – and no more frustrating experience than working with a dull one. Dull tools require more work and produce poor results. They are unsafe and difficult to control. Consequently, sharpening a cutting edge and keeping it sharp has always been an essential woodworking skill.

HOW A TOOL CUTS WOOD

To grind a keen cutting edge, it helps to understand how a tool cuts wood.

A DEFINITION OF CUTTING

Down at the level where the edge meets individual **wood fibers**[1], cutting is synonymous with breaking. The point of the tool presses against the wood fibers with enough force that they break, separating into two pieces.

A cutting edge concentrates all the force driving the tool at its point. And because a sharp edge contacts only a small amount of the wood surface, the resistance is confined to a tiny area. The keener the point, the smaller the resistance, and the smaller the force required to cut. The wood fibers separate along a narrow line described by the path of the tool, and the cut surface appears smooth and even.

A blunt or dull tool contacts a larger surface area. Consequently, there is more resistance and it requires more force to cut. The fibers fail along a wider, poorly defined line, and the cut is ragged.

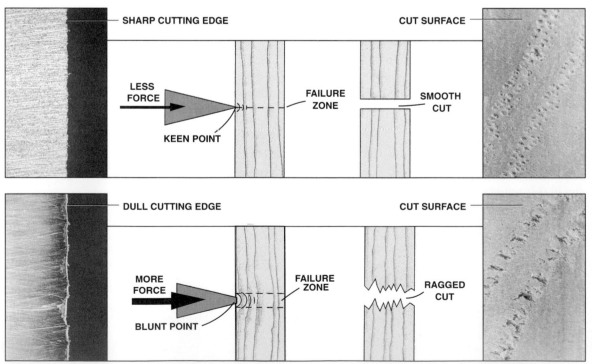

The point of a freshly whetted cutting edge is crisp and keen. It slices through wood easily, leaving a smooth surface. But as the edge wears, it grows dull and blunt, requiring more and more force to cut. As it dulls, the surface becomes more ragged.

CUTTING EDGE GEOMETRY

Sharpness isn't the only attribute that affects the cut. The angle at which the tool is sharpened, the angle at which it attacks the wood, and the shape of the cutting edge also determine how a tool cuts.

Every cutting edge has a *leading face* and a *trailing face*. The angle between the two is the *tool angle* – the smaller the angle, the less force required to cut. But if the angle is too small, there's too little metal to buttress the edge and it wears quickly.

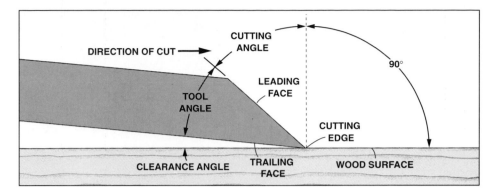

What tool angle is best? That depends on the tool and how it's used.

HAND-DRIVEN CHISELS, CARVING TOOLS — 15°–25°
MALLET-DRIVEN CHISELS, HAND PLANES — 25°–35°
JOINTER KNIVES, PLANER KNIVES — 35°–45°
ROUTER BITS, SHAPER CUTTERS, CIRCULAR SAW TEETH — 45°–60°
SCRAPING TOOLS — 60°–90°

MYTH *CONCEPTIONS*

TOOL ANGLE Tool angle is often confused with sharpness. It's not true that the smaller the angle, the sharper the tool. Sharpness refers to the *condition* of the edge, not its angle. A router bit, for example, has a high tool angle. But when the point is keen, the edge is sharp.

The angle at which the cutting edge meets the wood – the *cutting angle* – is measured from an imaginary line perpendicular to the wood surface. This, more than any other angle, controls how the tool cuts. At a *large* cutting angle, it lifts the wood fibers as it cuts them; at a *small* cutting angle, the tool compresses the fibers, then shears them off.

Because it's more difficult to compress fibers than lift them, the force required to remove a given amount of wood increases as the cutting angle decreases. Consequently, you must take progressively thinner shavings.

The angle between the trailing face and the work is the *clearance angle*. The size of this angle is not important, as long as there is one. Without a clearance angle, the cutting edge can't contact the wood.

These angles are affected by the shape or *grind* of the tool. There are three ways to grind a cutting edge – convex (*cannel* grind), concave (*hollow* grind) and flat. Chopping tools such as axes often have cannel grinds. The tool angle is high and

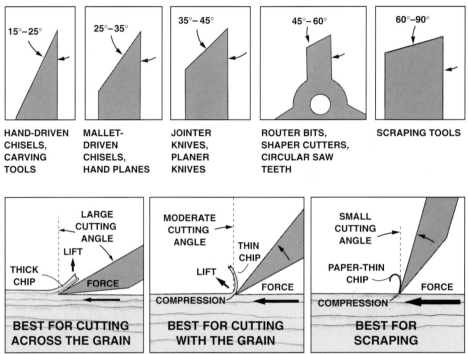

*When you drive a cutting tool through wood, it lifts **and** compresses the wood fibers. The force required depends on the cutting angle.*

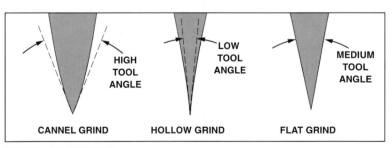

TYPES OF GRINDS

requires much force to cut, but the cutting edge is very durable. Light-duty tools such as carving chisels are sometimes hollow ground. This reduces the tool angle, making it easier to cut, but the cutting edge is less durable. A flat grind offers a good balance between cutting ease and durability.

SEE ALSO:
[1]Wood Grain 2

GROWING DULL: CHANGING GEOMETRY

As a cutting edge wears, the geometry changes. The edge rounds over – more in the trailing face than the leading face. As this happens, the tool angle increases while the cutting angle and clearance angles decrease. More and more force is needed to drive the tool through the wood, and the cut surface becomes rougher.

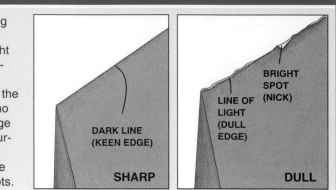

PRO *TIP*

If you suspect a cutting edge is growing dull, inspect it under a bright light. Because the surfaces of a sharp tool come to a crisp point, the cutting edge reflects no light. But once the edge wears, the rounded surface reflects a line of light. Nicks in the edge show up as bright spots.

DARK LINE (KEEN EDGE)

SHARP

LINE OF LIGHT (DULL EDGE)

BRIGHT SPOT (NICK)

DULL

CUTTING ANGLE

TOOL ANGLE

CLEARANCE ANGLE

SHARP TOOL

TOOL ANGLE

CUTTING ANGLE

CLEARANCE ANGLE

AFTER MODERATE WEAR

NO CLEARANCE ANGLE

TOOL ANGLE

CUTTING ANGLE

AFTER EXTREME WEAR

CHANGING TOOL GEOMETRY

SHARPENING KNOW-HOW

To sharpen a dull tool, you must do three things:

- Hone a keen point with progressively finer **abrasives**[1].
- Restore the edge to the proper tool angle.
- Grind it to the proper shape.

HONE A KEEN POINT

To create a crisp, keen cutting edge, *finish* the metal surfaces with progressively finer abrasives, making them as smooth as possible. If you use only coarse materials to sharpen, the edge will be rough. Instead, work up through finer and finer grits.

How fine should you sharpen? That depends on the tool and your personal preferences. For most applications, it's sufficient to grind and hone to between 500 and 700 (U.S.)

grit. But many craftsmen polish and strop to 1,200 grit and beyond for the keenest possible edge.

RESTORE THE TOOL ANGLE

To maintain the correct tool angle as you work your way through finer abrasives, use a *honing guide* or a *tool holder*. This eliminates the natural tendency to rock the chisel as

HONING GUIDE

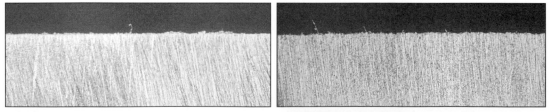

GRINDING (60 – 300 GRIT)

HONING (300 – 700 GRIT)

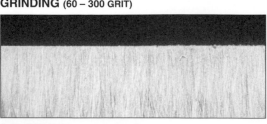

POLISHING (700 – 1,200 GRIT)

STROPPING (ABOVE 1,200 GRIT)

There are four sharpening levels, roughly defined by the abrasive grits used. As you sharpen with finer and finer grits, the cutting edge grows keener.
NOTE: The grits are graded according to the U.S. system.

you sharpen it, thereby rounding the face. You can get away without guides when you're just *touching up* a tool – polishing a slightly-worn edge – because you don't remove much metal. But even experienced sharpeners admit they can maintain the tool angle more precisely with a guide.

GRIND THE PROPER SHAPE

Most woodworking tools are ground flat by the manufacturers. There's rarely any reason to change to a cannel grind, but a hollow grind offers an advantage in some applications.

On a hollow grind, the *actual* tool angle (at the point) is 2 to 5 degrees less than the *apparent* tool angle (at the heel), depending on the radius of the abrasive wheel and the length of the hollow face. This reduces the force needed to drive the tool. However, there is a trade-off – a hollow-ground tool has less metal to buttress the cutting edge and it wears faster. For this reason, hollow-grind only *light-duty* tools such as carving knives and paring chisels. Others are best flat-ground.

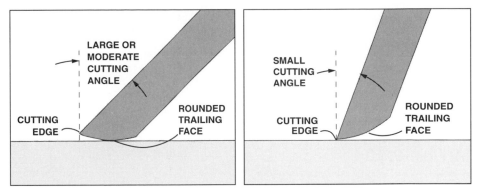

If you inadvertently round the trailing face when you sharpen a tool, the cutting edge will not meet the wood unless you decrease the cutting angle.

MICROBEVELS

You may also wish to add a *microbevel* to a cutting edge after sharpening it. A microbevel (also called a *secondary bevel*) is a tiny bevel at the point that increases the tool angle. It helps remove burrs and makes the edge more durable. (It does *not* make the edge sharper; that's a myth.) Because the microbevel is so small, the force required to make the cut increases only slightly.

To make a microbevel, sharpen the tool as you would normally. Then increase the tool angle a few degrees and make 2 or 3 passes – no more – over the finest abrasive. If the normal tool angle is 15 to 20 degrees, make the microbevel 5 to 7

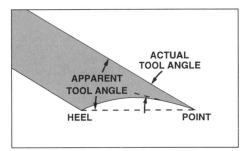

HOLLOW-GROUND CUTTING EDGE

degrees steeper. If it's more than 20 degrees, make it 3 to 5 degrees steeper. Tool angles of 30 degrees or more rarely need a microbevel; they are plenty durable without one.

SEE *ALSO:*

[1]Sharpening Materials   171

PRO *TIP*

Some craftsmen hollow-grind a face *before* they flat-grind the cutting edge. This practice doesn't change the force needed to drive the tool or the durability of the cutting edge. Instead, it reduces the amount of metal that must be removed to restore the edge and speeds the sharpening process.

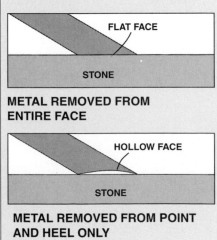

METAL REMOVED FROM ENTIRE FACE

METAL REMOVED FROM POINT AND HEEL ONLY

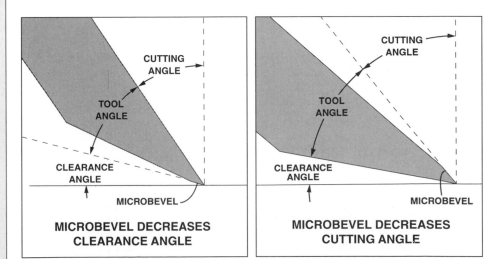

In most cases it's best to make a microbevel on the trailing face of a tool so it decreases the clearance angle. This is because the clearance angle is usually less critical than the cutting angle. However, if the clearance angle is extremely small, you will be better off making the microbevel on the leading face.

SHARPENING TOOLS

What sorts of sharpening tools and abrasives do you need? Should you sharpen by hand or use a **sharpening machine**[1]? That depends on the tools you need to sharpen, your experience, and your preferences.

BENCH STONES

A set of whetstones or *bench stones* is the core of most sharpening systems. These are available in different sizes, shapes, and grits. The materials are either natural stone or synthetic abrasives in a hard binder.

Many stones are used with oil or water. The liquid cleans the surfaces, floating away the *swarf* (metal particles) so it won't clog the abrasives. On sharpening machines, liquids also serve as a coolant, keeping the tool steel from overheating and losing some of its hardness.

Sharpening stones come in a variety of shapes and sizes to conform to the cutting edges of different tools.

MYTH *CONCEPTIONS*

ANTI-LUBRICANTS Liquids used to clean bench stones are traditionally referred to as *lubricants*, but this is misleading. A true lubricant reduces friction and abrasion, but you need to abrade the metal to sharpen a tool. These liquids clean and cool; they don't lubricate.

FILES

Many woodworking tools, especially hand saws and drill bits, are designed to be sharpened with **files**[2]. Although made of steel, files are hardened to a higher degree than wood cutting tools. Consequently, they will cut away the worn surfaces of a cutting edge.

STROPS

Strops are hard, flat, porous surfaces that can be loaded with ultrafine abrasives to polish cutting edges to a fine point. These abrasives include:

■ *Silicon-carbide powders* such as valve-grinding compound.

■ Natural *buffing compounds* like emery, Tripoli, or jeweler's rouge.

■ Synthetic *polishing compounds* like chromium oxide.

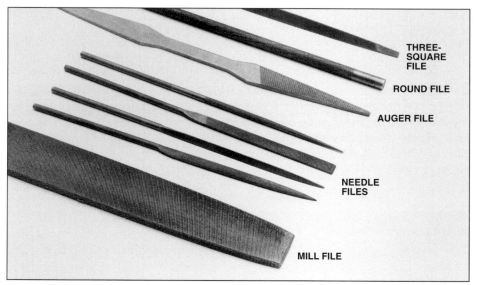

Several types of files are useful for sharpening. **Three-square files** *are made to fit saw teeth, while round files will fit hook teeth and chain saw teeth. You must have an* **auger file** *to sharpen drill bits.* **Needle files** *are handy for sharpening cutting edges with intricate shapes, and* **mill files** *are handy for flat, straight cutting edges.*

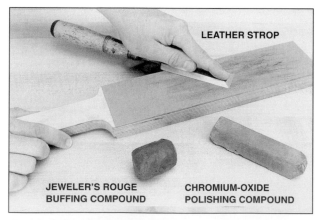

Traditionally, **sharpening strops** *are made of leather and backed with wood. However, you can use any hard surface that will hold fine abrasives.*

SEE ALSO:

[1] Sharpening Machines 115

[2] Files and Rasps 136

SHARPENING MATERIALS

MATERIAL TYPE AND GRIT (#)	COLOR	CLEANER	PREPARATION AND CARE	CHARACTERISTICS
NOTE: Grits are graded according to the U.S. system.				
ARKANSAS STONES Naturally-occurring novaculite (a type of quartz)		Light oil or water	Soak in cleaner prior to using first time. Wipe away dirty oil or water after each use; cover stone to keep from drying out; scrub clean with oil or kerosene.	Long wearing; produce an extremely keen edge; oil cleaner may contaminate wood surfaces if tools aren't wiped clean after sharpening.
Washita (350#)	Multicolored			
Soft Arkansas (500#)	Gray/green			
Hard White (700#)	White			
Hard Black (900#)	Black			
SYNTHETIC OILSTONES Aluminum oxide (India) and silicon carbide (Crystolon) bound in resin or sodium silicate.		Light oil	No preparation required; impregnated with oil. Wipe away dirty oil after each use; scrub clean with oil or kerosene.	Extremely hard and long wearing; inexpensive; produce serviceable edge but not extremely keen; oil cleaner may contaminate wood surfaces if tools aren't wiped clean after sharpening.
Coarse India (100#)	Brown or tan			
Coarse Crystolon (100#)	Gray or black			
Med. Crystolon (180#)	Gray or black			
Med. India (240#)	Brown or tan			
Fine India (280#)	Brown or tan			
Fine Crystolon (280#)	Gray or black			
WATERSTONES Aluminum oxide or silicon carbide bound in clay.	Either tan, brown, or gray	Water	Soak coarse and medium stones in water prior to using; fine stones need no preparation. Rinse stones after each use; if stones are stored submerged, change water occasionally and keep from freezing.	Many grades available; fast cutting; produce extremely keen edge; wears quickly; water may rust tools if tools aren't wiped dry after sharpening.
250 Extra Coarse (180#)				
800 Coarse (400#)				
1,000 Med. Coarse (500#)				
1,200 Medium (600#)				
4,000 Fine (900#)				
6,000 Extra Fine (1,000#)				
8,000 Ultrafine (1,200#)				
DIAMOND STONES Diamond dust embedded in nickel (or another soft metal) and fused to a steel plate.	All silver gray; bases are often color-coded to help identify grades	None required	No preparation required. Brush away filings as you work; wipe occasionally with damp cloth. Scrub clean with fiberglass abrasive pad and scouring powder.	Extremely long wearing; produce relatively keen edge; can be used to sharpen carbide tools; very expensive.
Coarse (240#)				
Medium (320#)				
Fine (600#)				
Extra Fine (1,200#)				
CERAMIC STONES Aluminum oxide embedded in ceramics and fused at 3,000°F.		None required	No preparation required. Wipe occasionally with damp cloth; scrub clean with fiberglass abrasive pad and scouring powder.	Extremely long wearing; produce extremely keen edge; no coarse grits available; can be used to sharpen carbide; moderately expensive.
Medium (600#)	Gray			
Fine (1,000#)	White			
Ultrafine (1,200#)	White			

MYTH *CONCEPTIONS*

A GRITTY COMPARISON Japanese waterstones appear to be finer than other sharpening abrasives because they have a higher grit number. However, the Japanese grading system is different from the one used in the United States. For example, 800 Japanese grit is equal to 400 American. Actually, waterstones are comparable to other materials.

SHARPENING CHISELS AND PLANE IRONS

The simplest tools to sharpen are those with straight cutting edges — flat **chisels**[1] and **plane irons**[2]. These tools have a *bevel* and a *back*. Initially, you must grind both surfaces, flattening the back and honing the bevel. But after the first sharpening, you need only sharpen the bevel.

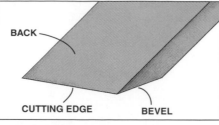

BACK

CUTTING EDGE   BEVEL

FLAT CHISEL

SHARPENING A CHISEL OR PLANE IRON

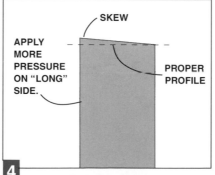

1 The first time you sharpen a chisel or a plane iron, **flatten** the back. Start with a coarse abrasive. Press the back against the stone and rub it back and forth until the scratch pattern covers the entire back. Work your way through finer stones, finishing the back to the same degree that you plan to finish the bevel.

NOTE: Once the back is flat, there's no need to grind it again. In fact, you shouldn't touch it except to briefly rub it across a fine stone or strop to remove burrs. If you grind the back each time you sharpen the chisel, the blade will grow thin and fragile.

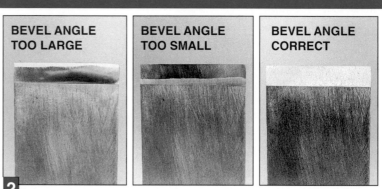

BEVEL ANGLE TOO LARGE

BEVEL ANGLE TOO SMALL

BEVEL ANGLE CORRECT

2 Mount the chisel in the tool holder or honing guide so the bevel rests against the abrasive. If you want to grind the bevel to a new angle, set that angle with the aid of a protractor. If you want to maintain the current bevel angle, set the tool so the bevel is flat on the stone. Make a few passes across the stone and inspect the bevel. If just the tip is scratched, the angle is too large. If just the heel is scratched, it's too small. When the entire bevel is scratched, the angle is right on the money.

BURR

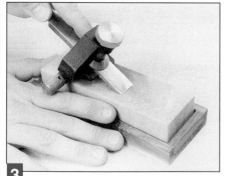

3 Start with a coarse abrasive and grind the bevel until the cutting edge appears keen and straight and all the nicks have disappeared. Move to a finer abrasive and hone the bevel at the same angle. For the sharpest possible edge, continue on through finer abrasives, polishing then stropping the bevel. How can you tell when it's time to move to a finer stone? Inspect the bevel — when the surface is an even color and texture with no dull areas or shiny spots, change to a finer grit.

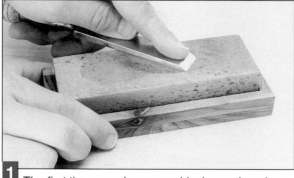

SKEW

APPLY MORE PRESSURE ON "LONG" SIDE.

PROPER PROFILE

4 As you sharpen, take care to preserve the profile of the blade — the cutting edge should be straight and perpendicular to the side. If you inadvertently grind a skew, you can easily correct it with some extra work and a judicious application of pressure.

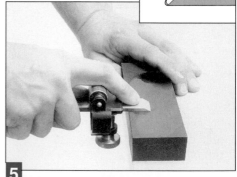

5 When you've finished the bevel, remove the burr that forms on the back. Turn the tool over and rub the back several times across the last abrasive used. Don't remove the honing guide or change the angle of the tool rest. To remove the last vestiges of the burr, it often helps to take a few more licks on the last stone or strop, alternating between the bevel and the back. Test the sharpness by cutting a thin slice **across** the grain of a wood scrap. Any traces of the burr will leave tiny lines of torn fibers in the cut surface.

SHARPENING SKEWS AND GOUGES

The steps for sharpening carver's skew chisels and **carver's gouges**[1] are roughly the same as they are for flat chisels. First, flatten the back of the skew or the *pod* (concave curve) of the gouge. Thereafter, sharpen the bevel, working your way up through finer and finer abrasives. Finally, remove the burr that forms at the cutting edge.

However, because the shapes of these tools are more complex than flat chisels, it's harder to maintain the bevel angle. You must either feel the angle or devise some method of holding the blade.

MORE *INFO*

Turners often grind back the ears on the **shaping gouges** they use to create spindles and bowls. This lets them cut concave shapes. **Roughing gouges,** on which the ears remain even with the nose, are used to round stock.

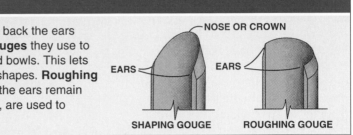

SHARPENING A CARVER'S SKEW

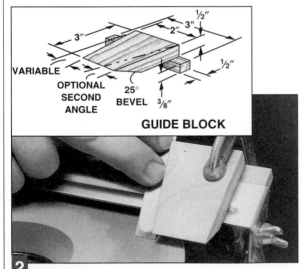

1 When sharpening a carver's skew **by hand,** you must grind without the benefit of a guide. **Feel** for the correct angle, resting the bevel flat on the stone. Then lock your wrist in place to maintain that angle as you sharpen. If you have trouble feeling the angle on a large stone, try a smaller slip stone. Press the stone against the bevel with your fingertips.

GUIDE BLOCK

2 When sharpening a skew **on a sharpening machine,** make a guide block with an angled side and clamp it to the tool rest. Hold the side of the chisel against the angled side as you work. The angle of the tool rest controls the bevel angle, and the angled side of the block controls the skew angle.
NOTE: When sharpening a skew chisel with a double bevel, such as a lathe skew, make a guide block with *two* angled sides, each side a mirror image of the other.

SHARPENING A CARVER'S GOUGE

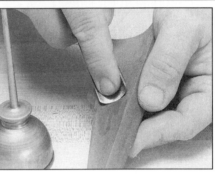

1 When **hand-sharpening** a carver's gouge, use a gouge slip. The rounded surfaces on the stone fit the curved cutting edge and pod of the tool. Put your fingertips in the pod opposite the bevel to help feel the angle.

GUIDE BLOCK

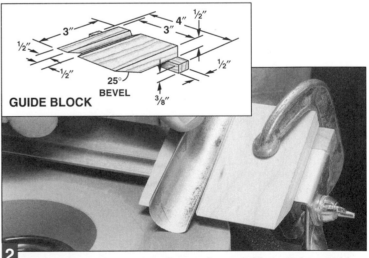

2 To sharpen a gouge **on a sharpening machine,** make a guide block with a V-groove and clamp it to the tool rest. Rest the blade of the gouge in the V and hold it there as you roll the tool from side to side. Press the tool forward gently to keep the cutting edge against the abrasive as the gouge rolls.

3 After finishing the bevel, use a round stone file to remove the burrs from the cutting edge of the gouge. Lightly stroke the concave surface of the pod with the file.

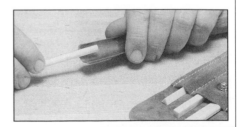

SHARPENING PARTING TOOLS

To sharpen a **carver's parting tool**[1] or V-tool, first check the profile. As they come from the manufacturer, many parting tools are ground with the nose slightly ahead of the ears. Because of this, the nose cuts the wood and begins to lift the chip before the ears have a chance to cut the sides of the groove. It makes more sense to let the ears lead the nose so the tool cuts the sides of the groove first, then cleans out the bottom.

When grinding the bevels, treat the tool as if it were two skew chisels joined at the sides. Each

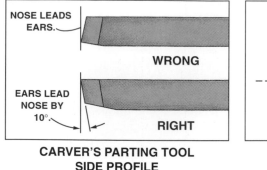

CARVER'S PARTING TOOL SIDE PROFILE

CARVER'S PARTING TOOL TOP PROFILE

bevel must be ground to precisely the same angle, and you must remove the same amount of stock from both. After grinding the bevels,

grind the nose (the point of the V) to the same angle as the bevels. This removes the small protruding *hook* that forms there.

SHARPENING A CARVER'S PARTING TOOL

FLATTEN EDGE, BUT MAINTAIN PROFILE.

1 *It's difficult to sharpen the bevels of a carver's parting tool and arrive at the correct side profile, with the ears leading the nose. Instead, grind the profile first by feeding the nose of the tool into a sharpening machine. This flattens and dulls the cutting edges, but you can use these flat edges as a guide to maintain the desired profile.*

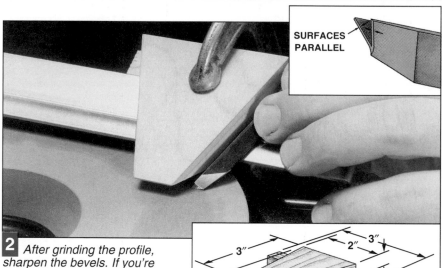

SURFACES PARALLEL

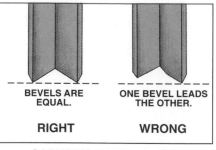

2 *After grinding the profile, sharpen the bevels. If you're using a sharpening machine, make a guide block with angled sides and clamp it to the tool rest. As you work, constantly check the flattened cutting edges. As the flats grow thinner, the inside and outside surfaces must remain parallel. Stop immediately when both flattened edges disappear. When this happens, the cutting edges are ground to a keen point, the bevels are equal, and the ears lead the nose.*

ANGLES EQUAL   25° BEVEL   ⅜″   **GUIDE BLOCK**

3 *As you sharpen, the nose of the V-tool will develop a slight protrusion or **hook**. Remove the hook by grinding the point of the V (where the bevels join) to the same angle as the bevels. Be careful not to grind too much; remove just enough metal to eliminate the hook.*

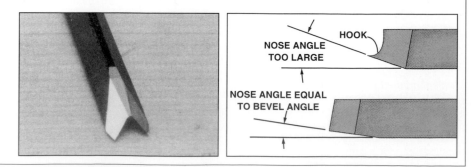

HOOK

NOSE ANGLE TOO LARGE

NOSE ANGLE EQUAL TO BEVEL ANGLE

SHARPENING KNIVES

Although a knife is perhaps the simplest of cutting tools, it can be deceptively complex to sharpen. The cutting edge is ground along the side of the blade rather than the tip, and the profile is often curved or crowned. Additionally, knives have a double-bevel and must be ground from both sides. Because of this, most craftsmen find it easier to hold the knife in their hands as they sharpen and maintain the angle by eye.

SHARPENING A KNIFE

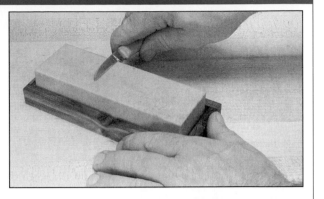

1 *To sharpen a knife **on a bench stone,** hold it roughly perpendicular to the length of the stone as you move it across the surface. Lock your wrist to maintain the angle. After sharpening one side of the bevel, turn the knife over and repeat for the other side.*

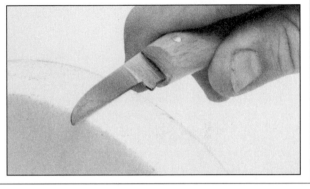

2 *To sharpen a knife **on an abrasive wheel,** lock your wrist at the desired angle and wipe the blade across the circumference, moving parallel to the wheel's axis. Use light pressure to keep from removing too much metal. Repeat for each side of the bevel.*

SHARPENING HANDSAWS

The teeth of **handsaws**[2] are sharpened with **files**[3]. You need a mill file to joint the teeth at the same height, and a three-square (triangular) file to sharpen the edges. Additionally, you'll need a *saw jointer* to hold the mill file and a *saw set* to set (bend) the teeth.

If the teeth are extremely worn or damaged, *joint* them flat and even with a mill file. Then recut or shape the teeth with a three-square file. Set the reshaped teeth alternately left and right, then sharpen them with a triangular file.

SHARPENING A HANDSAW

1 *Clean the handsaw and inspect the teeth. Compare the lightly used teeth near the heel of the saw with the heavily used teeth near the middle. If the middle teeth are worn down, or any teeth are damaged, joint the teeth with a mill file. Clamp the file in a saw jointer and run it along the saw until there's a small, shiny spot at the tops of all the teeth. When this happens, all the teeth are the same height.*

(Continued on next page)

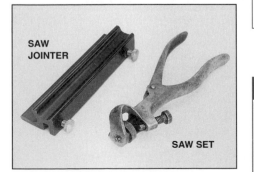

SAW JOINTER

SAW SET

SAW-SHARPENING TOOLS

PRO *TIP*

Sharpen dovetail saws that are used exclusively for cutting dovetails as *rip saws*. The saw will be easier to start and guide, and you'll get a smoother cut.

SHARPENING A HANDSAW — CONTINUED

RIP SAW

TOOTH LINE

TOOTH LINE

95°

75°

60°

CROSSCUT SAW

2 When jointing removes more than a third of the height of the teeth, recut the shapes with a three-square file. Clamp the saw between two long scraps and align the scraps about 1/16 inch below the old gullets. If you're sharpening a rip saw, cut hooked teeth with faces 95 degrees from the **tooth line.** For a cross-cut saw, cut sloped teeth with the faces 75 degrees from the tooth line. Stop cutting when the file reaches the scraps. Inspect the teeth — they should all be pointed with no shiny flat spots.

3 Saw teeth are bent slightly right and left so the kerf will be wider than the blade. This prevents the saw from binding in the cut. Bend the teeth with a saw set, adjusting it to bend each tooth about one-third of the blade thickness. Bend every other tooth to the right, then bend the teeth in between to the left.

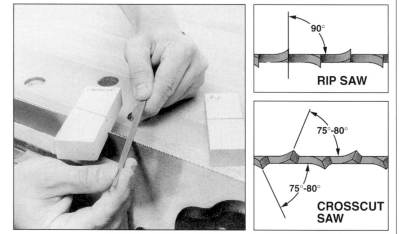

90°

RIP SAW

75°-80°

75°-80°

CROSSCUT SAW

4 After setting the teeth, sharpen them with a trian-gular file. File rip saw teeth straight across, perpendic-ular to the saw blade. For a crosscut saw, work at a 75- to 80-degree angle to the saw body. First file the teeth that are set to the right, working from the left side of the saw. Then switch sides and file the teeth that are set to the left.

JIGS & FIXTURES

SAW-SHARPENING GUIDES To help maintain the cor-rect angle when sharpening a handsaw, make a guide block for a rip saw and a crosscut saw. Position the guides over the saw teeth and hold the file parallel to the guide as you work.

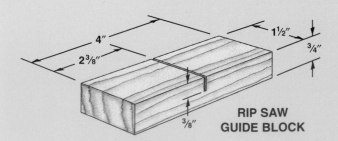

4"

2 3/8"

1 1/2"

3/4"

3/8"

RIP SAW GUIDE BLOCK

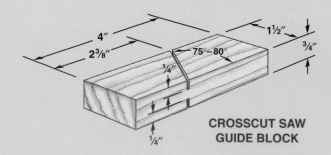

4"

2 3/8"

75°-80°

1/4"

1 1/2"

3/4"

1/4"

CROSSCUT SAW GUIDE BLOCK

SHARPENING DRILL BITS

The cutting edges of **augers**[1] and **drill bits**[2] are designed differently and require different sharpening procedures. However, the tools needed are all the same. You need an auger file, a mill file, a slip stone, and a set of ceramic files.

SEE ALSO:

[1] Hand Drills and Braces 134
[2] Drill Bits 107

SHARPENING AN AUGER BIT

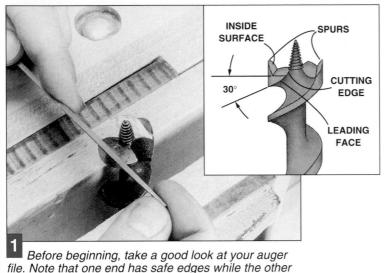

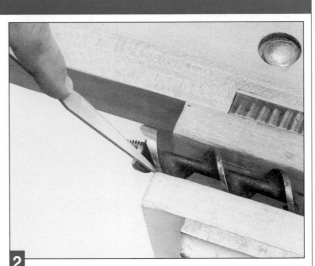

1 Before beginning, take a good look at your auger file. Note that one end has safe edges while the other has safe faces. (A safe file surface has no teeth.) File the **inside** surfaces of the spurs using the file end with safe edges. After filing, make sure both spurs are the same length. Twist the screw lead into a scrap, holding the body square to the surface. Both spurs should bite into the wood at the same time. If they don't, file the longer spur until it's even with the other.

2 After sharpening the spurs, file the leading faces of the cutting edges — the surfaces that face up as you bore a hole. For small augers, use the end of the file with safe faces; for larger ones, use the end with safe edges. Sharpen each cutting edge so the bevel angle is approximately 30 degrees. Afterward, bore a test hole. If one cutting edge takes a thicker shaving than the other, that edge is too long. File the long edge until the shavings are the same thickness.

SHARPENING A SPADE BIT

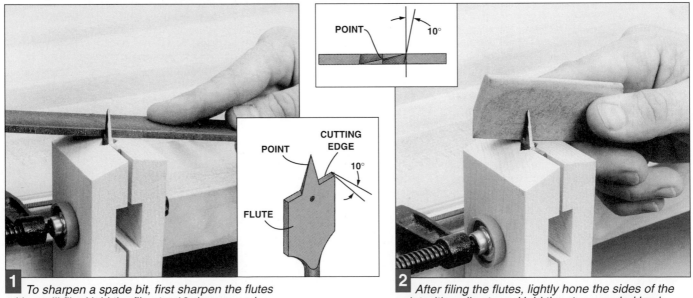

1 To sharpen a spade bit, first sharpen the flutes with a mill file. Hold the file at a 10-degree angle (approximately) and file the edges so the ears (outside corners) are even with each other.

2 After filing the flutes, lightly hone the sides of the point with a slip stone. Hold the stone angled back about 10 degrees. Count your strokes and hone each side the same amount to keep the point centered. **Don't hone too much!** Unless the bit is badly worn, each side should require only 5 or 6 strokes.

SHARPENING A BRAD-POINT BIT

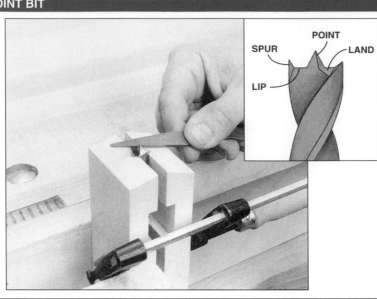

The procedure for sharpening a brad-point bit is similar to sharpening an auger. Use the end of an auger file with safe faces to file the spurs and the end with safe edges to file the cutting edge. There is one important exception, however. Instead of filing the leading face or **lip** of each cutting edge, file the trailing face or **land.**

PRO TIP

When sharpening a drill bit, *never* hone the outside edge or circumference of the bit. You'll change the diameter, and you may inadvertently grind the bit out-of-round.

SHARPENING A FORSTNER BIT

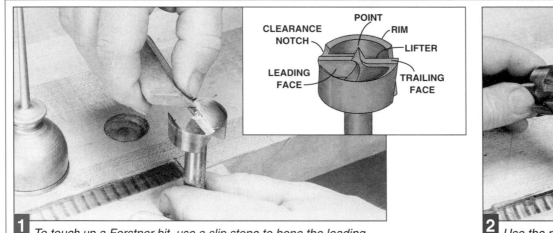

1 To touch up a Forstner bit, use a slip stone to hone the leading **and** trailing faces of each **lifter.** Hone the leading face first, pressing the stone flat against the surface. Then hone the trailing faces. The clearance notches on each side of the bit will let you reach them easily. Count your strokes and hone each side of the bit evenly.

2 Use the rounded edge of the slip stone to hone the **inside** edge of the **rim.** Roll the bit back and forth with your fingers while holding the stone against the rim.

JIGS & FIXTURES

DRILL BIT–SHARPENING GUIDE This guide holds both spade bits and brad-point bits, helping guide the file as you sharpen. When sharpening spade bits, use the angled end of the jaw that's cut 10 degrees off square. For brad-point bits, use the jaw that's 20 degrees off square.

Place the bit between the jaws and clamp them together. Position the bit with the thumbscrew so the flutes or lands are about 1/64 inch above the angled surface of the jaw. Sharpen the bit until the cutting edges are even with the jaw, holding the file or stone parallel to it.

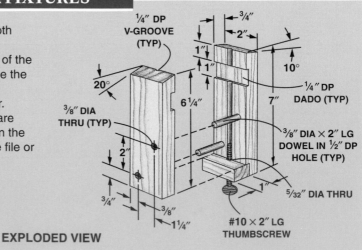

EXPLODED VIEW

SHARPENING SCRAPERS

Scrapers[1] have one or two cutting burrs on each cutting edge. To sharpen a scraping tool, you must remove the old burrs, square the edge, then raise new burrs. To do this, you need a bench stone and a mill file to condition the edges, and a *burnisher* to create the burrs.

SEE *ALSO:*

[1]Scrapers   136

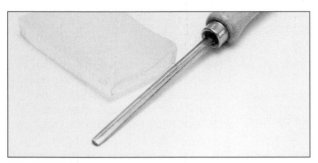

BURNISHER

SHARPENING A SHAVE HOOK

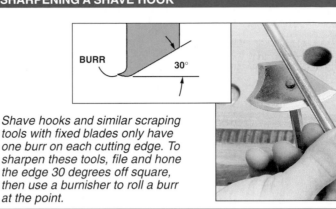

BURR   30°

Shave hooks and similar scraping tools with fixed blades only have one burr on each cutting edge. To sharpen these tools, file and hone the edge 30 degrees off square, then use a burnisher to roll a burr at the point.

SHARPENING A HAND SCRAPER

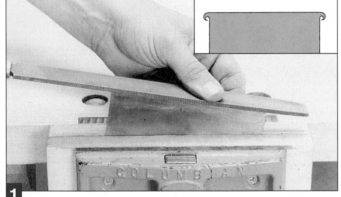

1 *Before you can sharpen a hand scraper, you must first remove the old burrs from the cutting edges. To do this, use a mill file to file the edges square to the blade. If you wish, mount the file in a saw jointer to keep it perfectly square to the scraper blade.*

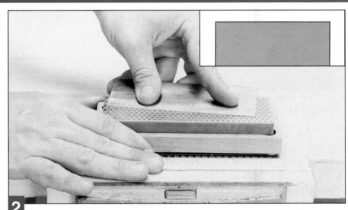

2 *After filing, hone the edges on a sharpening stone to remove any file marks. Then wipe the faces on the stone to remove any traces of the old burr, or any burrs left by the file.*

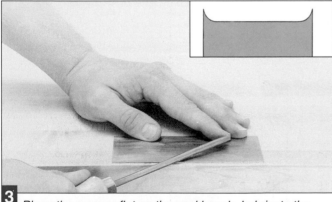

3 *Place the scraper flat on the workbench. Lubricate the burnisher by rubbing it with a candle or block of paraffin wax. Draw the waxed burnisher along each edge once or twice, pressing down hard enough that the burnisher makes a loud tick when it falls off the end of the scraper and hits the workbench. Turn the scraper over and repeat. This will raise two burrs on each cutting edge.*

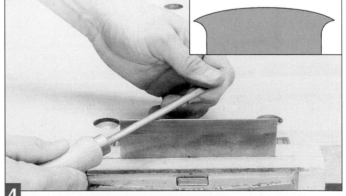

4 *Clamp the scraper in a vise with the edge up. Tilt the burnisher 10 to 15 degrees off horizontal and draw it along the edge once or twice, pressing down firmly. Then tilt the burnisher in the other direction and draw it along the edge again. Turn the scraper and repeat for the other cutting edges. This will roll the new burrs over so they are between 75 and 80 degrees from the face.*

TOUCHING UP HIGH-SPEED CUTTERS

Although you can sharpen high-speed tools in your workshop, it's not a good idea. The cutting edges are often tipped with carbide and ground to complex angles and shapes. These require special equipment to grind hard materials at precise angles.

More importantly, these tools are *balanced* to run at high speeds. Planer knives are ground to weigh

the same; saw blades are tensioned and straightened; router bits and shaper cutters are ground symmetrical. If they weren't, these tools would vibrate and wobble, leaving a rough surface in the wood.

You'll get better results from a reputable sharpening service with the proper equipment and know-how to sharpen high-speed blades, knives, bits, and cutters. However,

you can extend the time between sharpenings on power tools with *simple* cutting edges by touching them up occasionally.

PRO *TIP*

Before touching up or sharpening a high speed cutter, try cleaning it. The wood pitch that builds up on the cutting edges reduces the tool and the clearance angles, making the cutter seem dull. To remove the pitch, dissolve it with mineral spirits or oven cleaner. Wear eye protection and gloves when using oven cleaner.

TOUCHING UP JOINTER AND PLANER KNIVES

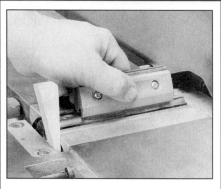

To touch up jointer and planer knives, **first unplug the machine.** Hone both the bevels and the backs of the knives with slip stones, feeling for the correct angles. You can also purchase special touch-up hones (shown) made especially for knives.

TOUCHING UP ROUTER BITS AND SHAPER CUTTERS

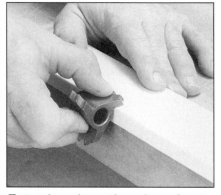

To touch up the cutting edges of router bits and shaper cutters, polish the **inside** faces on a fine stone. Rub each flute across the stone the same number of times to keep the bit balanced.

MORE *SOURCES*

The Complete Guide to Sharpening, by Leonard Lee, Taunton Press, 1995

How To Sharpen Every Blade in Your Woodshop, by Don Geary, Betterway Books, 1994

Sharpening, by Nick Engler, Rodale Press, 1994

TROUBLE *SHOOTING*

COMMON SHARPENING PROBLEMS

Problem	Possible Cause	Solution
Cutting edge overheats and becomes discolored.	Sharpening speed too high; holding edge against stone too long.	Use slower speed; hold tool against abrasive for short periods. Dip tool in water frequently to cool.
	Grit too fine for grinding.	Use coarser grit to grind.
Tool requires long time to sharpen.	Abrasive loaded with metal filings.	Clean abrasive; use sufficient water or oil while sharpening to float metal particles away.
	Grit too fine for grinding.	Use coarser grit to grind.
Cutting edge crowned or skewed after sharpening	Abrasive stone dished or worn.	Replace or resurface stone.
	Applying uneven pressure.	Apply even pressure to entire edge.
Tool won't cut at proper angle after sharpening.	Trailing edge rounded.	Use honing guide or tool holder to maintain angle.
	Tool angle too large.	Reduce tool angle.
Tool makes ragged cut after sharpening; needs too much force to cut.	Nicks remain in cutting edge.	Grind edge long enough to remove all nicks.
	Burrs not removed from cutting edge.	Polish or strop both leading and trailing surfaces to remove burrs.
	Cutting edge not keen enough.	Finish cutting edge with finer abrasives.
	Tool angle too large.	Reduce tool angle.
Tool wears quickly.	Tool angle too small.	Increase tool angle.

PART THREE

WOODWORKING TECHNIQUES

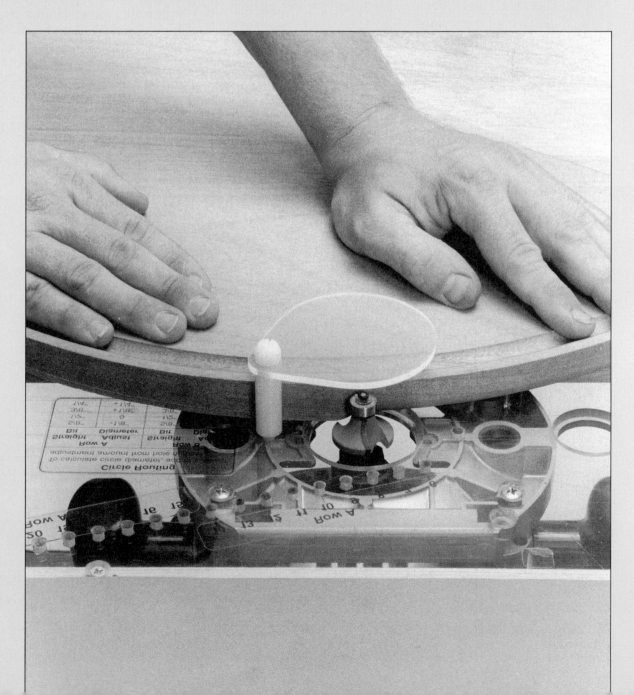

17

Jointing and Planing

To transform rough lumber into smooth, straight boards, you must consider the nature of the wood and your machinery.

Before you can build anything from wood, you must prepare your materials. Plane and joint the lumber true, making all the surfaces straight, flat, and square to one another. This is a critical step in any project, and although it sounds simple enough, it requires careful planning.

Think about what you're doing for a moment. You must take a material that grows naturally in rough, crooked, tapered cylinders (trunks and limbs) and transform it into smooth, straight rectangles (boards). As you do this, the material tends to move with every change in the weather. To accomplish this task, you must understand the **nature of wood**[1] and remember its special properties.

SELECTING LUMBER FOR SURFACING

Most craftsmen buy their materials from a lumberyard, a sawmill, or a retailer specializing in woodworkers' needs. Whatever your source, you usually have a choice of buying your wood rough or surfaced. Your choices may include:

■ Rough-sawn, with the surfaces untouched since leaving the mill

■ Surfaced on two sides (S2S), with both faces planed

■ Surfaced on four sides (S4S), with both faces planed and both edges jointed

*To keep this elegant **Shaker Lap Desk** as light as possible, the wood has been planed to between 3/16 inch and 3/8 inch thick. To make it strong, the corners are joined with through dovetails that were fitted to within 1/64 inch. To work such thin wood to such close tolerances, you must properly prepare the materials beforehand.*

SPECS: 6⅛″ high, 19⅜″ wide, 13″ deep
MATERIALS: Hard maple
CRAFTSMAN: David T. Smith Morrow, OH

ROUGH OR SURFACED?

Which should you choose? Ready-surfaced lumber saves you the time it takes to plane and joint. But if the wood should cup or bow, you'll have to live with the imperfections. Rough-sawn lumber gives you some extra stock so you can **true**[2] a slightly warped board, making the surfaces perfectly straight and flat.

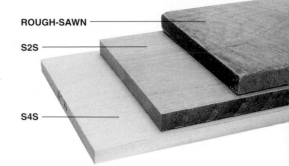

ROUGH-SAWN

S2S

S4S

*Commercial lumber comes unsurfaced (**rough-sawn**), face-planed only (**S2S**), or face-planed and edge-jointed (**S4S**).*

> ### PRO*TIP*
>
> When purchasing surfaced lumber, have it planed $\frac{1}{16}$ inch thicker than what you plan to use. The extra stock serves as a protective "wrapper." Wait until you're ready to work to plane the wood to its final dimension. You'll have a fresh surface, free of stains and dents.

Many craftsmen insist that you can get truly flat lumber only by surfacing it yourself. But this can be impractical, especially if you have a small shop and limited surfacing capabilities. Unless you have a wide jointer and a large planer, it makes sense to buy surfaced lumber (S2S) for noncritical parts that don't have to be perfectly true. When making critical parts such as door frame members and drawer sides, however, you should always start with rough lumber and true it.

S4S stock should be your last choice. It just isn't worth the money you pay for jointing the edges. Provided you have a jointer, you can make much straighter edges if you joint the parts as you cut them to size.

SHOP-DRYING

After purchasing the stock, let it rest in your shop for a week or two (per inch of thickness) before working with it. The same holds for stock you've stored in a building separate from your shop. Resist the temptation to get to work immediately – *you might have to do a lot of work over again!*

LET THE WOOD REACH EQUILIBRIUM

Wood typically expands or contracts whenever you change its location, due to differences in **relative humidity**[3]. When you first bring a board into your shop, it will be in motion. If you attempt to work it too soon, problems will result. The surfaces that you plane perfectly true today may be less than flat by tomorrow. Joints that fit beautifully on Monday may be nothing to crow about by Friday.

To avoid these problems, let the wood stabilize in its new environment. Stack it in a corner or on a rack until the moisture content of the wood reaches *equilibrium* with the relative humidity in your shop. This is called *shop-drying,* and it usually takes just a few days. Most craftsmen wait a week or more, to be safe.

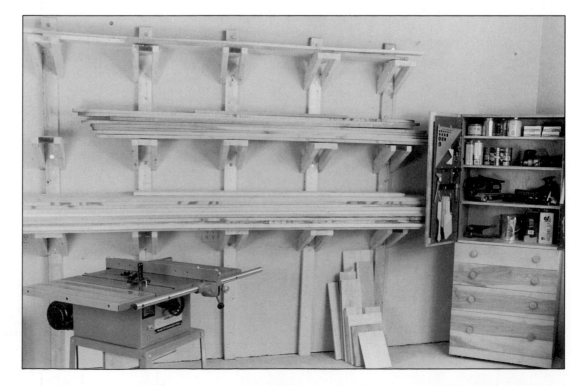

*Wood can shop-dry vertically for short periods of time, leaning against a wall. But if it sits for much longer than a few weeks, it should be stacked **horizontally** to keep it as straight as possible. This simple rack is designed for shop-drying lumber horizontally.*

Once the lumber has stabilized, joint and plane the surfaces straight, flat, and square to one another. Although jointing and planing are both surfacing operations, they are actually very different.

■ Jointing trues a surface and shaves it flat. It also cuts one surface at a precise angle (usually 90 degrees) to another.

■ Planing cuts one surface parallel to another and reduces the stock to a precise thickness.

JOINTING KNOW-HOW

The **jointer**[1] is a simple tool to use, but it must be aligned and adjusted perfectly for good results.

CHECK THE SETUP

Whenever you change or sharpen the jointer knives, check their height relative to the *outfeed* table. At the top of their rotation, they should be almost dead even with the table surface, maybe just 0.001 to 0.003 inch above it. If they're too high or too low, you can't make a straight cut. Whenever you move the fence, check its angle to the tables with a square or protractor.

> **PRO*TIP***
>
> Whenever possible, don't just check the tool setup. Make test cuts and check the *results*. Only then can you tell if the tool is adjusted properly.

CHECK THE STOCK

Because dirt is abrasive, clean dirty wood with a stiff brush before you joint it. This will help keep the knives sharp. Don't joint painted wood or plywood – these, too, contain abrasives that dull the knives. And avoid used lumber at all costs: It may contain embedded nails or broken screws that will nick the knives.

CHECKING THAT THE JOINTER CUTS STRAIGHT

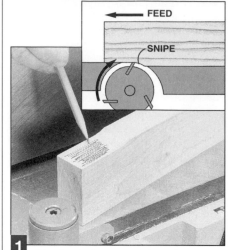

1 To check that your jointer is cutting a straight edge, joint the first 1 or 2 inches of a test board to create a snipe in the edge. Shade the snipe with a pencil.

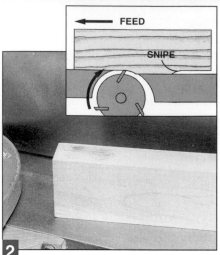

2 Turn the board around and joint the entire edge. (You should cut the snipe **last**.) Check the snipe — the knives should have shaved off most of the pencil marks, but they should still be barely visible. If the marks are untouched, the knives are too low in relation to the outfeed table. If they have been removed completely, the knives are too high.

CHECKING THAT THE JOINTER CUTS SQUARE

Make a test cut to determine that the jointer is cutting one surface square to another. Don't presume that just because the fence is square to the tables, you'll get a square cut. If the knives are cocked slightly, the jointer will still cut at an angle.

REDUCING MILL MARKS

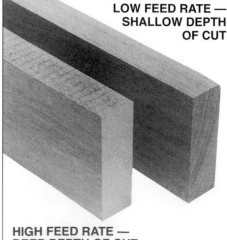

LOW FEED RATE — SHALLOW DEPTH OF CUT

HIGH FEED RATE — DEEP DEPTH OF CUT

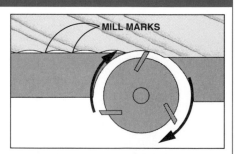

MILL MARKS

Because the jointer knives travel in an arc, each cut creates a scallop. The ridges between the overlapping scallops are known as **mill marks.** These can ruin the appearance of your project. To keep mill marks to a minimum, feed the work slowly and use a shallow depth of cut.

GOOD TECHNIQUE

As you work:

■ Adjust the height of the infeed table to control the depth of cut. Make deep cuts (greater than $1/16$ inch) only when you must quickly remove stock. Use shallow cuts (less than $1/32$ inch) to finish up – these leave a smoother surface.

■ Stand beside the jointer, opposite the fence, so if the wood kicks back, you'll be out of the way.

■ Keep the wood firmly against the jointer fence and the tables. Start with it pressed flat on the infeed table, then shift the pressure to the outfeed table as you feed the wood.

■ Feed the wood slowly. This creates the smoothest possible cut.

■ Cut *with* the grain so the wood doesn't chip or tear out.

■ Manipulate the wood with push shoes and push blocks to keep your hands away from the cutterhead.

■ If the board is cupped, joint the *concave* surface first.

SAFE *GUARDS*

When feeding the work, never place your hands directly over the cutterhead. If the wood kicks back severely, your hand could drop straight into the cutterhead.

JOINTING WITH THE GRAIN

*If the wood chips and tears as you cut it, you are cutting **against** the grain. (This is sometimes called "cutting uphill.") Turn the wood around and feed it in the opposite direction to cut **with** the grain ("downhill").*

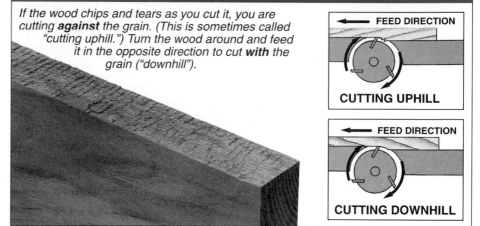

FEED DIRECTION
CUTTING UPHILL

FEED DIRECTION
CUTTING DOWNHILL

JOINTING SMALL PARTS

When jointing small parts (less than 12 inches long), fasten them to the bottom of a push shoe with double-faced carpet tape. This will help you handle them safely.
WARNING! Never joint anything shorter than three times the distance between the infeed and outfeed tables, or 6 inches minimum.

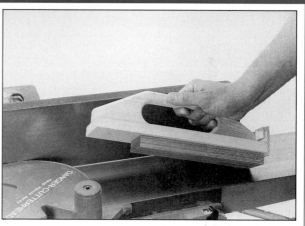

SEE *ALSO:*

[1]Jointers   102

JIGS & FIXTURES

ADJUSTABLE PUSH SHOE Push shoes let you hold a board firmly against a table or fence while protecting you from harm. Should you slip, the jig will fall into the cutter, not your fingers. Push shoes have soles to apply pressure and heels that you can hook over the work to feed it. This particular shoe has an *adjustable* heel that slides out of the way when you don't need it.

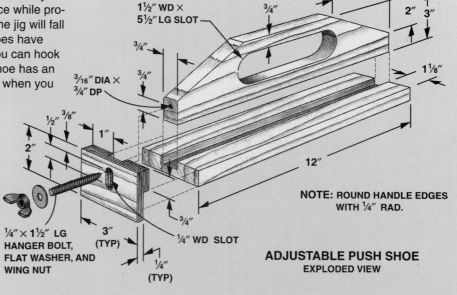

1½" WD × 5½" LG SLOT

¾"
¾"
¾"

³⁄₁₆" DIA × ¾" DP

3½"
2" 3"

¾"

1⅛"

½" ³⁄₈"
2"
1"

12"

NOTE: ROUND HANDLE EDGES WITH ¼" RAD.

¼" × 1½" LG HANGER BOLT, FLAT WASHER, AND WING NUT

3" (TYP)

¼" WD SLOT

¾"

¼" (TYP)

ADJUSTABLE PUSH SHOE
EXPLODED VIEW

JOINTING END GRAIN

To joint end grain, clamp the work to a large scrap to help support it. The scrap also backs up the stock, keeping the knives from chipping and tearing the trailing edge.

JOINTING AT AN ANGLE

*When jointing a bevel or a chamfer, tilt the fence **toward** the table. This captures the work and makes it easier to maintain an accurate angle. If you tilt the fence away from the table, the work tends to slip.*

PLANING WITH THE GRAIN

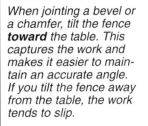

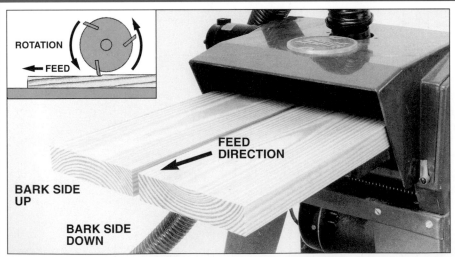

ROTATION

FEED

FEED DIRECTION

BARK SIDE UP

BARK SIDE DOWN

*To determine which direction to feed plain-sawn stock into a planer, look at the end grain and determine the **bark side** of the board — the side nearest the outside of the tree. Next, look at the "arrows" in the face grain. If the bark side is **up,** feed the wood in the same direction that the arrows point. If it's down, feed it in the opposite direction.*

PLANING KNOW-HOW

Many of the same concerns that you have when jointing also apply to **planing**[1].

CHECK THE SETUP

After changing or sharpening the knives in your planer, make a test cut. Using calipers, check the thickness of the board across the width. If the thickness isn't precisely the same at both edges, the knives are not parallel to the table. If the planer cuts a deep snipe at the beginning or end of a board, either the bed rollers aren't properly set or the feed roller pressure is not adjusted correctly.

CHECK THE STOCK

If necessary, clean the wood; avoid plywood and used wood. Set the feed rate and the depth of cut according to the wood species. The harder the wood, the slower the feed rate and the shallower the cut should be. The width of the stock should also affect your settings — use a slower feed and shallower cut for wide stock.

GOOD TECHNIQUE

As you work:

■ Stand on the same side of the planer as the switch. This lets you reach the switch easily and protects you from any kickback.

■ Pay careful attention to the motor speed as you plane. If the motor bogs down, the depth of cut is too deep or the feed rate is too fast.

■ To avoid chipping and tear-out, plane "downhill," cutting *with* the grain.

■ Remove stock as quickly as possible until you near the desired thickness. Then take shallow cuts at a slow feed rate. This will produce a smoother surface.

PRO*TIP*

Plane equal amounts of stock from each surface of a board. This will help prevent it from cupping if there are internal tensions in the wood.

PLANING THIN BOARDS

When planing a very thin board — thinner than the planer would ordinarily cut — rest it on top of a thicker board and send the two boards through the planer together.

MYTH *CONCEPTIONS*

PLANER LIMITATIONS Although a planer cuts one surface precisely parallel to another, it will not *true* lumber, removing cups and twists. The pressure of the feed rollers flattens the boards as they are cut. Once that pressure is released, the boards spring back to their former shape. The surfaces will be parallel, but any cup or twist will remain.

The easiest way to true lumber is with a jointer. You can also use a hand plane or the router planing jig shown on this page.

TRUING LUMBER

Preparing boards with surfaces that are perfectly straight, flat, and square to one another requires a combination of jointing *and* planing techniques.

BUSTING DOWN LUMBER

Start with thoroughly shop-dried stock. Measure and mark the parts of your project on the boards. As you do, leave extra stock, making the parts 1 to 2 inches longer and

½ to 1 inch wider than their final dimensions. **Cut and rip[2]** the boards, roughing out the parts.

Craftsmen refer to this as *busting down* rough lumber, and it relieves stresses in the wood. As the tree grows, it often buttresses itself against wind or gravity. **Drying[3]** may create further stress. These internal tensions remain until you release them by cutting the wood apart. As they are released, the **wood moves[4]**

slightly. But since you've cut the parts oversized, you have the extra stock needed to true them.

SEE *ALSO:*

[1]Thickness Planers	103
[2] Sawing	190
[3] Drying Defects	339
[4] Wood Movement	6

JIGS & FIXTURES

ROUTER PLANING JIG FOR FIGURED WOOD Figured wood doesn't have a consistent grain direction, making it difficult to joint or plane. No matter which way you feed the wood, you're planing *with* the grain part of the time and *against* it the other part. When you're planing against the grain, the knives tend to lift the wood fibers and tear them out, leaving the surface chipped and gouged.

A router, however, cuts the wood from a different angle and is not as likely to tear figured grain. With the aid of this jig, you can surface small and medium-sized boards. Secure the work in the trough with wedges, and fasten the router to the extended base. Mount a 1-inch straight bit in the router, rest the base on the sides of the trough, and adjust the height of the bit to cut the stock to the proper thickness. Turn on the router and slide it back and forth across the jig, shaving the surface of the wood.

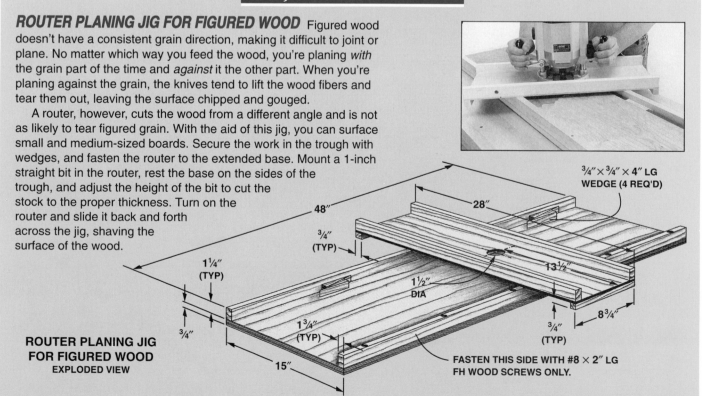

**ROUTER PLANING JIG
FOR FIGURED WOOD**
EXPLODED VIEW

48″

28″

¾″ × ¾″ × 4″ LG
WEDGE (4 REQ'D)

¾″
(TYP)

1¼″
(TYP)

13½″

1½″
DIA

8¾″

¾″
(TYP)

1¾″
(TYP)

¾″

15″

FASTEN THIS SIDE WITH #8 × 2″ LG
FH WOOD SCREWS ONLY.

USING A HAND PLANE

Although most contemporary craftsmen joint and plane on machine tools, **hand planes**[1] are still useful for trimming, removing mill marks, and taking mild cups or twists out of boards that are too wide to fit on your jointer. Besides, few experiences in woodworking are more satisfying than planing with a well-tuned bench plane. You just need to know a few simple tricks to make a hand plane sing for you.

TUNING A HAND PLANE

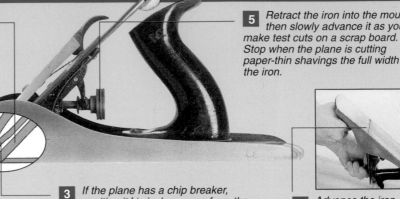

1 Sharpen the plane iron at 25 degrees for general work — a few degrees less if you work mostly with soft woods, a few degrees more for extremely hard woods or heavy-duty planing.

2 If the plane has an adjustable mouth, open it to ⅛ inch wide or more for rough cuts, ⅛ inch wide or less for fine cuts. You can also adjust it to control tear-out — close it down if the iron is tearing the wood grain.

3 If the plane has a chip breaker, position it ¹⁄₁₆ inch or more from the cutting edge for rough cuts, ¹⁄₁₆ inch or less for fine cuts. You may also want to adjust it for the type of wood — more for softwoods, less for hardwoods.

5 Retract the iron into the mouth, then slowly advance it as you make test cuts on a scrap board. Stop when the plane is cutting paper-thin shavings the full width of the iron.

4 Advance the iron until it's flush with the mouth, and adjust it so the cutting edge is parallel to the sole.

PLANING AT A SKEW

Keep the plane sole flat on the board as you cut. It's easier to push the plane — and you'll get a finer cut — if you hold the plane at a slight angle to its direction of travel. This effectively increases the cutting angle so the plane iron is shaving the wood from a lower angle.

STRAIGHT CUTTING PATH   **SKEWED CUTTING PATH**

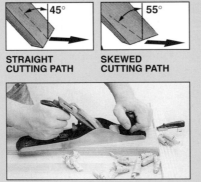

ROUGHING AND SMOOTHING

When you want to remove stock for a board quickly, plane at a steep diagonal to the wood grain. This is called a **roughing cut,** and it does not leave a particularly smooth surface. When a smooth surface is important, make a **smoothing cut** by passing the plane across the wood parallel to the grain.

ROUGHING CUT

SMOOTHING CUT

CHECKING YOUR WORK

To check that you're planing a flat surface, use the edge of the plane as a straightedge.

You can also sight along a pair of **winding sticks** to identify high and low spots.

PRECISION PLANING

To plane a board to a precise dimension, mark **all around** the outside of the board. Holding the plane at an angle, chamfer the corners of the board down to the lines you've marked. Then plane the surface of the board until the chamfers disappear.

TIP: Use a variation of this technique to cut a precise chamfer. Mark the chamfer on *both* adjoining surfaces, and plane down to the marks.

1

Mark dimension.

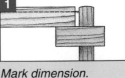

Chamfer to mark.

3

Plane until chamfer disappears.

PREPARING BOARDS

To true a rectangular board, first joint one face flat and true. Turn the board so the true face is against the fence and joint an edge. Plane the remaining face parallel to the jointed face, and **rip**[2] the remaining edge parallel to the jointed edge.

PREPARING SQUARE STOCK

To true square stock, joint two adjoining surfaces true and square to one another, as you do when truing a rectangular board. Mark these two jointed faces (so you remember which they are) and plane the remaining surfaces parallel to the jointed surfaces. Plane both remaining surfaces with the same *thickness adjustment*. The stock will be perfectly square.

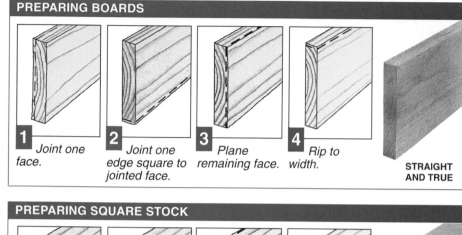

PREPARING BOARDS

1 Joint one face.

2 Joint one edge square to jointed face.

3 Plane remaining face.

4 Rip to width.

STRAIGHT AND TRUE

PREPARING SQUARE STOCK

1 Joint one surface.

2 Joint an adjoining surface square to the first.

3 Plane a remaining surface.

4 Plane the final surface. Do not change thickness.

STRAIGHT, SQUARE, AND TRUE

MORE SOURCES

BOOKS

Sanding and Planing, by Nick Engler, Rodale Press, 1994

The Complete Book of Stationary Power Tool Techniques, by R. J. DeCristoforo, Sterling Publishing, 1988

VIDEOS

Shop Planes with Roy Underhill, WTG Video

SEE ALSO:

[1] Surfacing and Trimming Planes   135

[2] Ripping   194

TROUBLE SHOOTING

COMMON JOINTING AND PLANING PROBLEMS

Problem	Possible Cause	Solution
Jointer cuts a slightly bowed surface.	Knives are too high or too low in relation to outfeed table.	Reset knives. Adjust outfeed table.
Jointed surfaces are not square.	Fence is not square to tables. Knives are not parallel to table surfaces.	Reposition fence. Reset knives.
Wood drifts to one side in planer.	Feed roller pressure is uneven.	Adjust roller pressure.
Wood thickness is not even.	Planer knives are not parallel to bed.	Reset knives.
Planer cuts snipe in ends of board.	Feed roller pressure is too low. Bed rollers are too high. Long board is not properly supported.	Increase roller pressure. Lower bed rollers. Support board with roller stand.
Machine bogs down, trips circuit breaker.	Depth of cut is too deep; feed rate is too high.	Reduce depth of cut or feed rate.
Wood is difficult to feed, seems to stick.	Planer bed or jointer tables require waxing. Planer feed roller pressure is too high. Planer bed rollers are too low.	Wax and buff bed or tables. Reduce roller pressure. Raise bed rollers.
Machine chips or tears wood grain.	Knives are cutting against the grain. Wood grain is figured. Knives are dull.	Reverse board end for end, or reduce feed rate or depth of cut. Reduce feed rate or depth of cut, or rout and sand stock to thickness. Touch up or replace knives.
Machine leaves noticeable mill marks.	Feed rate is too high. One knife is set too high.	Reduce feed rate. Reset knife.
Machine leaves raised lines.	Knives are nicked.	Sharpen or replace knives.

Sawing

In the course of a woodworking project, you are likely to make dozens of saw cuts using several tools and techniques.

As a woodworker, you spend much of your time in the shop sawing boards to specific sizes and shapes. Depending on the requirements of the projects, you may have to slice through the width, length, or thickness of the stock. Or, you must cut at an angle to the grain, follow a curve or contour, or create a three-dimensional shape. Each saw cut has its own special requirements, for which you must choose the proper sawing tools and techniques.

SAWING KNOW-HOW

Whatever equipment or methods you use, there are several important procedures that are common to all cutting operations.

■ Adjust the blade and the table for the proper angle and depth of cut.

■ Adjust the fence, miter gauge, stops, and any other accessories that you will use to guide the wood or control the cut.

■ Before you make a cut, check that the saw is set up correctly by making a *test cut.* Carefully measure the results.

■ Lay out the cut on the board. Sometimes, you can get away with just making a tick mark on the surface to indicate where to cut. But when the cut is

critical, mark all the cut lines. Use these to monitor your work as it progresses.

■ Align the layout marks on the board with the blade before turning on the saw.

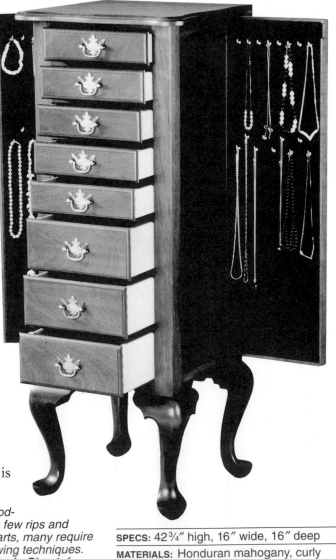

Photo by Dan Gabriel

*While almost every wood-working project takes a few rips and crosscuts to size the parts, many require more sophisticated sawing techniques. This **Jewelry and Lingerie Chest,** for example, required compound cutting to make the legs and duplicated cutting for the drawer parts.*

SPECS: 42¾" high, 16" wide, 16" deep

MATERIALS: Honduran mahogany, curly maple, hard maple

CRAFTSMAN: Jim McCann
Brookville, OH

■ Position your body to maintain control of the wood at all times. However, make sure you will always be out of the line of fire should the wood kick back. If you are performing an operation for the first time, go through a dry run without turning on the saw to make sure the operation feels comfortable and safe.

SAFE *GUARDS*

You must be able to reach the on/off switch for the power saw during the entire operation. If you must stand where you can't easily access the switch, use a foot switch or remote switch to turn the saw on and off.

■ Always wear eye protection. When sawing for long periods of time, also wear ear protection. Some high-speed blades and **universal motors**[1] generate loud, *high-frequency* sounds that can damage your ears even during a short exposure. When working with these tools, use ear protection at all times.

■ Use **push sticks**[2] or other safety tools to manipulate wood close to the blade.

ADJUSTING THE DEPTH OF CUT

When cutting through a board on a table saw, adjust the height of the blade so it just clears the top surface of the stock. Theoretically, the blade cuts smoother when the gullets clear the stock. Limiting the blade projection, however, is safer. If your hand should slip, only a small portion of the blade will protrude above the stock — enough to make a nasty cut, perhaps, but not enough to sever a finger.

PREVENTING CHIPS AND SPLINTERS

When the edge of a cut is ragged, it's often because the saw teeth lift and tear the wood fibers when exiting the cut. This is especially common when cutting plywood. To prevent chips and splinters, lay out the cuts with a marking knife. The knife severs the fibers on the surface of the wood and prevents the saw teeth from lifting them.

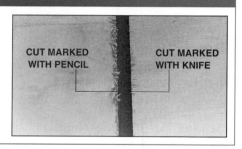

CUT MARKED WITH PENCIL

CUT MARKED WITH KNIFE

CUTTING SMALL WORKPIECES

To safely cut small work, attach the smaller piece to a larger scrap or a push block with double-faced carpet tape. The scrap serves as a handle to help feed and manipulate the small stock. Cut both the workpiece and the scrap, then remove the tape.

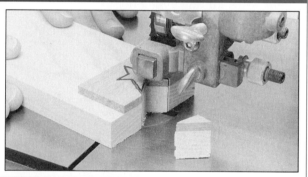

MAKING A ZERO-CLEARANCE INSERT

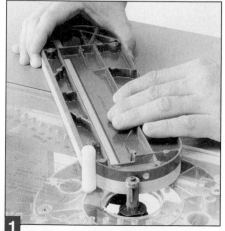

1 *To provide better support for a workpiece when making a cut, or to prevent small parts from dropping down past the blade, make a **zero-clearance insert**. Use the metal insert as a template to rout a wooden duplicate.*

2 *Lower the blade below the table surface and install the wooden insert. Press down on the insert with a pusher or featherboard. Turn on the saw and slowly raise the blade. This will cut a narrow slot in the wood, leaving almost no clearance between the blade and the insert.*

NOTE: Depending on the design of your saw, you may have to use a small-diameter blade to cut the slot.

SEE ALSO:

[1]Tool Buymanship   117
[2]Pushers   147

CROSSCUTTING

Crosscutting is sawing across the wood grain. (This is also called *cutting to length*.) While you can make a crosscut with almost any type of power saw, the three most common are the **radial arm saw, miter saw**[1], and **table saw**[2]. Whatever tool you use, it should be outfitted with a **crosscut or combination blade**[3], designed to cut across the grain.

A radial arm saw and a miter saw both crosscut long boards easily. The work remains stationary while you feed the blade through it, so the length of the stock matters little. But you have to watch the accuracy of a radial arm saw closely – the alignment tends to drift. And both saws have a limited crosscut capacity.

A table saw offers more precision and capacity, but you must feed the work past the blade. This can be difficult when cutting a long board. And the longer the board is, the more difficult it becomes. Attach an extension to your miter gauge or make a sliding table to cut long stock accurately.

CHECKING A SQUARE CUT

1 To check that a saw is cutting square to an edge, select a straight scrap about 18 inches long. If necessary, rip the scrap so both edges are parallel. Mark an X on the scrap near the middle, then saw through the mark.

2 Flip one part of the scrap over and butt the cut ends together. Align the edges with a straightedge. The seam between the parts should be tight. If it gaps at any point, the cut is not square.

CROSSCUTTING ON A RADIAL ARM SAW AND MITER SAW

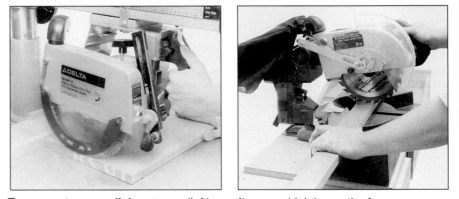

To crosscut on a **radial arm saw** (left) or **miter saw** (right), use the fence as a backstop. Place the board against the fence and slowly pull the saw through the cut. On a radial arm saw and a **sliding** miter saw, be careful that the blade doesn't **climb** as you cut, pulling itself through the board faster than you can control it. In some cases, you may have to push against the handle to prevent the blade from climbing.

MAKING DUPLICATE CROSSCUTS

To cut duplicate lengths, first cut one end of a board square. Attach a stop to the fence or miter gauge extension. Butt the square end of the board against the stop, and cut to length. Repeat as many times as necessary. As you work, brush away the sawdust to prevent it from building up between the stop and the board. Each cut-off part will be precisely the same length.

CROSSCUTTING ON A TABLE SAW

When making a crosscut on a table saw, take care that the board is well supported. The miter gauge is sufficient for feeding small boards, but you will need a miter gauge extension or a sliding table (shown) to guide longer stock accurately. If the board is extremely long, you must use a saw stand to support the end that hangs over the table.

SEE ALSO:

[1] Radial Arm Saws   100
[2] Table Saws   98
[3] Circular Saw Blades   101

JIGS & FIXTURES

SLIDING TABLE The Achilles' heel of every **table saw** [2] is that, as it comes from the factory, it's a marginal tool for making crosscuts. Unless the manufacturer provides something better than the usual miter gauge, you must make or purchase some sort of cutoff accessory to get the kind of accuracy you need. One of the most popular is the sliding table (also called a *sled*).

This particular sliding table travels back and forth in the left miter gauge slot.

The fence is 38 inches long to support long work, and a stop lets you make duplicate cuts. A short slot on the back of the fence holds the stop when it's not in use. Additionally, the fence pivots through 70 degrees for miter cuts.

When building the fence, cut the 3/4-inch-wide grooves in the inside faces of the fence halves *before* assembly, and the 1/4-inch-wide slots *after* assembly. The groove and slot in the front fence half is 2 inches long, while those on the back half are 32 inches long.

Position the guide so the right edge of the base and the right end of the fence will protrude 1/16 inch past the left side of the saw teeth. After assembly, cut the sliding table to its final size, trimming the base and fence. Adjust the fence stop so it holds the fence 90 degrees from the blade.

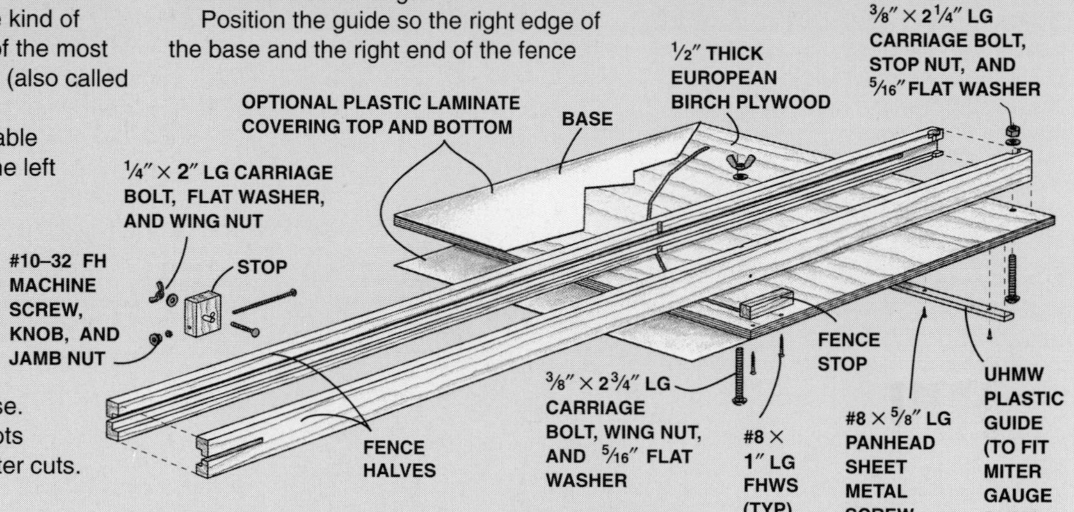
OPTIONAL PLASTIC LAMINATE COVERING TOP AND BOTTOM
BASE
1/2" THICK EUROPEAN BIRCH PLYWOOD
3/8" × 2 1/4" LG CARRIAGE BOLT, STOP NUT, AND 5/16" FLAT WASHER
1/4" × 2" LG CARRIAGE BOLT, FLAT WASHER, AND WING NUT
STOP
#10–32 FH MACHINE SCREW, KNOB, AND JAMB NUT
FENCE STOP
3/8" × 2 3/4" LG CARRIAGE BOLT, WING NUT, AND 5/16" FLAT WASHER
FENCE HALVES
#8 × 1" LG FHWS (TYP)
#8 × 5/8" LG PANHEAD SHEET METAL SCREW (6 REQ'D)
UHMW PLASTIC GUIDE (TO FIT MITER GAUGE SLOT)

EXPLODED VIEW

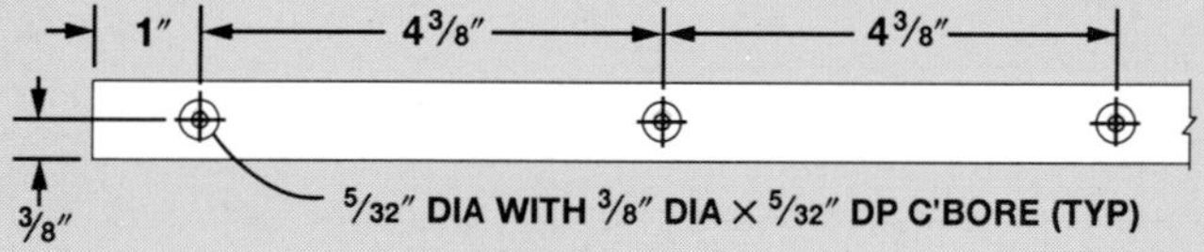
1"
4 3/8"
4 3/8"
3/8"
5/32" DIA WITH 3/8" DIA × 5/32" DP C'BORE (TYP)

GUIDE DETAIL

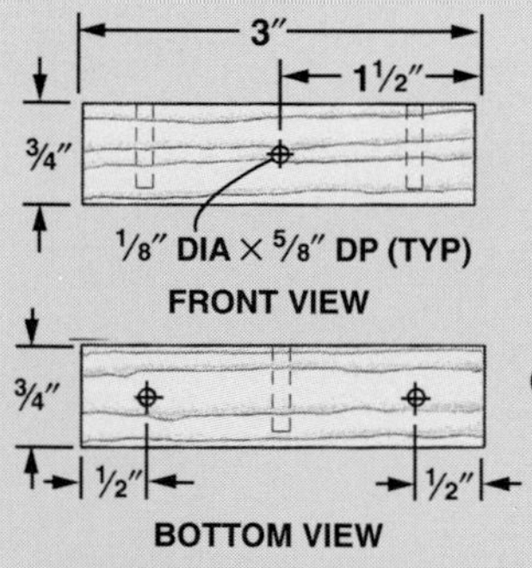
3"
1 1/2"
3/4"
1/8" DIA × 5/8" DP (TYP)
FRONT VIEW
3/4"
1/2"
1/2"
BOTTOM VIEW

FENCE STOP DETAIL

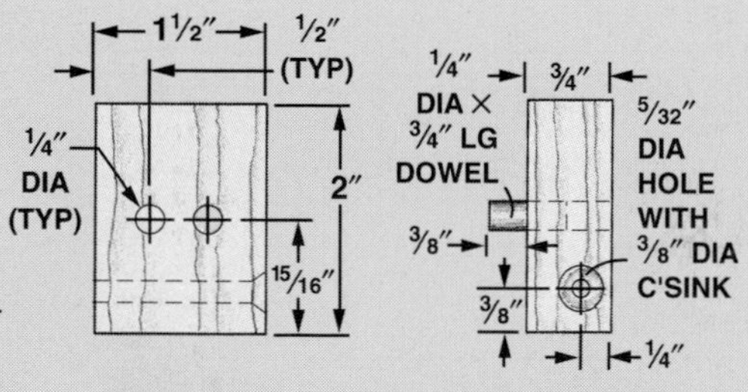
1 1/2"
1/2" (TYP)
1/4" DIA (TYP)
2"
15/16"
1/4" DIA × 3/4" LG DOWEL
3/4"
3/8"
5/32" DIA HOLE WITH 3/8" DIA C'SINK
3/8"
1/4"

FRONT VIEW

SIDE VIEW

STOP DETAIL

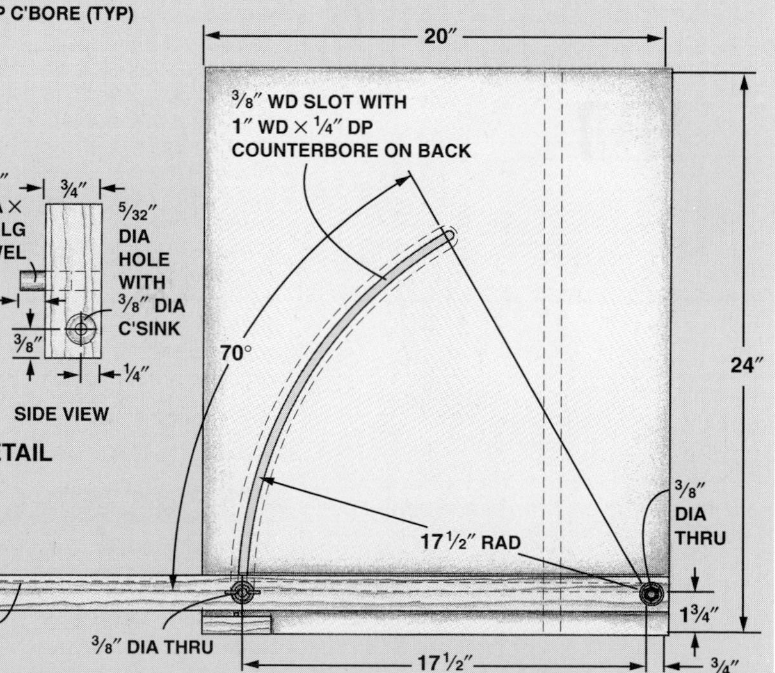
20"
3/8" WD SLOT WITH 1" WD × 1/4" DP COUNTERBORE ON BACK
70°
24"
17 1/2" RAD
3/8" DIA THRU
A
A
1 3/4"
3/4" WD GROOVES
3/8" DIA THRU
17 1/2"
3/4"

TOP VIEW

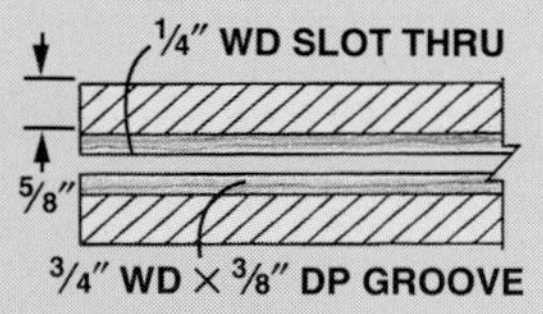
1/4" WD SLOT THRU
5/8"
3/4" WD × 3/8" DP GROOVE

SECTION A

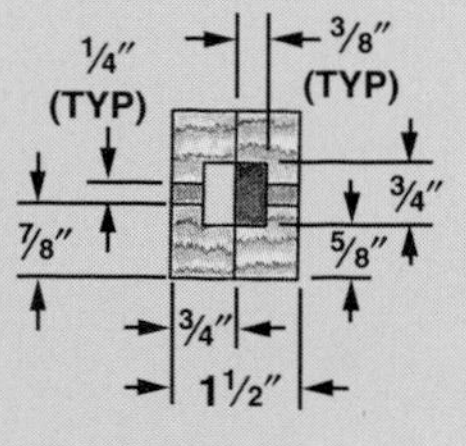
1/4" (TYP)
3/8" (TYP)
3/4"
7/8"
5/8"
3/4"
1 1/2"

END VIEW

FENCE DETAIL

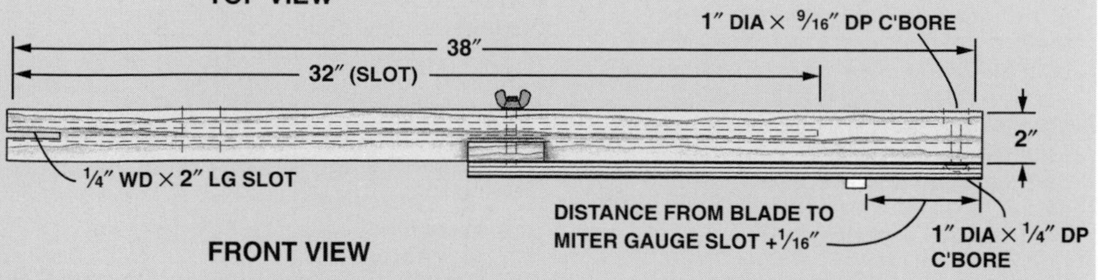
1" DIA × 9/16" DP C'BORE
38"
32" (SLOT)
2"
1/4" WD × 2" LG SLOT
DISTANCE FROM BLADE TO MITER GAUGE SLOT +1/16"
1" DIA × 1/4" DP C'BORE

FRONT VIEW

RIPPING

A *rip* cut is parallel to the wood grain. (This is also known as *cutting to width*.) You can rip with almost any power saw, but the two most common are the **radial arm saw**[1] and **table saw**[2]. Mount a rip or **combination blade**[3] on the tool arbor.

A table saw has a larger ripping capacity and is less trouble to use. To rip on a radial arm saw, you must break down the crosscut setup and reconfigure the machine for ripping. On a table saw, you simply put away the miter gauge and use the fence to guide the stock.

CUTTING A STRAIGHT EDGE IN CROOKED STOCK

Before you can make an accurate rip on either a table saw or radial arm saw, the board must have at least one straight surface to guide along the fence. In most cases, you can joint the edge straight. When you can't joint, attach a long, straight scrap to the board with double-faced carpet tape. One straight edge of the scrap should protrude past the crooked edge of the board. Use this protruding edge to guide the board along the fence as you cut a straight edge.

PROTIP

To check the fence position on a table saw, turn on the saw and guide the work along the fence until it just kisses the blade. Turn off the saw and measure from the board's edge to the tiny cut left by the blade.

RIPPING ON A RADIAL ARM SAW

*To rip a board on a radial arm saw, raise the track arm and rotate the cutterhead so the blade is parallel to the fence. Tilt the blade guard back so the back edge just clears the work. Adjust the width of the rip by moving the cutterhead along the arm until the blade is the desired distance from the fence. Lock the cutterhead in place, turn on the saw, and lower the arm until the blade bites into the table a fraction of an inch. Feed the wood against the rotation of the blade. **This is extremely important!** It's very dangerous to feed the wood in the wrong direction; the saw will throw the work like a missile.*

RIPPING ON A TABLE SAW

*To rip on a table saw, adjust the rip fence the desired distance from the blade, measuring from a tooth that's set **toward** the fence. Adjust the depth of cut so the blade clears the work, turn on the saw, and feed the work past the blade. If the work is extremely long, use a **saw stand** to support it on the outfeed side.*

RIPPING NARROW STOCK

When making narrow rips, you must be especially careful of kickback. If the wood is pinched between the blade and the fence, the saw will throw it back at you. To prevent this, feed the wood past the blade with a pusher. Don't stop pushing until the wood clears the blade completely.

NOTE: Guard is removed so you can see the cut.

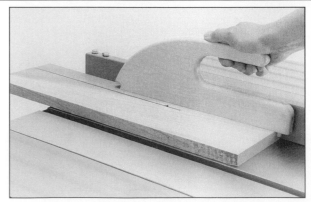

JIGS & FIXTURES

SAW STAND An adjustable saw stand is an essential tool in a small shop. It becomes the extra pair of hands you need to safely handle large or long workpieces.

This stand is "omnidirectional" — the transfer balls that support the work roll in any direction, allowing you to use the stand for crosscutting, ripping, even cutting curves and contours. The three-legged support always rests firmly on the floor. And the stand adjusts from 27¾ to 45¼ inches high, so it can be used with most stationary power tools.

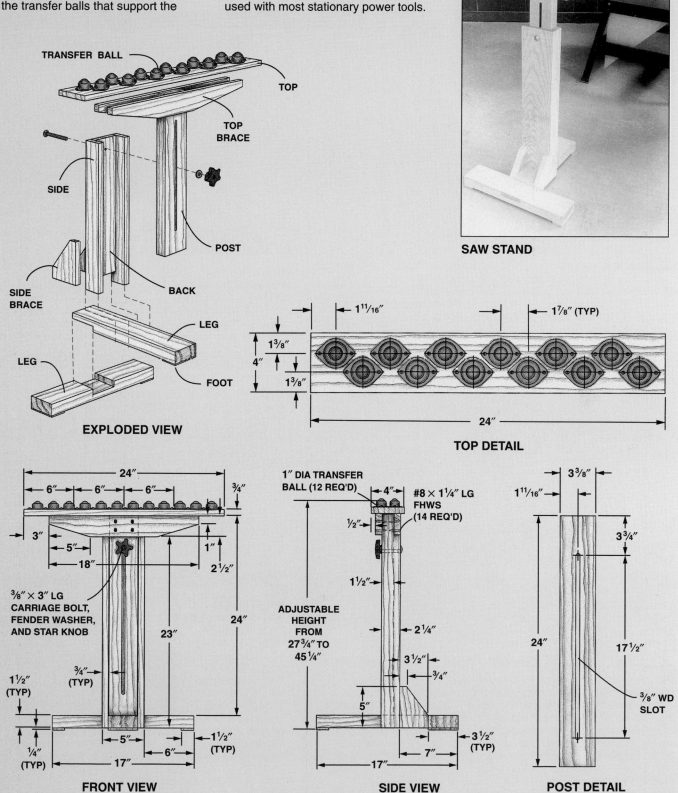

SAW STAND

TRANSFER BALL

TOP

TOP BRACE

SIDE

POST

SIDE BRACE

BACK

LEG

LEG

FOOT

EXPLODED VIEW

1¹¹⁄₁₆″

1⁷⁄₈″ (TYP)

1³⁄₈″

4″

1³⁄₈″

24″

TOP DETAIL

24″

6″   6″   6″

¾″

3″

5″

18″

1″

2½″

24″

³⁄₈″ × 3″ LG CARRIAGE BOLT, FENDER WASHER, AND STAR KNOB

23″

1½″ (TYP)

¾″ (TYP)

¼″ (TYP)

5″   6″   1½″ (TYP)

17″

FRONT VIEW

1″ DIA TRANSFER BALL (12 REQ'D)

4″

#8 × 1¼″ LG FHWS (14 REQ'D)

½″

1½″

2¼″

ADJUSTABLE HEIGHT FROM 27¾″ TO 45¼″

3½″

¾″

5″

3½″ (TYP)

7″

17″

SIDE VIEW

3³⁄₈″

1¹¹⁄₁₆″

3¾″

24″

17½″

³⁄₈″ WD SLOT

POST DETAIL

CUTTING SHEET MATERIALS

Cutting **plywood and particle-board**[1] is commonly referred to as a "ripping" operation because a fence guides the work. But otherwise, ripping solid wood and ripping sheet materials are two very different operations.

The most noticeable difference is the size of the stock. With the exception of a panel saw, there isn't a stationary tool made that will safely handle a 4 × 8-foot sheet as it comes from the manufacturer. Even if the machine has the necessary capacity, the work surfaces are

A **panel saw** is designed to cut full-sized sheets of plywood and particleboard safely and accurately. Unfortunately, these machines are expensive and require lots of shop space. Unless you work with sheet materials constantly, they may not be worth the money or the floor space.

USING EXTENSION TABLES

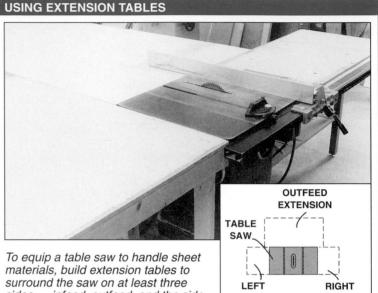

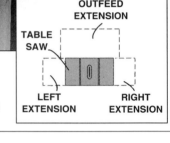

To equip a table saw to handle sheet materials, build extension tables to surround the saw on at least three sides — infeed, outfeed, and the side opposite the blade from the fence.

DOUBLE-CUTTING

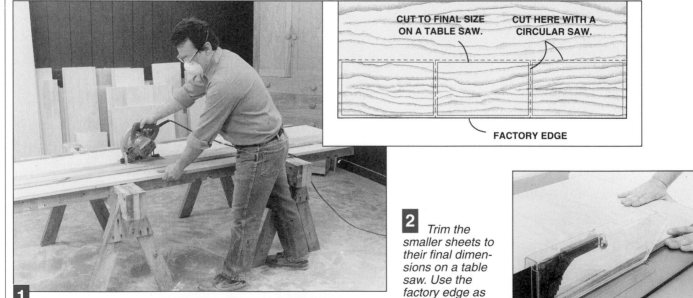

1 One of the easiest ways to saw sheet materials precisely is **double-cutting** — slice them into easily manageable sizes with a circular saw, then cut the pieces to their final dimensions on a table saw. To support an entire sheet as you cut it up, make a **cutting grid** of 2 x 4s and lay it across sawhorses. Lay out the cuts, making the parts slightly larger than needed. Also be sure that each part has at least one straight **factory edge.** Adjust the depth of cut so the circular saw will cut through the sheet but just bite a fraction of an inch into the cutting grid.

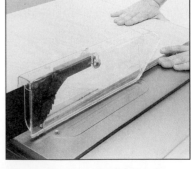

2 Trim the smaller sheets to their final dimensions on a table saw. Use the factory edge as the guiding edge for the first cut; thereafter, use either a factory edge or a table-sawed edge for the remaining cuts. You may want to make the first table saw cut slightly wide, then turn the stock and trim the factory edge. Although factory edges make good guides, they are often dented and chipped.

generally too small to support large sheets. This makes the stock difficult to handle. And the sheets often obstruct power switches, preventing you from turning off the saw should something go wrong.

There are three different strategies to overcome these shortcomings without investing in expensive panel-cutting equipment.

■ Surround your **table saw**[2] with extension tables to enlarge the work surface.

■ Cut the sheets to rough dimensions with a **circular saw**[3], then recut them to precise sizes on a table saw. This is called *double-cutting*.

■ Use a *circular saw guide* to cut sheets to precise sizes with a circular saw.

PRO *TIP*

To make a smooth finish cut with a circular saw, equip the tool with a high-quality combination or **plywood blade**[4]. You cannot make finish cuts with blades designed for construction work.

USING A CIRCULAR SAW GUIDE

To use a circular saw to cut sheet materials to their final size, guide the saw with a long straight-edge or a **circular saw guide.** *Clamp the guide to the work and press the shoe of the saw against it as you cut.*

JIGS & FIXTURES

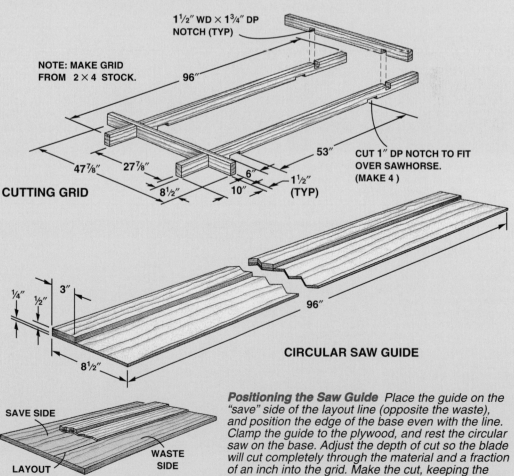

CUTTING GRID AND CIRCULAR SAW GUIDE To cut up sheet materials easily and accurately with a circular saw, you must *support* the work and *guide* the saw.

The **cutting grid** provides adequate support for a large sheet, preventing it from bowing in the middle no matter how you cut it up. Make the grid from 2 x 4s, then rest it on sawhorses when you need to use it.

The **circular saw guide** is an 8-foot-long straightedge that guides the circular saw. Cut the parts from plywood, making the base slightly wider than necessary. Glue the parts together, using the *factory edge* for the guiding surface of the straightedge. (Plywood edges are cut straight at the factory.) After the glue dries, cut the base to width using the same circular saw and blade you will use to cut sheet materials.

$1\frac{1}{2}$″ WD × $1\frac{3}{4}$″ DP NOTCH (TYP)

NOTE: MAKE GRID FROM 2 × 4 STOCK.

96″

53″

CUT 1″ DP NOTCH TO FIT OVER SAWHORSE. (MAKE 4)

$47\frac{7}{8}$″ $27\frac{7}{8}$″   6″ $1\frac{1}{2}$″ (TYP)

CUTTING GRID $8\frac{1}{2}$″   10″

$\frac{1}{4}$″ $\frac{1}{2}$″   3″

96″

$8\frac{1}{2}$″

CIRCULAR SAW GUIDE

SAVE SIDE

WASTE SIDE

LAYOUT LINE

Positioning the Saw Guide Place the guide on the "save" side of the layout line (opposite the waste), and position the edge of the base even with the line. Clamp the guide to the plywood, and rest the circular saw on the base. Adjust the depth of cut so the blade will cut completely through the material and a fraction of an inch into the grid. Make the cut, keeping the saw's sole firmly against the straightedge.

MITERS AND BEVELS

A *miter* cuts through the *width* of a board at an angle to an edge (and to the grain, typically). To make a miter, hold the work at an angle to the blade as you cut. A **combination blade**[1] works best.

A *bevel* cuts through the *thickness* of the board at an angle to a face. Instead of holding the work at an angle, tilt the blade or the table.

CUTTING A MITER

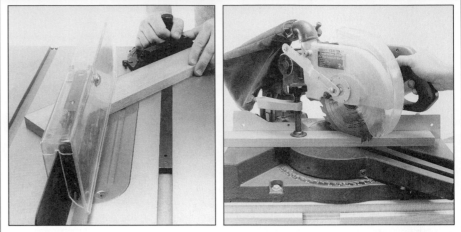

To cut a miter **on a table saw** (left), set the miter gauge at an angle. **On a miter saw** (right) or radial arm saw, swing the blade. Always angle the gauge or blade to keep your hands as far away from the sawteeth as possible.

CUTTING A BEVEL

To cut a bevel **on a table saw** (left), radial arm saw, or miter saw, adjust the blade angle. On other machines, such as **band saws** (right) and scroll saws, you must adjust the tilt of the worktable.

CHECKING A MITER OR BEVEL

To check a miter or bevel setup, make a small test frame. Cut all the parts exactly the same length, and fit them together. If any of the joints gap on the **inside** of the frame, **increase** the angle. If they gap on the **outside,** **reduce** the angle. Unless the gaps are extremely large, don't adjust the angle by more than ½ degree between each test.

CUTTING MATCHING MITERS AND BEVELS

When making a frame, you must cut matching right and left miters or bevels in the ends of the frame members. **To cut matching miters** (left), flip the boards end for end, keeping the same **edge** against the gauge or fence. **To cut matching bevels** (right), flip them end for end, keeping the same **face** against the worktable.

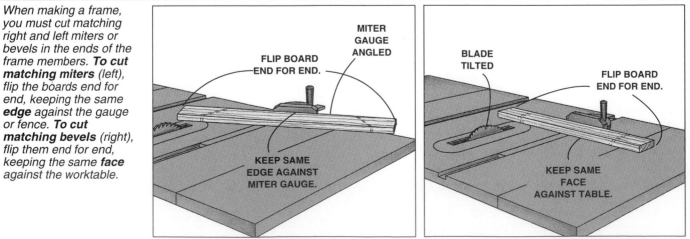

MITER GAUGE ANGLED

FLIP BOARD END FOR END.

KEEP SAME EDGE AGAINST MITER GAUGE.

BLADE TILTED

FLIP BOARD END FOR END.

KEEP SAME FACE AGAINST TABLE.

COMPOUND MITERS

In a *compound miter*, the sawed surfaces of the board are mitered *and* beveled. When joined by compound miters, the members of a frame "slope" rather than resting flat on an edge or a face. The angle of the slope and the number of sides in the frame determine the miter angle and bevel angle settings.

SEE *ALSO*:

[1]Circular Saw Blades   101

MAKING A COMPOUND MITER

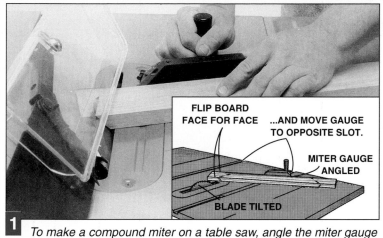

FLIP BOARD FACE FOR FACE   ...AND MOVE GAUGE TO OPPOSITE SLOT.

MITER GAUGE ANGLED

BLADE TILTED

1 To make a compound miter on a table saw, angle the miter gauge *and* tilt the blade. To make matching left and right compound miters, flip the board and move the miter gauge from one slot to the other. A **different edge** should rest against the miter gauge and a **different face** should rest against the table when cutting each end of the board.

2 To test a compound miter setup, make a small frame and tape the parts together. If the joints gap in the inside, decrease the blade tilt. If they gap on the outside, increase it. If the slope is greater than expected (as measured from horizontal), decrease the miter gauge angle. If it's less than expected, increase the angle.

COMPOUND MITER SETTINGS

To find the approximate miter and bevel settings for a compound miter, first decide how many sides the frame will have and what the *slope* of the sides will be. (The slope is measured from horizontal.) On the graph, find the arc for the number of sides and follow the arc to find the desired slope. Read the miter setting on the vertical scale and the bevel setting on the horizontal one. For example, if you wish to make a four-sided frame with a slope of 65 degrees, set the miter gauge to 71 degrees and tilt the blade to 41 degrees (approximately).

Or, use these formulas, substituting the number of sides for "N":

Miter angle =
$90° - [cos (\text{slope}) \times (360° \div 2N)]$

Bevel angle =
$sin (\text{slope}) \times (360° \div 2N)$

Owing to the complex geometry of a compound miter and the differences in sawing tools, these methods approximate the correct settings, but they may be a fraction of a degree off. For precise results, make test cuts and adjust the settings as needed.

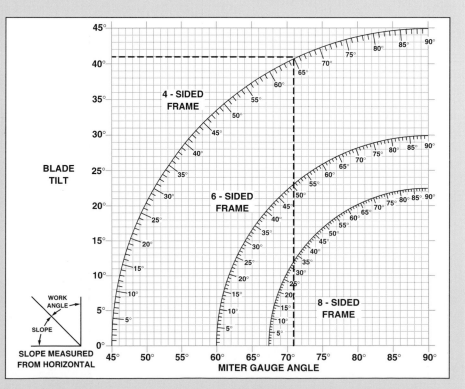

CUTTING EDGES AND ENDS

Now and then, you must cut the edges or ends of a board. To make a raised panel, for example, **bevel**[1] or chamfer all around the perimeter of the work. To make a **tenon**[2], cut several **rabbets**[3] in the end of the work. During these operations, the work must be balanced on an edge or end. Because typical fences and miter gauges are too short to support a wide board vertically, extend the guiding surface with a *tall extension* or a *tenoning jig*. When using a tall extension, you may also need a **featherboard**[4] to help control the work.

CUTTING A RAISED PANEL

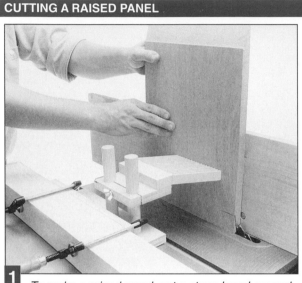

1 To make a raised panel, cut a steep bevel around the perimeter of a wide board. Attach a **tall extension** to the fence, and press the face of the stock against the extension as you work. Cut the ends first, sawing across the grain.

WARNING! You must remove the saw guard to perform this operation, so take extra care to keep your hands clear of the blade.

2 Then cut the edges, sawing with the grain. This keeps tear-out to a minimum — if the wood chips when cutting cross grain, the chipped surface will be removed when you cut with the grain.

NOTE: Raised panels often have a step between the *field* (the flat part of the panel) and the bevels — this emphasizes the profile. To make a step, position the tall extension so just the outside corners of the sawteeth break through the surface as you cut.

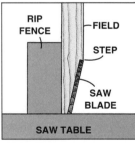

CUTTING A NOTCH

To create a notch in the edge or end of a board, attach a tall extension to a miter gauge. Clamp the board to the extension to prevent it from shifting as you cut.

CUTTING AN END GROOVE

To cut a groove in the end of a board, clamp it in a tenoning jig. Guide the jig along a rip fence as you cut.

JIGS & FIXTURES

TALL EXTENSION

TALL EXTENSION A *tall extension* extends a fence or a miter gauge vertically. The enlarged surface supports a wide board on its edge or end as you cut it.

The extension must be perfectly straight and flat to guide the work accurately. To ensure that it is, clamp the assembly face down on a flat surface (such as a saw table) as you glue the parts together. Attach the extension to the fence or miter gauge with bolts or screws and check that it's square to the worktable. If not, shim the extension with bits of paper or masking tape until it rests at the proper angle.

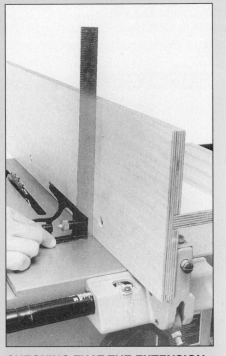

CHECKING THAT THE EXTENSION IS SQUARE TO THE TABLE

3/4" × 3/8" DP GROOVE

8"

RIP FENCE HEIGHT

30"

3"

3/4" (TYP)

TALL EXTENSION
EXPLODED VIEW

TENONING JIG

TENONING JIG A *tenoning jig* is a carriage that holds a board vertically as you cut an end. It's especially useful for holding narrow boards — too narrow to be supported safely or accurately by a tall extension.

When assembling the jig, don't attach the backstop permanently — just screw it in place. This lets you replace the backstop when it gets chewed up or when you need to hold the wood at a different angle. Assemble the rest of the jig with glue and screws. To use the jig, rest the board against the backstop and clamp it in place — this will keep the work from shifting. Guide the jig along a fence or a straightedge as you cut.

TENONING JIG WITH 45° BACKSTOP

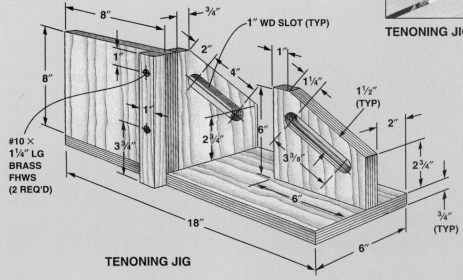

8"

3/4"

1" WD SLOT (TYP)

2"

1"

1"

4"

1 1/4"

1 1/2" (TYP)

8"

1"

1"

2"

6"

2 3/4"

3 3/8"

2 3/4"

3/4" (TYP)

#10 × 1 1/4" LG BRASS FHWS (2 REQ'D)

3 3/4"

6"

6"

18"

6"

TENONING JIG

CUTTING TAPERS

To taper a board, you must reduce its width or thickness gradually from one end of the board to the other. Mount the board in a *tapering jig* to hold its length at a slight angle to the blade, then rip the taper. A **rip or a combination blade**[1] works best.

CUTTING A TAPER

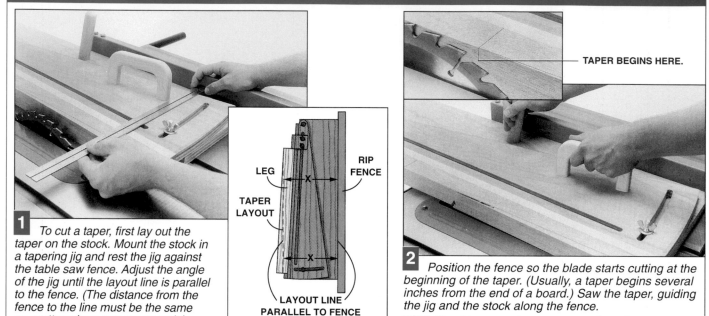

1 To cut a taper, first lay out the taper on the stock. Mount the stock in a tapering jig and rest the jig against the table saw fence. Adjust the angle of the jig until the layout line is parallel to the fence. (The distance from the fence to the line must be the same no matter where you measure it.)

LEG

RIP FENCE

TAPER LAYOUT

X

X

LAYOUT LINE PARALLEL TO FENCE

TAPER BEGINS HERE.

2 Position the fence so the blade starts cutting at the beginning of the taper. (Usually, a taper begins several inches from the end of a board.) Saw the taper, guiding the jig and the stock along the fence.

NOTE: Guard is removed so you can see the cut.

JIGS & FIXTURES

TAPERING JIG A *tapering jig* is a carriage that holds a board at an angle to the blade. The jig shown is adjustable, allowing you to cut at any angle between 0 and 15 degrees.

A clamp holds the stock by its ends to prevent it from shifting as you cut. Note that the jaws of the clamp have tiny "teeth" — cut-off nails that bite into the end grain for a better grip. To mount the work, place it in the jig between the clamp jaws. Tap the sliding jaw with a small mallet to drive the teeth into the ends, then tighten the wing nut that holds the sliding jaw in place.

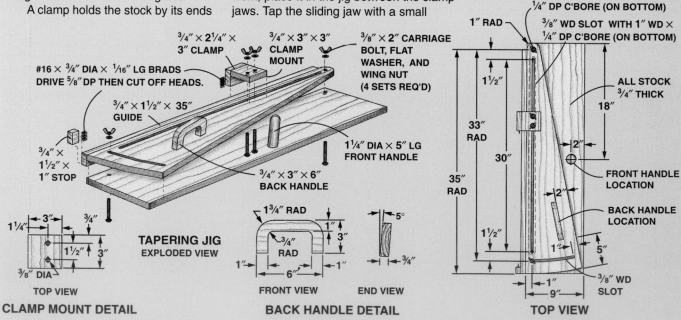

¾″ × 2¼″ × 3″ CLAMP

¾″ × 3″ × 3″ CLAMP MOUNT

⅜″ × 2″ CARRIAGE BOLT, FLAT WASHER, AND WING NUT (4 SETS REQ'D)

#16 × ¾″ DIA × 1/16″ LG BRADS DRIVE ⅝″ DP THEN CUT OFF HEADS.

¾″ × 1½″ × 35″ GUIDE

¾″ × 1½″ × 1″ STOP

1¼″ DIA × 5″ LG FRONT HANDLE

¾″ × 3″ × 6″ BACK HANDLE

TAPERING JIG EXPLODED VIEW

1¼″ 3″ ¾″

1½″ 3″

⅜″ DIA

TOP VIEW

CLAMP MOUNT DETAIL

1¾″ RAD

1″

3″

¾″ RAD

5°

1″ 6″ 1″

¾″

FRONT VIEW **END VIEW**

BACK HANDLE DETAIL

⅜″ DIA THRU WITH 1″ DIA × ¼″ DP C'BORE (ON BOTTOM)

1″ RAD

⅜″ WD SLOT WITH 1″ WD × ¼″ DP C'BORE (ON BOTTOM)

1½″

33″ RAD

35″ RAD

30″

1½″

ALL STOCK ¾″ THICK

18″

2″

FRONT HANDLE LOCATION

2″

BACK HANDLE LOCATION

1½″

5″

1″

9″

⅜″ WD SLOT

TOP VIEW

RESAWING

When you slice a board through its width, you are *resawing* the wood. Resawing makes two or more thin boards out of a thick one. It's a handy technique for reducing stock thickness, but it also has decorative applications. Resaw wood with **figured grain**[2] into thin sheets, then glue the sheets to ordinary lumber to create several matching panels. Or, resaw a board in half, open the halves like a book, and glue them edge to edge to create a "book-matched" panel.

Unless the stock is very narrow (less than 3 inches wide), resawing is best done on the **band saw**[3]. Use a **wide blade**[4] for this operation; it's less likely to bow or twist in the cut. Guide the stock past the blade along a **tall extension**[5] attached to the band saw fence. The extension

should be slightly shorter than the stock is wide so you can adjust the upper blade guide close to wood.

Position the fence parallel to the *blade lead*, not the blade body. Unlike circular saw blades, band saw blades rarely cut parallel to their bodies. The teeth usually cut more aggressively on one side than the other, and the blade "leads" a few degrees toward the aggressive side. To cut a straight line, the fence must guide the wood past the blade in the same direction that the blade leads.

When resawing long boards, you won't always be able to stand close enough to the saw to hold the board firmly against the tall extension. Instead, clamp a **featherboard**[6] to the saw table to hold the wood for you.

PRO*TIP*

Always make a test cut before resawing good stock. Resawing is one of those operations where you have to set your mouth differently each time you do it. Test cuts let you catch problems and adjust your technique without wasting wood.

FINDING THE BLADE LEAD

1 To find the blade lead, make a test cut in a long scrap. This scrap should be the same width and species as the stock you wish to resaw. Scribe a line down the center of the stock and begin cutting it on the band saw. Adjust the feed direction until the blade is cutting straight along the line, then stop cutting and turn off the machine. Don't let the scrap move!

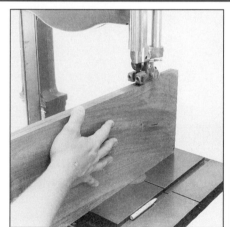

2 Use the scrap like a straightedge to mark a line on the table with a nonpermanent marker, such as a wax pencil. This is the **lead line** for that particular blade as it's presently mounted. When you change or readjust the blade, you must draw a new lead line.

RESAWING

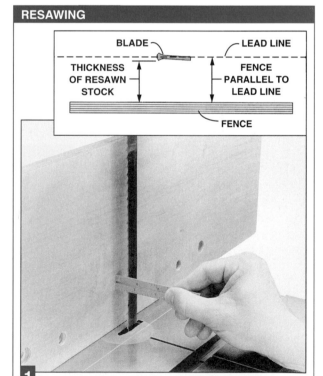

1 Attach the tall extension to the fence and position it so the distance from the blade to the fence is equal to the thickness you wish to cut. Adjust the fence parallel to the blade lead, measuring the distance from the fence to the lead line at both the infeed and outfeed edges of the table — the measurements should be the same. Check that the extension is parallel to the blade (vertically), measuring the distance from the blade to the extension near the top and bottom of the extension.

(continued)

RESAWING — CONTINUED

2 Joint at least one face and one edge of the board you will resaw. Scribe a line along the top edge of the stock to use as a reference.

3 Place the jointed edge on the saw table and the jointed face against the fence. Turn on the saw and feed the wood into the blade. Keep the feed rate slow and even. Watch the reference line as you cut — this will tell you if the blade drifts or wanders as it cuts.

4 If the blade bows backward from the pressure as you feed the wood, it will **cup** or **belly** in the cut, sawing a curved surface. Should this happen, try increasing the blade tension — you can safely tighten the blade one step above its indicated level on the tension scale, provided you do not collapse the tension spring. (For example, you can tighten a ¹/₂-inch-wide blade to a ³/₄-inch-wide level.) If cupping persists, use a wider blade or feed the wood more slowly.

5 A rough, uneven cut (often called **washboarding**) is caused by the blade slapping back and forth in the cut. This sometimes happens when you feed the wood at an uneven rate or use a narrow blade. Feed the wood steadily and slowly. If this doesn't eliminate the washboarding, use a wider blade.

JIGS & FIXTURES

FEATHERBOARD A *featherboard* (also called a finger-board) holds a workpiece flat against a fence or a table as you feed it past a blade. It also helps prevent kickback when used with a circular saw blade or other rotary cutter. Simply clamp it in place on the machine where you need it. Or, clamp it to the Self-Clamping Guide shown on page 219, then attach the guide to the tool. Position the featherboard to press against the wood *before* it gets to the blade. If it presses against the stock at the blade or behind it, the featherboard will pinch the sides of the kerf together. This, in turn, increases the drag on the blade and causes it to bog down.

Adjust the amount of pressure by flexing the feathers. The more they are flexed, the greater the pressure.

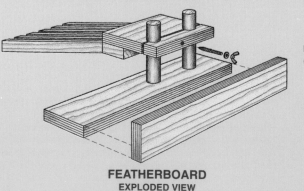

FEATHERBOARD
EXPLODED VIEW

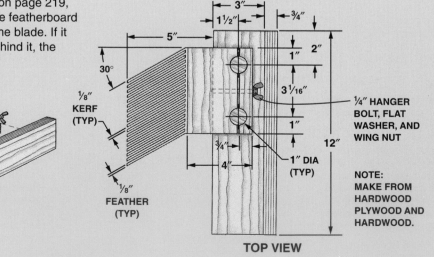

TOP VIEW

CUTTING CURVES AND CONTOURS

To cut a curved or contoured profile, use a tool with a narrow blade such as a **band saw**[1], **scroll saw**[2], or **coping saw**[3]. Because the blade is narrow, you can turn it in the kerf, changing the direction of the cut. Generally, the **narrower the blade**[4], the more you can turn it in the kerf and the smaller the radius that it will cut.

Create simple curves in a single step, following the line with the blade. Complex shapes require multiple cuts. Occasionally, you must *backtrack* (back the blade out of a cut) before you can make another cut. When this is the case, plan your cuts so you can backtrack the shortest possible distance.

CUTTING TIGHT CURVES

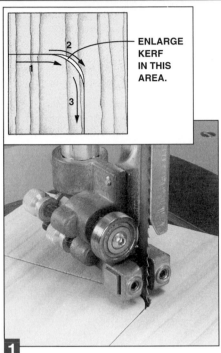

1 If the blade begins to drift in the cut, don't try to force it to follow the layout line. Instead, backtrack a short distance in the cut and shave the waste side of the kerf, making it wider. Then continue cutting the curve.

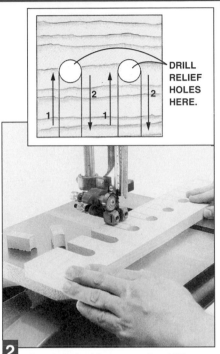

2 Cut tight inside curves by drilling relief holes in the waste. The radii of the holes should match the curves in the pattern.

PRO *TIP*

To cut a shape as accurately as possible, *shave* the layout line with the blade. Don't remove the line, just cut up to it. When you sand or file the cut edges, stop as soon as you remove the line.

SEE *ALSO:*

CUTTING A COMPLEX SHAPE

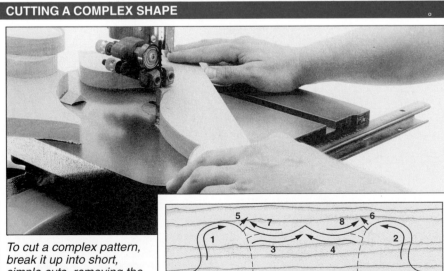

To cut a complex pattern, break it up into short, simple cuts, removing the waste in several steps.
Think through the operation and plan the sequence. For example, to cut the shape of this apron, you must make eight separate cuts, removing the stock in five pieces.

NIBBLING

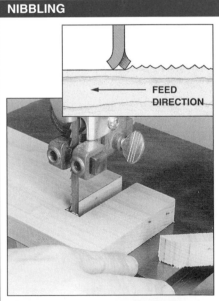

You can cut away the waste from any tight curve, inside or outside, by **nibbling** with the blade. Instead of feeding the wood parallel to the blade body, feed it perpendicular, using the teeth like a file. Feed very slowly and don't remove too much stock at once.

COMPOUND CUTTING

Create three-dimensional shapes with a **band saw**[1] or **scroll saw**[2] by cutting two patterns in the same workpiece and making each cut in a different plane. This is called *compound cutting*.

MAKING COMPOUND CUTS

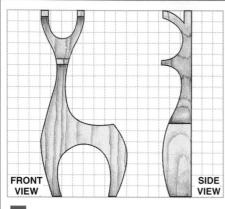

FRONT VIEW   SIDE VIEW

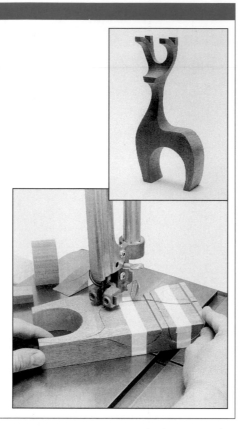

1 *Lay out patterns on two adjacent sides of a workpiece — in this case, the front and side profiles of a reindeer. Cut one pattern, saving the waste.*

2 *Tape the waste back to the block and cut the second pattern. (If necessary, mark the pattern over the tape so you can see it as you cut.) When you remove the tape and discard the waste, the workpiece will display **compound** contours. The intersecting contours form a three-dimensional shape.*

MORE *SOURCES*

BOOKS

Band Saw Handbook, by Mark Duginske, Sterling Publishing, 1989

Radial Arm Saw Techniques, by Roger W. Cliffe, Sterling Publishing, 1986

Table Saw Techniques, by Roger W. Cliffe, Sterling Publishing, 1985

Using the Band Saw, by Nick Engler, Rodale Press, 1992

Using the Table Saw, by Nick Engler, Rodale Press, 1992

VIDEOS

Mastering Your Band Saw with Mark Duginske, Taunton Books and Video

Mastering Your Table Saw with Kelly Mehler, Taunton Books and Video

TROUBLE *SHOOTING*

COMMON SAWING PROBLEMS

Problem	Possible Cause(s)	Solution(s)
Cut surfaces are rough or burned.	Saw is misaligned.	Align and adjust saw.
	Blade vibrates or chatters in cut.	Reduce feed rate; check blade condition.
	Blade is dull or loaded with pitch.	Clean blade. If no improvement, sharpen or replace.
	Blade has excessive run-out.	Replace or tune blade.
	Blade tension is too low (band saw only).	Increase blade tension.
	Work was not properly supported during cut.	Use support stands or extension tables.
Cut surfaces are not square to adjacent surfaces.	Saw is misaligned.	Align and adjust saw.
	Work is improperly prepared for cut.	Joint one face and one edge; use jointed surfaces to guide work.
	Machine setup is incorrect.	Readjust blade tilt, table tilt, or miter gauge angle.
Work is hard to feed or seems to stick.	Saw is misaligned.	Align and adjust saw.
	Table or fence requires wax.	Wax and buff guiding surfaces.
Work kicks back.	Saw is misaligned.	Align and adjust saw.
	Work is improperly prepared for cut.	Joint one face and one edge; use jointed surfaces to guide work.
	Machine setup is incorrect.	Setup mustn't trap cutoff between blade and fence.
	Work was improperly handled during cut.	Keep work firmly against table, fence, or miter gauge.
Saw bogs down in cut.	Feed rate is too fast.	Reduce feed rate.
	Kerf is closing behind blade.	Use splitter or wedges to prevent kerf from closing.

MAKING A CABRIOLE LEG

The most common application for compound cutting is making **cabriole legs**[3]. These graceful S-shaped legs come in many sizes and shapes, but they all have several features in common — *post, knee, ankle,* and *foot.*

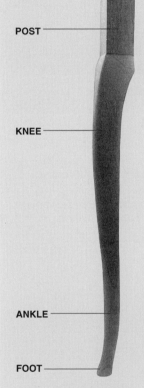

POST

KNEE

ANKLE

FOOT

CABRIOLE LEG

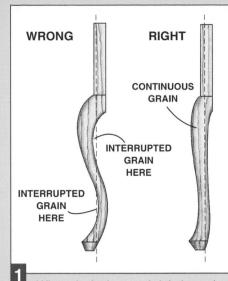

WRONG   RIGHT

CONTINUOUS GRAIN

INTERRUPTED GRAIN HERE

INTERRUPTED GRAIN HERE

1 When designing a cabriole leg, take care not to make the curves too pronounced. If the knee curves too far out or the ankle too far in, the wood grain will be broken into short segments and the leg will be weak. To keep the leg strong, lay out the curves so there is a narrow band of unbroken grain from the post to the foot.

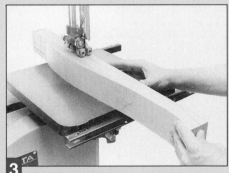

3 Cut the profile in one of the leg surfaces.

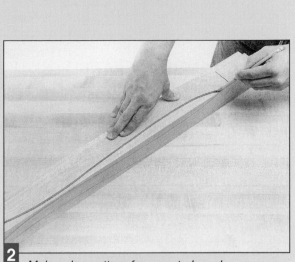

2 Make a leg pattern from posterboard or a scrap of thin plywood. Trace the pattern on two adjacent sides of the leg stock. Flip the pattern over when marking the second side so each layout is a **mirror image** of the other. Check that the parts of the patterns — post, knee, ankle, and foot — align horizontally.

4 Save the waste and tape it back to the stock. Turn the stock and cut the second profile. When you remove the waste, you'll have a cabriole leg with a square cross-section.

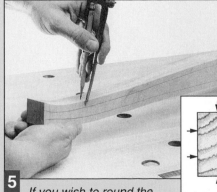

5 If you wish to round the cabriole leg, use a compass to mark guidelines parallel to the corners on the knee, ankle and foot.

MARK LEGS AT POINTS INDICATED.

SHAVE CORNERS DOWN TO MARKS.

BLEND SURFACES TOGETHER.

6 With planes, spokeshaves, and rasps, shave the leg down to these lines, giving it an **octagonal** cross section. Then blend the surfaces together, rounding them over.

19

Drilling and Boring

Almost every woodworking project has a few holes in it.

Look over a few woodworking projects and you're likely to find a wide variety of holes – holes to accommodate hardware, holes to create sockets and mortises, or holes just for decoration. Some holes require special cutters; others are drilled with general-purpose bits. Some are drilled square to a surface; others are bored at an angle. However, for all the different types of holes, all of them are made with remarkably similar techniques.

DRILLING KNOW-HOW

Most drilling operations are simple and straightforward. Select a bit, mount it in the drill, hold your mouth just so, and feed the bit into the wood. A few additional considerations, however, ensure good results.

SETTING UP

Before you begin, consider the *type* and *size* of hole you want to drill, as well as the *material* you're drilling. Those three factors will determine the proper **drilling equipment**[1] and techniques.

■ Select the **proper bit**[2] for the job. Brad-point drill bits serve well for most wood-drilling tasks, but other types of bits offer specific advantages. Spade bits and boring bits, for example, cut quickly. Forstner bits and multi-spur bits cut exceptionally smooth holes.

PRO*TIP*

When mounting a drill bit in a drill press or hand drill, tighten the jaws *twice,* in two different locations on the chuck's ring gear. This prevents the bit from slipping.

*While almost every woodworking project requires a few holes, some require more than others. This continuous-arm **Windsor Settee** is joined entirely with round mortises and tenons. Each hole or mortise is drilled at an angle.*

SPECS: 39″ high, 50″ long, 21″ deep
MATERIALS: Red oak, butternut, cherry
CRAFTSMAN: David Wright
          Berea, KY

■ Set the drill press or the hand drill to run at the proper speed. Different bit types, bit diameters, and work materials all require specific speeds. Generally, the larger the bit and the harder the materials, the slower the speed. Also, **drill end grain**[3] more slowly than long grain. If you're using a drill press, refer to the chart of "Drilling Speeds" below for recommended settings.

■ When using a drill press, check that the table is at the proper angle to the bit using a square or a protractor.

PREPARING THE WORK

To get the stock ready to drill:

■ Lay out the hole locations on the wood and create a small indentation at each mark to help start the drill bit.

■ Secure the work to prevent it from shifting when you drill.

MARKING HOLE LOCATIONS

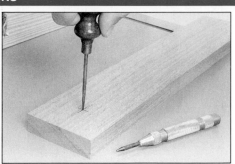

*To lay out the position of a hole, draw two intersecting lines. Where the lines cross, make a small indentation with an **awl** or a **prick punch.** The indentation prevents the bit from wandering off the mark before it begins to bite into the wood.*

SECURING THE WORK

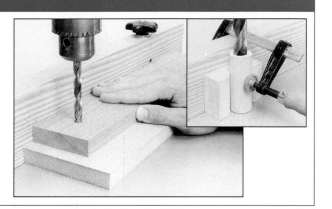

*Whenever possible, attach a fence to a drill press table and use it to help hold the work. It's easier to keep the work in one position when you can press it against the table **and** the fence. If necessary, clamp the work to the table or the fence to prevent it from moving or catching on the bit.*

PRO *TIP*

The wood shavings are the best indication that you are drilling at the proper speed. They should be a uniform size and must not clog the bit. If the shavings are powdery, the bit is cutting too slowly. If they become impacted around the bit, it may be cutting too fast.

SEE *ALSO:*

[1] Drill Presses   106
[1] Hand Drills and Drivers 118
[2] Drill Bits   107
[3] Drilling End Grain   214

DRILLING SPEEDS

These are recommended drilling speeds (in revolutions per minute) for drill presses with *hand-operated* feed mechanisms. Use them as a starting point. Drill several test holes, then adjust the speed up or down to get the results you want.

MATERIAL	DIAMETER	TWIST	BRAD-POINT	SPADE	BORING	FORSTNER	MULTI-SPUR
Softwoods	1/8″	2,400	1,800				
	1/4″	1,800	800	1,200		1,200	
	1/2″	800	800	800	1,200	800	800
	1″		400	800	800	400	800
	1 1/2″			400	400	400	400
	2″					400	400
Hardwoods	1/8″	1,200	1,800				
and Sheet	1/4″	800	800	800		800	
Materials	1/2″	800	800	800	800	800	800
	1″		400	400	400	400	400
	1 1/2″			400	400	400	400
	2″					400	400

GOOD TECHNIQUE

When you're ready to drill:

■ Advance the bit very slowly at first. Make sure the entire tip of the bit is cutting the wood, then gradually increase the feed pressure. If you feed too quickly before the bit has a chance to start the hole, the bit may wander off the mark.

■ If using a **bit with a lead point**[1], align the point of the bit with the indentation that marks the hole location *before* turning on the machine. This helps ensure that the hole is accurately positioned.

■ The bit may drift off center in hard materials or materials of uneven density. To prevent this, drill a small pilot hole, then gradually enlarge the hole to the necessary size with larger bits.

■ Clear away the sawdust as you work. Accumulated sawdust may interfere with the accuracy of drill press operations if it prevents the wood from resting flat against the work table or the fence.

MAKING LARGE HOLES

To drill a large hole (over 1½ inches in diameter), the best tool depends on the results you want. A multi-spur bit bores a smooth hole, while a *hole saw* cuts quickly and a *fly cutter* makes odd-sized holes.

DRILLING THROUGH

1 When drilling a hole completely through a board, place a scrap under the work. Drill through the work and partway into the scrap. This protects the workbench or the drill press table. It also supports the wood fibers where the bit exits the stock, preventing them from tearing out. This, in turn, helps create a clean exit hole.

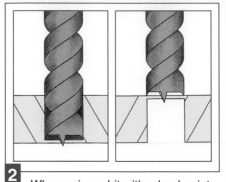

2 When using a bit with a lead point, feed the bit until just the point exits the wood (left). Turn the wood over and use the pinhole left by the lead point to reposition the bit and finish the hole (right). This completely eliminates tear-out because there is no exit hole — just two clean entry holes.

DRILLING STOPPED HOLES

To drill a hole to a specific depth on a drill press, extend the quill until the bit touches the workpiece — this is the "0" position. Adjust the depth stop to the desired measurement and lock it down. When using a hand drill, attach a **stop collar** to the drill bit. The collar halts the bit at the desired depth.

STOP COLLAR

USING A DRILL GUIDE

A **drill guide** helps you maintain an accurate angle when using a portable drill. These accessories are especially handy when you must drill precise holes in a workpiece that's too large to fit on a drill press.

MAKING LARGE HOLES

Use a **hole saw** (right) to make large holes quickly. These saws come in common fractional sizes (up to 6 inches in diameter) and mount in either a portable drill or a drill press.

If you need odd-sized holes, use a **fly cutter** (left). Because this tool is not balanced, it must be used in a drill press. It's notoriously grabby — it wants to catch the stock. To prevent this, clamp the wood to the worktable and run the press at a maximum speed of 500 rpm.

DRILLING DEEP HOLES

To drill a deep hole, use a long *extended* bit (also called an *installer* bit). You can also purchase *bit extensions* for spade bits. If you don't have an extended bit or bit extension, drill two matching holes that meet in the center of the stock.

MATCHING HOLES

On some assemblies you must match the holes in two or more parts. There are several methods:

■ Use a **fence**[2] and a stop to locate the parts on a drill press.

■ *Pad drill* the parts, making all the holes in one operation.

■ Locate the matching holes with a **doweling jig or dowel centers**[3].

■ Make a **template**[4] to locate the holes in precisely the same positions on each part.

CONNECTING HOLES

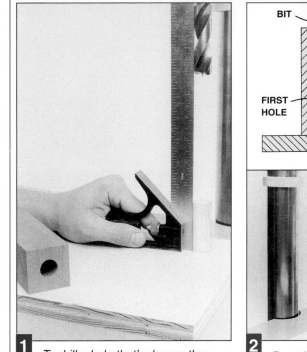

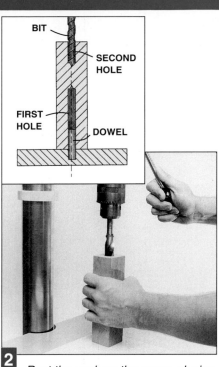

1 To drill a hole that's deeper than the bit is long, connect two holes in the middle of the stock. Drill the first hole in the work, then drill a hole the same diameter in a scrap. Insert a dowel in the scrap and center it under the bit.

2 Rest the work on the scrap, placing the first hole over the dowel and directly under the bit. When you drill the second hole, it will connect with the first.

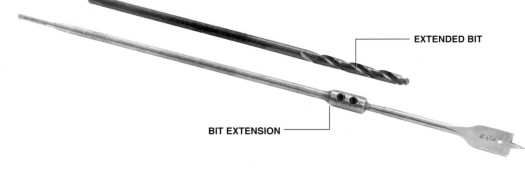

EXTENDED BIT

BIT EXTENSION

USING A STOP

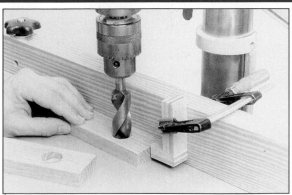

To drill matching holes in several identical parts, attach a fence and a stop to the drill press table. Position the stop to automatically locate the parts under the bit.

PAD DRILLING

If you must make matching through holes and the parts are thin enough, **pad drill** them. Stack the parts face to face and tape the stack together. Lay out the hole locations on the top part in the stack, then drill through all the parts at once.

DRILLING HOLES FOR HARDWARE

Pilot holes for **screws and nails**[1] guide the fasteners as you drive them and prevent the stock from splitting. *Shank holes* hold bolts and the unthreaded portions of screws. Often, the heads of these fasteners rest below the surface of the wood in *counterbores* and *countersinks*. Several special-purpose cutters are designed to drill pilot holes, shank holes, countersinks, and counterbores in one step.

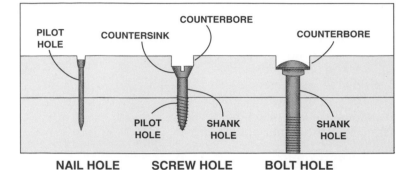

NAIL HOLE   SCREW HOLE   BOLT HOLE

PRO *TIP*

Drill pilot holes for small finish nails by *spinning* a nail into the wood. Cut the head off a nail and mount  the shank in a hand drill. Drive the nail into the wood like a drill bit. Pilot holes prevent the stock from splitting and prevent nails from bending.

USING A SCREW DRILL

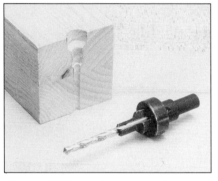

Screw drills *create a counterbore, countersink, shank hole, and pilot hole in one step. Use a stop collar to adjust the depth of the counterbore.*

USING SHELL COUNTERBORES AND COUNTERSINKS

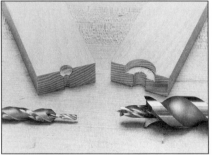

A **shell counterbore** *(left) or a* **shell countersink** *(right) slips over an ordinary drill bit to produce recesses for screw heads and bolt heads.*

COVERING SCREW HEADS

As useful as they may be, screws are unsightly. The heads interrupt the wood grain like a bad case of acne, detracting from the appearance of a project. Consequently, craftsmen often hide screw heads in counterbores and cover them with wooden plugs.

1 *When drilling screw holes, make the counterbores about 1/8 to 1/4 inch deep. After driving the screws into the wood, the heads should be well below the surface.*

1/8"–1/4"

2 *With a drill press and a* **plug cutter,** *cut plugs in a scrap of wood. Then cut them free from the scrap on a band saw. The scrap should be the same species and have the same grain pattern as the wood into which you have driven the screws.*

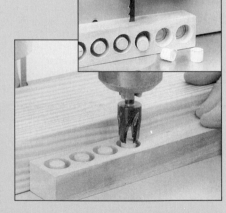

3 *Select the plug that covers each screw head to match the surrounding wood as well as possible. Dip the plug in glue and position it so the grain in the plug is parallel to the surrounding wood grain. Press the plug into the counterbore or tap it in with a small mallet.*

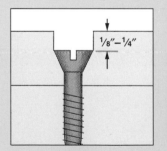

4 *Let the glue dry, then cut the plug flush with the wood surface. Sand the plug and the wood, removing any traces of glue. If you have closely matched the wood species, color, grain pattern, and grain direction, the plug should be almost invisible.*

MAKING EQUALLY SPACED HOLES

Holes for **shelving supports**[2] and similar hardware must be spaced equally. You can drill equally spaced holes with a **drilling template**[3]. Or, use a *stop* and a *pin* to position the work for each hole. This method lets you adjust the spacing between the holes.

MAKING ANGLED HOLES

To make **angled holes**[4] with a portable drill, start the hole approximately square to the surface, then angle the drill as soon as the bit is started. If you need to maintain a precise angle, use a **drill guide**[5].

To make angled holes on a drill press, tilt the table. Check the angle with a protractor, then fasten a fence on the *downhill* side of the bit – this will cradle the stock and keep it from slipping.

DRILLING EQUALLY SPACED HOLES

Clamp a stop to the fence about 1/16 inch above the work. Adjust its position so the distance from the stop to the bit equals the desired spacing. Drill a hole in the stock and insert a pin in it. Slide the work under the stop until the pin butts against it. Drill a second hole, move the pin to the new hole, and repeat.

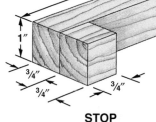

3″
1″
3/4″
3/4″
3/4″

STOP

DRILLING ANGLED HOLES

*When drilling at an angle on a drill press, feed the bit very slowly as you start the hole. **This is very important!** Because the stock is angled, the spurs or lips engage the wood before the lead point. If you feed too quickly at the beginning, the bit will walk toward the down side of the table. The hole won't be positioned properly, nor will it be at the proper angle. Wait until the lead point is engaged before you feed at the normal rate.*

MAKING SCREW POCKETS

One of the most common applications for angled holes is making *screw pockets* — angled counterbores and shank holes for screws that fasten the edge of one board to the face of another.

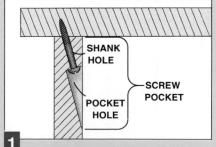

SHANK HOLE
SCREW POCKET
POCKET HOLE

1 *Screw pockets are typically used to attached aprons to table tops. The screw passes through an angled **shank hole** in the apron and into the table top. The head rests in a **counterbore**. Both holes are drilled at the same angle (usually 15 degrees), and the shank hole exits the edge of the apron halfway between the faces.*

2 *To drill a screw pocket, tilt the drill press table, attach a fence on the downhill side of the bit, and place a backup scrap on the table. The distance from the fence to where the lead point of the bit touches the scrap should equal one-half the thickness of the stock. Rest the work edge-down on the scrap and clamp it to the fence. Drill the counterbore first, stopping about 3/8 inch from the scrap.*

3 *Without changing the position of the work, switch bits and drill the shank hole through the center of the counterbore.*

NOTE: Make the shank hole slightly larger in diameter than the screw. This lets the table top expand and contract.

DRILLING END GRAIN

Drilling parallel to the **wood grain**[1] is more work than drilling across it. The bit must sever the wood fibers instead of shave them, which requires more power and creates more friction. To compensate, use a slow speed and a moderate feed rate.

HORIZONTAL BORING

When the work is so long that it won't fit on a drill press, use a portable drill to bore the end grain with the work held horizontally. The jig shown holds and positions both the work and the drill.

DRILLING PARALLEL TO THE GRAIN

How you drill end grain depends on the size of the board. If it's small enough, simply rest it on end on the drill press table and clamp it to the fence. For larger boards, tilt the table so the surface is vertical and clamp the board to it. Swing the table right or left to position the work under the bit.

DRILLING ROUND STOCK

When drilling holes in round stock, cradle the stock to prevent it from rolling around as you work. If you're working on a drill press, make a cradle by tilting the **table and the fence**[2]. Or, make a **V-jig**[3] to hold the round stock. When working with a portable drill, use a **drill guide**[4].

MORE *SOURCES*

The Drill Press Book, by R. J. DeCristoforo, TAB Books, 1991

Using the Drill Press, by Nick Engler, Rodale Press, 1995

DRILLING ROUND STOCK

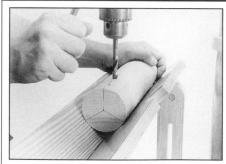

*To drill round stock **on a drill press,** tilt the table to 45 degrees. Attach a fence to the downhill side of the table to form a V-shaped cradle. Position the fence so the lead point of the bit is directly over the point of the V, where the fence meets the table. This ensures that the bit will pass through the center of the round stock.*

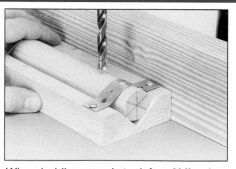

*When holding round stock **in a V-jig,** the same consideration applies: Position the jig so the point of the V is directly under the tip of the bit. To clamp the stock in the V-jig, make strap hold-downs from short lengths of hanger strap (a metal banding sold in the plumbing section of most hardware stores).*

*To drill precise holes in round stock **with a portable drill,** cradle the stock in a drill guide. Most guides incorporate V-shaped notches just for this purpose.*

JIGS & FIXTURES

HORIZONTAL BORING JIG This simple jig supports long workpieces while you drill the end grain. It also provides a flat surface to support a drill guide so you can drill holes at precise angles.

To use the jig, secure it to your workbench. Mark the location of the hole on the end of the board, and clamp the board to the horizontal support so the mark shows through the slot in the vertical support. Use the fence to hold the board at the proper angle. Attach your portable drill to a **drill guide**[4]. Place the base of the guide against the vertical support. Position the bit over the mark and drill the hole.

NOTE: MAKE FROM ¾"-THICK HARDWOOD PLYWOOD WITH HARDWOOD FENCE.

Position the stock so the mark shows through the slot.

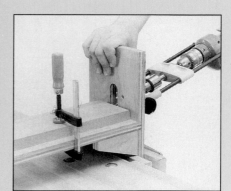

Use a drill guide to maintain a precise angle.

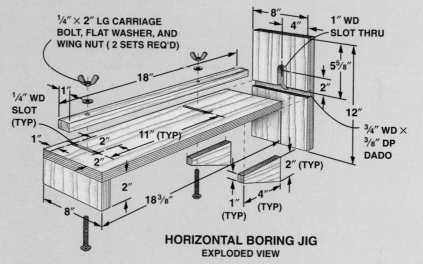

¼" × 2" LG CARRIAGE BOLT, FLAT WASHER, AND WING NUT (2 SETS REQ'D)

¼" WD SLOT (TYP)

18"

1"

1"

2"

11" (TYP)

2"

2"

8"

18⅜"

2"

1" (TYP)

4" (TYP)

2" (TYP)

8"

4"

1" WD SLOT THRU

5⅝"

2"

12"

¾" WD × ⅜" DP DADO

HORIZONTAL BORING JIG
EXPLODED VIEW

TROUBLE SHOOTING

COMMON DRILLING PROBLEMS

Problem	Possible Cause(s)	Solution(s)
Drill bit wanders; hole is not centered on mark.	Lips catch on stock, pull bit sideways.	Mark center with a punch; use a bit with a lead point.
	Feed rate is too fast at start of hole.	Feed bit very slowly until tip is cutting.
	Bit drifts in hole.	Drill small pilot hole, then enlarge to full size.
Bit overheats and burns wood.	Drill speed is too fast.	Reduce drill speed.
	Waste was not cleared from hole.	Reduce feed rate; retract drill often to clear wood chips.
	Drill bit is dull.	Clean and sharpen drill bit.
Sides of hole are rough or torn.	Drill speed is too slow or feed too fast.	Increase drill speed or decrease feed rate.
	Wrong type of bit for material	Drill test holes to determine best bit for material.
	Drill bit is dull.	Clean and sharpen drill bit.
Work chips or tears when bit exits stock.	Work was not backed up.	Back up work with scrap of wood.
	Material is brittle or fragile.	Drill holes from both sides to meet in center.
Bit catches on work, pulls it from your hands.	Feed rate is too fast.	Reduce feed rate.
	Work is not properly secured on drill press table.	Brace work against fence or clamp it to table.
Bit slips in chuck.	Sawdust is in chuck; bit shaft is galled.	Clean chuck; remove burrs from bit with emery cloth.
	Bit is not properly secured.	Tighten chuck at two locations on ring gear.

Routing

The router is a uniquely versatile tool. Use it hand-held or stationary, making joinery cuts as well as decorative shapes.

Perhaps the easiest and most accurate way to create shapes in wood is to rout them. This applies not only to decorative shapes such as coves and beads but also to more utilitarian shapes needed to assemble wooden parts. **Rabbets, dadoes, slots, and mortises**[1] can all be made with a router.

ROUTING KNOW-HOW

The **router**[2] gives you a unique choice: Use it as a stationary tool or hand-held. Pick whichever seems easier — generally, the easier an operation is to perform, the safer it will be. If the workpiece is small enough to handle comfortably, mount the router in a table and feed the work past the bit. If it's large and heavy, take advantage of the router's portability and pass the tool over the work.

SETTING UP

However you use the router, these general considerations apply:

■ If you have a variable-speed router, set it to the lowest speed that gives you a smooth cut. This prevents the bit from overheating and burning the wood.

■ When changing **bits**[3], blow the collet clean and check that the bit's shank is smooth. A little sawdust or a tiny burr will prevent the collet from gripping the shank securely, and the bit will creep out of the collet as you work.

*In many ways, the router has become the woodworker's Swiss Army knife, a multipurpose tool for joinery, shaping, pattern-cutting, and many other special operations. Both the joinery and the decorative molding on this **Keeping Box** were created with a router.*

SPECS:	12" high, 21" wide, 11" deep
MATERIALS:	Blistered poplar
CRAFTSMAN:	David T. Smith Morrow, OH

■ When you insert the bit in the collet, don't let the flutes touch it. If this happens, the collet may close around the *transition fillet*, where the shank flares out. This will also cause the bit to creep.

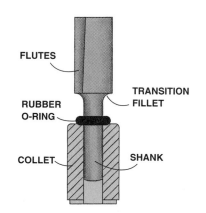

MOUNTING A BIT

As much as possible, rout with the grain. When you must rout across the grain, back up the wood where the bit will exit. This prevents the bit from tearing and chipping the wood.

■ How much of the shank should you insert in the collet? For the collet to safely grip ¼-inch shanks, insert at least ¾ inch of the length; for ½ inch shanks, 1 inch.

■ Make a test cut to check the setup. If an operation requires several routing setups, make enough test pieces at each stage to carry you through the entire procedure.

GOOD TECHNIQUE
As you rout:

■ Always wear eye *and* hearing protection. Not only do routers throw wood chips, they generate high-frequency noise, which damages your ears slightly with each exposure. After many routing sessions with no protection, you will lose part of your hearing.

■ Make shallow cuts, no more than ¼ inch deep.

■ Whenever possible, cut *against* the rotation of the bit. Use the rotation of the bit to hold the router

against the straightedge or to hold the work against the fence.

■ Occasionally you must *back-rout*, cutting with the bit rotation. It's much more difficult to control the work when back-routing. Take shallow cuts and feed slowly. Keep the router and the work steady; don't let the bit chatter.

■ When routing cross grain, back up the work with a scrap to prevent tear-out.

■ Keep the router or the work moving as you cut.

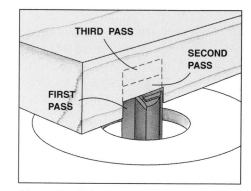

Never "hog" the cut when using a router; the tool is designed to remove only small amounts of stock at a time. For deep cuts, make several passes, cutting just ⅛ to ¼ inch deeper with each pass. (Generally, the denser the wood, the less you should remove on any one pass.)

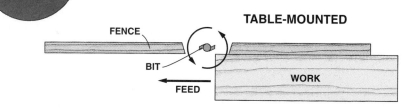

*When using the router as a hand-held tool, the bit rotates **clockwise** as you look at the router from the top. When the router is mounted in a table, the bit rotates **counterclockwise**. Plan the routing operation so you feed the router or the wood **against** the rotation of the bit as much as possible. It's much harder to control the router and the work when cutting with the rotation.*

If you feed the router bit too quickly, it will leave scallops or **mill marks,** as shown on the right. If you feed it too slowly, the bit will overheat and scorch the wood, as shown on the left. Keep the router or the work moving at a moderate pace.

GUIDING THE ROUTER

It's rarely a good idea to rout free-hand (with the router unguided). The router will pull itself all over the workpiece with unpredictable results. For safety and accuracy, guide the router.

USE A PILOTED BIT

A piloted bit has a ball bearing or bushing to guide the cut. These follow the surface of the work, keeping the width of the cut consistent. Typically, pilots are attached at the end of the bit, but some are positioned between the shank and flutes. (These are called *overbearings*.) When using a piloted bit, remember the pilot is meant to follow a surface. When you set the depth of cut, make sure the pilot will contact the wood.

USE A GUIDE COLLAR

A guide collar attaches to the base of the router. The collar follows a surface like a pilot bearing, and the bit protrudes through it. Guide collars aren't meant to follow the edge of a workpiece, however. They are designed to follow **templates**[1]. When using a guide collar, make sure the bit is centered in the collar and the flutes do not rub. That could ruin both the bit and the collar.

USE AN EDGE GUIDE

Edge guides are small fences that attach to the base of a router. They are designed to follow straight surfaces, although some come with a round guide to follow curves. When using an edge guide, adjust the horizontal distance between the bit and the guide to set the position of the cut.

*Because pilot bearings and guide collars are round, they cannot follow sharp **inside** corners. Any corners in the work or the template will be rounded off, as shown. To create a crisp corner, you must square the rounded shape with chisels or files.*

OVERBEARING

PILOT BEARING

*On a **piloted bit,** a bearing above or below the flutes follows the work surface, guiding the cut. Adjust the width of cut by changing the bearing. The larger the diameter of the bearing, the more it limits the bite of the flutes.*

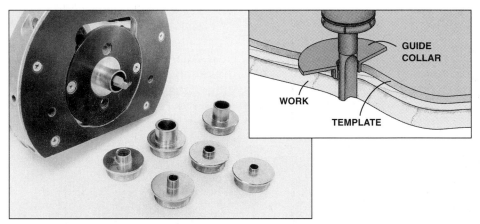

GUIDE COLLAR

WORK

TEMPLATE

***Guide collars** are designed to follow templates. As the collar traces the shape of the template, the bit cuts a similar shape in the work. Because the bit and the collar are not the same diameter, the routed shape will be a slightly different size than the template. When designing a template, you must adjust for this discrepancy.*

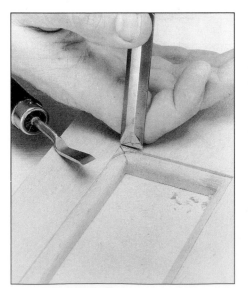

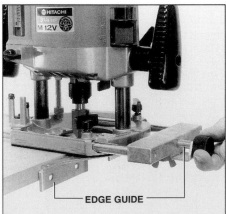

EDGE GUIDE

*An **edge guide** follows a straight edge. It can be positioned so the bit cuts the interior of the board, routing a slot or groove parallel to the edge.*

USE A STRAIGHTEDGE

Make a **straightedge**[1] by jointing the edge of a board straight. Clamp the straightedge to the work and guide the router along it. If the router sole has a flat side, keep this flat against the fence. If it's circular, paint a spot on the edge of the sole. Keep the spot turned toward you and away from the straightedge as you rout. The bit is never perfectly centered in the sole. If you allow the router to turn as you follow the straightedge, the cut will not be perfectly straight.

SEE ALSO:
[1]Fences and Guides   149

USING A STRAIGHTEDGE

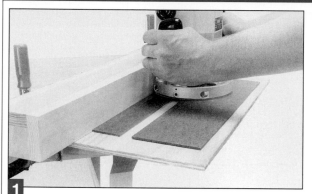

1 When guiding the router with a straightedge, make a gauge to help position the straightedge. Stick a thin piece of hardboard to a scrap with double-faced carpet tape. Rest the straightedge against one edge of the hardboard. Mount the bit you plan to use in the router. Rout through the hardboard, guiding the router along the straightedge. Save the strip of hardboard between the straightedge and the bit — this is your gauge.

2 Lay out the cut you want to make on the work. Position the straightedge on the work parallel to the edge of the cut and offset the width of the gauge.

3 Secure the straightedge to the work. Make the cut, keeping the router firmly against the straightedge as you feed it. TIP: Feed the router left to right as you face the straightedge. The rotation of the bit will help keep the router against the guiding surface.

JIGS & FIXTURES

SELF-CLAMPING GUIDE Most straightedges must be clamped in place, but this guide incorporates its own clamp. It's a wooden box that houses a pipe clamp. (The clamp shown is a Jorgenson pipe clamp, but other brands will work with modification.) Use the straight sides of the box to guide the router.

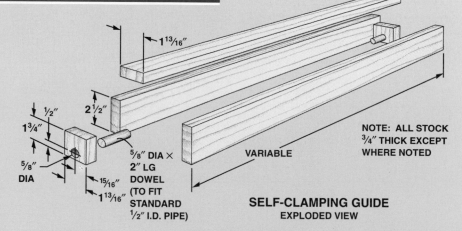

1¹³⁄₁₆″
½″
2½″
1¾″
⁵⁄₈″ DIA
¹⁵⁄₁₆″
1¹³⁄₁₆″
⁵⁄₈″ DIA × 2″ LG DOWEL (TO FIT STANDARD ½″ I.D. PIPE)
VARIABLE

NOTE: ALL STOCK ¾″ THICK EXCEPT WHERE NOTED

SELF-CLAMPING GUIDE
EXPLODED VIEW

PLUNGE ROUTING

Some operations require that you rout the interior of a board without cutting in from the edge. For example, when you rout a **mortise**[1], first make a small hole in the interior of the workpiece, then enlarge it.

To make this starter hole, you must lower or *plunge* the bit into the wood. You don't need a **plunge router**[2] to do this; craftsmen had been plunging with standard routers long before the tool was invented. But a plunge router does make this operation easier and more precise.

PLUNGE ROUTING

1 To make an interior cut with a standard router, set the router to the proper depth of cut. Rest the edge of the router sole on the wood, and brace it against a straightedge. Then rock the router into the work. After making a starter hole, guide the router along the straightedge.

2 A *plunge router* simplifies this operation. Adjust the depth stop to halt the bit at the proper depth of cut. Hold the router base against the straightedge and position the bit over the work. Turn on the router, release the height clamp, and push straight down until the router hits the stop. Lock the height clamp and guide the router along the straightedge.

JIGS & FIXTURES

ROUTER JACK Plunge routing is typically a simple operation — put both hands on the handles and push the bit into the wood. However, it sometimes requires more finesse. On occasion, the bit must be plunged slowly and precisely. Or, the router may be held in a position where you can't easily push on the handles. When this is the case, use a *router jack* to raise and lower the bit. This simple crank fits over the threaded post on a plunge router, enabling you to raise or lower the bit easily and accurately with one hand from almost any position.

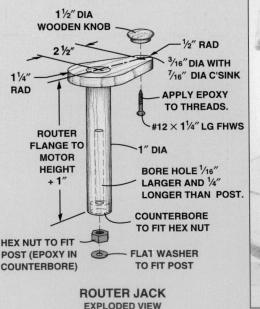

1½" DIA WOODEN KNOB

2½"

1¼" RAD

½" RAD

³/₁₆" DIA WITH ⁷/₁₆" DIA C'SINK

APPLY EPOXY TO THREADS.

#12 × 1¼" LG FHWS

ROUTER FLANGE TO MOTOR HEIGHT + 1"

1" DIA

BORE HOLE ¹/₁₆" LARGER AND ¼" LONGER THAN POST.

COUNTERBORE TO FIT HEX NUT

HEX NUT TO FIT POST (EPOXY IN COUNTERBORE)

FLAT WASHER TO FIT POST

ROUTER JACK
EXPLODED VIEW

BALANCING THE ROUTER

With the motor mounted above its base, the router is a top-heavy power tool. This makes it difficult to control in some operations. If the router is not properly supported, it may tip when routing near an edge or on a narrow surface. To prevent this, clamp scraps to the workpiece to enlarge the supporting surface, or attach an extended baseplate or offset baseplate to the router base.

SEE ALSO:

[1]Making a Mortise   238
[2]Routers   124

PRO TIP

The router platform from the Router Planing Jig on page 187 also serves as an extended baseplate, provided you remove the cleats from the ends.

BALANCING THE ROUTER ON A NARROW SURFACE

When routing a narrow workpiece, clamp scraps to the board to enlarge the surface on which the router rests. As a rule of thumb, at least half of the base should be supported at all times.

BALANCING THE ROUTER OVER AN EDGE

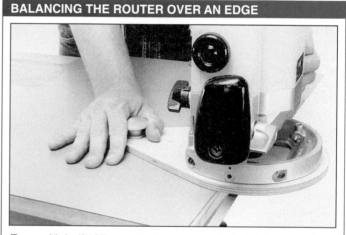

Even with half of the router base in contact with the wood surface, it can be difficult to keep the router from tipping. When you must hang the router over an edge during an operation, attach an **offset baseplate** to the base. Keep the offset portion of the plate over a solid surface and press down on it as you work.

JIGS & FIXTURES

OFFSET BASEPLATE An offset baseplate provides the leverage you need to keep a top-heavy router balanced. Cut the teardrop-shaped plate from ⅜-inch-thick plywood. The large diameter of the teardrop should be the same as the diameter of the router sole. Attach a wooden knob to the small end to serve as a handle. Drill mounting holes in the baseplate and attach it to the router base in place of the sole.

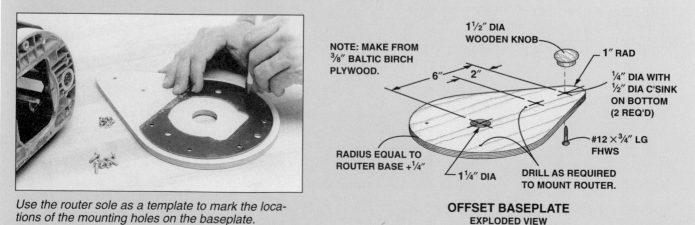

Use the router sole as a template to mark the locations of the mounting holes on the baseplate.

NOTE: MAKE FROM ⅜" BALTIC BIRCH PLYWOOD.

1½" DIA WOODEN KNOB

1" RAD

¼" DIA WITH ½" DIA C'SINK ON BOTTOM (2 REQ'D)

6"

2"

#12 × ¾" LG FHWS

RADIUS EQUAL TO ROUTER BASE +¼"

1¼" DIA

DRILL AS REQUIRED TO MOUNT ROUTER.

OFFSET BASEPLATE
EXPLODED VIEW

CIRCLE ROUTING

In addition to following edges with a pilot or pushing the router along a straightedge, you can guide it in a **precise arc**[1] to cut circles and curves. To do this, attach the router to a compass beam and swing it around a pivot.

FLUSH ROUTING

Rout one surface flush with another by mounting the router to a flush-cut jig. This is especially handy when cutting banding flush with a table top or panel. You can also use this technique to shave **screw plugs**[2] and protruding wooden parts flush with the surrounding surface.

ROUTING A CIRCLE

1 To cut a circle or an arc without drilling a pivot hole in the workpiece, secure a **pivot block** to the work with double-faced carpet tape. Mount the router to a **compass beam,** and attach the beam to the block with a pivot screw. The distance from the screw to the router bit must be equal to the radius of the circle you wish to rout. Drive the screw through the arm and into the block, but not into the work itself.

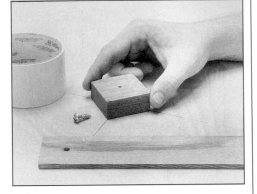

2 Swing the router around the pivot screw, cutting the circle. If necessary, make several passes, cutting a little deeper with each pass. When the circle is completed, remove the pivot block and discard the tape.

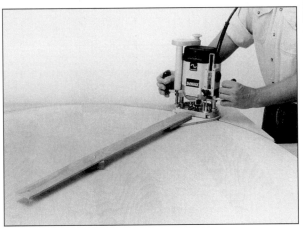

ROUTING FLUSH TO A SURFACE

1 Attach the router to a **flush-cut jig** — a small board that partially surrounds the bit. Mount a straight bit in the router and adjust the depth of cut so the tip of the bit is even with the bottom surface of the jig.

2 Turn on the router, rest the flush-cut jig on the surface, and pass the bit over the protruding parts that you want to rout flush.

JIGS & FIXTURES

ROUTER COMPASS BEAM AND PIVOT BLOCK This jig is designed to be used with the Offset Baseplate on page 221. Make the compass beam slightly longer than the radius of the circle you want to cut. Attach one end of the beam to the baseplate and the other to the pivot block.

FLUSH-CUT JIG Like the compass beam, the flush-cut jig attaches to the Offset Baseplate on page 221. Use a 1-inch straight bit or mortising bit to flush-cut.

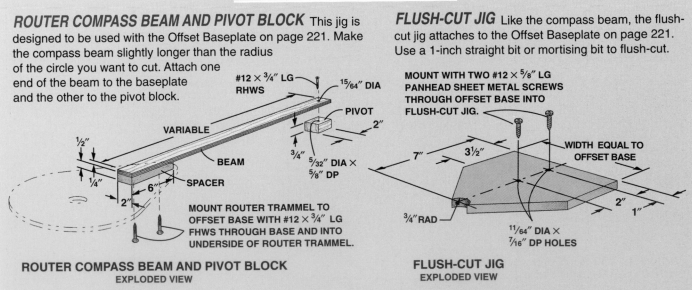

ROUTER COMPASS BEAM AND PIVOT BLOCK
EXPLODED VIEW

FLUSH-CUT JIG
EXPLODED VIEW

TABLE ROUTING

Many fixtures will hold a router stationary. Their design depends on *where* you want to hold the tool in relation to the work. An *overarm router*, for example, holds the router above the work. This is useful for some pattern-routing operations. A *joint maker* holds the router beside the work to make joinery cuts. The most versatile stationary routing jig, however, is a *router table*. This holds the router below the work.

ROUTER TABLE ANATOMY

On a router table, the *router* is attached to a **mounting plate**[3], made from thin plastic or metal. This plate is mounted flush with the surface of the *table*, suspending the router upside down below it. To use a table-mounted router, guide the work along a **split fence**[4] as you pass it over the bit. A *cutter guard* on the fence covers the bit as you work. Or, if you're using a piloted bit, begin the cut with the aid of a **starting pin**[5] attached to the mounting plate.

Besides these essential features, a router table may also have:

■ A **dust collector**[6] built into the fence to collect the waste as you work.

■ A *miter gauge slot* in the table so you can guide the work with a miter gauge.

■ **Moveable faces**[3] on the fence to adjust the opening for the router bit. Keeping the opening as small as possible provides more support for the work.

■ *Table inserts* that fit in the mounting plate and close down the space around the bit. These, too, help support the work.

OVERARM ROUTER

JOINT MAKER

DUST COLLECTOR

MOUNTING PLATE

CUTTER GUARD

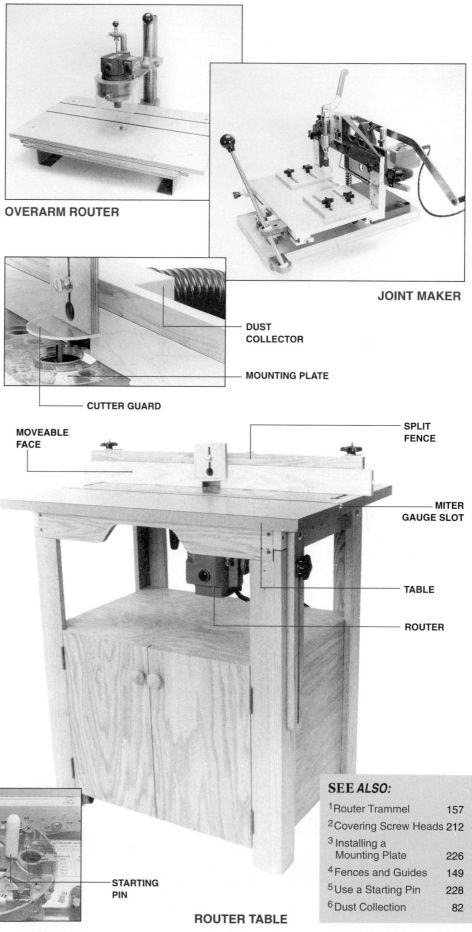

MOVEABLE FACE

SPLIT FENCE

MITER GAUGE SLOT

TABLE

ROUTER

ROUTER TABLE

TABLE INSERTS

STARTING PIN

JIGS & FIXTURES

LIFT-TOP ROUTER TABLE Most router tables have a fixed top, which makes them awkward to use. With the router buried beneath the work surface, you have to stoop or kneel to change the bits or adjust the depth of cut.

To save your knees and back, make a *lift-top* router table. The top swings up like the lid of a chest, allowing easy access to the router.

Turn a knob to lock it in place at a comfortable angle while you change bits or make adjustments *standing straight up.*

If you already have a router table, just make the storage stand. The stand is designed to support any 24-inch-deep, 32-inch-wide commercial router table top, converting it to a lift-top router table.

SAFE *GUARDS*

Some router table designs provide access to the router by leaving the mounting plate loose in the table. To reach the router, you lift the tool and the plate up and out. Unfortunately, it's unsafe to work with a loose router. Furthermore, the plate recess in the table wears as you remove and replace the router. It becomes enlarged, allowing the router to shift as you work. For safety and precision, secure the mounting plate in the table.

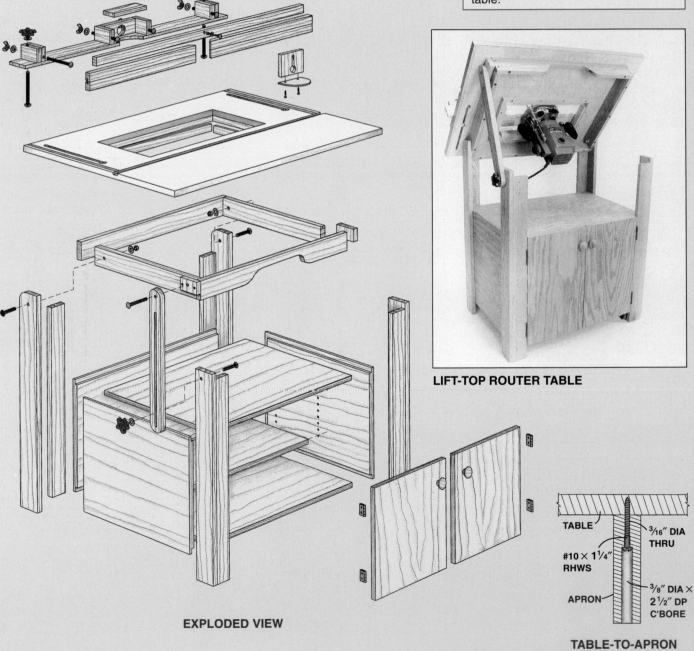

LIFT-TOP ROUTER TABLE

EXPLODED VIEW

TABLE

³⁄₁₆" DIA THRU

#10 × 1¼" RHWS

³⁄₈" DIA × 2½" DP C'BORE

APRON

TABLE-TO-APRON ASSEMBLY DETAIL

JIGS & FIXTURES

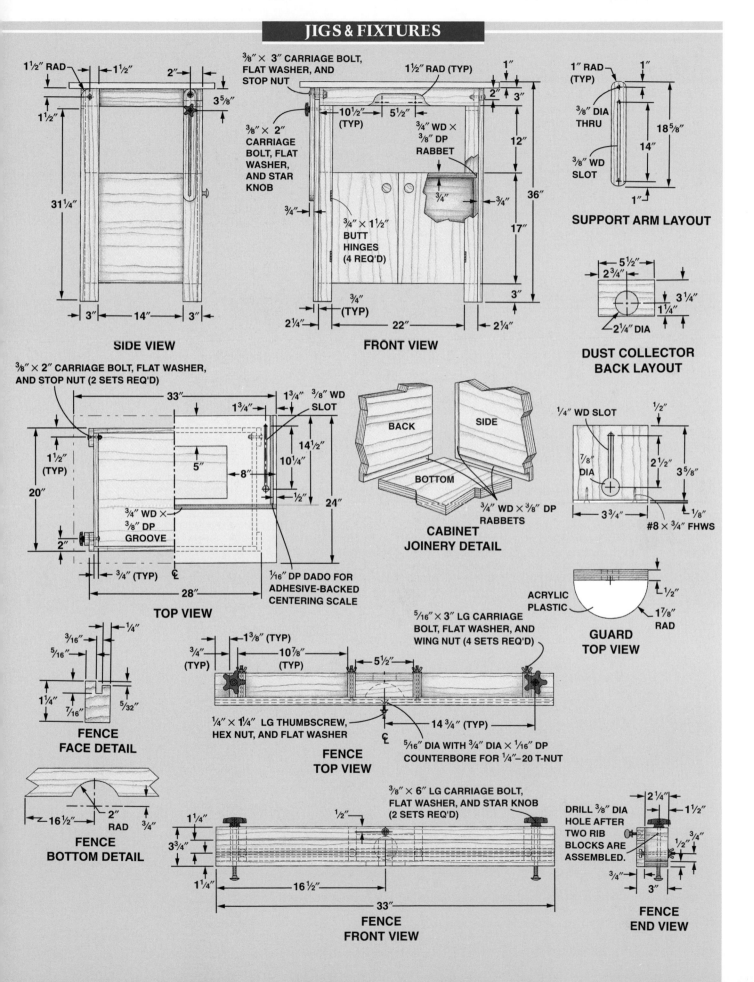

3/8" × 3" CARRIAGE BOLT, FLAT WASHER, AND STOP NUT

1 1/2" RAD

1 1/2"

2"

3 5/8"

1 1/2"

31 1/4"

3" **14"** **3"**

SIDE VIEW

1 1/2" RAD (TYP)

3/8" × 2" CARRIAGE BOLT, FLAT WASHER, AND STAR KNOB

10 1/2" (TYP)

5 1/2"

3/4" WD × 3/8" DP RABBET

1"

2"

3"

12"

36"

17"

3"

3/4"

3/4"

3/4"

3/4" × 1 1/2" BUTT HINGES (4 REQ'D)

3/4" (TYP)

2 1/4"

22"

2 1/4"

FRONT VIEW

1" RAD (TYP)

1"

3/8" DIA THRU

18 5/8"

14"

3/8" WD SLOT

1"

SUPPORT ARM LAYOUT

5 1/2"

2 3/4"

3 1/4"

1 1/4"

2 1/4" DIA

DUST COLLECTOR BACK LAYOUT

3/8" × 2" CARRIAGE BOLT, FLAT WASHER, AND STOP NUT (2 SETS REQ'D)

33"

1 3/4"

1 3/4" 3/8" WD SLOT

14 1/2"

10 1/4"

1 1/2" (TYP)

20"

5"

8"

24"

1/2"

2"

3/4" WD × 3/8" DP GROOVE

3/4" (TYP)

28"

1/16" DP DADO FOR ADHESIVE-BACKED CENTERING SCALE

TOP VIEW

BACK

SIDE

BOTTOM

3/4" WD × 3/8" DP RABBETS

CABINET JOINERY DETAIL

1/4" WD SLOT

1/2"

7/8" DIA

2 1/2"

3 5/8"

3 3/4"

1/8"

#8 × 3/4" FHWS

ACRYLIC PLASTIC

1/2"

1 7/8" RAD

GUARD TOP VIEW

1/4"

3/16"

5/16"

1 1/4"

7/16"

5/32"

FENCE FACE DETAIL

5/16" × 3" LG CARRIAGE BOLT, FLAT WASHER, AND WING NUT (4 SETS REQ'D)

1 3/8" (TYP)

3/4" (TYP)

10 7/8" (TYP)

5 1/2"

1/4" × 1/4" LG THUMBSCREW, HEX NUT, AND FLAT WASHER

14 3/4" (TYP)

5/16" DIA WITH 3/4" DIA × 1/16" DP COUNTERBORE FOR 1/4"–20 T-NUT

FENCE TOP VIEW

16 1/2"

2" RAD

3/4"

FENCE BOTTOM DETAIL

3/8" × 6" LG CARRIAGE BOLT, FLAT WASHER, AND STAR KNOB (2 SETS REQ'D)

1 1/4"

1/2"

3 3/4"

1 1/4"

16 1/2"

33"

FENCE FRONT VIEW

2 1/4"

1 1/2"

DRILL 3/8" DIA HOLE AFTER TWO RIB BLOCKS ARE ASSEMBLED.

1/2"

3/4"

3/4"

3"

FENCE END VIEW

INSTALLING A MOUNTING PLATE

When making or purchasing a mounting plate for a stationary router fixture, choose a stiff, thin **material**[1]. The material must not vibrate or sag with the router attached — acrylic plastic, phenolic plastic, and metal are all good choices. The plastics should be ⅜ inch thick; metals, ⅛ inch thick. Avoid polycarbonate plastics such as Lexan; these are too flexible.

To install the mounting plate in the fixture, follow these steps:

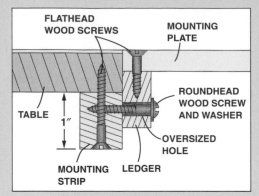

FLATHEAD WOOD SCREWS
MOUNTING PLATE
ROUNDHEAD WOOD SCREW AND WASHER
OVERSIZED HOLE
TABLE
1"
MOUNTING STRIP
LEDGER

MOUNTING PLATE INSTALLATION

1 Temporarily attach the mounting plate to the underside of the router table with two or three **small** pieces of double-faced carpet tape. Secure ¾ × 1-inch wooden **mounting strips** to the table around the perimeter of the plate. (Attach the **edge** of the strips so they stand 1 inch above the table.) Remove the mounting plate from between the strips.

2 Secure the table upside down to a large plywood scrap with double-faced carpet tape. Mount the router to an extended baseplate (such as the platform from the Router Planing Jig on page 187). Rout the cutout for the mounting plate with a 1-inch-long pattern-cutting bit, guiding the bit around the inside surface of the mounting strips. Cut completely through the table, then remove the plywood and the tape. Square the corners of the cutout with a file or a flush-cut saw.

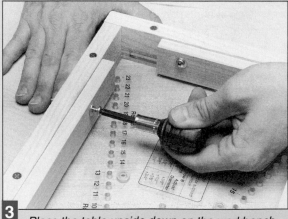

3 Place the table upside down on the workbench and insert the mounting plate in the cutout. Press down on the plate so the top surface will be flush with the top surface of the table. Secure ½ × ¾-inch **ledgers** to the mounting strips with roundhead wood screws. Make the shaft holes in the ledgers slightly larger than the shaft of the screws so you can adjust the ledgers up and down.

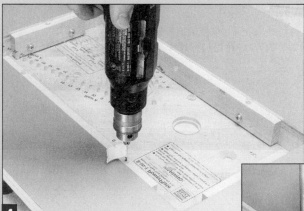

4 Drill and countersink mounting holes near the edges of the mounting plate. Secure the plate to the ledgers with flathead wood screws. (The heads of the screws **must** rest below the surface of the plate.) If necessary, adjust the ledgers so the plate is perfectly flush with the table.

GUIDING THE WORK

When working on a router table, there are several ways to guide the work over the bit.

USE A FENCE

Fasten a **split fence**[2] to the table, surrounding the router bit. Adjust the width of cut by moving the fence, exposing more or less of the bit as needed. Use **centering scales**[3] to help position the fence precisely. Joint the stock straight and guide the straight surface along the fence.

SAFE *GUARDS*

Whenever possible, "bury" the unused portion of the router bit in the fence. Avoid passing the work between the fence and the bit — this leaves too much of the bit exposed.

USE A MITER GAUGE

When routing the ends of narrow boards, feed the work with a miter gauge. Use the fence as a stop to prevent the rotation of the bit from pulling the board sideways.

PRO *TIP*

When making square cuts, it's often easier to use a square block of wood as a guide instead of a miter gauge. Hold the edge of the board against the block and push it along the fence as shown.

USING A FENCE

1 *To make large adjustments in the fence position, unlock **both** ends of the fence and slide it across the table. To make fine adjustments, unlock just one end and swing it, using the other end as a pivot. For every inch you move the loose end of the fence, the faces will move approximately ½ inch relative to the bit.*

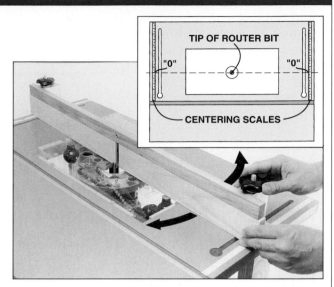

TIP OF ROUTER BIT

"0"   "0"

CENTERING SCALES

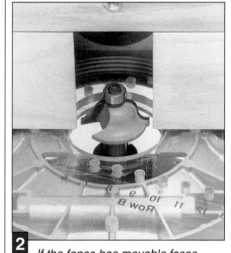

2 *If the fence has movable faces, make the bit opening as small as possible. Guide the stock along the faces, feeding it right to left (against the bit rotation) as you face the fence.*

3 *Occasionally, you need to advance the outfeed half of the fence slightly in front of the infeed half, similar to a shaper fence. To do this, attach a scrap of plastic laminate to the outfeed half with spray adhesive. This will advance the outfeed half ⅟32 to ⅟16 inch in front of the infeed half, and the two surfaces will remain parallel.*

USING A MITER GAUGE

Adjust the miter gauge to the desired angle. Position the fence to control the width of cut, making sure the faces are parallel to the miter gauge slot. Guide the wood over the bit with the miter gauge, keeping the end of the board against the fence.

USE A STARTING PIN

When working with **piloted bits**[1] in a router table, use a starting pin to help control the work. Start the operation with the work against the pin and rotate it into the bit. Feed against the rotation of the cutter, keeping the work pressed against both the pin *and* the pilot bearing. Otherwise, the operation is susceptible to dangerous kickback. The bit could easily catch on the work and pull it out of your hands.

MAKING INTERIOR CUTS

To make an interior cut on a router table, such as a **mortise**[2] or a blind slot, lower the work onto the bit to start the cut. The bit is hidden beneath the wood when you do this, making it difficult to know where to start routing and when to stop. To compensate, mark both the router table and the workpiece with indicator lines.

USING A STARTING PIN

1 A starting pin provides a leverage point to help control the workpiece as you feed it into the bit. Place the edge of the board against the pin, then gently pivot the wood into the spinning bit. Keep the wood firmly against both the pin and the pilot as you cut.

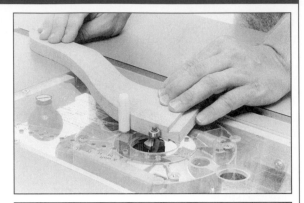

2 If you need the extra control when you finish the cut, stop cutting several inches before you get to the end of the board. Place the board against the opposite side of the pin, and rotate it into the cutter. Pull the board toward the pin, cutting the last few inches. This way, the board will rest against both the pin and the pilot bearing for the entire cut.

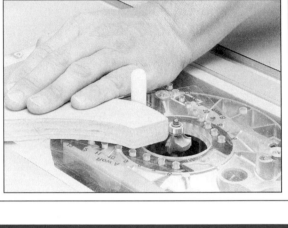

MAKING AN INTERIOR CUT

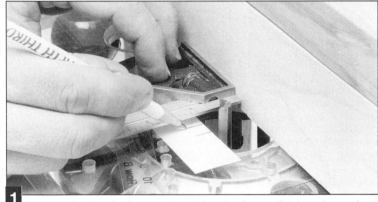

1 Adjust the depth of cut and position the fence. Stick a piece of masking tape to the worktable in front of the bit. Using a small square, make two marks on the tape to indicate the diameter of the bit.

2 Use the square again to transfer the layout lines that mark the beginning and end of the cut to a surface that will be visible when you rout.

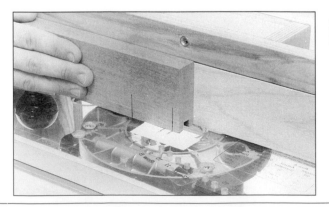

4 Once the bit is started, feed the workpiece horizontally across the table until the right-hand indicator line on the stock lines up with the right-hand indicator line on the router table. Back-rout in the opposite direction until the two left-hand marks align. When you remove the work from the table, the cut will begin and end at the indicated positions.

TROUBLE *SHOOTING*

COMMON ROUTING PROBLEMS

Problem	Possible Causes	Solutions
Routed surfaces are burned.	Feed rate is too slow.	Increase feed rate; keep router moving.
	Router speed is too fast.	Reduce router speed.
	Router bit is dull or loaded with pitch.	Clean bit, sharpen if necessary.
Routed surfaces are chipped or torn.	Bit is cutting against or across the grain.	Rout "downhill," with the grain. When this isn't possible, back up work with scrap to prevent tear-out.
	Bit is dull or loaded with pitch.	Clean bit, sharpen if necessary.
Routed surfaces have excessive mill marks.	Feed rate is too fast.	Decrease feed rate.
	Router speed is too slow.	Increase router speed.
Router bit creeps out of collet during operation.	Sawdust in router collet.	Clean router collet.
	Bit shaft is galled.	Remove burrs from shaft with file or emery cloth.
	Cutting away too much wood in one bite.	Decrease width or depth of cut.
Router bit chatters during operation.	Feed rate is too fast.	Decrease feed rate.
	Cutting away too much wood in one bite.	Decrease width or depth of cut.
Router or work is difficult to control; pushes or pulls in wrong direction.	Feeding router or work with rotation of bit.	Feed work against rotation of bit; use rotation to hold router or work against fence or guide.
	Cutting away too much wood in one bite.	Decrease width or depth of cut.
Cut is too wide, not straight, or not even.	Fence or straightedge drifting during operation.	Lock fence or straightedge in place.
	Pilot bearing not rubbing against surface.	Adjust depth of cut to engage pilot bearing.
Router tips over.	Router not properly supported and balanced.	Build up supporting surfaces or use offset router base.

3 *Place the workpiece against the fence, holding the portion where you want to make the cut above the bit. Turn on the router and lower the workpiece onto the bit, boring a starter hole.*

5 *Should you need to make the cut deeper, raise the bit a fraction of an inch and repeat. Because you're back-routing during part of this procedure, take very small bites. If you raise the bit 1/16 to 1/8 inch at a time, the work will be much easier to control and you'll get a more accurate cut.*

MORE *SOURCES*

BOOKS

Advanced Routing, by Nick Engler, Rodale Press, 1993

The New Router Handbook, by Patrick Spielman, Sterling Publishing, 1993

Routing and Shaping, by Nick Engler, Rodale Press, 1992

Woodworking with the Router, by Bill Hylton and Fred Matlack, Rodale Press, 1993

VIDEOS

Router Jigs and Techniques, with Bernie Maas and Michael Fortune, Taunton Books and Videos

Router Joinery, with Gary Rogowski, Taunton Books and Videos

SEE *ALSO:*

[1]Guiding the Router   218

[2]Making a Mortise   238

Making Wood Joints

Even the most complex joinery is made with simple cuts.

Much of the planing, sawing, drilling, and routing we do is aimed at making **wooden joints**[1] – fitting two or more pieces of wood together. There are hundreds of joints, some of which appear quite complex. However, the techniques required to make them are surprisingly simple and straightforward.

There are many ways to perform joinery operations, and I have room to show only a few here. These are accurate, effective techniques, but don't get the idea that they are necessarily the best method for every situation. Craftsman/author Bob Moran explained three different methods to perform many woodworking tasks in his book, *Woodworking: The Right Technique.* "I hope the title didn't mislead," he told me. "There is good technique and poor technique. But there is no technique that is always right."

This is good advice when planning a new wooden joint. Chances are, there are several effective ways to make it. The best is the way in which you feel the most comfortable and confident.

FIVE ESSENTIAL JOINERY CUTS

To make wooden joints, you must know just five **basic cuts**[2].

■ In a *butt cut,* the sawed edge, end, or face of the board is cut square to the adjoining surfaces.

The craftsmen show off their skills by making the mortises and tenons that join this **Arts and Crafts (or Mission) Desk** clearly visible. Although masterfully executed, these joints are relatively simple to make.

SPECS:	30" high, 72" wide, 36" deep
MATERIALS:	Cherry and ebony
CRAFTSMEN:	Kevin P. Rodel and Susan Mack Pownal, ME

■ A *miter cut* leaves the sawed surface at an angle other than 90 degrees to one or more of the adjoining surfaces.

■ A *rabbet cut* makes an L-shaped notch in the edge or end of a board. The cut surfaces of the rabbet are typically square to one another.

■ A *dado cut* creates a U-shaped channel in one surface. Like a rabbet, the surfaces of a dado are usually square to each other. *Note:* A dado runs perpendicular to the grain, while a groove is parallel to it. Both are made with dado cuts.

■ A *hole* or round mortise is a cylindrical cavity **bored**[3] into the wood. Holes can be made at any angle.

THROUGH AND STOPPED CUTS

When making joinery cuts, you can saw completely *through* the wood, or halt partway, making a *stopped cut* (sometimes shortened to *stop*). A stop rabbet is closed at one end; a stopped hole does not continue through the board.

Every woodworking joint, no matter how complex it may appear, is composed of these simple cuts. For example, a lap joint is made by fitting two dadoes together. The mortise in a mortise-and-tenon joint is a stop groove or dado; the tenon is formed from a butt cut (to cut the end of the tenon square) and two or more rabbet cuts. The trick in making a well-fitted joint is not in making difficult cuts but in making simple cuts precisely and in the proper sequence.

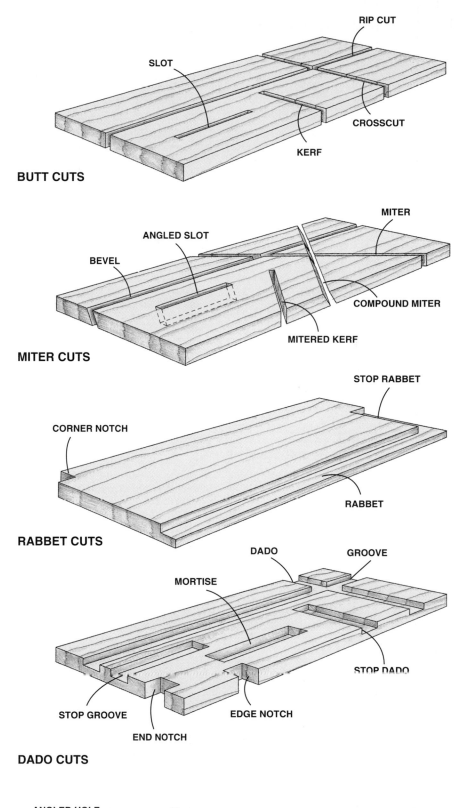

BUTT CUTS — RIP CUT, SLOT, CROSSCUT, KERF

MITER CUTS — MITER, ANGLED SLOT, BEVEL, COMPOUND MITER, MITERED KERF

RABBET CUTS — STOP RABBET, CORNER NOTCH, RABBET

DADO CUTS — DADO, GROOVE, MORTISE, STOP DADO, STOP GROOVE, END NOTCH, EDGE NOTCH

MORE *INFO*

The term *blind* is often used to describe stopped cuts. A stop rabbet is commonly called a blind rabbet. Technically, however, the term describes joints that can't be seen after assembly. A *blind mortise,* for example, disappears once the parts are joined. *Half-blind dovetails* can't be seen from one direction but can be seen from the other.

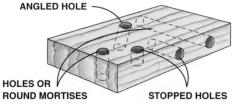

HOLES — ANGLED HOLE, HOLES OR ROUND MORTISES, STOPPED HOLES

MAKING SIMPLE JOINTS

Four of the five basic joinery cuts can be made on a table saw or radial arm saw. Use an ordinary **circular saw blade**[1] to make butt and miter cuts, and a *dado cutter* to make rabbets and dadoes. You can also use a **router**[2] (either hand-held or table-mounted) to make rabbets and dadoes. Straight bits, rabbeting bits, and mortising bits are all designed to make these basic cuts.

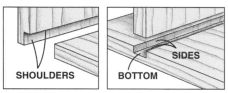

RABBET JOINT   **DADO JOINT**

When in doubt, choose the tool that gives you the **smoothest cut**[3]; the adjoining surfaces of a joint must be as flat as possible.

MAINTAINING ACCURACY

Whatever tool you use, it's likely that you'll make duplicate cuts. A **lap joint**[4], for example, requires identical dado cuts in the adjoining parts.

When making duplicate cuts, feed each board at the same rate and with the same pressure. Remember that a power tool, like any mechanical system, must have some "play."

Although a miter gauge rests snug in its slot, there has to be a little play or it wouldn't move. As you push the gauge forward, put a little sideways pressure to the left or right to eliminate this play. Remember how hard and in which direction you pressed, then do the same on the remaining cuts.

This is a very helpful technique. It ensures that duplicate cuts are precise copies and preserves the accuracy of your woodworking.

A **stacked dado cutter** cuts dadoes, rabbets, and grooves from $\frac{1}{4}$ to $\frac{13}{16}$ inch wide in $\frac{1}{16}$-inch steps. It's made up of two types of blades — outside **cutters** and inside **chippers**. Each blade is precisely $\frac{1}{4}$, $\frac{1}{8}$, or $\frac{1}{16}$ inch thick. To adjust the width of the cut, add or subtract chippers until the stack is the right width. For odd sizes that aren't divisible by $\frac{1}{16}$, insert **dado shims** between the blades. These come in thicknesses from 0.004 to 0.031 inch.

CHIPPERS

CUTTERS

DADO SHIMS

REDUCING TEAR-OUT

To reduce chipping and tearing when making joinery cuts, score the layout lines to cut the wood fibers. The top dado in this piece of plywood was laid out with a pencil. The grain is badly torn where the cutter lifted the veneer. The dado on the bottom was laid out with a knife and is much cleaner.

USING A DADO CUTTER

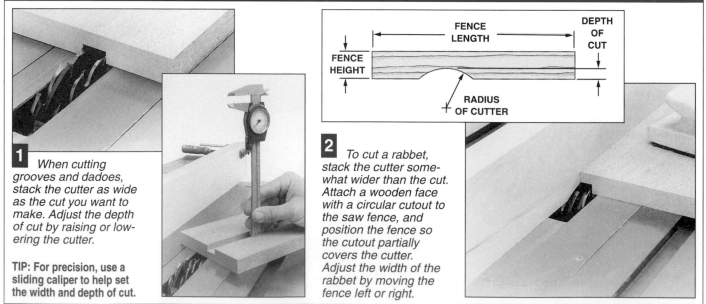

FENCE LENGTH

DEPTH OF CUT

FENCE HEIGHT

RADIUS OF CUTTER

1 *When cutting grooves and dadoes, stack the cutter as wide as the cut you want to make. Adjust the depth of cut by raising or lowering the cutter.*

TIP: For precision, use a sliding caliper to help set the width and depth of cut.

2 *To cut a rabbet, stack the cutter somewhat wider than the cut. Attach a wooden face with a circular cutout to the saw fence, and position the fence so the cutout partially covers the cutter. Adjust the width of the rabbet by moving the fence left or right.*

FITTING JOINTS

Because it's more difficult to add wood to a board than it is to cut it away, most craftsman make it a habit of cutting on the "long side" of their layout lines. This often makes it necessary to trim a cut to fit the joint. You can adjust the machine setup to shave this extra stock, but there are several **hand tools**[5] that will do it faster.

PRO *TIP*

When you fit a joint, aim for a "slip fit." There should be no slop in the joint, but you should be able to assemble it and take it apart without the aid of a mallet.

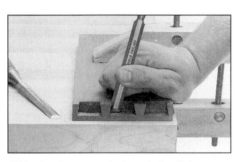

Chisels also come in handy for fitting cuts. A **mortising chisel** squares corners and shaves end grain in recesses; a **bevel-edge chisel** reaches into tight spaces. If the surfaces of a joint are less than 90 degrees from one another, clean it out with a **skew chisel** (shown).

TRIMMING RABBETS, DADOES, AND GROOVES

Several hand planes are made specifically for trimming and fitting joints.

1 Use a **rabbet plane** to shave the surfaces of a rabbet.

2 Trim the sides of grooves and dadoes with a **side rabbet plane.**

3 Clean out the bottoms of grooves, dadoes, and mortises with a **router plane.**

TRIMMING BUTT CUTS AND MITERS

Trim the sawed ends or edges of boards with a bench plane and a **shooting hook.** (See below.) Lay the plane on its side to shave the cut surface.

SEE *ALSO:*

JIGS & FIXTURES

SHOOTING HOOK This fixture combines two traditional workshop aids, a **bench hook** and a **shooting board.** A bench hook holds a workpiece while you cut it with a handsaw, and a shooting board holds it while you shave the cut end with a bench plane.

To use this fixture as a bench hook, hook the cleat over the edge of the workbench and hold a board against the backstop while you saw it. To use it as a shooting board, position the sawed end of the board even with the step in the base. Rest a plane on its side and guide it along the step, shaving the board. To "shoot" a miter, attach a 45-degree backstop to the base.

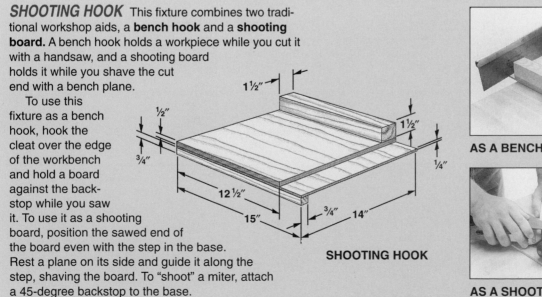

1½"
½"
1½"
¾"
¼"
12½"
15"
¾"
14"

SHOOTING HOOK

AS A BENCH HOOK

AS A SHOOTING BOARD

MAKING REINFORCED JOINTS

When you must reinforce a joint or need help in aligning it for assembly, add a third member to the joint such as a glue block, dowel, spline, or biscuit. Remember that all three wooden parts expand and contract – the reinforcing member must not restrict the **wood movement** [1].

USING GLUE BLOCKS AND CLEATS

Perhaps the easiest way to reinforce a joint is to attach a glue block or a cleat to the adjoining parts. As the name implies, glue blocks are attached with glue, while cleats are screwed or nailed in place.

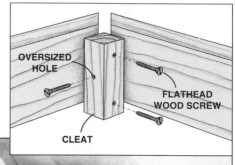

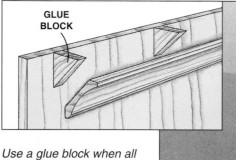

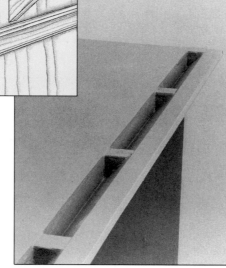

Use a glue block when all the parts expand and contract in the same direction or when the parts are small enough that the expansion and contraction are not a problem. (The glue joint should be less than 3 inches across the grain.) Triangular glue blocks hold the crown molding to this cupboard.

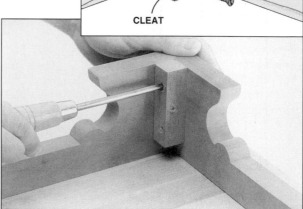

Use cleats when you don't want to restrict the wood movement. Drill oversized shaft holes to accommodate the expansion and contraction. The wood grain on the cleat that holds this bracket foot together is perpendicular to the grain in the adjoining parts. If the cleat were glued in place, it would restrict the movement.

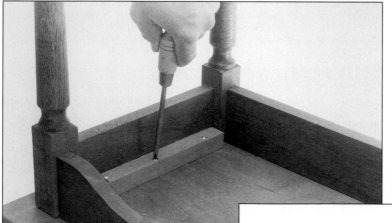

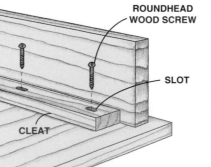

In some instances, you may want to glue a cleat to one member with parallel wood grain, and screw it to another with opposing grain. The strip of wood that holds this table top in place is glued to the aprons, where the wood grain runs in the same direction as the cleat. But it's screwed to the table top, where the grain is perpendicular to the cleat. The screws pass through slots in the cleats. This arrangement lets the top move without restriction.

*You can also reinforce a joint with a **gusset,** a block of wood or plywood that straddles the seam between adjoining parts. Gussets can be glued, screwed, or nailed in place. And although the term conjures up visions of ugly plywood squares holding roof trusses together, a gusset can be attractive. This decorative block, for example, is a wood gusset that reinforces a butt-jointed clock case.*

MAKING DOWEL JOINTS

A dowel spans a joint *inside* the wood, tying the adjoining members together. Typically, the dowels are hidden in stopped holes, and these **holes must match**[2] precisely. Use a *doweling jig* or *dowel centers* to align the holes.

■ If the wood grain of the assembled parts is opposed to the dowel grain, make the dowels as short as possible so as not to restrict the wood movement.

■ Drill the dowel holes about ¹/₁₆ inch deeper than needed to make room for the glue.

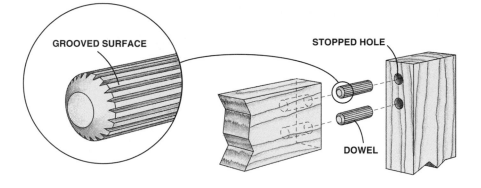
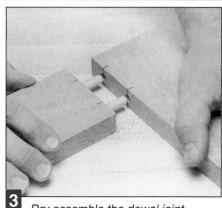

GROOVED SURFACE

STOPPED HOLE

DOWEL

■ Use dowels with grooves cut in the sides or score some grooves with an awl. These form a better

glue joint[3] and relieve the hydraulic pressure that builds up when you drive them into glue-filled holes.

USING A DOWELING JIG

1 To make a dowel joint in two boards of the same thickness, use a **doweling jig** to align the holes. Match up the mating surfaces of the two boards. Draw pencil lines across the seam between the boards wherever you want to install a dowel.

2 Align the doweling jig with a mark on one of the boards and clamp it in place. Bore a stopped hole with a twist bit or brad-point bit, using the jig to guide the bit. Repeat for each mark on each board.

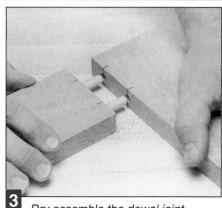

3 Dry assemble the dowel joint (without glue) to check the alignment of the dowel holes. If the holes are properly aligned, reassemble the joint with glue.

USING DOWEL CENTERS

1 When the boards are different sizes, use **dowel centers** to align dowel holes. Drill stopped holes in just one of the parts. Place the centers in the holes, align the adjoining parts, and press them together. If the wood is very hard, rap one part or the other with a mallet.

2 The dowel centers will make small indentations in the surface of the part that hasn't yet been drilled. Drill stopped holes at these marks, and then assemble the joint with dowels and glue.

SEE ALSO:

[1]Wood Movement — 6
[2]Matching Holes — 211
[3]Gluing and Clamping — 248

MAKING SPLINE JOINTS

A spline is a small strip of wood, usually just ⅛ to ¼ inch thick, that spans the joint between two boards. The spline rests in two matching grooves, one in each of the adjoining boards.

Make the splines from solid wood or plywood, as needed to accommodate the movement of the adjoining parts. If you make a spline from solid wood, cut it so the grain direction runs *across* the joint. If it runs parallel to the joint, the spline won't add any **strength**[1] to the assembly.

■ When cutting spline grooves in the edges of wide boards, use a **tall extension fence**[2] to help guide the work over the bit or cutter.

■ When cutting spline grooves in board ends, use a **tenoning jig**[3] to hold the board vertically.

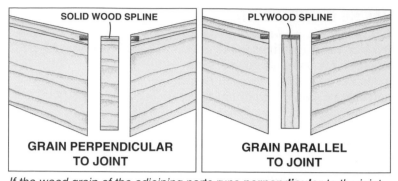

If the wood grain of the adjoining parts runs **perpendicular** to the joint, make the spline from solid wood. The grain will run across the joint and parallel to the grain in the parts. When the joint is assembled, the members will expand and contract together.

If the wood grain is **parallel** to the joint, use plywood. Plywood is relatively stable; so is wood parallel to the grain. When the joint is assembled, the spline and the wood surrounding it will move very little.

CUTTING SPLINE GROOVES

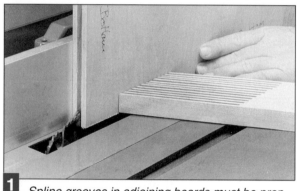

1 *Spline grooves in adjoining boards must be properly aligned. Mark the surfaces of the board so you know which surfaces are which, then cut the matching grooves with like surfaces facing in the same direction. For example, when attaching banding to a countertop, mark the top and bottom surfaces of the parts. Cut a spline groove in the **edges** of the countertop, keeping the bottom face turned away from the fence.*

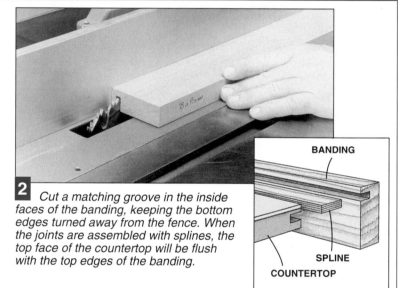

2 *Cut a matching groove in the inside faces of the banding, keeping the bottom edges turned away from the fence. When the joints are assembled with splines, the top face of the countertop will be flush with the top edges of the banding.*

MAKING SPLINE MITERS

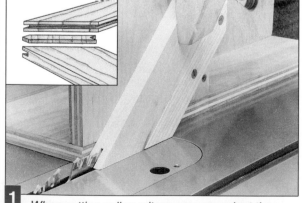

1 *When cutting spline miters, you can orient the splines parallel to the miter or perpendicular to it. If the parts are to be joined so the **faces** are flush (as in a picture frame), cut the grooves so the splines will be parallel.*

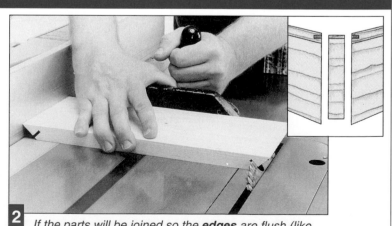

2 *If the parts will be joined so the **edges** are flush (like the sides of a small box), cut the groove so the splines will be perpendicular. Either hold the work or tilt the blade so it's 90 degrees from the mitered surface as you cut.*

MAKING BISCUIT JOINTS

Wooden plates or *biscuits* are short, football-shaped splines made of compressed wood. They are usually installed with a **biscuit joiner**[4], a portable power tool that cuts a groove with a semicircular bottom. The groove is slightly longer and wider than the biscuits themselves, letting you adjust the positions of the adjoining members when they're first assembled. **Water-based glues**[5] such as polyvinyl resin (white) glue or aliphatic (yellow) resin glue cause the compressed wood to swell, and the joint soon becomes tight.

Biscuits come in three sizes to reinforce small, medium, and large joints. Adjust the biscuit joiner to cut a groove to match the biscuit size you will use.

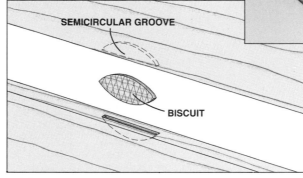

#0   #10   #20

SEMICIRCULAR GROOVE

BISCUIT

BISCUIT JOINT

MAKING A BISCUIT JOINT

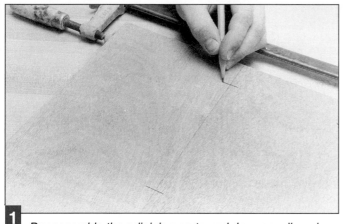

1 *Dry assemble the adjoining parts and draw pencil marks across the seam wherever you want to install a biscuit. Label the surfaces of the parts — top or bottom, inside or outside, front or back — as appropriate.*

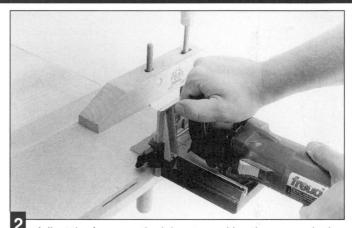

2 *Adjust the fence on the joiner to position the groove in the stock. Line up the indicator on the fence with one of the marks on the wood. Rest the fence flat on the wood surface and push the joiner forward, cutting a groove. Repeat for each mark on the adjoining parts. Always rest the fence on the **marked surface** so the groove will be properly aligned.*

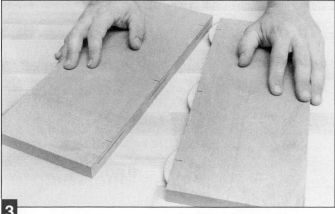

3 *Dry assemble the parts to check the alignment of the grooves and the fit of the biscuits. Don't worry if there's a little slop in the joints — the fit is supposed to be loose. Coat the adjoining surfaces and grooves with water-based glue, and assemble the parts. If the parts aren't aligned quite right, **quickly** reposition them before the biscuits swell.*

4 *If you wish to cut biscuit grooves in the face of a board, farther away from the edge than the biscuit joiner would ordinarily allow, remove the fence from the tool. Clamp a straightedge to the work to align the joiner for each cut.*

MAKING MORTISE-AND-TENON JOINTS

Although there are many **types of mortises and tenons**[1], the procedures for making them are very similar.

■ Make the mortise first, then fit the tenon to it. It's easier to shave down the tenon than it is to enlarge the mortise.

■ The wood grain must run *parallel* to the length of the tenon; otherwise, the **joint will be weak**[2].

■ When making a through mortise-and-tenon joint, make the tenon $\frac{1}{32}$ to $\frac{1}{16}$ inch longer than necessary. After assembly, sand the tenon flush.

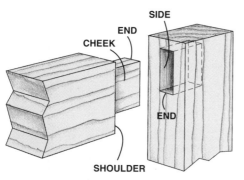

TENON   MORTISE

MORTISE-AND-TENON JOINT

MAKING A MORTISE

There are several common techniques for making a mortise.

■ **Bore**[3] a series of overlapping holes on a *drill press* to remove most of the waste, then clean up the sides of the mortises with a chisel.

■ **Rout**[4] a mortise with a *router* and a straight bit. If necessary, square the round corners with a chisel.

■ Cut the mortise by boring overlapping square holes with a hollow chisel *mortiser*.

CUTTING A MORTISE ON A DRILL PRESS

1 To make a mortise on a drill press, lay out the joint on the stock with a marking gauge and a marking knife. In addition to marking the perimeter of the mortise, scribe a line down the center to help position the drill bit.

2 Select a bit whose diameter matches the width of the mortise. Bore holes at the beginning and end of the mortise, then make overlapping holes between them to remove as much waste as possible.

3 Remove the remaining waste from the sides and end of the mortise with chisels. Use a bevel-edge chisel to clean up the sides and a mortising chisel to square the ends.

ROUTING A MORTISE

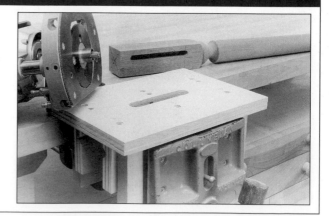

If you have a small number of mortises to make, rout them as you would a stop groove or a dado. However, if you must cut a large number of identical mortises, or you want the make the mortises precisely the same, make a mortising template. Clamp the template to the stock and follow it with a guide collar as you rout each mortise.

USING A MORTISER

1 To set up a mortiser, mount a hollow chisel in the holder. One side of the chisel must be square to the fence. Slide the bit inside the chisel and into the chuck. The spurs on the end of the bit must clear the chisel by 1/32 to 1/16 inch. If the clearance is too small, the bit will rub on the chisel and ruin it. If it's too large, the spurs won't break up the wood chips and they'll clog the chisel.

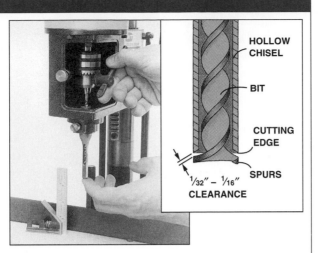

HOLLOW CHISEL

BIT

CUTTING EDGE

1/32" – 1/16" CLEARANCE

SPURS

2 Attach a hold-down to the fence to keep the stock on the table. Turn on the mortiser and feed the chisel slowly with firm pressure. Don't feed too fast; give the bit plenty of time to evacuate the chips. It also helps to retract the chisel frequently during a cut — plunge the chisel into the wood, hold the pressure for a few seconds, and repeat.

3 Form the mortise by drilling rows of overlapping holes. When drilling a single row, make the end holes first, then work your way from one end to the other. When drilling a double row, make the corner holes and then remove the waste between them. Ideally, the holes should overlap no more than one-quarter the width of the chisel; otherwise, the chisel may drift in the cut.

MYTH *CONCEPTIONS*

AND NOW FOR SOMETHING COMPLETELY USELESS...

Craftsmen who have never used one often have the mistaken idea that a *mortising attachment* for a drill press is a useful tool. This accessory pretends to convert a drill press to a mortiser and fails miserably in the attempt. A drill press lacks the leverage to drive a hollow chisel through anything but the softest of woods. If you need to drill square holes, invest your money in a dedicated mortiser.

JIGS & FIXTURES

MORTISING TEMPLATE To make a mortising template, cut an opening in plywood or hardboard to guide a router outfitted with a guide collar and straight bit. The opening must be slightly longer and wider than the mortise to compensate for the difference in diameters between the bit and the guide collar. How much longer and wider? Subtract the bit diameter (BD) from the collar diameter (CD) and add the result to the length (L) and width (W) of the mortise you wish to rout. This will give you the length and width of the opening in the template (TL and TW).

$$(CD - BD) + L = TL$$
$$(CD - BD) + W = TW$$

Attach cleats to the template to help position it and secure it to the work.

To rout a mortise in round stock, cut V-grooves in the cleats.

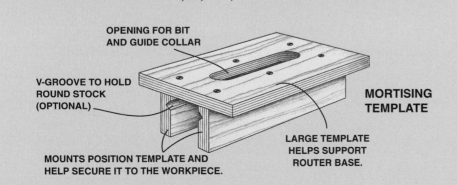

OPENING FOR BIT AND GUIDE COLLAR

V-GROOVE TO HOLD ROUND STOCK (OPTIONAL)

MORTISING TEMPLATE

MOUNTS POSITION TEMPLATE AND HELP SECURE IT TO THE WORKPIECE.

LARGE TEMPLATE HELPS SUPPORT ROUTER BASE.

HINGE MORTISES

If your woodworking project has a door or a lid, chances are you may have to cut mortises for the **hinges**[1]. The procedures are similar to cutting standard mortises, but there are important differences.

■ When setting a butt hinge or hinge with matching leaves, make *matching* mortises in the adjoining parts.

■ Cut the mortise very shallow, but deep enough that the wooden parts almost touch when the door or lid is closed. How deep? That depends on the hinge. For some, the depth of the mortise must equal the thickness of the hinge leaves; for others, half the diameter of the barrel.

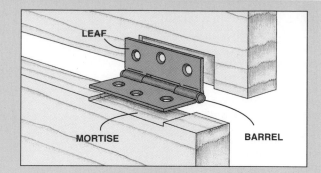

LEAF

MORTISE

BARREL

1 Mark the locations of the hinges on the case. If you're setting a lid, clamp it to the case. If you're hanging a door, wedge it in place with slivers of wood or cardboard. Transfer the marks from the case to the lid or door frame.

2 Remove the door or lid. Position the hinge leaf on the wood at the marks and trace around it. Cut the edges of the hinge mortise and remove most of the waste with a chisel.

3 Cut the bottom of the mortise to a uniform depth with a router plane. Drill pilot holes for the hinge screws and install the hinges.

4 You can also rout hinge mortises with a router and a mortising template. Use a guide collar to follow the template while a straight bit cuts the mortise. Shown is a commercial template for architectural door hinges.

5 European cabinet door hinges (such as Blum hinges) are set in round mortises. Manufacturers sell special boring bits (135 millimeters in diameter) to make the mortises.

TROUBLE *SHOOTING*

COMING UNHINGED? When you install a hinge slightly off-kilter, don't panic. To adjust its position, remove the screws and fill the pilot holes with toothpicks or matchsticks and glue. If necessary, enlarge the mortise slightly. After the glue is dry, drill new pilot holes beside the old ones and replace the hinge.

MAKING A TENON

Among the most common techniques for making a tenon:

■ Cut the cheeks and the shoulders in two steps on a table saw with an ordinary saw blade.

■ Cut each cheek and shoulder in one step with **dado cutter**[2] or a table-mounted router.

Should you need to hold the stock vertically while you cut or rout, secure it in a **tenoning jig**.[3]

PRO*TIP*

To get a tight fit between a mortise and a tenon, it often helps to **undercut** the shoulders of the tenon. Using a chisel, cut away a small amount of stock from each shoulder where it meets the cheek.

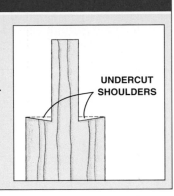

UNDERCUT SHOULDERS

CUTTING A TENON ON A TABLE SAW

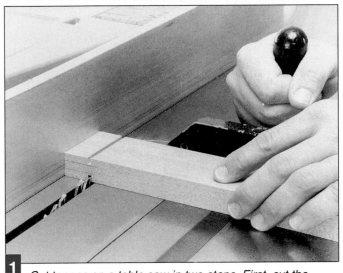

1 Cut tenons on a table saw in two steps. First, cut the shoulders. Guide the stock with a miter gauge, using the fence to position the stock.

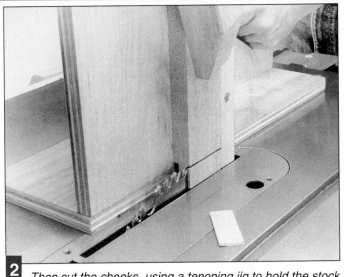

2 Then cut the cheeks, using a tenoning jig to hold the stock vertically as you slide the jig along the fence.

CUTTING A TENON WITH A DADO CUTTER

To cut a tenon with a dado cutter, use a miter gauge to guide the work over the cutter. If the tenon is longer than the cutter is wide, make several passes, removing a little more waste with each pass. Use the fence to position the work for the last pass.

CUTTING A TENON WITH A ROUTER

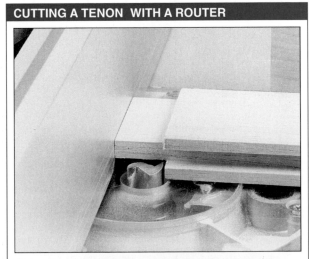

Cut a tenon on a router table by guiding the work past a wide straight bit with a miter gauge. As with a dado cutter, you may have to make several passes to create a long tenon. Use the fence to position the work and prevent the bit from pulling it sideways as you cut.

LOOSE TENON JOINTS

You can use mortising and tenoning techniques to create *loose tenon joints.* These are actually reinforced joints — the "tenon" is a large spline that spans the joint between two parts with matching mortises. But they are just as strong as traditional mortise-and-tenon joints and often require fewer setups.

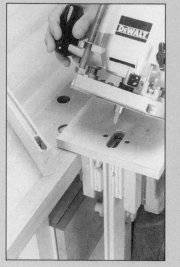

1 *Rout identical mortises in the two adjoining parts. Don't bother to square the corners. Then cut tenon stock as thick as the mortises are wide, and as wide as the mortises are long.*

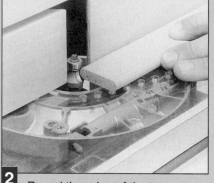

2 *Round the edge of the tenon stock to fit the mortises. Then cut the tenons to length. Score grooves in the sides of the tenons to relieve the hydraulic pressure that builds up when the glue is squeezed in the joint.*

3 *Apply glue to the mating surfaces and the mortises. Insert the tenon into the mortises, and clamp the parts together.*

MAKING ROUND MORTISES AND TENONS

Round mortises and tenons typically join turned parts, such as chair legs and rungs, although they can also be used to assemble rectangular boards. **Drill**[1] the mortises with a drill press or hand-held drill. **Turn**[2] the tenons or cut them with a *tenon cutter.*

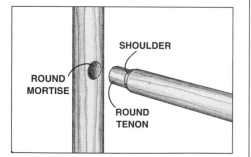

SHOULDER

ROUND MORTISE

ROUND TENON

ROUND MORTISE-AND-TENON JOINT

PRO *TIP*

For maximum strength, make round mortises and tenons at least 1½ times as deep and long as their diameter.

MAKING ROUND MORTISES

1 *When making round mortises in spindle turnings, it's often easier to drill the holes **before** you turn the shapes. Round the stock on the lathe, turning rough cylinders. Bore the mortises in the cylinders, then turn the finished shapes.*

2 *To drill mortises at an angle, mount a 6-inch length of coat hanger wire in a scrap of wood. Bend the wire to the angle you want and place it close to the mortise location. Drill the mortise with a portable drill, sighting along the wire and the bit to keep them parallel. Although you can drill at an angle by tilting the drill press table or using a drill guide, this method is quicker when you have a lot of mortises to make.*

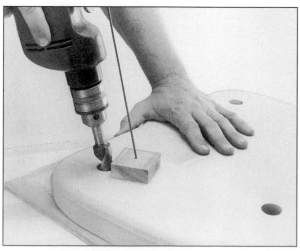

MAKING ROUND TENONS ON A DRILL PRESS

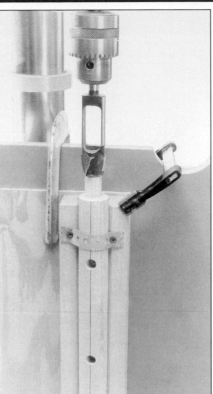

Cut a round tenon on a drill press with a **tenon cutter.** Tilt the drill press table vertically and attach a V-Jig to hold the end of a turning directly under the chuck. Clamp the turning in the V-jig and cut the tenon to the desired length with the cutter.

JIGS & FIXTURES

TENON GAUGE This gauge combines fixed calipers and a test hole. The initial opening of the calipers is 1/16 inch wider than the desired diameter, then it closes down to the correct diameter at a step inside the opening. This step is an early warning device, telling you when the turning is approaching the proper size.

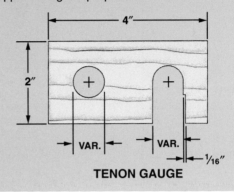

TENON GAUGE

SEE ALSO:

[1]Drilling Round Stock   214

[2]Lathe Turning   306

TURNING ROUND TENONS ON A LATHE

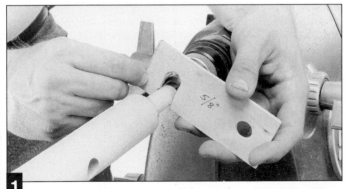

1 To turn a round tenon on a lathe, make a **tenon gauge** (see sidebar above) from a scrap of plywood to test the diameter. Turn the tenon, checking the work frequently with the gauge. When the calipers slip over the tenon up to the step, you know you're approaching the diameter.

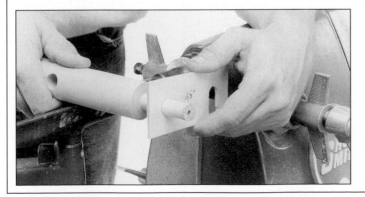

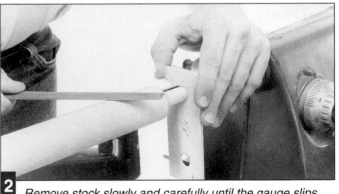

2 Remove stock slowly and carefully until the gauge slips over the tenon past the step. At this point, the tenon should be the correct diameter.

NOTE: Some craftsmen prefer to sand or file the tenon to its final diameter. This removes stock very slowly and reduces the risk of turning the tenon too small.

3 Turn off the lathe and dismount the turning. Test fit the tenon in the hole in the gauge — it should be a slip fit. If any further lathe work is required, mount the part back on the lathe.

TIP: Mark a spur on the drive center and the corresponding indentation on the turning. Should you need to mount the turning on the lathe again, line up the marks.

MAKING INTERLOCKING JOINTS

The common purpose of interlocking joints such as finger and dovetail joints is to **increase the gluing surface**[1]. This, in turn, makes a stronger joint.

MAKING FINGER JOINTS

Finger joints are interlocking tenons and notches in the ends of adjoining boards. Usually, the fingers are spaced evenly and are all the same width. This lets you cut them with a single setup, using a *finger joint jig*.

■ The width of the adjoining boards should be a multiple of the finger width so that there are no "half fingers" in the joint.

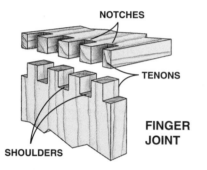

NOTCHES

TENONS

FINGER JOINT

SHOULDERS

■ Make the fingers $1/32$ to $1/16$ inch longer than the thickness of the adjoining board. After assembly, sand them flush.

■ Scribe the shoulders of the fingers and back up the board with a scrap to prevent the cutter from tearing the wood grain.

MAKING FINGER JOINTS

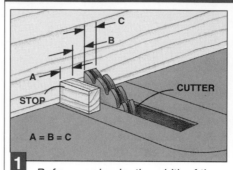

A = B = C

STOP

CUTTER

1 *Before you begin, the width of the stop on the jig and the width of the cutter must be precisely the same. Adjust the distance between the stop and the cutter equal to the width of the cutter (and stop).*

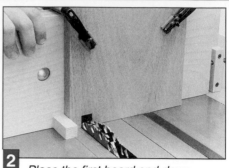

2 *Place the first board end-down against the face of the jig and slide it sideways until it butts against the stop. Clamp the board to the jig and slide it forward, cutting the first notch.*

3 *Place the second board against the first and align the edge with the side of the notch nearest the stop. Clamp the second board to the first and cut again.*

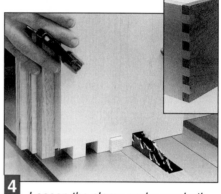

4 *Loosen the clamp and move both boards sideways until the notches you just cut fit over the stop. Tighten the clamp and cut another set of notches. Repeat until you have cut all the notches in both boards. Assemble the joint. If it's too tight, move the stop **toward** the cutter slightly. If it's too loose, move it **away** from the cutter.*

JIGS & FIXTURES

FINGER JOINT JIG

Mounted on a miter gauge, this fixture will work with either a table saw and a **dado cutter**[2] or a table-mounted router and a **straight bit**[3]. Make the stop the same size as the width of the fingers you plan to cut. Use the adjustment screw to fine-tune the position of the stop when setting up.

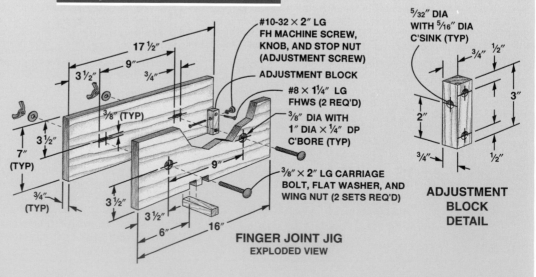

#10-32 × 2" LG FH MACHINE SCREW, KNOB, AND STOP NUT (ADJUSTMENT SCREW)

ADJUSTMENT BLOCK

#8 × 1¼" LG FHWS (2 REQ'D)

⅜" DIA WITH 1" DIA × ¼" DP C'BORE (TYP)

⅜" × 2" LG CARRIAGE BOLT, FLAT WASHER, AND WING NUT (2 SETS REQ'D)

17½"

9"

¾"

⅜" (TYP)

7" (TYP)

3½"

¾" (TYP)

3½"

9"

3½"

6"

16"

FINGER JOINT JIG
EXPLODED VIEW

⁵⁄₃₂" DIA WITH ⁵⁄₁₆" DIA C'SINK (TYP)

¾"

½"

2"

3"

¾"

½"

ADJUSTMENT BLOCK DETAIL

MAKING MACHINE-CUT DOVETAILS

You can cut dovetails on several different power tools, but it's easiest with a hand-held router and a commercial *dovetail jig*. Most are designed to cut only half-blind dovetails, commonly used to assemble drawers and boxes. A few jigs will also make through dovetails and other types of dovetail joints.

Use a **guide collar**[4] to follow the templates that come with the jig.

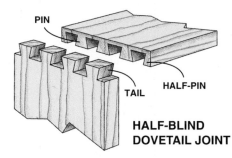

PIN

HALF-PIN

TAIL

HALF-BLIND DOVETAIL JOINT

Cut the sloped tails with a **dovetail bit**[3]. When cutting through dovetails, cut the pins with a **straight bit**[3].

SEE *ALSO*:

[1]Provide a Good Gluing
   Surface or Anchor   15
[2]Making Simple Joints   232
[3]Router Bits   125
[4]Guiding the Router   218

ROUTING HALF-BLIND DOVETAILS

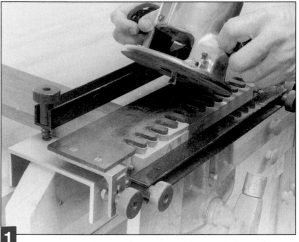

1 To rout a half-blind dovetail joint, secure both of the adjoining boards in the jig. The tail board is held vertically, its end flush with the top surface of the horizontal pin board. Cut both the tails and pins in one pass.

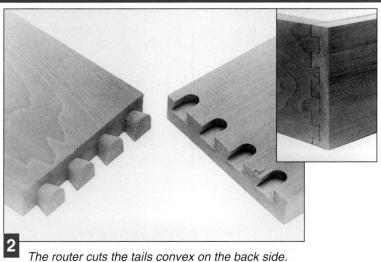

2 The router cuts the tails convex on the back side. These fit in the concave slots between the pins.

ROUTING THROUGH DOVETAILS

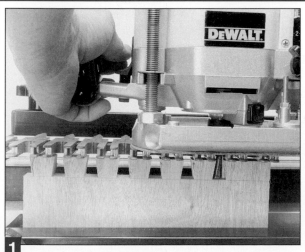

1 When routing through dovetails, make the joint in two steps. Secure the tail board vertically in the jig and rout the tails with a dovetail bit, guiding the router with the tail template.

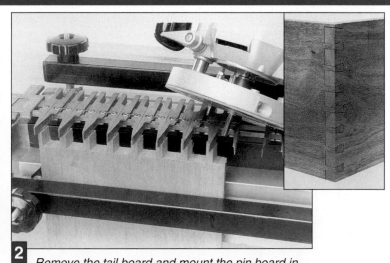

2 Remove the tail board and mount the pin board in its place. Fasten the pin template over it and rout the pins with a straight bit. Fit the pins to the tails by moving the template forward or back on the jig. This will change the size (but not the location) of the pins.

MAKING DOVETAIL JOINTS BY HAND

Although a router will cut a very respectable dovetail joint, many craftsmen still prefer to cut them by hand. No machine can match the wide, graceful tails and narrow, delicate pins of traditional handmade dovetail joints. These have become a hallmark of finely crafted furniture.

When making dovetail joints by hand:

■ Select **straight-grained wood**[1] for the members. It's difficult to hand-cut dovetails in wavy or irregular grain.

■ Keep the slope of the pins and tails between 8 and 12 degrees. When the slope is too shallow, the assembled joint slips. When it's too steep, the corners of the tails chip easily.

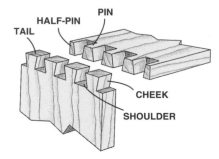

THROUGH DOVETAIL JOINT

■ Cut the cheeks with a **dovetail saw**[2] or **dozuki saw**.[3]

■ Always cut on the *waste* sides of the layout lines to ensure that the pins and tails fit snugly.

■ Make both the pins and tails $1/32$ to $1/16$ inch longer than the thickness of the adjoining boards. After assembly, sand them flush.

MAKING DOVETAIL JOINTS BY HAND

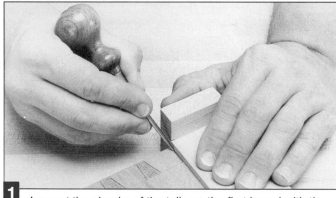

1 Lay out the cheeks of the tails on the first board with the **slope gauge/saw guide** and scribe the shoulders with a cutting gauge. Mark **both** sides of the board, shading the stock between the tails to indicate the waste.

2 Cut the sloping cheeks down to the shoulder line. Use the **slope gauge/saw guide** to start the cut.
NOTE: Dovetail saws used exclusively for cutting dovetails should be sharpened as *rip saws*.

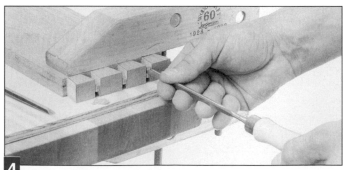

4 After cutting vertically, hold the chisel horizontally with its edge against the end about $1/16$ inch below the surface. Strike the chisel and split out a small amount of waste. Continue cutting and splitting with the chisel until you have removed the waste halfway through the board. Turn the board over and repeat, removing the remaining waste.

5 Use the completed tails to mark the pins. Position the tails over the end of the second board. Place the back of a chisel against a cheek of a tail and tap the chisel with a mallet. Repeat for each cheek, marking the ends of the pins on the board. Mark the cheeks of the pins and scribe their shoulder on both sides of the board. Shade the waste between them.

JIGS & FIXTURES

SLOPE GAUGE/SAW GUIDE This tiny jig simplifies the most difficult task in making hand-cut dovetails — sawing the sloped cheeks of the tails and pins. First use the jig to lay out the cheeks. When you're ready to cut, align it with a cheek line. Hold it against the wood with one hand and saw with the other. Keep the saw body flat against the jig, and the saw will follow the line precisely.

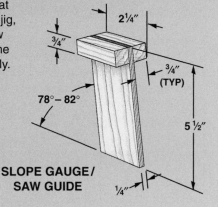

2¼"

¾"

¾"
(TYP)

78° – 82°

5 ½"

**SLOPE GAUGE/
SAW GUIDE**

¼"

TROUBLE *SHOOTING*

CLOSING THE GAP The most common problem in making dovetails — or any joint, for that matter — is when an over-zealous saw or chisel removes too much stock and **gaps**[4] appear.

1 To close the gaps, clean them out and widen them with a dovetail saw.

2 Glue wood slips or wedges in the gaps, carefully matching the wood color and grain direction. After the glue dries, cut and sand the wedges flush — no one will ever know.

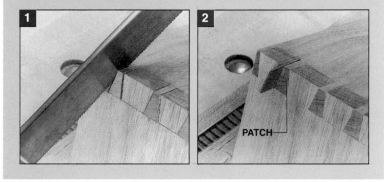

PATCH

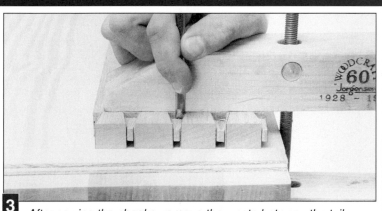

3 *After sawing the cheeks, remove the waste between the tails. Use a chisel alternately as a cutting tool and a wedge. Hold the chisel vertically with the cutting edge on the shoulder line. Strike the chisel lightly with a mallet, cutting about ¹⁄₁₆ inch into the wood.*

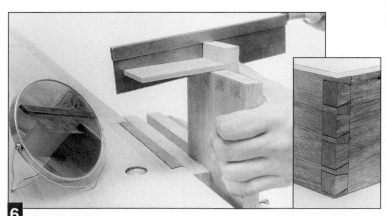

6 *Cut the pins in the same manner as the tails. Saw the cheeks, then remove the waste with a chisel. Fit the joint together. If the fit is tight, shave a little stock from the cheeks.*

MORE *SOURCES*

BOOKS

Encyclopedia of Wood Joints, by Wolfram Graubner, Taunton Press, 1992

Joining Wood, by Nick Engler, Rodale Press, 1992

Wood Joiner's Handbook, by Sam Allen, Sterling Publishing, 1990

Woodworking: The Right Technique, by Bob Moran, Rodale Press, 1995

VIDEOS

Dovetail a Drawer with Frank Klausz, Taunton Books and Videos

Making Mortise-and-Tenon Joints with Frank Klausz, Taunton Books and Videos

SEE *ALSO*:

[1]Grain Pattern	352
[2]Handsaws	131
[3]Japanese Saws	132
[4]Filling Gaps	249

22

Gluing and Clamping

Properly glued, the assembled parts of a project are stronger than if they were carved from a single piece of wood.

Woodworking, according to one tongue-in-cheek definition, is the act of cutting large boards into smaller boards, then gluing them back together again in the hopes of making something more useful than a board. Like all good jokes, there's more than a little truth to this statement. The usefulness of a project depends on many factors — good design, proper preparation of the stock, skilled joinery. But it all comes to naught if the little boards don't stay stuck. And although you can use nails and screws for assembly, gluing is the preferred method for permanently attaching one wooden part to another.

On the surface, it's a simple process — apply the glue to the adjoining surfaces, clamp the parts together, and wait for the glue to dry.

However, there's more to it. To get a strong, durable glue joint, you must fit the joint properly, pick the proper glue, and use the proper assembly methods for the task.

ANATOMY OF A GLUE JOINT

A *glue joint* attaches the surface of one piece of wood to another. When glued properly, any **stress**[1] applied to one board is transferred across the joint to the second, as if the two pieces were one.

*The ribbonlike inlays that weave themselves around this **Rolling Pin** were created by an ingenious gluing technique. The turner laminated contrasting layers of wood and cut the assembly at an angle — not once, but several times — prior to turning it on a lathe. Wherever the cylindrical shape of the pin intersects a layer of wood, it makes an elliptical line.*

SPECS: 2½″ diameter, 16″ long

MATERIALS: Walnut, cherry, marine plywood

CRAFTSMAN: Rude Osolnik
Berea, KY

COHESION AND ADHESION

The strength of the joint depends on two properties – the *cohesion* of the glue and its *adhesion* to the wood. The glue molecules in the *glue line* cohere to one another. Where they meet the wood, they adhere in two ways. The glue penetrates the pores and cell cavities in the wood, then hardens around these intricate structures, creating what glue chemists call an *interphase*. At the same time, the wood molecules and glue molecules attract one another because they have opposite electrical charges.

Several factors influence cohesion and adhesion in a glue joint:

- Type of wood or wood product
- Type of adhesive
- Environmental conditions in which the glue cures
- Total area of adjoining surfaces
- Orientation of the **wood grain**[2]
- Assembly technique
- Fit of the **joint**[3]

MAKING STRONG JOINTS

Of these factors, the most important is the fit of the joint. To form an interphase – and the strong bond that goes with it – the wood surfaces must contact each other *intimately*. When the glue cures, the glue line should be thin and uniform.

Gaps or voids in the glue line weaken the joint, as do areas where the glue is too thick. To form a strong joint, the parts should fit with about 0.005 inch of clearance. This is what craftsmen refer to as a **slip fit**[3] – there's no perceptible slop in the joint, but you can take it apart and put it back together without forcing it. When the joint is assembled with a water-based glue, the wood swells, closing the fit even tighter. The resulting glue line is 0.002 to 0.003 inch thick, no thicker than a piece of paper.

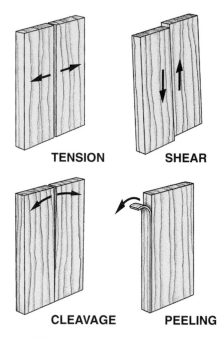

TENSION   **SHEAR**

CLEAVAGE   **PEELING**

A glue joint must withstand stress, transferring the load across the glue line so the adjoining parts share it. The four forces shown commonly tear apart weak joints.

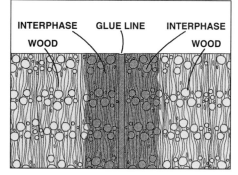

INTERPHASE   GLUE LINE   INTERPHASE
WOOD   WOOD

GLUE JOINT

FILLING GAPS

Inexperienced woodworkers sometimes try to fill gaps in joints with glue. Unfortunately, most glues are poor gap fillers. Glues are formulated from **resins and solvents**[4]. When the resin hardens, the solvent dissipates and the glue shrinks. The gaps reappear.

It's equally ineffective to mix glue with sawdust and use the resulting paste as a filler. The solvent in many popular glues is water, which causes the sawdust to swell. As the glue dries, the sawdust shrinks and the gaps return.

If you need to fill a gap, here are four effective techniques:

- Use epoxy cement to secure and fill the joint. Epoxy shrinks much less than other glues.
- Mix water-based glues with a substance that won't expand, such as **pumice or rottenstone**[5].
- Mix sawdust with glue that doesn't have a water base, such as model cement. This glue won't cause the sawdust to swell.
- Assemble the ill-fitting joint with glue. While the glue is still wet, press small wedges or slivers of wood into the gaps. Carefully choose these wedges to match the species, color, and grain direction of the adjoining parts. When the glue dries, cut and sand the wedges flush.

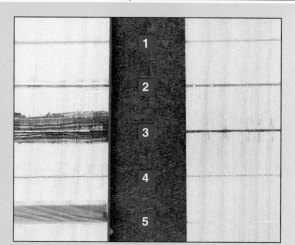

Which gap-filling method works best? The saw kerfs in these wood blocks were filled with aliphatic (yellow) glue (1), epoxy cement (2), polyvinyl (white) glue mixed with rottenstone (3), model cement mixed with sawdust (4), and a wooden wedge secured with glue (5). After the glues harden and you sand them flush, the wedge wins hands down.

ADHESIVE TYPES

Glues are simple concoctions, with just two major ingredients – a *resin* (or solid) and a *solvent* (to keep the resin in a liquid state until it's applied). Glues harden in several ways. Most simply harden as the solvent dissipates or evaporates. Others change chemically – the molecules cross-link, forming a strong matrix. A few are applied hot and harden as they cool.

Woodworking glues can be organized into four categories.

ONE-PART GLUES

One-part glues typically come ready to use in an applicator. A few must be mixed with water.

■ *Cooked hide glue* is boiled down from hides, hooves, bones, and sinews. Because it spoils easily, it comes as crystals. Mix these with water and apply them hot (125 to 140°F).

■ *Liquid hide glue* includes additives that keep it from spoiling and allow you to apply it at room temperature. It's slightly weaker than its cooked cousin.

MYTH *CONCEPTIONS*

STAYS STUCK Hide glues don't necessarily disintegrate with time, as many think. The resins are extremely stable. In fact, 3,000-year-old pieces of Egyptian furniture have been found with serviceable hide-glue joints.

■ *Polyvinyl resin glue* (white glue) is a general-purpose adhesive made from synthetic polyvinyl acetate (PVA) resin.

■ *Aliphatic resin glue* (yellow glue) is also made from PVA resin, but it's modified to be less runny, quicker-setting, and easier to sand. It's the preferred adhesive of most craftsmen.

■ *Urea-formaldehyde glue* (plastic resin glue) is made from a plastic resin. It comes as a powder that must be mixed with water.

■ *Cyanoacrylate glue* (such as the

*Traditional cooked **hide glue** must be applied hot. Although there are heated glue pots available for this task, a double boiler and an electric hot plate do just as well. Monitor the temperature with a candy thermometer.*

Super Glue brand) is made with an acrylic resin that hardens immediately upon contact with minute amounts of moisture. Purchase a formula that's made specifically to bond wood.

TWO-PART GLUES

Two-part glues come as a resin and a hardener. They must mixed before they can be used.

■ *Epoxy cement* is made from epoxy and polyamine resins and is available in two forms – slow-set and quick-set. It's strong and water-resistant, and there are formulas for gluing oily wood, gluing at low temperatures, and to adjust the color and texture. It can be used with or without clamps. All this makes epoxy the most versatile of woodworking adhesives.

■ *Resorcinol glue* consists of resorcinol and phenoresorcinol resins in liquid form with a powdered catalyst. This is the strongest glue available. It's also waterproof.

ELASTOMERS

Elastomer adhesives, when cured, remain flexible.

■ *Mastics,* such as panel adhesives, are made with latex, rubber, and other elastic resins. They hold rough, uneven surfaces better than other glues and are typically used in carpentry.

■ *Silicone caulk* is made from synthetic rubber and is useful for bonding nonporous materials. It's completely waterproof.

■ *Contact cement* is made from neoprene rubber, and is used to secure veneers, laminates, and other thin materials to wood.

THERMOPLASTIC GLUES

Thermoplastic glues change from solid to liquid when heated.

■ *Hot-melt glues* are made from polyethylene and polyvinyl resins. They are applied hot with a **special gun**[1], then harden as they cool. They are not particularly strong but are useful for temporary assemblies.

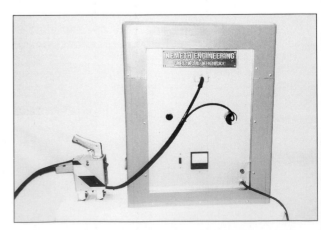

*Plastic resin glue is a favorite among manufacturers because of its long working times. Additionally, it can be cured in minutes by bombarding it with high-frequency radio waves. Shown is a hand-held **radio frequency (RF) gluing tool.***

Photo courtesy Nemeth Engineering, Crestwood, KY

ADHESIVE PROPERTIES

Each glue has characteristics or properties that suit it to specific woodworking operations.

WORKING PROPERTIES

Some properties determine the working quality of the glue.

■ *Shelf or pot life* – Ready-to-use glues have a shelf life, mixed glues, a pot life, after which their adhesive power degrades.

■ *Open assembly time* or working time – How much time do you have to spread the glue and assemble the project before the glue begins to cure? If the glue partially cures before assembly, it won't bond properly.

■ *Closed assembly time* or clamp time – How much time is required for the glue to cure sufficiently to remove the clamps holding the parts together?

■ *Cure time* – How long does it take for the glue to attain full strength? At this point the glue is hardened sufficiently so the joint can be machined or sanded.

■ *Sandability* – How likely is the glue to clog or **load**[2] the abrasive when sanded?

■ *Working temperature range* – What's the temperature range in which the glue cures properly?

GLUE DURABILITY

Other properties control how durable the glue is and what conditions the bond will endure.

■ *Strength* – This is the ability to withstand stress.

■ *Creep* – When put under constant stress, some glues will creep very slowly, allowing wooden parts to shift.

*Although **silicone caulk** is not used extensively in woodworking, craftsmen find it useful for specific tasks such as securing glass panes in doors. Because the caulk is an elastomer, it will allow the wood to expand and contract independently of the glass.*
NOTE: Silicone caulk won't hold a finish, so be careful not to get it on a surface you intend to finish.

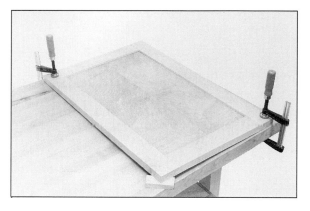

*Many glues will **creep**, allowing wood surfaces to shift under constant stress. You can sometimes use this property to your advantage. If a frame or case is not flat or square after glue-up, clamp it to apply pressure in the direction you'd like the wood to move. Check it every other day. After a while — sometimes weeks — the assembly will creep into alignment.*

■ *Water resistance* – Can the glue be dissolved by water? How quickly?

■ *Chemical resistance* – Can the glue be dissolved by other common chemicals, particularly **solvents in finishes**[3]?

■ *Heat resistance* – Many glues turn liquid when heated. How much heat must be applied to weaken the bond?

CHOOSING GLUES

To match a glue to a gluing task, ask yourself:

■ *How and where will you assemble the project?* Your shop environment is critical; most glues are temperature-sensitive. Some are affected by humidity, as well.

Surface contaminants may weaken the bond. Water-based glues won't spread properly on a material contaminated with wax or oil. If dust settles on contact cement before assembly, it will weaken the joint.

■ *What materials will you glue together?* Not all woods and wood products are equally bondable. Oily **extractives**[4] in some woods prevent the glue from bonding. **Wood density**[5] also plays a part. Generally, the denser the wood, the more difficult it is to bond.

■ How will the assembled project be used? In other words, how strong does the glue bond have to be and what sort of environment must it weather? The U.S. Forest Products Laboratory rates glues for strength and durability. Strong glues that resist stress for long periods of time without creep are *structural;* weaker ones are *semistructural* or *nonstructural.* Glues that stand up to moisture, heat, and common chemicals are *exterior* glues. Those that don't are *limited exterior* or *interior.*

PROPERTIES OF COMMON ADHESIVES

Type	Classification	Uses	Gap Filling	Sandability	Working Temperatures (F)
Cooked Hide Glue	One-Part, Nonstructural/ Interior	General interior woodworking, antique restoration and reproduction, veneering, joinery that can be easily disassembled	Fair	Good	Shop: 70°–100°, Glue: 125°–140°
Liquid Hide Glue	One-Part, Nonstructural/ Interior	General interior woodworking, complex assemblies requiring long open time, joinery that can be easily disassembled	Fair	Good	70°–90°
Polyvinyl Resin (White) Glue	One-Part, Nonstructural/ Interior	General interior woodworking	Fair	Poor	60°–90°
Interior Aliphatic Resin (Yellow) Glue	One-Part, Nonstructural/ Interior	General interior woodworking, gluing oily woods	Fair	Fair	45°–110°
Exterior Aliphatic Resin (Yellow) Glue	One-Part, Semistructural/ Exterior	General interior woodworking, gluing oily woods, kitchen and bathroom projects, outdoor furniture	Fair	Fair	45°–110°
Urea Formaldehyde (Plastic Resin) Glue	One-Part, Structural/ Limited Exterior	General woodworking, veneering, complex assemblies requiring long open time, architectural structures, bent laminations	Poor	Good	70°–100°
Cyanoacrylate (Super) Glue	One-Part, Nonstructural/ Interior	Small repairs, bonding nonporous materials, securing inlays	Poor to Fair	Fair	65°–180°
Quick-Set Epoxy Cement	Two-Part, Semistructural/ Limited Exterior	Small repairs, bathroom and kitchen projects, gluing oily woods, bonding nonporous materials	Good	Good	35°–200°, depending on formula
Slow-Set Epoxy Cement	Two-Part, Structural/ Exterior	Bathroom and kitchen projects, gluing oily woods, outdoor furniture, architectural structures, bent laminations, bonding nonporous materials	Good	Good	35°–200°, depending on formula
Resorcinol Glue	Two-Part, Structural/ Exterior	Bathroom and kitchen projects, outdoor furniture, architectural structures, bent laminations, complex assemblies requiring long open time	Good	Good	70°–90°
Mastics	Elastomer, Semistructural/ Limited Exterior	Securing paneling, wainscoting, flooring, non-load-bearing architectural structures	Good	Poor	65°–110°
Silicone Caulk	Elastomer, Nonstructural/ Interior	Bonding nonporous materials	Good	Poor	–35°–140°
Contact Cement	Elastomer, Nonstructural/ Interior	Veneering, bonding plastic laminates	Poor	Poor	65°–150°
Hot-Melt Glue	Thermoplastic, Nonstructural/ Interior	Small repairs, temporary assemblies, joinery that can be easily disassembled	Good	Poor	32°–160°

HIDE GLUES

POLYVINYL RESIN GLUE

ALIPHATIC RESIN GLUES

PLASTIC RESIN GLUE

SUPER GLUE

QUICK-SET EPOXY

Shelf Life/ Pot Life	Open Assembly Time	Closed Assembly Time	Cure Time	Comments
Indefinite unmixed/ 8–10 hours mixed	3–5 minutes	2 hours	12–16 hours	Develops tack almost immediately; nontoxic; don't heat glue above 160°F; clean up with water .
1 year	15–30 minutes	12–16 hours	1 day	Low toxicity; clean up with water.
Indefinite unopened/ 1 year opened	5–10 minutes	1 hour	1 day	Nontoxic; freezing may ruin uncured glue; clean up with water.
18–24 months	5–10 minutes	30 minutes	1 day	Develops tack in about 1 minute; low toxicity; freezing may ruin uncured glue; clean up with water.
1 year	4–8 minutes	1 hour	1 day	Critical times are slightly faster than interior formula; develops tack in about 1 minute; freezing may ruin uncured glue; clean up with water.
1 year unmixed/ 1–2 hours mixed	10–30 minutes	12–14 hours	1 day	Uncured glue is toxic; can be absorbed through skin; cured glue dust (from sanding) is toxic; use with adequate ventilation and protection; clean up with water.
Varies with formula	15–30 seconds	1 minute	2–4 hours	Water-resistant despite interior classification; bonds skin, but acetone dissolves bonds; vapors can irritate nose and eyes and may cause headaches; use with adequate ventilation.
Indefinite unmixed/ 5 minutes mixed	1–5 minutes	5 minutes	12–24 hours	No clamping pressure required; uncured glue is toxic; use with adequate ventilation and protection; resists moisture and chemicals but not heat; clean up with vinegar.
Indefinite unmixed/ 1 hour mixed	30–60 minutes	2–4 hours	12–24 hours	No clamping pressure required; uncured glue is toxic; use with adequate ventilation and protection; resists moisture and chemicals but not heat; clean up with vinegar.
1 year unmixed/ 1–4 hours mixed, depending on temperature	7–15 minutes	1–2 hours	1 day	Strongest of all glues; uncured glue is toxic; can be absorbed through skin; cured glue dust (from sanding) is toxic; use with adequate ventilation and protection; clean up with water.
Indefinite unopened	5–10 minutes	2–4 hours	1 day	May irritate skin, nose, and eyes; use with adequate ventilation and protection; clean up with mineral spirits.
Indefinite unopened	10–15 minutes	2–4 hours	1 day	Waterproof despite interior classification; may irritate skin, nose, and eyes; use with adequate ventilation and protection; clean up with mineral spirits.
1 year	15–30 minutes	Bonds on contact	1 day	Vapors are highly toxic; solvent-based formulas are flammable; use with adequate ventilation; clean up with acetone. Freezing ruins water-based formulas.
Indefinite	5–10 seconds	30–60 seconds	1 minute	Glue may break down when exposed to some finishing chemicals; tip of glue gun is extremely hot, so be careful not to touch.

SLOW-SET EPOXY **RESORCINOL GLUE** **MASTIC** **SILICONE CAULK** **CONTACT CEMENT** **HOT-MELT GLUE**

GLUING KNOW-HOW

The gluing process has several distinct steps. After *preparing a surface* for gluing, *dry assemble* the project (without glue) to check the fit of the joints. Spread glue and align the parts in *open assembly,* then apply clamps to *close* it. Finally, let the glue *cure.*

PREPARING SURFACES FOR GLUING

For the glue joint to be as strong as possible, the adjoining surfaces must **mate intimately**[1] with no perceptible gaps or voids. Additionally, the surface must be free of crushed fibers and chemical contaminants that might prevent the glue from spreading and penetrating.

Smooth knife-cut surfaces make the best glue joints. Wood cut with a planer, jointer, router, or shaper will glue up well. Some **high-quality saw blades**[2], such as hollow-ground planer blades and precision carbide-tipped blades, cut smoothly. However, most saws do not.

Planed or jointed surfaces make a strong glue joint. So do routed and sanded surfaces. Surfaces cut with ordinary saw blades may not be smooth enough, while those cut with a band saw are almost certainly too coarse.

> ### PRO *TIP*
>
> As a rule of thumb, a gluing surface should be at least as smooth as a surface sanded with 50-grit sandpaper. The smoother, the better.

Glue up as soon after cutting as you can – the same day, if possible. Otherwise, the wood surface starts to collect dust, oils, and other contaminants. It may also shrink or swell, ruining the fit of the joints. The bondability of some woods decreases the longer the surfaces are exposed to air.

DRY ASSEMBLY

Before applying glue, it's always advisable to *dry assemble* the parts, clamping them together without glue. Not only does this test the fit of the joints, it also allows you to adjust the clamps. If the assembly is complex, it provides a "clamping rehearsal." When it comes time to glue up, you can apply the clamps quickly and expertly.

OPEN ASSEMBLY

Apply glue in thin, even coats, using a brush, wood scrap, or some other tool to spread it. Fingers make handy glue spreaders, of course, provided you don't mind the mess

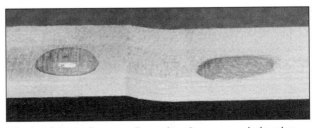

The surfaces of some oily and resinous woods harden when exposed to air. This prevents the glue from **wetting** the surface — that is, it won't spread or penetrate properly. The edge of this yellow pine was jointed and allowed to stand for a week. Afterward, a small portion of the edge was jointed again. As you can see, the freshly jointed surface absorbs liquids much faster than the other.

and provided the glue contains no irritants or toxins.

Just how thick or thin should you spread the glue? Thick enough that at least some glue squeezes out of the joint when you apply the clamps. You don't want to "starve" the joint for glue; this will make it weak.

> ### PRO *TIP*
>
> When gluing oily woods such as teak and rosewood, clean the surface with acetone or naphtha before applying the glue. This removes some of the oils near the surface and lets the glue penetrate.

APPLYING GLUE

Acid brushes and pipe cleaners make good, inexpensive glue applicators. Use a brush to spread glue over a surface, and a pipe cleaner to apply it in mortises, slots, and other recesses.

CLOSED ASSEMBLY

As soon as possible after spreading the glue, assemble the wooden parts and *apply pressure* to the joints with clamps. With the exception of **epoxy cement, contact cement, and cyanoacrylate glue** [3], wood glues must cure under pressure to form a strong bond. This squeezes the air out of the joint, brings the surfaces in intimate contact, and helps the glue penetrate the wood.

When gluing up broad or long surfaces, the pressure must be even across the joint. Apply enough pressure to close the joint down to a thin line but not so much that you crush wood fibers.

When working with water-based glues, clean up the excess glue (or *squeeze-out*) that oozes from the joint before it dries. Don't just wipe it from the wood: Thoroughly *wash* the surface with water. If you don't remove all the squeeze-out, it may prevent **stain and finishes** [4] from penetrating. This creates *glue stains* when you finish the wood.

PRO *TIP*

Check for **glue stains** before applying a finish by wetting the wood surface with water or naphtha.

CLEANING UP SQUEEZE-OUT

*Immediately after assembling a joint with water-based glue, clean up the squeeze-out with a **sopping** wet rag. Use enough water to dissolve the glue and float it away from the surface. After cleaning up the glue, wipe off the excess water.*

CURING THE GLUE

If you plan to sand or machine the assembly, you must wait for the glue to harden completely and develop full strength. Otherwise, the joint may come apart as you work. The cure time varies with the glue, but most dry completely in 24 hours. Check the directions.

AVOIDING SUNKEN JOINTS

*When curing water-based glues, you must **wait for the water to evaporate completely** before planing, jointing, or sanding the assembly.*

1 *Water swells the fibers around the joint.*

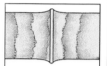

2 *If you sand the surfaces while they are still wet, you remove the high spots.*

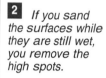
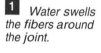

3 *When the wood dries, the surfaces surrounding the joint will sink.*

APPLYING CLAMPS

1 *To generate even pressure along a glue joint, space the clamps evenly, taking care that they're not too far apart. The pressure generated by each clamp is greatest directly under the jaws, and falls off to each side. If the clamps are too far apart, the pressure between them may be insufficient.*

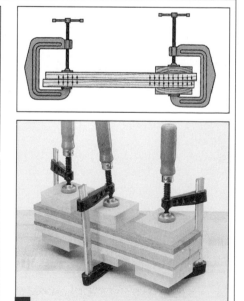

2 *Use thick, rigid hardwood **cauls** to help apply even clamping pressure. These wooden blocks distribute the pressure over a broader surface than the jaws alone. They also prevent the jaws from crushing the wood fibers directly beneath them.*

MYTH *CONCEPTIONS*

TOO MUCH PRESSURE?

You cannot starve a glue joint by applying too much clamping pressure. The glue will be absorbed into the wood long before too much of it will be squeezed out of the joint. The reason that excessive clamping pressure weakens a joint is that it crushes the wood fibers in and around the interphase. This, in turn, makes the wood more likely to break or split.

ASSEMBLY

Assembly techniques vary, depending on joinery, geometry, and, most of all, wood grain. As you glue up, keep two things in mind:

■ The **strongest bonds**[1] occur between long-grain surfaces; the weakest, between end grain.

■ **Wood moves**[2] across the grain, and flat-grain surfaces move more than quarter grain. If the adjoining surfaces move too much and the grain is mismatched, the assembly may distort or the joint may pop.

SIMPLE ASSEMBLIES

The simplest assemblies join identical surfaces, making stock wider, thicker, or longer.

■ *Gluing edge to edge* – To make wide stock from narrow boards, glue them edge to edge. To avoid **glue steps**[3], match the edge grain, gluing flat grain to flat grain or quarter grain to quarter grain. Should you need to align or reinforce the edge joints, use **biscuits, splines, or dowels**[4].

PRO *TIP*

One of the best ways to match edge grain is to cut the pieces from a single long board, then fold the edges back on themselves.

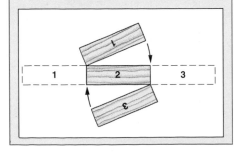

■ *Gluing face to face* – The importance of matching grain increases when gluing boards face to face. If the grain is mismatched, the boards expand and contract at different rates, and the assembly warps. Also consider that face joints have more surface area and require more clamping pressure.

GLUING EDGE TO EDGE

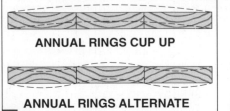

ANNUAL RINGS CUP UP

ANNUAL RINGS ALTERNATE

1 When arranging the boards, give some thought to how you will orient the annual rings. Usually the best-looking arrangement is with the boards turned so all the annual rings cup up — this shows the most heartwood. The assembly tends to cup, rising in the middle, but you can easily control this with bracework. However, if you can't brace the assembly, alternate the annual rings. The individual boards cup, but the overall assembly remains flat.

3 If you haven't already done so, joint the edges straight. Adjust and arrange bar clamps, then apply glue to **one** edge of each board (except the last one).

2 Once the boards are arranged, mark a large "V" across the seams. This shows you which edges to joint and helps you realign the parts for glue-up.

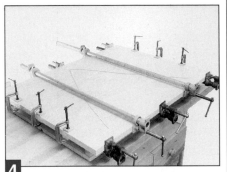

4 Apply the bar clamps, arranging them to alternate between the top and bottom faces. This evens out the pressure and keeps the assembly from buckling. If the boards shift or slide as you apply pressure, straddle the joints with C-clamps and cauls near the ends. Wrap the cauls in wax paper or plastic wrap to keep them from sticking.
WARNING! Don't let the iron parts of the clamps touch the wood where the glue squeezes out of the joints — they may leave black marks.

GLUING FACE TO FACE

PLAIN-SAWN

QUARTER-SAWN

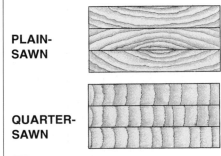

1 When gluing plain-sawn wood face to face, alternate the direction of the annual rings. This will balance the stress and keep the assembly from cupping. When gluing quartersawn lumber, the direction of the annual rings isn't important. But try not to mix plain-sawn and quartersawn — the two types of lumber expand and contract at different rates. Wide assemblies with mixed grain will cup.

2 To prevent the parts from shifting out of alignment when you clamp them, rub two sheets of 50-grit sandpaper together, sprinkling a **few grains** of grit on the wet glue. Press the parts together with enough force to embed the grit in the surfaces of both boards.
NOTE: If you plan to machine the assembly after glue-up, use ordinary sand in a salt shaker. Sand (quartz or silica) is much softer than most abrasives and does less harm to cutting edges.

MAKING A FINGER SCARF JOINT

Cut finger-scarf joints on a router table, using a special router bit. Carefully adjust the depth of cut to cut the adjoining ends precisely the same. When you flip one board and joint the ends together, the top and bottom faces must be flush.

GLUING UP LARGE BOXES

*Apply glue to the corners. As you assemble the parts, slide the bottom and top in place but **do not** glue them in their grooves; they must float. Apply bar clamps in a crisscross pattern to put even pressure on all sides.*

NOTE: To keep from fumbling with cauls, stick them to the wood surfaces with double-faced carpet tape.

GLUING UP SMALL BOXES

You can also use band clamps to assemble a box. Band clamps, however, do not generate as much pressure as bar clamps. They are best used for small or light constructions.

GLUING UP HEAVY FRAMES

*Apply glue to the corner joints. Slide the panel in place as you assemble the rails and stiles, but **do not** glue it. Arrange bar clamps in a crisscross pattern to create even pressure.*

GLUING UP LIGHT FRAMES

*Bar clamps may generate too much pressure when you're assembling light, open frames such as picture frames. And if the corners are mitered, the bar clamps could cause them to slip if the pressure isn't absolutely even. Instead, use **band clamps.** These clamps come with metal corner **cauls** that keep the corners aligned and distribute the pressure evenly to the frame members.*

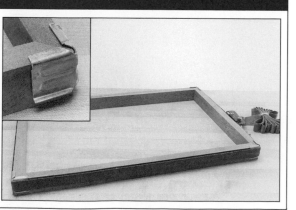

■ *Gluing end to end* – Occasionally you must glue the ends of boards together to create a longer assembly. End-grain joints are inherently weak, but you can strengthen them by increasing the gluing surface. Make a **scarf joint, scarf lap, or finger scarf**[5].

You can also make them stronger by **sealing the end-grain surfaces**[1] prior to assembly. This prevents the end grains from soaking up the glue and starving the joint.

COMPLEX ASSEMBLIES

Most assemblies, including box, frame-and-panel, leg-and-rail, and case **constructions**[6], join several types of wood surfaces and grain.

■ *Gluing up boxes, chests, and drawers* – In a typical box construction, the corners are joined rigidly, while the bottom and top (if there is one) float. Apply glue to the corners but not to the grooves that hold the top and bottom. After clamping, check that the corners are square and the assembly is flat.

■ *Gluing up frames and doors* – Frame-and-panel assemblies are similar to boxes – the corners are joined rigidly, while the panel floats. Consequently, the glue-up procedures are similar. Mitered frames are typically reinforced by **cross-nailing**[1] the corners.

> ### MORE *INFO*
>
> Unless you make a lot of picture frames, a commercial frame clamp is an unnecessary investment. A band clamp will do the same job and, in many cases, is easier to set up.

■ *Gluing up tables and chairs* – Most **leg-and-rail con-structions**[1] have eight or more parts, typically joined by **mortises and tenons**[2]. Fortunately, these joints don't have to be glued together all at once. Divide the construction into two separate and roughly symmetrical halves. Assemble each half, then join the halves.

■ *Gluing up cabinets and bookcases* – It also helps to divide complex **case constructions**[1] into several subassemblies. First, glue together the **frames**[3] – web frames, face frames, frame-and-panel sides. Then assemble the frames and other case parts.

As when gluing up other constructions, you'll find bar clamps and band clamps are the most useful assembly tools. However, some cases don't need to be clamped at all. Instead, **nail or screw**[4] the case together as you glue it up. The fasteners provide pressure while the glue dries.

PRO*TIP*

Conceal screws when assembling bookcases and cabinets by driving them from *underneath* a shelf or web frame and *inside* the case.

ASSEMBLING A CHAIR

1 *Divide chairs into left and right halves when assembling them. (If you divide them front and back, the angles of the side rungs will make it impossible to join the halves.) Join each set of front and back legs with the side rungs.*

2 *Then join the assembled halves with the remaining rungs and chair back.*

ASSEMBLING A CABINET

1 *If the cabinet includes any frame assemblies (such as web frames or a face frame), assemble these first.*

2 *Join a horizontal part to a case side to create a T-shaped assembly. Rest this assembly on its front edges — it will be stable enough to stand on its own. Add the remaining horizontal parts and side.*

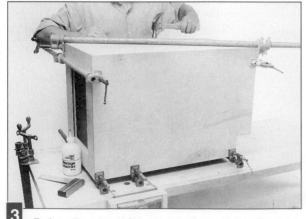

3 *Before the glue dries, square the corners, if necessary. Attach the back to the case to hold it square.*

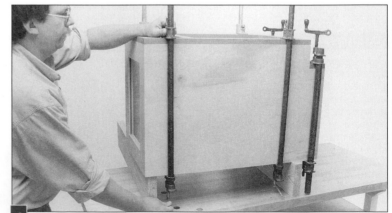

4 *Turn the case assembly over and attach the face frame and toe board.*

KEEPING ASSEMBLIES FLAT

To keep an assembly flat while the glue dries, clamp it or weigh it down to a flat surface. To check that it's flat, lay two **winding sticks** across the top and sight across them horizontally. If the sticks appear parallel to one another, the assembly is flat.

NOTE: Make the sticks from contrasting colors of wood.

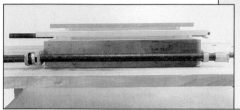

SQUARING ASSEMBLIES

To square up an assembly, straddle the acute corners with a **bar clamp.** Or, loosen the bar clamps that are already in place and shift the ends toward the acute corners. Slowly tighten the clamps until the corners are square. You can also hold the corners square with **miter clamps.**

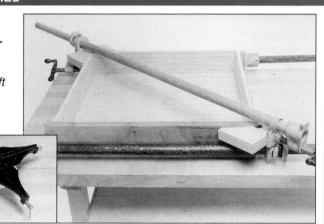

MORE *SOURCES*

Gluing and Clamping, by Nick Engler, Rodale Press, 1993

Gluing and Clamping, by Patrick Spielman, Sterling Publishing, 1986

Wood Handbook: Wood As an Engineering Material, by the U.S. Forest Products Laboratory, U.S. Government Printing Office, 1987

TROUBLE *SHOOTING*

COMMON GLUING PROBLEMS

Problem	Possible Cause(s)	Solution(s)
Weak or failed joints	Not enough gluing surface	Choose joinery to provide adequate surface area.
	Not enough glue (starved joint)	Apply more glue; if gluing end grain, seal end grain.
	Too little clamping pressure	Apply more clamps; space them evenly along joint.
	Poor-fitting joints	Fit joints so mating surfaces contact one another.
	Surface to be glued is too rough.	Cut or sand gluing surfaces smooth.
	Wrong glue for job	Choose appropriate glue for wood or wood product.
	Assembly requires too much time.	Choose glue with longer open assembly time, or divide assembly into shorter steps.
Joints give but don't fail completely.	Glue creeping under constant stress	Redesign joinery to better withstand stress; choose glue that is less likely to creep.
Assembly cups, twists, or distorts.	Adjoining parts moving in different directions or at different rates	Match type of grain and grain direction as closely as possible. Keep surfaces with opposing grain small.
Glue stains	Light stain — squeeze-out not cleaned from surface	Wash off excess water-based glue; let other glues dry, then scrape and sand; check by wetting surface.
	Dark stain — iron clamp in contact with joint as glue dries	Make sure pipes and cast iron or steel parts of clamps do not contact wet glue.
Gaps or voids in glue joint	Poor-fitting joints	Fit joints so mating surfaces contact one another.
	Surface to be glued is too rough.	Cut or sand gluing surfaces smooth.

23

Sanding, Scraping, and Filing

Woodworking can be hard on wood. Sanders, scrapers, and files repair the bruises, leaving a smooth, clean surface.

Sanding, scraping, and filing encompass a wide range of shaping and smoothing tasks. For example, you can sand the tails and pins flush after assembling a dovetail joint, or scrape away the mill marks after planing a board. Use rasps and files to shape a cabriole leg, then scrape and sand it smooth to prepare it for a finish.

What all these activities have in common is that you are removing a controlled amount of material from a wood surface. In each case, you want to sand, scrape, or file the surface flat (without any noticeable high or low spots) or — if the surface is contoured — fair (without awkward transitions in the surface curves). Additionally, you want to leave the wood *smoother* than when you began. In some instances, you create a different *shape* or contour at the same time.

INSPECTING THE SURFACE

Before you can smooth a surface, you must find the flaws in it. Some surface blemishes are fairly evident; others are less so. To find them all, you must know what to look for and how to look.

Photo by Leslie deBenedet

*The parts of this walnut **Blanket Stand** seem to flow into one another. Actually, they were all made from rectangular pieces of wood. The curves were rough-cut on a band saw, then carefully sculpted with rasps, files, scrapers, and sanders.*

SPECS: 24″ wide, 12″ deep, 36″ high

MATERIALS: Walnut

CRAFTSMAN: Dean deBenedet
Conifer, CO

FINDING THE FLAWS

Inspect the wooden surface from several angles under *a bright, oblique light.* Look for:

- *Saw marks* left by saw teeth
- *Mill marks* left by cutters
- *Torn grain* caused by **cutting uphill**[1], against the grain
- *Scratches* from sharp edges
- *Glue stains* from **excess glue**[2]
- *Dents* from hard objects
- *Checks,* where the wood is split
- *Gaps* in the joints and seams
- *Chips and gouges,* where wood is missing

In addition to looking, *feel* for those defects that you cannot easily see. Wipe the surface with a fine cloth or nylon stocking. It will snag or pull on tiny surface irregularities.

Continue this inspection as you sand and scrape. As you remove the more obvious flaws, you'll notice the smaller problems.

> ### PRO *TIP*
>
> Inspect the parts of a project and eliminate as many surface flaws as possible *before* assembly. In most cases, it's easier to sand and scrape single boards and simple subassemblies than it is to smooth the complex surfaces of an assembled project.

SURFACE REPAIRS

Once you identify the flaws, smooth them over. Most flaws can be removed with sandpaper, scrapers, files, or rasps. But several require that you *repair* the surface before you smooth it.

- Eliminate dents by applying water or steam to expand the crushed fibers.

> **SEE *ALSO*:**
> [1] Jointing Know-How   184
> [2] Gluing Know-How   254

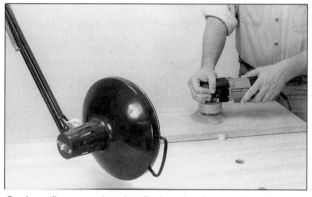

Surface flaws are hard to find under the overhead lighting in most shops: They just blend into the wood. Instead, shine a bright light across the wood so it rakes the surface. The irregularities in the surface will cast shadows, making them easier to see.

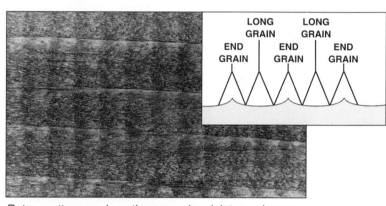

Rotary cutters, such as those used on jointers, planers, and routers, leave **mill marks** — tiny ridges in the wood. These marks show both **end grain** and **long grain.** Because end grain absorbs more finish than long grain, a finish will make these marks stand out, giving the surface a washboard appearance. Because mill marks are so hard to see, they are perhaps the most commonly overlooked surface flaws.

REPAIRING A DENT

1 To eliminate a dent, swell the crushed fibers back to their original condition. Cut a piece of clean cloth, slightly larger than the damaged area, soak it in water, and place it over the dent. Place a piece of aluminum foil over the cloth — this seals the water in.

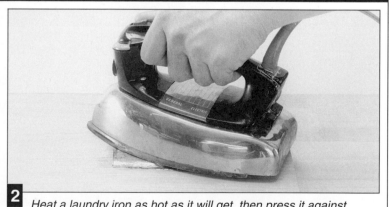

2 Heat a laundry iron as hot as it will get, then press it against the foil. Leave it there long enough for the water in the cloth to turn to steam, but not long enough to scorch the wood. The steam will penetrate the crushed wood fibers, causing them to expand. For deep dents or dents in hardwoods, you may have to repeat this process several times.

■ Fill large gaps in the joinery with **wedges or slips of veneer** [1]; fill smaller gaps with stick shellac or wax sticks. If you plan to paint the project, fill them with water putty.

■ Prevent checks from growing by gluing the split sections of the wood back together.

■ Disguise chips and gouges by splicing or inlaying new wood into the damaged surface. You can also drill out damaged areas and insert **wooden plugs** [2].

INLAYING NEW WOOD INTO A DAMAGED SURFACE

1 Using a hand-held router and a straight bit, rout a slot a little longer and wider than the damaged area. From the project scraps, cut a patch just a little larger than the slot. The grain direction and color on the patch must match the surface you're repairing.

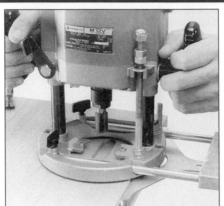

2 Bevel the edge of the patch to get a tight fit in the slot. Glue the patch in the slot, then sand it flush.

USING STICK SHELLAC

One of the quickest ways to fill small voids in a wood surface is with **stick shellac**. This material comes in dozens of colors. Select the one that most closely matches the **finished** wood. Heat an old, blunt knife with an alcohol lamp or propane torch. Carve a small amount of shellac from the stick with the hot tip, then melt the material into the void. If the knife cools, heat it up again. Sand the excess shellac off the wood surface as soon as it cools.

REPAIRING CHECKS AND SPLITS

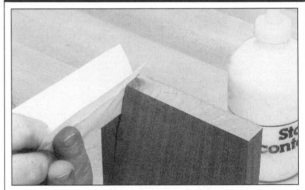

To repair wood that has checked or split, glue the pieces back together. If you must force the glue into a narrow space, put a dab of glue in the middle of a folded piece of paper and insert the fold in the crack. As if you were forcing toothpaste from a tube, squeeze the glue along the fold and into the crack.

SPLICING NEW WOOD ONTO A DAMAGED EDGE

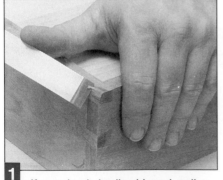

1 If an edge is badly chipped, splice a small piece of wood onto the damaged area. First, flatten the rough, broken surface with a chisel to create a level gluing surface.

2 From the project scraps, cut a small block or wedge slightly larger than needed. Glue it to the surface, carefully aligning the grain.

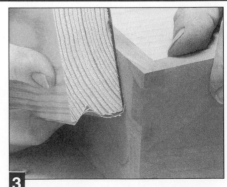

3 Let the glue dry, then sand the splice flush.

SCRAPING

Perhaps the easiest way to remove saw marks, mill marks, tiny scratches, glue spots, and minor surface imperfections is to shave the surface with a **scraper or shavehook**[3]. The burrs on the edges of these hand tools cut a paper-thin layer of wood and leave a smooth surface.

While the burr is sharp, it will turn wood curls like a bench plane.

*Scrapers and shavehooks have a thin metal blade with a **burr** on the edge. The burr is turned so when the blade is held at a slight angle to the wood, the burr shaves the surface. These tools perform well on all sorts of wood grain — not just straight grain but also uneven, wavy, interlocked, even figured grain.*

PRO*TIP*

Scraping saves an enormous amount of time. You can scrape a surface as smooth as you can sand it with 120- or 150-grit sandpaper in a fraction of the time. Experienced craftsmen scrape as much as possible, then sand with medium and fine abrasives.

But the burr wears quickly. The curls diminish and become dust. When this happens, **turn a new burr**[4].

FILING

Files and rasps[5] perform many smoothing tasks, but they are especially useful on contoured surfaces and small, hard-to-reach areas. Rasps remove wood quickly for shaping, rounding over, blending, and smoothing rough surfaces. Files cut more slowly and leave a smoother surface. Craftsmen often use them in tandem, following a rasp with a file to smooth the wood as much as possible before sanding.

USING A SCRAPER

Choose a blade to fit the surface you want to scrape. Hold it slightly off vertical, not quite square to the wood surface. Push or pull the blade in the direction you have tilted it, pressing down and varying the angle as you do so. When you feel the burr bite into the wood, hold that angle. Many craftsmen prefer to hold a scraper in two hands, flexing the blade as they push it. However, you can scrape one-handed or two-handed, flexing or not, whatever works best for the task at hand.

USING A SHAVEHOOK

Shavehooks are designed to scrape moldings and shaped surfaces. Grasp the handle, push the blade down on the stock, and pull it toward you. Vary the angle of the blade by raising or lowering the handle.

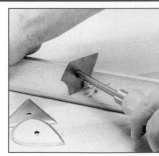

USING RASPS AND FILES

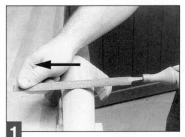

1 *There are three basic cuts you can make with a rasp or file. When you **crossfile**, hold the tool perpendicular or at an angle to the wood grain and push it forward, across the grain. This removes stock quickly.*

2 *To **flat-file**, hold the tool parallel to the grain and push forward, parallel to the grain. This makes a smoother cut.*

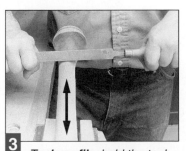

3 *To **draw-file**, hold the tool perpendicular to the wood grain, but push it sideways, parallel to the grain. This also makes a smooth cut.*

4 *When a rasp or file becomes clogged, clean it with a **file card**, brushing the tool parallel to its teeth. The card has hundreds of stiff wire bristles that dig down between the teeth and remove the impacted wood fibers.*

SANDING

Although you can create a smooth surface by scraping and filing, you must do some sanding to prepare a wood for a **finish**[1]. Scraping and filing shear the wood fibers, leaving a flat surface. Sanding scratches it, creating microscopic ridges and valleys or a *scratch pattern*. These increase the surface area, giving the finish more wood to hold on to so you get a stronger bond.

In addition to smoothing, you can shape wood with abrasives, grinding it to the desired size and contour. All of these tasks are remarkably straightforward, but you must select the right sanding tool and abrasive for the job.

SELECTING SANDING TOOLS

When should you use a power sander? When is it necessary to sand by hand?

Use **stationary power sanders**[2] for *precision* sanding. Worktables, fences, and miter gauges guide the stock and increase your control. You can sand at a specific angle or remove wood up to a layout line.

Use **portable power sanders**[3] when the stock is too large to hold comfortably. It's difficult to do precision tasks with these tools, but they save time.

When finesse and control are paramount, sand *by hand*. It's risky to use power sanders when you want to preserve a crisp edge or avoid sanding through a thin **veneer**[4]. Also rely on hand sanding to smooth areas that you cannot reach with a machine.

SELECTING ABRASIVES

What abrasive should you use? If you start with one that's too coarse, you may remove too much stock. If it's too fine, the sanding task will take too long. Or, the sanding dust will become impacted in the fine grit, clogging, or *loading*, the paper. Furthermore, power sanding tools are designed to work best within a specific *range* of abrasive grades:

■ Belt sander (portable) – 60 to 120 grit
■ Belt sander (stationary) – 36 to 120 grit
■ Detail sander – 100 to 320 grit
■ Disc sander – 12 to 120 grit
■ Drum sander – 60 to 150 grit
■ Palm sander – 100 to 320 grit

■ Random-orbit sander – 80 to 320 grit
■ Sander/polisher – 36 to 100 grit
■ Strip sander – 36 to 150 grit
■ Thickness sander – 12 to 60 grit

Although there are exceptions, these ranges are useful guidelines for general sanding tasks. If you don't get the result you want, it could be the grit is too coarse or too fine for the tool.

Also pay attention to the type of abrasive material, the coat, and the backing on which the abrasive is mounted. Each has a specific application.

Sanding machines differ markedly in their ability to remove stock. These three portable sanders were equipped with the same abrasive and were used to sand a board for five minutes. The belt sander has almost cut clear through the stock, the random-orbit sander has created a large gouge, and the palm sander has barely made a slight depression.

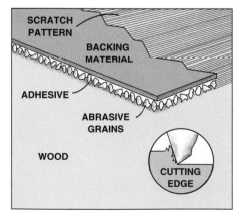

*Sandpaper is a scraping tool. The sharp edges of the abrasive grains scrape the wood surface, removing a small amount of stock. As they do so, they level the rough and uneven spots in the wood, leaving behind a uniform **scratch pattern**. The smaller the grains, the finer the scratch pattern, and the smoother the sanded surface appears to be.*

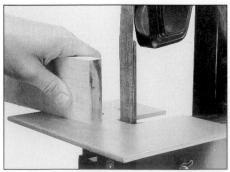

What happens if you use an abrasive grade on a machine that wasn't designed for it? You may not get the results you're after. This strip sander, for example, is running a 320-grit belt. This abrasive is intended for sharpening — it will remove metal, but it's much too fine for wood on this specific tool. The belt loads up, the friction and the heat increase, and the wood surface burns.

ABRASIVE MATERIALS

The smoothness and the quality of a sanded surface depend on the type of sandpaper used — the material, grade, backing, and coat.

ABRASIVE MATERIALS

Four types of mineral sand are commonly used in woodworking.

■ *Garnet* is preferred for hand sanding because it's very sharp and stays that way. The mineral is not particularly hard, but the grains fracture as you use them, constantly creating new cutting edges.

GARNET

■ *Aluminum oxide* is made by fusing bauxite in an electric furnace. Although it dulls eventually, the cutting edges are very sharp and durable. For this reason, it's used for machine sanding.

ALUMINUM OXIDE

■ *Silicon carbide* is made by heating silica and carbon. The color indicates its application — charcoal for wet and dry sanding; light gray for dry sanding only. Silicon carbide is preferred for **sanding finishes**[5] between coats or rubbing out the final coat.

SILICON CARBIDE

■ *Alumina-zirconia* (erroneously called "zirconium") is an alloy of aluminum oxide and zirconium oxide. It's an extremely tough abrasive and is typically used for heavy-duty surfacing operations, such as thickness-sanding. Like garnet, the grains fracture to produce new cutting edges, but only under extreme pressure.

ALUMINA-ZIRCONIA

ABRASIVE GRADES

Abrasives are graded according to the grain size or *grit* by sifting them through progressively finer sieves. If a grain falls through a sieve with 80 openings per inch, but won't fall through the next smaller sieve, it's considered 80 grit. Manufacturers also assign each grit a name (coarse, medium, fine, and so on), but these vary from brand to brand.

Hardware stores offer a wide selection of abrasive grades, from 50 to 600 grit. For most woodworking tasks, you don't need anything coarser or finer than this. But if you do, abrasives from 12 to 1200 grit are commonly available through mail-order companies. And some automotive and aviation supply houses sell abrasive materials up to 12,000 grit.

BACKING MATERIAL

The abrasive can be glued to either cloth (a cotton/polyester blend) or paper. Of the two, cloth is more durable. It comes in two *weights*. Thicker "X" backings are for heavy machine sanding; thinner "J" backings are for light-duty machine sanding and hand sanding.

Paper backings come in several weights, from "A" (lightest) to "F" (heaviest). Generally, the lighter papers are used for finer grits, and the heavier papers for coarser grits.

COATING

All abrasives are available in two coats.

■ *Open-coat* sandpapers have abrasives applied to just 50 to 70 percent of the surface. They don't load easily; the open spaces enable the paper to clear itself of dust.

■ *Closed-coat* papers are covered completely. Because there are more cutting edges per inch, they cut fast. However, when sanding soft or resinous surfaces, sawdust packs between the grit and loads the paper.

Sandpapers sometimes have *zinc stearate* coatings, a chemical treatment that prevents sawdust from sticking to the abrasive and loading the sandpaper.

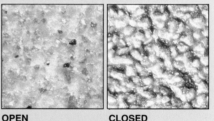

OPEN   CLOSED

ABRASIVE COATS

ABRASIVE TYPES

Material	Color	Uses
Garnet	Pink or red-brown	Hand sanding
Aluminum Oxide	Tan or brown	Machine sanding
Silicon Carbide	Charcoal (wet/dry) or gray (dry only)	Sanding finishes between coats and rubbing out final finish coats
Alumina-Zirconia	Green	Thickness-sanding, surfacing

ABRASIVE GRADES

Name	Grit	Uses
Extra Coarse	12, 16, 20	Grinding wood to shape
Very Coarse	24, 30, 36	Grinding wood to shape, rough thicknessing
Coarse	40, 50	Leveling surfaces, removing stock, final thicknessing
Medium	60, 80, 100	Smoothing surfaces, sanding joints flush and clean
Fine	120, 150, 180	Preparing surfaces for "building" finishes, such as varnish and polyurethane
Very Fine	220, 240, 280	Preparing surfaces for "penetrating" finishes, such as wiping oil
Extra Fine	320, 360, 400	Sanding finishes between coats
Ultra Fine	500, 600, 1,000	Rubbing out final finish coat

GENERAL SANDING KNOW-HOW

No matter what sanding tool or abrasive you use:

■ Brush off the wood frequently as you sand. This lets you see the surface and prevents the sandpaper from loading.

■ Place the stock on an old towel or a rubber mat. Whenever you switch grits or change sandpaper, shake out the towel or mat. This protects the wood from dents and scratches.

■ Don't press too hard as you sand. If you press down, the sander will cut more quickly for a few moments, but the abrasive will rapidly clog with sanding dust. Some tools will bog down or stop. Sanders cut faster if you keep the pressure light.

■ Don't set sander speeds too high, especially when using fine grits. The resulting friction will heat the wood and burn it.

■ Keep the sander or the stock moving. If the abrasive dwells on any one area for too long, it will dig in and create a low spot.

How do you know when it's time to change to the next higher abrasive grade? When the **scratch pattern**[2] on the surface is consistent. To monitor the scratch pattern as it develops, sand under a **bright, oblique light**[3].

How fine do you sand? That depends on the finish you will apply. For a **building finish**[4], you can stop at 150 or 180 grit. For a **penetrating finish**[4], continue to 220 grit.

PRO *TIP*

Apply a finish immediately after the final sanding. The wood surface will be as clean as it's going to get, and the finish will bond better. If you can't apply a finish quickly, delay sanding until you can.

REMOVING GLUE BEADS

*Before you sand the surfaces of a glued-up assembly, remove the glue beads with a **glue scraper**. Most wood glues are thermoplastic — when you heat them, they become a gooey liquid. The friction from sanding heats the glue and liquefies it. The liquid glue sticks to the sandpaper, solidifies as it cools, and clogs the abrasive.*

MASKING ADJACENT SURFACES

Mask off areas of the project that you don't want to sand. When hand sanding, cover these areas with masking tape. When using power sanders, cover them with wood scraps. Clamp the scraps in place or stick them down with double-faced carpet tape.

SANDING DIRECTION

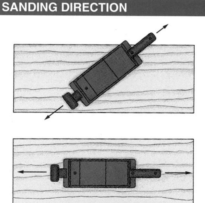

To remove stock quickly, sand at an angle to the wood grain. To smooth the surface and prepare it for a finish, sand with the grain. When you sand at an angle to the grain, the abrasive tears the wood fibers and the surface looks ragged and fuzzy. Sanding with the grain combs the fibers.

CREATING A CONSISTENT SCRATCH PATTERN

Use consecutive grades of sandpaper, working your way from coarse to fine. Remember, the grains create a scratch pattern in the surface. The coarser the grade, the larger the scratches. When you move to the next finer grade, you trade one set of scratches for slightly smaller ones.

If you skip grades, the fine abrasive may be too small to level all the coarse scratches. The wood will be left with an uneven scratch pattern.

RAISING THE GRAIN

CRUSHED CELLS
SEVERED FIBERS
BEFORE WETTING

WHISKERS
RAISED GRAIN
AFTER WETTING

*To provide the best possible surface for a finish, **raise the wood grain** before you sand it with the finest abrasive. Wet the wood surface with a damp rag. This swells crushed wood cells and makes any severed fibers or **whiskers** stand up. After the wood dries, sand off the whiskers and the raised grain.*

POWER SANDING KNOW-HOW

When changing abrasives, pressure sensitive adhesives (PSA) and hook-and-loop systems make it easier to mount sandpaper to a pad or disc. The differences between the two are expense and durability. PSA-backed abrasives are relatively inexpensive, but they can be mounted only once. Hook-and-loop-backed abrasives cost more, but they can be mounted over and over.

MORE *INFO*

When mounting an abrasive to metal, clean the surface and make sure it's at room temperature. Spray adhesives and adhesive-backed sandpapers won't stick securely to cold surfaces.

When sanding with a **stationary power sander**[5]:

■ Use a worktable, fence, or miter gauge to support the work whenever possible. This makes the setup safer and the results more precise.

SAFE *GUARDS*

To keep pinch points to a minimum, adjust worktables and backstops to within ⅛ inch of the abrasive.

■ Control the amount of stock you remove with a *disc sander* by working with different areas of the disc. Near the outside edge, the abrasive is traveling faster and removes stock quickly. Approaching the center, the abrasive travels more slowly and is less aggressive.

■ Keep the stock moving to cover the whole width of a *belt sander*. If you dwell in just one area, the abrasive wears unevenly and the belt drifts to one side.

■ Use the "soft" side of a *belt sander* (the side without the platen) or remove the platen from a *strip sander* to sand gentle contours and round over edges.

■ Always sand against the rotation of a *drum sander*. If you feed the work in the same direction as the drum revolves, the tool tries to pull the wood out of your hands.

KEEPING THE WORK IN PLACE

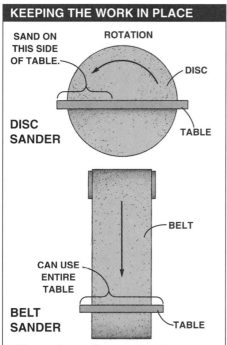

When using a disc sander, always sand on the side of the disc that rotates **down** toward the table. When using a belt sander, set up the backstop so the belt travels **down or back,** toward the backstop. In both cases, the motion of the abrasive holds the work against the support.

PAD SANDING

When you must sand several parts identically, stack them together. Use masking tape or double-faced carpet tape to prevent the stack from shifting, and sand all the parts at once.

SANDING SMALL PARTS

Sanding a small part on a stationary sander may bring your fingers uncomfortably close to the moving abrasive. To prevent this, attach the part to a push block or a large wood scrap with double-faced carpet tape. Use the block or scrap to maneuver the part as you sand it.

PATTERN SANDING

You can also sand precise shapes with a drum-sanding accessory for a drill press. Cut a guide disc the same diameter as the drum sander and mount it to a sheet of plywood. Center the disc beneath the drum and clamp the sheet to the drill press table. Adjust the height of the drum about 1⁄16 inch above the disc. Make a pattern template from stock that's about ¼ inch thicker than the guide disc. Attach the template to the workpiece with double-faced carpet tape. Sand the edge of the work, guiding the template against the disc.

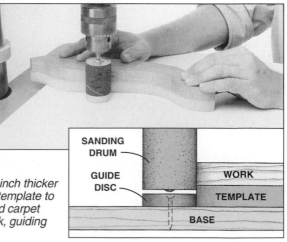

When using a **portable power sander**[1]:

■ Hold the work stationary as you sand. Place it against a **bench stop**[2] or clamp it between **bench dogs**[2].

■ Use the entire pad or disc; don't tip the sander on its edge. The sander cuts faster and more evenly when you use all of the available abrasive surface. If you use the edge, the sander may dig low spots in the surface, and the abrasive at the edge will wear out long before the rest.

■ To prevent sanding corners and edges overmuch, work from the edges in rather than the center out.

PRESERVING A CRISP EDGE

Portable sanders and hand-sanding blocks have a tendency to rock when you sand close to the edges of a board. This will round over the edges. If the work is veneered, it may cut through the veneer at the edge. To prevent this, keep the pad, disc, or block flat on the sur-face. If necessary, back up the edges with scraps of wood.

PAD SANDER ROCKS, ROUNDS EDGE.

BACK UP EDGE WITH SCRAP.

CONTOUR SANDING

1 *Soft-sided drum sanders, such as this **pneumatic drum,** allow you to sand three-dimensional curves and contours. Control the firmness of the abrasive by changing the air pres-sure inside the drum. The softer the surface, the easier it is for the drum to conform to curves. It also becomes more aggressive (removes stock faster).*

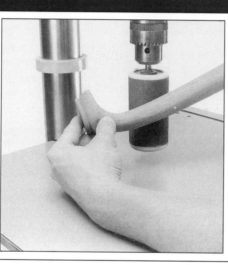

2 *For complex surfaces, use an **abrasive mop, flutter sheets,** or a **flap sander** mounted in a drill press or portable drill. All of these accessories reach into crevices and conform to the shape of the work.*

HAND SANDING KNOW-HOW

When sanding a surface by hand:

■ Use a padded sanding block to back up the sandpaper whenever possible – this is less tiring and produces a more even surface. If you must rely on your fingers as a backup, fold the paper to get a better grip.

■ When sanding hard-to-reach surfaces, use sanding sticks and abrasive cords to reach into cracks and crevices.

■ Clean the sandpaper often by tapping the block on the work-bench. This clears the sanding dust and prevents loading.

CLEANING A POWER ABRASIVE

*When an abrasive belt, pad, or disc loads with sanding dust, clean it by holding a rubber abrasive cleaner against the moving abrasive. The rubber digs between the abrasive grains and pops out the impacted dust. It **does not,** however, sharpen a dull abrasive. If the abrasive cuts slowly and tends to burn the wood after you clean it, replace the abrasive.*

USING SANDING BLOCKS

When hand sanding, back up the sandpaper with a block that's shaped to conform to the wood's surface. To sand a complex surface, use sev-eral simple shapes. Or, cut a complex shape out of foam and glue sand-paper to it.

FOLDING SANDPAPER

When using your fingers to back up sandpaper, cut standard size sandpaper sheets in quarters and fold the quarter sheets into thirds, as shown. Not only does this give you a good grip, you can use the entire sheet, turning or refolding the paper when one area wears out.

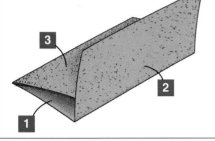

STORING SANDPAPER

Paper-backed sandpaper curls because the uncoated side of the paper absorbs moisture faster than the coated side. The uncoated side swells, and the paper curls toward the coated side. To prevent this, store the sandpaper between boards and place a brick or a weight on the top board.

MYTH *CONCEPTIONS*

TRUE GRIT Worn sandpaper is *not* the equivalent of the next finer grade. You can't use worn-out 100-grit paper and expect it to perform like 120-grit. When the abrasive is dull, it doesn't cut quickly and cleanly. Worn 100-grit paper requires more work and leaves a rougher surface than sharp 120-grit paper.

SEE *ALSO:*

[1]Hand Sanders   123

[2]Stops, Dogs, and Holdfasts   92

JIGS & FIXTURES

SANDING BLOCK This wood block fits the hand comfortably and holds a quarter sheet of sandpaper. The paper is held in place by a rubber band. Cover the bottom of the block with felt or leather to cushion the paper — this helps prevent the sanding dust from packing between the abrasive grains.

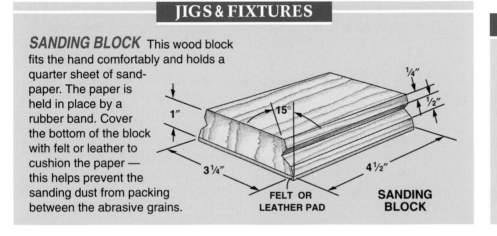

FELT OR LEATHER PAD   SANDING BLOCK

MORE *SOURCES*

The Complete Book of Portable Power Tool Techniques, by R. J. DeCristoforo, Popular Science Books, 1986

The Complete Book of Stationary Power Tool Techniques, by R. J. DeCristoforo, Sterling Publishing, 1988

Sanding and Planing, by Nick Engler, Rodale Press, 1994

TROUBLE *SHOOTING*

COMMON SANDING PROBLEMS

Problem	Possible Causes	Solutions
Takes too long	Wrong tool or abrasive for the job	Pick tool for job; match abrasive to tool.
	Starting with a fine grit	Start sanding with a coarser grit.
	Sandpaper is loaded or dull.	Clean sandpaper; replace if necessary.
Sanded surface burned	Sanding grit is too fine.	Use a coarser grit.
	Sanding too long in one spot	Keep sander or work moving; don't dwell.
	Too much pressure when sanding	Use only light pressure; don't force sander or work.
	Sandpaper is loaded or dull.	Clean sandpaper; replace if necessary.
Sanded surface scratched	Skipping grits when sanding	Work up through consecutive grits.
	Not sanding sufficiently with each grit	Sand with each grit until scratch pattern is even.
	Loose grit on workbench	Place work on towel or rubber pad; shake out often.
	Sanding across grain	Sand with wood grain.
Sanded surface dented	Project bumps into hard surfaces or tool on bench top.	Place work on towel or rubber pad.
Sanded surface not flat or fair	Sanding too long in one spot	Keep sander or work moving; don't dwell.
	Sandpaper not backed up properly	Back up sandpaper with sanding block.
Sandpaper loads quickly.	Glue on wood surface	Remove glue with scraper before sanding.
	Wood is soft or resinous.	Use open-coat or stearated-coated sandpaper.
	Too much pressure when sanding	Use only light pressure; don't force sander to work.

24 Finishing

Finishing is a decision-making process. The more information you have, the better your decisions – and your finishes.

There are two reasons why craftsmen apply a finish to a project. The coating (1) protects the wood and (2) enhances its appearance. A finish resists abrasion, scratches, and other wear and tear. It's a barrier to grime, spills, and other substances that might discolor or harm the surface. It also slows the absorption and release of moisture caused by changes in the weather. This, in turn, slows the **movement of the wood**[1] and reduces the stress that it causes to the **joinery**[2].

Furthermore, the finish improves the look and feel of the wood. It makes the **wood grain**[3] at the surface translucent so it catches the light. You can adjust the color and the luster to your own tastes. And once polished, the finish eliminates irregularities in the wood surfaces, making it smooth to the touch. To see how a finish affects a specific wood, refer to the chart of "Physical Properties of Wood" on pages 353–360.

SELECTING A FINISH

The term *finish* encompasses hundreds of finishing materials and processes, each with its own distinct effect. Walk into any hardware store or thumb through a finishing catalogue and you're likely to find these popular choices:

■ *Drying oils* – naturally occurring oils that cure to form a film

■ *Shellac* – a resin produced by the Indian lac bug, dissolved or "cut" in alcohol

■ *Lacquers* – synthetic nitrocellulose resins dissolved in powerful solvents

Photo by Jonathan Bizen

*While planing, sawing, drilling, routing, jointing, and sanding are all essential to good craftsmanship, it's the finish that everyone notices right off the bat. For this reason, many craftsmen take as many pains to finish a project as they take to build it. That's evident in this reproduction **Kast,** a Pennsylvania German linen press. The craftsman mixed his own milk paint and vinegar paint, then covered those with shellac and varnish, building layer upon layer.*

SPECS: 72″ wide, 23″ deep, 93″ tall

MATERIALS: Tulip poplar

CRAFTSMAN: Kendl Monn
Christiana, PA

- *Varnishes* – made by cooking drying oils and resins (typically synthetic alkyd or phenolic resins)
- *Polyurethane* – extremely tough varnishes made with polyurethane resin
- *Wiping oils* – polymerized (modified) oils, thinned varnishes, and oil/varnish blends
- *Water-based finishes* – resin (typically acrylic or polyurethane) suspended in water with a small amount of a powerful solvent
- *Conversion finishes* – two-part finishes that must be mixed before they will cure
- *Oil paints* – chemically similar to varnishes, with colored pigments added
- *Latex paints* – similar to water-based finishes, with pigments added

You'll also find stains, dyes, fillers, sealers, waxes, and dozens of other materials. Despite the large number of choices, however, there are more similarities between finishes than differences.

FINISHING CHEMISTRY

At its simplest level, a finish is a chemical mixture that forms a thin *film*, penetrating and coating the wood surface. Almost every finish has two basic ingredients – *resins* (which cure or harden) and *solvents* (which don't).

There are other chemicals, of course. Many finishes include *driers*, heavy metal salts that speed drying. *Flatteners* are colorless powders that give the finish a flat or "satin" look. Binders, extenders, hardeners, and so on, all affect the characteristics of a finish.

It's not important that you know the name or purpose of every ingredient. What is important is that some of these materials are *volatile;* others are *nonvolatile.* The volatile chemicals are, for the most part, solvents that keep the finish liquid as you wipe, brush, or spray it on the wood. After the finish is applied, the volatile chemicals dissipate or evaporate, and what's left is everything else – the nonvolatile resins, hard-

ened oils, flatteners, driers, and so on. These form the film.

FORMING THE FILM

More important than the ingredients, or even the type of finish, is how the liquid hardens to form a chemical film. There are four possible reactions.

- *Solvent-releasing* – As the solvents evaporate, the solids form a solid matrix on the wood surface. There is no molecular change; the solids can be easily dissolved again. A fresh coat of finish partially dissolves the old one, and the two coats blend.
- *Reactive* – When exposed to oxygen, the solids form crosslinks, joining in complex molecular matrices. The hardened film is chemically different from the liquid finish, and the reaction cannot be easily reversed. The film cannot be dissolved by the same solvent that delivered it.

- *Catalyzing* – The resin in a two-part finish reacts with a hardener (catalyst) in much the same way reactive solids respond to oxygen. The molecules form extremely stable matrices, impervious to most solvents.
- *Coalescing* – As the water and the solvent in a water-based finish evaporate, the resins coalesce into a film and harden. The resulting coating resists water, but it can be dissolved by the solvent.

When choosing a finish, it's useful to know how the various types form films. This process affects compatibility with other finishing materials, methods of application, drying times, and other characteristics.

SEE *ALSO:*

[1]	Wood Movement	6
[2]	Let the Wood Move	13
[3]	Wood Grain	2

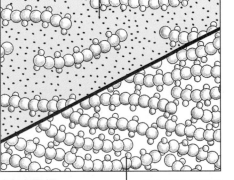

SOLVENT-RELEASING — LIQUID FINISH — HARDENED FILM

REACTIVE — LIQUID FINISH — HARDENED FILM

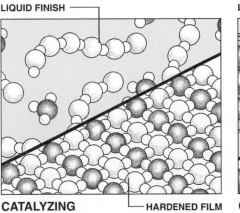

CATALYZING — LIQUID FINISH — HARDENED FILM

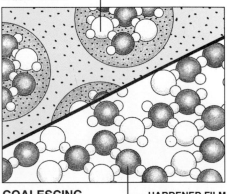

COALESCING — LIQUID FINISH — HARDENED FILM

FINISHING PROPERTIES

Every finish has a unique blend of properties that define how it protects and beautifies the wood.

The properties that help the finish *protect* the wood include:

■ *Hardness* – The better a finish resists wear and tear, the harder it's said to be. However, if it's too hard, it may be brittle or inflexible.

■ *Permeability* – The longer it takes moisture to pass through a finish, the less permeable it is. Low permeability slows **expansion and contraction**[1], making the wood more stable.

■ *Heat resistance* – The temperature at which a finish softens and separates from the wood determines heat resistance.

■ *Water resistance* – Some water-sensitive finishes allow the wood to soak up water; others exclude water but become cloudy when they contact it. Water-resistant finishes keep the water out of the wood and keep their good looks.

■ *Chemical resistance* – Some finishes are sensitive to caustic chemicals in household cleaners, acids in fruits and vegetables, and alcohol from beverages.

■ *Durability* – How long does a finish protect? The longer it lasts, the more durable it is.

Properties that *enhance* the appearance of the wood include:

■ *Penetration* – The depth to which a finish penetrates the wood affects its looks and texture. Penetrating finishes form a thin film, preserving the natural texture. Those that build up to a thick film replace the natural texture with a smoother one.

■ *Depth* – The film thickness of a building finish increases with each application, and the visible distance from the finish surface to the wood surface grows.

■ *Luster* – A film will either reflect light back at you or scatter it. Some films can be rubbed to a highly reflective *gloss*. A surface that scatters the light appears *flat*. If it's somewhere in between, it has a *satin* look.

■ *Tint* – All but a few finishing materials **alter the natural color**[2] of the wood. Many transparent finishes "warm up" the wood with an amber tint. Those with colored dyes and pigments change the color dramatically.

■ *Opacity* – As a finish becomes less transparent and more opaque, the more it obscures the wood grain.

Additionally, there are two miscellaneous properties that can be important in selecting a finish:

PROPERTIES OF COMMON FINISHING MATERIALS

Type of Finish	Examples	Chemistry	Protecting Properties
Drying Oils	Boiled linseed oil, pure tung oil, walnut oil	Reactive	Very soft and permeable; ineffective barrier to water; chemical- and heat-sensitive; not durable.
Shellacs	Orange shellac, white shellac	Evaporative	Medium hard, non-permeable; not a great water barrier; chemical- and heat-sensitive; fairly durable.
Lacquers	Spray lacquer, brush lacquer, lacquer paint	Evaporative	Medium hard, semi-permeable; acceptable water barrier; somewhat sensitive to heat, chemicals; fairly durable.
Varnishes	Tung oil varnish, spar varnish, varnish stains	Reactive	Hard, almost non-permeable; good water barrier; chemical- and heat-resistant; durable.
Polyurethanes	Polyurethane varnish, polyurethane stain	Reactive	Very hard, non-permeable; excellent water barrier; chemical- and heat resistant; very durable.
Wiping Oils	Most "tung oil" finishes, antique oil, Danish oil	Reactive	Medium-hard, semi-permeable; acceptable water barrier; chemical- and heat-resistant; fairly durable.
Water-Based Finishes	Water-based varnish, water-based lacquer	Coalescing	Very hard, semi-permeable; good water barrier; somewhat sensitive to heat, chemicals; durable.
Conversion Finishes	Bar-top finish, epoxy resin, catalyzed lacquer	Catalyzing	Very hard, non-permeable; excellent water barrier; chemical- and heat-resistant; very durable.
Oil Paints	Spray paint, house paint, artist's oils	Reactive	Hard, almost non-permeable; good water barrier; chemical- and heat-resistant; durable.
Latex Paints	Interior latex, exterior latex, artist's acrylics	Coalescing	Hard, semi-permeable; good water barrier; chemical- and heat-resistant; durable.
Wood Stains	Oil stain, gel stain, water-based stain	Reactive or Coalescing	Provides no protection by itself; meant to be applied under a clear finish.
Wood Dyes	Aniline dye, spirit stain	Evaporative	Provides no protection by itself; meant to be applied under a clear finish.
Waxes	Paste wax, furniture wax	Evaporative	Provides no protection by itself; meant to be applied over a finish.

■ *Method of application* – Can the finish be **wiped**[3], **brushed**[4], or **sprayed**[5]? Each method has different requirements, as we shall see.

■ *Toxicity* – How toxic is the finish film after it's dried? If the project comes in contact with food, skin, or children, you may need a **nontoxic finish**[6].

TESTING FINISHES

If you can't decide between finishes, make a *test board*. Tests are also useful if you've never used a finish before or never applied it to a specific wood.

Prepare the surface of the test board as you did the project. *This is important!* If you don't sand and scrape in the same manner, the results will be misleading. If you are unsure how to prepare the surface, make it part of your test – prepare different areas of the board in different ways.

Carefully label the types of finishes, number of coats, and other pertinent information so you can duplicate the finish precisely if the results are to your liking.

This **test board** was used to prepare several possible stain and finish combinations. The materials were applied in a grid, with the stains running in one direction and the finishes running in the other. Not all the finishes bonded properly to every stain — some combinations were incompatible.

Enhancing Properties	Application	Toxicity	Comments
Penetrating; flat and will not take a gloss; amber tint; fairly transparent.	Wipe on or brush on	Low, nontoxic	Slow to dry, has little value as finish except where nontoxicity is needed.
Building; can be rubbed to a high gloss; clear to deep amber tint; transparent.	Brush on or spray on	Nontoxic	Fast-drying, easy to apply and repair. Traditional finish for classic furniture.
Building; can be rubbed to a high gloss; clear to slight amber tint; very transparent.	Brush on or spray on	Low	Fast-drying, easy to repair. Fumes highly dangerous and unhealthy. Spray-on sensitive to humidity.
Building; can be rubbed to a low gloss; amber tint; very transparent.	Brush on or spray on	Low	Fairly slow to dry, difficult to repair. Fumes unhealthy.
Building; can be rubbed to a low gloss; slight amber tint; transparent.	Brush on or spray on	Low	Can be slow to dry, difficult to repair. Fumes unhealthy.
Penetrating; can be rubbed to a satin look (after many coats); amber tint; transparent.	Wipe on or brush on	Low, nontoxic	Easy to apply, easy to repair. Film very thin, requires multiple coats.
Building; can be rubbed to a low gloss; clear (some are tinted); transparent.	Brush on or spray on	Low	Fast-drying, fairly easy to apply and repair. Sensitive to silicone, oil, and wax.
Building; can be rubbed to a gloss; clear to slight amber tint; very transparent.	Brush on or spray on	Medium	Must apply quickly, very difficult to repair. Skin contact may be unhealthy.
Building; can be rubbed to a gloss; may be any color (pigmented); opaque.	Brush on or spray on	Low, medium	Fairly slow to dry, difficult to repair. Fumes unhealthy.
Building; can be rubbed to a low gloss; may be any color (pigmented); opaque.	Brush on or spray on	Low, nontoxic	Fairly quick to dry, easy to repair. Sensitive to oil and wax.
Penetrating; may be any color (pigmented, may have dyes added); semi-opaque.	Wipe on or brush on	Low	Can be slow to dry, color "bleeds" into some transparent finishes.
Penetrating; may be any color; transparent.	Wipe on or brush on	Low, nontoxic	Fast-drying, color vivid and permanent, slow to fade.
May be tinted; semi-opaque (transparent after buffing).	Wipe on, buff off	Nontoxic	Gives finish an oily sheen, pleasant feel and smell.

FINISHING HAZARDS

Like many woodworking tools, if used recklessly, finishes can be dangerous.

Organic Solvents

Most finishes are made with *organic* solvents, so called because they break down organic hydrocarbons like oils, resins — and you, if you're exposed long enough. Some of the names you might run across:

■ *Alcohols* — ethanol, methanol, isopropanol

■ *Aliphatic hydrocarbons* — naphtha, kerosene, mineral spirits

■ *Aromatic hydrocarbons* — toluol, xylene

■ *Chlorinated hydrocarbons* — methylene chloride

■ *Ketones* — acetone, methyl-ethyl ketone, methyl-isobutyl ketone

■ *Others* — turpentine, glycol ether, diglycidyl ether

SAFE GUARDS

Pregnant and breast-feeding women should avoid all organic solvents. Exposure may be especially dangerous during the first three months of a pregnancy.

Physical Effects

Most of these chemicals attack the central nervous system, but some damage the lungs, liver, kidneys, and blood as well. They may irritate the skin, eyes, nose, and throat lining, producing both acute and chronic effects.

The acute effects last only a short time. An overexposure to high concentrations of finishing chemicals may cause dizziness, shortness of breath, headache, nausea, confusion, uncoordination, and irrational behavior. These pass as soon as you begin to breathe clean air again.

The chronic effects don't pass. They're caused by frequent exposure to low concentrations of chemicals. The effect of each exposure is minor, but the damage is cumulative. As it mounts, the symptoms listed above become a daily ritual.

Protecting Yourself

To prevent adverse effects, don't contact the chemicals or breathe their fumes.

■ *Ventilate the finish area.* Open windows; use a fan to move the air.

■ *Wear a respirator* when exposed to concentrated fumes — a close-fitting mask with filter cartridges for organic vapors.

■ *Wear a face shield and rubber gloves* when there is danger of splashing or when working with these chemicals for long stretches.

Preventing Fires

In addition to posing health risks, these chemicals are *flammable.* To reduce the chance of fire:

■ *Keep finishing chemicals in sealed metal containers.* Store the containers in a metal cabinet. Professional craftsmen often store finishes in a ventilated cabinet to keep fumes from accumulating.

■ *Dispose of rags and paper towels saturated with finishes in sealed metal containers.* Rags saturated with linseed oil and other **reactive**[1] or **catalyzing**[1] finishes may ignite spontaneously from the heat caused by chemical action.

■ *Don't wad rags up* when using them; hang them flat over the edges of a workbench or trash can. This will prevent fumes and heat from accumulating in the folds.

■ *Use an explosion-proof spray booth* when **spraying**[2] flammable finishes. The booth is ventilated, and the lights, switches, and motors are shielded to prevent an electric spark from igniting the fumes.

MORE INFO

If you need more information on the hazards of a specific finish, request a *Materials Safety Data Sheet* from the manufacturer. This lists hazardous ingredients, fire and explosion hazards, dangerous reactions with other chemicals, and health hazards.

NONTOXIC FINISHES

While most finishes are health hazards before they dry, most harden to relatively benign substances with low toxicity. However, projects that come in contact with food and children and those that are in prolonged contact with the skin require *nontoxic* finishes and **woods**[3]. These include cutting boards, bowls and other eating utensils, toys, infants' furniture, and wooden jewelry.

The traditional nontoxic finish is *mineral oil.* Tradition aside, this is no finish at all. It doesn't harden and does little to protect or beautify the wood. Instead, consider:

■ *Walnut oil,* which does dry but does not form a hard film. It must be reapplied from time to time.

■ *Salad bowl finishes,* which are manufactured from FDA-approved chemicals. They're durable but do not form especially hard films.

■ Some brands of *water-based finishes,* which are marketed as nontoxic. Because they chip and flake, however, they are not recommended for eating utensils.

■ *Shellac,* which is so benign the FDA approves its use in medicines.

■ *Food dyes,* which when diluted with water make good stains. They are surprisingly colorfast.

MORE INFO

Your best finish for a cutting board may be no finish at all. Wood appears to contain a natural antibacterial agent which kills the creepy things in meat and vegetable juices. Tests at the University of Wisconsin–Madison showed that *unfinished* wood cutting boards were more sanitary than plastic. When the wood was finished, however, the two materials were about neck-and-neck.

APPLYING A STAIN

Color is an important component of good design; a change in color can profoundly alter the visual effect of a project. Lighter woods seem contemporary and casual; darker tones are traditional and formal.

When the natural wood tones don't convey the effect you want, stain the wood. You can do this in one step with a tinted finish or *finish stain*. However, most experienced craftsmen prefer to stain, then finish wood. This gives you more control over the color and penetration.

TYPES OF STAIN

There are three common staining materials.

■ *Pigment stains* are opaque, colored powders suspended in a "binder." This may be a drying oil, varnish, lacquer, or water-based finish. It may be as thick as paste or as thin as water. When applied to the wood, the binder adheres the pigment to the surface.

■ *Wood dyes* are liquid coloring agents that penetrate the wood surface and bond to the wood fibers. They can be mixed with water, alcohol, or oil.

■ *Chemical stains* react with the wood or each other, altering the wood color. They are usually dissolved in water.

STAIN PROPERTIES

When choosing a stain, consider these characteristics:

■ *Color* – There are many colors of dyes and pigments, and you can mix them to produce any hue. Of the two, dye colors are more vibrant, rich, and colorfast, although they will fade in time. Chemical stains are more limited – each chemical produces only one color in any given wood species.

■ *Penetration* – Dyes and chemical stains penetrate the wood; pigments rest on top of it. If you scratch the surface, it's more likely

that a pigment stain will show raw wood through the damage.

But there are times when you don't want a stain to penetrate. Stain will penetrate **end grain**[4] deeper than **flat grain or quarter grain**[4]. In some species, it will penetrate the **springwood**[4] deeper than the **summerwood**[4]. The deeper a stain penetrates, the darker it appears. If the wood absorbs stain unevenly, the color will be blotchy. The exception to this rule is a chemical stain. Chemicals penetrate deeply and create a remarkably even color.

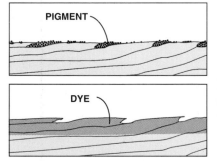

How a stain colors the wood affects the appearance of the wood as much (or more!) than the natural wood color. Wood dyes and chemical stains penetrate the wood, coloring the fibers beneath the wood surface. Pigment stains cover the surface. The particles of pigments collect in pores, microscopic grooves left by sandpaper, and other irregularities in the surface.

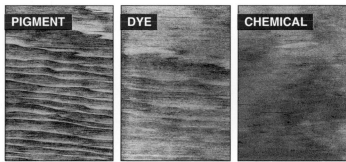

Sometimes you want an even color. The pigment stain on this pine board highlights the bands of springwood and summerwood. The wood dye does a better job of disguising them, and the chemical stain (nitric acid) hides them completely.

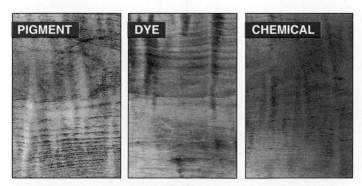

Sometimes you don't want an even color. Here the dye highlights the figure in this curly maple, while the pigment stain and chemical stain (nitric acid) do little to enhance it.

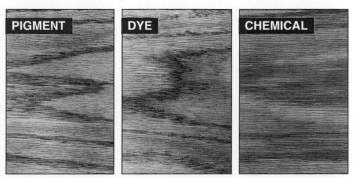

And sometimes it's a toss-up. The pigment stain highlights the strong grain in this red oak; the dye shows it, but not so dramatically; and the chemical stain (nitric acid) mutes it.

■ *Clarity* – Because pigments are opaque, they cloud the wood surface, partially obscuring the grain. Dyes are more transparent, and the grain remains distinct.

■ *Compatibility* – Is the binder in the stain compatible with the finish you will apply over it?

PRO *TIP*

You can sometimes use two incompatible finishing materials by insulating the layers with a **wash coat** [1] of shellac.

Incompatible stains may "bleed" into a clear finish or prevent it from drying. If you don't know for sure, make a test board.

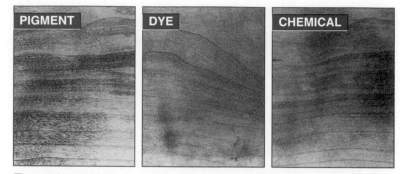

These pieces of cherry contain light-colored sapwood (at the bottom) and darker heartwood (at the top). The pigment stain only slightly masks the color difference. The dye does a much better job, and the chemical stain (nitric acid) does the best of all.

APPLYING PIGMENT STAINS

To apply a pigment stain, brush it on and wipe off the excess with a clean rag. If the surface is irregular and has a lot of crevices, wipe off the stain with a dry brush, then wipe off the brush on a rag.

PRO *TIP*

You can also adjust the tone by how you sand the wood. The coarser the sanding grit, the deeper the surface scratches. More pigment collects in the deeper scratches, and the wood appears darker.

COARSE

MEDIUM

FINE

Wiping evens out the stain color and controls the tone. The harder you wipe, the more stain you pick up and the lighter the tone becomes.

If you need to adjust the color or deepen the tone, add pigments to the stain. Add artist's oil paints to oil-based stains and artist's acrylics to water-based. Or, purchase "universal" pigments in powder form.

Oftentimes you can produce a more even color by limiting the penetration of a pigment stain. However, the overall tone will appear lighter. The piece of softwood plywood on the right was covered with a wash coat of shellac before it was stained. The color is more even, but somewhat lighter, than the piece on the left.

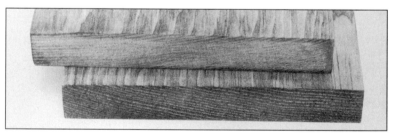

Apply a wash coat of shellac to end grain to control the penetration of both pigment stain and wood dye. On the untreated board (bottom), the stained end grain is much darker than the flat grain. On the treated board (top), the tones are even.

APPLYING WOOD DYES

The most common types of wood dyes are aniline dyes. These come as powders and must be mixed with a solvent. Adjust the tone when you mix them. For darker colors, add more dye to the solvent. For a lighter color, add more solvent.

If you're applying a water-soluble dye, raise the wood grain with clear water before you apply the dye. Let the surface dry completely and lightly sand it. The grain will raise again when you apply the stain but not nearly as much as the first time.

Wipe or brush the dye on the wood. Keep the surface wet, overlapping the brush strokes as little as possible. If necessary, blend the stained areas with a solvent-soaked rag before the dye dries.

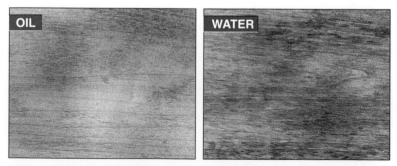

You can limit the penetration of a wood dye by using a thicker solvent. Oil-soluble aniline dyes won't penetrate as deeply as water-soluble. However, there is a wide difference in tone, and the denser the wood, the wider this difference becomes. The maple board on the left was stained with an oil-soluble dye, and the one on the right with the same color in a water-soluble dye.

APPLYING CHEMICAL STAINS

Because chemical stains aren't as versatile or colorful as pigments and dyes, they aren't used as much. But there are several that still come in handy, especially for reproducing antique styles.

■ *Nitric acid* – When applied to most woods, nitric acid speeds up the aging process. The surface grows darker, developing an artificial **patina**[2]. Purchase laboratory-grade nitric acid from a chemical supply house, then mix a 14 percent solution by adding 1 part acid to 7 parts water.

With a nylon bristle brush, paint the diluted acid on the wood. Let it soak a few minutes, then warm the surface with a heat gun. The wood color will "develop" like a photo-

Nitric acid will not darken wood on its own. The color must be "developed" with a heat gun.

graph. Neutralize the acid with a mixture of 1 tablespoon baking soda and 1 pint water. Let the surface dry completely and sand the raised grain.

■ *Lye,* or sodium hydroxide (available at most hardware stores as a drain opener), will darken cherry, oak, and many other woods. Dissolve a tablespoon in a cup of distilled water. Paint it on the wood with a nylon bristle brush and let dry. Neutralize the lye with a solution of 1 part white vinegar and 1 part water.

■ *Hydrated lime,* or calcium oxide (available from any nursery), will darken oak, cherry, walnut, and mahogany, leaving white specks in the **pores**[3]. This "limed" or "pickled" look was stylish early in the twentieth century. Mix the lime with enough water to make a paste and paint it on the wood. Let the paste dry overnight, then scrape the residue off the surface and wipe it

with a damp rag. Let the surface dry completely and lightly sand the raised grain.

■ *Potassium dichromate* is sometimes used in marquetry. It reacts with tannic acid, darkening the acid-rich woods in a design (mahogany, walnut, cherry) but not those with low amounts of acid (holly, boxwood, satinwood). This heightens the contrast between the woods. Mix and apply the chemical as you would a water-soluble aniline dye. It's available from finishing supply companies.

BLEACHING WOOD

While stains typically add color to the wood or darken the tone, you can remove the color and lighten the wood with wood *bleach*. Bleaches are highly reactive chemicals that attack the coloring agents or **extractives**[4] in the wood, breaking them down.

Most bleaches are two part "A/B" solutions. Typically, solution A is 25 percent sodium hydroxide (lye), and B is 35 percent hydrogen peroxide.

Apply the sodium hydroxide (A) first. Let it soak into the wood, then apply the hydrogen peroxide (B). In some cases, you may get better results if you apply B immediately after A, mixing them on the surface. The chemicals will foam slightly. When they stop foaming, the wood will be lighter in color. Repeated applications will remove more color. When the wood is as light was you want it, wash the surface thoroughly with water.

You can also apply a little chlorine bleach while solutions A and B are foaming to give the chemical reaction a little kick and make it work faster.

FILLING WOOD

Scraping and sanding will not always produce as smooth a surface as you could wish for. Many wood species have **open pores**[1] and other surface irregularities that cannot be leveled completely. If you want a smooth finish, you must *fill* the wood grain.

Paste wood fillers are made from quartz powder or silica mixed in a binder (oil, varnish, lacquer, or water-based finish). They are available in a variety of colors, or you can tint them with dyes or pigments to suit yourself.

Thin the filler with the appropriate solvent to the consistency of thick cream, and brush a thick coat on the wood. Let it dry to a dull sheen, then wipe it off *across* the grain with a piece of burlap. The burlap will be too coarse to remove all the excess, so follow with a clean

cloth. Let the filler dry overnight, then sand *lightly*. Don't sand too much; you don't want to open up new pores.

SEALING WOOD

A sanding sealer is a multipurpose finishing material. As the name implies, it's a sanding aid. It hardens the microscopic fibers or **whiskers**[2] on the wood surface, allowing you the sand them off for a super-smooth base. It will fill tiny irregularities in the surface of closed-grain woods. A sealer creates a barrier, preventing chemicals from penetrating and keeping whatever chemicals are already in the wood from bleeding out. And it serves as a primer for compatible finishes.

A **wash coat**[3] of shellac makes an excellent sealer for many finishes.

MORE *INFO*

Fillers and sealers are meant to be used with building finishes, such as varnishes, lacquers, and water-based finishes. They should not be used with penetrating finishes, like wiping oils, because they prevent these materials from soaking into the wood.

You can also purchase special sealers for lacquer and water-based finishes. Brush the sealer on in a *thin* coat, let it dry completely, and sand it with a fine grit. Some craftsmen prefer to *wet sand* the sealer with **silicon carbide sandpaper**[4], using water or mineral spirits. This prevents the sealer from clogging the sandpaper. After wet sanding, clean the surface with a dry rag.

The solids in a wood filler lodge in the wood pores and other surface irregularities, leveling it.

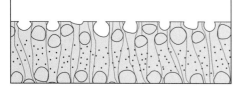

BEFORE FILLING

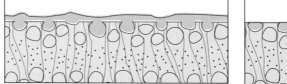

IMMEDIATELY AFTER FILLING

AFTER SANDING

When you're applying a building finish, such as lacquer or varnish, to an open-grain wood, the large pores will create dimples, interfering with the smoothness and luster of the finish. In some cases, they may prevent the finish from forming a continuous film. The ash on the left of this photo was not filled before it was finished with lacquer; the ash on the right was filled.

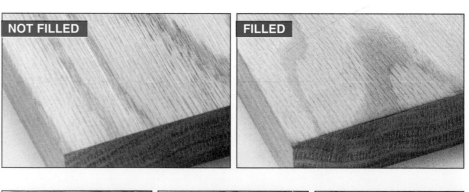

NOT FILLED

FILLED

You can achieve a variety of effects with tinted wood fillers. The oak board on the left has not been treated. The one in the middle was treated with a filler that matches the wood tone, while the one on the right was treated with a dark filler. The light filler mutes the strong grain, while the darker one accents it.

NOT FILLED

NATURAL FILLER

DARK FILLER

APPLYING A FINISH

There are three common methods for applying finishes – wipe, brush, and spray. Although the techniques differ, each follows the same general formula – apply a coat of finish, let it dry, sand it smooth, and repeat as needed.

GENERAL FINISHING KNOW-HOW

No matter what method you use, some considerations apply to *all* finishes.

■ *The finishing area should be the proper temperature,* typically between 70 and 80°F.

■ *Cover the wood surface with a thin, uniform coat* – thin enough that it doesn't run or sag but not so thin it doesn't "flow out" to an even depth.

■ *Cover all wood surfaces evenly,* inside and out, top and bottom. If you don't finish both sides of a board, the two surfaces will **absorb moisture**[5] at different rates, and the board will warp.

■ *Remove any runs or sags before the finish dries.* If runs develop in a partially cured finish, work them out using your fingertip and a little thinner.

■ *Sand the finish between coats.* This levels out the high spots, removes dust, and prepares the surface for the next application.

■ *Clean the surface before each coat* to remove dust that may cloud the finish or prevent it from flowing evenly.

■ *Always follow the manufacturer's directions.* The tips and techniques presented here are *supplements*.

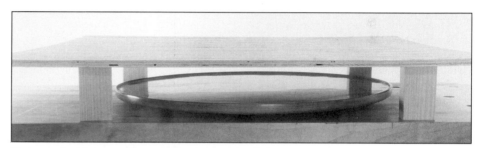

To keep dust from settling on a project as the finish dries, make a **dust umbrella** from a scrap of plywood or particleboard.

CLEANING THE SURFACE

1 *Clean the wood surface thoroughly before you apply a finish and after sanding each coat. Begin by vacuuming the surface to remove as much dust as possible. Don't brush or blow the wood clean: This throws dust into the air, and it will settle on the wet finish afterwards.*

2 *Wipe the surfaces with a tack cloth to remove the microscopic dust. You can purchase ready-made tack rags, but these are sometimes made with waxes and other chemicals that interfere with some finishes. It's safer to make your own. Simply sprinkle a little of the finish you intend to use on a piece of cheesecloth and work it in until it's tacky.*

WIPING ON A FINISH

Wipe-on finishes require little effort – simply wipe them on, then wipe off the excess. Because they are more dilute and slower to dry than other finishes, you can apply an extremely even coat with no lap marks. The drawback is that each coat is very thin – sometimes less than 0.001 inch thick. You must apply many more coats to achieve the depth and degree of protection provided by brush-on and spray-on finishes.

MORE *INFO*

Craftsmen often prefer wipe-on finishes with tung oil in the formula. When used as part of a varnish or oil/varnish blend, tung oil dries harder and has more luster and more water resistance than other materials. Unfortunately, not all "tung oil" finishes contain tung oil. Manufacturers use the term generically to indicate a wipe-on finish.

WIPING KNOW-HOW

Use a rag, sponge, brush, or even your hand to apply a wipe-on finish. What you use to wipe the finish on the wood is not nearly as critical as what you use to wipe it off. Employ a clean, lint-free cloth to remove the excess finish and spread it out in an even coat.

Because wipe-on finishes are so thin, the first one or two coats will penetrate the surface. The penetrating coats may bleed back out of the wood for several hours. (This is a problem particularly with **open-grain woods**[1].) If you don't wipe off the bleed-back, it will create shiny "scabs" on the surface. If necessary, continue wiping the surface every hour or so until the bleeding stops.

Some woodworkers "sand in" the penetrating coats with 320- or 400-grit wet/dry **silicone carbide sandpaper**[2]. Sanding creates a slurry of sawdust and finish that fills the pores and other minute imperfections on the surface. It will also fill small gaps in the joinery. Some fin-

If you choose to sand a wipe-on finish into the wood, wipe off the resulting finish across the wood grain, as you would a paste wood filler. This helps force it into the wood grain.

ishers advise against this technique because the fine sawdust partially obscures the wood grain and disguises the pores. Part of the advantage of a penetrating finish, after all, is that it preserves the natural texture of the wood. But sanding does create a smoother appearance without the fuss of applying a filler. It's one more option you can consider.

To build a film on top of the surface, either for additional protection or to add depth and luster, apply additional coats of finish. Some finishers add a small amount of spar varnish (1 tablespoon per cup) to help the finish build. Let each coat dry thoroughly, then sand with 400-grit sandpaper or abrasive pads between coats.

PRO *TIP*

You can sand between coats *and* apply the next coat in one step by sanding with wet/dry sandpaper, using the finish itself as a lubricant. Wipe off the excess finish with a clean cloth after sanding.

MAKING WIPE-ON FINISHES

Although there are dozens of ready-mixed wipe-on finishes, some woodworkers like to make their own. Follow this time-tested recipe for "wiping varnishes" and it's hard to go wrong.

Mix an oil-based building finish, a drying oil, and a compatible thinner. (Linseed oil can be used as either a drying oil or a thinner.) The classic mixture is 1 part varnish, 1 part boiled linseed oil, and 1 part turpentine, but you can create an original brew, picking from the ingredients in the chart.

WIPING VARNISH INGREDIENTS

Choose one from each column.

Building Finish	Drying Oil	Thinner
Varnish (regular or spar)	Boiled linseed oil	Boiled linseed oil
Polyurethane	Pure tung oil	Turpentine
Polymerized tung oil	Walnut oil	Mineral spirits

BRUSHING ON A FINISH

The majority of finishes – shellacs, varnishes, polyurethanes, paints, brushing lacquers, and some water-based finishes – are formulated to be brushed onto the wood surface.

BRUSHING KNOW-HOW

Don't apply the finish directly from the can. If there is dust or dirt on the surface of your project, the brush will pick it up and transfer it to the container, contaminating the contents. Instead, pour out the amount you need in a separate container.

If you haven't applied a sealer, dilute the first coat one-to-one with the appropriate solvent to make a primer. This helps the finish penetrate the wood and aids in sanding the first coat smooth.

Don't apply a thick finish. The thinner the coat, the less likely it is to run or sag. Also, thin coats cure faster. However, the coat must be thick enough to "flow out" and form a smooth surface.

PRO*TIP*

To prevent runs and sags on intricate surfaces, apply the finish with a partially loaded brush — sometimes called a *dry* brush. Dip the brush in finish, wipe some off on a piece of scrap wood, then apply what remains to the project.

If the air bubbles in the finish don't rise to the surface and dissipate, thin the finish slightly with the appropriate solvent.

If a bristle comes loose from the brush, pick it out before the finish dries. You may want to keep a pair of tweezers handy for this eventuality.

If you apply too much finish to an area, spread it out or remove it with a dry brush before it cures.

As much as possible, brush with the grain. But don't brush too much. If the finish is slow to dry, you'll work air bubbles into the film. If it dries fast, you'll leave lap marks or brush marks.

Let the finish dry for the recommended time before applying another coat. Don't use a fan or warm air to speed drying. Not only does this stir up the dust, it may cause the finish to *skin over* – the molecules on the surface cure before those beneath them. This skin may sag or wrinkle.

PRO*TIP*

To see if a finish has cured or hardened completely, test it with your thumbnail. If you can leave an indentation in the surface, it needs to dry longer.

If the chemical film is hard when it dries (as varnish, polyurethane, and water-based finishes are), sand between coats with 250- to 320-grit sandpaper. If the film is soft (as shellac and lacquer are), use 400-grit sandpaper. The finer grit will keep you from sanding through the soft film. If the paper loads quickly, stop sanding – the finish probably hasn't hardened sufficiently.

When applying a **solvent-releasing finish**[3] (such as shellac and lacquer) that partially dissolves preceding coats, you don't always need to sand between coats. Some craftsmen prefer to sand every second or third coat to allow the film to build faster. However, the more coats you apply before sanding, the more uneven the finish becomes.

USING A BRUSH

1 *Dip the brush less than halfway into the finish. If you load too much finish on the brush, it will flood the wood surface, creating runs. If the brush is overloaded, don't wipe it on the sides of the container. This loosens the bristles and creates air bubbles. Instead, let the excess finish drip off the brush or press it against the side of the container to squeeze the finish out of the bristles.*

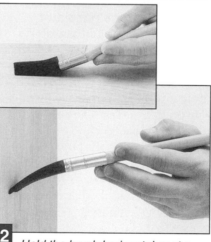

2 *Hold the brush horizontal or at a slight angle as you apply the finish. This prevents the finish from flowing out of the bristles too quickly.*

WET SANDING A FINISH

Once the surface is well sealed, use wet/dry sandpaper to sand between coats, lubricating the paper with either mineral spirits or water, as appropriate. The lubricant keeps the sandpaper from clogging so that it cuts faster. You get a smoother surface in less time.

SPECIAL BRUSHING METHODS

Depending on the type of finish you apply, there may be several special brushing methods.

■ *Shellac* – When stored as a liquid, shellac degrades quickly. For this reason, many craftsmen prefer to mix a fresh batch for each project. Use 95 percent denatured *ethyl* alcohol to dissolve the shellac solids. Too much methyl alcohol reduces the finish quality.

Pay attention to the *cut* – the ratio of solids to alcohol. One pound of shellac flakes dissolved in 1 gallon (8 pounds) of alcohol is a 1-pound cut. You may prefer to think in smaller quantities – 1 ounce of shellac flakes in 1 cup (8 ounces) makes a 1-pound cut. One-to 2-pound cuts are used for wash coats and primers, 2- and 3-pound cuts for successive "top" coats.

■ *Varnishes* – Of all the brush-on finishes, varnish is the slowest to dry. Depending on the temperature and humidity, you can wait 48 hours or more between coats. This has its advantages. You can "work" a varnish finish with a brush for a much longer time than other finishes, getting it as even as possible. Some finishers brush the varnish on, then use the soft tip of the brush to gently wipe the liquid film smooth. (This is sometimes referred to as *tipping.*) The slow drying time also gives you a longer window to remove runs.

■ *Polyurethane* – Polyurethane has a sensitive time "window" in which you must apply the next coat. For most polyurethanes, this is 8 to

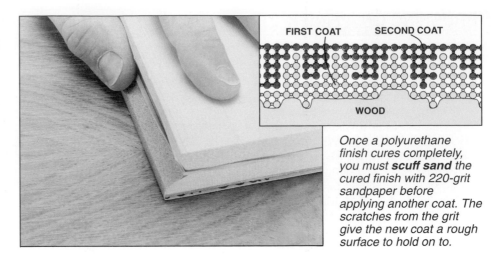

Once a polyurethane finish cures completely, you must **scuff sand** the cured finish with 220-grit sandpaper before applying another coat. The scratches from the grit give the new coat a rough surface to hold on to.

12 hours. (However, check the directions– sometimes the window lasts as long as 2 days.) If you don't let it dry long enough, the finish will not be hard enough to sand the surface. But if you wait too long, it will become too hard for another coat to bond to it.

■ *Brushing lacquers* – Brushing lacquers are mixed with highly volatile solvents and produce extremely unhealthy fumes. As a precaution, wear a **respirator**[1], even when working in a well-ventilated area.

Although you can sometimes apply other finishes over lacquer, it's rarely a good idea to apply lacquer over other finishes. The solvents dissolve many reactive and coalescing films. This also applies to stains and fillers. Use special lacquer-compatible materials, or seal the surface with a wash coat of shellac.

Brushing lacquers are tricky to apply evenly; it's easy to get lap

MORE *INFO*

Lacquer dissolves the extractives in some imported hardwoods. The colors in rosewood and closely related species bleed into the lacquer, clouding the finish.

marks. For this reason, finishers often reserve them for small projects, applying super-thin coats.

■ *Water-based finishes* – When applying water-based finishes, use a nylon bristle brush. Natural bristles absorb water and swell. Dampen the bristles to help load the finish on a clean brush.

Use distilled water to thin water-based finishes. The impurities in hard water can precipitate "gel specks" in the finish. If the finish dries too fast, add a small amount of retarder. Propylene glycol is often used as a *retarder,* but check the directions.

Store water-based finishes at room temperature; don't let them freeze. Once frozen, these finishes no longer dry properly.

When disposing of old water-based finishes, don't think that just because it cleans up with water you can pour it down a drain. Hard water turns these materials into a sticky glop that clogs pipes.

DISPOSING OF FINISHES

Be careful how you dispose of finishing chemicals. Depending on the toxicity of the solvent, a single cup — no more than you'd use to clean a single brush — can pollute thousands of gallons of water!

■ Save used solvent, let the solids settle out of it, pour the clear liquid into another container, and use it again. Mineral spirits and turpentine can be recycled over and over again.

■ When you must throw away a chemical, call your local municipal government or county clerk. Ask how small amounts of hazardous wastes are handled in your community.

■ If you don't have a collection or disposal program in your area, pour the liquids in a shallow pan. Let the solvents evaporate, then throw away the hardened solids.

SEE *ALSO:*

[1] Finishing Hazards   274

CHOOSING AND CARING FOR A BRUSH

A good brush makes a finishing job much easier. But how can you tell a good brush from a mediocre one?

The most important part, of course, is the bristles. These should be slender, slightly tapered, with the wide end at the ferrule. When viewed from the side, the brush should have a wedge shape, tapering to a point. The ends of the bristles should be trimmed at a slight angle, not cut square.

The tips of the bristles should be split or *flagged.* The flags help control the finish flow and diminish the brush marks. The bristles should also be springy but not so stiff that they won't bend easily. Finally, they should be half again as long as the brush is wide.

Inexpensive, disposable foam brushes serve well for many finishes. They hold a lot of finish, and they don't leave brush marks. But it's easier to regulate the flow of finish with a bristle brush. Also, solvents in shellac and lacquer will dissolve foam.

HANDLE

FERRULE

FLAGGED TIPS   TAPERED BRISTLES

HANDLE

BRISTLES

TIP

HEEL

FOAM

BRISTLE BRUSH   **FOAM BRUSH**

1 To prepare a new bristle brush, eliminate any loose bristles. Strike the brush against your hand sharply. A few bristles may fall out, but as you continue striking, this will stop and the remaining bristles will hold fast. (If the bristles continue to fall out, get your money back.)

2 If you've purchased a natural bristle brush, it will require a short break-in period. Suspend the brush in mineral spirits or turpentine for a day or two. Wipe the brush on scrap wood for a few minutes, and clean it with soap and water.

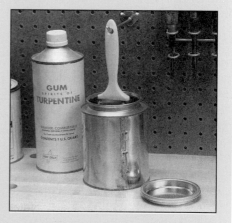

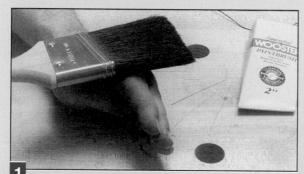

3 Always clean a bristle brush immediately after using it. Wipe off the excess finish on scrap wood or paper. Swirl the bristles in solvent and work them against the sides of the can. Groom the bristles with a **brush comb** and swirl them in clean solvent. Finally, wash with soap and water.

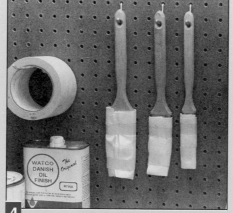

4 Store a brush by hanging it with bristles down — never rest it on its bristles. Wrap the bristles in paper to help them hold their shape. Don't use plastic; this won't allow the bristles to dry. The bristles must dry completely between each finishing job or they will lose their spring.

PRO*TIP*

If the finish hardens on the bristles, don't throw the brush away. You can save it with this super brush cleaner. Mix:

- 2 parts toluol or xylene
- 1 part acetone
- 1 part denatured alcohol

Let the brush soak in this overnight, and comb the hardened finish out of the bristles. Rinse the brush in fresh cleaner, then wash it with soap and water.

SPRAYING ON A FINISH

Two types of finish are commonly applied by spraying – lacquer and water-based finishes. However, you can spray almost any finishing material, provided you mix it to the proper consistency. Once you acquire the spraying knack, the finish goes on very evenly with no brush strokes.

SPRAY GUN

SPRAY EQUIPMENT

There are two types of sprayers commonly used for wood finishing – low-volume, high-pressure (LVHP) systems, and high-volume, low-pressure (HVLP) systems.

An LVHP system is driven by an air compressor. When you pull the *trigger* of the spray gun, you open the upper end of the *siphon*. High-pressure air blowing through the gun draws a steady stream of finish from the reservoir or *cup* and blows it out the nozzles, *atomizing* the finish (reducing it to tiny droplets) in the process.

An HVLP system uses a turbine, blowing a large volume of air through the gun to atomize the finish. There are also *conversion-air* systems, which convert high-pressure compressed air to high-volume air to power an HVLP spray gun.

The advantage of an LVHP sprayer is that it will handle big jobs. It delivers a lot of finish in a short amount of time. But when you are spraying medium-sized or small projects, there's a lot of *overspray* – finish that ends up on the floor and the walls. An HVLP sprayer has a much higher *transfer efficiency*. About two thirds of HVLP-delivered finish ends up on the wood, versus one quarter with an LVHP system.

To contain the overspray, you need a *spray booth* – a ventilated room or enclosure. This applies whether you spray lacquers or water-based finishes. There is a misconception among craftsmen that you don't need a spray booth to apply water-based finishes because they contain fewer organic solvents. Unfortunately, *all* finishing materials produce dangerous vapors that must be evacuated, especially if you're using an LVHP system. Unlike lacquers, however, water-based finishes don't require **explosion-proof wiring**[1] in the finishing area.

> ### MORE *INFO*
>
> You can also use inexpensive "airless" spray guns to finish wood. However, these don't atomize the finish as finely as LVHP and HVLP sprays. Typical spray lacquers and water-based finishes dry before the coarse droplets flow together, and the finish appears rough. To get acceptable results, you must use slow-drying paints or varnishes.

PREPARING TO SPRAY

Before you spray a finish, you must prepare the finish and the spray gun to achieve the proper atomization and spray pattern. If the atomization is too coarse, the droplets dry before they flow together, creating a rough *orange peel* appearance. If they are too fine, the droplets dry before they hit the wood, and the finish looks dusty. This is a *dry spray*.

■ *Assemble the spray gun.* Spray guns have interchangeable *air nozzles*, *fluid nozzles*, and *needle-valve stems* to help control air and finish flow. In some cases, manufacturers recommend specific nozzles and stems for their finishes.

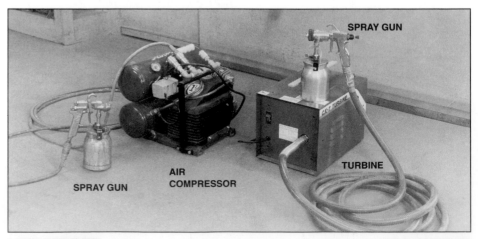

LVHP SPRAYER   HVLP SPRAYER

■ *Mix the finish.* If the manufacturer recommends doing so, thin the finish to the proper viscosity for spraying. You may also have to adjust the viscosity for temperature and humidity. A warm environment causes the finish to dry quickly and develop orange peel. Add a *retarder* to the mix to control this. Retarder also helps on humid days when the finish *blushes*, developing milky spots. If the wood surface is contaminated, the finish may not flow evenly, resulting in dimples or *fish-eyes*. A *flow-out agent* (sometimes called a "fish-eye eliminator") may correct this if the contamination isn't too bad. Flow-out agents can also help with orange peel.

■ *Adjust the spray gun.* When the finish is mixed, spray a test piece. Adjust the *fluid-control knob* to control how much finish is delivered, and the *fan-width control knob* to change the spray pattern. As you increase the airflow, the pattern changes from a circle to an ellipse or *fan.* Alter the orientation of the ellipse by turning the *horns* of the air nozzle. (The long dimension of the elliptical fan is always perpen-

dicular to the horns.) Adjust the pattern so you can finish the surface in the fewest possible number of passes.

SPRAYING KNOW-HOW
As you spray:

■ Start with the nozzle pointing to one side; don't pull the trigger with it aimed directly at the wood.

■ Keep the gun moving at an even speed to deposit the finish evenly.

■ Keep the nozzle a constant distance from the wood surface – 6 to 12 inches, typically.

■ Spray surfaces in long passes, working either side to side or up and down.

■ Coat the edges, turnings, and small surfaces first, then spray wide, flat areas.

■ If you must stop for more than a few minutes, spray solvent through the gun to clear it of finish. Otherwise, the finish may harden and clog the gun.

■ After completing the finish, take the gun apart and clean each piece thoroughly. Some craftsmen store nozzles and stems in solvent.

SPRAY FINISH PROBLEMS

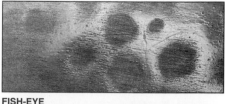
FISH-EYE

ORANGE PEEL

DRY SPRAY

BLUSH

SEE ALSO:
[1] Finishing Hazards   274

SPRAYING ON A FINISH

1 Adjust the nozzle to get a wide, elliptical spray pattern or **fan.** This pattern deposits more finish in the middle of the fan than toward the ends. To compensate, overlap each pass about one-third the width of the fan.

OVERLAP EACH PASS.

THIN / AREA OF GREATEST COVERAGE / THIN — FAN

2 Move your arm from side to side in a straight line. This keeps the nozzle the same distance from the project, so the spray pattern remains the same size and the finish is deposited evenly. Don't swing your arm in an arc; the finish coat will be thin at the beginning and end of the arc, and too thick in the middle. Where it's thin, the coat may **orange peel.** Where it's thick, it will run or sag.

6"–12"

RIGHT

WRONG

WORK YOUR WAY BACK. → MAKE THE LONGEST POSSIBLE PASSES.

WORK YOUR WAY DOWN.

3 When spraying a surface, work your way down or back. It's easiest to move the spray gun from side to side when spraying broad **outside** surfaces. For **inside** surfaces, move in the direction that allows the longest possible pass.

FINISHING THE FINISH

Once you've applied the final coat, most finishes – especially building finishes – require that you *rub out* the tiny flaws, polishing with finer and finer abrasives.

RUBBING OUT A FINISH

Before you can rub out a finish, it must harden completely. Partially hardened films simply clog the sandpaper. Furthermore, the degree of hardness determines how much you can polish. The harder a finish, the finer the **scratch pattern**[1] it will accept. You can polish harder finishes with finer abrasives, creating a higher gloss.

It requires much more time for a finish to harden completely than it does to dry between coats. And different finishes require different periods to reach full hardness – check the directions.

Once the finish hardens sufficiently, determine what degree of **luster**[2] you want. This will determine the final abrasive grit or material you should use.

■ For a *flat* look, polish to between 320 and 600 grit.

■ For *satin*, work up to between 600 and 1000 grit.

■ For *gloss*, continue beyond 1000 grit.

MORE *INFO*

"Satin" finishes contain flatteners to control the luster. However, even if you use a satin finish, you must rub out the surface or it will look duller than expected.

Finishers commonly use sandpaper for rubbing as far as 600 grit, then switch to powdered stone – *pumice* for a satin look, then on to *rottenstone* for gloss. However, there are other abrasive materials that work well.

■ #000 *steel wool* produces a flat look; use #0000 for satin.

■ *Fiberglass abrasive pads* (also called synthetic steel wool) are impregnated with abrasives. The gray pads (roughly equal to 320-grit) create a flat finish. The white pads (about 1000-grit) produce a satin look.

■ *Rubbing compounds* are abrasives suspended in paste. They are available from automotive stores in several grits for a range of lusters, from satin to high gloss.

APPLYING PASTE WAX

As a final step, many finishers apply a coat of paste wax to a finish. This is not absolutely necessary – wax is softer than any finish and provides no additional protection to the wood. It does, however, lubricate the surface, protecting the finish from wear and abrasion. It also fills tiny scratches and increases luster.

There are two ways you can apply wax – with and without abrasives. Many finishers use paste wax as part of a final rub-out, applying it with steel wool or abrasive pads. This polishes and waxes the surfaces at the same time. Or you can apply wax with a damp cloth *after* the rub-out. In either case, wait for the wax coat to haze over, then wipe off the excess with a clean cloth. Buff with chamois or other soft cloth.

MYTH *CONCEPTIONS*

WAX FACTS Paste wax does not "feed" a finish, nor does it replace wood oils. It does not stop wood from breathing, nor is it a moisture barrier — it's much too thin. You cannot build up coats of wax — every time you apply a new coat, you dissolve the old one. After buffing, the wax layer is never more than a few molecules thick.

SEE *ALSO:*

[1] Sanding   264
[2] Finishing Properties   272

MORE *SOURCES*

BOOKS

Finishing, by Nick Engler, Rodale Press, 1992

Understanding Wood Finishing, by Bob Flexner, Rodale Press, 1994

The Woodfinishing Book, by Michael Dresdner, Taunton Press, 1992

VIDEOS

Wood Finishing with Frank Klausz, Taunton Books and Videos

The Woodfinishing Video with Michael Dresdner, Taunton Books and Videos

USING POWDERED STONE

Wrap a piece of felt around a sanding block. Dip the felt in water, linseed oil, or paraffin oil, then sprinkle a little pumice or rottenstone on it.

USING RUBBING COMPOUNDS

Apply rubbing compounds with a felt block or a sander/polisher. Don't use rubbing compounds with open-grain woods that haven't been filled — the paste lodges in the pores, leaving a light-colored residue.

TROUBLE *SHOOTING*

COMMON FINISHING PROBLEMS

Problem	Possible Cause(s)	Solution(s)
General		
Finish cures slowly or not at all.	Incompatible finishing materials, or oils in wood are incompatible with finish.	Prepare test board to find compatible materials; try insulating incompatible materials with wash coat of shellac.
	Finishing area is too cold, hot, or humid.	Apply finish between 70° and 80°F; dehumidify area.
Dust trapped in finish leaves tiny bumps.	Dust in air settles on finish.	Use dust umbrella and a damp shop mop to keep dust down; apply finish in clean room.
Finish runs or sags.	Applying too much finish; coat is too thick.	Apply thin, even coat.
Staining		
Stained surface is uneven and blotchy.	Wood grain or density is uneven; stain penetrates unevenly.	Seal wood with wash coat of shellac; use pigment stain in oil or gel base that doesn't penetrate wood.
	Pigment stain was not wiped off evenly.	Wipe carefully, blending areas to make them same tone.
	Water-based stain was wiped off too soon.	Allow stain to penetrate completely before wiping.
Stain highlights surface imperfections.	Stain penetrates deeper into exposed end grain in problem areas.	Carefully scrape and sand surface, removing mill marks. Scratch pattern from abrasives must be even.
End grain is darker than other surfaces.	Stain penetrates deeper into end grain than flat or quarter grain.	Coat end grain with wash coat of shellac before staining.
Stain is too dark.	Too much pigment remains on surface.	Sand with finer abrasive; wipe more aggressively.
	Dye is too saturated or penetrates too deeply.	Dilute dye or use oil-soluble dye.
Stain is too light.	Too little pigment remains on surface.	Sand with coarser abrasive; wipe less aggressively; add more pigment to stain.
	Dye is too dilute or doesn't penetrate enough.	Add more dye or use water-soluble dye.
Stain color bleeds into finish.	Stain was partially dissolved by finish.	Prepare test board to find compatible finish; try insulating stain from finish with wash coat of shellac
Stain shows streaks or lap marks.	Stain is drying too quickly during application.	Apply stain more quickly; keep surface wet. Or, use stain that dries more slowly.
Stain raises the wood grain.	Water-based finishing materials cause wood grain to swell.	Before staining, wet wood grain with clear water, let dry, and sand lightly.
Wiping On a Finish		
Finish appears very flat, has no luster.	Normal appearance of all drying oils and first two coats of wiping oils	Apply multiple coats of wiping oils to build film on surface. Or, add small amount of compatible varnish to oil.
Finish must be reapplied each year or so.	Normal for all drying oils and thin applications of wiping oils	Apply multiple coats of wiping oils to build more durable film. Or, add small amount of compatible varnish to oil.
Finish forms bumps or scabs.	Finish bleeds out of wood after applying. Common with open-grain woods.	Wipe off bleed-back every hour or so until it stops.
Finish uneven, builds up in crevices.	Not all excess finish is wiped off after each coat.	Wipe more thoroughly; use dry brush to reach into crevices.
Brushing On a Finish		
Finish doesn't flow into pores.	Normal for open-grain woods	Fill pores with wood filler, then sand smooth.
Finish shows brush marks or lap marks.	Finish is drying too quickly during application.	Apply more quickly or use slower-drying finish.
Air bubbles in finish	Normal, caused by brush action	If bubbles don't rise and pop, thin finish slightly.
Spraying On a Finish		
Finish develops a white haze or blush.	Finishing area is too humid; moisture is drawn into film as solvent evaporates.	Thin lacquer with retarder to slow evaporation.
Fish-eyes or tiny craters appear in finish.	Surface is contaminated with oil or silicone.	Add flow-out agent to finish. Or, try sealing surface with wash coat of shellac.
Finish is rough like an orange peel.	Atomization is too coarse; finish is too thick; finish is drying too fast.	Adjust air flow and/or thin finish. Retarder and flow-out agent may also help.
Finish looks dusty.	Atomization is too fine; finish is drying in air.	Adjust air flow, hold spray gun close to surface. Retarder may help.

25

Shaping and Molding

Applied molding and shaped edges add detail, emphasize design, and make a project more formal and polished.

M oldings and shaped edges have decorative profiles that create visual interest. By applying moldings or shaped edges, you can frame panels and openings, emphasize planes and shapes, and make surfaces look shorter, taller, thinner, or thicker.

Molding and shaping techniques are simple and straightforward. To make a molding, simply cut a profile in a long, narrow strip of wood. To apply it, cut the strip to fit the surface you wish to decorate, then attach the pieces with nails or screws. Shaping an edge is even easier – just cut the profile with the appropriate cutter or bit. But there are additional concerns. What shapes should you use? How do you create a pleasing profile? To choose the best shapes for a particular project, you need to understand what molded shapes are available and how to combine them.

A MOLDING PRIMER

Open any tool catalog to the **shaper cutter**[1] or **router bit**[2] section, and you'll find whole pages of shapes, all in a jumble. However, there is some order in this chaos.

BASIC SHAPES

Despite the profusion of bits and cutters, there are really only three shapes in any molding profile – a bead (convex curve), a cove (concave curve), and a flat (straight) line. Each of these are subdivided into a few

*The trim on the case of a classic **Grandfather Clock** converts what would otherwise be a tall, uninteresting rectangular box into a triumph of design and craftsmanship. Instead of just telling time, the clock becomes an eye-popping display of lines and forms.*

SPECS: 93″ high, 24″ wide, 14″ deep

MATERIALS: Curly cherry

CRAFTSMAN: Leonard Marsharck
Bedminster, PA

Photo by Whitney Photography

basic shapes that can be cut with a simple bit or cutter, as shown in "Common Molding Profiles" below. All moldings are variations on or combinations of these shapes.

COMBINING SHAPES

There are no hard and fast rules dictating how to combine shapes or how to use them. However, you may find these guidelines useful:

■ Use simple shapes when a molding is subject to heavy use, such as a base molding or table edge. Complex shapes soon show the wear.

■ Vary the shapes in a complex molding; don't repeat them over and over. The classic bed molding, which incorporates a cove and bead, is an old favorite. But you hardly ever see a molding with a double cove or double bead.

■ To make the moldings more dramatic, use sharp, crisp transitions between the molded shapes. Make the curves and flats meet at distinct angles, or use fillets (small, flat steps) and grooves to separate the shapes. A bed molding is more dramatic than an ogee because the curves are divided by a fillet.

Strong grain patterns fight with the lines of complex molding profiles. The intricate shapes of the crown molding are easy to discern in the mahogany. But they are much less distinct in oak.

MAHOGANY CROWN MOLDING **OAK CROWN MOLDING**

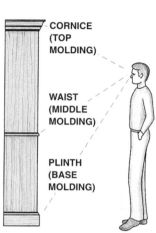

CORNICE (TOP MOLDING)

WAIST (MIDDLE MOLDING)

PLINTH (BASE MOLDING)

Consider where people will stand when viewing moldings. The molded shapes on this corner cupboard angle toward you so they can be seen and enjoyed.

SEE ALSO:

[1] Shaper Cutters   111
[2] Router Bits   125

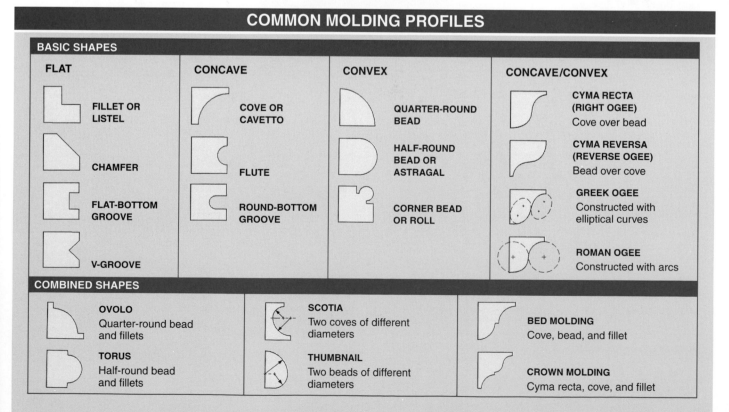

COMMON MOLDING PROFILES

BASIC SHAPES

FLAT

- FILLET OR LISTEL
- CHAMFER
- FLAT-BOTTOM GROOVE
- V-GROOVE

CONCAVE

- COVE OR CAVETTO
- FLUTE
- ROUND-BOTTOM GROOVE

CONVEX

- QUARTER-ROUND BEAD
- HALF-ROUND BEAD OR ASTRAGAL
- CORNER BEAD OR ROLL

CONCAVE/CONVEX

- CYMA RECTA (RIGHT OGEE)
  Cove over bead
- CYMA REVERSA (REVERSE OGEE)
  Bead over cove
- GREEK OGEE
  Constructed with elliptical curves
- ROMAN OGEE
  Constructed with arcs

COMBINED SHAPES

- **OVOLO**
  Quarter-round bead and fillets
- **TORUS**
  Half-round bead and fillets
- **SCOTIA**
  Two coves of different diameters
- **THUMBNAIL**
  Two beads of different diameters
- **BED MOLDING**
  Cove, bead, and fillet
- **CROWN MOLDING**
  Cyma recta, cove, and fillet

SETTING UP A SHAPER

Although there are several power tools you can use to cut molding profiles and shape edges, the **shaper**[1] is the only machine designed especially for this job. It's used in a similar manner as a router table is, but there are important differences. A shaper commonly has more muscle and stamina than a router. It's typically powered by a large **induction motor**[2], built for hours of continuous use.

1 If necessary, place an insert on the shaper table opening to close down the space around the cutters as much as possible. This will provide better support for the work as you feed it past the cutter.

2 To mount a shaper cutter, place the hub over the spindle, place a keyed washer over the hub, and lock them in place with a nut. You can also stack two or more cutters on a spindle to create combined shapes. If you wish, add rub collars to the stack to limit the depth of cut and help guide the stock, like a pilot bearing on a router bit.

3 Shaper cutters are **reversible.** You can flip them over to cut in either direction — some cutters are made to cut one shape with one side of the flutes and another with the opposite side. If you stack cutters, make certain the cutting edges all face in the same direction. Set the motor to rotate in the direction that the cutters face.

NOTE: Guard is removed so you can see the cut.

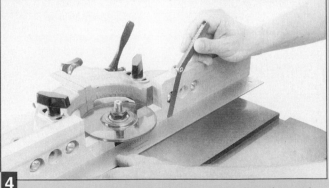

4 When using a fence to guide the work, adjust the position of the split faces. These faces move independently both front to back and side to side. Set the front-to-back positions first. For some operations, you'll want both faces even with one another. For others, you'll want to **offset** the outfeed face in front of the infeed face to properly support the work after some of the stock has been removed. No matter what their relative positions, make sure the faces remain parallel.

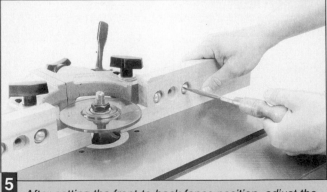

5 After setting the front-to-back fence position, adjust the side-to-side positions so there's as little space as possible between the faces. This will provide the maximum amount of support for the work.

SHAPING KNOW-HOW

When making shaping cuts on a shaper or a router table:

■ Make test cuts to check your setup. If a profile requires multiple passes, make enough test pieces to carry you through the entire procedure.

■ Always cut *against* the rotation of the cutter.

■ Feed the work slowly for a smooth cut, but keep stock moving steadily.

■ When using large wing cutters (over 2 inches in diameter) on a router table, slow the router.

■ Cut with the grain whenever possible. When you must rout cross grain, **back up the work**[3] with a scrap to prevent tear-out.

SAFE *GUARDS*

When cutting stock on a shaper, use featherboards and push shoes to help feed the stock. **Push sticks are NOT recommended.** The stick tends to catch on the cutter, whipping it around and flinging it back at you like a spear.

SHAPING STRAIGHT EDGES

When shaping the edge of a board:

■ **Joint**[4] the edge straight and smooth. Any irregularities in the edge will show up in the shaped profile.

■ Use a fence to guide the work.

■ When making a small molding, shape the edge of a large board, then rip the molding free.

SHAPING FLAT SURFACES

You can also shape the face of a board, provided it's narrow enough and the cutter will reach the area where you want to make a decorative profile. For wider boards, use a *molding head*. This shaping accessory mounts on a table saw.

SEE *ALSO*:

[1] Shapers — 111
[2] Tool Buymanship — 117
[3] Routing Know-How — 216
[4] Jointing Know-How — 184

SHAPING NARROW MOLDINGS

To cut small or narrow moldings, shape the edge of a larger board, then rip the moldings free. Don't try to shape narrow stock; it's likely to splinter as you cut it. The shaper or the router table will catch on the splintered wood and kick it back at you.

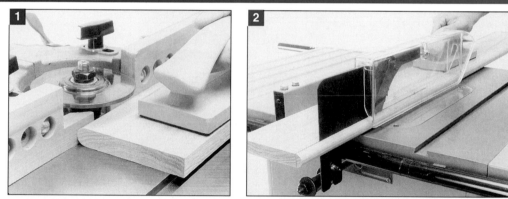

SHAPING NARROW ENDS

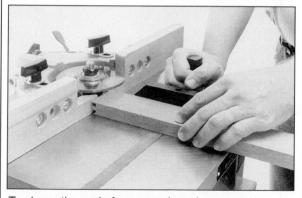

To shape the end of a narrow board, use a miter gauge and a fence to guide the work. The fence must be precisely parallel to the miter gauge slot. You may find it easier to clamp the work to the edge of a square scrap. Then push the work and the scrap along the fence, past the cutter.

USING A MOLDER

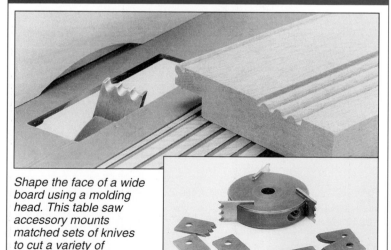

Shape the face of a wide board using a molding head. This table saw accessory mounts matched sets of knives to cut a variety of molded shapes. Guide the work along the fence.

SHAPING CURVED SURFACES

When shaping a curved edge or end, sand the surface smooth. The curve must be *fair*, without any flat spots or sharp transitions. If you're using a router table, mount a bit with a **pilot bearing**[1] to guide the work. If you're using a shaper, mount a rub collar on the spindle with the cutter – this serves the same purpose. Also mount a **starter pin**[2] on one side of the bit or cutter, and use it to help feed the work past the cutter.

MORE *INFO*

Solid metal rub collars may burnish the wood, crushing the fibers. This, in turn, will prevent stains and finishes from penetrating the wood. To prevent this, purchase a set of *ball-bearing* collars. These are available from shaper cutter distributors.

SEE *ALSO:*

[1] Use a Piloted Bit 218
[2] Use a Starter Pin 228
[3] Circular Saw Blades 101

GUIDING CURVED WORK

Guide curved workpieces along a pilot bearing or a rub collar. Adjust the height of the cutter so that at least ⅛ inch of the wood contacts the bearing or collar; otherwise the work will be difficult to control. Feed against the rotation of the cutter, keeping the edge of the work pressed against the guide. Use a starter pin as a leverage point to help start the cut and feed the work into the cutter.

CUTTING CURVED MOLDING

1 To make a curved molding, such as the "gooseneck" molding on a grandfather clock, first cut the curve that you wish to shape in a large board. Sand the curved edge smooth, then shape it.

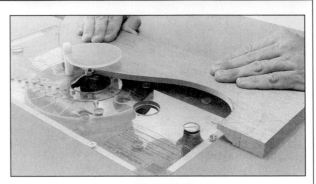

2 Cut the molding free of the larger board with a band saw or coping saw.

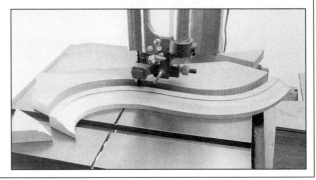

SHAPING RAISED PANELS

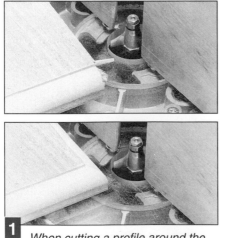

1 When cutting a profile around the perimeter of a panel, shape the ends first, then the edges. If the cutter tears the wood when it exits the end cuts, it won't matter: The edge cuts will remove the torn areas of the wood.

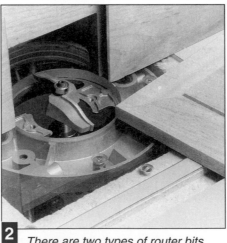

2 There are two types of router bits that cut raised panels. **Wing cutters** cut with the work resting on its face. Use them with a fence to cut straight surfaces, or with a pilot bearing to cut curved surfaces.

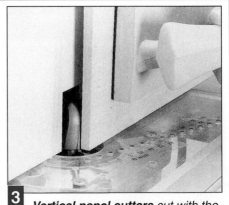

3 **Vertical panel cutters** cut with the board resting on its edge and its face against the fence. They are taller than wing cutters but have a much smaller diameter. Because of this, the speed of the cutting flutes is lower and they are safer to use. However, they will shape only straight surfaces. You cannot shape curved edges with them.

MAKING COVE CUTS

To cut a cove molding with a larger radius than is commonly available in router bits and shaper cutters, use a table saw. Pass the molding stock over a **combination blade**[3], guiding it along a straight-edge at an angle to the blade. The depth of the cove is determined by the height of the blade, and the width of the cove by the angle and position of the straightedge.

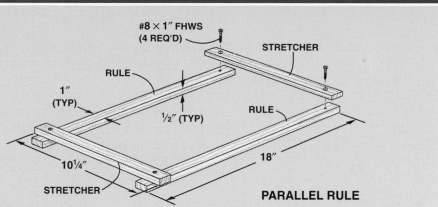

#8 × 1" FHWS (4 REQ'D)

STRETCHER

RULE

1" (TYP)

½" (TYP)

RULE

10¼"

18"

STRETCHER

PARALLEL RULE

1 To find the coving angle — the angle at which the work must cross the blade — make a simple **parallel rule** from four strips of wood. Adjust the saw to the desired depth of cut, and set the rule to the desired width of the cove. Place the rule on the saw table, straddling the blade. Turn it at various angles to the blade while rotating the blade by hand. Find the position where the teeth of the saw brush both the front and back strips. Using a grease pencil, trace the **inside edge** of each strip, making two lines on the table.

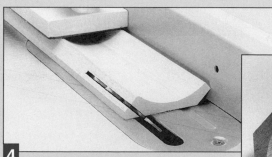

MIDDLE LINE

STOP LINE

START LINE

2 Measure the distance between the front and back lines, then draw a third line halfway between and parallel to them. This marks the center of the cove cut. Use all three lines as references to determine the angle and position of the straight-edge that guides the work. For example, if you want to cut a cove down the middle of a 5-inch-wide board, the straightedge must be parallel to and 2½ inches away from the middle reference line. Fasten the straightedge to the saw table with double-faced carpet tape.

3 Adjust the saw blade so it projects no more than ¹⁄₁₆ inch above the saw table. Turn on the saw and place the work against the straightedge. Slowly feed the stock from the infeed side of the saw, **against** the rotation of the blade. After completing the first pass, raise the saw blade another ¹⁄₁₆ inch and make a second pass. Repeat until you have cut the cove to the desired depth and width.

TIP: On the last pass, make a shallow cut and feed the wood very slowly. This will make the surface of the cove as smooth as possible and reduce the amount of scraping and sanding needed.

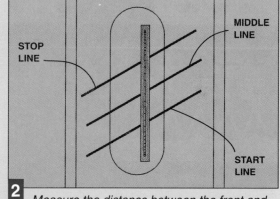

4 If you are making a **sprung molding** (a molding that will lean out from the surface to which it's attached), double-bevel the edges of the molding stock on the table saw.

TIP: The two mounting faces of a sprung molding can be cut at any angle, but the two angles must add up to 90 degrees.

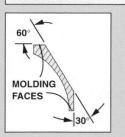

60°

MOLDING FACES

30°

COMPLEX PROFILES

Complex molding profiles combine several **simple shapes**[1] to enhance the visual effect. There are two ways to do this. You can either make multiple cuts in a single board or cut simple shapes in several boards, then glue them together.

MAKING MULTIPLE CUTS

When making multiple cuts in a molding, consider which bits or cutters to use to cut what shapes. There may be several cutters in your selection that will produce a single shape. Some cutters will produce two or more shapes in a single pass. What cutters will work best? That depends on the order in which you make the cuts.

Carefully think through this order. Each cut should leave enough stock to adequately support the work during the succeeding cuts. The rules of thumb are to make small cuts before large ones, and remove stock from the center of a surface before removing it from the corners or edges.

BUILDING UP MOLDINGS

This is the simplest way to make complex shapes. You aren't limited by the size of molding stock that your tools will handle; you can build up an assembly as large as you need. Massive **architectural moldings**[2] are made in this manner. So are complex cornices (top moldings) on classic case pieces.

MAKING COMPLEX MOLDINGS

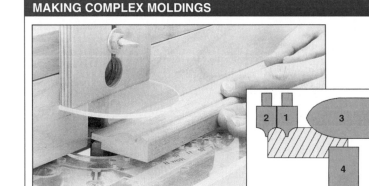

1 When making a complex molding, plan the sequence of cuts so the stock remains as stable as possible. For instance, to cut this picture frame molding, cut the half-round bead in the face **before** the cove. If you cut the cove first, the stock may rock when making the bead. Leave the rabbet until last. A solid edge provides additional support as you hold it against the fence.

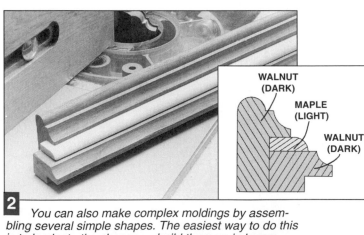

WALNUT (DARK)

MAPLE (LIGHT)

WALNUT (DARK)

2 You can also make complex moldings by assembling several simple shapes. The easiest way to do this is to laminate the shapes — build them up in layers. But you can also join the shapes with dadoes, rabbets, and grooves. Furthermore, the shapes that you glue together don't have to be the same species. Glue up contrasting colors of wood to emphasize the shapes, if you wish.

COMMON MULTIPLE-CUT MOLDINGS

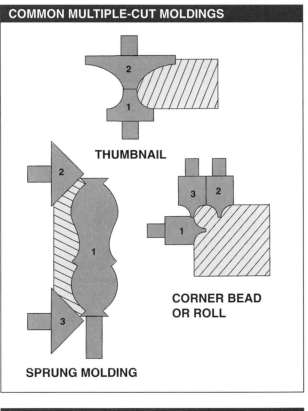

THUMBNAIL

SPRUNG MOLDING

CORNER BEAD OR ROLL

COMMON BUILT-UP MOLDINGS

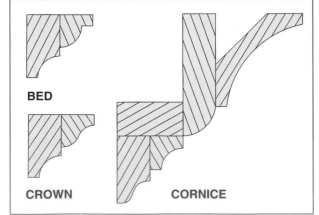

BED

CROWN

CORNICE

MAKING COPED JOINTS

Moldings and frame members with shaped edges are joined at right angles with **miter joints**[3] or *coped joints*. In a coped joint, both of the adjoining surfaces are shaped. The surface that joins the molding or shaped edge is a mirror image or *reverse* of the profile.

There are two common ways to make a coped joint. You can cut the molding profile and its reverse with two matched router bits or shaper cutters. The coped joints that join door and window frame are typically routed or shaped.

Or, you can cut the reverse shape with a coping saw or a scroll saw. Architectural moldings are joined in this manner.

APPLYING MOLDINGS

Once you've made a molding, you must secure it to the surface you wish to decorate – either attach it to a piece of furniture or install it in a room.

ATTACHING MOLDINGS TO FURNITURE

When applying molding to furniture, cut the stock to fit the assembly, mitering the adjoining ends where the molding turns a corner. Pay close attention to the **grain direction**[4] of the surface to which you will attach the molding. If the wood grain runs parallel to that of the molding, glue the molding in place. If not, attach the molding with screws or nails so it won't restrict the **wood movement**[5] across the grain.

SAWING A COPED JOINT

To join moldings, either miter the adjoining ends or cope the **one** end, cutting a reverse shape. To do this accurately, first miter the end of the part you wish to cope. With a coping saw or a scroll saw, cut along the edge where the mitered surface meets the profile.

TIP: Mount a *spiral blade* (a blade that cuts in all directions) in your scroll saw. This will enable you to cut the cope without turning the molding.

SHAPING A COPED JOINT

1 To join frame members with shaped edges, rout or shape coped joints with matching cutters. First, cut the decorative profile in the inside edges of the stiles and rails.

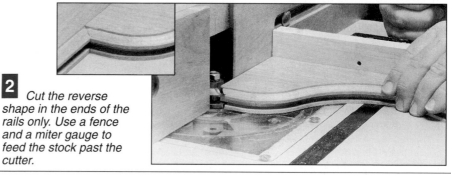

2 Cut the reverse shape in the ends of the rails only. Use a fence and a miter gauge to feed the stock past the cutter.

INSTALLING FURNITURE MOLDINGS

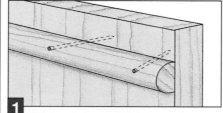 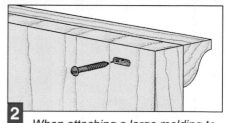

1 When attaching a small molding to a wide surface with opposing wood grain, **don't** glue it in place. This will restrict the wood movement. Instead, attach it with small finishing nails or wire brads. These bend slightly as the wood expands and contracts.

TIP: Drive the nails at slight angles, alternating the angle with each nail. This prevents the molding from coming loose.

2 When attaching a large molding to a wide surface with opposing wood grain, cut slots in the case for the screw shafts. The long dimension of the slots must be perpendicular to the wood grain. This will allow the wood to move. Drive the screws from inside the case so they can't be seen.

TRIMMING A ROOM

The trim or **casing**[1] that surrounds windows and doors is attached to the **jambs**[2] with **casing nails**[3]. Cut and install the vertical members first, then the horizontal members.

When trimming floors, walls, and ceilings, the rule of thumb is to miter *outside* corners and cope *inside* corners. Butt **baseboards and chair rails**[4] to casings. If necessary, fit the edges of the moldings to uneven surfaces; don't try to bend them around bumps and hollows in ceil-ings and floors. Where you must splice two moldings end to end to make a longer one, use a simple **scarf joint**[5]. When ending a molding, *return* it with a shaped cap.

TRIMMING DOORS AND WINDOWS

1 When trimming a window or door, mark the **reveal** on the jamb, drawing a line to show how much of the jamb will show. Make a **reveal gauge** from a block of wood to help mark a consistent reveal.

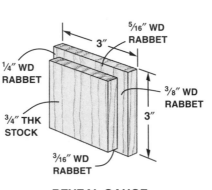

REVEAL GAUGE

2 Cut the casing to frame the reveal. Install the vertical casing members first, tacking them in place temporarily. Fit the horizontal members to them. If the casing is butt-joined, cut the horizontal members to span the reveal **and** the vertical members.

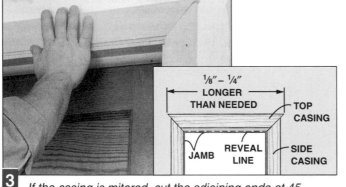

3 If the casing is mitered, cut the adjoining ends at 45 degrees, but make all members ⅛ to ¼ inch longer than needed. Tack them in place with the edges parallel to the reveal lines. Inspect the miter joints. If they're tight, cut them to the proper length, mitering the ends at 45 degrees. If the joints gap, adjust the miter angle to eliminate the gaps.

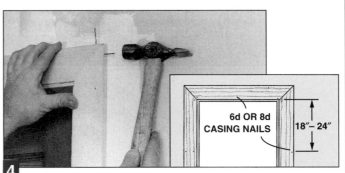

4 When you're satisfied that the members fit, secure the casing with casing nails. Space the nails 18 to 24 inches apart and stagger them, driving one into a jamb and the next into the surrounding framing. If the casing members are mitered, **cross-nail** the corners to lock them together.

FITTING MOLDING

If the floor or ceiling is uneven, cut the edge of the molding to fit it. Measure the widest gap between the molding and the surface it rests against. Adjust a compass so the distance between the point and the scribe is equal to that gap. Scribe the edge of the molding with the compass, following the uneven surface with the point. Saw or plane the molding edge to the mark.

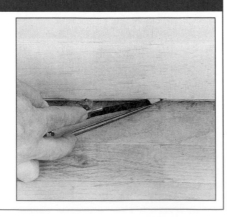

EXTENDING AND ENDING MOLDING

To extend a length of molding, join two shorter pieces with a **scarf joint**. To end a molding, make a **return**. Miter the end, then make a mitered cap from a scrap with the same profile. Glue or nail the cap to the mitered end.

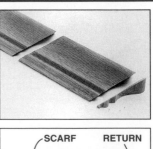

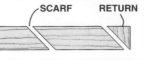

SCARF   RETURN

MITERING AN OUTSIDE CORNER

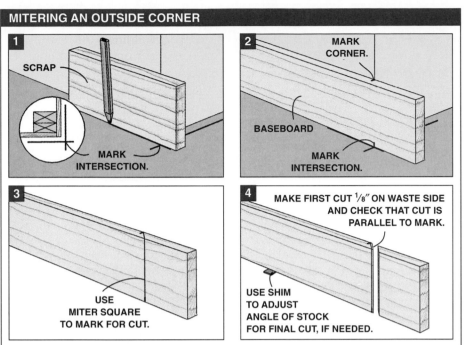

1 SCRAP

MARK INTERSECTION.

2 MARK CORNER.

BASEBOARD

MARK INTERSECTION.

3 USE MITER SQUARE TO MARK FOR CUT.

4 MAKE FIRST CUT ⅛" ON WASTE SIDE AND CHECK THAT CUT IS PARALLEL TO MARK.

USE SHIM TO ADJUST ANGLE OF STOCK FOR FINAL CUT, IF NEEDED.

To miter molding to turn an outside corner, use a scrap of the molding to mark the floor or ceiling where the outside surfaces will meet. Hold the baseboard in place and mark the inside of the miter at the corner of the wall. Mark the outside where the lines on the floor intersect. Make a miter cut about ⅛ inch wide of the marks to see if the saw will pass through both. If it won't, eyeball the correct angle, then either adjust the saw or use a shim (as shown) to reposition the molding on the saw.

MORE SOURCES

Furniture Mouldings, by E. J. Warne, Linden Publishing, 1995

Routing and Shaping, by Nick Engler, Rodale Press, 1992

The Shaper Handbook, by Roger W. Cliffe and Michael Holtz, Sterling Publishing, 1990

Trim Carpentry Techniques, by Craig Savage, Taunton Press, 1989

TROUBLE SHOOTING

COMMON SHAPING PROBLEMS

Problem	Possible Cause(s)	Solution(s)
Cutter leaves burn marks on shaped surface.	Feed rate is too slow; dwelling in one spot.	Keep work moving at a steady rate; don't stop.
	Removing too much stock in one pass	Take small bites, removing just a little stock with each pass.
	Cutter speed is too fast.	Reduce router speed.
	Cutter is dull or loaded with pitch.	Clean or sharpen cutter.
Cutter chips wood along shaped edge.	Cutting uphill, against the wood grain	If possible, reverse wood to cut downhill, with wood grain. If not, reduce feed rate and depth of cut.
Cutter tears out wood at end of cut.	Cutting end grain	Back up wood with scrap.
Cutter leaves mill marks in shaped surface.	Feed rate is too fast.	Reduce feed rate.
	Cutter speed is too slow.	Increase router speed.
Shaper cuts snipe in molding at end of cut.	Fence not properly adjusted; infeed fence too far forward or outfeed fence too far back	Retract infeed fence or advance outfeed fence in small increments until snipe disappears.
Shaped surface is irregular.	Inconsistent pressure against fence or table when feeding work	Feed the work with steady pressure, holding it against table, fence, pilot bearing, or rub collar.
	Work is warped or bowed.	Joint surfaces to be shaped flat and straight. Sand curved surface smooth.
Work kicks back at start of cut.	Removing too much stock in one pass	Take small bites, removing just a little stock with each pass.
	Not using starter pin to begin cut	Install starter pin to one side of bit or cutter.
Work is difficult to hold.	Not enough surface bearing against pilot bearing or rub collar	Adjust cutter so at least ⅛ inch of work surface bears against bearing or collar.

26

Scrollwork

Lacy patterns and light, airy designs make solid wood seem a little less solid.

Scrollwork is intricate two-dimensional patterns sawed from wood. There are several types of patterns, including lacelike fretwork, architectural gingerbread, cut-out signs, and pictorial scenes. Scrollwork patterns may be *in relief* (applied to a solid surface) or used as *openwork,* without backing. All are exclusively decorative. And although a scrollwork part may be used in the structure of a project, the pattern itself has no other function than its intrinsic beauty.

Scrollwork is a craft in its own right, and many craftsmen make it their specialty. However, it's also a useful skill for folks who do general woodworking. Architecture and furniture designs sometimes incorporate scrollwork trim or parts. **Chippendale and Federal style**[1] chair backs, for example, are scroll sawed, then carved to a final shape.

MORE *INFO*

Scrolling is an excellent way to introduce children to woodworking. Although all power tools present a degree of danger, the **scroll saw**[2] is one of the safest and simplest to operate. Kids of grade school age can be taught to make intriguing shapes with a fair degree of competence in an afternoon.

SPECS: 39″ high, 23″ wide, ¾″ thick

MATERIALS: Curly cherry

DESIGNER: Mary Jane Favorite
West Milton, OH

CRAFTSMAN: Chris Walendzak
Centerville, OH

The intricate shapes of this **Fretwork Mirror** were cut with a scroll saw, then attached to the mirror frame. These "cloud forms," as they were once called, are formed from ellipses and S-curves. They were very popular among craftsmen who worked in the Chippendale style.

CHOOSING MATERIALS

Although the scroll saw will cut a wide variety of substances, most scrollwork is done with wood, plywood, or particleboard. Some of these materials are better suited for scrolling than others.

HARDWOOD AND SOFTWOOD

Look for a species with a tight, uniform grain pattern. **Closed-grain**[3] woods, such as white pine, basswood, and poplar, work best, followed by medium-grain woods, such as maple, cherry, birch, and beech. **Open-grain**[3] woods, such as oak and ash, tend to split.

> ### PRO *TIP*
> Another reason for avoiding open-grain woods is that the strong grain pattern often fights with the intricate scrollwork pattern, "pulling the eye."

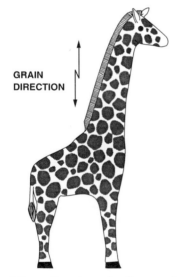

GRAIN DIRECTION

Orient the pattern to make the wood grain as continuous as possible. This will make the pattern as strong as it can be. For example, the wood grain must run vertically in this giraffe silhouette. Otherwise the neck and legs will be weak.

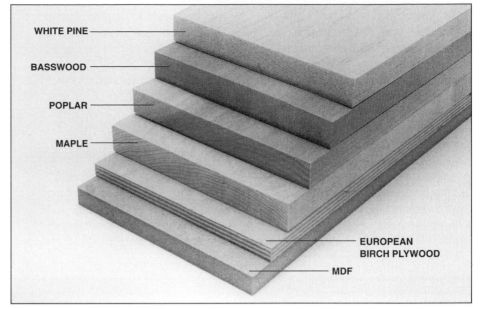

WHITE PINE

BASSWOOD

POPLAR

MAPLE

EUROPEAN BIRCH PLYWOOD

MDF

SCROLLWORK MATERIALS

Also choose clear, straight-grained woods with an even **density**[4]. Avoid woods with dense knots, burls, or large differences in density between **springwood and summerwood**[5], such as yellow pine or Douglas fir. The flexible blade is easily deflected by the harder portions, making the material frustrating to cut.

PLYWOOD AND FIBERBOARD

Solid wood splits easily along the grain, and complex scrollwork patterns have many weak points where the grain runs across the width of an appendage. Plywood, however, is much less likely to break. Choose a hardwood plywood, relatively free of voids. **Marine plywood and European birch**[6] are best. **Medium-density fiberboard**[7] (MDF) is a good choice for patterns in relief. It's not strong enough, however, to be used for openwork.

LAYING OUT A PATTERN

The first step in any scrollwork project is to lay out the pattern on the material.

MAKE IT STRONG

Decide how you will orient the pattern. If you're using plywood or fiberboard, you needn't be too concerned about orientation. But it's extremely important when using solid wood. Remember, **wood is stronger**[4] when the grain is continuous. You may have to make do with some weak areas in the finished project, but you can eliminate many of them with a little planning.

When laying out openwork, remember that all the parts of the pattern must be connected somehow. Plan unobtrusive *bridges* whenever an interior area needs support.

*When laying out an openwork pattern with interior parts, connect these parts to the surrounding stock with slender **bridges** or they'll fall away.*

BRIDGES

TRANSFER THE PATTERN

When you have decided the best way to orient a pattern, transfer it to the wood.

■ If the pattern is full-sized, photocopy the original and adhere the copy to the wood surface.

PRO *TIP*

You can transfer a photocopied pattern to a wood surface as many as four times by ironing it with a hot, dry iron. The pattern will be reversed, so position it on the back of the stock rather than the front.

■ Or, trace the original pattern onto the wood with carbon paper.

■ If the pattern will be used over and over again, photocopy it and attach the copy to thin acrylic plastic. Cut the plastic on the scroll saw and sand the sawed edges. This will create a durable *template.*

■ If the pattern must be enlarged, blow it up to the desired size with an enlarging/reducing copier. (These are available at most quick-print shops.)

■ You can also use a *pantograph* to enlarge the pattern.

■ Or, use the traditional *squares method,* transferring the pattern from a small grid to a larger one.

PRO *TIP*

Never cut the *original* pattern, even if you intend to use it only once. Keep it intact in case something goes wrong while you're sawing.

■ After applying or transferring the pattern to the wood, shade the pattern so it's easy to identify the waste.

ENLARGING PATTERNS

1 *A* **pantograph** *is a drafting tool that looks like a flexible parallelogram with pivots on the corners. A stylus is attached to one corner, and a pencil is mounted at the end of one arm. As you trace the pattern with the stylus, the pencil draws an enlarged copy. Adjust the percentage of enlargement by moving the pivots. Pantographs are available through most art supply stores.*

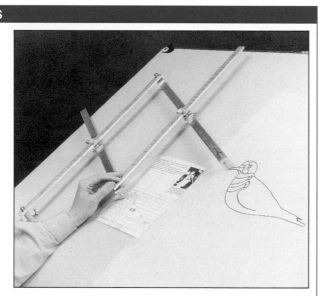

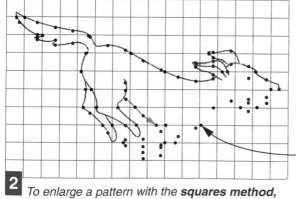

2 *To enlarge a pattern with the* **squares method,** *draw a small grid over the pattern and draw a scaled-up grid on a separate sheet of paper. For example, if you want to enlarge a pattern three times, each square on the larger grid should be three times the size of those on the smaller one. Also, there should be the same number of horizontal and vertical lines in both grids. (To help keep track, number the lines.) Wherever a pattern line meets one of the smaller grid lines, make a dot in the corresponding position on the larger grid. Then connect the dots.*

ADHERING A PATTERN

Perhaps the easiest way to transfer a pattern is to copy it, then apply the copy with **spray adhesive.** *(This is available at most art and office supply stores.) Spray the paper only, then press it in place. Cut the wood and the paper, then peel the paper off the wood. Remove any residue left by the adhesive with acetone.*

SHADING PATTERNS

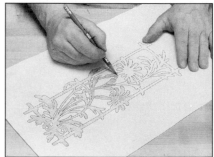

Shade intricate patterns to help remember what to cut away and what to leave in place. It's too easy to saw through a bridge or eliminate an important part of the design when the waste and the pattern look the same.
TIP: Don't make the shading too dark or the blade will be difficult to see.

SCROLLING KNOW-HOW

Although scrollwork procedures are relatively simple, you must pay close attention to the details when setting up the scroll saw.

MOUNT A BLADE

Choose the largest (widest and thickest) **blade**[1] that will do the job. When cutting plywood or thin veneers that are prone to splintering, chose a **reverse skip-tooth blade**[1]. For an extremely smooth cut, use a **double skip-tooth blade or precision-ground skip-tooth blade**[1].

Brush or blow the sawdust from the **blade clamps**[2] to prevent the blade from slipping. Secure the blade so the teeth face down. When mounting a reverse skip-tooth blade, one or two of the reversed teeth should rise above table at the top of the stroke.

Tension[3] the blade, pulling it taut. How much tension should you apply? Generally, the blade needs

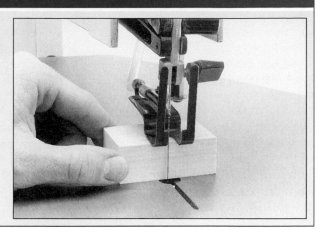

To check that a blade is square to the table, make a shallow cut in the surface of a wood block. Turn the scrap around and slip the back of the blade into the cut. If you can do this without tilting the scrap, the table is square to the blade.

just enough to remain straight in the cut. If the blade wanders or cups, it's too loose. If it breaks frequently, you're applying too much tension.

ADJUST THE TABLE ANGLE

To make a square cut, set the table 90 degrees to the blade. To check the angle, rest a small square on the table and hold it against the side of

the blade. If you wish to cut at an angle other than 90 degrees, set the table tilt with a protractor.

SEE _ALSO:_
[1] Scroll Saw Blades   113
[2] Scroll Saws   112
[3] Tensioning   162

At least two, preferably three teeth should remain in contact with the wood as you cut. If there are fewer than that, the cut may be difficult to control. To check that you've selected the right blade, multiply the thickness of the stock times the number of saw teeth per inch (tpi). The answer should be 2 or more.

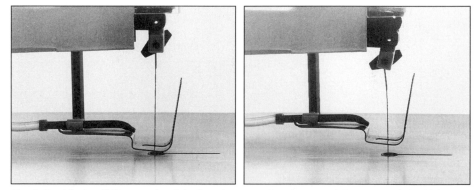

Push the blade all the way back in the clamp and make sure it hangs straight. If the blade is secured toward the front of the clamp or at an angle, it's much more likely to slip. And even if it doesn't slip, it will bow toward the front or back, quickly become fatigued, and break.

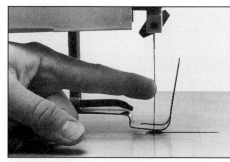

To tension a blade, tighten the tension adjustment while applying **moderate** pressure against the back of the blade with your index finger. When you can't flex the blade any more than ⅛ inch, it's tight enough.

Check that the clamps are aligned and the blade is parallel to the stroke. If the clamps are offset from one another, the blade will be skewed and will cut an unnecessarily wide kerf. Since it must remove more stock, this slows down the cutting process and puts more wear and tear on the blade.

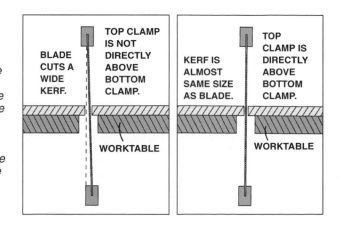

MAKING A CUT

When you get ready to make a cut on the scroll saw, get comfortable. Scrollwork takes a long time and it can't be rushed. Also, make sure you have plenty of light to see the pattern.

■ Adjust the **pressure foot**[1] to press lightly on the stock. You should still be able to slide the work under the foot easily, but the blade mustn't lift the work off the table.

■ For most cuts, set the saw to run at high speed (1,200 to 1,800 strokes per minute); for extremely thin stock, use a slow speed (400 to 800 strokes per minute).

PRO *TIP*

Turn the saw off and on with a **foot switch**[2]. This allows you to keep both hands on the work at all times.

CUTTING INSIDE CORNERS

There are two ways to cut sharp inside corners with wide blades (number 5 or wider).

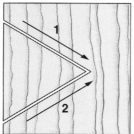

1 *Saw to the corner, cutting along one of the converging lines. Stop at the corner, backtrack out of the cut, and start again, cutting along the second line until you meet the first at the corner.*

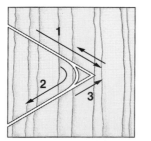

2 *Or, saw to the corner along one line, then backtrack a short distance. Turn around in the waste, and cut along the second line until you exit the stock. Finish by making a third cut along the second line to the corner.*

■ Begin sawing across the grain if you can – it's easier to start the cut.

■ Feed the work slowly, using gentle pressure. Don't feed so fast that the blade bows backward.

■ To cut a straight line, you may have to feed the work at a slight angle to the blade. The saw teeth are not milled precisely, so one side of the blade is likely to cut more aggressively than the other. Because of this, the blade will drift to one side of the cut if the wood is fed parallel.

MAKING CONTINUOUS CUTS

Whenever you can, start cutting at a point or corner in the layout. When you start in the middle of a line or curve, you must make a second cut to complete that portion of the pattern. It's difficult to make two cuts meet perfectly in the middle of a line; the result is likely to be a step or bump in the sawed edge.

SAW CURVE IN ONE CONTINUOUS CUT.

CUTTING OUTSIDE CORNERS

There are three common methods for cutting outside corners with wide blades (number 5 or wider).

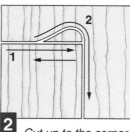

1 *Cut past the corner, then loop around so the blade crosses its own path at the corner, and continue cutting.*

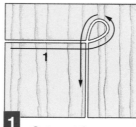

2 *Cut up to the corner, backtrack a short distance, and cut away from the pattern line. Curve around to meet the cut at the corner and continue cutting.*

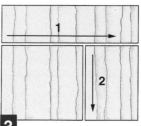

3 *Cut past the corner to the outside edge of the workpiece. Remove the scrap, then start cutting again at the corner.*

■ The narrower the blade, the smaller the radius you can cut. Blades smaller than a **number 5**[3] (0.038 inch wide) will turn inside their own kerf. This allows you to make *zero-radius turns*, pivoting the work around the blade.

■ To **cut tight corners**[4] with wide blades, make two or more cuts. Make the first cut, then carefully *backtrack* in the kerf, and cut again from another direction.

NIBBLING

*You can **nibble** away stock with a scroll saw blade, using the teeth like a tiny rasp. Gently press the edge of the wood against the teeth, moving it sideways as the teeth nibble the wood. This technique is handy for smoothing steps and cleaning out tight corners.*
NOTE: Raise the hold-down for this operation.

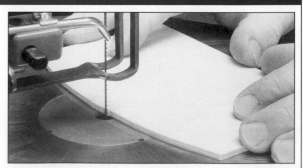

MAKING INTERIOR CUTS

An interior cut is one that doesn't begin or end at the perimeter of the workpiece. You begin somewhere in the middle of the stock and cut away waste from the interior without sawing through to an edge or end. To do this, drill a starter hole or *saw gate*, thread the blade through it, and cut. It's this unique ability to make interior cuts that makes the scroll saw valuable for general woodworking as well as for decorative scrollwork.

DRILLING RELIEF HOLES

To cut tight inside curves with a blade that's too wide to make them, drill relief holes in the waste. The radius of the hole must match that of the curve. Cut along the pattern line until you enter the hole, turn the workpiece, then cut away from the hole, continuing along the line.

NOTE: Hold-down is raised so you can see the cut.

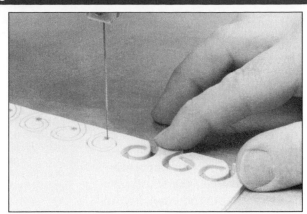

MAKING INTERIOR CUTS

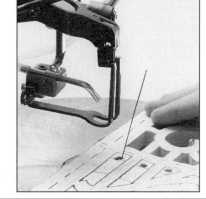

1 *To make an interior cut, drill a small hole or* **saw gate** *in the waste. Release one end of the blade from its clamp, thread it through the gate, and secure the free end in the clamp again.*

2 *Cut out from the saw gate to the pattern line. Cut the interior pattern, removing the waste. When you've completed the cut, release one end of the blade from its clamp and pull the blade from the cutout.*

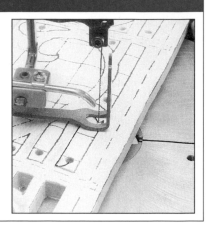

CUTTING ON A BEVEL

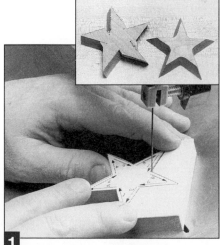

1 *To cut a consistent bevel in a pattern, make all the cuts in the same direction — clockwise or counterclockwise — around the pattern. On this star pattern, for example, the sides must be sloped so the bottom face is larger than the top. To do this, tilt the table to the left and cut clockwise. If you cut a portion of the pattern counterclockwise, parts of the star will be beveled in the opposite direction.*

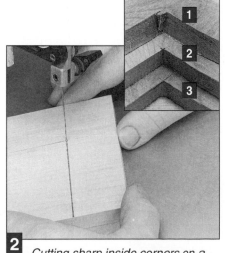

2 *Cutting sharp inside corners on a bevel is tricky — you must make a zero-radius turn to keep the cut moving in the proper direction. If you make two separate cuts that meet at the corner, one of two things will happen: (1) The cuts will meet on one surface but not the other, or (2) the cuts will cross each other on one surface. (3) If you make a zero-radius turn, the corner will be sharp on one surface and rounded on the other.*

CUTTING ON A BEVEL

To cut a beveled edge with a scroll saw, tilt the table to the proper angle and begin cutting. Although this sounds simple enough, it requires careful planning. You must make all the beveled cuts in the *same direction* around the pattern. This is necessary for both interior and outside cuts.

WOOD INLAY

You can inlay one piece of wood in another by stacking two boards and cutting both of them at a **bevel**[1]. Fit the part that you've cut from the interior of one board (the *inlay*) into the hole in the other board (the *field*).

Both the inlay and the field must be beveled because the scroll saw blade leaves a kerf. If you cut the parts at 90 degrees, there will be a small gap around the inlay. If you tilt the worktable slightly, the inlay will be slightly larger than the hole in the field, and the two parts will fit with no visible gaps.

INLAYING WOOD

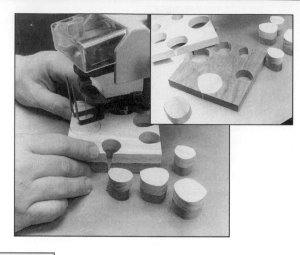

1 The trick to inlay is to saw at the right bevel angle. This will depend on the thickness of the stock and the size of the blade, and you must make a few test cuts to find it. Stack two scraps face to face, tilt the table, and cut a circle in both scraps. Fit the circular piece from the top scrap in the hole in the bottom scrap. If the test inlay drops below the surface of the field, increase the tilt. If it won't drop down flush with the field, decrease the tilt.

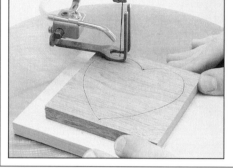

2 Once you have found the proper bevel angle, stack the inlay stock on top of the field stock. Fasten the two pieces together with carpet tape to keep them from shifting. If necessary, drill a tiny saw gate to start the cut. Cut the shape of the inlay, sawing around the perimeter of the pattern in one direction only. Separate the pieces and discard the tape.

TROUBLE *SHOOTING*

COMMON SCROLLWORK PROBLEMS

Problem	Possible Cause(s)	Solution(s)
Blade breaks often.	Blade is too fine for thick or hard stock.	Use a larger blade.
	Blade is too loose or too taut.	Adjust blade tension as needed.
	Too much pressure against the blade	Feed work using gentle pressure.
	Twisting blade in cut	Don't try to turn corners that are too tight for blade.
Blade wanders from pattern line.	Blade is too loose.	Increase blade tension.
	Blade is too large for thin stock.	Use finer blade. At least 2 teeth should remain in contact with wood during cut.
	Too much pressure against the blade	Feed work using gentle pressure.
	Blade is deflected by knots or hard portions of stock.	Use clear wood with even density.
	Blade is dull.	Replace blade.
Blade cuts very slowly.	Blade is too fine for thick or hard stock.	Use a larger blade.
	Blade clamps are misaligned.	Align blade clamps so blade is parallel to stroke.
	Blade is dull.	Replace blade.
Blade bows in the cut.	Blade is too loose.	Increase blade tension.
	Blade is deflected by knots or hard portions of stock.	Use clear wood with even density.
Work lifts off the table or chatters.	Pressure foot is not holding stock on table.	Adjust pressure foot to apply more pressure.
Cuts do not meet precisely at corners.	Table is not square to blade.	Adjust table tilt.
	Changing directions when bevel cutting	Cut in one direction only.

3 Test fit the inlay in the field. You may have to do a little handwork with a file to fit it properly. When it fits to your satisfaction, glue the inlay in the field. Let the glue dry, then sand the surfaces flush.

MYTH *CONCEPTIONS*

NO CURE FOR THE SHAKES

The standard cure for the annoying vibrations that a scroll saw produces is to rest it on a rubber mat. However, despite the claims of advertisers, these "anti-vibration pads" don't reduce the vibration of a scroll saw or any other machine. They only isolate it. The pads work much the same as the rubber engine mounts in your car — the mounts isolate the engine vibration from the chassis without reducing it. Anti-vibration pads cause a machine to run quieter because it no longer shakes the stand that it rests upon. But when the pad isolates the machine from the stand, it often shakes worse than before. The best way to combat vibration in a scroll saw is to add *mass* — mass helps dampen vibration. Mount the saw to a heavy stand. If you have a bench-top machine, bolt it to the bench top directly over a leg. Or, build the "Vibration-Reducing Mount" shown below.

MORE *SOURCES*

BOOKS

Scroll Saw Fretwork Techniques and Projects, by Patrick Spielman and James Reidle, Sterling Publishing, 1990

Scroll Saw Handbook, by Patrick Spielman, Sterling Publishing, 1986

Using the Scroll Saw, by Nick Engler, Rodale Press, 1994

PATTERNS

Nelson Designs
P.O. Box 422
Dublin, NH 03444

Spielman Publishing
P.O. Box 867
Fish Creek, WI 54212

Wildwood Designs
P.O. Box 676
Richland Center, WI 53581

SEE *ALSO:*
[1] Cutting on a Bevel   303
[2] Scroll Saws   112

JIGS & FIXTURES

VIBRATION-REDUCING MOUNT

More than any other stationary tool, the scroll saw is plagued by vibration. The **frame arms**[2] reverse direction on each stroke, causing the machine to vibrate excessively. This, in turn, interferes with its accuracy, generates noise, and makes the saw tiring and unpleasant to use.

One way to reduce this vibration is to add a massive stand to the scroll saw — mass dampens vibration. Or, you can employ an old turner's trick and *sandbag* your scroll saw. (Turners sandbag lathes to reduce vibration when making delicate turnings.) Sand not only adds mass, it has the unique physical property of *hysteresis* — it actually absorbs the vibrations. This special mount for a bench-top scroll saw is a box filled with sand to suck up the vibrations.

1 Fill the box with sand to within 1 inch of the top edge. Level the sand, then place the lid over the studs. The lid should fit within the box sides and rest on the sand.

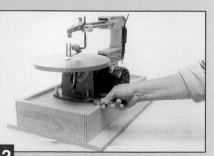

2 Place the scroll saw on the lid so the base fits over the studs. Secure the scroll saw with nuts and washers.

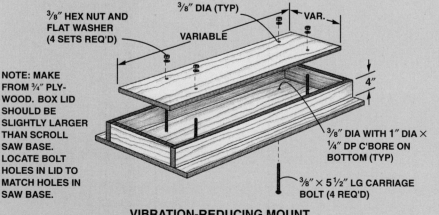

3/8" HEX NUT AND FLAT WASHER (4 SETS REQ'D)

3/8" DIA (TYP)

VAR.

VARIABLE

4"

NOTE: MAKE FROM 3/4" PLYWOOD. BOX LID SHOULD BE SLIGHTLY LARGER THAN SCROLL SAW BASE. LOCATE BOLT HOLES IN LID TO MATCH HOLES IN SAW BASE.

3/8" DIA WITH 1" DIA × 1/4" DP C'BORE ON BOTTOM (TYP)

3/8" × 5 1/2" LG CARRIAGE BOLT (4 REQ'D)

VIBRATION-REDUCING MOUNT

Lathe Turning

Lathe work is like carving a spinning block of wood. Just shave away the stock until the wood assumes a shape that pleases you.

Lathe turning is a craft in its own right. The **lathe**[1], after all, is one of the few woodworking tools on which you can create a project from beginning to end *with a single setup!* Mount a block of wood between the centers, turn it to the desired shape, sand it smooth, and apply a finish – all without removing it from the lathe. Many turners spend their entire careers exploring the intricacies of this process.

More often, craftsmen use a lathe to make the turned parts of a larger project, such as the legs of a table or the spindles in a staircase. For these woodworkers, lathe turning is a special procedure rather than a separate craft. Whatever your turning ambitions, however, the methods are exactly the same.

TURNED SHAPES

At its heart, turning is a *reductive* technique – shave a piece of wood with a chisel, removing stock until it assumes the shape you're after. Although there are an infinite number of patterns you can create on a lathe, they are all built up from just three shapes:

- A convex curve or *bead*
- A concave curve or *cove*
- A *flat,* such as a short **fillet**[2], a long cylinder, or a tapered cone

*The delicately curved parts that make up this tiny **Box** were all turned on a lathe, then glued together. The intricate pattern on the inside of the lid was created with a "chatter tool," a special lathe chisel that vibrates as you turn.*

SPECS:	3″ diameter, 2″ high
MATERIALS:	Pink ivory wood, boxwood, and ebony
CRAFTSMAN:	Judy Ditmer Tipp City, OH

TURNING TECHNIQUE

There are two basic techniques for creating these shapes on a lathe, depending on the **cutting angle**[3] of the tool.

SCRAPING

Scrape[4] the wood, peeling away the paper-thin layers of wood with a burr on the edge of the chisel. Hold the chisel at a small cutting angle to the turning. This is the easiest of all turning methods. However, it's also the slowest way to remove stock from a turning and produces the roughest surfaces.

SHEARING

Shear the wood, using the chisel to shave the surface. Hold the chisel at a large angle to the wood, with the cutting edge skewed to the direction of rotation. This skew increases the effective cutting angle of the chisel in the same way that holding a **bench plane**[5] at a skew increases its cutting angle.

Shearing removes stock quickly and produces an extremely smooth surface. However, it takes practice. This technique requires more control to create the shapes, and there is danger that the cutting edge of the chisel will dig into the wood.

IN BETWEEN

Think of scraping and shearing as two ends of a wide spectrum of cutting angles you can use. Adjust this angle as you work to find the one that produces the best results. Creating the shapes on a single turning often requires that you approach the wood from many angles. The best angle for a specific job will depend on the shape you're making, the tool used to make it, and your turning experience.

MYTH *CONCEPTIONS*

SHEARERS VS. SCRAPERS
Some experienced turners convey the impression to beginners that shearing is somehow a better method than scraping. This shearing chauvinism is a holdover from the days when master craftsmen expected their apprentices to learn efficient production techniques. Shearing saves time over scraping, but that's all. There is no difference between a scraped table leg and sheared leg once they are sanded and finished.

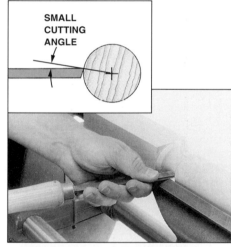

SCRAPING WITH A ROUNDNOSE CHISEL

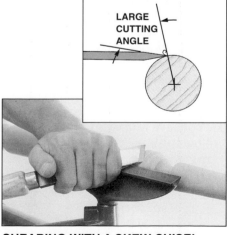

SHEARING WITH A SKEW CHISEL

BASIC LATHE SHAPES

BEAD   COVE   FLAT

COMMON TURNED PATTERNS

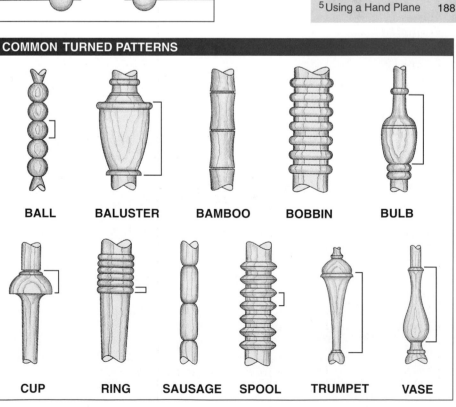

BALL   BALUSTER   BAMBOO   BOBBIN   BULB

CUP   RING   SAUSAGE   SPOOL   TRUMPET   VASE

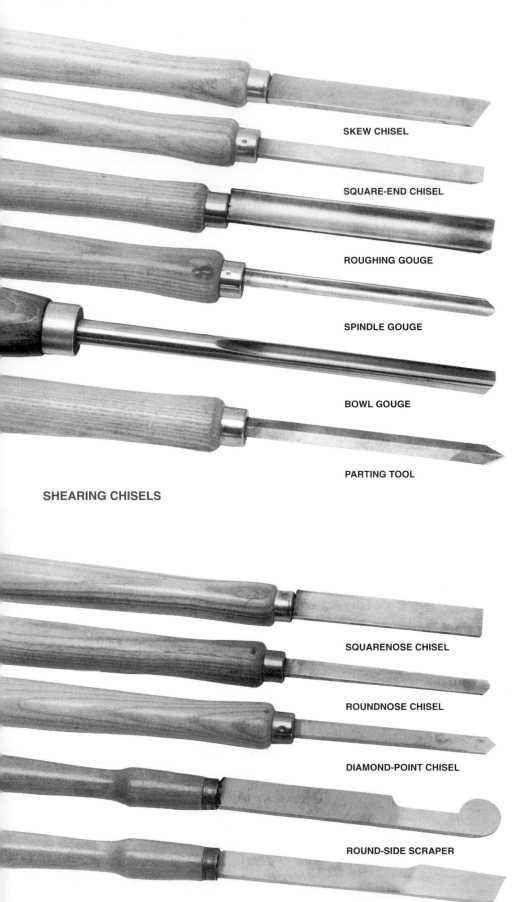

SKEW CHISEL

SQUARE-END CHISEL

ROUGHING GOUGE

SPINDLE GOUGE

BOWL GOUGE

PARTING TOOL

SHEARING CHISELS

SQUARENOSE CHISEL

ROUNDNOSE CHISEL

DIAMOND-POINT CHISEL

ROUND-SIDE SCRAPER

STRAIGHT-SIDE SCRAPER

SCRAPING CHISELS

TURNING TOOLS

To cut shapes on a lathe, you must use specially designed *turning chisels*. The thick, sturdy blades are fitted with long handles to provide leverage and to make them easy to control. The cutting edge of each chisel is forged and ground for a specific purpose.

SHEARING CHISELS

Shearing chisels have small **tool angles**[1] to better cut or shave the stock. These include:

■ *Skew chisels* for cutting beading and V-grooves and for smoothing tapers and flats

■ *Square-end chisels* for smoothing tapers and flats

■ *Roughing gouges* for reducing square or octagonal turning blocks to rough cylinders

■ *Spindle gouges* for cutting and smoothing coves

■ *Bowl gouges* for cutting coves and hollows in end grain

> **MORE** *INFO*
>
> Spindle and bowl gouges are often referred to as *shaping* gouges.

■ *Parting tools* for cutting small flats, cutting to diameter, or cutting through the stock

SCRAPING CHISELS

As you might expect, *scraping* chisels have much larger tool angles so they can better scrape the wood. These include:

■ *Squarenose chisels* to scrape flats and beads

■ *Roundnose chisels* to scrape coves and hollows

■ *Diamond-point chisels* to scrape flats, V-grooves, and corners

■ *Round-side scrapers* to scrape the concave interiors of bowls and hollow turnings

■ *Straight-side scrapers* to scrape straight and convex interiors

MEASURING TOOLS

A turner also needs special measuring tools:

■ A *center finder* helps mark the rotational center of square or cylindrical turning stock. **Combination squares**[2] often come with a center head that does the same job.

■ *Inside calipers* measure the inside diameter of a turning.

■ *Outside calipers* measure the outside diameter.

■ A *sizing tool* mounts on a parting tool. When hooked over the turning, it guides the chisel to cut a precise diameter.

SHARPENING TURNING CHISELS

The cutting edge of each chisel is **sharpened**[3] at a specific **tool angle**[1], depending on how it's used. Shearing chisels are normally sharpened at between 30 and 45 degrees. The more punishment the chisel is expected to withstand, the larger the tool angle. Roughing gouges, for example, see extremely heavy duty when knocking the corners off turning stock. Consequently, they are typically sharpened at 45 degrees.

Grind a scraping chisel at 75 to 80 degrees. Then **raise a burr**[4] on the cutting edge with a burnisher. It's the burrs on these chisels that cut the wood, similar to hand scrapers.

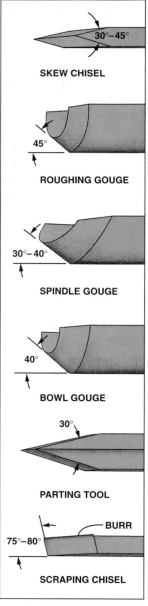

MEASURING TOOLS

TURNING TOOL ANGLES

SKEW CHISEL 30°–45°

ROUGHING GOUGE 45°

SPINDLE GOUGE 30°–40°

BOWL GOUGE 40°

PARTING TOOL 30°

SCRAPING CHISEL 75°–80° BURR

MORE *INFO*

Turning chisels often come from the manufacturer ground at a tool angle of 45 degrees. This is a *multipurpose* angle that will serve for shearing and scraping. However, you'll get better results and the chisels will be much easier to handle if you regrind the cutting edges for specific tasks.

SHARPENING A SCRAPING CHISEL

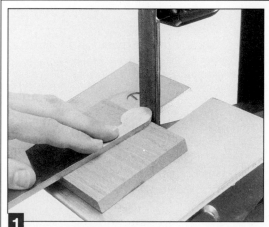

1 *Grind the blades of scraping chisels at a 75 to 80 degree angle on a sander (shown), hollow grinder, or flat grinder. Grinding will form a small burr or **wire edge** on the cutting edge. Some turners prefer to stop sharpening at this point and use this burr to cut with.*

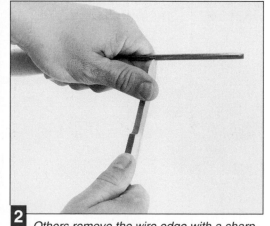

2 *Others remove the wire edge with a sharpening stone, then "raise" a burr with a burnisher. To do this, draw the burnisher along the cutting edge once or twice, pressing down firmly. The advantage of raising a burr is that you can better control its size and angle. Some craftsmen contend that a raised burr lasts longer than a wire edge when turning.*

TURNING KNOW-HOW

More so than any other wood-working skill, the way you stand and hold your body affects your turning technique.

BASIC TOOL CONTROL

Build a stand[1] that holds the lathe at a comfortable working height. For most craftsmen, the **centers**[2] should be at the same height as their elbows.

Grip the turning chisels with both hands, one hand on the handle and the other on the blade. When doing rough work, use an *overhand grip,* wrapping your fingers over the chisel blade just behind the **tool rest**[2]. For delicate work, use an *underhand grip,* holding the chisel between your thumb and fingers.

Stand close to the machine with your feet apart and the chisel tucked close to your body. Move your body with the tool so the tool travels in a straight line, slowly and steadily. Don't just move your arms — the chisel will tend to swing in an arc. This, in turn, makes it difficult to feed the chisel properly.

PRO *TIP*

To help the chisel glide across the tool rest, dress the rest with a file, removing all nicks and burrs. If the chisel has a rectangular blade, slightly round the corners with a sharpening stone so they won't dig into the rest.

INITIATING A CUT

Before you begin cutting, adjust the tool rest. For a scraping cut, it should be just below the turning axis. For shearing, it should be just below the top surface of the turning. Position the rest as close to the work as possible. (This reduces the **pinch point**[2].)

To start the cut, lay the chisel on the tool rest. If you're *shearing,* lay the blade across the turning, then draw it toward you while lifting up on the handle until the cutting edge begins to cut. To *scrape,* slowly advance the chisel into the stock. Make shallow cuts, moving right or left along the tool rest.

UNDERHAND GRIP

OVERHAND GRIP

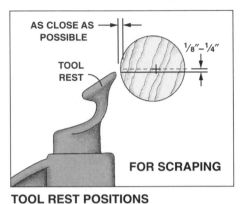

AS CLOSE AS POSSIBLE

TOOL REST

1/8"–1/4"

FOR SCRAPING

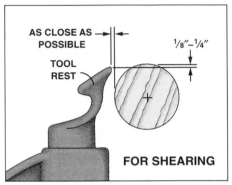

AS CLOSE AS POSSIBLE

TOOL REST

1/8"–1/4"

FOR SHEARING

TOOL REST POSITIONS

STARTING A CUT

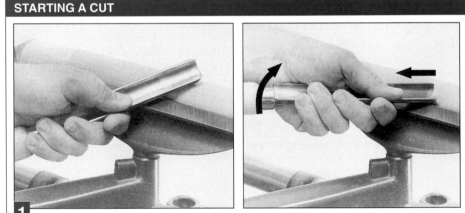

1 *Initiate a cut by laying the blade across the tool rest **and** the rotating turning. (The cutting edge must not contact the turning at this point.) Slowly draw the chisel toward you and lift up on the handle until the nose begins to cut. Incline the chisel in the direction of the cut.*

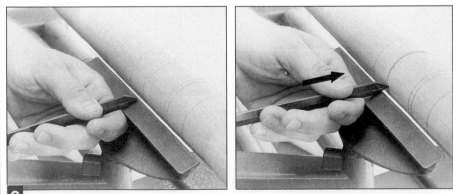

2 *Or, rest the blade on the tool rest close to (but not touching) the stock. Slowly feed the chisel toward the turning until the nose starts cutting.*

SPINDLE TURNING

When you mount stock between centers – the drive center and the cup center – you can create a long, cylindrical *spindle turning*.

MOUNTING SPINDLE STOCK

Find the rotational centers on either end of the stock. Stamp one end to make an impression for the drive center and the other to impress the cup center. If the stock is fairly large (over 3 inches square), cut or joint the stock to an octagonal shape. This will save you time when rounding it.

Mount the stock between centers, applying enough pressure to hold it securely. If you're using a "dead" cup center (one that doesn't rotate on bearings), wax the cup center to prevent it from burning the wood. Set the lathe to the proper **roughing speed**[3] and cut the stock to a rough cylinder with a roughing gouge.

SAFEGUARDS

When gluing up turning stock, let the glue dry for at least 24 hours. Otherwise, the assembly may come apart on the lathe.

TURNING SHAPES

Mark the location of the coves, beads, and flats along the length of the spindle. Using a parting tool, turn down to the appropriate diameter at each mark. Increase the **lathe speed**[3] and cut the shapes, working your way from large features to delicate details. Stop cutting when you reach the diameter you first turned with the parting tool.

PROTIP

After turning to a diameter with a parting tool, shade the bottom of the groove with a pencil. When you turn the shape, stop cutting when you begin to shave the pencil marks.

TURNING A SPINDLE

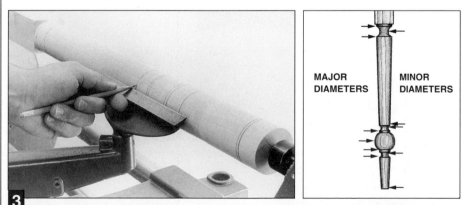

1 To locate the lathe centers on the ends of square turning stock, draw diagonal lines from corner to corner. Drill small holes about ½ inch deep where the lines cross — these will hold the points of the centers. Cut shallow kerfs along the lines on the drive end, then tap the drive center into it so the spurs bite into the kerfs. Tap the cup center into the opposite end.

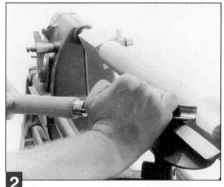

2 Secure the centers in the lathe, then mount the stock between them with enough pressure to hold the turning secure. Turn on the lathe at low speed and carefully cut the corners off the stock with a roughing gouge. Slowly cut the stock down to a rough cylinder slightly larger than the largest diameter in the spindle profile you plan to turn. To avoid splintering the corners, work from the center of the stock out to the ends.

MAJOR DIAMETERS **MINOR DIAMETERS**

3 Consult the plan of the turning and determine the **major** and **minor** diameters. The major diameters include the crests of beads, flats, and the widest portions of tapers. Minor diameters include the bottoms of coves and the narrowest portions of tapers. With a pencil, mark the locations of these major and minor diameters along the length of the spindle stock.

4 At each mark, turn the leg to the appropriate diameter with a parting tool. Use outside calipers or a sizing tool (shown) to gauge the diameter as you work. The parting tool will cut a narrow groove only a little wider than a saw kerf.

(continued)

TURNING A SPINDLE — CONTINUED

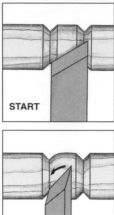

START

FINISH

5 Cut beads with a skew chisel or a diamond-point chisel. Start at the top of the bead (the major diameter), then roll the chisel down, shaving and rounding the curved sides of the bead.

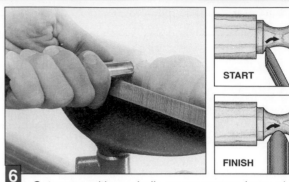

START

FINISH

6 Cut coves with a spindle gouge or roundnose chisel, slowly feeding the tool into the wood until you reach the minor diameter. To widen the cove and smooth the surface, "sweep" the gouge downhill along the sides of the cove. Always work from the high sides of the cove toward the middle — the gouge tends to dig in when you cut uphill.

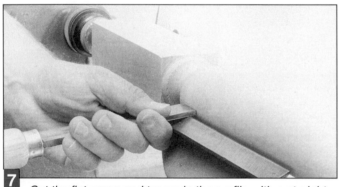

7 Cut the flat areas and tapers in the profile with a straight cutting edge, such as a skew or squarenose chisel. If the flat is long, adjust the tool rest parallel to it. Draw the chisel slowly along the rest, using your hand as a "depth stop" so the cutting edge moves parallel to the edge of the tool rest.

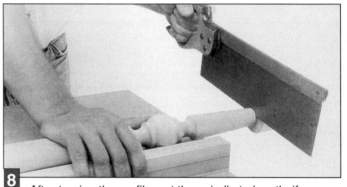

8 After turning the profile, cut the spindle to length, if necessary. Cut partway through the turning with a parting tool, leaving a narrow "neck." Dismount the turning from the lathe and finish sawing through the neck with a handsaw.

JIGS & FIXTURES

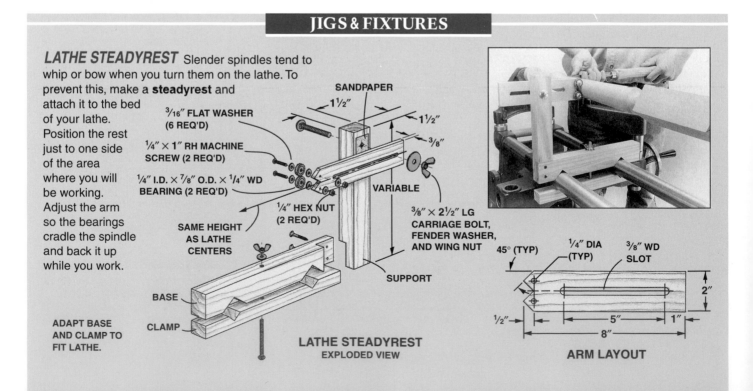

LATHE STEADYREST Slender spindles tend to whip or bow when you turn them on the lathe. To prevent this, make a **steadyrest** and attach it to the bed of your lathe. Position the rest just to one side of the area where you will be working. Adjust the arm so the bearings cradle the spindle and back it up while you work.

SANDPAPER

1½"

1½"

3/16" FLAT WASHER (6 REQ'D)

¼" × 1" RH MACHINE SCREW (2 REQ'D)

¼" I.D. × 7/8" O.D. × ¼" WD BEARING (2 REQ'D)

3/8"

VARIABLE

¼" HEX NUT (2 REQ'D)

SAME HEIGHT AS LATHE CENTERS

3/8" × 2½" LG CARRIAGE BOLT, FENDER WASHER, AND WING NUT

SUPPORT

BASE

CLAMP

ADAPT BASE AND CLAMP TO FIT LATHE.

LATHE STEADYREST
EXPLODED VIEW

45° (TYP)

¼" DIA (TYP)

3/8" WD SLOT

2"

½"

5"

1"

8"

ARM LAYOUT

LATHE SPEEDS

Turning Diameter	Roughing Speed (rpm)	Shaping Speed (rpm)	Sanding Speed (rpm)
Up to 2″	900–1,300	2,400–2,800	3,000–4,000
2″–4″	600–1,000	1,800–2,400	2,400–3,000
4″–6″	600–800	1,200–1,800	1,800–2,400
6″–8″	400–600	800–1,200	1,200–1,800
8″–10″	300–400	600–800	900–1,200
Over 10″	200–300	300–600	600–900

DUPLICATING TURNINGS

You can duplicate spindles with a fair amount of accuracy *without* an expensive lathe duplicator. Just combine some common spindle turning techniques.

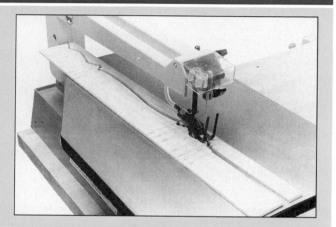

1 *Draw a full-sized plan of the spindle you wish to duplicate. Attach a copy to a thin piece of plywood, hardboard, or plastic. Using a band saw or a scroll saw, cut a negative of the profile, making a **reverse template.** Mark the major and minor diameters on the template.*

TIP: If you cut the template on a scroll saw with a number 5 (or smaller) blade, you can create both a standard and a reverse template. The standard template lets you see the contours before you cut them.

2 *Round the stock, then use the template to mark the locations of the major and minor diameters.*

TIP: Many turners shade the beads and coves, making the beads lighter and the coves darker. The flats and tapers are left unshaded. This eliminates confusion when turning a complex profile.

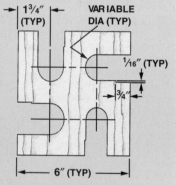

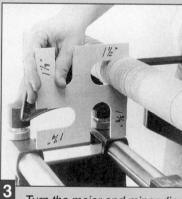

3 *Turn the major and minor diameters with a parting tool.*

TIP: To keep from constantly having to change the setting of your calipers, make a set of *fixed calipers* from thin plywood or hardboard that correspond to the diameters in your profile.

4 *Turn the beads, coves, and flats. As the spindle evolves, compare it to the reverse template. When the profile is complete, the template should fit against the turning with very little daylight showing between them. By carefully marking and turning the shapes to the same diameters on each piece, the spindles will turn out remarkably similar to one another. There will be some minor differences, of course, but these won't be distracting.*

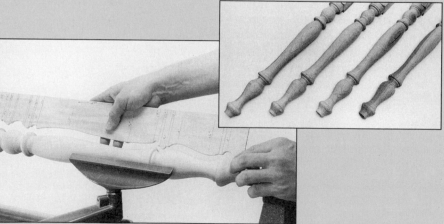

FACEPLATE TURNING

To turn bowls and discs, you must turn the face or end of the turning as well as the sides. To do this, mount the stock to the **lathe arbor**[1] with a special mounting plate. This is called turning with one center, or *faceplate turning*.

MOUNTING STOCK ON A FACEPLATE

To mount a faceplate turning, cut the stock to a rough cylinder on the band saw. Glue the stock to a mounting disc roughly the same diameter as the faceplate, let the glue dry overnight, then screw the faceplate to the disc. Secure the entire assembly on the lathe arbor.

TURNING A BOWL

Turn the outside of the bowl first, then the inside. As you turn the

inside, measure the thickness of the side frequently to keep from cutting it too thin. When the shape of the bowl is complete, remove the mounting disc from the bottom of the bowl.

PRO *TIP*

When gluing a mounting disc to turning stock, insert a piece of paper between the two parts to make it easier to separate them. When the turning is complete, align the cutting edge of a chisel with the glue joint and tap it with a mallet. The joint will separate cleanly.

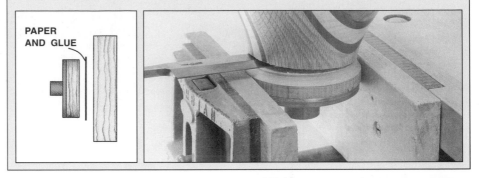

PAPER AND GLUE

SAFE *GUARDS*

When turning the face of the stock, work on the half of the turning that rotates *down*. This will hold your chisel safely on the rest.

TURNING A BOWL

1 To mount bowl stock on the lathe, first glue the stock to a mounting disc, then screw a faceplate to the disc. (If you attach the faceplate directly to the bowl stock, the screws will leave holes in the bottom of the turning.) Align the rotational centers of the stock, disc, and faceplate as you assemble them.

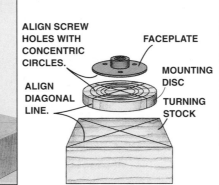

ALIGN SCREW HOLES WITH CONCENTRIC CIRCLES.

FACEPLATE

MOUNTING DISC

ALIGN DIAGONAL LINE.

TURNING STOCK

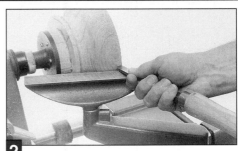

2 Position the tool rest at the side of the stock and turn the outside shape of the bowl. Make the beads, coves, and flats in the same manner as a spindle turning.

3 Attach a drill chuck and a bit to the lathe tailstock. Drill a hole in the center of the bowl to the same depth that you want to turn the interior of the bowl. If you don't have a chuck accessory, remove the faceplate/ stock assembly from the lathe and bore the hole on a drill press.

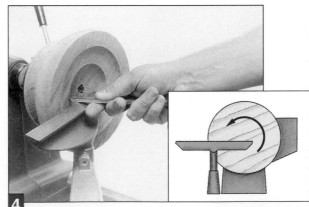

4 Reposition the tool rest at the face of the stock, as shown. Scrape away the waste inside the bowl, working from the outside of the bowl toward the center. Stop cutting when you reach the bottom of the hole that marks the depth of the interior.

5 As you work, use outside calipers to gauge the thickness of the side. Cut it to a uniform thickness, but don't turn the side too thin.

USING A LATHE CHUCK

You can also turn with one center using a *lathe chuck*. This is much like faceplate turning, but there's no need to glue the stock to a mounting disc or screw it to a faceplate. Instead, the turning is held in a large chuck. Most lathe chucks are *reversible*. That is, the jaws expand and contract. When the jaws contract, they grip the outside surface of the stock much like a drill chuck grips a bit. When they expand, the jaws press outward, gripping the inside surfaces of a shape.

JAWS

REVERSIBLE LATHE CHUCK

SEE *ALSO:*
[1] Lathes   114

As the jaws contract, they grip the outside surface of the turning.

As the jaws of a lathe chuck expand, they grip the inside surface of the turning. This particular lathe chuck also has jaw extensions (shown) to grip large-diameter turnings from the inside.

JIGS & FIXTURES

WOODEN LATHE CHUCK You can make your own contracting lathe chuck with a faceplate, a hose clamp, and a scrap of wood. Fasten the scrap to the faceplate and scoop out the interior, turning the inside diameter to match the stock you want to hold. Turn the outside diameter so the side is 1/8 to 1/4 inch thick. Make several saw kerfs in the side, dividing it into flexible fingers.

Place the hose clamp around the fingers, insert the stock in the chuck, and tighten the clamp.

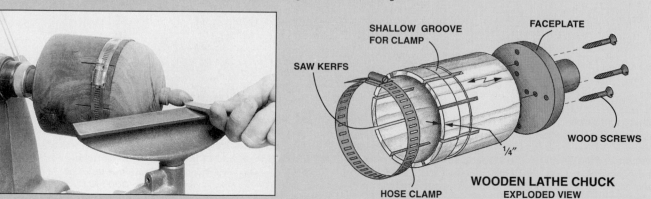

SHALLOW GROOVE FOR CLAMP

FACEPLATE

SAW KERFS

WOOD SCREWS

1/4"

HOSE CLAMP

WOODEN LATHE CHUCK
EXPLODED VIEW

FITTING A LID

A lathe chuck enables you to fit a lid to a turned box. Make the box as a **faceplate turning**[1] and carefully measure the inside opening with inside calipers. Mount the lid stock in the lathe chuck and turn a lip on the inside surface, fitting it to the box. Then turn the stock around in the chuck and turn the outside shape of the lid.

FITTING A LID

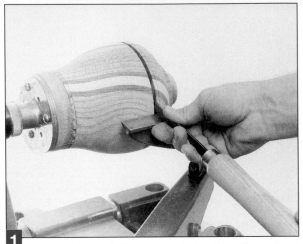

1 *Attach the stock to a faceplate and turn the outside shape of the box and* **most** *of the lid. Don't turn the very top. Instead, turn a plug on the top of the lid to fit the lathe chuck. Separate the lid from the box.*

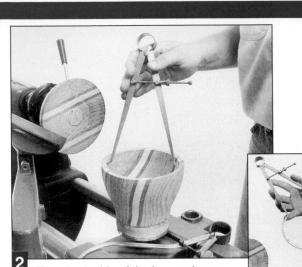

2 *Turn the inside of the box and measure its diameter with inside calipers. Transfer this measurement to outside calipers.*

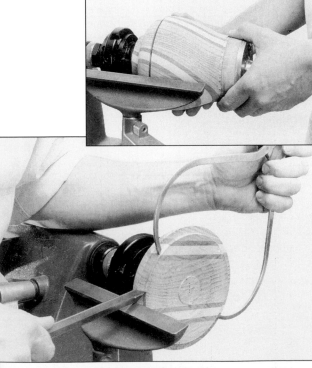

3 *Mount the lid in the chuck, tightening the jaws so they contract around the plug — the underside of the lid should face out. Turn a lip in the underside of the lid. The outside diameter of the lip should be equal to (or just a hair smaller than) the inside diameter of the box. Test the fit of the lid on the bowl. If you wish, hollow out the inside of the lid.*

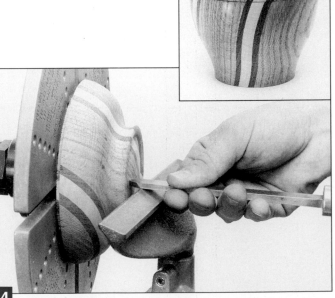

4 *Remove the lid from the chuck and turn it around so the top of the lid faces out. Mount it in the chuck again, tightening the jaws so they press against the inside of the lip. Complete the outside shape of the lid.*

TIP: If you wish, turn the plug to form a handle.

SANDING TURNINGS

It's much easier to sand both spindle turnings and one-center turnings while they are still mounted on the lathe. The **sanding rules**[2] are the same as for any other project – keep the sandpaper moving, don't press too hard, and work your way through progressively finer grits.

Increase the turning **speed**[3] for a smoother surface.

You can also sand between finish coats on the lathe, if you wish. However, think twice before you apply finish to a spinning bowl or spindle – it will fling finish everywhere.

SAFE *GUARDS*

Before you sand on the lathe, remove the tool rest. Otherwise you may pinch your fingers between the rest and the turning.

SEE *ALSO:*

[1]Faceplate Turning	314
[2]General Sanding Know-How	266
[3]Lathe Speeds	313

SANDING FLAT AREAS

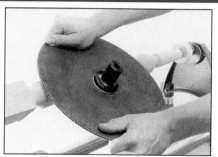

To sand cylinders and tapers perfectly straight, mount a piece of sandpaper to a flat scrap of wood. Or, use a stiff sanding disc (shown).

SANDING HARD-TO-REACH SPOTS

To reach into crevices or narrow areas, fold the sandpaper or use abrasive cord especially designed for this purpose.

AVOIDING HEAT

As you sand on the lathe, the sandpaper heats up and becomes painful to hold. To protect your fingers, wrap the sandpaper around a fiberglass abrasive pad.

MORE *SOURCES*

BOOKS

The Lathe Book, by Ernie Conover, Taunton Press, 1993

The Practical Woodturner, by Frank Pain, revised by James A. Jacobson, Sterling Publishing, 1989

Woodturning: A Guide to Advanced Techniques, by Hugh O'Neill, Crowood Press, 1995

VIDEOS

Bowl Turning with Del Stubbs, Taunton Books and Videos

Turning Wood with Richard Raffen, Taunton Books and Videos

Twists and Advanced Turnings with Dennis White, GMC Publishing

TROUBLE *SHOOTING*

COMMON TURNING PROBLEMS

Problem	Possible Cause(s)	Solution(s)
Lathe vibrates excessively or turning chatters.	Speed is too high.	Reduce lathe speed.
	Work is out of balance.	Mount work on center.
Wood splinters during roughing cuts.	Starting the cut at end of stock	Work from center out to ends.
	Feeding chisel too fast	Feed chisel slowly; don't rush.
Chisel digs into work.	Feeding chisel too fast or holding it at wrong angle to wood	Feed chisel slowly; pay attention to cutting angle and point of chisel.
Spindle turning whips or bows.	Spindle is too slender.	Support spindle with one or more steadyrests.
Work stops turning or slips.	Spindle is not secured between centers.	Increase pressure between centers.
	Drive center has torn end of spindle.	Cut off damaged area, re-seat drive center.
Work burns at cup center.	Too much friction at cup	Wax cup center or switch to ball-bearing cup center.
Sanding leaves scored lines on work.	Skipping grits	Work through progressively finer grits.
	Sanding too long in one spot	Keep sandpaper moving.

Bending Wood

Wood can be made flexible and bent to almost any shape. The trick is getting it to stay that way.

You can't always cut a curved part from a straight board. When you do, you shorten the wood grain and **weaken**[1] that part. You also change the appearance of the grain – a curved surface cut from a straight board will show end grain in some areas and long grain in others. This, in turn, makes it more difficult to finish. To preserve the strength and the appearance of the wood, you sometimes have to *bend* a straight board to make a curved part.

There are two ways in which you can make wood bendable.

■ *Thin the wood.* The thinner the stock, the more flexible it becomes. Bend the thin stock, then attach it to a brace or glue several layers together to hold its new shape.

■ *Plasticize the wood.* Heat the wood or treat it with chemicals to make the **lignin**[2] soft and pliable. As you bend the wood, the **cellulose fibers**[2] (which are bound by the lignin) will slip past one another. Hold the wood in position until it cools or the chemicals dissipate. As the lignin hardens again, the wood will assume a new shape.

STRESSES IN BENT WOOD

When you bend a piece of wood, the outside or convex surface stretches, while the inside is compressed. When planning a bend, it's important to know that you can compress wood much more easily than you can stretch it. Wood will compress 25 to 30 percent parallel to the grain but can

*The back, posts, and spindles on this elegant **Postmodern Armchair** are bent from straight-grained stock. The flowing lines not only add visual interest, they also make the chair more comfortable and preserve the strength of the assembly.*

SPECS: 40″ high, 24″ wide, 22″ deep

MATERIALS: Cherry and white oak

CRAFTSMAN: Phillippus S. Sollman
Bellefonte, PA

be stretched only 1 or 2 percent. This isn't a big deal when bending thin stock – the forces of **tension and compression**[3] are too small to stress the wood to the point where it breaks. But it becomes increasingly important as the wood get thicker. You must design your bending jigs to compress the wood into the curve, stretching it as little as possible.

BENDING STOCK

Some woods bend better than others. You will always have a certain number of failures because it's hard to predict which boards will break and which won't. But some species break less often than others.

WOOD SPECIES

In general, **hardwoods**[4] bend better than **softwoods**[4]. Some species seem particularly well suited to bending. These include ash, beech, birch, elm, hickory, red gum, mahogany, maple

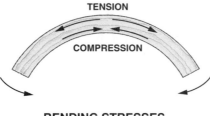

TENSION

COMPRESSION

BENDING STRESSES

(both hard and soft), oak (both red and white), and walnut. The chart below right compares the bending properties of several woods, mostly species that are commonly used for making bent parts. It also lists a few woods that aren't especially bendable, for comparison.

PREPARATION

Green woods bend more easily than seasoned woods. If you work with a seasoned wood, it mustn't be too dry; the drier the wood, the more likely it is to fail. But it mustn't be too wet, either. Woods bend best near their **fiber saturation point**[5]

(28 percent moisture content), but they take a long time to dry. A good compromise seems to be 12 to 20 percent moisture content. The smaller the radius, the higher the moisture content should be. Additionally, **air-dried**[6] woods are less likely to fail than **kiln-dried**[6].

Wood should be absolutely clear, with no defects. Even a tiny knot may cause a failure. Some craftsmen report better results bending **plain-sawn**[2] boards rather than **quartersawn**[2].

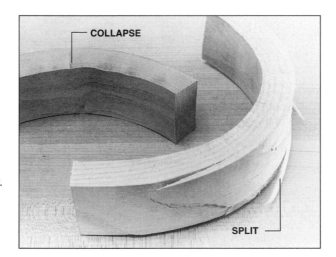

There are two types of failure common in bending. The outside of the curve may split or shake due to tension. Or, the inside may collapse because of compression.

COLLAPSE

SPLIT

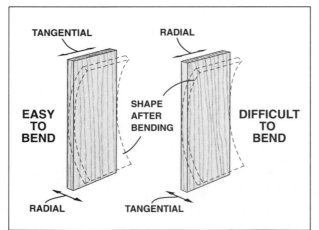

*In some species, it may be easier to bend wood along a plane that's **tangent** to the annual rings than one that's **radial** to them. If the stock breaks consistently during bending, or it won't hold its bend, check the orientation of the rings.*

TANGENTIAL — RADIAL

EASY TO BEND

SHAPE AFTER BENDING

DIFFICULT TO BEND

RADIAL — TANGENTIAL

COMPARING BENDING STOCK

Which wood is best for bending? The U.S. Forest Products Laboratory conducted tests in which they bent hundreds of boards from dozens of different species. Some failed, some didn't. The rating is the percentage of boards from a particular species that bent successfully, without splitting or collapsing.

Ash	67
Basswood	2
Beech	75
Birch	72
Chestnut	56
Elm	74
Gum, Red	67
Hackberry	94
Hickory	76
Magnolia	85
Maple, Hard	57
Maple, Soft	59
Oak, Red	86
Oak, White	91
Poplar, Yellow	58
Sycamore	29
Walnut	78
Willow	73

NOTE: Mahogany was not tested, although it is known to have excellent bending properties.

KERF-BENDING

Perhaps the easiest way to bend a piece of wood is to make saw kerfs in one face, almost cutting through the board. The board is very thin at each kerf. This, in turn, makes it flexible.

To determine the correct depth for the kerf, cut test boards. It's a good idea to thin most hardwoods down to $3/16$ inch, but you may have to cut deeper depending on the species. The spacing between the kerfs depends on the radius of the curve and the width of the kerfs. The smaller the radius and the narrower the kerfs, the closer the kerfs should be. Don't make kerfs too far apart, however. The closer the kerfs, the smoother the bend will appear.

Cut the kerfs on a table saw, radial arm saw, or miter saw. If just a portion of the board is to be bent, you only need to cut kerfs in that portion. Use this formula to determine length of a bent section, where R is the *radius* of the bend and A is the *arc* or number of degrees of the bend:

$$(3.1416 \times 2R) \times (A \div 360)$$

After cutting the kerfs, bend the wood around a curved brace. Or, glue two kerfed boards back to back in a *bending form*. (See the opposite page for how to make a bending form.)

KERF-BENDING

1 To find the minimum kerf spacing for a bend, cut a scrap as thick as the wood you want to bend and about a foot longer than the radius of the bend. Cut a kerf in the board about 6 inches from one end. Measure and mark the length of the radius out from the kerf. Clamp the end of the board to your workbench. Lift up on the other end until the kerf closes. The distance between the board and the bench top at the radius mark is the **minimum** kerf spacing.

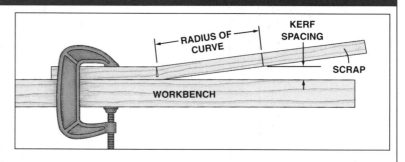

2 To space the kerfs evenly, attach an auxiliary face to your table saw's miter gauge. Cut a single kerf and drive a finishing nail in the auxiliary face, near the bottom edge. The distance from the nail to the blade should be equal to the kerf spacing. Place the kerf you just cut over the nail and cut another. Repeat until you have cut all the kerfs.

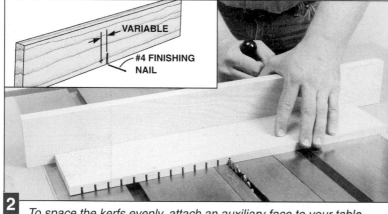

3 Bend the kerfed wood around a curved brace with the solid surface facing out. To hold the bend, attach the wood to the brace.

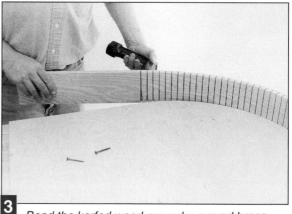

4 You can also laminate two kerfed pieces of wood back to back, clamping them to a curved form while the glue dries. When you remove the clamps, the laminated parts will hold their curve.

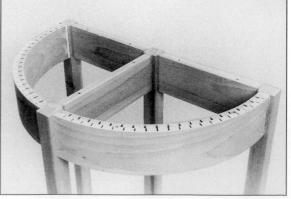

LAMINATION-BENDING

To make a bent lamination, glue up thin layers of wood in a curved form. Unlike kerf-bent boards, which are fairly weak, bent laminations are solid and strong. However, the glue lines may be visible at edges, especially if the tone and grain pattern of the laminate layers don't match.

GLUING UP

Resaw[1] the laminate strips from the same board, and number the strips as you cut them. Or, use **numbered veneers**[2] from the same **flitch**[2]. This will ensure that the wood grain in the assembly matches as well as possible.

Laminate the strips with a glue that has a long **working time**[3] to give yourself time to assemble the strips in the form. Apply pressure along the entire length of the lamination. *You must close all the gaps!* If the strips shift when you tighten the clamps, press them back into place. A little **abrasive grit between the layers**[4] prevents shifting.

LAMINATION-BENDING

Dry assemble the strips without glue to check that the wood grain matches as well as possible. The grain in the layers should all run the same direction. Apply glue to the adjoining faces and clamp the assembly in the form. If you're using a one-part form, start clamping at the center of the assembly and work your way toward both ends. Let the glue dry overnight before you remove the clamps.

TIP: Use a glue with a long working time, such as slow-set epoxy or plastic resin glue.

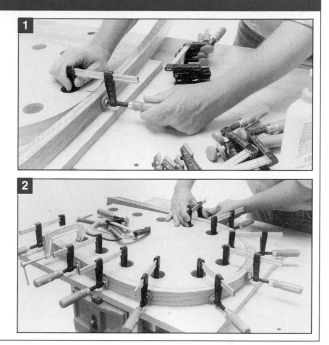

JIGS & FIXTURES

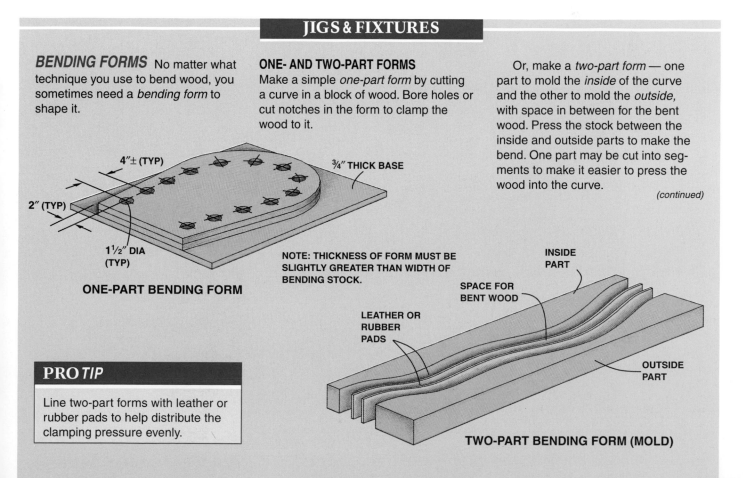

BENDING FORMS No matter what technique you use to bend wood, you sometimes need a *bending form* to shape it.

ONE- AND TWO-PART FORMS
Make a simple *one-part form* by cutting a curve in a block of wood. Bore holes or cut notches in the form to clamp the wood to it.

Or, make a *two-part form* — one part to mold the *inside* of the curve and the other to mold the *outside,* with space in between for the bent wood. Press the stock between the inside and outside parts to make the bend. One part may be cut into segments to make it easier to press the wood into the curve.

(continued)

4"± (TYP)
¾" THICK BASE
2" (TYP)
1½" DIA (TYP)

ONE-PART BENDING FORM

NOTE: THICKNESS OF FORM MUST BE SLIGHTLY GREATER THAN WIDTH OF BENDING STOCK.

INSIDE PART
SPACE FOR BENT WOOD
LEATHER OR RUBBER PADS
OUTSIDE PART

TWO-PART BENDING FORM (MOLD)

PRO *TIP*

Line two-part forms with leather or rubber pads to help distribute the clamping pressure evenly.

JIGS & FIXTURES — CONTINUED

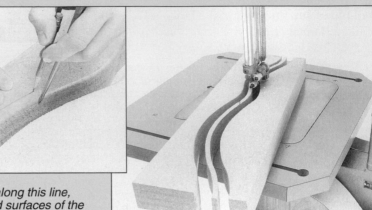

To make a two-part form, glue up a large enough block to make both parts. Lay out the outside curve of the wood. Add to this the thickness of *one pad* — this is the outside curve of the form. Cut the outside curve of the form, separating the block into two halves. Use a compass as shown to make a line for the inside curve on the inside part. The distance from this line to the curved edge must be equal to the wood thickness *plus* two pad thicknesses. Cut along this line, then adhere leather or rubber pads to the curved surfaces of the inside and outside parts.

WIDE FORMS

Forms don't have to be cut from solid stock. When bending large sheets or panels, solid forms grow heavy and cumbersome. To make a *wide form,* cut several ribs to the shape you want to bend. Also cut "reverse" ribs. Face both sets of ribs with thin plywood. If necessary, kerf the plywood so it bends to fit the shape of the ribs.

THREE-DIMENSIONAL FORMS

To make three-dimensional curves, such as the curve on a continuous-arm **Windsor chair**[1], combine several one-part forms, joining them at the desired angles. The three-dimensional form shown below includes two forms for bending the curves of the arms and a third for bending the curve of the back. As the wood is laid in the form, it's given a partial twist where it makes the transition from one curve to another.

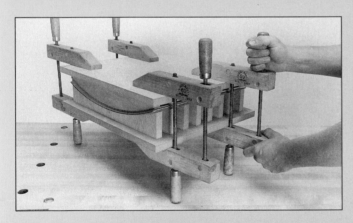

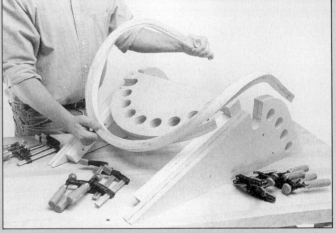

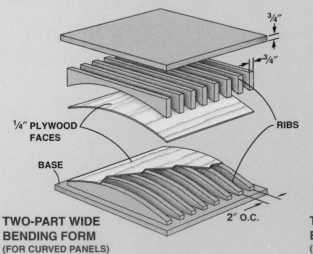

3/4"

3/4"

1/4" PLYWOOD FACES

RIBS

BASE

2" O.C.

TWO-PART WIDE BENDING FORM
(FOR CURVED PANELS)

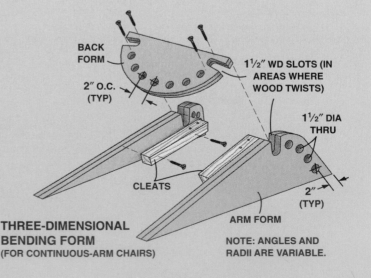

BACK FORM

2" O.C. (TYP)

1½" WD SLOTS (IN AREAS WHERE WOOD TWISTS)

1½" DIA THRU

CLEATS

2" (TYP)

ARM FORM

THREE-DIMENSIONAL BENDING FORM
(FOR CONTINUOUS-ARM CHAIRS)

NOTE: ANGLES AND RADII ARE VARIABLE.

DRY HEAT–BENDING

Bend thin, narrow strips of wood without a form of any sort by pressing them against a hot pipe. As the surface that rests against the pipe heats up, the lignin softens. This allows the hot wood to bend as you press down. This technique is often used to make curved parts for musical instruments.

SEE *ALSO:*

[1]Folk Tradition, 1725 to 1935   56
[2]Wood Movement   6

DRY HEAT–BENDING

1   Cut the strips you want to bend no thicker than ¼ inch. Hold the wood against a hot pipe, rolling it back and forth to heat a long section. Press down firmly as you do this. After a bit, you'll feel the wood give. Bend it to the radius you want, then move on to the next section.

2   To reverse the bend and make an S-shaped curve, flip the wood over and heat the other side. TIP: Hold a strip of paper between the wood and the pipe to prevent scorch marks. If the paper scorches immediately upon contact with the pipe, or the wood scorches through the paper, the pipe is too hot.

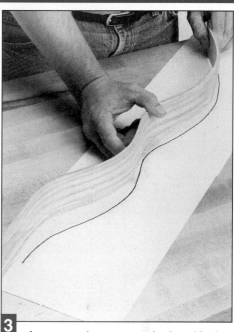

3   As you work, compare the bend in the wood to a full-sized drawing or template. If you make a radius too small or bend the wood in the wrong place, use the hot pipe to unbend it.

JIGS & FIXTURES

DRY HEAT–BENDING JIG

Traditionally, dry heat–bending was done on a hot stovepipe. However, few woodworking shops have wood-burning stoves these days. Substitute an iron plumbing pipe, at least 1½ inches in diameter. Secure the pipe to a base and heat it from the inside with a propane torch. Secure the torch to the jig with a rubber band or length of surgical tubing.

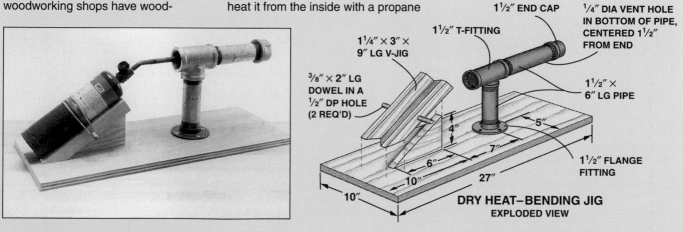

1¼″ × 3″ × 9″ LG V-JIG

1½″ T-FITTING

1½″ END CAP

¼″ DIA VENT HOLE IN BOTTOM OF PIPE, CENTERED 1½″ FROM END

⅜″ × 2″ LG DOWEL IN A ½″ DP HOLE (2 REQ'D)

1½″ × 6″ LG PIPE

4″

5″

7″

6″

10″

27″

1½″ FLANGE FITTING

10″

DRY HEAT–BENDING JIG
EXPLODED VIEW

STEAM-BENDING

With steam heat, you can bend almost any size of board, provided you get it hot enough. Heat the wood evenly in a *steamer*. How long should you heat it? The rule of thumb is to heat **seasoned wood**[1] one hour for every inch of thickness, or **green wood**[1] a half-hour per inch. These times may change depending on the species and radius of the bend – experiment with scrap wood before bending good stuff.

Remove the wood from the steamer and place it in a *bending strap*. This strap has a stop on each end to prevent the wood from stretching around the curve. Instead, the stops compress the wood as you bend it around a **one-piece form**[2]. Clamp the wood to the form and wait for it to cool and dry.

SEE *ALSO:*
[1] Bending Stock   319
[2] Bending Forms   321

MORE *SOURCES*

BOOKS

Fine Woodworking on Bending Wood, Taunton Press, 1985

Understanding Wood, by R. Bruce Hoadley, Taunton Press, 1980

The Complete Manual of Woodworking, by Albert Jackson, David Day, and Simon Jennings, Alfred A. Knopf, 1989

VIDEOS

Bending Wood with Marc Adams, Marc Adams Videos

PRO *TIP*

Don't heat the wood in a high-pressure steamer. You'll get better results from low-pressure steam. The idea is to heat the wood, not to cook it.

MORE *INFO*

Oftentimes the wood springs back, unbending slightly when you release the clamps. The amount of *springback* depends on the radius of the bend and the wood species. To compensate, make the radius of the form a little smaller than the radius you want to bend.

STEAM BENDING

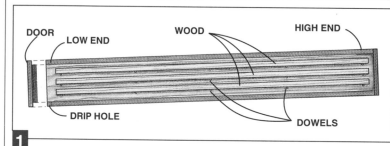

1   When steaming the wood, mount the **steam box** at a slight angle so the condensed water runs out. To allow the steam to circulate on all sides of the board, rest it on dowels inside the steamer. Don't let it touch the sides. If you stack several pieces of wood in the steamer at once, separate them.

2   Secure the form so it can't move. When the wood is hot enough, place it in a bending strap and draw it around the form using lots of pressure. Work quickly; you have only a minute or two before the wood cools.

3   Clamp the wood and the bending strap to the form. After the wood cools, remove the strap but leave the wood clamped in the form. Let it dry for two to four weeks, depending on its thickness. (The thicker the wood, the longer you should let it dry.)

SAFE *GUARDS*

When steam-bending, observe these safety rules:
■ Don't overtighten the steam generator's filler cap.
■ Vent the steam box.
■ Don't let the generator run dry.
■ Don't reach inside the steam box; use tongs to manipulate the wood.
■ Wear thick gloves when handling hot wood.
■ Keep the steam generator's heat source away from flammable materials.

JIGS & FIXTURES

STEAM-BENDING JIGS To steam-bend wood, you need a *wood steamer* to heat the stock and a *bending strap* to compress the hot wood around the form.

■ The **wood steamer** shown is a box made from exterior plywood. Load the wood through a small door at one end and rest it on dowels inside the box. Build the box to any size to accommodate the boards you want to bend — there should be about 1 inch of space between the boards and the sides of the box on the inside.

Generate the steam by boiling water in a large, covered container over a propane burner or electric hot plate. Pipe the steam from the container into the box. Or use a wallpaper steamer (available from most tool rental businesses) as a steam generator.

■ The **bending strap** is a length of flexible steel with handles and stops at either end. The distance between the stops must be precisely the same as the length of the wood you wish to bend. This strap has removable stops so you can adjust that distance.

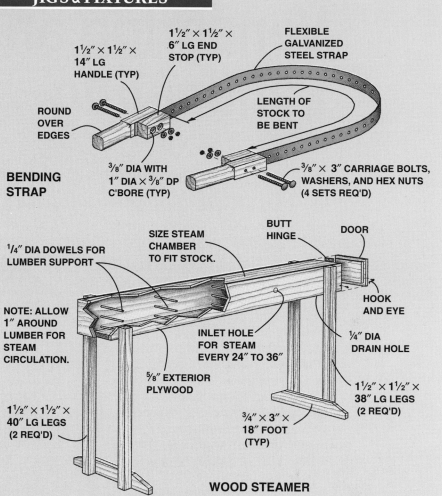

1½" × 1½" × 14" LG HANDLE (TYP)

1½" × 1½" × 6" LG END STOP (TYP)

FLEXIBLE GALVANIZED STEEL STRAP

ROUND OVER EDGES

LENGTH OF STOCK TO BE BENT

BENDING STRAP

⅜" DIA WITH 1" DIA × ⅜" DP C'BORE (TYP)

⅜" × 3" CARRIAGE BOLTS, WASHERS, AND HEX NUTS (4 SETS REQ'D)

¼" DIA DOWELS FOR LUMBER SUPPORT

SIZE STEAM CHAMBER TO FIT STOCK.

BUTT HINGE

DOOR

HOOK AND EYE

NOTE: ALLOW 1" AROUND LUMBER FOR STEAM CIRCULATION.

¼" DIA DRAIN HOLE

INLET HOLE FOR STEAM EVERY 24" TO 36"

⅝" EXTERIOR PLYWOOD

1½" × 1½" × 40" LG LEGS (2 REQ'D)

¾" × 3" × 18" FOOT (TYP)

1½" × 1½" × 38" LG LEGS (2 REQ'D)

WOOD STEAMER

TROUBLE *SHOOTING*

COMMON BENDING PROBLEMS

Problem	Possible Cause(s)	Solution(s)
KERF-BENDING AND LAMINATION-BENDING		
Wood breaks consistently.	Wood species is difficult to bend.	Use species with better bending properties.
	Wood isn't thin enough.	Increase kerf depth or reduce stock thickness.
Wood unbends slightly.	Not letting glue dry completely	Cure glue overnight before removing clamps.
	Glue moves or "creeps."	Use glue less likely to creep under stress.
DRY HEAT–BENDING AND STEAM-BENDING		
Wood splits or collapses consistently.	Wood species is difficult to bend.	Use species with better bending properties.
	Wood is not hot enough.	Heat wood longer before bending, increase pipe temperature, add more steam.
	Moisture content is too low.	Use green wood or soak wood in water.
Wood splits consistently on convex side of curve.	Wood is stretched around curve.	Design bending fixture to compress wood as it's bent.
Wood collapses consistently on concave side of curve.	Radius of bend is too small.	Use species with better bending properties or increase radius.
Wood unbends slightly.	Not letting wood cool or dry completely	Let wood cool and dry for several weeks before removing it from form.
	Normal for wood species	Decrease radius of form to compensate.

Veneering and Laminating

Properly applied, veneers and laminates increase the beauty, strength, and durability of a woodworking project.

Since the beginnings of woodworking, craftsmen have used thin slices of exceptionally beautiful woods to dress up mundane surfaces. These slices were glued in place, making an otherwise ordinary project look as if it were made from extraordinary lumber. From this practice, the craft of *veneering* developed.

Why not simply make the project from extraordinary wood in the first place? For three reasons:

■Truly striking **grain patterns**[1] are rare. Slicing exceptional woods into thin **veneers**[2] conserves this resource and makes it go further.

■Figured woods aren't as strong or as stable as straight-grained lumber – you sacrifice strength for beauty. Veneering lets you have both.

■Veneering makes it possible to repeat wood grain and **create patterns**[3] that don't occur in nature – bookmatches, herringbones, diamonds, and so on.

More recently, craftsmen have begun to cover surfaces with materials that make them more *durable*. Soon after the discovery of plastics early in the twentieth century, manufacturers developed **plastic laminates**[4] – veneer-thin sheets of tough, waterproof, chemical-resistant materials. These are applied to surfaces using methods very similar to veneering.

Photo by Joel Breger and Associates

*It's a table — a Federal-style **Card Table,** to be precise — but you hardly notice for the spectacular display of veneering. Federal masterpieces such as this were often decorated with figured veneers, banding, striping, and inlay.*

SPECS:	36″ diameter, 28″ high
MATERIALS:	Mahogany and poplar, with veneers and inlays cut from crotch mahogany, walnut, rosewood, holly, curly maple, and ebony
CRAFTSMEN:	Walter Raynes and Carl Clinton Baltimore, MD

PREPARING THE CORE

The **core material**[5] or ground to which you apply veneers and laminates must be as smooth as possible; otherwise the defects will "telegraph" through the surface. Fill all holes, voids, and gouges, then sand the surface smooth. To increase the holding power of the adhesive, make fine scratches in the core surface.

PREPARING VENEER

Sheets or **leaves**[6] of **common veneer**[2] are likely to buckle as they dry. This is normal, but you must flatten the leaves before you can use them. To do this, wet them with a damp cloth or foam brush and press them between sheets of plywood.

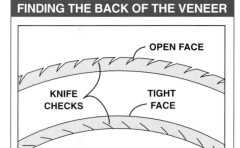

PRO *TIP*

If the veneer is brittle or heavily buckled, wet it with a solution of 4 parts water, 2 parts white glue, 1 part denatured alcohol, and 1 part glycerin. Press it between sheets of nylon window screen and allow it to dry 3 or 4 days. This will make the leaves more pliable.

If the leaves are all from the same **flitch**[6] (cutting), they were probably stacked in the order they were cut. Number them as you take them off the stack; this will help you match grain patterns when you apply them. Mark on the *open* face – the face with knife checks from the slicing process. The opposite face (the *tight* face) is the surface that you probably want to show when applying the veneer.

PREPARING THE CORE

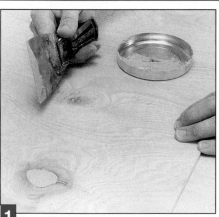

1 To make the core as smooth as possible, level any surface defects with stick shellac, water putty, or auto body filler (shown). Let the filler material harden, then sand it flush with the core surface.

2 To increase the holding power of the adhesive, scratch shallow grooves in the surface of the core materials. Traditionally, this is done with a **toothing plane,** but a 6-inch length of hacksaw blade fastened to the edge of a board works just as well.

FLATTENING VENEER

To flatten leaves of buckled veneer, wet them and press them between sheets of plywood. To prevent the leaves from splitting, add a little wallpaper paste or hide glue to the water before you wet them. Blot up extra water with newspaper. Separate the leaves with nylon window screen to prevent them from sticking together. Let them dry completely.

FINDING THE BACK OF THE VENEER

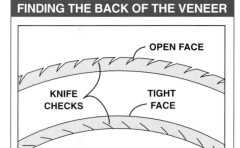

1 When veneer is sliced, the knife creates tiny splits or checks in one face, called the **open** face. The opposite face (called the **tight** face) has none. To find the tight face, roll the veneer parallel to the grain. If it rolls easily, the outside or convex surface of the roll is the face with knife checks. If it resists rolling, it's the tight face. Mark the open face. In most veneering projects, this will be the back — the surface that will be adhered to the core.

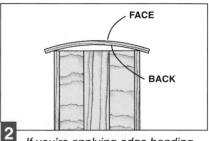

2 If you're applying edge banding, look to see which way the veneer strip cups. If it's not cupped, wet both sides to see which way it curls naturally. Mark the concave side — this is the back.

CUTTING AND MATCHING VENEER

Leaves of veneer are rarely the right size to cover a surface. They must be cut and joined to make a sheet the proper size. You can cut veneer with a utility knife or a *veneer saw*. Simply guide the knife or the saw along a straightedge to make a straight cut.

Cut the veneer about ½ inch longer and wider than the surface you plan to cover. Should you need to join two or more leaves, overlap the adjoining edges and cut both of them at once. Join the leaves with gummed veneer tape, then glue the seam together.

If the veneer leaves are all from the same **flitch**[1], you can create many different patterns with the grain. Arrange them side by side in the order they were cut to make a *slip match*. Or open the flitch like the pages of a book to make a *book match*. Or, cut four sheets at an angle, then arrange them so the grain forms a *diamond match*.

CUTTING VENEER

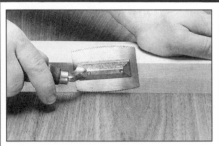

To cut veneer with a **veneer saw,** place a straightedge along the layout line. Push or pull the saw along the straightedge, pressing down lightly. It typically takes several passes to saw completely through the veneer.
NOTE: A *veneer* saw isn't really a saw at all, but a knife with a serrated edge.

MATCHING VENEER LEAVES

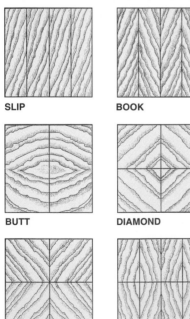

SLIP   BOOK

BUTT   DIAMOND

REVERSE DIAMOND   BUTT-AND-BOOK

JOINING VENEER

1 To join two leaves of veneer, overlap the edges you want to join. Tape the pieces together on the front and the back faces so they won't shift, then cut through **both** leaves at the same time. Even if you don't make a straight cut, the edges should match perfectly.

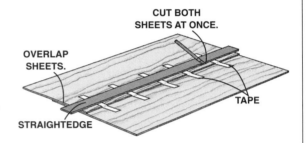

CUT BOTH SHEETS AT ONCE.

OVERLAP SHEETS.

TAPE

STRAIGHTEDGE

2 Assemble the leaves before gluing them to the core material. Arrange them on a sheet of plywood with the side that you want to show facing up. Hold them in place with veneer pins. (These look like push pins, but they leave smaller holes.) Make sure the edges butt together with no gaps, then cover the seams with gummed veneer tape. Wet the tape to soften the gum, and press it in place. Let the tape dry, then remove the pins.
NOTE: *Don't* use masking tape; it sometimes tears the grain when you remove it.

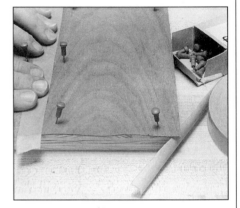

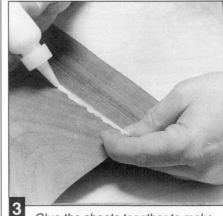

3 Glue the sheets together to make stronger seams. Fold the leaves at the seams to expose the edges. Carefully apply glue to one edge, then lay the leaves flat again.

4 Wipe off the excess glue that squeezes out of the seam with a damp rag. Don't worry about glue stains — this is the side of the veneer that will face **down**.

APPLYING VENEER

The proper technique for applying veneer depends on the **adhesive**[3] used. Almost any adhesive will bond veneer; but cooked hide glue, contact cement, and sheets of hot-melt glue are the most commonly used in small shops. Other glues require veneer presses, large clamping devices designed to apply pressure over a large area.

HAMMER-VENEERING

To apply veneer with **cooked hide glue**[3], you need a laundry iron and a *veneer hammer*. Cook the hide glue, but be careful not to get it too thick. Test it by dipping a brush into it – the glue should run from the bristles without breaking into droplets.

Apply glue to both the veneer and the core. Let it cool and dry partially, then place the veneer on the core. Heat the veneer (and the glue) with a hot iron, then smooth it with the broad end of the veneer hammer as it cools. Let the glue dry overnight, then trim the veneer to size.

Wet the veneer tape to soften the gum, then peel it away. Scrape the veneer smooth, and *lightly* hand sand the surface. Avoid sanding too much; you don't want to sand through the thin veneer.

PRO *TIP*

Be careful not to let the sanding block tip when sanding near an edge of a veneered surface. If the block tips, it will cut more aggressively at the edge and may go through the veneer.

TROUBLE *SHOOTING*

REMOVING BLISTERS To get rid of a blister or a lump of foreign matter under the veneer, make a small V-shaped cut, creating a small flap. Carefully lift the flap, remove the lump, and glue the flap back in place. The repair will be almost invisible.

SEE ALSO:

[1] Slicing Veneer   369

[2] Preparing Veneer   327

[3] Adhesive Types   250

HAMMER-VENEERING

1 Brush cooked hide glue onto both the veneer and the core. Let it cool and dry until it turns tacky.

2 Position the veneer on the core. Although tacky, the glue won't bond on contact. You will be able to shift the veneer into position. If necessary, hold it with veneer pins. Wipe a small area of veneer (about 2 or 3 square feet) with a damp rag. This closes the pores so the glue can't squeeze up through them. Heat the dampened area with a hot electric iron set to a low temperature.

3 Using the broad end of a veneer hammer, press the hot veneer down firmly, rubbing with the grain. If you must rub across the grain, press gently. (If you press too hard across the grain, the veneer will stretch and split.) Continue pressing while the glue cools. As the temperature drops, the hide glue develops a great deal of tack, enough to hold the veneer flat until it cures completely. Continue dampening, heating, and rubbing until the entire sheet is bonded to the core. Let the glue dry overnight.

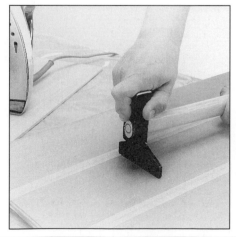

4 When the glue is dry, trim the overhanging veneer with a sharp knife or a veneer saw. Cut across the grain first, then cut with the grain. This prevents the veneer from splitting at the corners.

CONTACT-VENEERING

Contact cement[1] lets you apply veneer to curved as well as flat surfaces. You can use it to apply both common veneer and **reinforced veneer**[1]. However, it's not recommended for brittle or highly figured veneers that are prone to splitting.

PRO *TIP*

Contact-veneered edges are more fragile and prone to damage. To increase the durability of the edge, use a solid wood banding rather than a veneer strip.

Apply contact cement to both the core and the veneer, then let it dry completely. Place a sheet of paper over the core and position the veneer over the paper. Slide the paper out from under the veneer and press down on the sheet.

CONTACT-VENEERING

1 *Apply thin, even layers of contact cement to both the veneer and the core with a brush or roller. Cover the surfaces evenly and completely with **one** pass. Don't try to spread the glue out or go over it a second time: The partially dried glue will start to ball up, and you'll find it impossible to get rid of the lumps. Let the glue dry until it's no longer tacky.*

2 *Because contact cement bonds on contact, it's important that you position the veneer precisely before you press it down on the core. Lay strips of paper across the core to separate it from the veneer until you're ready. Rest the veneer on the paper and adjust its position. Remove a single paper strip and lightly press a small amount of the veneer against the core. Check that the veneer is where you want it to be. (If not, carefully dissolve the glue bond with acetone or the recommended solvent and try again.) When the veneer is positioned correctly, remove the spacers one at a time, pressing the veneer down as you go.*

3 *You can't generate enough pressure with your hands to create a strong bond between the veneer and the core. Hand pressure alone may also leave some air bubbles under the veneer. So after you've pressed the veneer in place, roll it out with a **veneer roller**, pressing as hard as you possibly can. Roll the entire surface **with** the grain as much as possible.*

THERMAL-VENEERING

Manufacturers of **hot-melt glue**[1] make this adhesive in large, thin sheets called *glue film*. These are simple to use – all you do is place the veneer and the glue on the core and heat them with an electric iron. This technique is not recommended for **common veneers**[2], but it's well suited for covering small surfaces with reinforced veneer.

THERMAL-VENEERING

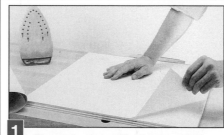

1 *To apply glue with sheets of hot-melt adhesive, you must heat the glue **twice.** First, position the glue film over the core and heat it with an electric iron (set to a high temperature) to tack it down. Let the glue cool, then peel off the backing paper.*

2 *Place the veneer over the glue film and wet it with a damp rag. Iron the veneer until the glue beneath it melts and sticks to the veneer. If necessary, continue to dampen the veneer to prevent the hot iron from scorching it.*

BANDINGS AND INLAYS

You can add ready-made decorative banding and inlays to veneered surfaces by attaching them to the veneer leaves when you assemble the panels. Like veneers, these decorative pieces are taped in place, then applied to a core with an adhesive. However, the panels are assembled in a slightly different manner, as shown below.

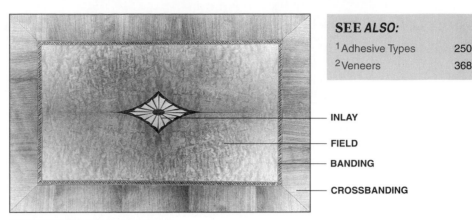

INLAY

FIELD

BANDING

CROSSBANDING

BANDED AND INLAID PANEL

SEE ALSO:

[1] Adhesive Types   250

[2] Veneers   368

ADDING BANDING TO VENEERED SURFACES

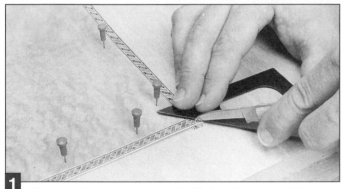

1 *To assemble a veneer panel with banding around the perimeter, tack a rectangular piece of veneer to a sheet of plywood with veneer pins. (This will serve as the* **field.***) Tack bandings in place along the edges and ends. Where the bandings overlap, make miters with a utility knife, cutting through both strips at once.*

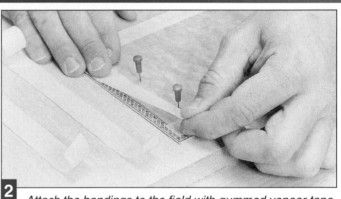

2 *Attach the bandings to the field with gummed veneer tape.*
NOTE: The bandings must be approximately the same thickness as the veneers.

3 *If you wish, add strips of* **crossbanding** *on the outside edges of the bandings. Cut these pieces from common veneer so the grain in the crossbanding is perpendicular to the edge to which it's attached.*

ADDING INLAY TO VENEERED SURFACES

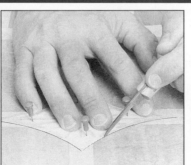

1 *To add an inlay to a panel, tack the inlay in place on the veneer with veneer pins. Trace around the shape of the inlay with a sharp knife, cutting through the veneer.*

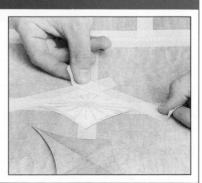

2 *Lift out the cutout you've made, and insert the inlay in its place. Assemble the parts with gummed veneer tape.*

APPLYING LAMINATES

Plastic laminates[1] are applied to core materials in a similar manner as veneers, with some important differences.

CUTTING LAMINATES

You can cut laminates on a table saw, but it's sometimes difficult. Because the sheets are so thin and flexible, they often wedge themselves under the fence, or the blade chips the laminate. It's much easier to size laminates by cutting a groove with a scoring knife, then snapping the sheet in two along the score line.

When you need to cut a clean edge or joint a laminate, use a router and a carbide-tipped straight bit[2]. Guide the router along a straight-edge as you cut.

JOINING LAMINATES

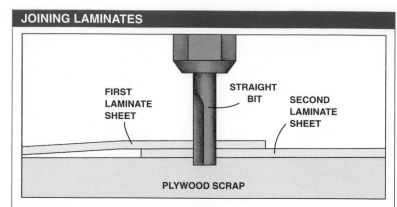

FIRST LAMINATE SHEET

STRAIGHT BIT

SECOND LAMINATE SHEET

PLYWOOD SCRAP

To join two sheets of laminate, joint the edges with a router and a straight bit. Lap the sheets where you want to join them, lay a straightedge along the joint, and rout them, cutting through both sheets at the same time. The routed edges will mate perfectly. Assemble the sheets before you apply them, taping the seams together with masking tape on the face side of the laminate.

CUTTING LAMINATES

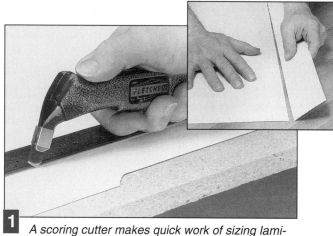

1 A scoring cutter makes quick work of sizing laminates. Using a straightedge to guide the cutter, press down firmly and score a line in the decorative or **face** side of the laminate. Then bend the laminate at the score line, folding the face side in on itself. The laminate will break along the line.

2 To cut laminate with a router, first place a sheet of plywood over the workbench to protect the top. Lay the laminate on the plywood and position a straightedge over the laminate. Clamp the straightedge to the laminate and the plywood, then rout through the laminate (and partway into the plywood), using the straightedge as a guide.

TIP: Always rout the laminate with the *face side down* to protect it from scratches.

JIGS & FIXTURES

LAMINATE-CUTTING JIG This simple jig helps cut and joint laminates quickly and accurately. Joint a strip of hardwood to make a straightedge, then glue it to a strip of ¼-inch plywood. Rout a groove in the plywood with the router and a ¼-inch straight bit that you will use to cut laminates. To use the jig, position it over the "save" side of the cut line (opposite the waste). Align the *inside* edge of the groove with the line.

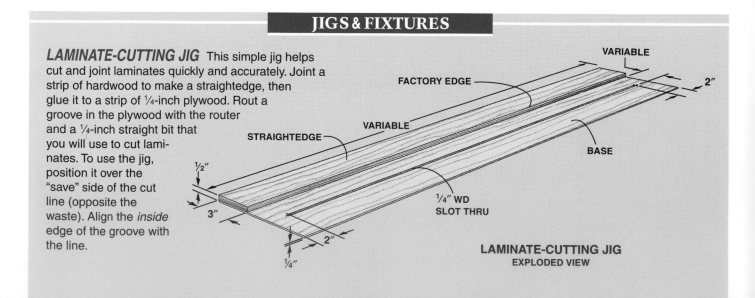

VARIABLE

FACTORY EDGE

2″

VARIABLE

STRAIGHTEDGE

BASE

½″

3″

2″

¼″

¼″ WD SLOT THRU

LAMINATE-CUTTING JIG
EXPLODED VIEW

LAMINATING VERTICAL SURFACES

Cover the edges (vertical surfaces) of the core first. Cut a piece of laminate slightly larger than the vertical surface to be covered and apply contact cement to the core and the laminate. Let the cement dry, then press the laminate in place. Trim the overhang with a router and a **flush-trim bit**[2]. This bit cuts a square edge, allowing you to lap the horizontal laminate over it.

LAMINATING HORIZONTAL SURFACES

After covering the vertical surfaces, apply laminate to the top or horizontal surfaces. The process is similar, but the surface area is typically much larger. Use strips of paper or wood or dowels to separate the core and the laminate until you're ready to press it into place. Afterwards, trim the overhang with a bevel-trim bit to "soften" the edge.

PRO TIP

In addition to covering the visible face of a large, unsupported panel with plastic laminate, apply a **backing laminate**[1] to the opposite face. Otherwise, the surfaces of the panel will **absorb and release moisture**[3] at different rates and the panel will warp.

SEE ALSO:

LAMINATING A COUNTERTOP

1 When covering a countertop, begin with the vertical edges. Cut a laminate strip (called a **self edge**) about ½ inch wider and longer than needed. Apply contact cement to the edge of the countertop and the back of the laminate. Let the cement dry until it's no longer tacky, then press the self edge in place with your hands. Start at one end of the strip and work toward the other. To get a good bond, apply additional pressure with a veneer roller.

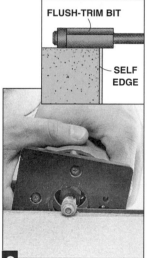

FLUSH-TRIM BIT

SELF EDGE

2 Trim the portion of the self edge that overhangs the surface using a router and a flush-trim bit. This cuts a square edge on the laminate.

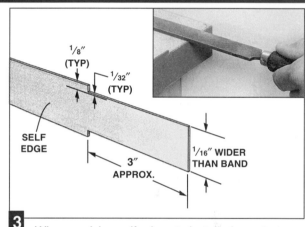

⅛" (TYP)

1/32" (TYP)

SELF EDGE

3" APPROX.

1/16" WIDER THAN BAND

3 When applying self edges to installed countertops, portions of the edges may be too close to the wall to reach with a router. When this is the case, notch the end of the self edge, as shown, where it will butt against the wall. After you've applied the self edge, trim this notched portion with a file.

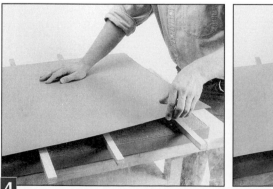

4 To cover the top surface of the countertop, apply cement to the laminate and core and let it dry. Lay strips of wood or paper over the core, then lay the laminate over the strips. The paper strips keep the laminate from bonding while you adjust its position. Once the laminate is positioned, remove the strips one at a time. As you do so, gently press the laminate in place.

5 Because laminate is much harder and thicker than veneer (and hard, stiff materials distribute pressure over a broader area), rolling the top laminate may not produce enough pressure to create a strong bond. Instead, **pound** the surface to generate the necessary pressure. Place a block of wood over the laminate to protect it, then hit the block with a mallet. Move the block a few inches and repeat. Continue until you have pounded the entire surface.

(continued)

LAMINATING A COUNTERTOP — CONTINUED

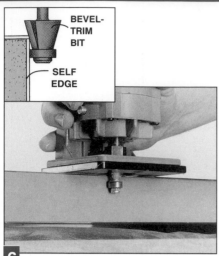

6 After applying laminate to the top surface of the counter, trim the overhang with a bevel-trim bit. This cuts the laminate to size and bevels the edge at a slight angle. A bevel edge feels softer and won't chip as easily. For an even softer edge, **lightly** file the arris, rounding it over slightly.

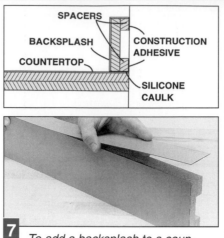

7 To add a backsplash to a countertop, cut a strip of plywood or particleboard to serve as the core. Cover the front (vertical) surface with laminate first, then the top (horizontal) edge. Fasten the laminated backsplash to the wall behind the counter with construction adhesive. Seal the seam between the backsplash and the countertop with epoxy or silicone caulk.

MORE SOURCES

BOOKS

Gluing and Clamping, by Patrick Spielman, Sterling Publishing, 1986

The Veneering Book, by David Shath Square, Taunton Press, 1995

Veneering, Marquetry, and Inlay, Taunton Press, 1996

VIDEOS

Laminates with Marc Adams, Marc Adams Videos

Making Kitchen Cabinets with Paul Levine, Taunton Books and Videos

TROUBLE SHOOTING

COMMON VENEERING AND LAMINATION PROBLEMS

Problem	Possible Cause(s)	Solution(s)
Veneer splits or breaks.	Veneer is fragile or brittle.	Apply thin solution of wallpaper paste or hide glue to back of veneer.
	Pressing or rolling veneer across grain	When applying pressure to bond veneer, press or roll with the grain as much as possible.
Gaps appear between leaves or veneer buckles after it's applied.	Taped seam doesn't hold when veneer is applied.	Tape *and* glue seams before applying veneer.
	Wood core expanding and contracting	Use quartersawn wood for core; apply veneer so grain is parallel to core grain.
	Veneer damp; shrinks when applied	Allow veneer to dry completely before applying.
Air pockets form under veneer.	Veneer not properly applied or pressed down.	Cut small slit in pocket to release air, press veneer flat with hot iron.
Lumps of sawdust or foreign material trapped under veneer	Veneer or core contaminated during glue-up.	Cut V-shaped flap in veneer; raise flap to remove material; glue flap down.
Veneer or laminate is not positioned correctly on core.	Veneer or laminate bonds to core before you can adjust position.	Separate veneer or laminate from core with paper strips until position is correct.
	Veneer shifts when applied.	Hold veneer in place with veneer pins.
Portions of veneer or laminate separate from core.	Glue was not evenly applied; too thin in some areas.	Carefully lift veneer or laminate and apply more glue under it; clamp until glue dries.
	Veneer or laminate not pressed in place with sufficient pressure.	Heat veneer or laminate with hot iron to soften glue; apply pressure until glue cools.
Panel warps after laminate is applied.	Laminate is applied to one surface, blocks moisture on one face only.	Apply laminate to both faces of the core so they absorb and release moisture evenly.
Trimming bit shaves away decorative surface of laminate.	Router tilts when trimming laminate.	Hold router firmly on surface; use offset baseplate for better balance.
	Face is not square to edge.	Cut edge square.

PART FOUR

WOOD AND WOODWORKING MATERIALS

Sawing and Preparing Lumber

To get the best lumber for your money, you need to know how trees are made into boards.

Although craftsmen have been building furniture and other useful items from wood for over 5,000 years, lumber is a recent development. Boards were either hand-sawn or *riven* (split) from logs until the first water-powered sawmill was built in Germany in 1321.

It's impossible to overestimate the effect that the sawmill had on woodworking. Can you imagine how little woodworking you'd get done if you had to split a log from end to end, then work the riven boards down to the necessary thickness with a hand plane every time you wanted to build something? Sawmills made boards affordable. Before the fourteenth century, only rich folks had furniture, and much of that was pretty crude. But by the time America was settled, all but the poorest homes were furnished, and furnituremaking was a flourishing craft.

SAWYERING

Today, lumber is made from trees in a complex manufacturing process known as *sawyering,* which includes milling, drying, and grading.

*Some of the most appealing projects showcase the sawyer's skills as well as the woodworker's. This Chippendale **Piecrust Table** is a striking example. The 33-inch-diameter top is a single board, live-sawn from an ancient walnut tree.*

SPECS: 33″ diameter, 30″ high (with top horizontal)

MATERIALS: Walnut

CRAFTSMAN: George Reid Dayton, OH

MILLING THE LOGS

In a large commercial sawmill, the logs are processed through several different saws and cutters. The first step is a *debarker,* which chews the bark off the logs. Then they're sent through a *metal detector* to sort out logs with bits of metal inside them, since a single nail can ruin a mill blade. From there, they are loaded onto a log carriage and fed past the *head saw* to make the first cuts.

If the log is to be **plain-sawn or live-sawn**[1], the first cut is a *slab cut,* removing part of the round surface and creating a flat side on the log. If it's to be **quartersawn**[1], the log is cut into quarters or *bolts.* After making the initial cuts, the sawyer begins to slice lumber from the log or bolts. At a small mill, all the boards are cut at the head saw. In larger operations, the slabbed logs or bolts are sent to a *resaw* to be sawed into *slabs.*

The thickness of a slab is measured in quarter inches. A slab that's 1 inch thick is 4/4 (four-*quarter*) stock. Slabs that are 1½ inches thick are 6/4; 2-inch-thick slabs are 8/4; and so on. Some of the larger mills that do business overseas also cut lumber in millimeters.

TRIMMING THE SLABS

The fresh-cut slabs go to an *edger saw,* which puts straight edges on them, then to a *trimmer saw,* where they are cut to standard lengths (multiples of 2 feet). The final stop in a large mill is the *grading station.* Here, someone with a trained eye inspects each board and assigns a preliminary **grade**[2].

SEE *ALSO:*

[1]Wood Grain   2

[2]Softwood Lumber
Grades   340

[2]Hardwood Lumber
Grades   341

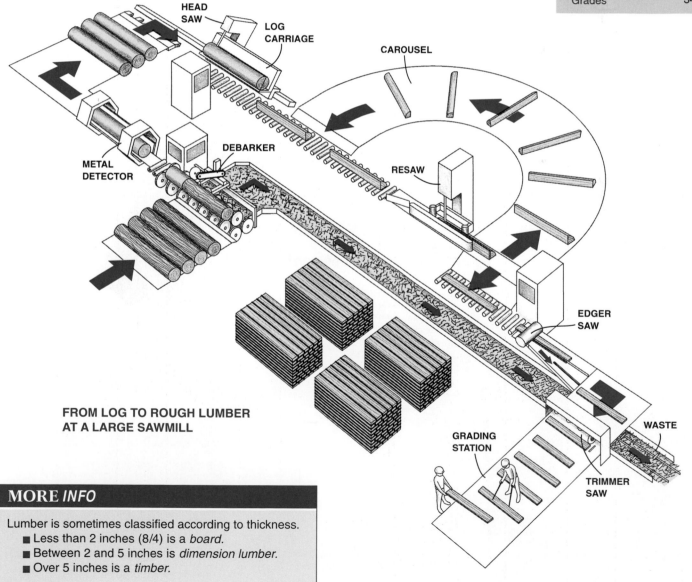

FROM LOG TO ROUGH LUMBER AT A LARGE SAWMILL

MORE *INFO*

Lumber is sometimes classified according to thickness.
■ Less than 2 inches (8/4) is a *board.*
■ Between 2 and 5 inches is *dimension lumber.*
■ Over 5 inches is a *timber.*

DRYING LUMBER

After the lumber is milled and trimmed, it's dried either in the open air or in a special *kiln*.

SEASONING

To prepare the lumber for drying, the boards are stacked with evenly spaced *stickers* (narrow sticks) between them to allow the air to circulate on all sides. Once stacked, the ends of the boards are sealed with paint – this keeps the ends from drying faster than the rest of the board. The stacks are *seasoned*, resting outdoors for one to four months until the wood loses most of its **free water**[1].

AIR-DRYING

Afterwards, the boards may be covered or moved to a sheltered area (under roof, but not indoors) to *air-dry*. With time, the wood loses most of its **bound water**[1], eventually

reaching a **moisture content**[1] more or less at rest with the **prevailing relative humidity**[1].

KILN-DRYING

Complete air-drying can take a year or more, so most commercial lumber is kiln-dried instead. The wood is stacked in an oven and baked at a low temperature (between 110 and 180°F) for one to four weeks. This reduces the moisture content to an average percentage for the geographic location.

MORE *INFO*

Both air-dried and kiln-dried wood must be **shop-dried**[2] for a week or more in your workshop. This lets the moisture content reach equilibrium with the relative humidity in the shop, and prevents the wood from expanding and contracting overmuch as it's worked.

In most parts of the United States, lumber is kiln-dried to approximately 8 percent moisture content, but it may be as high as 11 percent in humid areas of the South and as low as 6 percent in dry regions of the Southwest. These percentages represent the **average** *moisture content for wood in a particular location. They are not necessarily a stable moisture content — the lumber must still be acclimated to the specific conditions in your shop.*

KILN-DRIED MOISTURE CONTENT

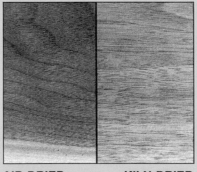

When stacking wood for seasoning, the position of the stickers is extremely important. They must be aligned vertically; otherwise the boards will dry with crooks and bows.

A **wood kiln** *looks like an ordinary garage, but it's actually a huge, low-temperature oven. The heat for this particular kiln is produced by burning the sawdust and wood scraps from the sawmill.*

WOOD DEFECTS

Once the lumber is dried, it's inspected a final time. Graders look for *defects*. Some of these are caused by improper drying; others are inherent in the wood.

DRYING DEFECTS

Both air-drying and kiln-drying must be done carefully and not too fast. Poor drying can create problems such as:

■ *Cracking* – The most common drying defects are *checks, splits,* and *shakes*. The ends and the exterior of the board lose moisture faster than the middle and interior. As they do, they shrink and crack. Some cracking is normal. But lots of small cracks or wide, long cracks indicate improper drying.

> **MORE** *INFO*
>
> A *check* is a crack that does not go all the way through a board, while a *split* does. Both are roughly perpendicular to the growth rings. When a crack follows a ring, it's a *shake*.

■ *Case-hardening* – If the wood is dried too quickly, it will case-harden and check on the surface. In severe cases, it will *honeycomb,* checking on the inside. A case-hardened board also has internal stresses. When you cut the board, you relieve some of this stress, and the wood reacts by warping or bowing.

■ *Instability* – If the wood isn't dried long enough, the moisture content may not be low enough for it to stabilize. Normal shop-drying won't allow enough time for the wood to reach equilibrium with the

> **MORE** *INFO*
>
> Some internal stresses are inherent. Trees on a steep hillside buttress themselves against gravity; in windy areas, they brace themselves against the prevailing wind. In both cases, one side of the trunk is under **tension**[5], while other side feels the effects of **compression**[5]. This is called **reaction wood**[1].

surrounding relative humidity, and the lumber will continue to expand or contract as you work it. Or, the moisture content will be uneven, and the wood will warp or twist after it's worked.

■ *Pitch pockets* – Softwood that's not properly dried retains pockets of resin that ooze or bleed out of the wood after it's worked. This can make the board extremely difficult to sand, stain, and finish.

INHERENT DEFECTS

Some problems are inherent in the log but are not apparent until the wood is milled. These include:

■ *Knots* – Knots occur wherever the trunk shoots out branches. If the branch is living and growing at the time the tree is harvested, it will form a *tight knot* in the lumber. If the branch dies and the tree grows around it, the dead branch will appear as a *loose knot* or a *knothole*.

■ *Bore holes* – Insects such as powder-post beetles, carpenter ants, and termites dig tunnels through the wood, which appear as holes in the lumber.

■ *Stains* – Wood mold, fungi, and bacteria can discolor the wood.

COMMON WOOD DEFECTS

SURFACE CHECKS

END SPLIT

SHAKE

TIGHT KNOT

KNOTHOLE

BLUE STAIN

BORE HOLES

Blue stain is a common discoloration caused by mold.

■ *Wood rot* – If the critters that eat the wood aren't stopped in time, they will damage the wood structure, causing it to decay.

The wood fibers in green wood are evenly saturated with moisture. As the board dries, it loses moisture near the surface first. If the moisture evaporates too quickly, the wood on the outside shrinks too fast, **case-hardening** *and developing surface checks. In severe cases, the board's hardened outside prevents the inside from shrinking normally, causing interior checks or* **honeycomb.**

GREEN WOOD

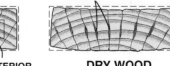

SURFACE CHECKS

WET INTERIOR   DRY EXTERIOR

INTERIOR CHECKS

DRY WOOD

The grader scores each board according to the number of defects he finds. The fewer the defects, the higher the grade. **Hardwoods and softwoods**[1] are graded differently.

SOFTWOOD LUMBER GRADES

Softwood is graded for *appearance,* by inspecting the best face of the board. There are three grades, and several categories within each grade.

SELECT
The *Select* grades are the best soft-wood boards.
■ *C and Better Select* is the clearest softwood available. It may contain small spots of torn grain, fine checks, or tiny sap pockets.
■ *D Select* may have some sound defects such as small, tight knots.
■ *Molding Stock* offers long, clear (but narrow) rippings useful for making moldings.

COMMON
The *Common* grades are utility wood.
■ *Number 2 and Better Common* may have tight knots, but no loose ones.
■ *Number 3 Common* has tight knots and is allowed a single structural defect such as a loose knot or knothole.

SHOP
Shop grades may have structural defects, but they must yield a min-imum percentage of *clear cuttings* — small boards, at least 3 inches wide and 18 inches long.
■ *Number 3 Clear* must yield at least 70 percent clear cuttings; only 30 percent can be waste.
■ *Number 1 Shop* must yield 50 percent clear cuttings.
■ *Number 2 Shop* only has to yield 33 percent clear cuttings.

MORE *INFO*

Softwood that's 5/4[2] and thicker is scored somewhat differently than 4/4[2] and thinner, and the rules vary for different species. But the grades remain the same.

SELECT (C AND BETTER SELECT)

COMMON (NUMBER 2 AND BETTER COMMON)

SHOP (NUMBER 1 SHOP)

HARDWOOD LUMBER GRADES

Hardwoods are assigned *cutting grades* based on the amount of clear wood (with no defects) that can be cut from each board. The grader envisions the rectangular shapes, or clear cuttings, that can be cut from a board. Those with defects are waste.

FIRSTS AND SECONDS

Firsts and Seconds (FAS) is the best hardwood grade. Each board must have no more than 16 percent waste (as scored on the *worst* side of the board), and the clear cuttings must be no smaller than 3 inches wide and 7 feet long, or 4 inches wide and 5 feet long. The boards themselves must be at least 6 inches wide and 8 feet long.

On rare occasions, firsts and seconds are scored on the *best* side of the board. These are designated *FAS 1-Face.*

SELECTS

Selects are similar to Firsts and Seconds, but the board can be smaller – as narrow as 4 inches and as short as 6 feet.

NUMBER 1 COMMON

Number 1 Common (also called *Thrift*) can have up to 33 percent waste. The clear cutting must be no smaller than 4 inches wide and 2 feet long, or 3 inches wide and 3 feet long. The boards must be at least 3 inches wide and 4 feet long.

MORE *INFO*

There are other hardwood grades with more waste, but they are rarely used in fine woodworking and are not commonly available.

SEE *ALSO:*

[1] Hardwoods and Softwoods   344

[2] Milling the Logs   337

FIRSTS AND SECONDS

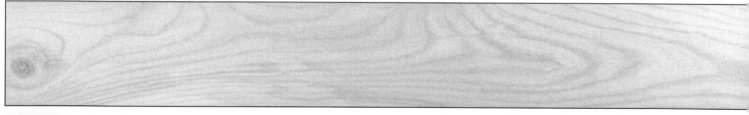

SELECTS

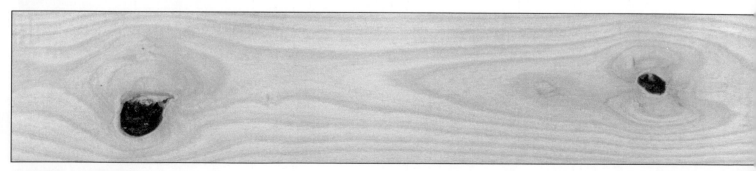

NUMBER 1 COMMON

PURCHASING LUMBER

Lumber is sold by the *board foot*. A board foot is a measure of *volume* – 144 cubic inches of wood. On 12-inch-wide, 1-inch-thick (4/4 or **four-quarter**[1]) stock, a board foot would be 12 inches long ($1 \times 12 \times 12 = 144$).

When you purchase lumber, you must decide what **grade**[2] you want, what thicknesses you need, and the number of **board feet required**[3].

Often the grade is the least of your worries – in most cases, it's decided for you. Many wood retailers offer only one hardwood grade (usually FAS); others mix FAS with Selects and call it *Selects and Better*. Any of the three grades of softwood may be available at building supply centers, but they are not always labeled as such. The Selects are sorted out, but you frequently find Common and Shop grades mixed.

Sort through the bins, choosing individual boards you think you can use, regardless of their grade. Discard those with defects that will detract from the appearance or weaken the structure of your projects.

PRO *TIP*

Purchase a mix of wood grain patterns. Straight grain works easily, but it's visually uninteresting. A range of grain patterns gives you more choices when you lay out a project.

CUTTING AND DRYING YOUR OWN LUMBER

Many craftsmen cut and dry their own lumber, not just to save money, but to make sure they get exactly what they want. You don't need a sawmill or a woodlot to do this – just a dry place to stack a small quantity of lumber.

FELLING AND SLABBING

Fell your trees during the autumn or winter when they aren't full of sap. The lumber takes less time to dry and isn't as susceptible to **molds or bacteria**[4]. Take the logs to a small

This lightweight band saw is powered by a gasoline motor, similar to a chain saw motor. The band saw has an adjustable guide that rides along a flat surface, letting you cut a log into slabs. Chain saw mills work in a similar manner, but the guidance system attaches to the chain saw bar.

mill that does custom cutting. Or have the sawyer come to you. Many small lumber operations have portable band saw mills that can be set up on site. If you don't have your own trees, purchase individual logs from a mill and have them cut to order.

If you'd rather do your own sawing – but you don't want to invest in a sawmill – you can purchase *chain saw mills* and *portable band saw mills* that will slab a log where it lies. Or, you can **resaw**[5] small logs on your workshop band saw.

SLABBING ON A BAND SAW

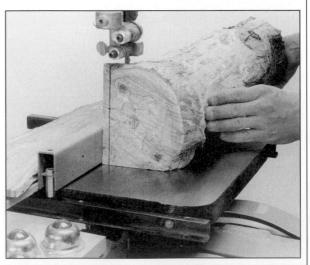

#12 × 2" FHWS TO HOLD LOG IN CARRIAGE

¾" PLYWOOD

85% DIAMETER OF LOG

85% DIAMETER OF LOG

1 To slab a small log on a band saw, hold the log in a plywood carriage to keep it from rolling around. Cut a flat side on the log, turn the log (and the carriage) 90 degrees, and cut another.

2 Remove the log from the carriage and **resaw** the remainder of the log, resting the log on one flat side and guiding the other along the fence.

STACKING AND DRYING

Stack the green lumber on a rack outdoors. Let the **free water**[6] evaporate, seasoning the stack for three to four months during a time when the average temperature is above freezing. Then move the stack to a sheltered (but *unheated*) location inside a barn, storage shed, or garage to remove the **bound water**[6]. The wood is ready to **shop-dry**[7] when the moisture content drops below 12 percent.

FIGURING MOISTURE CONTENT

How long does this take? The rule of thumb is that wood should dry one year for every inch of thickness, but many species dry faster.

Test the **moisture content**[6] of your lumber with a *moisture meter.*

Or, cut a small piece of wood from the *center* of a board in the stack. (*Don't* take it from the ends.) Weigh the sample, then bake it in an oven at 200°F for two to three hours to remove all the moisture. Weigh the sample again immediately.

Subtract the oven-dried weight (DW) from the initial weight (W) and divide the result by the oven-dried weight. Multiply by 100 to find the moisture content (MC).

$$[(W - DW) \div DW] \times 100 = MC$$

For instance, if the sample weighs 5 ounces initially and 4 ounces after drying, the moisture content is 25 percent: $[(5 - 4) \div 4] \times 100 = 25$. Those of you who remember grade school math are thinking, "Wait a minute! Shouldn't I divide by the

initial weight to get a true percentage?" Well, that's true. But what can I say? The U.S. government devised this formula.

MORE *SOURCES*

The Conversion and Seasoning of Wood, by William H. Brown, Linden Publishing, 1989

Understanding Wood, by R. Bruce Hoadley, Taunton Press, 1980

Wood Handbook: Wood As an Engineering Material, by the U.S. Forest Products Laboratory, U.S. Government Printing Office, 1987

Wood and Woodworking Materials, by Nick Engler, Rodale Press, 1995

DRYING LUMBER

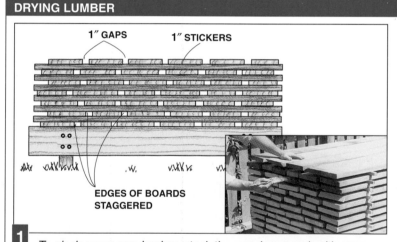

1" GAPS   1" STICKERS

EDGES OF BOARDS STAGGERED

1 To air-dry your own lumber, stack the wood on a rack with space between the edges of the boards. Stagger the edges with each layer; don't line them up. Place 1-inch-thick stickers between each layer, arranging the stickers so they are vertically aligned. This will provide even support and allow the air to circulate around the boards. Paint the ends to keep the boards from drying too fast.

2 Put a final layer of stickers on top of the stack, then cover it with sheets of exterior plywood. The sheets keep most of the rain off the lumber and protect it from direct sunlight. Weight the plywood down with concrete blocks (the more weight, the better). This prevents the top layers of boards from distorting. Place another sheet on the windward side of the stack to prevent the wind from blowing through it and drying the lumber too quickly.

NOTE: Do *not* cover the stack with a tarp. A tarp traps moisture and causes the wood to mold.

JIGS & FIXTURES

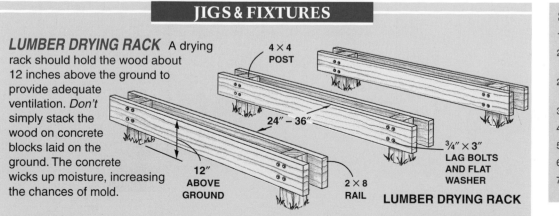

LUMBER DRYING RACK A drying rack should hold the wood about 12 inches above the ground to provide adequate ventilation. *Don't* simply stack the wood on concrete blocks laid on the ground. The concrete wicks up moisture, increasing the chances of mold.

4 × 4 POST

24" – 36"

¾" × 3" LAG BOLTS AND FLAT WASHER

12" ABOVE GROUND

2 × 8 RAIL

LUMBER DRYING RACK

Hardwoods and Softwoods

There are over 250 species of wood available to craftsmen, each with unique characteristics that affect every aspect of your work.

Wood is commonly divided up into hardwoods and softwoods. This has little to do with their relative hardness, although as a group, hardwoods rank harder than softwoods. Rather, it denotes a botanical difference between lumber from trees with encased seeds and leaves versus those with cones and needles.

For a woodworker in North America, there are actually three types of wood – domestic hardwoods, domestic softwoods, and imported woods or "exotics." Most imports are hardwoods, but we have come to think of them as a class by themselves. However you wish to divide them up, there are over 250 types of lumber com-mercially available in the United States and perhaps as many as 1,000 worldwide. Even if you work with just a few species that are available locally, it's useful and exciting to know about the incredible variety of available woods.

WOOD BOTANY

When selecting a wood species for a project, it helps to know some of the botanical traits that set hardwoods and softwoods apart from each other. It's commonly believed that hardwoods come from *deciduous* trees and softwoods come from *conifers*. Basically, this is true, but there's more to it than that.

Photo by Bill Parsons

*This decorative bowl was turned from a redwood **root**. Tree roots — particularly tap roots — often contain hard, stable, highly figured wood.*

SPECS: 19" diameter, 7½" high

MATERIALS: Redwood root burl

CRAFTSMAN: Robyn Hutcheson Horn, Little Rock, AR

ANGIOSPERMS

Hardwoods come from angiosperms, which means the plant seeds are encased in a "seed vessel" like a fruit or a nut. There are two types of angiosperms: *monocots* (such as palm and bamboo) and *dicots* (such as oak and rosewood). Almost all hardwoods come from dicots.

Most dicots in temperate climates are *deciduous,* meaning they lose their leaves during winter dormacy. Dicots in warmer parts of the world don't lose their leaves – at least, not all at once. So, contrary to the standard definition, not all hardwoods come from deciduous trees.

GYMNOSPERMS

Softwoods come from *gymnosperms,* plants with naked seeds. As the seeds develop on the cones, they are not encased in any tissue. Within this botanical group, there is a subdivision of *conifers,* which are characterized by needle- and scale-like foliage. All softwoods come from coniferous gymnosperms.

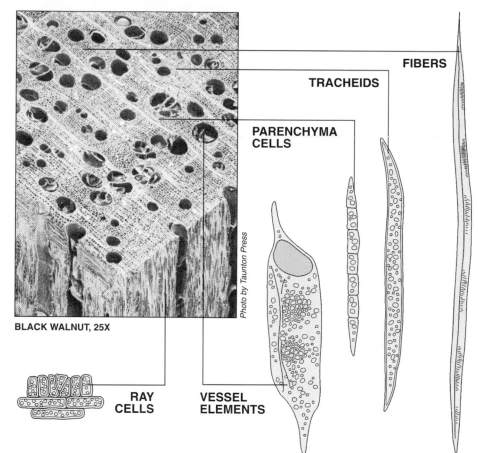

BLACK WALNUT, 25X

Photo by Taunton Press

RAY CELLS

PARENCHYMA CELLS

VESSEL ELEMENTS

TRACHEIDS

FIBERS

MICROSCOPIC ATTRIBUTES

These botanical categories, while interesting, make little difference to most craftsmen. To find the traits that affect your woodworking, you must look closer.

HARDWOOD CELL STRUCTURE

Study a piece of hardwood under a microscope and you'll find five major types of cells. Four of these are longitudinal cells, running parallel to the length of the trunk or limb.

■ Most hardwood tissue is composed of *fibers* 100 times longer than they are wide. These have thick cell walls, sometimes appearing almost solid.

■ Interspersed among the fibers are *vessel elements.* These appear much larger in diameter and shorter than fibers, and they are always aligned to form long, longitudinal

pipelines. When sliced open, they appear as *pores* in the wood surface.

■ You may also find a small number of *tracheids* and *parenchyma cells* with much thinner cell walls than fibers. These are few and far between and are completely missing in some hardwood species.

The fifth cell type runs perpendicular to the others:

■ *Ray cells* form radial pipelines running out from the center of the tree.

HARDWOOD GRAIN

The appearance of a hardwood's **grain**[1] depends on the size, shape, and number of each cell type. And because there are so many possible combinations, hardwood grain is enormously varied. For example, the rays can grow quite large, producing a pronounced **ray fleck**[2] in some species. In quartersawn oak, for example, the rays are the first thing you see. In other woods, they are barely noticeable.

WHITE OAK

SYCAMORE

LACEWOOD

*The quarter grain of wood with large ray cells shows pronounced **ray fleck.***

Grain differs with the distribution of cells in the growth rings. When the cells in the **summerwood**[1] are roughly the same size and density as the **springwood**[1], the wood has an even grain texture. When the summerwood cells are noticeably smaller and denser than those in the springwood, the texture is uneven.

Vessel elements and the pores they create also have a conspicuous effect. Hardwoods with large pores are said to have an *open grain*. Those with extremely small pores (too small to be seen with the naked eye) have a *closed grain*.

EVEN GRAIN TEXTURE
(HONDURAN MAHOGANY)

UNEVEN GRAIN TEXTURE
(RED OAK)

SOFTWOOD CELL STRUCTURE

Softwoods have a much simpler structure. Between 90 and 95 percent of the wood is composed of tracheids, while the rest are ray cells. There may also be a small number of parenchyma cells. There are no fibers or vessel elements, although some softwoods have *resin canals* lined with *epithelial cells*.

SOFTWOOD GRAIN

Because there are no fibers in softwoods, they tend not to be as dense or as hard as most hardwoods. And because there are fewer types of cells, there is less variety in the grain and appearance. For example, the absence of vessel elements eliminates the pores on softwoods. The grain is neither open nor closed – these terms don't apply to softwoods.

CHEMICAL ATTRIBUTES

Although most wood tissue is composed of strands of cellulose fibers stuck together with lignin, there are many other chemicals and minerals embedded in this matrix.

WOOD EXTRACTIVES

Extractives, as the embedded substances are known, differ from species to species. A particular mix is what gives wood its characteristic color. But color is just one of the effects of extractives.

■ Extractives can effect the density and strength of the wood

species. The more extractives that are embedded in the fibers, the denser and stronger the wood.

■ Many extractives are minerals. These act as fine abrasives, dulling your cutting tools as you work.

■ Some are resinous and waxy substances. These build up as *pitch* on the cutting surfaces of power tools and interfere with the cutting action. They can also make a wood difficult to glue or finish.

■ Many are antibiotics, killing molds and bacteria that would cause disease and rot. Woods high in these chemicals are resistant to decay.

■ A few of these antibiotic chemicals are **toxic to humans**[2] as well as microbes and have been known to cause or aggravate allergic reactions, respiratory ailments, and other health problems.

These botanical, microscopic, and chemical attributes all combine in a wood species to give it distinct characteristics or *properties*. These can be divided into two general categories, *mechanical* properties and *physical* properties.

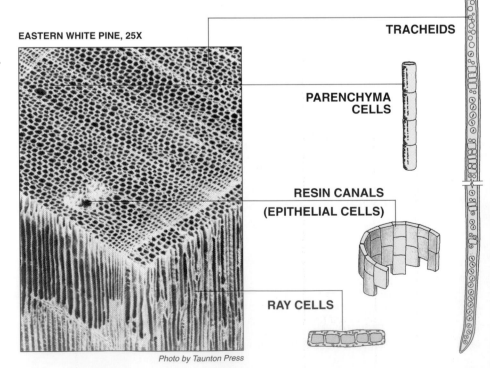

EASTERN WHITE PINE, 25X

TRACHEIDS

PARENCHYMA CELLS

RESIN CANALS
(EPITHELIAL CELLS)

RAY CELLS

Photo by Taunton Press

MECHANICAL PROPERTIES

The mechanical properties are those that affect the performance of the wood species and the ease with which you can work it. Is the wood sufficiently hard, strong, and stable for your project? Can you cut, assemble, and finish it easily? To answer these questions, refer to the appropriate categories in the chart of "Mechanical Properties of Wood" on pages 348–351. This chart includes the following categories.

SPECIFIC GRAVITY

Although **specific gravity**[3] is technically a physical property, it's usually included with mechanical properties. It's a reasonably reliable indicator of the wood strength and ease with which it can be worked. Woods with high specific gravities are generally stronger and more difficult to work.

HARDNESS

The **hardness**[3] is the ability of the wood surface to resist damage. This is an important consideration when choosing woods for projects that will be subject to abrasion or heavy use.

STRENGTH

Strength[3] is the sum of compressive strength, bending strength (also called the modulus of rupture), and stiffness (modulus of elasticity). This is a concern when the wood must withstand high amounts of stress.

MOVEMENT AND STABILITY

Wood changes dimension[4] tangentially (across flat grain) and radially (across quarter grain). This movement is measured by determining the percentage that wood shrinks from when it's green (freshly cut) to completely dry. The lower the percentage, the less the wood moves and the more stable it is. Additionally, a big difference between tangential and radial movement indicates that the wood is susceptible to warping, twisting, and bowing.

WORKING CHARACTERISTICS

Before buying a wood species that you've never worked before, it helps to know how difficult it is to surface the wood with a hand plane or a thickness planer. Does it lend itself to strong glue joints? Is it incompatible with common finishes?

These working characteristics depend on many factors. If the wood is extremely dense, it's harder to cut. Irregular grain patterns make planing more difficult. The cell structure of some woods makes them prone to splitting and chipping. Waxy or resinous extractives interfere with cutting, gluing, and finishing.

The chart of "Mechanical Properties of Wood" rates the following:

■ The relative ease of working a wood species with *hand tools*

■ The ease of working it with *power tools*

■ The tenacity with which common *wood glues* hold it together

■ The facility with which it accepts a *finish*

COMMON USES

Finally, nothing helps so much in deciding whether or not to use a wood species for a project as knowing how other craftsmen use the same wood.

MORE *INFO*

Many useful wood species, especially those from fragile environments such as rain forests, are severely depleted from overuse and poor management. These are specified as "Endangered" in the Comments section of the chart of "Mechanical Properties of Wood" on pages 348-351. If you work with these species, purchase them from a responsible supplier who respects their sensitive environments. For a list of these suppliers, ask for the "Good Wood" list from:

Good Wood Alliance
289 College Street
Burlington, VT 05401

In yellow birch (top), there is a large discrepancy between the tangential movement (8.1%) and radial movement (3.6%). Consequently, the species is prone to warping, twisting, and bowing. In Honduran mahogany (bottom), on the other hand, the discrepancy is very small (4.1% versus 3.0%). This wood is much more likely to remain flat.

MECHANICAL PROPERTIES OF WOOD

Species and Origin	Specific Gravity	Hardness	Strength	Tangential Movement	Radial Movement	Hand Tools	Power Tools
DOMESTIC HARDWOODS							
Alder, Red Western North America	0.41	Very Soft	Weak	7.3%	4.4%	Difficult	Difficult
Ash North America	0.60	Hard	Strong	7.8%	4.9%	Very Easy	Easy
Aspen North America	0.38	Very Soft	Very Weak	6.7%	3.5%	Very Easy	Easy
Basswood Eastern North America	0.37	Very Soft	Weak	9.3%	6.7%	Very Easy	Easy
Beech Eastern North America	0.64	Hard	Strong	11.9%	5.5%	Easy	Easy
Birch, Yellow Eastern North America	0.62	Hard	Very Strong	8.1%	3.6%	Easy	Moderate
Butternut Northeastern North America	0.38	Very Soft	Weak	6.4%	3.4%	Very Easy	Very Easy
Cherry Eastern North America	0.50	Medium	Medium	7.1%	3.7%	Very Easy	Easy
Chestnut, Wormy Southeastern North America	0.43	Very Soft	Weak	6.7%	3.4%	Very Easy	Very Easy
Elm, Red Eastern North America	0.50	Soft	Medium	9.5%	4.2%	Difficult	Difficult
Gum, Red Southeastern North America	0.52	Medium	Strong	10.2%	5.3%	Difficult	Easy
Hickory Eastern North America	0.72	Very Hard	Very Strong	10.2%	7.0%	Very Difficult	Difficult
Holly Southeastern North America	0.50	Hard	Strong	9.9%	4.8%	Very Easy	Very Easy
Maple, Hard Eastern North America	0.63	Hard	Very Strong	9.9%	4.8%	Difficult	Easy
Maple, Soft Eastern North America	0.54	Medium	Strong	8.2%	4.0%	Difficult	Easy
Oak, Red North America	0.63	Very Hard	Strong	8.9%	4.2%	Easy	Easy
Oak, White North America	0.68	Very Hard	Very Strong	10.5%	5.6%	Easy	Easy
Osage Orange North America	0.77	Very Hard	Strong	N/A	N/A	Difficult	Moderate
Poplar, Yellow Eastern North America	0.42	Soft	Medium	8.2%	4.6%	Very Easy	Very Easy
Sassafras Eastern North America	0.46	Soft	Weak	6.2%	4.0%	Easy	Very Easy
Sycamore Eastern North America	0.49	Soft	Medium	8.4%	5.0%	Difficult	Difficult
Walnut Eastern North America	0.55	Medium	Strong	7.8%	5.5%	Very Easy	Very Easy
Willow Eastern North America	0.39	Very Soft	Very Weak	8.7%	3.3%	Very Easy	Very Easy
DOMESTIC SOFTWOODS							
Cedar, Aromatic Red North America	0.47	Medium	Very Weak	5.2%	3.3%	Easy	Very Easy
Cedar, Western Red Western North America	0.32	Very Soft	Very Weak	5.0%	2.4%	Very Easy	Very Easy
Cypress Southeastern North America	0.46	Soft	Medium	6.2%	3.8%	Easy	Very Easy
Fir, Douglas Western North America	0.48	Soft	Very Strong	7.3%	4.5%	Easy	Very Easy
Hemlock Western North America	0.45	Soft	Strong	7.9%	4.3%	Very Easy	Very Easy

Gluing	Finishing	Common Uses	Comments
Good	Good	Utility wood for upholstered furniture because it holds tacks well	Grain tears easily. Blends with walnut, cherry, and mahogany when stained.
Excellent	Excellent	Ball bats, tool handles, bentwood furniture, food containers	Popular for food containers because wood imparts no taste to food. Easy to bend. Resists shock loads.
Good	Poor	Utility wood, papermaking	Almost indistinguishable from Cottonwood.
Excellent	Excellent	Carvings, toys, boxes, beehives	Preferred by many woodcarvers.
Excellent	Excellent	Cabinets, bentwood furniture, tool handles, boxes, flooring, workbenches	Easy to bend. Sometimes substituted for hard maple.
Good	Excellent	Furniture, bentwood furniture, turnings, flooring, plywood	Easy to bend. Sometimes substituted for hard maple. Prone to warping and twisting.
Excellent	Excellent	Carving, furniture, paneling	Once a common source of dye for "butternut" jeans. Sometimes referred to as white walnut.
Excellent	Excellent	Furniture, cabinets	Premium furniture wood.
Excellent	Excellent	Furniture, antique reproduction	Most living trees destroyed by fungus in early twentieth century. New lumber is salvaged from dead trees.
Adequate	Adequate	Bentwood furniture, chair seats, boats, barrels, baskets	Fairly easy to bend. Has an outstanding resistance to shock loads.
Excellent	Excellent	Inexpensive furniture, cabinets, plywood, trim, boxes	Also known as Sweet Gum. Bark produces balsam used in medicines.
Excellent	Excellent	Tool handles, ladder rungs, chair parts, pegs	Fairly easy to bend. Also used to smoke meats.
Excellent	Excellent	Inlays, marquetry, musical instruments	One of the few evergreen dicots — doesn't lose its leaves seasonally.
Adequate	Excellent	Furniture, chair parts, turnings, flooring, musical instruments, toys	Premium furniture wood, curly figure and bird's-eye figure common. Easy to bend.
Good	Excellent	Furniture, turnings, boxes, toys	Utility furniture wood, curly figure common.
Good	Excellent	Furniture, cabinets, flooring, trim	Quartersawn stock has "silver" figure. Sawdust is potential irritant.
Good	Good	Furniture, flooring, trim, barrels	Similar to red oak in most respects, but has finer texture and darker color. Potential irritant.
Adequate	Good	Archery bows, canes, fence posts, cart and buggy wheels	Resists decay. Source of yellow, tan, and khaki dyes. Potential irritant.
Excellent	Good	Furniture, patternmaking, turning, boxes, eating utensils, trim, plywood	Although not considered a premium wood, it's very versatile — not much it can't be used for.
Excellent	Good	Furniture, boats, boxes, barrels	Root bark used for tea and flavoring for medicine. Sawdust is potential irritant.
Excellent	Good	Furniture, musical instruments, food containers	Quartersawn stock has "lacy" figure due to rays. Curly figure also common.
Good	Excellent	Furniture, cabinets, gun stocks, boats, clock cases	Premium furniture wood, produces a wide variety of figured grain, fairy easy to bend. Potential irritant.
Good	Excellent	Furniture, boxes, toys, beehives, artificial limbs, plywood	Sometimes stained to simulate walnut.
Good	Good	Boxes, chests, liners for closets and storage units	Has strong but pleasant odor. Despite folklore, no evidence that odor or wood oil repels insects.
Excellent	Good	Doors, windows, interior and exterior trim, boats, outdoor furniture	Decay resistant, sawdust is a potential sensitizer.
Excellent	Good	Outdoor furniture, boats, liners for closets and storage units	Decay resistant. Not to be confused with "Genuine Cypress," a hardwood depleted earlier in this century.
Good	Difficult	Construction, windows, doors, trim, flooring, boats, plywood	More veneer and plywood are made from this species than any other. Sawdust is potential irritant.
Excellent	Excellent	Construction, broom handles, papermaking	No relation to the poisonous herb.

(continued)

MECHANICAL PROPERTIES OF WOOD — continued

Species and Origin	Specific Gravity	Hardness	Strength	Tangential Movement	Radial Movement	Hand Tools	Power Tools
DOMESTIC SOFTWOODS — CONTINUED							
Pine, Ponderosa Western North America	0.40	Very Soft	Weak	6.2%	3.9%	Easy	Very Easy
Pine, Sugar Western North America	0.36	Very Soft	Very Weak	5.6%	2.9%	Easy	Very Easy
Pine, Eastern White Northeastern North America	0.35	Very Soft	Weak	7.4%	4.1%	Very Easy	Very Easy
Pine, Southern Yellow Southern North America	0.59	Medium	Very Strong	6.1%	2.1%	Easy	Easy
Redwood Western North America	0.35	Very Soft	Weak	4.9%	2.2%	Very Easy	Very Easy
Spruce, Sitka Western North America	0.40	Very Soft	Medium	7.5%	4.3%	Easy	Easy
IMPORTED WOODS							
Balsa Central and South America	0.16	Very Soft	Very Weak	7.6%	3.0%	Very Easy	Very Easy
Bocote Central and South America	0.55	Medium	Medium	N/A	N/A	Easy	Easy
Bubinga West Africa	0.71	Very Hard	Very Strong	8.4%	5.8%	Easy	Moderate
Cocobolo Central America	1.10	Very Hard	Very Strong	5.7%	2.9%	Difficult	Moderate
Ebony, Gaboon Central Africa	1.03	Very Hard	Very Strong	6.5%	5.5%	Difficult	Difficult
Goncolo Alves South America	0.84	Very Hard	Very Strong	N/A	N/A	Difficult	Difficult
Jelutong Indonesia, Malaysia	0.36	Very Soft	Very Weak	N/A	N/A	Very Easy	Very Easy
Lacewood Europe	0.62	Medium	Medium	N/A	N/A	Easy	Moderate
Mahogany, African West Africa	0.42	Soft	Medium	4.5%	2.5%	Moderate	Easy
Mahogany, Honduran Central America	0.45	Soft	Medium	4.1%	3.0%	Very Easy	Very Easy
Mahogany, Philippine, Lauan Indonesia, Malaysia	0.54	Soft	Strong	8.0%	3.8%	Very Easy	Very Easy
Mahogany, Philippine, Meranti Malaysia	0.67	Medium	Medium	N/A	N/A	Easy	Easy
Padauk West Africa, Indonesia	0.72	Medium	Strong	N/A	N/A	Easy	Very Easy
Purpleheart Central and South America	0.67	Hard	Very Strong	6.1%	3.2%	Moderate	Difficult
Rosewood, Bolivian South America	0.80	Very Hard	Very Strong	4.6%	2.9%	Difficult	Difficult
Rosewood, Honduran Central America	0.96	Very Hard	Strong	N/A	N/A	Difficult	Difficult
Rosewood, Indian India, Indonesia	0.75	Very Hard	Very Strong	5.8%	2.7%	Difficult	Difficult
Teak Southeast Asia, Indonesia	0.55	Medium	Strong	5.8%	2.5%	Moderate	Moderate
Tulipwood South America	0.96	Very Hard	Very Strong	N/A	N/A	Difficult	Difficult
Wenge Central Africa	0.88	Very Hard	Strong	N/A	N/A	Moderate	Easy
Zebrawood West Africa	0.74	Hard	Strong	N/A	N/A	Easy	Difficult

Gluing	Finishing	Common Uses	Comments
Adequate	Good	Construction, trim, paneling, doors, windows, boxes, informal furniture	Also known as Knotty Pine.
Excellent	Good	Interior trim, boxes, toys, carving, light construction	Not durable.
Good	Excellent	Informal furniture, carving, trim, light construction, boats, musical instruments	Once the most commercially important timber type in America, but overuse has depleted supply.
Good	Adequate	Construction, exterior trim, flooring, boats, boxes	Suitable for heavy construction. Also used to make turpentine and pitch.
Excellent	Good	Construction, decking, coffins, vats	Resists decay, holds nails and screws poorly. Trees are up to 350 feet high and 4,000 years old.
Excellent	Excellent	Construction, boats, airplanes, musical instruments, trim, boxes	Sawdust is a potential irritant.
Excellent	Poor	Modelmaking, insulation, floats, lifebelts, buoys, boxes, toys	The softest and lightest hardwood available commercially.
Adequate	Excellent	Cabinets, furniture, inlay, boats, tool handles	Many tool manufacturers substitute this for Rosewood on top-of-the-line hand tools.
Poor	Excellent	Furniture, turnings, eating utensils, knife handles	Gum pockets in the wood make gluing difficult, may also cause pitch to build up on cutters. *Endangered.*
Poor	Good	Tool handles, knife handles, turnings, wooden jewelry	Dulls cutting edges, may react with some oil-based and lacquer finishes. Potential irritant. *Endangered.*
Good	Excellent	Tool handles, piano keys, musical instruments, turnings, inlay	Dulls cutting edges, chips easily. Potential irritant and sensitizer. Supplies severely depleted. *Endangered.*
Good	Excellent	Furniture, cabinets, turnings, knife handles	Interlocking and irregular grain make it difficult to work. Potential sensitizer. *Endangered.*
Excellent	Excellent	Carving, patternmaking	Has become a favorite among wood carvers. Is similar to Basswood but more stable.
Excellent	Excellent	Furniture, inlay, turnings, boxes, paneling	Quartersawn grain shows unique ray fleck. Related to American Sycamore.
Good	Excellent	Furniture, cabinets, boats, trim.	Quartersawn grain shows ribbon figure. Similar properties and appearance as Honduran Mahogany.
Excellent	Excellent	Furniture, cabinets, boats, caskets, pianos, carving	Most cherished furniture wood in world, preferred for classic styles. Resists decay. *Endangered.*
Excellent	Good	Furniture, cabinets, boats, trim, boxes, paneling, plywood	Waterproof, resists decay. Premium furniture and boat-building wood.
Good	Excellent	Furniture, boats, flooring, plywood	Sometimes substituted for Honduran Mahogany, but texture is coarser.
Good	Excellent	Furniture, cabinets, turnings, tool and knife handles, carvings, flooring	Very stable, resists decay. Potential irritant. *Endangered.*
Good	Good	Furniture, turnings, boats, tool handles, billiard tables, inlay, construction	Resists decay. Alcohol-based finishes dissolve purple color, lacquer finishes preserve color.
Poor	Poor	Furniture, cabinets, pianos, inlay, musical instruments, knife handles	Best substitute for Brazilian Rosewood, which is depleted. Resists decay. Potential sensitizer. *Endangered.*
Poor	Poor	Furniture, pianos, musical instruments, billiard tables, turnings.	A fair substitute for Brazilian Rosewood. Resists decay. Potential sensitizer. *Endangered.*
Adequate	Good	Furniture, inlay, musical instruments, turnings, boats	Resists decay. Potential sensitizer. *Endangered.*
Good	Good	Furniture, cabinets, boats, outdoor furniture, vats	Very stable, resists decay. Potential sensitizer. *Endangered.*
Good	Excellent	Cabinets, coffins, turnings, inlay	Stable, resists decay. Potential sensitizer. Member of the Rosewood family.
Poor	Good	Carving, inlay, turnings, flooring, carving	Stable, resists decay. Sometimes substituted for Ebony.
Good	Excellent	Cabinets, inlay, turnings	Stable. Interlocking grain makes it difficult to plane and joint.

PHYSICAL PROPERTIES

The physical properties of a wood species are those that affect its appearance, weight, feel, and smell. Most craftsmen aren't especially concerned about feel and smell, since these change considerably when you apply a finish. But appearance is paramount. Weight can also be important if the project is meant to be moved or carried. The chart of "Physical Properties of Wood" on pages 353–360 describes the appearance and weight of common species.

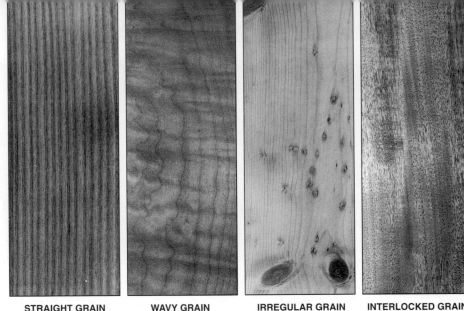

| STRAIGHT GRAIN | WAVY GRAIN | IRREGULAR GRAIN | INTERLOCKED GRAIN |

TYPES OF WOOD GRAIN

WOOD COLOR

The unique color of a wood species is determined by the **chemical extractives**[1] embedded in the cell walls. But the initial color of the raw, freshly cut wood doesn't remain unchanged.

This color darkens somewhat when you apply a finish, even if that finish appears clear and colorless. Most finishes also change the hue, making it more amber. Craftsmen describe this as "warming up" the wood color. In the chart of "Physical Properties of Wood," you can see how common finishes affect color.

Unfortunately, what you can't see is that the wood also changes color with age. As the surface of the wood is exposed to air, it slowly oxidizes. Some woods are *photosensitive* – exposure to ultraviolet light alters the extractives. Both reactions change the wood color at the surface. This

Cherry is a photosensitive wood. The escutcheon that once adorned this cherry drawer front blocked the light. Consequently, the patina where the escutcheon once was is much lighter than the surrounding wood.

thin layer of color-changed wood, sometimes only a few thousandths of an inch thick, is the *patina*.

The patina of most woods grows darker with age. However, in two species – walnut and mahogany – it grows lighter. As they age, their patina becomes a soft gray color.

PRO*TIP*

When restoring or refinishing antiques, be careful not to sand through the patina. If you do, the wood may appear *blotchy* — darker in some areas than in others.

WOOD TEXTURE

Texture depends on the size of the longitudinal cells. In hardwoods, this refers to the size of the fibers and the vessel elements; in softwoods, it's the tracheids. Fine-textured woods have small cells, while coarse woods have larger ones.

GRAIN PATTERN

The normal orientation of the longitudinal cells determines a species' characteristic grain pattern. There are four categories.

■ In *straight grain*, the longitudinal cells grow fairly straight and parallel to the axis of the trunk.

■ In *wavy grain*, the cells undulate in short, even waves. This sometimes produces curly figure.

■ In *irregular grain*, the cells undulate in no discernible pattern.

■ In *interlocked grain*, the cells spiral around the trunk, reversing direction every few growth rings. This produces ribbon figure.

WOOD WEIGHT

The weight of a species can be gauged from its **specific gravity**[2] The higher the specific gravity, the heavier the wood. To figure the precise weight of a board foot (1 × 12 × 12 inches) of a wood, multiply its specific gravity by the weight of a cubic foot of water, 62.5 pounds, then divide by 12. The weight of cherry, for example, is 2.6 pounds per board foot:

$$0.50 \times 62.5 \div 12 = 2.6$$

SEE *ALSO:*

| [1]Chemical Attributes | 346 |
| [2]Wood Strength | 9 |

MORE *SOURCES*

Good Wood Handbook, by Albert Jackson and David Day, F & W Publishing, 1993

Red Oaks and Black Birches, by Rebecca Rupp, Storey Communications, 1990

Wood and Woodworking Materials, by Nick Engler, Rodale Press, 1995

World Woods in Color, by William A. Lincoln, Linden Publishing Co., 1986

PHYSICAL PROPERTIES OF WOOD

UNFINISHED	FINISHED WITH:				
	TUNG OIL	ORANGE SHELLAC	POLYURETHANE	SPRAY LACQUER	WATER-BASED VARNISH

DOMESTIC HARDWOODS

ALDER, RED ● WESTERN NORTH AMERICA ● FINE TEXTURE ● STRAIGHT GRAIN ● 2.14 LB/BF

ASH ● NORTH AMERICA ● COARSE TEXTURE ● STRAIGHT GRAIN ● 3.13 LB/BF

ASPEN ● NORTH AMERICA ● MEDIUM TEXTURE ● STRAIGHT GRAIN ● 1.98 LB/BF

BASSWOOD ● EASTERN NORTH AMERICA ● FINE TEXTURE ● STRAIGHT GRAIN ● 1.93 LB/BF

BEECH ● EASTERN NORTH AMERICA ● MEDIUM TEXTURE ● STRAIGHT GRAIN ● 3.34 LB/BF

BIRCH, YELLOW ● EASTERN NORTH AMERICA ● MEDIUM TEXTURE ● STRAIGHT AND WAVY GRAIN ● 3.23 LB/BF

BUTTERNUT ● NORTHEASTERN NORTH AMERICA ● MEDIUM TEXTURE ● STRAIGHT AND IRREGULAR GRAIN ● 1.98 LB/BF

(continued)

PHYSICAL PROPERTIES OF WOOD — CONTINUED

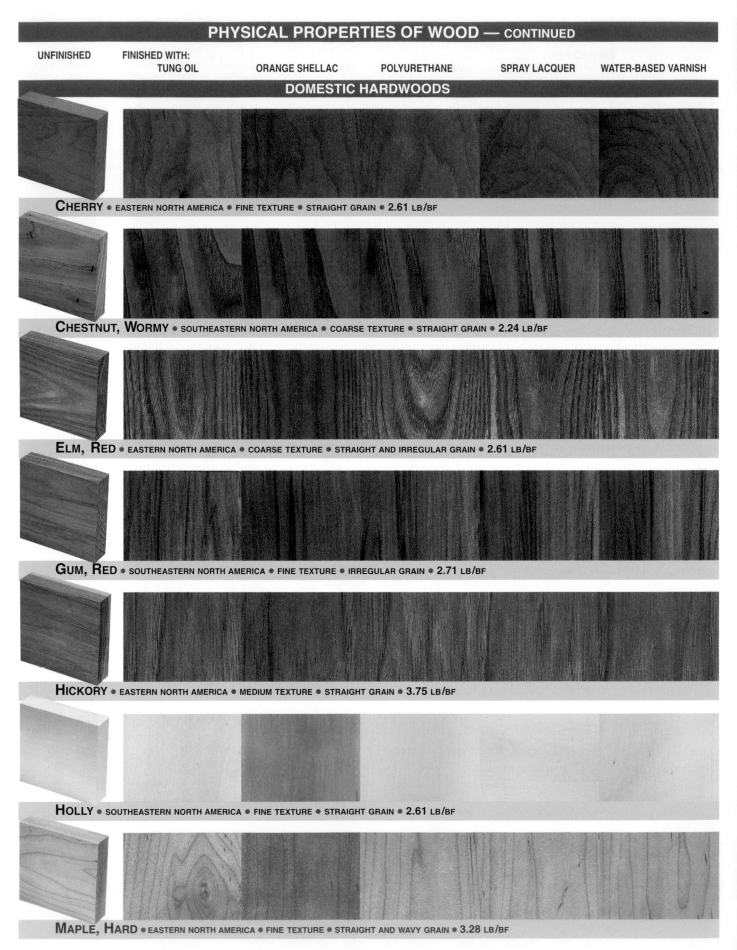

| UNFINISHED | FINISHED WITH: TUNG OIL | ORANGE SHELLAC | POLYURETHANE | SPRAY LACQUER | WATER-BASED VARNISH |

DOMESTIC HARDWOODS

CHERRY ● EASTERN NORTH AMERICA ● FINE TEXTURE ● STRAIGHT GRAIN ● 2.61 LB/BF

CHESTNUT, WORMY ● SOUTHEASTERN NORTH AMERICA ● COARSE TEXTURE ● STRAIGHT GRAIN ● 2.24 LB/BF

ELM, RED ● EASTERN NORTH AMERICA ● COARSE TEXTURE ● STRAIGHT AND IRREGULAR GRAIN ● 2.61 LB/BF

GUM, RED ● SOUTHEASTERN NORTH AMERICA ● FINE TEXTURE ● IRREGULAR GRAIN ● 2.71 LB/BF

HICKORY ● EASTERN NORTH AMERICA ● MEDIUM TEXTURE ● STRAIGHT GRAIN ● 3.75 LB/BF

HOLLY ● SOUTHEASTERN NORTH AMERICA ● FINE TEXTURE ● STRAIGHT GRAIN ● 2.61 LB/BF

MAPLE, HARD ● EASTERN NORTH AMERICA ● FINE TEXTURE ● STRAIGHT AND WAVY GRAIN ● 3.28 LB/BF

PHYSICAL PROPERTIES OF WOOD — CONTINUED

UNFINISHED	FINISHED WITH: TUNG OIL	ORANGE SHELLAC	POLYURETHANE	SPRAY LACQUER	WATER-BASED VARNISH

DOMESTIC HARDWOODS

MAPLE, SOFT ● EASTERN NORTH AMERICA ● MEDIUM TEXTURE ● STRAIGHT AND WAVY GRAIN ● 2.81 LB/BF

OAK, RED ● NORTH AMERICA ● MEDIUM AND COARSE TEXTURE ● STRAIGHT GRAIN ● 3.28 LB/BF

OAK, WHITE ● QUARTERSAWN ● NORTH AMERICA ● MEDIUM AND COARSE TEXTURE ● STRAIGHT GRAIN ● 3.54 LB/BF

OSAGE ORANGE ● NORTH AMERICA ● FINE TEXTURE ● IRREGULAR GRAIN ● 4.01 LB/BF

POPLAR, YELLOW ● EASTERN NORTH AMERICA ● MEDIUM TEXTURE ● STRAIGHT GRAIN ● 2.19 LB/BF

SASSAFRAS ● EASTERN NORTH AMERICA ● COARSE TEXTURE ● STRAIGHT GRAIN ● 2.40 LB/BF

SYCAMORE ● QUARTERSAWN ● EASTERN NORTH AMERICA ● MEDIUM TEXTURE ● IRREGULAR GRAIN ● 2.55 LB/BF

(continued)

PHYSICAL PROPERTIES OF WOOD — CONTINUED

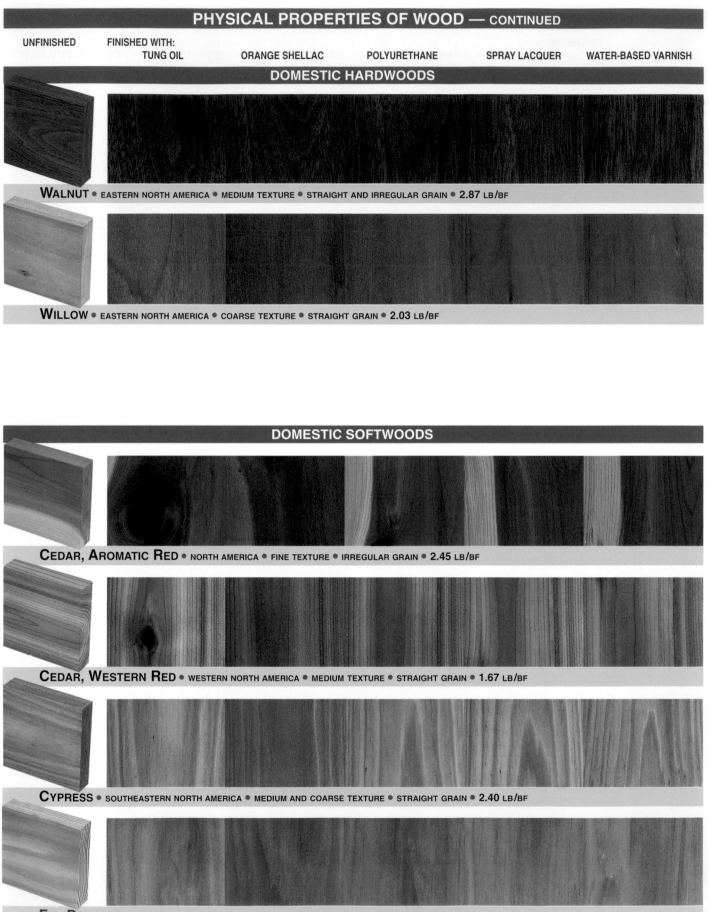

UNFINISHED	FINISHED WITH: TUNG OIL	ORANGE SHELLAC	POLYURETHANE	SPRAY LACQUER	WATER-BASED VARNISH

DOMESTIC HARDWOODS

WALNUT ● EASTERN NORTH AMERICA ● MEDIUM TEXTURE ● STRAIGHT AND IRREGULAR GRAIN ● 2.87 LB/BF

WILLOW ● EASTERN NORTH AMERICA ● COARSE TEXTURE ● STRAIGHT GRAIN ● 2.03 LB/BF

DOMESTIC SOFTWOODS

CEDAR, AROMATIC RED ● NORTH AMERICA ● FINE TEXTURE ● IRREGULAR GRAIN ● 2.45 LB/BF

CEDAR, WESTERN RED ● WESTERN NORTH AMERICA ● MEDIUM TEXTURE ● STRAIGHT GRAIN ● 1.67 LB/BF

CYPRESS ● SOUTHEASTERN NORTH AMERICA ● MEDIUM AND COARSE TEXTURE ● STRAIGHT GRAIN ● 2.40 LB/BF

FIR, DOUGLAS ● WESTERN NORTH AMERICA ● COARSE TEXTURE ● STRAIGHT GRAIN ● 2.50 LB/BF

PHYSICAL PROPERTIES OF WOOD — CONTINUED

UNFINISHED	FINISHED WITH: TUNG OIL	ORANGE SHELLAC	POLYURETHANE	SPRAY LACQUER	WATER-BASED VARNISH

DOMESTIC SOFTWOODS

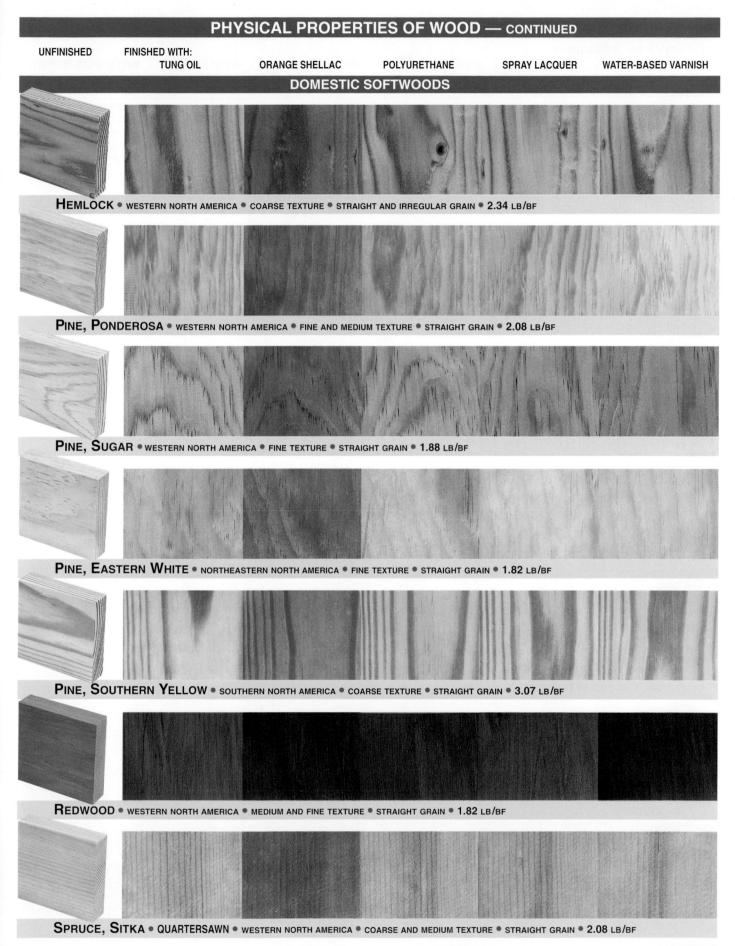

HEMLOCK • WESTERN NORTH AMERICA • COARSE TEXTURE • STRAIGHT AND IRREGULAR GRAIN • 2.34 LB/BF

PINE, PONDEROSA • WESTERN NORTH AMERICA • FINE AND MEDIUM TEXTURE • STRAIGHT GRAIN • 2.08 LB/BF

PINE, SUGAR • WESTERN NORTH AMERICA • FINE TEXTURE • STRAIGHT GRAIN • 1.88 LB/BF

PINE, EASTERN WHITE • NORTHEASTERN NORTH AMERICA • FINE TEXTURE • STRAIGHT GRAIN • 1.82 LB/BF

PINE, SOUTHERN YELLOW • SOUTHERN NORTH AMERICA • COARSE TEXTURE • STRAIGHT GRAIN • 3.07 LB/BF

REDWOOD • WESTERN NORTH AMERICA • MEDIUM AND FINE TEXTURE • STRAIGHT GRAIN • 1.82 LB/BF

SPRUCE, SITKA • QUARTERSAWN • WESTERN NORTH AMERICA • COARSE AND MEDIUM TEXTURE • STRAIGHT GRAIN • 2.08 LB/BF

(continued)

PHYSICAL PROPERTIES OF WOOD — CONTINUED

UNFINISHED	FINISHED WITH: TUNG OIL	ORANGE SHELLAC	POLYURETHANE	SPRAY LACQUER	WATER-BASED VARNISH

IMPORTED HARDWOODS

BALSA • CENTRAL AND SOUTH AMERICA • COARSE TEXTURE • STRAIGHT GRAIN • 0.83 LB/BF

BOCOTE • CENTRAL AND SOUTH AMERICA • MEDIUM TEXTURE • STRAIGHT AND INTERLOCKED GRAIN • 2.87 LB/BF

BUBINGA • ENDANGERED • WEST AFRICA • FINE TEXTURE • STRAIGHT GRAIN • 3.70 LB/BF

COCOBOLO • ENDANGERED • CENTRAL AMERICA • MEDIUM TEXTURE • INTERLOCKED GRAIN • 5.73 LB/BF

EBONY, GABOON • ENDANGERED • CENTRAL AFRICA • FINE TEXTURE • STRAIGHT AND IRREGULAR GRAIN • 5.37 LB/BF

GONCOLO ALVES • ENDANGERED • SOUTH AMERICA • COARSE TEXTURE • INTERLOCKED GRAIN • 4.38 LB/BF

JELUTONG • INDONESIA, MALAYSIA • FINE TEXTURE • STRAIGHT GRAIN • 1.88 LB/BF

PHYSICAL PROPERTIES OF WOOD — CONTINUED

UNFINISHED	FINISHED WITH: TUNG OIL	ORANGE SHELLAC	POLYURETHANE	SPRAY LACQUER	WATER-BASED VARNISH

IMPORTED HARDWOODS

LACEWOOD • QUARTERSAWN • EUROPE • COARSE TEXTURE • STRAIGHT GRAIN • 3.23 LB/BF

MAHOGANY, AFRICAN • QUARTERSAWN • WEST AFRICA • MEDIUM TEXTURE • INTERLOCKED GRAIN • 2.19 LB/BF

MAHOGANY, HONDURAN • ENDANGERED • CENTRAL AMERICA • MEDIUM TEXTURE • STRAIGHT AND IRREGULAR GRAIN • 2.34 LB/BF

MAHOGANY, PHILIPPINE, LAUAN • INDONESIA, MALAYSIA • COARSE TEXTURE • STRAIGHT AND INTERLOCKED GRAIN • 2.08 LB/BF

MAHOGANY, PHILIPPINE, MERANTI • QUARTERSAWN • MALAYSIA • FINE AND MEDIUM TEXTURE • STRAIGHT AND IINTERLOCKED GRAIN • 2.08 LB/BF

PADAUK • ENDANGERED • WEST AFRICA, INDONESIA • COARSE TEXTURE • STRAIGHT AND INTERLOCKED GRAIN • 3.75 LB/BF

PURPLEHEART • CENTRAL AND SOUTH AMERICA • FINE TEXTURE • STRAIGHT AND WAVY GRAIN • 3.49 LB/BF

(continued)

PHYSICAL PROPERTIES OF WOOD — CONTINUED

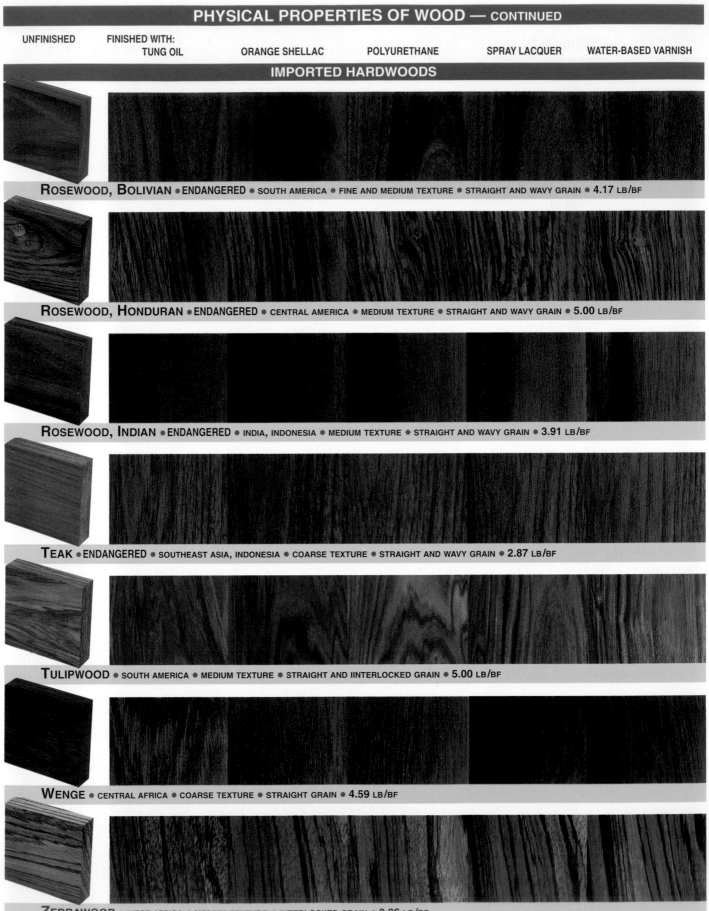

UNFINISHED	FINISHED WITH: TUNG OIL	ORANGE SHELLAC	POLYURETHANE	SPRAY LACQUER	WATER-BASED VARNISH

IMPORTED HARDWOODS

ROSEWOOD, BOLIVIAN ● ENDANGERED ● SOUTH AMERICA ● FINE AND MEDIUM TEXTURE ● STRAIGHT AND WAVY GRAIN ● 4.17 LB/BF

ROSEWOOD, HONDURAN ● ENDANGERED ● CENTRAL AMERICA ● MEDIUM TEXTURE ● STRAIGHT AND WAVY GRAIN ● 5.00 LB/BF

ROSEWOOD, INDIAN ● ENDANGERED ● INDIA, INDONESIA ● MEDIUM TEXTURE ● STRAIGHT AND WAVY GRAIN ● 3.91 LB/BF

TEAK ● ENDANGERED ● SOUTHEAST ASIA, INDONESIA ● COARSE TEXTURE ● STRAIGHT AND WAVY GRAIN ● 2.87 LB/BF

TULIPWOOD ● SOUTH AMERICA ● MEDIUM TEXTURE ● STRAIGHT AND IINTERLOCKED GRAIN ● 5.00 LB/BF

WENGE ● CENTRAL AFRICA ● COARSE TEXTURE ● STRAIGHT GRAIN ● 4.59 LB/BF

ZEBRAWOOD ● WEST AFRICA ● MEDIUM TEXTURE ● INTERLOCKED GRAIN ● 3.86 LB/BF

HEALTH HAZARDS FROM WOODS

Like many other plants, trees produce antibiotic chemicals to protect themselves from the organisms that cause disease and decay. These may also have an unpleasant effect on craftsmen who come in intimate contact with the wood.

WOOD-RELATED AILMENTS

Chemicals in wood have been found to cause or contribute to:
- Nausea and headaches
- Kidney and liver malfunction
- Skin rashes and eye irritation
- Asthma, emphysema, and other respiratory problems
- Nasal cancer

This can be a problem for craftsmen, but it shouldn't be blown out of proportion. Not everyone is affected by the potentially toxic chemicals in wood. Only 2 to 5 people out of 100 develop an unhealthy sensitivity to them, although woodworkers have an increased risk. And not many woods contain enough chemicals to be dangerous. There are just a few troublesome species, listed in the chart below.

IRRITANTS AND SENSITIZERS

There are two common ways that a wood may affect your health – as either an *irritant* or a *sensitizer*. Irritants bother most craftsmen, at least to a small degree. These effects may be mechanical rather than chemical – fine sawdust tickles your nasal passages and makes you sneeze. More often, though, it's the chemicals in the sawdust that irritate you. The tannic acid in oak, for example, is a powerful irritant.

Sensitizers affect only those people who are allergic to them. Allergic reactions range from a runny nose and watery eyes to hives and asthma. Furthermore, repeated exposure often causes greater sensitivity, and the reaction becomes more severe.

A very few woods contain chemicals which cause *systemic* reactions, affecting the stomach, nerves, kidneys, even the heart. Oleander and yew, for example, contain chemicals similar to digitalis, a heart drug.

LIMITING EXPOSURE

What can you do to limit your exposure? Quite a bit.
- Wear a dust mask. The most common way you get wood chemicals into your body is by inhaling them.
- Use a dust collector when running power tools.
- Ventilate your shop and clean it frequently.
- Keep your shop cool. Heat causes you to perspire. This mixes with sawdust and releases more toxic chemicals.

Just as important, you should not expose other people. Never use potentially toxic woods to make cutting boards, bowls, or eating utensils. Also avoid them for toys, jewelry, and items that someone might put in their mouth or rub against their skin.

One more precaution: See a doctor if you have recurrent nosebleeds or persistent sinus infections when you work wood. These are causes for special concern.

MORE *SOURCES*

AMA Handbook of Poisonous and Injurious Plants, by Dr. Kenneth Lampe and Mary Anne McCann, American Medical Association, 1985

Woods Injurious to Human Health, by Bjorn M. Hausen, Walter de Gruyter Inc., 1981

TROUBLESOME WOODS

Species	Irritant	Sensitizer	Species	Irritant	Sensitizer
Cedar, Western Red	No	Yes	Oleander	Yes	No
Cocobolo	Yes	No	Padauk	Yes	No
Ebony	Yes	Maybe	Peroba Rosa	Yes	Maybe
Fir, Douglas	Yes	Maybe	Rosewood, Bolivian	No	Yes
Goncolo Alves	No	Yes	Rosewood, Honduran	No	Yes
Ipe	No	Yes	Rosewood, Indian	No	Yes
Iroko	Yes	Maybe	Sassafras	Yes	Maybe
Kingwood	No	Yes	Satinwood	Yes	No
Lacewood	Yes	Maybe	Spruce	No	Yes
Mansonia	Yes	Yes	Teak	No	Yes
Myrtle, Oregon	Yes	Maybe	Tulipwood	No	Yes
Oak, Red	Yes	No	Walnut	Yes	Maybe
Oak, White	Yes	No	Yew	Yes	No

32

Plywood and Particleboard

Sheet materials offer unique properties that aren't available in lumber, simplifying and expanding the scope of your woodworking.

In the mid-nineteenth century, John Henry Belter, a German immigrant working in New York, began to produce **Victorian Rococo Revival**[1] furniture. This style was extremely elaborate, in both construction and decoration. In need of a strong, stable material that he could carve with delicate decorations, Belter invented a method of laying up veneers in **curved shapes**[2]. In effect, Belter made the first plywood furniture.

Belter's techniques were widely imitated, and American craftsmen soon found that plywood offered other advantages. Turning trees into plywood produced larger quantities of useful material than sawing them into lumber. By the early twentieth century, plywood was an indispensable woodworking material, commonly available in sheets of standard sizes.

Other engineered wood products soon followed as sawyers found new ways to create large panels from smaller and smaller pieces of wood. Today, there are dozens of sheet materials made from wood products of every size, from large chips to individual fibers.

Photo by Jonathan Barber

*Many modern furniture forms would be difficult or impossible to make without sheet materials. This Art Deco **Platform Bed and Headboard,** for example, depends on plywood and particleboard to provide the strength and stability needed to support vast expanses of figured veneer.*

SPECS:	42″ high, 104″ wide, 81″ long
MATERIALS:	Cherry, padauk, ebonized cherry, ebony, cherry veneer, eucalyptus veneer, maple plywood, and medium-density fiberboard
CRAFTSMAN:	Andrew Pate Greenwich, NY

PLYWOOD COMPOSITION

Plywood is a laminated panel, made up of several thin layers (or *plies*) glued face to face. Every sheet has a veneer *face,* the side that shows the highest-quality wood grain. The opposite side is the *back,* and the material in between makes up the *core.* These are glued up in broad sheets and typically trimmed to 48 inches wide and 96 inches long.

GRAIN DIRECTION

The face and back are always **wood veneer**[3], but the inside layers may be other materials such as **particleboard or fiberboard**[4]. The grain direction in the veneer plies alternates – each layer is perpendicular to the adjacent layers. Those layers in which the wood grain runs opposite the face and back are *crossbands.* This arrangement restricts the **wood movement**[5] and prevents it from expanding and contracting as much as it would otherwise.

NUMBER OF PLIES

Plywood typically has an odd number of plies so the wood grain in the face and back are parallel to one another. More importantly, this arrangement keeps the assembly *balanced* so it doesn't warp or twist. If, for some reason, the plywood has an even number of plies, the wood grain in the two middle plies are parallel so they behave as one. If the plywood has a particleboard or fiberboard core, it's sandwiched between face and back veneers, making an odd number of layers.

PLYWOOD CHARACTERISTICS

Because of its crossbanded composition, plywood has several important characteristics.

■ *Stability* – Plywood is more stable *across its width* than solid wood. However, it's not completely stable; it *does* move. It expands and contracts across its thickness every bit as much as solid wood, and there is a small amount of movement along its length, generally between 0.1 and 0.2 percent. A 48-inch-wide sheet may expand and contract about 1/16 inch over the course of a year.

> **PRO** *TIP*
>
> **Shop-dry**[6] your plywood, even though it's more stable than wood. Large sheets are still subject to significant movement.

■ *Strength* – Contrary to a popular misconception, plywood is not necessarily stronger than the wood from which it's made. Its *shear strength* is greater – it will not split as easily. But it's not as **stiff**[7] as solid wood.

■ *Gluing and fastening* – Plywood can be glued easily and forms as strong a bond as solid wood. But it differs in its ability to hold nails and screws. If you drive the fasteners through the plies, plywood will hold them better than wood because of the crossbanding. But when driven parallel to the plies, the fasteners don't hold as well.

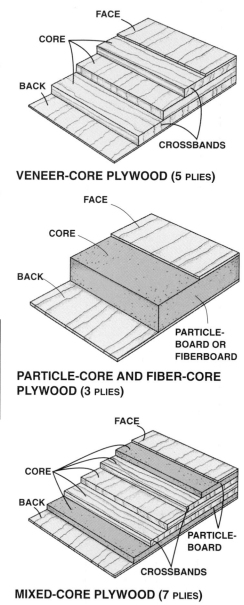

VENEER-CORE PLYWOOD (5 PLIES)

PARTICLE-CORE AND FIBER-CORE PLYWOOD (3 PLIES)

MIXED-CORE PLYWOOD (7 PLIES)

> **PRO** *TIP*
>
> For a better hold in plywood and particleboard, use twin-threaded *utility screws.*

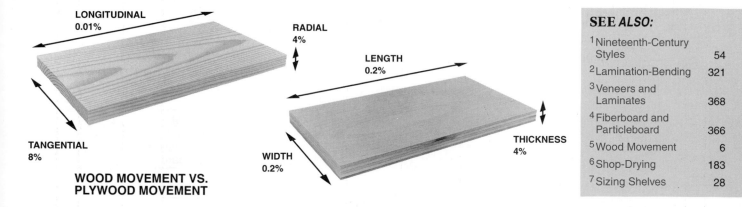

WOOD MOVEMENT VS. PLYWOOD MOVEMENT

LONGITUDINAL 0.01%

TANGENTIAL 8%

RADIAL 4%

LENGTH 0.2%

WIDTH 0.2%

THICKNESS 4%

PLYWOOD TYPES

There are two general categories of plywood – *construction* and *cabinet*. Construction plywood is used almost exclusively in the building trades; most woodworkers work with the cabinet variety. Cabinet plywood is classified by several criteria.

THICKNESS

Cabinet plywoods are anywhere from 1/8 to 3 inches thick, but the commonly available thicknesses are 1/4, 3/8, 1/2, and 3/4 inch. These are *nominal* thicknesses only; most plywood is 1/32 inch thinner than the label would have you believe.

CORE CONSTRUCTION

There are four types of plywood cores commonly available:

■ *Veneer-core plywood* is the most common and provides the greatest stability.

■ *Particle-core plywood* has a **particleboard**[1] core. This is the weakest and least expensive type.

■ *Fiber-core plywood* has a core made from **hardboard**[1] or **medium-density fiberboard**[1]. It's weak but very stable and perfectly flat.

■ *Mixed-core plywood* is made from both veneers and particleboard, a compromise between strength and economy.

ADHESIVES

The adhesives used to bond the plies are classified according to their ability to resist moisture.

■ *Exterior plywood* can be used inside or out. It won't fall apart in a wet environment.

■ *Interior plywood* is intended for inside use only. It's made with moisture-resistant adhesives that take some wetting but delaminate if constantly exposed.

CORE SPECIES

Plywood cores are made from both **hardwoods and softwoods**[2].

■ *Softwood plywood* is normally used for construction, but some of the better grades are suitable for cabinetry.

■ *Hardwood plywood* is generally higher in quality and is preferred for fine woodworking.

PLYWOOD GRADES

Plywood is graded with a two-character code. The first indicates the quality of the veneer face, and the second the back. Softwood and hardwood plywoods are graded differently.

■ *Softwood plywood grades* – The face and back veneers are graded with letter codes. N, A, and B provide a smooth surface. C-plugged, C, and D have increasing numbers of defects.

■ *Hardwood plywood grades* – The *face* veneers of domestic hardwood plywood are graded with letter codes. AA, A, and B are best; C, D, and E are utility grades. The *back* veneers are graded with number codes – 1 and 2 are smooth and sound; 3 and 4 have increasingly more defects.

■ *Imported plywood grades* – Hardwood plywoods made overseas are graded differently than those made in America. The face veneers are graded BBPF, BB, CC, and OVL, in descending order of quality. The back veneers are A or B, with A being better.

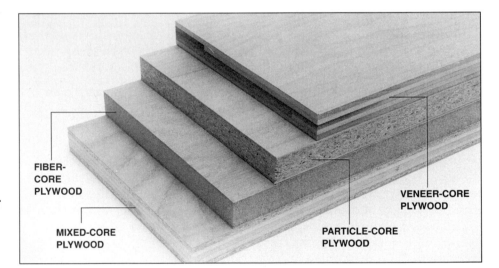

FIBER-CORE PLYWOOD

MIXED-CORE PLYWOOD

VENEER-CORE PLYWOOD

PARTICLE-CORE PLYWOOD

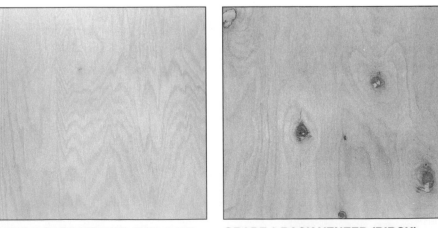

GRADE B FACE VENEER (RED OAK)

GRADE 3 BACK VENEER (BIRCH)

SPECIAL-PURPOSE PLYWOOD

Some plywoods are designed for special purposes:

■ *Painting – Medium-density overlay* (MDO) plywood has a thin, resin-impregnated paper overlay on one or both sides to provide a smooth base for paint. It's made with exterior adhesive and is often used for outdoor signs.

■ *Outdoor projects – Marine plywood* is a top-quality, cabinet-grade exterior plywood. It has A- and B-grade faces and a core with no voids, and it is laminated with waterproof glue.

■ *Bending –* You can curve **bendable plywood**[3] around a corner. This material has only three plies – a thick face and back laminated to a thin veneer core.

■ *Strength and stability –* **European birch plywood**[4] is made from high-quality veneer layers with few voids. The layers are thinner than average, they are all the same thickness, and there are more of them. These characteristics increase the strength and stability of the material. In Europe, this is referred to as *multi-ply*.

MORE INFO

Unlike American plywood, European birch comes in sheets approximately 60 inches square. The thicknesses are metric, but they roughly correspond to the thicknesses of domestic sheet materials.

BENDABLE PLYWOOD

EUROPEAN BIRCH PLYWOOD

MEDIUM-DENSITY OVERLAY

MARINE PLYWOOD

READING GRADE STAMPS AND STICKERS

Most plywood has a *grade stamp* or a *grade sticker* to show the species and the quality of the veneers. In addition, the stamp or sticker may also indicate **how the face veneer was cut**[5]. ROT indicates a *rotary cut* — the face was sliced from the log in a continuous tangential cut. This shows unnaturally wide bands of **springwood and summerwood**[6]. FLAT indicates veneers that look more like ordinary boards joined edge to edge. Depending on the manufacturer, these veneers may be *slip-matched* or *book-matched*.

NOTE: Construction plywood is stamped on its back, but cabinet plywood is stamped or stickered on the edge to keep the veneer surfaces clean.

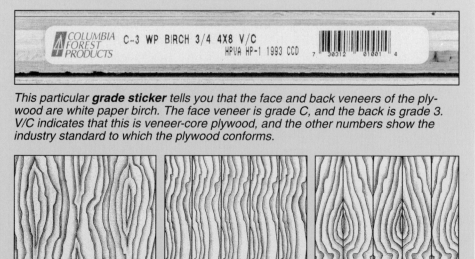

COLUMBIA FOREST PRODUCTS   C-3 WP BIRCH 3/4 4X8 V/C   HPVA HP-1 1993 CCD   7 30312 01001 4

*This particular **grade sticker** tells you that the face and back veneers of the plywood are white paper birch. The face veneer is grade C, and the back is grade 3. V/C indicates that this is veneer-core plywood, and the other numbers show the industry standard to which the plywood conforms.*

ROTARY-CUT VENEER   **SLIP-MATCHED VENEER**   **BOOK-MATCHED VENEER**

FIBERBOARD AND PARTICLEBOARD

Two additional sheet materials are commonly used in woodworking:

■ *Fiberboard* is made by reconstituting **wood fibers**[1].

■ *Particleboard* is formed from small pieces of wood glued together.

FIBERBOARD

To make fiberboard, the wood is chopped, ground, and heated until it separates into individual fibers. To bond them back together, they are compressed and heated at the same time – a process known as *interfelting*. This turns the **lignin**[1] on the outside of the **cellulose**[1] fibers semi-liquid and sticks them to one another. Occasionally glues and other binders are added to improve the bond, as well as other chemicals to improve the strength, durability, water resistance, and fire resistance of the sheet material.

There are four common types of fiberboard:

■ *Insulation board* is a lightweight material used mostly in construction for sheathing, ceiling tiles, and similar products.

■ *Hardboard* is much heavier. There are two types – *tempered* and *standard*. Tempered hardboard is sprayed with resin after it's interfelted, then baked to make the material harder, stronger, and more water-resistant. Standard hardboard is not treated, and it's softer and easier to bend.

■ *Medium-density fiberboard* (MDF) has resin added before it's interfelted. It's very stable, remains **perfectly flat**[2], and offers a smooth surface that can be shaped and molded like solid wood.

■ *Laminated paperboard* is made in two steps. First the fibers are made into paper, then layers of paper are pressed together. Often, the outside layers are printed with a pattern, color, or simulated wood grain.

PARTICLEBOARD

Particleboard is made from wood particles of all sizes, from sawdust to large chips. After being chipped, planed, or ground up, the particles are sprayed with adhesive resin and pressed into sheets.

The characteristics of a sheet are determined by the adhesive used, the density of the material, and the size and shape of the particles. Consequently, particleboard is graded with a three-letter code that corresponds to these factors.

ADHESIVE

■**1** indicates interior use only.

■**2** means the material can be used on the exterior and in wet locations.

DENSITY

■**H** denotes high density (over 53 pounds per cubic foot).

■**M** indicates medium density (38 to 53 pounds).

■**L** is low density (less than 38 pounds).

PARTICLE SIZE

■**1** indicates the material is made from extremely small particles (fiber bundles).

■**2** is run-of-the-mill sawdust.

■**3** denotes large particles such as planer shavings.

■**F** stands for flakes.

■**W** tells you the material is made from large wafers or strands.

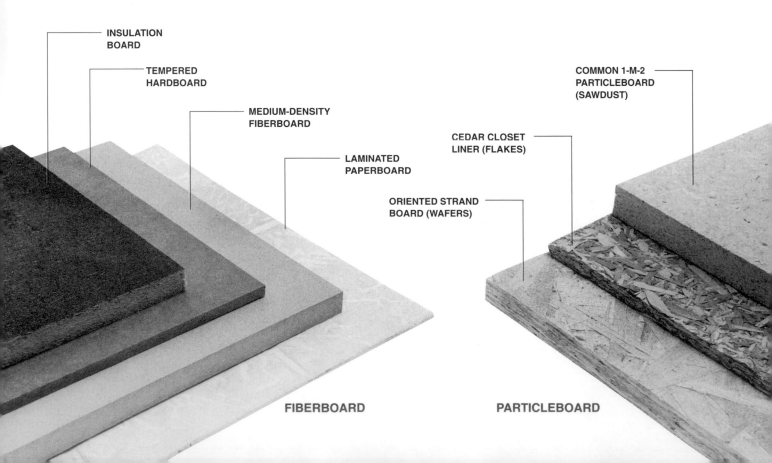

INSULATION BOARD

TEMPERED HARDBOARD

MEDIUM-DENSITY FIBERBOARD

LAMINATED PAPERBOARD

COMMON 1-M-2 PARTICLEBOARD (SAWDUST)

CEDAR CLOSET LINER (FLAKES)

ORIENTED STRAND BOARD (WAFERS)

FIBERBOARD

PARTICLEBOARD

Larger particles result in a rougher surface but greater strength and stiffness. Particleboard made from F- and W-sized particles is strong enough to be used for structural panels in construction. Manufacturers further increase the strength by aligning the wood grain in the particles. *Oriented strand board* is made from W-sized particles laid down in layers. The wood grain in each layer is perpendicular to the adjacent layers. It's not as strong as plywood, but it's much stronger than ordinary particleboard.

Most of the particleboard used in woodworking is made with interior glue and has a medium density. The most important factor is particle size. If you need a smooth surface for painting or **veneering**[3], choose materials made with 1- or 2-sized particles. When choosing a core for **plastic laminates**[4], look for 2- or 3-sized particles. There are also sheets made with special *resin-impregnated paper coatings* (such as Melamine) that are designed especially for cabinets, shelves, and built-ins.

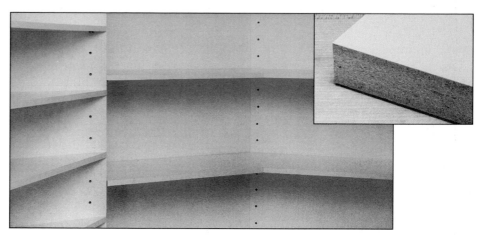

The particleboard used to make the shelving in this storage closet is coated with plastic resin–impregnated paper, about 1/100 inch thick. Although extremely thin, this produces a smooth, hard finish. It's also waterproof and chemical resistant.

MORE *SOURCES*

Wood Handbook: Wood As an Engineering Material, by the U.S. Forest Products Laboratory, U.S. Government Printing Office, 1987

Wood and Woodworking Materials, by Nick Engler, Rodale Press, 1995

SEE *ALSO:*

JIGS & FIXTURES

SHEET CADDY Plywood, fiberboard, and particleboard are all somewhat unwieldy. Large sheets — especially *thick* sheets — can be difficult to move around your shop. This **sheet caddy** makes it easier. Ropes attached to the caddy hook around the bottom corners of a sheet, allowing you to lift and carry even full-sized (4 × 8 feet) sheets in a comfortable position.

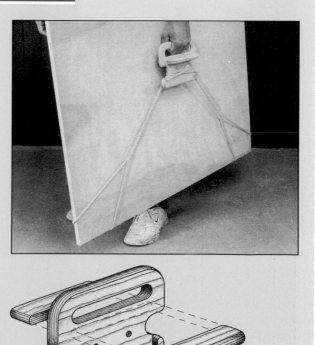

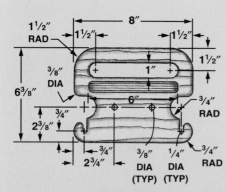

1½" RAD — 1½" — 8" — 1½" — 1½"
1"
3/8" DIA
6 3/8"
6"
2 3/8"
3/4"
3/4" RAD
3/4" RAD
2 3/4"   3/8" DIA (TYP)   1/4" DIA (TYP)

FRONT VIEW

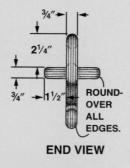

3/4"
2 1/4"
3/4" — 1 1/2"
ROUND-OVER ALL EDGES.

END VIEW

NOTE: USE 1/4" HOLLOW-BRAID POLY-ROPE, 16' LONG WITH 24" LOOPS AT END AND 6"-LONG SPLICE.

SHEET CADDY

EXPLODED VIEW

Veneers and Laminates

In woodworking, as elsewhere, beauty is only skin deep.

Although veneers have been used in woodworking for thousands of years, only recently have they become commonplace. The earliest veneers were split or sawn from exceptional woods, then hand-scraped paper-thin – a laborious process that few could afford. It wasn't until the seventeenth century that the invention of the *veneer saw* – a slender, fine-tooth blade in a wooden frame – made it possible to produce veneer economically. Much of the **classic furniture**[1] from the eighteenth and early nineteenth centuries is decorated with sawed veneers.

Since then, the use of veneer has expanded tremendously. Not only do contemporary craftsmen use veneers to **enhance plain surfaces**[2], they also laminate veneers to make **plywood sheets**[3] and **curved shapes**[4]. Additionally, we have developed artificial veneers or *plastic laminates* made from paper and plastic resin. These not only decorate surfaces, they make them waterproof, chemically resistant, and remarkably durable.

VENEERS

Although veneers were once sawed, nowadays all but the most brittle woods are sliced. This, in fact, is the modern definition of the word – a *veneer* is a thin slice of a log or timber.

Photo by John Kane

*You can produce striking visual effects with veneers that you can't create with solid woods, as this Studio-style **Writing Table and Chair** show. The grain directions on the table aprons and chair rails are **vertical** for a dramatic look. If they were solid wood, this would make them weak. But what you see is veneer, applied over a strong, solid core.*

SPECS:	31″ high, 18″ wide, 18″ deep (chair)
	29″ high, 21″ wide, 50″ long (table)
MATERIALS:	English brown oak solids and veneer, leather
CRAFTSMAN:	James Shriber New Milford, CT

VENEER THICKNESSES

How thin is veneer? There are several standard thicknesses, each with specific uses.

- $1/128$- to $1/100$-inch-thick slices are used to make *reinforced veneers* (also called flexible veneers). These super-thin slices are typically bonded to sheets of paper, cloth, or plastic, depending on how and where the veneer will be used. Reinforced veneers are often applied to tightly curved surfaces.

- $1/40$- to $1/28$-inch-thick slices are *common veneers*. These either dress up flat surfaces in furniture and cabinets, or they are used as **face or back veneers**[3] in making plywood.

- $1/10$- to $3/16$-inch-thick veneers make up the middle plies or **cores**[3] of plywood.

Although it's possible to slice wood into considerably thicker pieces, anything over $1/4$ inch is not considered to be a veneer. Instead, it's known as *slicewood*. This is sometimes used in the manufacture of plywood and other sheet materials.

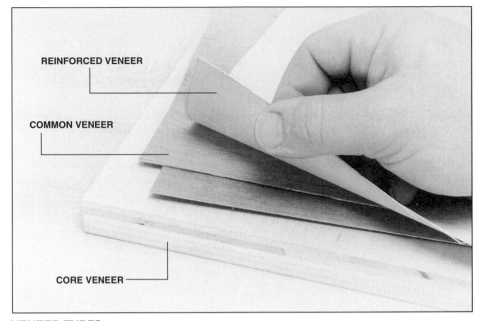

VENEER TYPES

REINFORCED VENEER
COMMON VENEER
CORE VENEER

MORE *INFO*

Common veneers sliced from inexpensive, ho-hum woods are used as *utility veneers*. These may be applied under a decorative face veneer to smooth the surface, or on the back side of a veneered panel to stabilize it.

SLICING VENEER

Veneer is sliced hot and green – high temperature and moisture content soften the wood fibers so the knife makes smooth cuts. Often, the logs are stored in ponds or pools to keep them from drying out, then cooked for several days prior to cutting.

There are three different methods for slicing veneer from a log.

ROTARY CUTTING

A whole log is mounted between the *centers* of a *veneer lathe*. This machine spins the log like a giant spindle turning. As the log rotates, a long *knife* shaves the circumference and produces a continuous ribbon of veneer, as wide as the log is long. A *pressure bar* presses against the log just ahead of the cut to prevent the veneer from splitting. This is a fast and efficient way to produce veneer. However, because the knife makes a continuous **tangential**[5] cut, rotary cut sheets show **flat grain**[5] only. Furthermore, the bands of **springwood and summerwood**[5] are unnaturally wide.

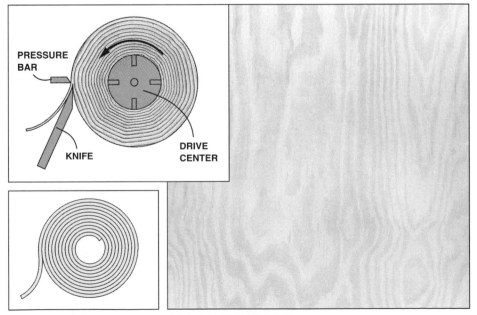

PRESSURE BAR
KNIFE
DRIVE CENTER

ROTARY CUTTING   **ROTARY-CUT VENEER**

FLITCH CUTTING

The log is halved or quartered into pieces known as *flitches*. The flitches are mounted on a *veneer slicer,* held to a *carriage* by two sets of *dogs.* The carriage moves the flitches past a *knife,* slicing a sheet of veneer. As with rotary cutting, a *pressure bar* keeps the veneer from splitting as it's cut. Depending on how the flitch is held, the slices will show flat grain, quarter grain, or anything in between. Consequently, flitch-cut veneer looks a lot like solid wood when it's applied to a surface.

STAY-LOG CUTTING

The log is mounted off-center on an *eccentric chuck* and swung past a *knife* and *pressure bar,* slicing an arc through the wood. In many cases, the logs are sawn into flitches first, then the flitches are mounted and swung. As with flitch-cutting, this method produces several grain patterns, depending on how the log or flitch is held in relation to the knife.

MORE *INFO*

Flitch cutting and stay-log cutting both produce *leaves* of veneer. Often the leaves from a single flitch are sold together as a *book* of veneer. This lets the buyer match them for color and grain.

FLITCH-CUT VENEER

STAY-LOG-CUT VENEER

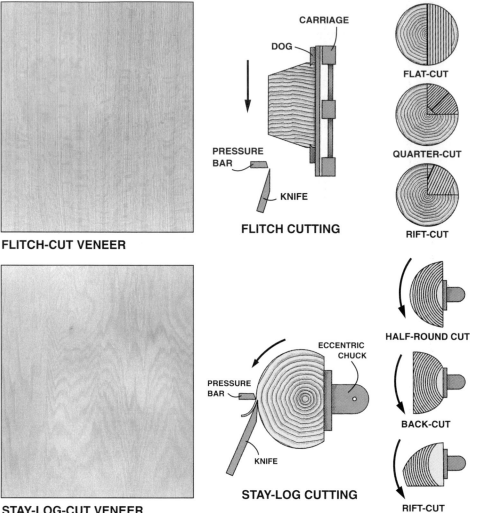

CARRIAGE

DOG

PRESSURE BAR

KNIFE

FLITCH CUTTING

FLAT-CUT

QUARTER-CUT

RIFT-CUT

HALF-ROUND CUT

ECCENTRIC CHUCK

PRESSURE BAR

KNIFE

STAY-LOG CUTTING

BACK-CUT

RIFT-CUT

After the logs or flitches are sliced, the green veneer is dried on a hot platen (a large metal plate) or in a kiln. Unlike lumber, which can take a week or more to dry, veneer is processed in just 10 to 20 minutes.

VENEER CORES

The material to which you apply the veneer is called the *core material* or the *ground.* Take care in selecting and preparing the core – it must be relatively stable and perfectly smooth. If it's not stable, or it expands and contracts at a different rate or in a different direction than the veneer, it may cause the veneer to split or buckle. If it's not smooth, imperfections will "telegraph" or show through the veneer. Some natural characteristics of specific woods will also telegraph. For instance, the difference in density between **springwood and summer-wood**[1] in **Douglas fir**[2] will create ridges in the veneer.

Hardwood plywood[3] makes a smooth, strong core. **Hardboard and medium-density fiberboard**[4] (MDF) are also good choices, although not as strong as plywood. If you use solid wood, select **quartersawn**[1] stock – it's more stable.

HARDWOOD PLYWOOD

HARDBOARD

MEDIUM-DENSITY FIBERBOARD

QUARTERSAWN WOOD

VENEER CORES

LAMINATES

Plastic laminates[5] are made by laminating multiple layers of paper. The back and core (middle) papers are bonded with *phenolic resin,* a durable plastic. This makes the laminates waterproof and highly resistant to chemicals, heat, and wear. The top paper layer is typically thicker than the others. It's printed with a decorative design or color and impregnated with clear *melamine resin* that lets the decoration show through. In some laminates, the decorative layer is covered with one or more super-thin, transparent paper layers to protect it from wear and tear.

Plastic laminates are available in many different colors, patterns, thicknesses, even textures.

LAMINATE TYPES

Five types of plastic laminates are commonly available:

■ *General-purpose* laminates are $1/16$ inch thick. They are intended for surfaces that see a good deal of use, such as the tops and edges of counters.

■ *Vertical-surface* laminates are $1/32$ inch thick and are used for the sides and other outside surfaces of cabinets that see less wear than the counters.

■ *Post-forming* laminates are no more than $1/32$ inch thick and are made with flexible resins that allow you to bend them around curved surfaces. Typically, you must warm these materials with a heat gun to fit them to their curved cores.

■ *Backing* laminates are just $1/50$ inch thick and do not come in colors or designs. They are applied to the backs of panels to **control warping**[4].

■ *Liner* laminates are similar to backing laminates, but they are available in colors. They are used to line the interiors of cabinets.

All of these types are available in large sheets of various sizes, from 24 to 48 inches wide and up to 12 feet long. The two most common sizes are 4 feet by 8 feet and 30 inches by 10 feet.

LAMINATE CORES

Like veneers, laminates are applied to core materials. A core must be reasonably smooth – laminates aren't as likely to telegraph surface imperfections as veneer, but large dents, gouges, and other imperfections will show through.

Stability is extremely important. Because a laminate doesn't move at all, the core must be as stable as possible. The best materials are **hardwood plywood**[1] **medium-density fiberboard, and particleboard**[2]

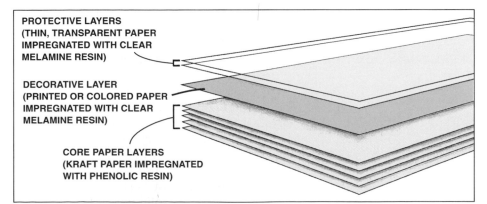

PROTECTIVE LAYERS
(THIN, TRANSPARENT PAPER
IMPREGNATED WITH CLEAR
MELAMINE RESIN)

DECORATIVE LAYER
(PRINTED OR COLORED PAPER
IMPREGNATED WITH CLEAR
MELAMINE RESIN)

CORE PAPER LAYERS
(KRAFT PAPER IMPREGNATED
WITH PHENOLIC RESIN)

PLASTIC LAMINATE COMPOSITION

MORE *SOURCES*

Understanding Wood, by Bruce Hoadley, Taunton Press, 1980

Wood Handbook: Wood As an Engineering Material, by the U.S. Forest Products Laboratory, U.S. Government Printing Office, 1987

Wood and Woodworking Materials, by Nick Engler, Rodale Press, 1995

Woodworking Hardware

You can't make every project from wood alone. Sometimes you need something a little harder.

Hardware includes all the fasteners and fittings required to make a woodworking project. For the most part, these are made from metal (hence the name), although an increasing number are made from plastic.

NAILS

A nail wedges itself between the wood fibers as you drive it into a board. Usually made from steel, nails may be coated with zinc to prevent them from rusting, or with glues to increase holding power.

COMMON NAIL
General-purpose; used mostly for construction; 1″ to 5″ long.

FINISHING NAIL
General-purpose; used when you want to bury or set the head in the wood to hide it; 1″ to 3″ long.

WIRE BRAD
Small, slender finishing nail, $\frac{3}{4}$″ to $1\frac{1}{4}$″ long.

CASING NAIL
Slightly larger head than a finishing nail; used to attach door and window casings; $1\frac{1}{4}$″ to $3\frac{1}{2}$″ long.

CUT NAIL
Used like common nails; some special shapes for flooring and casings; rectangular shank prevents splitting; $1\frac{1}{4}$″ to $3\frac{1}{2}$″ long.

PANEL NAIL
Used to attach sheet paneling; ribbed shanks provide extra holding power; available in colors to match paneling; 1″ to $1\frac{5}{8}$″ long.

CUT TACK
Used to attach fabric to upholstery frame in areas that will be hidden; $\frac{1}{2}$″ to $1\frac{1}{4}$″ long.

UPHOLSTERY NAIL
Used to attach fabric to a frame in areas that will remain visible; decorative head $\frac{1}{8}$″ to $\frac{1}{2}$″ in diameter.

DOWEL NAIL
Used for hidden nail joints; pointed on both ends; $1\frac{1}{2}$″ to 2″ long.

CORRUGATED FASTENER
Used to reinforce miter and butt joints; $\frac{7}{8}$″ to $1\frac{1}{4}$″ long.

MORE *INFO*

The sizes of some nails are given in *pennies* (abbreviated "d"). In the 1880s, this referred to the cost per hundred. You could buy 100 sixteen-penny (16d) nails for 16 cents. They cost a little more nowadays.

SCREWS

Screws are miniature clamps that pull the boards together as you drive them. They are usually made from a steel alloy but are also available in brass, bronze, aluminum, and stainless steel. They may be coated with chromium, zinc, cadmium, or bronze to prevent corrosion.

Screws are sold by length and gauge (the diameter of the shank). The higher the gauge number, the larger the diameter. The most common gauges are 4 ($^7/_{64}$ inch) through 14 ($^1/_4$ inch).

PRO *TIP*

To make screws easier to drive in hard or dense wood, apply wax or soap to the threads.

FLATHEAD WOOD SCREW
Used when screw head must be flush with wood; requires cutting a countersink in the wood.

ROUNDHEAD WOOD SCREW
Typically used for fastening decorative hardware.

OVAL-HEAD WOOD SCREW
Also used to attach hardware; sometimes used with a *screw cup.*

LAG SCREW
Used for heavy construction; has hex head.

SHEET-METAL SCREW
Used in woodworking for joining plywood or to join sheet metal, plastic, and fabric to wood; available with flat, round, oval, and pan heads.

UTILITY SCREW
Used to join sheet materials; coarse twin threads provide extra holding power.

DOWEL SCREW
Used for hidden screw joints.

FINISHING WASHER
Used in upholstery; provides a finished look for flathead and oval-head screws.

KNOCK-DOWN FITTINGS

Knock-down fittings are used to assemble furniture that may have to be dismantled from time to time. They are especially suited for pieces made from sheet materials.

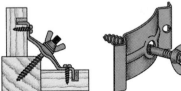

HANGER BOLT
Typically used with corner brackets to attach legs to aprons; has screw thread on one end, bolt thread on the other.

CORNER BRACKET
Used with hanger bolts to fasten legs to aprons; attaches to inside corner.

CROSS DOWEL AND BOLT
Used to attach right-angle joints; hardware is hidden inside wood.

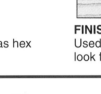

BLOCK JOINT
Also used to attach right-angle joints; attaches to inside corner.

CABINET CONNECTOR
Used to joining parts face to face.

PANEL CONNECTOR
Used to join panels edge to edge.

CAM CONNECTOR
Used for both corner and edge joints; extremely easy to connect, just turn cam.

TAPER CONNECTORS
Used to hang cabinets and join heavy framed components.

HIDING NAIL HEADS

1 *To completely hide a nail head, lift a sliver from the wood surface with a veiner or small gouge.*

2 *Drive the nail into the depression and set the head, then glue the sliver back in place.*

HINGES

A traditional hinge consists of two metal *leaves* joined by a pivot or *pin*. Each leaf is attached to a separate wooden part so one part or the other can pivot. There are many variations on this fundamental design, but the purpose remains the same.

BUTT HINGE
General-purpose; leaves are typically recessed in mortises.

LOOSE-PIN HINGE
General-purpose; pin can be removed to detach hinged doors or lid from case.

FLUSH HINGE
General-purpose; leaves fold into one another, do not require mortise; not recommended for heavy doors and lids.

OFFSET HINGE
Used for lipped cabinet and cupboard doors.

EUROPEAN CABINET HINGE
Typically used for contemporary cabinets; door leaf set in a round mortise; completely concealed when installed.

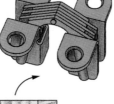
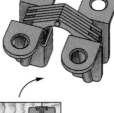

CONCEALED HINGE
General-purpose; set in routed mortises; completely concealed when installed.

BARREL HINGE
Used for light-duty applications; set in round mortises; completely concealed when installed.

DROP-LEAF HINGE
Used for rule joints; joins folding leaves to table.

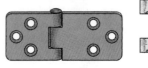

KNIFE HINGE
Light-duty; recessed into top and bottom edges of doors; almost completely concealed when installed.

PIANO HINGE
Used for heavy-duty applications; available in lengths up to 6 feet.

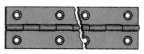

STAYS AND SUPPORTS

Stays and supports hold doors and lids open, and folding leaves horizontal.

LOCKING STAY
General-purpose; folds in the middle when door, lid, or drop front closes, locks straight when open.

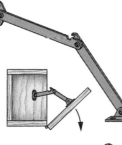

FRICTION STAY
Light-duty; slides open and closed, friction holds lid or door in any position.

SLIDING STAY
Light-duty; slide is recessed in routed mortise, completely concealed when installed.

TOY BOX LID SUPPORT
Used for heavy-duty applications and safety; prevents heavy lids from closing unexpectedly; often rated for the amount of weight it will support.

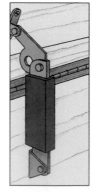

DROP-FRONT SUPPORT
Used as both a hinge and a support for drop-front desk surfaces.

DROP-LEAF SUPPORT
Used to hold folding table leaves horizontal.

LOCKS AND CATCHES

Locks and catches hold doors, drawers, and lids closed when not in use.

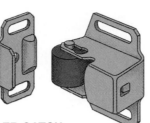

ROLLER CATCH
Used for cabinet doors; spring-loaded rollers capture head of striker.

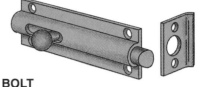

BALL CATCH
Used for light-duty applications; spring-loaded ball is captured in depression in striker plate.

MORTISED KEY LOCK
General-purpose; installed in a mortise in the door or drawer.

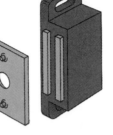

MAGNETIC CATCH
Used for cabinet doors; magnets hold steel plate.

BOLT
Used for doors; end of bolt slides into striker plate.

TUMBLER LOCK
General-purpose; set in a round mortise.

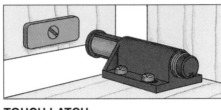

TOUCH LATCH
For cabinet doors without pulls; push door against latch to close or open.

ELBOW CATCH
Used for cabinets with double doors (two doors in one opening); holds one door closed.

PULLS

Pulls provide a grip or purchase so you can open doors and drawers.

KNOB
General-purpose; may be round, oval, or square; made from wood, metal, porcelain, or plastic.

RING PULL
General-purpose, ring-shaped pull hangs from escutcheon.

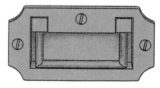

BIN PULL
Used for small drawers; fingerhold is made from wood, plastic, or metal.

OPEN PULL
General-purpose; may be C-shaped or D-shaped; made from wood, metal, or plastic.

BAIL PULL
Used for drawers; D-shaped handle or bail hangs from two small plates.

FLUSH PULL
General-purpose; plate is set in mortise, ring or bail rests flush with plate until needed.

DROP PULL
General-purpose; teardrop-shaped pull hangs from plate or escutcheon.

BAIL-AND-ESCUTCHEON
Used for drawers; bail hangs from escutcheon.

RECESSED PULL
General-purpose; wood or metal finger-hold set in mortise.

STANDARDS AND BRACKETS

Standards, brackets, clips, and pins hold fixed and adjustable shelves.

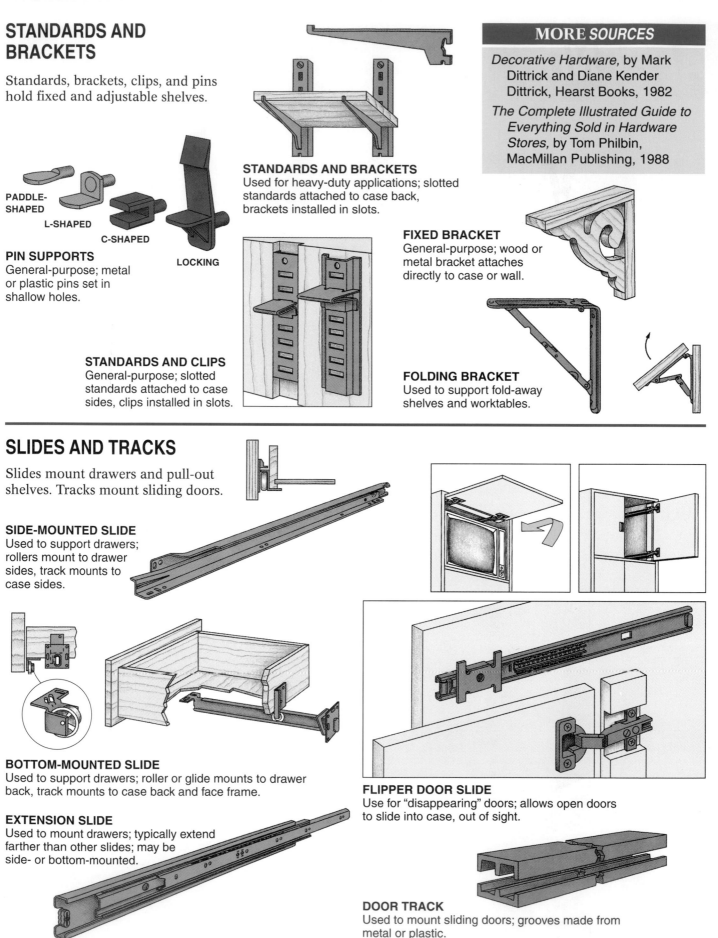

MORE SOURCES

Decorative Hardware, by Mark Dittrick and Diane Kender Dittrick, Hearst Books, 1982

The Complete Illustrated Guide to Everything Sold in Hardware Stores, by Tom Philbin, MacMillan Publishing, 1988

PADDLE-SHAPED

L-SHAPED

C-SHAPED

LOCKING

PIN SUPPORTS
General-purpose; metal or plastic pins set in shallow holes.

STANDARDS AND BRACKETS
Used for heavy-duty applications; slotted standards attached to case back, brackets installed in slots.

FIXED BRACKET
General-purpose; wood or metal bracket attaches directly to case or wall.

STANDARDS AND CLIPS
General-purpose; slotted standards attached to case sides, clips installed in slots.

FOLDING BRACKET
Used to support fold-away shelves and worktables.

SLIDES AND TRACKS

Slides mount drawers and pull-out shelves. Tracks mount sliding doors.

SIDE-MOUNTED SLIDE
Used to support drawers; rollers mount to drawer sides, track mounts to case sides.

BOTTOM-MOUNTED SLIDE
Used to support drawers; roller or glide mounts to drawer back, track mounts to case back and face frame.

EXTENSION SLIDE
Used to mount drawers; typically extend farther than other slides; may be side- or bottom-mounted.

FLIPPER DOOR SLIDE
Use for "disappearing" doors; allows open doors to slide into case, out of sight.

DOOR TRACK
Used to mount sliding doors; grooves made from metal or plastic.

WOODWORKING SOURCES

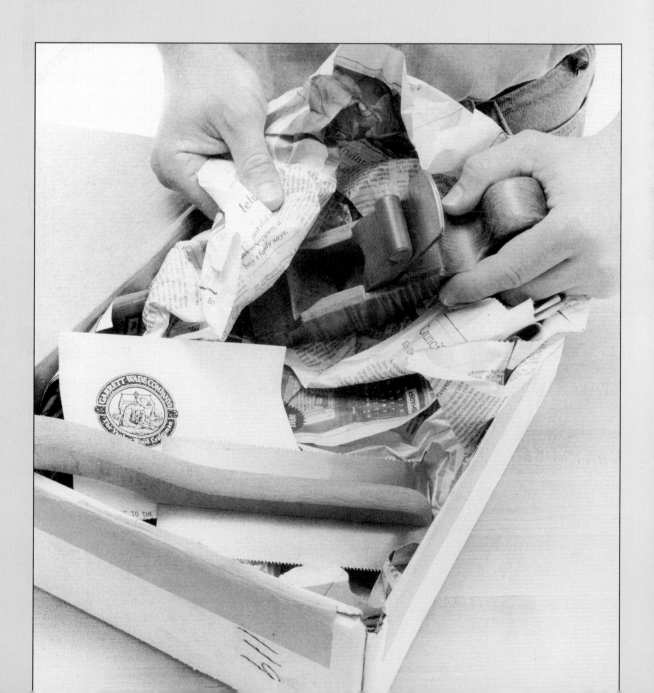

Woodworking Publications

MAGAZINES AND NEWSLETTERS

These periodicals offer information and projects of *general* interest to woodworkers. To find a publication that caters to your special woodworking interests, consult *Ulrich's Periodical Directory* or *Standard's Periodical Directory* at your local library. you can also ask to see the EBSCO's *Librarian's*

Handbook – this is kept behind the desk; you won't find it in the reference section.

Also use the directories to update information on these general-interest periodicals, should you need to. Magazines change phone numbers, subscription services, even publishers from time to time.

American How-To
12301 Whitewater Drive
Minnetonka, MN 55354
(612) 936-9581

American Woodworker
2915 Commers Drive, Suite 700
Eagan, MN 55121
(651) 454-9200

Decorative Woodcrafts
606 Spine Road
P. O. Box 54696
Boulder, CO 80323-4696
(800) 477-4271

Fine Woodworking
Taunton Press
63 S. Main Street
P. O. Box 5507
Newtown, CT 06470-5507
(800) 888-8286

Home Furniture
Taunton Press
63 S. Main Street
P. O. Box 5507
Newtown, CT 06470-5507
(800) 888-8286

Popular Woodworking
F&W Publications
1507 Dana Avenue
Cincinnati, OH 45207
(800) 283-0963

ShopNotes
August Home Publishing Co.
2200 Grand Avenue
Des Moines, IA 50312
(800) 333-5854

Today's Woodworker
4365 Willow Drive
Medina, MN 55340
(612) 478-8212

Weekend Woodcrafts
EGW Publishing Company
1041 Shary Circle
Concord, CA 94518
(800) 676-5002

Wood
P.O. Box 55050
Boulder, CO 80322-5050
(800) 374-9663

Woodshop News
35 Pratt Street
Essex, CT 06426
(860) 767-8227

Woodsmith
August Home Publishing Co.
2200 Grand Avenue
P.O. Box 50312
Des Moines, IA 50312
(800) 333-5075

Woodwork
Ross Periodicals, Inc.
42 Digital Drive
Suite 5
Novato, CA 94949
(415) 382-0580
or
Ross Periodicals, Inc.
42 Digital Drive
P.O. Box 1529
Ross, CA 94949

Woodworker's Journal
4365 Willow Drive
Medina, MN 55340
(612) 478-8255

Woodworker West
P.O. Box 452058
Los Angeles, CA 90045
(310) 216-9265

Workbench
August Home Publishing Co.
2200 Grand Avenue
Des Moines, IA 50312
(515) 282-7000

MORE *INFO*

Should you need to find a specific article, or want to read all the available articles on a certain subject, there are three extensive indices of general woodworking magazines to help you locate information.

The Guide to Published Woodworking Plans and Techniques
KnotWhole Publishing
5629 Main-Street-Putney
Stratford, CT 06614
(203) 386-1270

Infoware
Infodex Services
10609 King Arthur's Court
Richmond, VA 23235-3840
(804) 320-4704

Woodfind
P.O. Box 2703
Lynnwood, WA 98036
(425) 743-6605

All three indices are available as database search-and-find programs for IBM-compatible computers. The Guide and *WOODFIND* are also available in a printed format.

BOOKS

While many publishers offer how-to titles, those listed here are especially active in woodworking publishing. For a complete listing of current woodworking books, consult the "Subject Guide" of R.R. Bowker's Books in Print at your local library.

PRO *TIP*

If the book you want is not in print and your local library doesn't have it, request it through interlibrary loan. This service locates an institution that has the book, which sends it to your library, and your library then lends it to you. Not only is this a great way to obtain out-of-print titles, but you can also evaluate books in print before you buy them.

MORE *INFO*

Looking for a bookstore that caters exclusively to woodworkers, with over 1,700 titles to browse? Try:

Manny's Woodworker's Place
555 South Broadway
Lexington, KY 40508
(606) 255-5444

Betterway Books
F&W Publications
1507 Dana Avenue
Cincinnati, OH 45207
(513) 531-2222

Dover Publications
31 E. Second Street
Mineola, NY 11501
(516) 294-7000

**Guild of Master
Craftsman Publications**
166 High Street
Lewes, East Sussex
BN7-IXU ENGLAND
(800) 225-9262

Linden Publishing
336 West Bedford
Suite 107
Fresno, CA 93711
(800) 345-4447

**Meredith Corporation
Book Group**
1716 Locust Street
Des Moines, IA 50309
(800) 678-8091

Reader's Digest Association
Reader's Digest Road
Pleasantville, NY 10571
(914) 244-7445

Sterling Publishing
387 Park Avenue South
New York, NY 10016
(800) 367-9692

Taunton Books and Videos
63 S. Main Street
Newtown, CT 06470-5507
(800) 888-8286

**U.S. Government
Printing Office**
Superintendent of Documents
Washington, DC 20402-9325
(202) 512-1800

Woodworking Institutions and Organizations

These organizations exist to share information on specific woodworking subjects. I only have room for a few of the most interesting, but there are many more listed in the *Encyclopedia of Associations* in your local library. And don't think that any area of woodworking interest is too specialized for a fullblown association – it pays to check. When I was putting together the "Photographic History of American Furniture Styles" on pages 57-64 and needed a photo of a Wooton desk, I was delighted to find there was a Society of Wooton Desk Owners!

**American Association of
Woodturners (AAW)**
3200 Lexington Avenue
Shoreview, MN 55126
(651) 484-9094
Journal: American Woodturner
Lathe turning

**American Forest & Paper
Association (AFPA)**
1111 19th Street NW, Suite 700
Washington, DC 20036
(202) 463-2700
Wood products

**APA - The Engineered
Wood Association**
P.O. Box 11700
Tacoma, WA 98411-0700
(253) 565-6600
Ext. 189 for literature list
Plywood, engineered wood products

**Certified Forest
Products Council**
14780 SW Osprey Drive,
Suite 285
Beaverton, OR 97007
(503) 590-6600

Forest Products Laboratory
(see sidebar on page 380)

Guild of American Luthiers
8222 S. Park Avenue
Tacoma, WA 98408-5226
(253) 472-7853
Journal: American Lutherie
Stringed musical instrument-making

Hand Tools Institute
25 N. Broadway
Tarrytown, NY 10591
(914) 332-0040
Hand tool use

Hardwood Plywood and Veneer Association
P.O. Box 2789
Reston, VA 20195-0789
(703) 435-2900
Cabinet-grade plywood

International Guild of Miniature Artisans
P.O. Box 2320
Malta, NY 12020
1-800-711-IMGA

International Wood Collectors Society (IWCS)
2300 W. Rangeline Road
Greencastle, IN 46135
(317) 653-6483
Hardwoods and softwoods

Marquetry Society of America
32-34 153rd Street
Flushing, NY 11354
Marquetry and parquetry

National Hardwood Lumber Association
6830 Raleigh La Grange Rd.
Memphis, TN 38134
(901) 377-1818
Hardwoods

National Woodcarver's Association
7424 Miami Avenue
Cincinnati, OH 45243
(513) 561-0627
Journal: Chips/Chats
Woodcarving

North American Plywood Corporation
351 Manhattan Avenue
Jersey City, NJ 07307
(201) 420-0440
Plywood, sheet materials

Southern Forest Products Association (SEPA)
P.O. Box 641700
Kenner, LA 70064-1700
(504) 443-4464
Softwoods

Western Wood Products Association (WWPA)
522 S.W. Fifth Avenue
Suite 500
Portland, OR 97204-2122
(503) 224-3930
Softwoods

Wood Moulding & Millwork Producers Association
507 First Street
Woodland, CA 95695
(513) 661-9591
Wood molding products, literature

Wood Turning Center
P.O. Box 25706
Philadelphia, PA 19144
(215) 844-2188
Newsletter: Turning Point
Lathe turning

THE U.S. FOREST PRODUCTS LABORATORY

The Forest Products Laboratory (FPL) is an arm of the U.S. Department of Agriculture, occupying 13 buildings and 22 acres at the University of Wisconsin in Madison. It brings together over 200 specialists from all facets of the woodworking industry and is the largest research facility ever built to study wood and wood materials.

But research is only half its mission. The other half is *information*. The scientists at the FPL occupy much of their time sharing what they've learned. They have published hundreds of reports, articles, and handbooks on wood-related topics.

If you ask, the FPL will send you a list of their publications. Write:

Information
Forest Products Laboratory
One Gifford Pinchot Drive
Madison, WI 53705

Or contact them through the internet:
http://www.fpl.fs.fed.us/

Woodworking Schools

If you'd like to learn woodworking or a specific woodworking subject from an accomplished craftsman, there are many courses available at institutions throughout the United States and Canada, from short seminars to four-year college degrees. This is a list of some of the more active woodworking schools; you can find much more complete lists at several sites on the Internet. (For example, *The Woodworks' Forum* at **http://www.woodforum.com** maintains an extensive list of woodworking schools online.) Or, check the listings of classes and courses in the "upcoming events" section of most woodworking magazines. You might also call local colleges and vocational schools and ask whether they offer woodworking training.

Marc Adams School of Woodworking
5504 East 500 North
Franklin, IN 46131
(317) 535-4013
Woodworking

Alpine School of Woodcarving, Ltd.
225 Vine Avenue
Park Ridge, IL 60068
(847) 692-2822
Chip Carving

Arrowmont
P.O. Box 567
Gatlinsburg, TN 37738
(423) 436-5860
Woodworking, woodcrafts

Berea College Department of Technology
CPO 2347
Berea, KY 40404
(606) 986-9341
Woodworking

Brigham Young University
Technology Education and
Construction Management
230 SNLB
Provo, UT 84602
(801) 378-2021
Woodworking

Center for Furniture Craftsmanship
25 Mill Street
Rockport, ME 04856
(207) 594-5611
Design, woodworking

Chicago School for Violin Making
3636 Oakton
Shokie, IL 60076
(847) 673-9545
Violin Making

College of the Redwoods Fine Woodworking Program
1211 Del Mar Drive
Fort Bragg, CA 95437
(707) 964-7056
Fine furniture making

Conover Workshops
18125 Madison Road
P.O. Box 679
Parkman, OH 44080
(440) 548-3491
Woodworking, turning

Dana Robes Wood Craftsmen
Lower Shaker Village
P.O. Box 70
Enfield, NH 03748
(800) 722-5036
Woodworking

Elston Woodworking School
2228 N. Elston Avenue
Chicago, IL 60614
(773) 342-9811
Woodworking

Haywood Community College
1 Freelander Drive
Clyde, NC 28721
(828) 627-4500
Woodworking

The Hymiller School
783 N. Clayton Street
Lawrenceville, GA 30245
(770) 521-0146
Woodworking

North Bennet Street School
39 N. Bennet Street
Boston, MA 02113
(617) 227-0155
Woodworking

Northwest School of Wooden Boatbuilding
251 Otto Street
Port Townsend, WA 98368
(360) 385-4948
Boatbuilding

Oregon College of Arts & Crafts
8245 S.W. Barnes Road
Portland, OR 97225
(503) 297-5544
Woodworking, crafts

Orth Furniture Apprenticeship
1107 Chicago Avenue
Oak Park, IL 60301
(708) 383-4399
Furniture making

Penland School of Crafts
P.O. Box 37
Penland, NC 28765
(828) 765-2359
Design, Woodworking

Peters Valley Craft Center
19 Kuhn Road
Layton, NJ 07851
(973) 948-5200
Woodworking

Purdue University
Dept. of Forestry and Natural Resources
West Lafayette, IN 47907-1159
(765) 494-3591
Woodworking, production

Rockingham Community College
P.O. Box 38
Wentworth, NC 27375
(919) 342-4261
Woodworking

School of Classical Woodcarving
319 Dolan Avenue
Mill Valley, CA 94941
(451) 381-9474
Woodcarving

Southern Union State College
P.O. Box 2268
Opelika, AL 36803-2268
(334) 745-6437
Woodworking

The University of the Arts
320 S. Broad Street
Philadelphia, PA 19102
(800) 616-ARTS
Woodworking

University of Cincinnati
Wood Technology Program
OMI College of Applied Science
2220 Victory Parkway
Cincinnati, OH 45206
(513) 556-6567
Woodworking

University of Rio Grande
College of Technology
Rio Grande, OH 45674
(740) 245-7311
Woodworking

Warwick County Workshops
P.O. Box 665
Warwick, NY 10990
(914) 986-6636
Woodworking

John Wilson, Boxmaker
500 E. Broadway Highway
Charlotte, MI 48813
(517) 543-5325
Boxmaking

Windsor Workshop
1332 Harlem Blvd.
Rockford, IL 61103
(815) 965-6677
Chairmaking

Woodenboat School
P.O. Box 78
Brooklin, ME 04616
(207) 359-4651
Boatbuilding

The Wood Turning Center
P.O. Box 25706
Philadelphia, PA 19144
(215) 844-2188
Lathe turning

**The Woodworking Center
of Ontario**
299 Doon Valley Drive
Kitchner, Ontario
N2G 4M4 CANADA
(519) 748-5220, Ext. 466
Woodworking, production

Worcester Center for Crafts
25 Sagamore Road
Worcester, MA 01605
(508) 753-8183
Woodworking

**Yestermorrow Design/Build
School**
189 Vermont Route 100
Warren, VT 05674
(802) 496-5545
Design, cabinetmaking

Woodworking Tool Manufacturers

These are some of the major players among the woodworking tool makers. Not all of them sell direct, but if you're interested in their products, ask for the name of a nearby distributor.

Adjustable Clamp Company
417 N. Ashland Avenue
Chicago, IL 60622
(312) 666-0640

**American Machine and
Tool Company**
400 Spring Street
Royersford, PA 19468-2519
(610) 948-0400
Stationary tools and accessories

Black & Decker, Inc.
701 E. Joppa Road
Towson, MD 21286
http://www.blackanddecker.com

Borden
180 E. Broad Street
Columbus, OH 43215-3799
(800) 848-9400
Adhesives

Bridge City Tool Works
1104 N.E. 28th Avenue
Portland, OR 97232
(800) 253-3332
Measuring and layout tools

Cooper Tools
Cooper Hand Tool Division
P.O. Box 30100
Raleigh, NC 27622
(919) 781-7200
Hand tools

**Delta International
Machinery Corp.**
246 Alpha Drive
Pittsburgh, PA 15238
(800) 438-2486
Stationary power tools

DeWalt Tool Company
626 Hanover Pike
Hampstead, MD 21074
(800) 4-DEWALT
Portable power tools

Forrest Manufacturing Company, Inc.
457 River Road
Clifton, NJ 07014
(800) 733-7111
Saw blades

Franklin International
2020 Bruck Street
Columbus, OH 43207
(800) 877-4583
Adhesives

Freud, Inc.
218 Feld Avenue
High Point, NC 27264
(800) 472-7307
Blades, cutters, bits

General Manufacturing Company, Ltd.
835 Cherrier Street
Drummandville, Quebec
J2B 5A8 CANADA
(819) 472-1161
Stationary power tools

Grizzly Imports, Inc.
2406 Reach Road
Williamsport, PA 17701
(800) 523-4777 (East) or
P.O. Box 2069
Bellingham, WA 98227-2069
(800) 541-5537 (West)
Stationary power tools

Hitachi Koki U.S.A. Ltd.
3950 Steve Reynolds Blvd.
Norcross, GA 30093
(770) 925-1774
Portable power tools

Jet Equipment and Tools
P.O. Box 1349
Auburn, WA 98071-1349
(253) 351-6000
Stationary power tools

Klingspor Abrasives
P.O. Box 2367
Hickory, NC 28603-3737
(800) 645-5555
Abrasives

Lie-Nielsen Toolworks
Route 1
Warren, ME 04684
(800) 327-2520
Hand tools

Makita U.S.A., Inc.
14930 Northam Street
La Mirada, CA 90638
(800) 462-5482
Portable power tools

Milwaukee Tool Corporation
13135 W. Lisbon Road
Brookfield, WI 53005
(414) 781-3600
Portable power tools

Norton Company
1 New Bond Street
Box 15008
Worcester, MA 01615-0008
(508) 795-5000
Abrasives

Olson Saw Company
16 Stony Hill Road
Bethel, CT 06801
(800) 272-2885
Band saw and scroll saw blades

Porter-Cable
4825 Highway 45 N.
Jackson, TN 38302
(800) 487-8665
Portable power tools

Powermatic
619 Morrison Street
McMinnville, TN 37110
(800) 248-0144
Stationary power tools

Record Tools, Inc.
1920 Clements Road
Pickering, Ontario
L1W 3V6 CANADA
(905) 428-1077
Hand tools

Ryobi American Corporation
P.O. Box 1207
Anderson, SC 29622
(800) 525-2579
Portable power tools

Sears Roebuck & Company
20 Presidential Drive
Roselle, IL 60172
(800) 377-7414
Stationary and portable power tools, hand tools

Shopsmith, Inc.
6530 Poe Avenue
Dayton, OH 45414-2591
(800) 543-7586
Stationary power tools

Stanley Tools
600 Myrtle Street
New Britain, CT 06052
(860) 225-5111
Hand tools

U.S. Safety
8101 Lenexa Drive
P.O. Box 15965
Lenexa, KS 66285-5965
(800) 821-5218
Safety products

Vermont-American Tool Company
P.O. Box 340
Lincolnton, NC 28093-0340
(704) 735-7464
Blades, bits, hand tools

General Woodworking Supplies

Some of the major mail-order woodworking suppliers:

Constantine
2050 Eastchester Road
Bronx, NY 10461
(800) 223-8087

Craftsman Wood Service
1735 W. Cortland Court
Addison, IL 60101-4280
(312) 629-3100

Eagle America
P.O. Box 1099
Chardon, OH 44024
(800) 872-2511

Garrett-Wade Company
161 Avenue of the Americas
New York, NY 10013-1299
(800) 221-2942

Harbor Freight Tools
3491 Mission Oaks Boulevard
P.O. Box 6010
Camarillo, CA 93011-6010
(800) 423-2567

Highland Hardware
1045 N. Highland Ave, NE
Atlanta, GA 30306
(800) 241-6748

Leichtung Workshops
1108 N Glenn Road
Casper, Wyoming 82601
(800) 321-6840

McFeely's Square Drive Screws
P.O. Box 11169
Lynchburg, VA 24506
(800) 443-7937

Northern
P.O. Box 1219
Burnsville, MN 55337-0219
(800) 533-5545

Penn State Industries
2850 Comly Road
Philadelphia, PA 19154
(800) 377-7297

Tool Crib of the North
P.O. Box 14930
Grand Forks, ND 58208-4040
(800) 582-6704

Trend-Lines
135 American Legion Highway
Revere, MA 02151
(800) 877-7899

Woodcraft
210 Wood County Industrial Park
P.O. Box 1686
Parkersburg, WV 26102-1686
(800) 225-1153

Woodworkers' Store
4365 Willow Drive
Medina, MN 55340
(800) 279-4441

Woodworker's Supply Inc. of New Mexico
1108 North Glenn Rd
Casper, Wyoming 82601
(800) 645-9292

Specialty Woodworking Supplies

A sampling of companies that offer specialized woodworking materials:

Ball and Ball
463 W. Lincoln Highway
Exton, PA 19341
(800) 257-3711
Brass and Iron hardware

Belcher Carving Supply
6205 E. State Route 40
Tipp City, OH 45371
(937) 845-0346
Carving supplies

Bob Morgan Woodworking Supplies
1121 Bardstown Road
Louisville, KY 40204
(502) 456-2545
Wood, veneers

Cherry Tree
P.O. Box 369
Belmont, OH 43718
(800) 848-4363
Woodcrafting supplies

Jesada Tools
310 Mears Boulevard
Oldsmar, FL 34677
(800) 531-5559
Router bits and tools

Colonial Hardwoods
7953 Cameron Brown Court
Springfield, VA 22153
(800) 466-5451
Hardwoods, supplies

Durst Lumber Company
2450 W. Eleven Mile Road
Berkley, MI 48072
(248) 542-2010
Hardwoods

Horton Brasses
Nooks Hill Road
Cromwell, CT 06416
(860) 635-4400
Brass hardware

Japan Woodworker
1731 Clement Avenue
Alameda, CA 94501
(800) 537-7820
Japanese tools

Klingspors Sanding Catalogue
856 21st Street Drive SE
Hickory, NC 28602
(828) 327-7623

Klockit
P.O. Box 636
Lake Geneva, WI 53147
(800) 556-2548
Clockmaking supplies

Wood Finish Supply
P.O. Box 86
Mendocino, CA 95460
(800) 245-5611
Finishes

W.D. Lockwood & Company
81-83 Franklin Street
New York, NY 10013
(212) 966-4046
Wood dyes

Maple Specialties, Inc.
43306 S.E. North Bend Way
Suites 1 and 2
North Bend, WA 98045
(800) 409-9663
Figured maples, turning blocks, thin lumber

Meisel Hardware Specialties
P.O. Box 70
Mound, MN 55364-0070
(800) 441-9870
Woodcrafting plans and supplies

Mohawk Finishing Products
4715 State Highway 30
Amsterdam, NY 12010
(800) 545-0047
Finishes

Nelson Designs
P.O. Box 422
Dublin, NH 03444
(603) 563-8306
Scrollwork patterns and books

Old Mille Cabinet Shoppe
1660 Camp Betty
Washington Road
York, PA 17402
(717) 755-8884
Antique finishes

Packard Woodworks
P.O. Box 718
Tryon, NC 28782
(800) 683-8876
Lathe turning tools and supplies

Paxton Beautiful Woods
6311 St. John Avenue
Kansas City, MO 64123
(800) 333-7298
Hardwoods, plywoods

Rare Earth Hardwoods
6778 E. Traverse City,
Traverse City, MI 49684
(616) 946-0043
Imported hardwoods

Renovator's Supply
Millers Falls, MA 01349
(800) 659-3211
Antique hardware

Sandy Pond Hardwoods
921-A Lancaster Pike
Quarryville, PA 17566
(800) 546-9663
Figured hardwoods

Seyco
P.O. Box 1900
Rockwall, TX 75087
(800) 462-3353
Scrollwork tools and supplies

Shaker Workshops
P.O. Box 8001
Ashburnham, MA 01430
(800) 840-9121
Chairmaking supplies

Smoky Mountain Knife Works
P.O. Box 4430
Sevierville, TN 37864
(800) 251-9306
Knife-making supplies

Steve Wall Lumber Company
P.O. Box 287
Mayodan, NC 27027
(800) 633-4062
Hardwoods

Stewart-MacDonald
Box 900
Athens, OH 45701
(800) 848-2273
Musical instrument supplies

Tropical Exotic Hardwoods
P.O. Box 1806
Carlsbad, CA 92018
(760) 434-3030

Wood Carvers Supply, Inc.
P.O. Box 7500
Englewood, FL 34295-7500
(800) 284-6229
Carving tools and supplies

Woodhaven
501 W. First Avenue
Durant, IA 52747-9743
(800) 344-6657
Routing tools

INDEX